Human Intimacy

Marriage, the Family and Its Meaning

Human Intimacy
Marriage, the Family and Its Meaning

Fourth Edition

Frank D. Cox
Santa Barbara City College

West Publishing Company
St. Paul   New York   Los Angeles   San Francisco

Copyediting: Loralee Windsor
Design: Janet Bollow
Illustrations: Barbara Barnett, Brenda Booth, John Foster, Sue Sellars
Production Coordination: Janet Bollow Associates
Composition: Janet Hansen & Associates Graphics
Cover photo: Paul Nehrenz, © 1981 The Image Bank

Library of Congress Cataloging-in-Publication Data

Cox, Frank D.
 Human intimacy.

 Bibliography: p.
 Includes index.
  1. Family—United States. 2. Marriage—United
States. 3. Sex customs—United States. I. Title.
HQ536.C759 1987   306.8'0973   86–32472
ISBN 0–314–30393–6

Acknowledgments

p. 21 Published in the April 28, 1985 issue of *Parade*. Copyright © by Claire Safran, 1985.

p. 43 From *Marriage and Alternatives: Exploring Intimate Relationships*, edited by Roger Libby and Robert N. Whitehurst. Copyright © 1977 by Random House, Inc. Reprinted by permission of the publisher.

p. 63 From *Marriage: East and West* by David and Vera Mace. Copyright © 1959, 1960 by David and Vera Mace. Reprinted by permission of Doubleday & Co., Inc.

p. 67 "Love Birds" by Cynthia Moorman. Reprinted by permission of Cynthia Moorman, Santa Monica, California.

p. 71 © 1983 Ann Landers and News America Syndicate.

pp. 76–79 Adaptation of Chapter 5, "The Six Basic Styles of Loving" by Marcia Lasswell and Norman Lobsenz. Copyright © 1980. Reprinted by permission of Doubleday & Co., Inc.

p. 109 Adapted from Ridley, Peterman and Avery, 1978, pp. 135–136.

p. 174 From Richard Hunt and Edward Rydman, *Creative Marriage* (Boston: Halbrook, 1976) pp. 50–51. Reprinted by permission.

pp. 189–190 (Dialog between Ralph and Betsy, pp. 55–58) from *The Intimate Enemy* by Dr. George R. Bach and Peter Wyden. Copyright © 1968, 1969 by George R. Bach and Peter Wyden. By permission of William Morrow & Co.

p. 215 Macleod, *The Village Voice* (February 11, 1971).

pp. 228–229 Alice G. Sargeant, *Beyond Sex Roles*. St. Paul, Minn.: West, 1977, p. 87.

pp. 330–331 John Leo, "On the Trail of the Big O," Time Magazine, March 3, 1983, p. 12. Reprinted by permission of Time Inc. © 1983.

pp. 390–391 Wallis, "A Surrogate's Story," Time Magazine, September 10, 1984, p. 53. Reprinted by permission of Time Inc. © 1984.

(continued following Subject Index)

Contents in Brief

Contents

Chapter 4

Dating, Sexual Mores, and Mate Selection   93

Inset 4.1
Questions for Couples Contemplating
Living Together   109

Inset 4.2
Couple Wed So They Know What to
Call Each Other   114

**Marriage, Intimacy, Expectations, and the Fully Functioning
    Person   137**

Chapter 5

Communication in Intimate Relationships   167

Chapter 6

Chapter 7

People Liberation: Changing Masculine and Feminine Roles   201

Chapter 8

The Family as an Economic System   239

The Dual-Worker Family: The Real American Revolution   281

Chapter 9

Human Sexuality   311

Chapter 10

Chapter 11

Family Planning   357

Preface

Continuing editions of a textbook are always exciting for an author. First they mean that the book has been well enough received that new editions are warranted. Second they mean that the author has a great deal of new input coming from the many people who have used the book. With such input a new edition cannot help but be improved. Third in a field as complex and rapidly changing as marriage and the family, the need to update is perhaps more pressing than in many other fields. Finally the writer can rethink his or her basic assumptions and the writing that has gone before. I believe that such rethinking leads to a better, more up-to-date, thorough, interesting, readable, and exciting textbook.

Human Intimacy: Marriage, the Family and Its Meaning was written to stimulate thinking about the meaning and function of marriage and family in American life and, in particular, in the reader's own personal life. Criticizing marriage and the family has always been popular and easy, yet despite this, marriage and family life remain a prominent and important part of the American scene. Most of us grow up in families, and over 90 percent of us will be marriage partners at some time in our lives. This high percentage places America among the most marrying nations in the world. I believe that intimacy is still most often found within the family setting and that the family is functioning better than doomsday critics would have us believe.

It is difficult for the newly married to concentrate on improving the marital relationship. Yet a marriage does not naturally take care of itself, and "love" will not make a marriage successful. After all most divorced people married their former spouses out of "love." What happened? Why didn't their relationship work? *Human Intimacy stresses the point that every person has the ability to improve his or her intimate relationships.*

Human Intimacy takes a positive view of the potentials inherent in the marital relationship. Indeed the first chapter, *Human Intimacy: The Strengths of the Successful Relationship*, is wholly new to this edition. Social scientists are at last scientifically studying families that are strong and successful, and from this research we are beginning to gain an understanding of the characteristics needed by all families to build and maintain successful and enduring relationships. Thus this fourth edition starts on a very positive note, looking at family characteristics that lead to successful, enduring, and satisfying human relationships. More than previous editions, this edition tries to emphasize how the characteristics of strong and successful families can be nurtured in all intimate relationships so that a couple's, a family's, full potential can be realized. In addition the book examines and discusses the entire field of family life in a positive and constructive manner, trying to weave throughout the text the lessons we have learned from studying strong and successful families.

One advantage of American society is the wide spectrum of choice it offers individuals in most aspects of life. Although family patterns have been somewhat limited in the past, a wider variety of intimate lifestyles is becoming acceptable. For example, the loosening of traditional sex roles allows individuals greater freedom to adapt their marriages to their own needs and make their intimate relationships unique and vital. Marriage is now seen to involve personal satisfaction rather than just the proper fulfillment of duties and specific roles. Since greater freedom of choice brings the freedom to err, however, becoming knowledgeable about marriage and the family is more important than ever.

I hope that *Human Intimacy* will contribute to your ability to make intelligent, satisfying choices about intimate relationships. Individuals who are able to make satisfying choices in their lives are most apt to be fulfilled persons. And fulfilled persons have the best chance of making their marital relationships exciting and growth producing.

The fourth edition of *Human Intimacy* has become an even more positive statement about marriage and the family. It realistically reflects the place of marriage and the family in today's American society. It tries to offer hope for tomorrow's family by emphasizing what the family ideally can become as well as what it currently is. The beauty of the institution called family is that it is adaptable and flexible. People with knowledge of themselves, the family, and their culture have the opportunity in America to build a marriage and family that will suit their own needs. Families can change for the better; intimate relationships can become more deeply satisfying and fulfilling. *Human Intimacy* was written with these ends in mind.

This book has several features designed to aid your reading:

- Each chapter is preceded by a comprehensive outline that gives an overview of the material to follow. The outline is also an excellent study guide and tool of review.
- "Insets" supply interesting detail, allow hypothesizing, and present controversy. They also add variety to the reading much as an aside adds variety to a lecture.
- Because the field of marriage and family is fraught with controversy and divergent opinions, "Scenes from Marriage" appear at the end of each chapter. These are essentially condensed excerpts and discussion from other sources that add new dimensions and/or conflicting viewpoints to each chapter. Of the sixteen insets, twelve are new to this edition, including a large and informative "Scene" discussing acquired immune deficiency syndrome (AIDS) in detail.
- To add life and realism, many case studies are scattered throughout the book. They highlight the principles being discussed and illustrate how a principle might be applied in everyday life. Most of the cases are composites, built on real-life experiences shared by my students over the years.

Several major changes have been made in this fourth edition.

- As already noted, the totally new opening chapter makes the present edition even more positive and constructive than past editions. The chapter, indeed the whole fourth edition of *Human Intimacy*, emphasizes the strengths to be found in successful intimate relationships and how to build such strengths.
- Much of the material that was found in the appendixes in the third edition has been brought into the body of the text. Although extensive appendix material seemed like a good idea at the time of writing the third edition, experience with that edition indicates that many readers simply do not attend to appendix material.
- "Issues" is a new type of presentation in which some controversial topic, such as the single-parent family or comparable pay, is debated by arguing both a "pro" and a "con" side of the topic. Taking definite stands on both sides of

controversial topics, should make the discussions more lively and thought provoking.

■ It goes without saying that the whole book has been updated, and much new material has been added throughout.

As with all such undertakings, many more people than myself have contributed to *Human Intimacy*. The most important contributors are the many family members with whom I have interacted all my life, including parents, grandparents, aunts, uncles, cousins, siblings, and, of course, my immediate family—Pamela, Randy, and Michelle. Many fine researchers and writers have also influenced and contributed to my thoughts, including the direct reviewers of the previous edition, without whom *Human Intimacy* could not exist. To them I wish to extend a special thanks.

Arlene Chandler, Cuesta College, California

Richard D. Carr, Ball State University, Indiana

John W. Hoskins, Furman University, South Carolina

Ray Goldberg, SUNY—Cortland

George Mann, University of Lethridge, Alberta, Canada

Leslie A. Koepke, University of Wisconsin, Stout

Judy Winkelpleck, University of Iowa

Barbara Lindemann, Santa Barbara City College

Henry Bagish, Santa Barbara City College

John Bowman, Santa Barbara City College

Although *Human Intimacy* has my name on it, the actual production of the book rests with Clyde Perlee of West Publishing; Janet Bollow, the designer; the wonderful editorial staff at West Publishing; and above all those oft-forgotten production people at West Publishing who turn the final copy into a beautiful book and place it in the hands of the many teachers and students who use it. Please know that I am always grateful for your fine work and consider *Human Intimacy* to be *our* book not mine alone.

Frank D. Cox

The Eloquent Story of Life in Ancient Symbols

	Man
	Woman
	Man and woman united
	Woman becomes pregnant
	And bears a child
	The family: Man, woman, and children
	Friendship between men
	Men quarrel and fight
	Man dies
	The widow and her children
	The mother dies
	Surviving children bearing within themselves the seeds of new families

Chapter 1

Human Intimacy: Strengths of Successful Relationships

Contents

The study of intimate relationships is both essential and exciting because we live in a society where such relationships are important to social, psychological, and emotional survival. What better way to begin this journey than by examining the strengths exhibited by successful and ideal intimate relationships, families in particular. What could my intimate relationships be like if I could make them the best possible? Even if I succeed in solving the major problems that will surely arise in my marriage, can I build a marital relationship that is better than just satisfactory? Can my mate and I create an intimate relationship that is at the same time secure and comfortable and growing and exciting? Will my family be able to rear children that care about themselves and the community of which they are a part, children who will grow into adults who are capable of being intimate, caring, and loving human beings?

Why start with the ideal? Won't we all fall short of the ideal? Yes, of course we will. But ideals can be goals, and goals give us something at which to aim. They give us direction in life. They motivate us. They can be the rudder that keeps us on course as our ship sails through life.

To have a vision of what we want ourselves, our relationships, our families, our children, our society, and our world to be is of the utmost importance to human beings. It is the ability to visualize the ideal that allows human beings to change. Without this vision of what could be, there would be little if any change. If all of our behaviors were inborn, biologically determined, preordained, nothing could change and no vision of the ideal would be necessary to survive.

So we will begin by examining the ideal qualities of strong families because it is within families that all of us learn about intimate relationships. Our family of origin is after all the first seat of our learning and the essence of the family is human relationship.

Researchers have begun to study strong, healthy, successful families. Those doing the research point out that volumes have been written about what is wrong with the family but little has been written about what is right in the successful family (Mace, 1983). "We don't learn how to do anything by looking only at how it shouldn't be done. We learn most effectively by examining how to do something correctly and by studying a positive model" (Stinnett, 1979, p. 24).

The basic thrust of *Human Intimacy* is to create and develop an ideal vision of what the strong family is and to weave this image throughout the book. Of course, we will spend time discussing family problems, because all families (all people for that matter) have problems. But by holding out an ideal vision of what a family can be, we take the first and perhaps most important step toward resolving problems that will most certainly arise throughout our lives.

Vera and David Mace coined the phrase "family wellness" to describe the strong family that is functioning at a high level (Mace & Mace, 1985; Mace, 1983). For the Maces the quality of life in our communities is determined by the quality of relationships in the families that make up communities. The quality of life in our families is decided by the quality of relationships between the couples who found those families.

We take the view that family wellness, in its full and true meaning, grows out of marriage wellness. A family begins when a marriage begins. We do not mean that a one-parent family cannot be a well family. It can. But since four out of five one-parent families are really in transition between marriages, and most of them are one-parent families because the first marriage broke down, it is the marriage relationship that is still the foundation stone. So the key to nearly everything else is to enable marriages to be what they are capable of being and what the people involved want them to be. (Mace & Mace, 1985, p. 9).

What are the qualities of a couple relationship that lead to family strength and wellness? Numerous researchers have sought answers to this question and, to date, there has been considerable agreement among their findings.

The research suggests six major qualities shared by all strong, healthy families (Stinnett, 1979; Stinnett & DeFrain, 1985).

1. *Commitment*: The major quality of these strong families is a high degree of commitment. They are deeply committed to promoting each others' happiness and welfare. They are also very committed to the family group, as reflected by the fact that they invest much of their time and energy in the family. "The individual family member is integrated into a web of mutual affection and respect. By belonging and being committed to something greater than oneself, there is less chance that individualism will sour into alienation or egocentrism" (Gardner, 1981, p. 94).

   Some of the most informative research on commitment has been done in communes. One of the main differences found between successful and unsuccessful groups was commitment. The most successful, longest-lasting, most-satisfying communes in terms of relationships are those in which there is a great deal of commitment to each other and to the group. Commitment in communes is reflected in the amount of time the members spend together. The same is true with strong families.

   An important point about strong families is that they take the initiative to structure their lifestyle in a way that enhances the quality of their family relationships and their satisfaction. They are on the "offensive." They do not just react; they make things happen. There is a great deal that families can do to make life more enjoyable. These strong families exercise that ability.

2. *Appreciation*: This quality emerged from the research in many ways and seemed to permeate the strong family. The family members appreciate one another and make each other feel good about themselves. Each of us likes to be with people who make us feel good. Yet many families fall into interactional patterns in which they make each other feel bad. In strong families members are able to find good qualities in one another and to express appreciation for them.

3. *Good communication patterns*: Strong families have good communication patterns. They spend time talking with each other. Family therapist Virginia Satir has stated that often families are so fragmented and busy and spend so little time together that they communicate with each other only through rumor. By this she means that the families often communicate indirectly by hearsay, assumption, guesswork, and innuendo rather than directly by using good communication techniques (see Chapter 6).

Another important aspect of communication is that these families listen well. By being good listeners, they are saying to one another, "You respect me enough to listen to what I have to say. I'm interested enough to listen too."

Another factor related to communication is that when these families fight they fight fairly (see Chapter 6, p. 189). They get angry at each other, but they get conflict out in the open and are able to discuss the problem. They share their feelings about alternative ways of dealing with the problem and of selecting a solution that is best for everybody.

4. *Desire to spend time together*: Strong families do a lot of things together. It is not a "false" or "smothering" togetherness. They genuinely enjoy being together. Another important point is that these families structure their lifestyles so that they can spend time together. They make it happen. And this togetherness exists in all areas of their lives—eating meals, recreation, and work—and much of their time together is spent in active interaction rather than in passive activities such as watching television.

5. *A strong value system*: Members of a strong family share a strong value system. Stinnett and DeFrain (1985) found this quality most often expressed as a high degree of religious orientation. This finding agrees with research from the past forty years, which shows a positive relationship between religion, marriage happiness, and successful family relationships. The old saying, "A family that prays together stays together," appears to be based on more than wishful thinking. Of course, strong values can be demonstrated in other areas, such as education and work. Perhaps the underlying factor is not necessarily an overt religious orientation but a strongly held and shared value system.

Family members believe in something and those beliefs are shared by all family members.

6. *Ability to deal with crises and stress in a positive manner:* Strong families have the ability to deal with crises and problems in a positive way. Not that they enjoy crises, but they are able to handle them constructively. They manage, even in the darkest of situations, to look at the situation; see some positive element, no matter how small; and focus on it. For example, in a particular crisis it may be that they rely to a greater extent on each other and the trust they have developed in each other. They are able to unite in dealing with the crisis instead of being fragmented by it. They deal with the problem and support each other.

Families having a high degree of these six characteristics are pleasant to live in because members learn beneficial ways of treating one another. They can count on one another for support and love. Members of strong families feel good about themselves both as individuals and as members of a family unit or team. They have a sense of "we." However, this sense of belonging does not overpower their individuality. Rather the family supports and respects individuality. Perhaps strong families can best be defined as creating homes we enter for comfort, development, and regeneration and from which we go forth renewed and charged with power for positive living (Stinnett, 1985, p. 8). Within the strong healthy family, individuals learn how to be intimate and close with family members. This sets the stage for successful future intimate relationships.

It does not seem unreasonable that family members exhibit such characteristics as we have listed. We usually start our family with mutual appreciation, wanting to spend time together, feeling committed, and trying to communicate well. Yet many families seem to lose these characteristics as time passes. How can a family keep these characteristics? How can families get them back if they start to lose them? The first step is to improve our understanding of the ideal characteristics and how they operate. Let us, therefore, examine each of these six characteristics of the strong family in more detail.

Commitment

Commitment in the strong family is multifaceted. There is first of all *commitment to the family unit itself.* Support is offered to other family members because it is recognized that if one member is in trouble and hurting, all family members will be in trouble and hurting. Commitment is experienced by each family member as trusting that the family can be depended on for support, love, and affirmation. It is also experienced as willingness to support the family if trouble arises. The well-being of all family members is a major goal of the family. In fact, the commitment is so strong that it may be described as "irrational" (Curran, 1983, p. 71). Support is offered for the squeaky concert presented by the third-grader just learning a musical instrument as well as for the college student who is playing at a professional level.

It is not just parents who are committed to offer support; all members of the family offer support to one another. Olson (1983; 1986) suggests that the strong family is "enmeshed," that is, it has a high degree of cohesion and togetherness. Thus another facet of commitment is that commitment is offered to each other as individuals as well as to the family as a whole. An overworked mother may experience this commitment as the children pitching in to help her clean up the house. Perhaps a brother or sister will give up plans in order to help a sibling in need. The general idea that the family is a team of individuals working together to achieve individual as well as team goals is felt by all members of the strong family. To cooperate as a team often is the most efficient way to achieve individual goals as well as group goals.

Another facet of commitment is that the *commitment is long-lasting*. It is this quality that creates family stability (Barnhill, 1979). Family members can count on support today, tomorrow, and next year. "I love you today" is a wonderful thought, but it is not worth much if the people to whom it is said have no idea whether you will love them tomorrow. If they cannot be reasonably sure about your feelings tomorrow or next week, they can only feel insecure and fearful of what tomorrow may bring. There can be no stability of relationship only fear of instability. Commitment that isn't long-lasting really isn't commitment at all because it robs people of their enthusiasm for the future; of their ability to plan for the future; of future stability; and, most important of all, of their own ability to commit to the relationship. If one is robbed of his or her ability to commit, one will be robbed of all possibility of an enduring intimate relationship.

Another facet of commitment for the strong family is that the *commitment to family overrides all other commitments*, even the commitment to work. Stinnett (1985, pp. 27–28) relates the following story told by a member of one of the 3000 strong families he studied:

> I was off on my usual weekly travel. Business took me away from home three or four days a week. I'd left a teenager disappointed because I would miss her dance recital. My wife felt swamped. She'd described herself as a "de facto" single parent. I had a growing sense of alienation from my family; sometimes I missed chunks of their lives. Indignantly, I thought, "Yeah, but they don't mind the money I make. I have work to do. It's important!" Then the flash of insight came. What frontier was I crossing? I wasn't curing cancer or bringing world peace. My company markets drink mixer. Drink mixer! Granted we sell it all over Ohio and are moving into other markets, but how many gallons of mixer for my family? I didn't quit. I enjoy sales and it's a good job. I make good money. I did learn to say "no" to some company demands. And I plan my travel to leave more time at home. Sometimes now I take my wife or a child along. In a few years I'll retire and within a few months I'll be forgotten in the mixer business. I'll still be a husband and a father. Those will go on until I die.

This does not mean to imply that other things can't, at times, take precedence over the family. The key phrase is "at times." As important and necessary as work is to family well-being, a parent married to his or her job will have a difficult time being married to his or her family. Everyone understands something else at times being more important than a given relationship. But if these times become all times, then those in relationships with that person can only begin to feel secondary and question the depth of commitment. To know that your mate or parent always puts other things ahead of you can only erode your self-esteem and confidence.

The fact that commitment to one's family is strong should not be confused with loss of individuality and "belonging to" others. The healthy family is committed to helping family members maintain their individuality. Barnhill (1979) suggests that strong families support **individuation** of their members. *Individuation* refers to independence of thought, feeling, and judgment of individual family members. It includes a firm sense of autonomy, personal responsibility, identity, and boundaries of the self.

In her interviews with family professionals Curran (1983, p. 186) found yet another facet of commitment, healthy families exhibit a sense of shared responsibility. Family members help each other recognize the responsibilities that commitment creates. They may at times help each other shoulder these responsibilities. They will at other times allow a family member to live with the consequences of irresponsibility. Without responsibility, commitment becomes a meaningless state. "If I can't depend on myself, if others can't depend on me, then protestations of commitment aren't helpful."

Note that parents in strong families allow their children the freedom to experience the cost of irresponsibility. It is difficult for good parents to see their child fail or act irresponsibly. Our commitment to the child makes us want to jump right in and help, guide, and protect them from negative consequences. Yet a child is not born a responsible being. Children must learn about the consequences of their actions, and this is often best done by letting them experience those consequences. If we always remove the negative consequences of children's irresponsible actions, they have no way to learn and thus change their behavior.

> *Recently my daughter failed to set the emergency brake on her car properly when she rushed in to fetch something she had forgotten before driving to school. The car rolled down our slightly inclined driveway and knocked down part of the neighbor's fence. The neighbor came to the door very upset and demanded immediate repair of the fence. As the father, I explained that our daughter (eighteen years of age) would have to take the responsibility. The neighbor was sure that my daughter couldn't do a good job and that I should repair the fence for her. I assured the neighbor that she would have to do a job that he approved of and that he should tell her if the job was unsatisfactory. I indicated to my daughter the neighbor's concern and said that if she didn't know how to repair the fence, I'd be glad to help her by sharing my knowledge, but that the actual repair and cost was up to her. She bent a good number of nails and scratched her arms and legs on the shrubbery but with some direction managed to do a decent job rebuilding the fence. I doubt if she will ever again fail to set her emergency brake properly.*

It would have been an easy job for the father to do since he often did and enjoyed repair work around the house, and certainly the father indicated that he felt sorry for his daughter and was tempted to help her directly as he watched her struggle. Yet in this case it was better to allow the child to assume her own responsibility. Naturally, direct help may be offered when children are too young to assume respnsibility for their actions or if a real danger can result from their actions.

In summary, commitment has many sides to it. Basically the members of a strong family experience commitment to the family as trust, support, affirmation, acceptance, belonging, love, and enduring concern about their personal well-being as well as that of the family.

Appreciation

It is astounding to realize that people often treat the ones they claim to love worse than they might treat a stranger. Most of us would excuse ourselves if we bumped into a stranger in a crowded department store. Yet when we bump into our brother at home, we may say, "Why don't you look where you are going? You're so clumsy." In strong families the expression of appreciation permeates the relationship (Stinnett & DeFrain, 1985, p. 44). Stinnett (1986) defines appreciation with the help of a story he calls "Dirt and Diamonds."

> Diamond miners spend their working lives sifting through thousands of tons of dirt looking for a few tiny diamonds. Too often, we do just the opposite in our intimate relationships. We sift through the diamonds searching for dirt. Our strong families are diamond experts.

> Many young people report that they can be "good" and obey all of the family rules for weeks on end, yet when finally there is a breach of conduct, that seems to be all that their parents remember.

> *When I was a teenager and started to date, my parents set 11 P.M. as the time I had to return from a date. For the first six months I dated, I was always home on time. Finally, I got home one Friday evening at midnight and they blew a fuse. It was all I heard about for the next three months. It was as if my six months of getting home on time counted for nothing. One slip had cost me the entire six previous months. It made me wonder why I had even bothered to get home on time during those previous months.*

Somehow many families take each other for granted until something happens to upset the routines. Parents often forget to let their children know how much their good behavior is appreciated. Too often children fail to let their parents know how nice it is to come home to a good meal, a clean house, a regular allowance. Each forgets to find the diamonds. It is amazing how far a little appreciation goes in a family where there is little of it. When discussing appreciation I sometimes suggest to my classes that a simple phone call home to say that you had a wonderful day in school and really appreciated your parents' support could do wonders. Recently one student reported that she had done this after class. When she returned home on the weekend, she found her parents ecstatically happy over the call. They told her that they had never realized that she even recognized their efforts on her behalf much less that she appreciated them. She said that the weekend home turned out to be the best time she had spent with her family in some time.

The ability to appreciate others starts with appreciation of oneself. When we don't feel good about ourselves, it is difficult to feel good about others. And of course we learn to feel good about ourselves by having others appreciate us. Thus strong families seem able to start a circular process of "I appreciate and respect you, you learn to appreciate and respect yourself, which leads you to appreciate and respect me." Many families start what we call a **vicious circle** pattern of behavior instead. "I don't appreciate you, you don't learn enough self-respect to appreciate others." A vicious circle is a pattern of behavior in which one negative behavior provokes a negative reaction, which in turn prompts more negative behavior.

At Delaware's White House Conference on Families, Nelson and Banonis (1981) identified *respect* as another important quality of strong families. Schlesinger (1984) also found that "respect" was ranked high by strong families in his Canadian study. We can't appreciate what we don't respect. Curran (1983, pp. 90–111) suggests that respect is shown in many ways in strong families. First the family respects individual differences. Parents for example don't expect that all their children will be just the same. Nor do they expect their children to be carbon copies of themselves. They respect each other's privacy. The family accords respect to all groups, even those with whom they may not agree. A general attitude of respect permeates the family in that family members also respect those outside the family, the property of others, and the institutions of their society. For example, parents who ridicule the school system as inadequate and failing can hardly expect their children to go happily to school. Do not take this to mean that there can never be criticism. Of course, there can and should be constructive criticism not only of society's institutions but also of the family and its members as long as appreciation is also shown. The key word here is *constructive*, which we will discuss in Chapter 6 on communication.

Respect for privacy deserves an additional word or two. Family teamwork does not necessarily mean that everything about every member of the family is shared. Perhaps a parent has a particular problem that is shared only with the spouse. Perhaps a child does something wrong that does not affect others in the family, so the parent may keep it just between the particular child and him- or herself. In addition, even in large families each family member needs some place and times for privacy. Fathers and mothers employed outside the home rarely have any time to themselves at home. When they are home, there is always someone else there. Parents might take turns allowing each other some private time around the house by taking the rest of the family elsewhere.

We have spoken mainly about giving appreciation but members of strong families realize that the ability to receive appreciation gracefully is also of importance. When we offer a sincere compliment to another person only to have it rejected, we can be made to feel stupid. "My, you look handsome today." "Well, I feel ugly today." Now what do you say? Inability to give or accept compliments stifles the flow of appreciation.

Communication

Stinnett and DeFrain (1985) report on an enlightening research study in which couples were wired with portable microphones and all of their verbal communications recorded. The average couple spent only about seventeen minutes a week in conversation (McGinnis, 1979). As we shall see in the next chapter, one of the real changes in the American family has been the widespread entrance of the wife and mother into the workforce. The dual-worker family (Chapter 9) has now become the norm rather than the exception. When both partners work, two of our six factors are strongly affected, communication and time spent together. Strong families make an effort to communicate and do in fact spend a lot of time conversing, both about trivial aspects of their lives and about deeper, more important issues.

Communication of support, affirmation, appreciation, caring, respect, and interest in other family members is the lifeblood of the successful family system. Almost all couples that come in for counseling or start divorce proceedings or indicate serious problems in their relationship start by describing their inability to communicate. "He never listens to me." "All she does is nag." "I never know what he is feeling." "She expects me to read her mind." "He never talks to me." All of these are common statements made by couples in trouble.

If we examine the other five characteristics of the strong family, it is clear that they cannot exist on a foundation of poor communication. A husband who does not listen to his wife talk about her day, a parent who doesn't listen to a child talk about his or her problems in school is obviously expressing disinterest in the person talking, and disinterest is a sign of lack of respect and appreciation. The wife or husband who doesn't share his or her workday, a child who doesn't share school problems is expressing a lack of trust and therefore a lack of respect and appreciation for other family members. Parents who do not attend to the day-today activities of their children can hardly expect their children to come to them with major problems such as drugs or sex. "Why didn't you come to me with this before it became a problem?" is a frequent parental comment to a child. Yet if the parent turns a deaf ear to day-to-day trivia, such as how the child did in tennis class or on the history exam, it is clear to the child that they probably won't listen to problems either.

Poor communication within a family is often manifested in a number of ways. First the family members suffer from a constant feeling of frustration, of not being understood, of not getting their message across. This usually leads to a preoccupation with escape, a need to go out, to be constantly on the phone, to have the television set turned on all the time, to keep one's headphones in place throughout family time together. Poor communication leads to the often-quoted parent-child interaction: "Where are you going?" "Out." "What are you going to do?" "Nothing."

Poor communication often leads to sharp words, quarrels, misunderstandings. The poorly communicating family tends to bicker and conflict a great deal. Sometimes this becomes so unpleasant that family members simply cease to talk, and silence becomes the norm. Some people confuse silence with lack of communication. However, silence may be one of the most devastating forms of communication. Think back on the last time someone gave you the silent treatment and how you reacted to it to understand just how strong a communication silence can be.

Chapter 6 discusses communication in detail so we won't go further with it at this time. We will next address the strong family characteristic of spending time together, because without spending time together there can be no communication. In fact, having enough time together profoundly affects all the characteristics.

Desire to Spend Time Together

Stinnett (1985) and his colleagues do an exercise with their subject families that they call "The Journey of Happy Memories." They ask their subjects to close their eyes and spend five minutes wandering through childhood memories and then to tell the happiest ones. I tried this with my classes and found as did Stinnett that the memories recalled almost always had to do with things that the students had done with their families.

My favorite memory is climbing the big rocks that were in the campground where my grandfather would take me and my cousins camping for two weeks each summer.

It's hard to believe, but I'll never forget my grandmother coming into the bathroom to scrub me whenever I was in the tub. I'm sure she'd be doing it to this day if she was still alive.

The family would go to the sand dunes by the beach and dad would always be disappearing, making us play hide and seek with him. We'd be walking along and suddenly he wouldn't be there and we'd run off to find him. We'd try to keep an eye on him but he was very good at disappearing.

At Christmas time, dad and mom would always get out the old 8mm family movies and although we'd all say, "Oh, not the movies again," we always loved to see mom and dad as little kids and especially ourselves growing up.

What Do You Think?

1. What is your favorite childhood memory?
2. What do you think your siblings' favorite memories would be?
3. Are they the same or different from yours? Why do you suppose this is so?
4. What do you suppose your parent's favorite memories are?
5. If you have children what do you suppose your children's favorite memories are?

It is clear that family time together is of great value at least in retrospect to most people. Yet family time together is becoming increasingly difficult to find. Perhaps the major revolution in family structure in recent years has been the advent of the dual-earner family (see Chapter 9), the family in which both father and mother are employed outside the home. It is obvious that in such a home family time together will be at a premium. Indeed Curran (1983, p. 135) goes so far as to state, "Lack of time might be the most pervasive enemy the healthy family has."

As family time has become more scarce, many have argued that it is not the quantity but the quality of time together that counts. There is certainly truth in the argument. I may be with my partner or my child physically but does that do much good if I am not there mentally? The stereotypical picture of the husband at breakfast hidden behind the newspaper and the wife trying desperately to get his attention comes immediately to mind. On the other hand, the argument often seems to ignore the fact that quality and quantity of time together are interrelated. There must be enough time for quality to surface. It seems, too, that the argument is sometimes used to soothe the guilty conscience of a spouse or parent who is spending very little time with the family.

When we examine the daily pattern of many dual-earner families, it is clear that there is often too little time available for it to be quality time.

Jane and Murray have two children, aged five and seven. Jane remained home with the children until the second child started preschool at age two and has worked since that time. Their first child leaves for school at 8 A.M. and Jane drops the second child off at preschool in time to get to work at 9 A.M. Murray leaves about 7:45 to commute to his 9 A.M. job. Jane arises about 6:30 A.M. to get everyone organized. The hour and fifteen minutes that they are all together in the morning passes quickly and with little communication since everyone is preoccupied with getting ready for his or her day. The oldest child is watched over by a neighbor in the afternoon after school is out, and the second child is picked up by Jane about 5:15 P.M. Murray arrives home about 6 P.M. After a long day, the family members are tired, yet they must face preparing the evening meal as well as other family chores. The youngest child is in bed by 8 P.M. and the oldest child follows around 9 P.M. Thus the whole family is together for a maximum of two to three hours at the end of the day and it is clear that there is little quality time to communicate when household chores must be done and everyone is already fatigued from a long day. It is only after 9 P.M. that Murray and Jane may have time for themselves. It is little wonder that the family feels that time is their most sought after commodity.

Whether there can be quality family time with such a daily routine is open to serious question.

The above description fails to take into account the many other kinds of activities that may drain a family's time together. Most families spend time on such things as Little League baseball, PTA meetings, children's music lessons, church socials, and money-raising events such as school newspaper collections. Certainly for some families, the children's school years make great time demands on the parents.

Curran (1983, p. 143) points out that a family needs time to play together. Periodically, the family needs to get away from work and responsibility and simply play and enjoy life. The couple needs to do this alone and away from the children as well as with the children. Also the family must be careful not to "work" at playing. Some families plan and organize their play time to such a degree that it turns into work rather than play. Curran suggests that the hallmark of the strong family seems to be its absence of guilt at times of play. Further, they schedule play into their calendar rather than hoping for free time to occur magically. They do not hide behind, "Someday we will . . ."; "When we get time . . ."; or "When we have the money. . . ." They deliberately make the time to play.

Strong families seem to have the ability to work, play, and vacation together without smothering one another. During the 1950s there was a great deal of criticism of the idea of togetherness in a marriage. Too much togetherness between partners meant individuality was lost. Yet today the opposite problem is more prevalent. There seems to be too little marital togetherness to maintain family

strength. The emphasis on individuality too often overrides commitment to the family as a team. Thus the idea of a family spending time together is one in which there is a balance of time spent between the needs of the family and the needs of individual members of the family.

Also time spent together does not necessarily mean that the time is spent with all members of the family at once. Perhaps mom and dad spend some time playing, then dad takes his son or daughter on an outing, then sister and brother take a short vacation together, and so forth.

Spending time together also allows a family to develop an identity, a group unity, and a sense of family history. This feeling of belonging helps family members find an identity. The need for adolescents to turn to their peer group for support and identity is reduced if they have a strong sense of family.

Although strong families spend time together doing many different kinds of activities, almost all strong families indicate that at least one meal a day is reserved as a time of family togetherness. It is usually the evening meal and everyone in the family living at home is expected to attend on a regular basis.

Perhaps the importance of spending enough quality time together is best summed up by a recent student comment:

> My brother and two sisters are my best friends and my mom and dad are not only my mom and dad but my pals as well. I always look forward to doing things with the family because we have so much fun together. We have fun but I also know that if I need help they will all pitch in and give me the help I need.

Both Stinnett and Curran found that strong families had a strong sense of values, often manifested in religious behavior. Stinnett now calls this characteristic *spiritual wellness.* He defines it as a unifying force, a caring center within each person that

A Strong Value System

Inset 1-1
"Shhh, I'm Watching TV"

Television is a powerful force in the lives of most American families. Many families report that they spend time together, but further questioning reveals that much of that time is spent silently watching television. Although a television program might foster discussion and debate among family members, this is not often the case. In fact, many families now have multiple television sets so that watching television may be done alone by each family member separately.

Curran (1983, p. 40) lists family control over television as her second major point in discussing successful family communication patterns. The term *television widow* is no joke to many families. A woman remarked on a talk show, "I can't get worried about whether there's life after death. I'd be satisfied with life after dinner in our home."

It is interesting to note that many families place the TV in the "family room." R. G. Goldberg suggests that this is a misnomer since talking and communicating among family members is usually discouraged when the TV is being watched. The family room containing a TV set might more aptly be named the "antifamily room."

Many families simply have the TV on whenever anyone is in the house. It is like background noise. The only problem is that because it activates two senses, hearing and sight, it is far more difficult to avoid attending to it than to noise alone. I'm sure we've all had the experience of visiting someone who leaves the television on during our visit. Communication is next to impossible even though one tries to converse. Eyes keep wandering to the television. In a sense, leaving the television on when someone comes in to converse is the not-so-subtle message, "Television is more important than your communication."

A. C. Nielsen Company estimates that the average American television set is on approximately forty-four hours per week. With scarcity of time being one of the American family's major problems, it is clear that television often usurps what little togetherness time a family may have.

---

promotes sharing, love, and compassion for others. It is a force that helps a person transcend self and become part of something larger (Stinnett & DeFrain, 1985, p. 102).

Research has long demonstrated a relationship between family stability and religious orientation. For example, Glenn and Supancie (1984) found a strong negative correlation between attendance at religious services and divorce. Among white males the adjusted marital dissolution rate is three times greater for those who said they never attend than for those who said they attend church at least two or three times a month.

Curran (1983) finds that a strong value system shows up in three of her fifteen strong family traits. She finds that the strong family teaches a sense of right and wrong, has a shared spiritual core, and values service to others. She also found that members of many strong families do not talk directly about their values but simply behave in ways that reflect those values. For example, if the work ethic is a major family value, the individual family members all tend to work hard. If religious values are central to a family, family members tend to be active in church-related functions.

Family members state that they couldn't live with someone who didn't believe in some value that they honor. It does not mean that all family members share all the same values or that the values can't be influenced by experience and learning or shown in different behaviors. For example, the family's value system might include the idea that growth and change are important life goals. In this case, deliberate change in some values might be sought as a way for the family and its members to grow.

Shared values seem to give a family purpose and direction. Sharing values makes one feel supported, which leads to increased freedom and reduced conflict. If I know that my spouse shares my value of loyalty, I am comfortable when my spouse interacts with strangers knowing that there is no need for jealousy. Shared values help family members predict how the other members will act. The values add stability and predictability to family interactions both within and outside the family.

Sharing the same basic values doesn't necessarily mean that behaviors will be the same.

Susan and Scott both value helping others. Susan volunteers two nights a month at the homeless shelter. She feels it is important to people who are down and out to know that someone cares about them. Scott feels that giving something such as shelter to a person for free is doing them a disservice by taking their self-respect. He feels it is better to help people get a job so they can assume responsibility for their own shelter. Scott makes an effort to support job-training programs for the chronically un-employed by volunteering time to teach.

What Do You Think?

1. What communication behaviors did your parents model for you?
2. In light of our discussion, did these behaviors help you learn to communicate effectively?
3. What major value did your parents model?
4. Has this value become important to you?
5. How do your parents show affection to one another?
6. Do you show affection in the same way?

A sense of right and wrong seems best taught to children by parents who share a consensus of important values. Although Curran (1983, p. 214) points out that one of the most destructive forces in a marriage is that of significant different value systems held by the two partners, she goes on to point out that healthy couples who disagree seem to do so in such a way that their children know that people can disagree on some values and still care for and respect one another. Sharing a value system does not mean that each family member is a carbon copy of every other member.

However, strong families do have clear and specific guidelines about correct behavior and try to help their children live up to these guidelines. One way by which strong families do this is to hold their children responsible for their behavior. This was demonstrated in the example given earlier in which the daughter repaired the fence damaged by her car. The family also points out the importance of intent as part of correct behavior. When one accidentally or unknowingly does something that the family considers wrong, the error is treated differently from an action involving deliberate intent.

Curran mentioned finding that strong families seem to extend their values to others outside the immediate family. The families seem to be empathetic with the problems of others. Family members may volunteer to help with social problems outside the family as Susan and Scott do in the example above. After finishing her training on a closed mental health ward one nursing student enlisted family members and friends to help her make small Christmas packages of sweets for all those patients confined to the ward over the Christmas holidays. In general strong families can extend themselves into the society and to others because they are safe and secure in their beliefs (whatever they might be).

Ability to Deal with Crises and Stress in a Positive Manner

Strong successful families have problems just like any other family. Where they seem to differ from weak unsuccessful families is in their ability to deal with the problems and crises that come their way. They deal with them from a position of strength and solidarity. They can unite and deal with problems as a team if necessary. They are able to pull together. They do not squander energy on intrafamily differences and conflicts but focus on the problem at hand. Each family member's attitude seems to be, "What can I do to help?" By planning and working together strong families often head off crises, so life runs smoothly and is generally free of emergencies.

Strong families also seem to remain flexible, and their adaptability helps them weather the storms of life (Stinnett & DeFrain, 1985, p. 135). They bend, change, and adapt; when the storm is over they're still intact. A crisis is a turning point for such a family rather than a disaster. Because the family is strong it not only works to solve the crisis but also learns and builds further strengths from having dealt with the situation successfully.

It is clear from perusing this data on strong families that such families have a pool of resources on which to draw when times become difficult. In contrast unhealthy families are worn out and depleted on a daily basis by the stress of poor relationships. When a crisis comes along, the unhealthy family must add it to the burden they already carry. It is no wonder that a crisis sometimes destroys the already unhealthy family (Lewis, 1979).

Curran (1983, p. 292) finds that the strong family expects problems and considers them a normal part of family life. They seem to have the ability to find the positive even in the most negative of situations and do not expect the family to be perfect. Unlike families of yesteryear, today's strong families do not often write off problems or family members as lost causes.

> How did our ancestors cope with the problems we know they had? They coped in a way modern parents can't and don't want to use. They wrote off the people owning the problem as different. They used the term *black sheep* and this flock of sheep came in many forms. The spouse who was unfaithful or alcoholic was labeled "ne'er-do-well" by the community, thus sparing the family both responsibility and shame for his/ her behavior. The depressed woman was "going through her time" or "in the change" and her family was thus alleviated from blaming itself for her problem. The teenage boy who wanted a slice of life bigger than his local community had to offer had "itchy feet," and if he decided to go off for a year or two to find himself, his parents weren't castigated for pushing him out. Always he was the problem not they. Old people got "ornery," children who were heard as well as seen were dismissed as "young upstarts," and women that wanted more out of marriage than cooking and children were considered suspect. A child with an emotional or learning problem was "not quite right," and those who questioned approved mores and customs were "just plain crazy." In sum, the problems of the family of the past were attributed solely to the individual, never to the family (Curran, 1983, p. 293).

Thus the family of the past only seemed perfect because family problems were blamed on individuals rather than the family. There are, of course, individual problems but strong families tend to see the problems of their individual members as family problems too.

Because strong families recognize that problems are a normal part of life, they tend to develop problem-solving skills. They also recognize when they may need extra outside help and are able to seek such help (Chapter 17).

Inset 1-2

Strong Families and Healthy Individuals

What Keeps a Marriage Going?

Here are the top reasons respondents gave, listed in order of frequency.

Men	Women
My spouse is my best friend.	My spouse is my best friend.
I like my spouse as a person.	I like my spouse as a person.
Marriage is a long-term commitment.	Marriage is a long-term commitment.
Marriage is sacred.	Marriage is sacred.
We agree on aims and goals.	We agree on aims and goals.
My spouse has grown more interesting.	My spouse has grown more interesting.
I want the relationship to succeed.	I want the relationship to succeed.
An enduring marriage is important to social stability.	We laugh together.
We laugh together.	We agree on a philosophy of life.
I am proud of my spouse's achievements.	We agree on how and how often to show affection.
We agree on a philosophy of life.	An enduring marriage is important to social stability.
We agree about our sex life.	We have a stimulating exchange of ideas.
We agree on how and how often to show affection.	We discuss things calmly.
I confide in my spouse.	We agree about our sex life.
We share outside hobbies and interests.	I am proud of my spouse's achievements.

Lauer & Lauer, 1985.

Although we have focused our discussion on dealing with major family problems, it is clear that small day-to-day frustrations often cause as much trouble in a family as major crises. No spouse will complain if her or his partner occasionally leaves a little toothpaste on the sink. However, if there is toothpaste to clean up every time the partner brushes, tolerance will soon turn to anger. Successful families work out ways to cope with the minor irritations before they grow into major confrontations. Naturally part of the solution is the respect and appreciation that each family member has for the others in the family.

Summary

It is clear from our discussion of these six characteristics of the strong family that few families can live up to these ideals all of the time. Indeed these six characteristics can be thought of as traits of the mentally healthy individual as well as of the healthy family (see Chapter 5). Just as an individual must work to achieve mental health and become fully functioning, so family members must work to move their relationships toward the ideals.

Strong families have problems. Strong families sometimes break up. Strong families are the first to tell you that they are not perfect families. No child has ever had a perfect parent; no parent has ever had a perfect child. Yet strong families tend to make the most of their relationships. They seem to cope with living in productive ways. Such families tend to turn out children who become successful (defined in any terms the reader desires) and healthy adults.

Thus to understand what the characteristics of the strong family are gives each of us a goal at which to aim. We have the ability to change and move our imperfect family relationships in a positive direction. As long as our relationships are growing in positive directions there is hope that intimate relationships of all kinds will be successful.

The remainder of the book examines many aspects of intimate relationships and supplies information that the author hopes will help move the reader in directions that will result in fulfilling and successful intimate relationships both within and outside the family.

Why More People Are Making Better Marriages

Americans are happier in marriage than their parents were. Despite gloomy predictions regarding the institution of marriage, that's the surprising fact that emerges from *Parade*'s new survey on marriage in the eighties.

An impressive 70 percent of the husbands and wives in our survey tell us that they are "happily married," while only 51 percent would say the same about their parents.

Most of the 799 people who filled out the survey are married for the first time, have two children and live in major cities or their suburbs. Their median age is thirty-six, meaning that half are younger than that and half are older. They are better educated than the average American (more than 70 percent have been to college) and more affluent (with an average family income of $30,000 a year).

The Importance of Laughter

Marriage is a serious affair, the experts tell us. But the husbands and wives in this survey insist that it also ought to be fun. Three out of four people say that their number one reason for choosing their mate is "our ability to laugh and have fun together." Significantly, these people have happier and more sexually satisfying marriages than other couples. Fifty-five percent of those surveyed consider "a sense of humor very important" to marital happiness. They rate it ahead of "sex," which only 32 percent call "very important."

New Reasons for Getting Married

Along with shared laughter, people say they decided to marry because of

"strong sexual/physical attraction" (63 percent), "our ability to share thoughts and feelings" (59 percent), "the many things we had in common" (51 percent), and "desire for emotional security" (46 percent).

"Those reasons add up to a good definition of love," says Donald Riley, director of clinical services at the Family Service Association of Greater Bos-

ton. "They show a healthier orientation toward marriage than we might have expected."

The reasons for marriage have changed with the generations. Only one in three people says that "a desire to have children" was a factor, and those who say it are more likely to have been married at least a decade. "Financial security," once an important consideration for women, hardly is mentioned. A simple "desire to be married" was a factor for 54 percent of the longtime marrieds but only 41 percent of those recently married.

How Marriage Is Changing

The new ideas of the sixties and seventies—the sexual revolution, the women's movement, the two-paycheck family—are changing marriage in the eighties. Fifty-nine percent of those surveyed say that "the new ideas about men's and women's roles" have had a positive or very positive effect on their relationship. They are less certain about the sexual revolution. Forty-one percent see it as a positive influence; 21 percent see it as a negative influence; and the rest aren't sure how it applies to them.

The Impact of Children

Marriage counselors often warn that the birth of a child, especially the first one, can turn a marriage upside down. But 60 percent of the people we surveyed say that the birth of their first child had a positive or very positive effect on their marriage. As children grow, they continue to be a happy influence in most marriages, bringing the most marital joy as toddlers and the rockiest times as teenagers.

What Pushes People Apart

At one time or another, two-thirds of these husbands and wives have thought seriously about divorce or separation. Of this group, 21 percent did separate for a time and 15 percent are still considering it.

When people are at the brink of divorce, there seem to be three major causes. About 70 percent of those surveyed blamed "lack of communication," "feeling that the marriage isn't as happy or fulfilling as it should be," and "frequent arguments." Counselors like Suzanne Garb of Family and Mental Health Services in Chicago worry about that second cause. "Many people still have unrealistic expectations of marriage," she says. "They expect a spouse to fill needs that no one can fill for them."

Sexual fidelity is "important" or "very important" to 91 percent of these husbands and wives, yet infidelity is no longer a major reason to end a marriage. Only 13 percent say a partner's infidelity was grounds for thinking about divorce, while 12 percent considered divorce after their own infidelity.

What Keeps Them Together

Commitment and hope are the glues that keep a rocky marriage together. "The good in our marriage outweighed the bad," say 52 percent. "I keep hoping the marriage will get better," says 51 percent. For 42 percent of those who waited out the marital storm, it did get better.

Forty-three percent say they stayed together "for the sake of the children." People over forty and the longtime marrieds—the ones who are more likely to have married in order to have children—also are most likely to stay together for the children's sake. A minority of husbands and wives stay in a faltering marriage out of fear. Thirty-six percent say they're afraid of being alone or starting over; 28 percent worry that the family income can't support two separate households.

For almost everyone in our survey, it's "important" or "very important" to "keep romance and excitement alive." With time, some of that excitement fades, and both sexes—though it's somewhat truer for women than men—say that they miss the thrill of the early days.

The men in our survey put a bit more importance on sex than do the women. The women place a great deal more importance on "sexual fidelity." Judging by the results of other polls, those surveyed are more faithful than average. Only 21 percent of the women and 28 percent of the men say they have had extramarital sex. Only 19 percent of the women and 12 percent of the men think that their spouses may have strayed.

One secret to sexual happiness does emerge from this survey. Among the very satisfied sexually, 50 percent say they share equally in the responsibility for initiating sex. This happens with a scant 6 percent of those who are very dissatisfied sexually.

Men versus Women

Equality is the new wave in marriage, but men tend to think there's more of it than do women. In those marriages where household tasks *are* shared, more husbands than wives—by a two-to-one margin—believe they're doing it fifty-fifty. The wives agree that the men are sharing, "but not equally."

The gender gap in marriage is a perception gap, a difference in the way men and women look at what's happening. On marital issues such as how to spend money, how often to see the in-laws, how to spend leisure time, men consistently see more agreement than women do. "It could be that the wife isn't speaking up, so he doesn't *know* that she disagrees," says counselor Suzanne Garb. "Or it could be that the husband isn't paying enough attention to what the wife is signaling or even saying out loud."

Husbands and wives also disagree on how much talking together they're doing, according to our survey. Men think there's more communication than women do. Women, on the other hand, are the ones who want that communication and who are more likely to say it's "very important" to their marital happiness.

Profile of a Happy Marriage

For a happy marriage, it helps to have the right role model. Our survey shows that those who grow up with parents who are happily married are more likely to be happily married themselves. More than other people, contented husbands and wives tend to marry people like themselves, with similar backgrounds, and to have many mutual interests. They're also more likely to make the time to "do things as a couple," yet they tend to give each other more "time and space to be separate individuals" and to appreciate that apartness.

Communication, according to our survey, is the key to marital happiness. Most couples, happy or not, say they are quick to share good news with each other. The happily married, however, also share the bad news, turning to each other when they feel sad or depressed.

Not surprisingly, happy couples argue less than unhappy ones. That's especially true of disagreements over money, the number one cause of marital arguments in our survey.

When they do disagree, happily married people know how to fight fair. An overwhelming majority—four out of five—of people whose marriages either changed for the better last year or stayed the same tell us that they can usually arrive at a compromise when they disagree with their partners. Scarcely any of those whose marriages changed for the worse last year can do that.

Happily Ever After

These husbands and wives tell us that a marriage works only when you work at it. The great majority of them have been to the edge of divorce—and drawn back. Part of what kept the couples together is an understanding that marriage has its ups and downs. As almost all of them—98 percent—agree, "A marriage is a process, constantly changing."

Source: Safran, 1985.

Chapter 2

The Family and Its Meaning

Contents

Intimate relationships: what an exciting and essential field of study. Communicating and caring. Boyfriend/girlfriend. Husband/wife. Parent/child. Grandmother/grandfather. Family and friends. The relationships that give meaning to life. The relationships that give us a sense of identity, of well-being, of security, of being needed. The relationships that ward off loneliness and insecurity. The relationships that allow us to love and be loved. Without intimacy where would the human be? Perhaps the *human* part of "human being" would disappear and we'd all simply "be"—automatons similar to our home computers, able to solve problems and deliver information, but lacking in those markedly human qualities of loving, caring, and compassion. In a word, characteristics that allow human beings to become intimate.

In the first chapter we tried to set ideals at which we could aim as we establish our own intimate relationships, our marriage, our families. We tried to see what an ideal intimate relationship could be. In this chapter we will describe what American families are like in reality.

Can we study "intimacy"? (See p. 42 for a definition.) Yes, we can if we study relationships that can be and often are intimate. Within marriage and the family is where we most often find intimacy. It is true that intimacy can exist between any two people, but it is within the family that most of us learn to be intimate, caring, loving people. Thus to study the family is also to study intimacy, and it is the family and the relationships within it that will be the central focus of this book.

The study of the family deals with many topics, as the table of contents of this book reveals. It is clear that such a study cuts across many disciplines: psychology, sociology, anthropology, home economics, and so on (see Figure 2-1). To identify the study of marriage and family more clearly, we will use the term *family science* (NCFR Report, 1985).

Because each of us is born into a family (the family of orientation) and over 90 percent (U.S. Bureau of the Census, 1985, p. 1) of us marry and establish a family at some time in our lives, we usually have strong feelings about marriage, families, love, and intimacy. Such feelings are natural. Yet we must examine our feelings about such an intimate relationship as our family in order to understand just how our own personalities have been influenced by our upbringing. Thus to study family science is also to study one's own feelings about the institutions of marriage and family. A piece of data may appear simple and clear (one in two American marriages will break up), yet its meaning will vary with individuals according to their family experiences. This is why there seems to be so little agreement about how marriages and families are changing and what the changes mean.

Some Americans feel that today's families are in deep trouble because they are different from their family of orientation. Others feel the broader variety of acceptable relationships now available to Americans allows people to create families that are best for themselves. This, in turn, will improve the quality of family life. Some people see the high divorce rate as sounding the death knell of marriage. Others see it as normal behavior in a society that emphasizes personal happiness. One must no longer endure an unhappy marriage but is free to find happiness through divorce. Regardless of what you may feel about the changes taking place in American marriages and families, it is clear that all individuals interpret the data in a personal manner based in part on their own family experiences.

Figure 2-1   Family science involves the study of many disciplines.

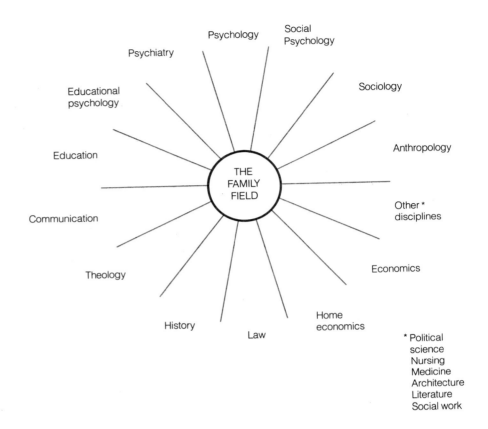

Lest one take this to mean that there are *only* personal opinions about family institutions, let me hasten to add that there is, indeed, a broad and rich foundation of scientific information about this most personal and intimate of relationships. People who know the scientific facts as well as their personal feelings about marriage and family are in a better position to understand themselves and build successful and satisfying intimate relationships. It is toward this end that this book has been written.

The Basic Assumptions

As we mentioned, all people hold certain beliefs about marriage and the family, and this includes authors. Because these beliefs color an author's writing, it is important to recognize and make clear just what they are. Let me state clearly the major assumptions on which this book is based; the remainder of this chapter will be organized around them. The discussion of each assumption in this chapter is of necessity short and cursory. Therefore when appropriate, I have listed the chapter or chapters within the text where additional information can be found.

Each assumption is supported by some facts that also introduce many of the basic statistics about American families. Remember, an assumption is a belief that may or may not be well supported by the facts. Although I believe that the various assumptions are supported with some facts, acceptance is left to the reader's discretion.

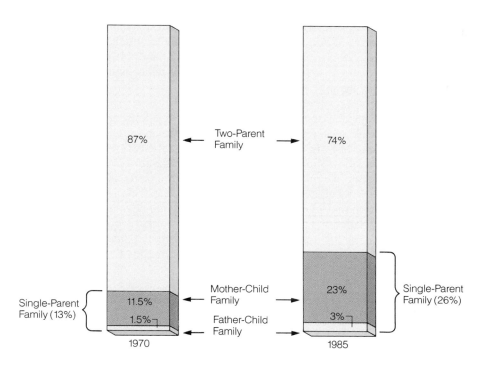

Figure 2-2 Families with children (Source: Norton and Glick, 1986.)

The American Family: Many Structures and Much Change

Assumption 1:   A free and creative society offers many structural forms by which family functions, such as childrearing, can be fulfilled (Chapters 5, 8, and 16).

Mom and Dad, Sissy and Junior, a dog, and maybe a cat represent the stereotypical American **nuclear family**. Yet to talk of the American family perpetuates the myth that one family structure represents the American family. If we examine the structure of the family, we find that there are, in fact, many kinds of American families. (By structure we mean the parts of which a family is composed and their relationships to one another. The nuclear family has a mother, a father, and their children. On the other hand, a single-parent, mother-headed family has just a mother and her children.)

For example, the single-parent family has been one of the fastest-growing family structures during the past decade (see Figure 2-2). In 1985 single-parent families accounted for 26 percent of the 33.3 million families with children, in contrast to 1970 when they accounted for only 13 percent. During this period the number of families that included children under eighteen years of age increased by 3.6 million. During the same period, however, the number of two-parent families declined by 1.2 million, while the number of one-parent families increased by 4.8 million (U.S. Bureau of the Census, September, 1986, 9).

It is true that single-parent families tend to be temporary, but the fact is that this family structure accounts for a significant number of American families. The large increase can be accounted for by the greatly increased divorce rate in America. To a lesser extent the greater social acceptance of the unwed mother who keeps her child has also contributed to the increasing number of single-parent families.

Nuclear family

A married couple and their children living by themselves

Reconstituted family

A husband and wife, at least one of whom has been married before, and one or more children from previous marriage(s)

Divorce is a good example of changing family structure within a single family. The family begins as a nuclear family, becomes a single-parent family, and then, in most cases, becomes a **reconstituted family** when the single parent remarries. These kinds of changes signal the end of the initial relationship, at least as an intimate love relationship.

However, even a relationship that remains intimate changes structure over time. Such a relationship usually begins as a couple relationship and then broadens to include children, sons- and daughters-in-law, and finally grandchildren. When the children leave home, the couple returns to a two-person household. Table 2-1 indicates how many structural forms families take in various cultures.

The 1970s were a period when Americans experimented widely with different family structures. In fact, a popular cliché was that marriage as we had known it was dead. Communal living, multiple sex partners, cohabitation, childlessness, and other family experiments blossomed and were quickly reported and dramatized in the mass media. Some experiments, such as cohabitation, have become for some Americans a relatively permanent family structure. Other experiments, such as "swinging," have lost much of their appeal.

The criticism of the family was thought by many Americans to be new. Yet throughout the twentieth century there have been continued criticisms of marriage and the family. Suggestions for "new" family forms have always been made by critics of the status quo. For example, in 1936 Bertrand Russell saw marriage collapsing as a social institution unless drastic changes were made:

> In the meantime, if marriage and paternity are to survive as social institutions, some compromise is necessary between complete promiscuity and lifelong monogamy. Although it is difficult to decide the best compromise at a given time, certain points seem clear:
>
> Young unmarried people should have considerable freedom as long as children are avoided so that they may better distinguish between mere physical attraction and the sort of congeniality that is necessary to make marriage a success.
>
> Divorce should be possible without blame to either party and should not be regarded as in any way disgraceful.
>
> Everything possible should be done to free sexual relations from economic taint. At present, wives, just as much as prostitutes, live by the sale of their sexual charms: and even in temporary free relations the man is usually expected to bear all the joint expenses. The result is that there is a sordid entanglement of money with sex, and that a woman's motives not infrequently have a mercenary element. A woman, like a man, should have to work for a living, and an idle wife is no more intrinsically worthy of respect than a gigolo. (Reprinted in 1957, pp. 171–172)

Perhaps the major contribution of the turmoil of the 1960s and 1970s for the family was the increase in available alternatives for intimacy. If a couple decides not to have children, that is all right; divorce doesn't mean the end of the world; a cohabitation experience does not make one unmarriable.

Modern America is remarkably tolerant of multiple forms of intimate relationships. Other cultures have had different marital systems, but they have usually disallowed deviance from the current system. A free and creative society, however, offers many structural forms of the family by which its functions, such as childrearing and meeting sexual needs, may be fulfilled. The reasons for America's permissiveness are partly philosophic but mainly economic. Marriage forms were historically limited because women were economically tied to the men who supported them and the family. Industrialization and affluence made it more

---
Table 2-1
Different Family Structures

Kind	Composition	Functions
Types of Marriage		
Monogamy	One spouse and children.	Procreative, affectional, economic consumption.
Serial monogamy	One spouse at a time but several different spouses over time. Married, divorced, remarried.	Same.
Common-law	One spouse. Live together as husband and wife for long enough period that state recognizes couple as married without formal or legal marriage ceremony. Recognized by only a few states.	Same.
Polygamy	Multiple spouses.	Same.
Polygyny	One husband, multiple wives.	Any, power vested in male.
Polyandry	One wife, multiple husbands.	Any, power vested in female.
Group	Two or more men collectively married to two or more women at the same time.	Any, very rare.
Types of Families		
Nuclear family	Husband, wife, children.	Procreative, affectional, economic consumption.
Extended family	One or more nuclear families plus other family positions such as grandparents, uncles, etc.	Historically might serve all social, educational, economic, reproductive, affectional, and religious functions.
Composite family	Two or more nuclear families sharing a common spouse.	Normally those of the nuclear family.
Tribal family	Many families living together as a larger clan or tribe.	Usually those of the extended family.
Consensual family (cohabitation)	Man, woman, and children living together in legally un-recognized relationship.	Any.
Commune	Group of people living together sharing a common purpose with assigned roles and responsibilities normally associated with the nuclear family.	Can provide all functions with leadership vested in an individual, council, or some other organized form to which all families are beholden.
Single-parent family	Usually a mother and child. Father/child combination less common.	Same as monogamy without a legally recognized reproductive function.
Concubine	Extra female sexual partner recognized as a member of the household but without full status.	Usually limited to sex and reproduction.
Reconstituted (blended)	Husband and wife, at least one of whom has been previously married, plus one or more children from previous marriage or marriages.	Any.
Authority Patterns		
Paternalistic	Any power vested in male.	Any.
Maternalistic	Any power vested in female.	Any.
Egalitarian	Powers divided in some fair manner between spouses.	Any.

---

possible to consider alternate lifestyles and marital forms. For example, affluence allows people to further their education and thus exposes them to new ideas and knowledge. Affluence also brings mobility and mobility brings contact with new people and new lifestyles. If a person discovers greater personal satisfaction in some alternate lifestyle, affluence makes it possible to seek out others who have the same interests. Affluence often enables people to postpone assuming adult responsibility (earning one's own living), thus increasing experimentation and lessening the consequences of failure. Affluence has also given rise to the mass media, which have spread the news about various lifestyles and experimental relationships and helped create new lifestyles by portraying them as desirable, exciting, or "in."

In part then because of America's affluence, the young have a broader choice of acceptable relationships (family structures) than their grandparents did. Perhaps by choosing wisely the roles that best fit them as individuals, couples will be able to create growing intimate relationships that are more fulfilling than those of the past. On the other hand freer choice involves greater risks.

In the past, we knew more clearly what our roles would be. Sons often followed in their father's footsteps. Women became wives and mothers and ran the home. But today the pattern has changed. Individuals now must make their own choices about their lifestyles, vocations, marriages, and families. If one doesn't consciously make such choices, the choices are made by default. The idea that love will automatically make such decisions for us is the source of much disappointment. One goal of this book is to help the reader make conscious, knowledgeable decisions about intimate relationships rather than leaving them to chance.

The major risk in opening up choice is error in choice. When choices open up, one must carefully consider priorities. The older restricted system exacted a price; it often placed a person in a mold which did not enable him [her] to choose a lifestyle that would allow maximum self-growth and social contribution. In a more open system, people run the risk of acting impulsively. . . . Thus, the price of a more open system is the greater need for a rational examination of the alternatives.

The old system had many people trapped in a rut; the new one may have many people constantly running from one style of life to another, unable to choose wisely (Reiss, 1972, p. 246).

It may be that freedom will encourage people to run from one lifestyle to another as Ira Reiss suggests. On the other hand, it may also encourage experimentation that leads to better decisions. Free inquiry leading to reasoned decisions with opportunities to test one's decisions is the way of science. There is no reason why this method should not improve the intimate life of people just as it has improved their material life. Moreover, free choice of a lifestyle can counteract feelings of entrapment that are often expressed by long-married couples.

Certainly then, one characteristic of today's American society is that people are offered more structural alternatives by which to build their intimate relationships and families. Thus the ability to know and understand the alternatives and to choose well has become increasingly important to living a successful life and building a strong family.

Change within Continuity and Uniqueness within Commonality

Assumption 2:   There is continuity to the changes that take place in families.

Assumption 3:   Each family is unique but also has characteristics in common with all other families in a given culture.

As you try to understand the family and what is happening to it, remember that the American family covers a vast territory and is far from uniform in design. Everyone is conscious of how family life has changed, and yet the central core of family life continues much the same as it has for many generations. Grasping the two ideas—*change within continuity* and *uniqueness within commonality*—will help you cope with the seeming riddles of the American family (see Inset 2-1).

Some examples of diverse data interpretation will help clarify what we mean by these two principles. For example, as we noted, the divorce rate has risen steadily throughout this century. In 1900 there was about one divorce for every twelve marriages. Today there is about one divorce for every two marriages, although the dramatic upsurge in divorce (starting about 1965) has slowed in the past five years. Many use these statistics to support their contention that the institution of the family in America is in real trouble and will soon be dead and buried. Yet many others see these statistics as positive. Americans will have better marriages and more fulfilling family lives because they must no longer put up with the dissatisfactions of empty-shell marriages that previous generations accepted. Indeed, remarriage statistics indicate that divorced persons have even higher marriage rates than single, never-married persons. Most divorced persons leave a particular mate but not the institution of marriage.

A second example also illustrates the conflict evoked by statistics about changing family characteristics. America's birthrate has generally been falling for the past 200 years with the major exception of the baby boom between about 1945 and 1957, which was related to the dislocations and prosperity caused by World War II. However, the birthrate has fallen more dramatically since 1960, reaching a low of about 14.5 births per thousand population in 1975. In 1983 that figure had risen to 16.0 per thousand but dropped again by 1986 to approximately 15.7 per thousand, still relatively low compared with earlier levels (U.S. Bureau of the Census, March 1986). Many suggest that the decreased birthrate resulted because many young women decided not to have children. "Having children is no longer an important part of marriage." "Careers are more important and children are only troublesome to the pursuit of one's own goals." The proportion of women who stated they expected to remain childless did go up between 1967 and 1974, but there is a difference between a statement made when one is eighteen years of age and what one actually does later in life. A high proportion of those women born between 1952 and 1956 stated that they did not want to have children. Yet they are now members of the only group that experienced a substantial increase in fertility between 1980 and 1984 (U.S. Bureau of the Census, November 1985). The birthrate is decreasing not because more women are remaining childless, but because mothers are having fewer children. The average mother born between 1846 and 1855 had 5.7 children. Women born between 1931 and 1935 had an average of 3.4 children. Women born between 1940 and 1945 average fewer than 3 children. Although it is too early to tell for sure, it appears that women born between 1950 and 1955 will average even fewer.

Thus the decreasing birthrate may not mean that couples are abandoning parenthood at all. Rather it seems to mean that families are having fewer children, which is probably positive for the children. Evidence suggests that children do better in smaller families, where they receive more adult time and attention. After reviewing much demographic data about the family and children, Mary Jo Bane concluded (1976, p. 23):

> In short, the major demographic changes affecting parents and children in the course of this century have not much altered the basic picture of children living with and being cared for by their parents. The patterns of structural change so often cited as evidence of family decline do not seem to be weakening the bonds between parents and children.

Inset 2-1
The Family Riddle

Marriage, children, forever together, mom, dad, apple pie, love, Sunday softball in the park, grandmother's for Sunday dinner—The American Family.

Cohabitation, childlessness, divorce and remarriage, stepdad, stepmom, junk food, child abuse and wife beating, spectator sports in front of the TV, Pizza Hut for Sunday dinner—The American Family.

Student: "But these two descriptions can't both be of the American family."
Friend: "Oh, but they are, and, indeed, there are infinite other descriptions that also would fit. American families, each and every one, are unique and representative of the individuals and their interactions within the family."
Student: "But how then can we study the American family if each is unique?"
Friend: "Because they all have certain things in common. They are all alike in some ways."
Student: "But they can't be. You just said they were all different and unique."
Friend: "They are and they are also always changing."
Student: "But how can you study something that is unique and also always changing?"
Friend: "Because change occurs in the midst of continuity and continuity can remain despite change."
Student: "You are saying then that each family is unique but has things in common with all other families and, besides, families are always changing but have continuity."
Friend: "Yes."
Student: "It sounds like a riddle."
Friend: "It is a riddle because in order to understand the family one must be able to live with and understand two abstract principles:

1. Change can occur within continuity, and
2. Uniqueness can exist within commonality."

These two examples (divorce and birth rates) help point out just how confusing and controversial interpretation of marriage and family data can be. Further, they demonstrate both principles stated in Inset 2-1.

Both examples show change within continuity. The divorce rate has increased dramatically in the past few years, which is indicative of change. Yet those divorcing return to marriage rather quickly (close to 50 percent are remarried within three years), indicating continuity of the marriage institution. Families are having fewer children, a change from the past. But they are indeed having and rearing children as families have always done, again indicating continuity.

Both examples also demonstrate uniqueness within commonality. Two married couples share the commonality of being married. Each partner of one marriage is in his or her first marriage. One partner of the other marriage is in his or her second marriage. Thus each couple, although sharing the characteristic of being married, is also unique in previous marriage experience. Some couples opt for no children, others for one, two, or three. All couples share the opportunity to have children in their marriage but are individual in the way they use the opportunity.

Many changes are occurring in the American family. As we discuss these changes, keep in mind the continuity. The year 1982 was the seventh consecutive year that the total number of marriages grew, and that total was the largest ever: 2.5 million. There were 2,425,000 marriages in 1985, but because the population grew, the marriage rate per thousand population has dropped from 10.8 in 1982 to 10.2 in 1985 (U.S. Bureau of the Census, March 1986). So we see that marriage remains popular and that most Americans still spend the greater share of their lives in family units even though the rate of marriage has dropped.

Inset 2-2 points out some of the changes in the American family. For example, we noted earlier the rapid rise of single-parent families. Yet America has always had single-parent families. In fact, the proportion of such families remained about one in ten for the 100 years between 1870 and 1970. Early single-parent families were generally the result of the premature death of a parent rather than divorce as is true today. Although the 1970s saw a large increase in the single-parent family structure, the structure itself is not new to American society.

An examination of other items in Inset 2-2 demonstrates clearly the principle of change within continuity. Ostensibly the inset shows great changes taking place in the American family. How great are the changes? Unmarried couple cohabitation increased 282 percent from 1970 to 1985, yet in actual numbers these couples still account for only 4 percent of the total number of married couples (2 million cohabiting couples compared with 50 million married couples). Change (an increase in unmarried cohabitation) yet continuity (most couples living together are married) is clearly demonstrated in these statistics. And how new is cohabitation to the American society? Not so new. During the 1920s common-law cohabitation involved about one in five couples (Ramey, 1981); (see Inset 2-3).

Single-parent families increased by 60 percent between 1970 and 1985, yet 78 percent of all children still live with two parents. Change (more children live with one parent than before), yet continuity (most children still live with two parents) is again shown.

Perhaps the biggest change of all is the increasing acceptance of various forms of intimate relationships. We are, after all, a pluralistic society, a society made up of diverse groups. Thus it seems natural that different family structures may become accepted.

Family: The Basic Unit of Human Organization

Assumption 4: The family is the basic unit of human organization. If defined functionally the family is essentially universal. However, its form and strength vary greatly across cultures and time.

The term *family* is used here in the broadest possible sense: It is defined as whatever system a society uses to support and control reproduction and human sexual interaction. This broad definition solves many apparent conflicts over the meaning of changes presently taking place in family functions and structure. For example, within this definition Israeli kibbutzim are families, even though major childrearing responsibilities are assumed by persons other than parents.

Most authors give a narrower definition. For example, Robert Winch (1971, pp. 10–11) says the family is "a set of persons related to each other by blood, marriage, or adoption, and constituting a social system whose structure is specified by familial positions and whose basic societal function is replacement." Lucille Duberman (1977, p. 10) says the family is "an institution found in several variant forms, that provides children with a legitimate position in society and with the nurturance that will enable them to function as fully developed members of society." Narrow definitions like these seem to limit family functions to childrearing.

Part of the reason for the debate over the health of the American family is confusion between the functions of the family institution and the structure by

---

Inset 2-2

Marriage and Family Statistics Summarized

Statistics about marriage and the family are included in the appropriate sections of this chapter and throughout the book. However, to help the reader better understand just where today's marriages and families are, we include here a list of pertinent statistical facts. As you peruse these facts it is well to keep in mind, as the Skolnicks (1986) suggest, that researchers have found that when the statistics of family life are plotted for the entire twentieth century, a surprising fact emerges: *today's young people appear to be behaving in ways consistent with long-term historical trends* (Cherlin, 1981; Masnick & Bane, 1980). The recent changes in family life appear deviant only when compared to what people were doing in the 1940s and 1950s. The now middle-aged adults who married young, moved to the suburbs, and had three or more children, were the generation that deviated from twentieth century trends. "Had the 1940s and 1950s not happened, today's young adults would appear to be behaving normally" (Masnick & Bane, 1980, p. 2)

■ Proportions of never married women aged fifteen to nineteen years who have had sexual intercourse have increased to 40 percent among whites and 58 percent among blacks in 1982, up from 23 percent and 52 percent respectively in 1971. Since 1980 the rates have leveled off for white women and actually decreased slightly for black women (Pratt et al., 1984).

■ The fertility rate has fallen from a high of 122 per 1000 women aged fifteen to forty-four in 1957 to 66.1 in 1985. A low point was reached in 1976 (62) and then the fertility rate increased slowly until 1983, at which time there was a small drop with the rate remaining between 65 and 67 to 1986.

■ The average number of children already born to ever-married women aged fifteen to forty-four years dropped from 2.2 in 1973 to 1.9 in 1982 (Pratt et al., 1984).

■ Single-parent families account for 26 percent of all families with children, up from 11 percent in 1970. 89 percent of these families are mother headed. 33 percent of these mother-child families were black but only 12 percent of all families with children under eighteen years of age are black (Norton & Glick, 1986).

■ Families maintained by never-married mothers increased 500 percent between 1970 and 1984 and account for 20 percent of all mother-child families (Norton & Glick, 1986). In 1984 17 percent of all women who had a child were unmarried, up from 14 percent in 1980. Approximately half of all black births are to unmarried women (U.S. Bureau of the Census, November 1985).

■ 24 percent of all children under 18 years of age, 57 percent of those in one-parent families, and 60 percent of those in mother-child families were economically below the poverty line in 1983 (Norton & Glick, 1986).

■ Children living with only one parent increased 60 percent between 1970 and 1985 but in 1985 78 percent of all children under eighteen years of age still live in two-parent families.

■ The number of cohabiting couples has increased by 282 percent between 1970 and 1985, but account for only 4 percent of the total number of married couples. For the first year since 1970, the numbers of cohabiting couples did not increase in 1985 (U.S. Bureau of the Census, Nov., 1986, 14).

■ 54 percent of all American women over age sixteen are working. 56 percent of working women are married. 60 percent of all mothers with children under eighteen are in the labor force (U.S. Department of Labor, 1985).

■ Life expectancy has increased dramatically. In 1900 the life expectancy for white American men was 48.2 years and for white American women, 51.1 years. By 1985 the figure was 72 years for men and 79 years for women. Thus the family life cycle has been greatly lengthened, leading to two new periods in the average family life cycle. There is a new period of couple togetherness after the last child leaves home. There may be a long period of widowhood.

■ 76 percent of men and 58 percent of women aged 20 to 24 are single.

---

which these functions are fulfilled. Many structures can fulfill the responsibilities of the family. In modern America the duties and thus the functions of the family have been reduced, and new structures, or alternative family forms, are being tried to fulfill some functions. Let us take a closer look at these functions.

Inset 2-3

Tricky Statistics: Cohabitation and Rejection of Marriage

The news media always interpret the cohabitation statistics to mean that more and more young couples are living together in a sexually and emotionally intimate relationship without being married. However, the U.S. Bureau of the Census states clearly in all of their publications covering cohabitation data that they do not ask questions regarding the nature of the couple's personal relationship.

In fact, the census bureau goes further and states that many cohabiting households undoubtedly contain couples where there is no emotional or sexual involvement. For example, a young male college student who rents a room in the home of an elderly widow

causes that household to show up under cohabitation data. Whenever there are hard times economically, such as the recession of 1982–1983, many people double up in their living arrangements. Thus a man and a woman who live together for economic reasons only would also show up in the cohabitating data.

In fact 1985 was the first year since 1970 that the number of cohabitating couples did not increase (U.S. Bureau of the Census, October 1985; 1986). Perhaps this is because the economy was much improved by 1985 and the economic necessity to double up one's living arrangements was not as pressing.

Despite the clarity of the census bureau's statement that cohabitation data say nothing about the couple's personal relationship, the media tend to present cohabitation data as a rejection of marriage by America's young people. Yet just what percentage of cohabitating couples see their relationship as a permanent rejection of marriage is impossible to determine. Studies of cohabitation indicate that most intimately cohabitating couples either break up or marry with time (see Chapter 4).

Family Functions   The family serves both the society and the individual. Sometimes, of course, there is a conflict between social and individual needs, as with the recent one-child-per-family laws in China. Although having more children may benefit a particular family, the Chinese government believes that too many children harm the larger society. For the family to remain a viable social institution, it must meet the needs of society and society's individual members and must hold conflict between the individual and the society to a minimum.

The family has handled a broad range of functions in different times and societies. In some primitive societies the family is synonymous with society itself, bearing all the powers and responsibilities for societal survival. As societies become more complex and elaborate, social institutions form to take over many responsibilities that formerly belonged to the family.

Robert Winch (1971) identifies the following functions as necessary for the maintenance of society:

1. Replacements for dying members of the society must be produced.
2. Goods and services must be produced and distributed.
3. Provision must be made for accommodating conflicts and maintaining order internally and externally.
4. Newborn human replacements must be socialized to become participating members of the society.
5. Individual goals must be harmonized with the values of the society, and there must be procedures for dealing with emotional crises and maintaining a sense of purpose.

Although the American family is still involved with all five of these functions, other social institutions have assumed the primary responsibility for some of them. For example, the family is no longer a production unit per se. Individuals within the family may work to produce goods and services, but this is usually done outside the family setting in a more formalized job situation. The family is still an economic unit, however, in that it demands goods and services and is the major consumption unit in the United States (see Assumption 8). The courts and police maintain external order, although the family is still primarily responsible for maintaining order within its own boundaries. Formal education now trains children to become participating members of society, although the family begins and maintains the socialization process.

Thus we find that the contemporary American family is left with two of Winch's primary functions: (1) *providing a continuing replacement of individuals so that society continues to exist, and* (2) *providing emotional gratification and intimacy to members, helping them deal with emotional crises so they grow in the most fulfilling manner possible.*

Despite sperm banks and surrogate mothers, human beings are still being conceived and born in the age-old, time-honored fashion. Thus the family's importance as the means of replenishing the population remains. The family is also the most efficient way of nurturing the human newborn, who is physically dependent during the first years of life. Without some kind of stable adult unit to provide child care during this long period of dependence, the human species would have disappeared long ago.

Sexual Regulation

Each family structure, then, has reproduction as its primary function. An extension of this function is the regulation of sexual behavior. In the animal world sex and reproduction are, for the most part, handled automatically and instinctively. When the female is in estrus (ready to conceive), the male responds and impregnates her. Most of the mechanisms and behaviors of sex and reproduction are built into the biology of the animal. There are fixed periods of sexual readiness, and the animal has little choice in its sexual behavior.

Human beings of course are different. Sexual behavior may be sought and enjoyed at any time, regardless of the stage of the female reproductive cycle. Humans are free to use sex not only for reproduction but also for pleasure. As in so many other aspects of human life, however, freedom of choice is a mixed blessing. Humans must balance their continual sexual receptivity and desire with the needs of other individuals and with the needs of society as a whole. They must find a system that provides physical and mental satisfaction in a socially acceptable context of time, place, and partner.

No matter what system is worked out to handle sexuality, humans seem to be comfortable only when they can convince themselves that the system is proper, just, and virtuous. When each culture has established a satisfactory system, it bolsters this system with a complex set of rules and punishments for transgressions. However, our society has evolved to a point where the old rules no longer work well, so we are faced with trying to create new ethics to control sexuality. Western literature on marriage and the family is filled with arguments about the proper sexual system for humans. Were men and women originally promiscuous, **polygamous**, or **monogamous**? We have even applied Darwin's theory of evolution

Polygamy
Having multiple spouses

Monogamy
Having one spouse in a sexually exclusive relationship

to the male-female relationship in an effort to demonstrate that the monogamy of Western cultures is the highest and therefore the only proper form of relationship. Yet close and objective study of the multiple methods devised by humans to work out their sexual and family life tends to destroy most of the historical arguments for any straight-line evolutionary theory of family development. In their book *The Family in Various Cultures* (1974, pp. 3–5), Stuart Queen and Robert Habenstein conclude that because there is such variance among family patterns and the way sexuality is controlled, "no single form need be regarded as inevitable or more 'natural' than any other." They further state: "We assume that all forms of the domestic institution are in process, having grown out of something different and tending to become something still different. But there is no acceptable evidence of a single, uniform series of stages through which the developing family must pass."

New Family Functions

Although consensus has it that the modern family has lost some functions, it may also be true that it has gained new ones. For example, F. I. Nye (1974) suggests that three new roles are present in the middle-class American family:

1. *The recreational role*: Family members spend their leisure time, especially vacation time, together.
2. *The therapeutic role*: Each family member assists the others in solving individual problems that may either originate in the family or be external to it. As we become more isolated from the larger ongoing society, such support becomes more crucial.
3. *Changed sexual roles*: Traditionally it was the woman's role to meet her husband's sexual needs. Now the feminist movement has emphasized the equal importance of the husband's meeting his wife's sexual needs, thereby placing a new responsibility on the man, and changing the female role also.

We have seen the family's functions changing over time. And we can certainly assume that its functions will continue to change. Do changing functions mean that the family as we know it will disappear? Not necessarily. The family's secret to survival over the past centuries has been its flexibility and high adaptive capability. The family is a system in process rather than a rigid unchanging system. As John Crosby has pointed out:

> No one can yet foresee what the structure of the future family will look like because no one can know with certainty what the functions and needs of the future family will be. It is likely, however, that the needs for primary affection bonds, intimacy, economic subsistence, socialization of the young, and reproduction will not yield to obsolescence. To the extent that human needs do not change drastically, the family structure will not change drastically. (1980, p. 40)

Family: A Buffer against Mental and Physical Illness

Assumption 5: The family becomes increasingly important to its members as social stability decreases and/or people feel more isolated and alienated. Indeed, the healthy family can act as a buffer against mental and physical illness.

Note that one of Winch's remaining family functions was providing emotional gratification and intimacy to family members. And Nye added the function that each family member assists others in solving individual problems. In general as the pace of life quickens and people become increasingly alienated from their larger society, the family can become more important as a refuge and source of emotional gratification for its members. The family has been called the "shock absorber" of society—the place where bruised and battered individuals can return after doing battle with the world, a nurturing place for vital beings, the one stable point in an ever-changing environment. If you do not belong to a family, where do you turn for warmth and affection? Who cares for you when you are sick? What other group tolerates your failures the way a devoted wife, husband, mother, or father does? The family can serve as "portable roots," anchoring one against the storm of change. Furthermore, the family can provide the security and acceptance that give a person the inner strength to behave individually rather than always conforming with one's peers. The family can be a source of security, a protective shield against environmental pressures.

To the degree that environmental stress on individual family members can be reduced, the family can act as a buffer against mental and physical illness of its members. It is important that we emphasize the word *can*. The family can act as a buffer only if it is healthy, well integrated, fully functioning, and successful. This status is an ideal and we realize that few families will achieve it. Yet as noted in Chapter 1, ideals are important because they give us goals toward which we can direct our lives.

As families have become smaller and more isolated from societal supports because of industrialization and alienation processes, intimate relations within the family have become more intense, more emotional, and more fragile. For example, if a child has no significant intimate relationships with adults other than his or her parents, this emotional interaction becomes crucial to the child's development. If the interaction is positive and healthy, the child develops in a healthy manner; if it is not, the child is apt to develop in an unhealthy manner. The family, in a sense, is a hothouse of intimacy and emotionality because of its close interaction and intensity of relationships. It has the potential to do either great good or great harm to its members. Because of the potential for harm, it becomes even more important to understand how to create a strong and healthy family that can help its members toward health.

We will all spend a good part, if not all, of our lives in a family unit. Within this setting most of us will achieve our closest intimacy with other persons—the shared human intimacy that promotes feelings of security and self-esteem. Such feelings lead to improved communication, and good communication tends to be therapeutic. According to Carl Rogers (1951, p. 1), "the emotionally maladjusted person is in difficulty first, because communication within himself has broken down, and second, because, as a result of this, his communication with others has become damaged." To the degree that our family can help us become good communicators, it can help us toward better life adjustment.

When one compares health statistics on married, single, divorced, separated, and widowed people, it is clear that married people are the healthiest. Lois Verbrugge (1979) surveyed a great deal of data on six general health indicators: (1) incidence of acute health conditions; (2) percentage of people limited in activity by a chronic condition; (3) percentage of people with a work disability; (4) rates

of restricted activity, bed disability, and work loss; (5) average number of physician (or dental) visits per year; and (6) percentage of people with a hospital stay in the past year, average length of stay, and hospital discharge rates. She adjusted rates for age and found that significant differences existed between the various groups. Divorced and separated people clearly appeared least healthy, while married people appeared overall to be the most healthy.

The American Council of Life Insurance reports that divorced white American males under 65 had a death rate from strokes and lung cancer that was double that of married men, seven times greater for cirrhosis of the liver, double for stomach cancer and heart disease, and five times greater for suicide.

Interpretation of such data is complex and controversial. The differences between various marital groups, however, are substantial enough to suggest that they are real rather than simply chance. The fact that married persons generally appear most healthy, and divorced and separated persons least healthy suggests that the family may have a strong influence on health. The successful family operates to improve its members' health, while the unsuccessful family may do the opposite. If this is true, it becomes a matter of health to work toward improved family functioning and increased levels of intimacy.

The Need for Intimacy Seeking physical, intellectual, or emotional closeness with others seems to be a basic need of most people (Fromm, 1956; Maslow, 1971; Morris, 1971; Murstein, 1974). To feel close to another, to love and feel loved, to experience comradeship, to care and be cared about are all feelings that most of us wish and need to experience. Such feelings can be found in many human relationships. It is within the family, though, that such feelings ideally are most easily found and shared. I say "ideally" because it is apparent that in many families such feelings are not found. Families that do not supply intimacy are usually families in trouble, and often these families disintegrate because members are frustrated in their needs for meaningful intimate relationships. A successful family, then, supplies intimate relationships to its members and through this intimacy contributes to their health.

The term **intimacy** generally covers all of the feelings mentioned in the preceding paragraph as well as being a commonly used euphemism for sexual intercourse. Because of the many meanings, a clear and concise definition is difficult to make. For our purposes we will use Carolynne Kieffer's (1977) definition: *"Intimacy is the experiencing of the essence of one's self in intense intellectual, physical and/or emotional communion with another human being"* (p. 267).

The primary components of intimacy are choice, mutuality, reciprocity, trust, and delight (Calderone, 1972). Two people like one another and make overtures toward establishing a closer relationship. They have made a choice. Their act, of course, must be mutual for an intimate relationship to develop. As confidence in each other grows, each reveals more and more thoughts and feelings. *Reciprocity* means that each partner gives to the relationship and to the other: sharing, confidences, caring, and feelings expressed. This sharing nurtures acceptance and *trust*, which in turn increase the sharing, which eventually leads to the experience of *delight* in one another that true intimates always share.

B. J. Biddle (1976) suggests that intimacy must be considered on each of three dimensions: breadth, openness, and depth. *Breadth* describes the range of activities shared by two people. Do they spend a great deal of time together? Do they share occupational activities, home activities, leisure time, and so on? *Openness* implies that a pair share meaningful self-disclosures with one another. They feel secure enough and close enough to share intellectually, physically, and emotionally. They trust each other enough that they can be honest most of the time, and this encourages further trust in one another. *Depth* means that partners share really true, central, and meaningful aspects of themselves. Self-disclosure leads to deeper levels of interaction. In the ultimate sense both are able to transcend their own egos and fuse in a spiritual way with the essence or central being of their partner. Such an experience is difficult to attain, yet many believe that it is in the deepest intimate experiences that love and potential for individual growth are found. Abraham Maslow (1968), for example, holds that each individual must find deep intimacy to become a self-actualizing and fulfilled person.

Kieffer (1977) adds to Biddle's three dimensions the age-old idea of intellectual, physical, and emotional realms of action. A totally intimate relationship would have breadth, openness, and depth in each activity realm. Table 2-2 describes a highly intimate relationship. Of course, as Kieffer cautions, such a description is simplistic and does not include the numerous psychological processes that characterize the interaction of the partners and brought them to their level of involvement. In addition, she reminds us that intimacy is a process, not a state of being. Thus this description only indicates where this particular couple is at one particular time.

In the past intimacy was maintained throughout one's life by the geographical and physical proximity of the family. However, as the economic pattern changed in this country, and as increasing geographical mobility separated people from their families, social emphasis shifted from family closeness to individual fulfillment. Many people have found the achievement of intimacy more difficult because of this shift (see Inset 2-4).

What Do You Think?

1. Is intimacy a goal for you?
2. If it is, why is it difficult for you to be intimate?
3. In what action realm (intellectual, physical, emotional) do you share intimacy most easily? Why?
4. Which realm is most difficult? Why?
5. In what ways is your relationship with your parents intimate? Why?
6. In what ways can you not be intimate with your parents? Why?

_____ **Table 2-2** _____

Intensity Matrix for the Analysis of an Intimate Relationship*

	Intellectual	Physical	Emotional
Breadth (Range of Shared Activities)	Telling of the meaningful events in one's day	Dancing	Phone calls providing emotional support when separated
	Participating in a political rally	Caressing	Experiencing grief in a family tragedy
	Years of interaction resulting in the sharing of meanings (phrases, gestures, etc.) understood only by the partners	Swimming	Witnessing with pride a daughter's graduation from college
		Doing laundry	Resolving conflict in occasional arguments
		Tennis	
	Decision making regarding management of household	Shopping	
		Gardening	
		Sexual intercourse	
		Other sensual/sexual activities	
Openness (Disclosure of Self)	Disclosing one's values and goals	Feeling free to wear old clothes	Describing one's dreams and daydreams
	Discussing controversial aspects of politics, ethics, etc.	Grooming in presence of the other	Feeling free to call for "time out" or for togetherness
	Using familiar language	Bathroom behavior (elimination, etc.) in presence of the other	
	Not feeling a need to lie to the partner	Nudity	Maintaining openness (disclosure) regarding one's emotional involvement with other intimates
	Sharing of secrets with the partner and using discretion regarding the secrets of the partner	Few limitations placed on exploration of one's body by the partner	Telling of daily joys and frustrations
		Sharing of physical space (area, possessions, etc.) with few signs of territoriality	Emotional honesty in resolving conflict
			Expressing anger, resentment, and other positive and negative emotions
Depth (Sharing of Core Aspects of Self)	"Knowing" of the partner	Physical relaxation, sense of contentment and well-being in the presence of the other	Committing oneself without guarantee, in the hope that one's love will be returned
	Having faith in the partner's reliability and love		
	Occasional experiencing of the essence of one's self in transcendental union		Caring as much about the partner as about oneself
	Working collectively to change certain core characteristics of the self and of the partner		Nonjealous supportiveness toward the other intimate relationships of the partner

Source: From _Marriage and Alternatives: Exploring Intimate Relationships_ by Roger W. Libby and Robert N. Whitehurst. Copyright © 1977 by Scott, Foresman and Company. Reprinted by permission.

*You can use this matrix to analyze your own intimate relationships or to compare levels of involvement or discern patterns among your various relationships.

But life today offers many different opportunities for fulfilling intimacy needs. Marriage is no longer seen as the only avenue to intimacy. If we examine our lives, we will probably find we have what Carolynne Kieffer calls a "patchwork intimacy." By this Kieffer means that most people are involved in a multitude of intimate relationships of varying intensity.

We can see this idea more clearly if we examine the concept of "open marriage." Nena and George O'Neill propose (1972) that the old idea of marriage expected both partners to fill all of their intimacy needs within the marriage. In an "open marriage," on the other hand, a partner may limit physical intimacy to the marriage relationship but share intellectual intimacy with, perhaps, some work colleagues.

Inset 2-4

Why Do We Avoid Intimacy?

To seek and find intimacy with another is highly rewarding. Yet people often avoid intimacy for many reasons. To open ourselves to another invites intimacy but also risks hurt. What if we open ourselves to others, trust them to reciprocate, and they do not? Each of us has probably had such an experience. Who hasn't liked someone and been rejected by that person? We may now be able to laugh at some of our early failures with intimacy (label them "puppy love," and so forth), yet each time we fail at intimacy, we become more guarded and apprehensive.

Fear of rejection is one of the strongest barriers to intimacy. Each time we are hurt by another, it becomes more difficult to be open, trusting and caring in a new relationship. To be the first to share our innermost feelings, to say "I like you" or "I love

you" leaves one open to rejection. The first steps toward an intimate relationship are especially hard for the insecure person who lacks self-confidence. To build an intimate relationship, one must first be intimate, accepting, and comfortable with oneself. To the degree that we are not these things with ourselves, we will probably be fearful to enter an intimate relationship.

Intimacy demands active involvement with another. Often passive spectator roles seem more comfortable — let the other person supply the intimacy. Our society teaches us to be spectators via television. Society often conditions us to play roles, always to please others, to deny our feelings. We shall see how intimacy is avoided when we play our stereotypical masculine and feminine roles (macho males don't cry or show caring emotions, for example).

Anger can be another barrier to intimacy if it is not dealt with openly. When we suppress, deny, and disguise anger, we do not rid ourselves of it. Rather the anger lingers as growing hostility. Of course, we all become angry on occasion with our most intimate loved ones. Anger does not destroy intimacy. Suppressed anger, though, leads to hostility and will, over time, tend to destroy intimacy. Remember that intimacy implies openness between intimates. Suppressed anger is unexpressed, thus keeping us closed rather than open. Suppressing anger also implies lack of trust in the partner. Without trust there cannot be intimacy.

Fear of rejection, nonacceptance of ourselves, spectator roles, and unexpressed anger are four of the strongest barriers to intimacy.

What Do You Think?

1. With which people in your life do you find it easiest to be intimate?
2. Why is it easier with each of these persons than with others?
3. Is it easier for you to be intimate with men or women? If there is a difference, what do you think that difference is?
4. Is your family of orientation generally close and intimate?
5. Do your friends generally consider you to be a person with whom they can be intimate?
6. If so, why? If not, why not?

Also, the partners are free to spend time away from each other, with other companions.

If one is secure in a marital relationship of deep intimacy, enough trust may develop so that each partner can encourage the other to seek fulfillment through intimacy even outside the relationship. Such trust must be earned and respected; it is not easy to come by.

If intimacy is as rewarding as we have suggested and if American society allows each person to seek it in ways other than marriage, we need to develop an ethic for intimates. For example, how do we keep the quest for individual intimacy and fulfillment within acceptable boundaries to our spouse? How do we keep the quest from lapsing into the selfish pursuit of "doing your own thing"? Questions like these must be considered by all couples seeking intimacy.

The Family as Interpreter of Society

Assumption 6:   The attitudes and reactions of family members toward environmental influences are more important to the socialization of family members than the environmental influences themselves (Chapters 5 and 6).

A family with small children is watching the evening news describe an atomic power plant protest. The parents either support or criticize the actions of the protesters. The parental reaction to this social event is more influential on the children than the event itself because the parents are the models by which young children build their attitudes and behaviors.

We have seen that the family supplies the society's population by reproducing children. But the family also physically and psychologically nurtures the offspring into adulthood. Because humans have such a long period of dependence before becoming independent adults, the family is the main source for **socialization** of young children to their culture. Formal education takes over part of the job of socializing the young when they reach school age, but the family retains the greatest overall influence on preschool children. Indeed the family's continuing formal and informal socialization of its children may supply the most deeply lasting lessons. However, with increasing numbers of mothers joining the work-force when their children are young, formal preschool child-care programs and television are decreasing the family's influence even with preschoolers.

Social learning theory has long pointed out the importance of modeling in learning, especially for young children (Bandura, 1969). **Modeling** is learning by observing other people's behavior. Parents and other family members are the most significant models for young children. How they react to their society is often more important than what they formally teach their children about it. If, for instance, a father teaches his children the importance of obeying rules and then asks them to watch for policemen when he exceeds the speed limit, he is teaching them that not getting caught breaking rules is more important than obeying them.

Social problems—depression, inflation, unemployment, poverty—also greatly influence families. General social upheavals, such as the protests against the Vietnam War in the 1960s and the continuing battles for minority rights, affect the family drastically. For example, if a child is to be bused twenty miles into a new neighborhood and school to promote racial equality, there will certainly be consequences within the family. The parents will lose some control over the child. The distance to school may mean that they cannot participate in school activities such as PTA and class parties. They will not know the families of the child's playmates. The child will be exposed to different social mores and expectations that they may or may not find acceptable.

Yet more important than the political fact of busing will be the family's reaction to it. Will the family accept and support it? Will it picket, riot, and protest? Will it transfer children from public into private school? Each family's reaction to busing teaches its children values about minority groups, racial prejudice or tolerance, law, and authority.

An additional function of the family, then, is to help family members interpret social influences. This function also brings the possibility that an individual family may teach an interpretation unacceptable to others in the society as a whole.

Socialization
Acquiring skills necessary to survive as an individual and as a member of society

Modeling
Learning vicariously by observing others' behavior

Unique Characteristics of the American Family

Assumption 7:   The American family, especially the middle-class family, has certain characteristics that make it unique. Among these, the following four stand out (Chapters 4, 8, and 9):

a. *Relative freedom in mate and vocational selection.*   Most cultures, historically at least, believed that mate and vocational selection were too important to be left to inexperienced people. The decisions that would influence one's entire life were often made long before a child reached puberty. To this day in many countries children enter the labor market early. Whether tending the family's goats in Morocco or tying the thousands of knots in an Iranian carpet, children contribute to their family's economic well-being and learn their lifetime vocation early.

Western society, especially the United States, long ago rejected child labor. As America became increasingly child centered and affluent, childhood (an historically recent concept) became a protected period of freedom from adult responsibility. Today children whose parents value education and have the means to supply it are encouraged to educate themselves and to seek out vocations for which they are best suited. Families may make suggestions about possible vocations, but the final decision is usually left to the child.

This freedom is even more evident in mate selection. As we shall see in Chapter 4, unstructured dating as a method of mate selection is a relatively new American contribution. When Americans are asked why they marry, invariably they list "love" as their most important reason. To marry for romantic love is another American contribution to the mate selection process. Although romantic love has always been recognized historically, it has almost never served as a basis for marriage. Marriages were contracted by parents for their children. The contracts were made for economic, political, power, and prestige reasons, not for love. If love were to appear in the contracted relationship, generally it would have to grow as time passed. The lyrics to the song "Do You Love Me?" from *Fiddler on the Roof* exemplify a contracted marriage.

Tevye to his wife Golde

Do you love me?
Do I what?
Do you love me?
Do I love you? With our daughters getting married and this trouble in town, you're upset, you're worn out. Go inside, go lie down. Maybe it's indigestion. Golde, I'm asking you a question: Do you love me?
You're a fool!
I know, but do you love me?
Do I love you? Well, for twenty-five years I've washed your clothes, cooked your meals, cleaned your house, given you children, milked the cow. After twenty-five years why talk about love right now?
Golde, the first time I met you was on our wedding day. I was scared, I was shy, I was nervous.
So was I.
But my father and mother said we'd learn to love each other, and now I am asking, Golde, do you love me?
I'm your wife.
I know, but do you love me?
Do I love him? For twenty-five years I've lived with him, fought with him,

starved with him. Twenty-five years my bed is his; if that's not love, what is?
Then you love me.
I suppose I do.
And I suppose I love you too.
It doesn't change a thing, but even so, after twenty-five years it's nice to know.

b. *Relative freedom within the family, fostered by a high standard of living, physical mobility, lack of broader familial responsibilities, and the pluralistic nature of American society.* Freedom of vocational choice and mate selection stem from the general freedom that exists for the young within the American family and society. We have already examined the role that societal affluence plays in allowing broader choice of family structure.

c. *High economic standards and abundant personal possessions.* As we saw, affluence, increased education, and mass media proliferation all combine to allow America's young wider experiences. Such experiences increase youth's freedom both within the family and in the life choices that all youth must make. Of course such freedom increases the need and the responsibility for decision making. Freedom also means freedom to make mistakes. Thus the freedom of American youth tends to increase their anxiety and insecurity. This increased anxiety and insecurity may partially explain the interest of some young Americans in cults, most of which ask their members to give up freedom and live by strict rules.

d. *An extremely private character.* The private character of the American family is another result of the general affluence of our society. In most of the world housing is in short supply. Many families are fortunate if they have more than one room. Living quarters often house not only the nuclear family but also many more distant relatives.

The average size of American families living together has decreased over the years. In 1790 the average American household included 5.6 persons. In 1970 the size had dropped to 3.14 persons, and in 1985 it had dropped further to just 2.69 persons (U.S. Bureau of the Census, September, 1986, 1). This decrease is accounted for mainly by the loss of the additional relatives that used to live with families and the low birthrate.

The number of single persons living alone has also increased. Households containing just one person have jumped 90 percent since 1970, compared to a 37 percent increase in households overall (U.S. Bureau of the Census, October 1985). Shrinking household sizes and growing numbers of persons living alone are possible only in a society affluent enough to supply abundant housing. An American family living in a 1400-square-foot, three-bedroom, bath-and-a-half house uses enough space to house approximately twenty people in a country such as Afghanistan. It is this ability of the American nuclear family to live separately from relatives, neighbors, and even each other that has allowed it to become private. Such privacy is a luxury of economic affluence. Our society's privacy brings both advantages and disadvantages. Living with fewer people increases individual freedom, but living privately also increases the opportunity for spouse or child abuse because others aren't around to observe such abuse. And although living alone certainly increases privacy, it also increases the chances of loneliness.

Family: The Consuming Unit of the American Economy

Assumption 8:   The family in modern America is the basic economic unit for the society (Chapters 8 and 9).

Early American farm family members were also production workers. The industrial revolution removed much of the economic production from the American family. Family members remained production workers, but the production was moved from the home into factories and did not necessarily include all family members. The money earned by outside work supported the family. Thus the family's economic well-being became more subject to the whim of an anonymous marketplace than to the industry of individual family members. Rather than each family producing what it needed to survive, each had to go to the marketplace and buy what it needed. Thus the family became the consuming unit of society's agricultural and industrial output.

The family, of course, still provides services to its members. Such services as meal preparation and keeping the house in repair require productive work from family members. However, such production is largely unpaid and unrecognized by the larger society. Some feminists suggest that those who provide the services—mainly women—be paid. Payment for such family services would probably have a significant impact on husband-wife relationships, as family power relates in part to who earns the money. Estimates based on current wage scales of cooks, baby-sitters, and so forth place the value of services provided by the full-time mother-housewife at from $25,000 to $45,000 per year. Feminists suggest that such productive work be recognized not only by the woman's husband but also by the government for the granting of social security benefits.

Family consuming—consumer spending—is important to the health of the economy. When consumer spending drops as it did during the recession of 1981–1983, the economy suffers. Thus the family also acts as an economic foundation block of American society.

Some Words about Marriage and Family Data

Hard and fast data in such an intimate field of study as the family are difficult to produce. Most of the data come from surveys and from clinicians who work in the field.

Survey data are often problematic for three reasons. The first problem is that the sample may not be representative of the population in which you are interested. For example, if you are interested in the cohabiting behavior of college students, which college students do you survey? Certainly state university students will give different answers from students at a small denominational college where dormitory residence is required. You must always ask whether the sample surveyed accurately represents the population about which you want to draw conclusions.

A second problem with survey data is who actually responded. The researcher will, in most cases, set up a representative sample. However, responding to surveys is not mandatory but depends on voluntary cooperation. Although 100 percent of the sample may indeed be representative of the population about which you want to generalize, you will be fortunate if 50 to 80 percent of those in the sample cooperate. Thus you need to know if those who cooperated with the survey are the same as those who didn't. For example, Alfred Kinsey and his associates worked hard to draw a representative sample of Americans to interview about sexual behavior. They took people from all geographic areas and from various social classes. But can we be sure that the people who volunteered to discuss their most intimate sexual behavior with the interviewers behaved the same sexually as those who did not volunteer? Of course we can't, and thus there will always be a question about how representative of Americans the two monumental Kinsey studies really are.

The third problem with surveys is the difficulty of validating the respondents' answers. Are they telling the truth? The more intimate the questions, such as those about marriage or sex habits, the more likely the respondents are to hedge their answers or perhaps not to answer at all. Researchers try to overcome this problem by making surveys anonymous, but, again, we can never really be sure that an answer is true. Also, while respondents might not actually lie, sometimes memories are inadequate, or what we think we'd do in a hypothetical situation is not at all what we would actually do in real life. Thus always be careful about uncritically accepting all data that surveys yield.

Clinicians such as marriage counselors, clergy, psychologists, psychiatrists, and others who work with families also supply data to the research field. These data are usually anecdotal (storytelling), and unfortunately the clinicians' conclusions may be overgeneralized. And because they work with those seeking help, they may see only troubled families. After working eight hours a day over long periods with people who have problems, clinicians may come to hold an overly pessimistic view of the family.

Data on individual cases are usually valid for those cases, but can such data be generalized to the entire population? In most cases probably not. Also, group data does not accurately predict what an individual will do. For example, data from large group studies indicate that the chances of divorce go up if one's parents are divorced. Yet we all know persons who are long married and indeed have worked harder to make their marriage succeed because their parents were divorced. Does this mean that the group data are incorrect? Not at all. The statistics are correct for the group but cannot predict the behavior of any specific individual within the group. As Sherlock Holmes (in *The Sign of the Four*) said, "While the individual man is an insoluble puzzle, in the aggregate he becomes a mathematical certainty. You can never foretell what any one man will do, but you can say with precision what an average number will be up to. Individuals vary but percentages remain constant."

In general, then, remember to be cautious about immediately accepting all supposed facts in the field of marriage and family research.

In recent years people have started to study the effect that government policies and laws have on the family. After all the family exists within a society that is governed by laws. The family is affected by those laws.

Senator Daniel Patrick Moynihan tried unsuccessfully in 1965 to awaken government to the importance of considering the effects that changing government policies have on the American family. He was roundly criticized and largely ignored at the time, probably because his report focused on the breakdown of the

Family and Nation: Government Family Policy

nonwhite family. President Carter tried through the White House Conference on Families in 1980 to alert the nation to the importance of examining the effects of governmental policy on the family. Unfortunately the conference was so absorbed in bickering about a definition of the term *family*, abortion issues, gay rights, and so forth that it failed to evolve a coherent government family policy. The conference did, however, cite as its primary concern the sensitivity or insensitivity of federal, state, and local government toward families. Policies covering tax, welfare, and foster care were among policies critics claimed ignored or undermined families (White House Conference on Families, 1981).

In 1986 Moynihan published *Family and Nation*, in which he reiterated the need for the nation to consider the effects of government policy on the family. He noted that white families seemed to be breaking down at rates comparable to those for black families back in 1965 when he first raised the alarm (p. 146). For example, in 1965 the number of nonwhite mother-child families reached 21 percent of all nonwhite families. By 1984, mother-child white families had reached the same percentage, while over 50 percent of nonwhite families were mother-child families. Overall single-parent families accounted for 26 percent of all American families in 1984. Moynihan pointed out that "what was a crisis condition for one group in 1965 is now the general condition" (p. 146).

As one example of the harm that government action can do the family, Moynihan cited the diminishing income tax exemptions allowed for family members. In 1948 the exemption was $600 per person while in 1984 it had risen to $1000 per person. However, if the exemption had been indexed for inflation it would have been $2589 per person in 1984. As a result of this reduction of family member exemptions the federal government is now taxing the family at levels without equal in history. All told, combining federal income and Social Security taxes, an American family of median income in 1948 paid about 4.4 percent of its income to the federal government. By 1982 the federal government was claiming 18 percent of the median family's income (p. 161).

In fact, considering the official poverty level of $10,166 for a family of four and federal tax liability commencing at $8783 in 1983, the government was actually taxing poor families, that is, taking money away from one hand and returning it with the other in various welfare forms (p. 160). Taxes actually pushed economically marginal families below the poverty line.

Had family exemptions simply been indexed to inflation, families falling below the poverty line would be exempted from taxes. Such a simple change would drastically reduce various welfare payments to families because exemption from taxes would leave them with more spendable income.

Moynihan pointed out that government policy has recognized the elderly for some time and has wrought a miraculous transformation: the virtual disappearance of poverty among the elderly. While 30 years ago the elderly were, in the words of the Economic Report to the President (Council of Economic Advisors, 1985), "a relatively disadvantaged group," their income levels have increased so dramatically since then that "poverty rates for the elderly were lower than poverty rates for the rest of the population."

If government policy can help the elderly, it seems obvious that government policies ought to be able to help the American family. Although such a conclusion seems reasonable, it is not always easy to understand the effects of a change in policy on the family or general society for that matter. Recently the government has tried various *income maintenance* (guaranteeing all families a minimum income) experiments that ensure support to all members of a family even if the marriage is terminated. One rationale for these experiments was that a family that survives economically is less apt to break up than one that does not. Yet in actuality another effect was also discovered—the independence effect (Steiner, 1979). If women are guaranteed an income for themselves and their dependent children, divorce is sometimes the outcome because the guaranteed income allows them to be independent of their husbands. In surveying these experiments, Suzanne M. Bianchi and Reynolds Farley (1979, p. 548) conclude:

> The net outcome of the opposing effects (increased stability versus increased independence) depends upon the magnitude of the support level and the income of the family in the absence of support. Most discussions of the negative income tax or other income maintenance programs envision modest levels of support which would be focused upon families near the poverty level. The experiments conducted thus far suggest that, in such circumstances, the independence effect will far outweigh the income effect and rates of family dissolution will increase.

Family policy research is aimed at uncovering these kinds of practical relationships between governmental actions and the family.

Americans have mixed feelings about government formally declaring an interest in the family. Many fear it will lead to more governmental interference in their lives. On the other hand, intentionally or not, the government is a part of every family.

Conclusion: Marriage, a Resilient Institution

It is easy and popular to attack marriage and suggest alternatives to current practices. But such attacks tend to imply that marriage is a rigid relationship that has passed relatively unchanged into our modern culture. In reality "marriage has undergone dramatic change, and is still steadily changing, as it adapts itself to today's world" (Mace & Mace, 1977, p. 391).

Changes in the family because of modernization have led some critics of marriage to long for "the good old days." This suggests that there was some lost golden age of the family. Study of family history, however, fails to uncover any such golden age. Arlene and Jerome Skolnick (1986, p. 17) point out that those condemning modernization may have forgotten the problems of the past. Our current problems inside and outside the family are genuine, but we should remember that many of these issues derive from the benefits of modernization— benefits too easily taken for granted or forgotten in the fashionable denunciation of modern times. In the past there was no problem of the aged because most people died before they got old. Adolescence wasn't a difficult stage of the life cycle because it didn't exist; children worked and education was a privilege of the rich. When most people were hungry illiterates, only aristocrats could worry about sexual satisfaction and self-fulfillment. Modernization surely brings its troubles, yet how many of us would trade the troubles of our era for the ills of earlier times? David and Vera Mace note that the family has changed from "formal," "authoritarian," "rigidly disciplined" institution with "rigid sex roles" to a pattern characterized by "interpersonal relationships," with "mutual affection," "sympathetic understanding," and "comradeship."

Surely the first group of terms represents precisely the values in marriage which the counterculture has deplored, and the second group the very values which it has extolled.

What we are saying is that the monogamous marriage and nuclear family function far better in the companionship mode than they ever did in the institutional pattern; and that they can adapt very easily . . . to the new emphasis on personal and relational growth and development. (Mace & Mace, 1977, pp. 393–394)

Our discussion has been about family life in general. Yet for most Americans it is within a creative and changing marriage that they will find intimacy and satisfaction. Despite the popularity of attacking marriage as an institution, most Americans spend the bulk of their lives within a marriage and family relationship. This indicates that we need to expend more energy on making marriage viable and fulfilling than we spend on suggesting alternatives to it. As the Maces point out (1977, p. 392):

The possibilities for better marriage are exciting. In what we now call the marriage enrichment movement, we are experimenting with new tools and getting encouraging results. In skillfully led couple groups, we are seeing significant and lasting changes taking place in dull, superficial marriages as they break loose and embark on new growth. We are becoming aware that the majority of marriages in North America are functioning far below their potential. But we now realize that couples need no longer accept this miserable yield. With proper help and guidance they can appropriate the locked-up capacity for depth within the relationship that has been there all the time, but that no one helped them to actualize.

In short, we are at last beginning to provide the services to marriages which should have been available a generation ago, when the new alternative companionship style was emerging to replace traditional marriage.

"Working toward family wellness is the wave of the future" (Mace & Mace, 1985, p. 3).

The family remains because it is a flexible institution with great resilience. It can be pressed, stretched, and bent but always seems to recover its strength, spirit, and buoyancy. Despite the many criticisms of it, the family remains the basic unit of society. When functioning well, the strong, healthy family is the individual's greatest source of love and intimacy.

Summary

Human intimacy is based on eight major assumptions about marriage and the family in America.

1. A free and creative society offers many structural forms by which family functions, such as childrearing, can be fulfilled.
2. There is continuity to the changes that take place in families.
3. Each family is unique but also has characteristics in common with all other families in a given culture.
4. The family is the basic unit of human organization. If defined functionally the family is essentially universal. However, its form and strength vary greatly across cultures and time.
5. The family becomes increasingly important to its members as social stability decreases and/or people feel more isolated and alienated. Indeed, the healthy family can act as a buffer against mental and physical illness.

6. The attitudes and reactions of family members toward environmental influences are more important to the socialization of family members than the environmental influences themselves.
7. The American family, especially the middle-class family, has certain characteristics that make it unique. Among these, the following stand out:
   a. Relative freedom in mate and vocational selection
   b. Relative freedom within the family, fostered by a high standard of living, physical mobility, lack of broader familial responsibilities, and the pluralistic nature of American society
   c. High economic standards and abundant personal possessions
   d. An extremely private character
8. The family in modern America is the basic consuming economic unit for the society.

American Subgroup Families

The United States is made up of a great variety of peoples. In the 1980 census over 14 million Americans were foreign born. All races and nationalities are represented in the American population.

Although the American ideal is a social "melting pot," in fact "like tends to marry like." For example, among those Asians whose families have long been in America, interracial outmarriage (any marriage in which one partner is non-Asian) still remains a minority phenomenon. In 1979 in Los Angeles county, outmarriage rates for Japanese were 49.9 percent, for Chinese, 30.2 percent and for Koreans, 19.2 percent (Kitano, 1984). Although interracial marriages of all kinds have doubled since 1969, they still accounted for only 2 percent of all marriages in 1982 (Wilson, 1984).

Thus rather than the great American "melting pot," what we really have are numerous familial subgroups: the Chinese-American family, the black family, the Spanish-origin family, etc. Each of these subgroup families share familial characteristics with all American families but also have specific characteristics unique to themselves.

Although this book tends to focus on aspects of family life that are common to all families regardless of race or nationality, it is important to note that *each* family is not *all* families. Table 2-3 compares a few demographic characteristics for four different family groups. This is followed by a brief discussion of Asian-American, Black, and Spanish-origin families. These discussions are not meant to be exhaustive. Rather they are aimed at alerting the reader to the fact that America is made up of diverse family groups representing many subcultures.

Asian-American Families

In 1965 the discriminatory immigration quotas against Asians were lifted. Since then a large number of Asians, mainly those dislocated by the wars in Vietnam and Cambodia, have entered the United States. These latest Asian immigrants have largely avoided assimilation, setting up their own subcommunities and maintaining many of their family traditions.

As with any group of immigrants, however, those Asians who came early to this country (mainly Chinese, Japanese, and Koreans) have slowly become acculturated. Thus their families have become increasingly similar to American families in general.

Compared to the rest of American society, Asians generally have more conservative family and sexual values, a lower fertility rate, fewer out-of-wedlock births, and more traditional attitudes toward the roles of women. Their households tend to be larger because they more often have relatives living with the nuclear family. Despite acculturation, Asians seem to feel a strong duty and obligation to their families and still believe in restraining strong feelings and being polite to others.

Verbal communication within Asian-American families is relatively restrained compared to that in Anglo families. This verbal reticence is not only rooted in traditional cultural norms but may also have been strongly reinforced by racial discrimination. On the other hand, there appears to be much greater utilization of nonverbal and indirect modes of communication. Family members generally become quite sensitive to using nonverbal cues and to reading between the lines of indirect statements.

Unlike traditional Asian families, contemporary Asian-American families are not dominated by parent-son relationships. The strongest relationships appear to be those between husband and wife and between the mother and her children. Husbands and wives appear to enjoy much closer companionship today than in previous years. Since mothers continue to assume most of the responsibility for childrearing they develop the closest relationships with their children. Fathers still tend to maintain some distance from their children in order to engender respect and obedience. While fathers play with the children, they do not try to become close companions in the way that Anglo fathers do. Parents are more likely to show affection for their children in indirect ways (for instance, by sacrificing their own needs for their children's), rather than with words or overt displays of affection, such as hugging or kissing.

These relationships have made the Asian-American family a close-knit social unit. This cohesiveness is reflected in the social activities of Asian-American families, which tend to be more family-centered than those of Anglo families. Children are more likely to be included in Asian-American social gatherings since parents appear less comfortable about leaving them at home with baby-sitters.

Childrearing

While acculturation toward Anglo middle-class patterns has taken place, many aspects of traditional Asian childrearing practices appear to be continued among contemporary Asian-American families. The early years of childhood are still characterized by close, nurturant care by the mother, who tends to be more permissive with the young infant than her Anglo counterpart. Infants are seldom allowed to cry for prolonged periods before they are picked up by their mothers. Mothers tend to feed their infants on demand rather than by scheduling. On the average, weaning takes place at a later age than for Anglo infants. Toilet training is also more gradual. Parents often allow the young child to sleep with them, occasionally tolerating such behavior even after the child begins school.

Such an approach to childrearing develops close, affective ties within the family and the child's sense of belonging to the family. It also makes the children strongly dependent on the mother to satisfy their needs and, in turn, enables the mother to use various deprivation techniques to control the child's behavior. Moreover, even as the Asian-American mother caters to the needs of her child, she inculcates the child with a sense of obligation, which she continues to reinforce as the child grows older. Consequently, she is able to use shame and guilt to control behavior by appealing to this sense of obligation whenever the child deviates from her expectations.

Kinship and Community

The nuclear family consisting of the parents and their children is the norm today among Asian-American families. However, close ties are still maintained with many relatives outside the immediate residential family through frequent visits and telephone calls, mutual assistance, reciprocal gift giving, and various social get-togethers. The bonds appear particularly strong between married sisters and between

Table 2-3
Some Demographic Variables for Four Family Groups: 1984

Variable	Asian-American[3]	Black	Spanish-Origin	White
Percent population*	2.1% (5 million)	12% (27 million)	6.5% (15 million)	
Percent married-couple families[2]	62.2%	37%	60%	61%
Birth rates per thousand[1]	58	72.2	86.1	64.4
Percent women childless 18–44 years[1]	37%	30%	29.1%	38.8%
Percent one parent families[2]	12–14%	59%	23%	20%
Children under 18 Living with:				
2 parents	88%	41%	70%	81%
1 parent	12%	53%	27%	17%
mother only	10%	50%	25%	15%
father only[2]	2%	3%	2%	2%
Median Family Income (1985)	$28,000 (est.)	$16,786	$19,027	$29,152
Divorces per 1000 married persons with spouse present[2]	50 68	155 269	159 219	84 (men) 129 (women)
Percent high school graduates among males aged 25–29[3]	90 + %	73.8%	58.4%	87.2%

*The population of the United States was approximately 240 million on January 1, 1986.
[1]U.S. Census Bureau. "Fertility of American Women: June 1984." *Current Population Reports.* Series P-20, No. 401. Washington, D.C.: U.S. Government Printing Office. November, 1985.
[2]U.S. Census Bureau. "Marital Status and Living Arrangements: March 1984." *Current Population Reports.* Series P-20, No. 398. Washington, D.C.: U.S. Government Printing Office. April, 1985.
[3]Many of the Asian-American figures are best possible estimates. Gardner, R. W., et al., "Asian Americans: Growth, Change, and Diversity." *Population Bulletin.* Washington, D.C.: Population Reference Bureau. 40. 4 October, 1985. 1980 Census, Chapter D. Detailed Population Characteristics. Part I, Section A. Tables 253–310.

a mother and her married daughters. While grandparents generally do not live with their married children, they often live nearby and become quite involved with their children's families.

Strongly complementing family ties are the extensive networks of affiliations and communications that exist in the Asian-American communities. These include both informal networks, such as family friends and social groups, and formal networks, such as ethnic newspapers, churches, family and business associations, recreational clubs, and various other community organizations.

It is these networks that made the Asian-American communities very close-knit social entities. They strongly reinforce the sanctioning techniques of the family for controlling behavior by serving as effective channels for gossip and news about both misdeeds and achievements of individuals in the community. Through such communications, the "good families" and "bad families" are readily identified. Thus, community members are quite aware that their actions will become widely known and ultimately reflect on their families' reputations.

In sum, culture seems to be the key element in Asian family life. Their traditional culture stressed the importance of the family unit at the expense of the individual, and socialization processes in the family created patterns of self-control that facilitated the achievement of societal goals. These cultural values were very consonant with traditional American values and made them adaptable to the American family system. Class membership does not seem as important since many of the Asian immigrants brought with them values associated with the middle class: that is, an emphasis on education and a capitalist orientation.

Black-American Families

Black-American families have a history unlike that of any other minority. The fact that blacks were first brought to this country as slave labor and their family relationships were ignored by their white owners effectively destroyed many of their tribal traditions and identities. They were traded and sold as individuals rather than as family units. Thus the modern breakdown of the black family so widely decried by social scientists really has its roots in the nonrecognition of the black family by early slave traders and owners.

Black Americans make up the largest minority (12 percent of the population) in America. Because their early transportation to America as slaves was rooted in economics, it is appropriate that we start our discussion with the modern black family's economic circumstances. Per capita income for blacks was up from 60 percent of that for persons of all races in 1970 to 63 percent in 1979. About 15 percent of all American families, but 31 percent of black families, fell below the poverty line in 1984 (Moynihan, 1986, p. 111) if various government welfare and subsidy programs are excluded.

However, family poverty in the United States ties closely to the number of single-parent households found in any group. In fact, a White House task force report on families indicated that, "The poverty issue . . . would disappear almost entirely with the improved economy (1981) except that the rates of divorce and formation of single-parent households remains high (Moynihan, 1986, p. 114)." And it is here that the black families vary the most from the norm. As Table 2-3 (p. 55) pointed out, the 1984 divorce rate for blacks was almost twice as high as for other American families. Children living in single-parent families account for 53 percent of all black families but only 26 percent of all American families (see "Children Having Children," p. 395).

It appears as if the black families' economic problems are at least partially rooted in this pattern of single parenthood. In 1985, Dorothy I. Height, president of the National Council of Negro Women, commented that

. . . while early marriage was common in the black community in previous times and hence early motherhood, the statistical facts have changed dramatically in one area: Today an overwhelming majority of all black children are born to single teenage mothers. It must be regarded as a natural catastrophe in our midst, a threat to the future of black people without equal. (Moynihan, 1986, p. 167)

Interracial outmarriage (any marriage when one partner is nonblack) among blacks tends to be low. In 1982 all interracial marriages accounted for only 2 percent of all marriages. White wife–black husband were the most common outmarriage among blacks and accounting for .5 percent of all marriages between 1968 and 1980 (Wilson, 1984).

Interracial married couples have a greater probability of having a short marriage than married couples with the husband and wife of the same race. Of first marriages that were contracted in 1950 and were still intact twenty years later, 90 percent of the white husband-wife and 78 percent of the black husband-wife couples were still living together. But only 63 percent of black husband–white wife and 47 percent of white husband–black wife marriages were still together (Glick, 1981).

Ball and Robbins (1986) report that the overall levels of perceived well-being for black men and women are nearly identical to levels found among all Americans despite the economic difficulties. Unlike other groups, however, marriage is not associated with the highest satisfaction levels. In fact, marriage is associated with the lowest satisfaction levels for black men.

A number of factors may account for this. Black families face both economic and social discrimination problems. Thus black men more than others face difficulty with the provider role, which may lead to difficulty in spousal relations. As income levels increase for black men, there is more marital satisfaction and intact first marriages increase (Glick, 1981). There are also disparities in education and in the sex ratio between black men and women. Spanier and Glick (1980) found that black women have a more restricted field of marriage eligibles than do white women, and to compensate, they often marry less-educated men. This reversal of the generally expected relationship may have a negative impact on marital satisfaction for both partners (Ball & Robbins, 1986, p. 393).

Both the high number of black mother-child families and the black husband's low marital satisfaction levels might be accounted for by disproportionate numbers of black women compared to black men. Guttentag and Secord (1983, p. 201) point out that in 1970, for example, there were severe shortages of black men in every age category from twenty to forty-two years

of age such that 20 or more out of every 100 black women did not have a potential partner in the marriage pool. Because of the high number of available women, many black men may simply seek and find more-rewarding, less-demanding relationships outside of marriage.

Gary et al. (1986) conducted a study of black families in Washington, D.C. (Equal numbers of husband-wife and mother-child families) to identify black family strengths. The researchers found the same kind of strengths in strong black families as were described in Chapter 1. In addition, the researchers found:

- a love for children and general acceptance of children born out of wedlock
- a high religious orientation
- general enthusiasm for life
- pride in their own accomplishments and those of black people generally
- strong kinship bonds
- family unity

Like Spanish-origin families, black families tend to have higher proportions of three-generation families than white families. Often it is an aging parent living in the family (11.3 percent of black families had a parent living with them sometime between 1966 and 1976 for an average of four years). However, more often it was a grandchild (28.1 percent of families had a grandchild with them sometime between 1966 and 1976 for an average of 4.2 years) (Beck & Beck, 1984). The strong family bonds (especially among black women) help lend stability to the family.

Black families are an important subculture of American society. They differ in many ways from other Amer-

ican families, but strong black families possess value systems, patterns of behavior, and institutions that can be understood and appreciated for their own strengths and characteristics (Peters, 1978).

Spanish-Origin Families

Spanish-origin families comprise 6.5 percent of the American population. This subpopulation has been growing rapidly, especially in the Southwest and in Florida. It is composed mainly of people from Mexico, Puerto Rico, Cuba, and Central and South America. The percentage of population figure may be higher than found by the census in 1980 due to the fact that many Spanish-origin persons, especially those from Mexico, enter the country illegally and do not participate in the census.

Families of Spanish origin tend to have a higher birth rate than either Asian, black, or white families but divorce rate, percentage of married couples and single families do not differ significantly from the general population (see Table 2-3, p. 55).

In general, Spanish-origin families tend to place strong emphasis on the importance of the family (familism). Relatives play a large part in family functions and recreation. Extended family members tend to be the best friends of one another. The families tend to be patriarchal (male dominated) and the "double standard" for sexual behavior persists (Mirande, 1977).

Most researchers see familism as the most significant characteristic of the Spanish-origin family. Children tend to develop close bonds with grandparents, aunts, uncles, cousins, and other extended family members. Friends of the family who are not directly related are often symbolically incorporated into the family. Thus for the children, there may be lots of unrelated aunts, uncles, and godparents. This Spanish custom is termed "compadrazgo" and remains a part of many Spanish-American families.

Another characteristic of the Spanish-origin family is "machismo" of the men. This is the idea that the man must adhere to male ideals of strength and power. Much of this role is fulfilled among male peers. The younger Spanish-American male often relates closely with his male friends, sometimes forming gangs in the large urban areas. Much of the social activity of the male even after he marries and reaches middle-age involves his male friends.

Because this ideal of male power and strength is widespread in the Spanish culture, many see it as the basis of a highly patriarchal family structure. Yet studies examining the power structure and decision-making processes within Spanish-origin families uncover a much more egalitarian relationship between mother and father than expected (Hawkes & Taylor, 1975; Ybarra, 1977; Baca Zinn, 1980; Cromwell & Cromwell, 1978). Some suggest that the Spanish-origin family is in actual practice "mother centered" but presents a façade of patriarchy to support the machismo of the male outside of the home (Baca Zinn, 1975, 1976).

Although outmarriage (marriage to a person of non-Spanish origin) has increased rapidly since World War II and is much higher than Asian or Black rates, the trend to outmarriage seems to be stabilizing (Staples & Mirande, 1980). After examining outmarriage trends Murguia and Frisbie (1977, p. 387) concluded that the Spanish-origin American population will endure as a distinct sociocultural entity for some time to come.

The Center on Budget and Policy Priorities has found that poverty is worsening among Hispanics. The median income of Hispanic-Americans dropped 9.8 percent between 1973 and 1985; while median income of all American families fell 4.9 percent during this period. Thus, as with Black families, economic problems loom large for Spanish-origin families.

Most of the material on Asian-American families has been adapted from two sources:
1. Suzuki, B. "Asian-American Families." In *Parenting in Multicultural Society*, edited by M. D. Fantini and R. Cardenas. New York: Longman, 1980.
2. Staples, R., and Mirande, A. "Varieties of Family Experience." *Journal of Marriage and the Family* (November 1980):157–173.

American Ways of Love

Contents

*When God would invent a thing
apart from eating or drink or
game or sport, and yet a world—
restful while in which our
minds can melt and smile. He
made of Adam's rib an Eve
creating thus the game of
love.*

Piet Hein

To most Americans, love and marriage are like hand and glove, apple pie and ice cream, bacon and eggs: They belong together. Where there is one, there should be the other. Of course, we all know of marriages without love, and romantic literature is full of examples of love without marriage. But the traditional ideal, the ultimate in human relationships for most Americans, is the time-honored combination of love and marriage.

When Americans are asked: Why do you want to marry? they often reply, "Because I love. . . ." So we Americans marry for love. But doesn't everyone? What other reasons could there be? There are several other reasons; indeed love as a basis for marriage may be a unique American contribution to the world. As Ralph Linton pointed out many years ago, "All societies recognize that there are occasional violent emotional attachments between persons of the opposite sex, but our present American culture is the only one which has attempted to capitalize on these and make them the basis for marriage" (Linton, 1936, p. 175).

In most societies love has historically been an amusing pastime, a distraction, or, in some cases, a godsent affliction. For example, courtly love began as a diversion among the feudal aristocracy. It exalted both chastity and adultery. Courtly love glorified love from afar and made a fetish of suffering over love affairs. It made a great game of love in which men proved their manliness on the jousting field in the name of love and a woman's honor. Adultery was an integral part of courtly love. The intrigue and excitement of adultery added to the sport and made the love even more sweet. Marriage was not considered the proper place for courtly love. Married love was too mundane and unexciting.

> The story of the knight Ulrich von Lichtenstein highlights courtly love, which seldom found consummation in marriage. At an early age Ulrich pledged his love and admiration to an unnamed lady. He accepted every challenge in an effort to prove himself worthy of serving his love. He was filled with melancholy and painful longings for his lady, a condition which he claimed gave him joy. The heartless lady, however, rejected his admiration even after his ten years of silent devotion and his many feats of valor. Undaunted, perhaps even inspired by her rebuffs, he undertook a stupendous journey in 1227 from Venice north to Bohemia during which he claimed to have broken the incredible total of 307 lances fighting his way to Vienna and his lady love. It comes as something of a shock when by his own statement he stopped off for three days to visit his wife and children. For the fact is that this lovesick Galahad, this kissless wonder, this dauntless knight-errant had long had a wife to lie with when he had the urge, and a family to live with when he felt lonely. He even speaks of his affection for his wife, but, of course, not his love; to love her would have been improper and unthinkable to the ethic of courtly love. (Hunt, 1959, pp. 132–139)

On the other hand, ancient Japan felt love to be a grave offense if not properly sanctioned, for it interfered with proper marriage arrangements. Etsu Sugimoto describes this in *A Daughter of the Samurai* (1935, pp. 115–116):

When she was employed in our house, she was very young, and because she was the sister of father's faithful Jiya, she was allowed much freedom. A youthful servant, also of our house, fell in love with her. For young people to become lovers without the sanction of the proper formalities was a grave offense in any class, but in a samurai household it was a black disgrace to the house. The penalty was exile through the water gate—a gate of brush built over a stream and never used except by one of the Eta, or outcast class. The departure was public and the culprits were everafter shunned by everyone. The penalty was unspeakably cruel, but in the old days severe measures were used as a preventative of law-breaking.

As surprising as it may be, such attitudes are still widespread. Marriage in many cultures has been and still is based on considerations other than love. In India, as Inset 3-1 demonstrates, the Hindu place responsibility for finding a suitable mate on the parents or older relatives. The potential mate is judged by his or her economic status, caste, family, and physical appearance. These criteria are not by any means simple snobbery; they reflect the couple's prospects for rapport, financial stability, and social acceptance, all valid concerns in marriage. Even in the United States such considerations are often found hidden in the ephemeral concept of love, as we shall see in Chapter 4.

The American Myth That Romantic Love Should Always Lead to Marriage

John Crosby (1985) suggests that the American idea that romantic love should lead to marriage is a myth (p. 295). The myth implies that love alone is the one indispensable ingredient that should determine whom and when one marries. A corollary to the myth states that if there is love, never mind the obstacles, such as lack of commonality, meshing of personality, and so on, because love will overcome every obstacle, every difference of opinion, every personality conflict.

He goes on to say that the reader may protest, "Oh, but nobody really goes to that extreme! People don't really marry just because they fall in love, and if they do, they know there are other important factors in the selection of a mate." Yes, it appears that people are more thoughtful than the myth suggests, yet when it comes to behavior, our emotions tend to cancel out and override our reasonableness. Who in the midst of falling in love is always reasonable? Indeed, the myth suggests that if you are always reasonable about being in love, you probably really aren't "in love."

Because Americans tend to believe this romantic myth that love must lead to marriage, numerous marriages are contracted that have little other than "love" going for them. So little, that within a short time the union dissolves because there is no basis on which to build a lasting relationship. Crosby goes further (p. 296):

> In the name of "falling in love" with another man or woman, many a triangle is born; and many a marriage, destroyed. In the name of "falling in love," many a career has been abandoned, and many an education disrupted, postponed, or aborted. In the name of "falling in love," many a fetus has been conceived and then followed with the nuptial ritual giving legal status to an unplanned pregnancy. In the name of "falling in love," many a family has been torn with strife because an adolescent insists on marriage with the person they love when it is clear to all others except the person blinded by love that a mistake is being made.

_____ **Inset 3-1** _____

I Certainly Don't Want the Responsibility of Picking My Own Mate

David Mace, a marriage scholar, reports the following conversation with a group of coeds in India:

"Wouldn't you like to be free to choose your own partners, like the young people in the West?"

"Oh no!" several voices replied in chorus.

"Why not?"

"For one thing," said one of them, "Doesn't it put the girl in a very humiliating position?"

"Humiliating? In what way?"

"Well, doesn't it mean that she has to try to look pretty and call attention to herself, and attract a boy, to be sure she'll get married?"

"Well, perhaps so."

"And if she doesn't want to do that, or if she feels it's undignified, wouldn't that mean she mightn't get a husband?"

"Yes, that's possible."

"So a girl who is shy and doesn't push herself forward might not be able to get married. Does that happen?"

"Sometimes it does."

"Well, surely that's humiliating. It makes getting married a sort of competition in which the girls are fighting each other for the boys. And it encourages a girl to pretend she's better than she really is. She can't relax and be herself. She has to make a good impression to get a boy, and then she has to go on making a good impression to get him to marry her."

Before we could think of an answer to this unexpected line of argument, another girl broke in.

"In our system, you see," she explained, "we girls don't have to worry at all. We know we'll get married. When we are old enough, our parents will find a suitable boy, and everything will be arranged. We don't have to enter into competition with each other."

"Besides," said a third girl, "how would we be able to judge the character of a boy we met and got friendly with? We are young and inexperienced. Our parents are older and wiser, and they aren't as easily deceived as we would be. I'd far rather have my parents choose for me. It's so important that the man I marry should be the right one. I could so easily make a mistake if I had to find him for myself."

Another girl had her hand stretched out eagerly.

"But does the girl really have any choice in the West?" she said. "From what I've read, it seems that the boy does all the choosing. All the girl can do is say yes or no. She can't go up to a boy and say 'I like you. Will you marry me?' Can she?"

We admitted that this was not done.

"So," she went on eagerly, "when you talk about men and women being equal in the West, it isn't true. When our parents are looking for a husband for us, they don't have to wait until some boy takes it into his head to ask for us. They just find out what families are looking for wives for their sons, and see whether one of the boys would be suitable. Then, if his family agrees that it would be a good match, they arrange it together."

For Crosby, to believe that the love attraction should inevitably lead to wedlock is folly. To believe that wedlock could possibly be sustained by the love attraction alone is more than folly. It is the first step toward destroying the relationship.

Lest the reader feel that such strong criticism means that love should play no role in marriage, it must be pointed out that love does indeed play a role in all lasting intimate relationships. Even in the arranged marriages of India, couples who marry with no intense love present often build a loving relationship over time. Much of the confusion about the love-as-a-basis-for-marriage myth has to do with the many definitions of love. Love does not take one form; it assumes many forms. I love my wife. I love my child. I love Mozart. I love a T-bone steak. Obviously love is many things.

Defining Love

Trying to define love has kept poets, philosophers, and sages busy since the beginning of history. What is this phenomenon that causes two people to react to one another so strongly? Is it physical? Spiritual? A mixture of the two? Why does it only occur with some people and not others? Is it the same as infatuation? The questions are endless, yet we speak of love, seek it, and recognize it when it happens even if we can't define it.

Twenty-five centuries ago the Greek poet Sappho described the physical state of love:

> For should I but see thee a little moment,
> Straight is my voice hushed;
> Yea, my tongue is broken, and through and through me
> 'Neath the flesh impalpable fire runs tingling;
> Nothing see mine eyes, and a noise of roaring
> Waves in my ear sounds;
> Sweat runs in rivers, a tremor seizes
> All my limbs, and paler than grass in Autumn,
> Caught by pains of menacing death, I falter
> Lost in the love-trance.

The Greeks divided love into three elements: eros (carnal or physical love), agape (spiritual love), and philos (brotherly or friendly love).

Eros
The physical, sexual side of love; termed "Cupid" by the Romans

Eros is the physical, sexual side of love. It is needing, desiring, and wanting the other person physically. Sappho's poem describes the effect of eros. The Romans called eros Cupid, and, as we know, Cupid shoots the arrow of love into our hearts. Eros is the aspect of love that makes our knees shake, upsets our routines, and causes us to be obsessed with thoughts of our lovers.

Agape
Greek term for spiritual love

Agape is the altruistic, giving, nondemanding side of love. It is an active concern for the life and growth of those whom we love. It is most clearly demonstrated by a parent's love for a child. Agape is an unconditional affirmation of another person. It is the desire to care, help, and give to the loved one; it is unselfish love.

Theologian Paul Tillich sees the highest form of love as a merging of eros and agape (1957, pp. 114–115):

> No love is real without a unity of eros and agape. Agape without eros is obedience to moral law, without warmth, without longing, without reunion. Eros without agape is a chaotic desire, denying the validity of the claim of the other one to be acknowledged as an independent self, able to love and to be loved.

Philos
Greek term for the love found in deep, enduring friendships; a general love of mankind

Philos is the love found in deep and enduring friendships. It is also the kind of love described in the Bible as: "Love thy neighbor as thyself." It can be deep friendship for specific people, or it can be a love that generalizes to all people. Philos is often nonexclusive, whereas eros and agape are often exclusive.

The philos element of love is most important to a society's humanity. A loving person creates loving relationships, and enough loving relationships make a loving society. A society that has a high level of philos among its members fosters the other elements of love. Lack of this kind of love creates a society of alienated and isolated individuals. When people are alienated and isolated from one another, the chance of dehumanized conflict between them escalates. Crime statistics in the United States make it clear that the Christian command to "love thy neighbor" (philos) is often ignored in our society. This kind of love turns strangers into friends, and it is more difficult to perpetrate a crime against a friend than against a stranger.

Theories of Love

Probably there are as many theories of love as there are persons in love, although it should be noted that such theories do not enjoy much empirical support. However, it is worthwhile to examine a few of them, even if only superficially. Learning how other thoughtful people have theorized about love will help us understand our own feelings and thoughts. And, as we shall see, the better we know our own attitudes and definitions of love, the better we will become in making long-lasting intimate relationships.

In his classic book *The Art of Loving*, Erich Fromm defines love as an active power that breaks through the walls that separate people from each other. In love we find the paradox of two beings becoming one yet remaining two (Fromm, 1956). Like the Greeks, Fromm discusses several kinds of love, including brotherly and maternal love. Brotherly love is characterized by friendship and companionship with affection. Maternal love is characterized by an unselfish interest in your partner and a placing of yourself second to your partner's needs. For Fromm mature love includes attachment plus sexual response. More importantly it includes the four basic elements necessary to any intimate relationship: care, responsibility, respect, and knowledge. People who share all of the elements of mature love are pair-bonded. The relationship is reciprocal. Fromm goes on to suggest that a person's need to love and be loved in this full sense arises from our feelings of separateness and aloneness. Love helps us escape these feelings and gain a feeling of unitedness.

Taking off from this idea, Lawrence Casler (1969) considers that love develops in part because of our human needs for acceptance and confirmation. These needs are heightened in a society as competitive and individualized as ours. Thus it is a relief to meet someone whose choices coincide with our own, who doesn't try to undermine us in some way. We tend to attach ourselves to such a person because he or she offers us validation, and such validation is an important basis for love (see Rubin, 1973, ch. 7).

Casler points out that American dating may provoke love feelings in the partners more as a by-product than from some innate attraction. For example, a person pretends to like a date more than he or she really does for any number of reasons including simple politeness. The date, also seeking validation, responds favorably. This favorable response makes the first person feel good and feel fondness for the one who has made him or her feel good. As one person's feelings increase, the other's are likely to also. Obviously, it is easier to love someone who loves you than someone who is indifferent.

Of course, falling in love is more complex than in this example because of our many needs besides validation. Sex is another of these needs:

> Society emphasizes the necessity for love to precede sex. Although many disregard this restriction, others remain frightened or disturbed by the idea of a purely sexual relationship. The only way for many sexually aroused individuals to avoid frustration or anxiety is to fall in love—as quickly as possible. More declarations of love have probably been uttered in parked cars than in any other location; some of these are

What Do You Think?

1. What do you personally mean when you say, "I love you"?
2. What do your parents mean when they say, "I love you" to each other? To you?
3. Does saying "I love you" carry a commitment to marriage? To sexual intercourse?
4. How do you recognize if a person is sincere in saying that he or she loves you?
5. How does love make you feel physically?

surely nothing more than seduction ploys, but it is likely that self-seduction is involved in most cases. (Casler, 1969, p. 33)

In more general terms Casler's sources of love are: (1) the need for security, (2) sexual satisfaction, and (3) social conformity. If these are the causes of love, what are its consequences?

First Casler says, "Being in love makes it easier to have guilt-free sex, to marry, and to view oneself as a normal healthy citizen." Being in love also creates the error of overevaluation (romanticized ideal images; see Chapter 5) of the love object. Love will foster dependency on the love object to the extent that the love object is relied on for gratification.

The love of a child for a parent is a result mainly of the child's dependence on the all-powerful parent. To the degree that one's love of the partner is dependent, it remains immature and childlike. Mature love tends to create interdependence between the couple. Each member is an independent person with self-esteem and enough security to give and relate emotionally to the partner. Too much independence results in separateness and the inability to relate intimately to another person. In a sense love that stresses independence above all else is similar to the adolescent period in which the effort to achieve personal identity impels one to rebel against most close relationships.

Ira Reiss (1960) suggests the wheel as a model of love (see Figure 3-1). In the rapport stage (Stage 1) the partners are struck by feelings that they have known each other before, that they are comfortable with one another, and that they both want to deepen the relationship. These feelings lead to Stage 2—self-revelation—during which more and more intimate thoughts and feelings are shared. This sharing deepens the relationship because such sharing is only done with special people. As the sharing becomes more and more intimate, a feeling of mutual dependency develops (Stage 3). With it comes a feeling of loss when the partner is not present. More and more personal needs are being met (Stage 4) as the couple deepens their relationship. Reiss suggests that it was perhaps the hope of having these deeper needs met that caused the initial rapport.

Figure 3-1 The Wheel of Love

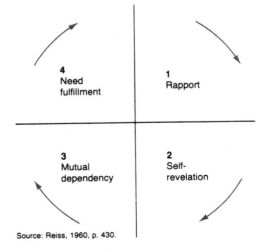

Source: Reiss, 1960, p. 430.

Inset 3-2

Love Is . . .

Love is such a tissue of
paradoxes, and exists in
such an endless variety of
forms and shades that you
may say almost anything
about it that you please,
and it is likely to be correct.

Henry Fink
Romantic Love and Personal Beauty

Love is patient and kind;
love is not jealous or boastful;
it is not arrogant or rude.
Love does not insist on its own
way; it is not irritable and
resentful; it does not rejoice
at wrong, but rejoices in the right.
Love bears all things,
believes all things, hopes all
things, endures all things.

I Corinthians 13:4–7

How do I love thee? Let me count the ways.
I love thee to the depth and breadth and height
My soul can reach, when feeling out of sight
For the ends of Being and ideal Grace.
I love thee to the level of everyday's
Most quiet need, by sun and candle-light.
I love thee freely, as men strive for Right;
I love thee purely, as they turn from Praise.
I love thee with the passion put to use
In my old griefs, and with my childhood's faith.
I love thee with a love I seemed to lose
With my lost saints—I love thee with the breath,
Smiles, tears, of all my life!—and, if God choose,
I shall but love thee better after death.

Elizabeth Barrett Browning

Let me not to the marriage of true minds
Admit impediments. Love is not love
Which alters when it alteration finds,
Or bends with the remover to remove.
O, no! It is an ever-fixed mark,
That looks on tempests and is never shaken;
It is the star to every wandering bark,
Whose worth's unknown, although his height be taken.
Love's not Time's fool, though rosy lips and cheeks
Within his bending sickle's compass come;
Love alters not with his brief hours and weeks,
But bears it out even to the edge of doom.
If this be error and upon me proved,
I never writ, nor no man ever loved.

William Shakespeare
Sonnet 116

Love birds burn in the sky,
The Flame of Passion carries them high.
Beaks touching as one,
Wings beginning to melt, as they ride the crest of the flames.
With nothing to hold them in their flight
They fall
Into the inferno
Of their own passion.

Cynthia Moorman

These four processes are in a sense really one process for when one feels rapport, he/she reveals him/herself and becomes dependent, thereby fulfilling his/her personality needs. The circularity is most clearly seen in that the needs being fulfilled were the original reason for feeling rapport. (1960, p. 143)

Borland (1975) changes the model slightly, likening it to a clock spring rather than a circle.

As these four processes occur and lead one into the other, they wind themselves toward a closer and more intimate relationship with an understanding of the real inner self of the other person. As this occurs, the individuals form an increasingly tighter bond to one another in much the same way as a clock spring tightens as it is wound. (p. 291)

Goldstine (1977) suggests that love occurs in three stages. Stage I, Falling in Love, is characterized by excitement, emotional highs, good feelings both about oneself and one's partner and the belief that this new love will transform one's life. Both partners strive to put their best foot forward and each perceives the other through "rose-colored" glasses, that is, they see the good points and are blind to the negative aspects of their partner. Unfortunately, Stage I is brief and fleeting at best. Over time, satiation dilutes the intense pleasure the partners originally found in each other. Real-life obligations encroach on the relationship and evidence of each other's shortcomings accumulates. Delightful in itself, Stage I doesn't necessarily ensure that a relationship will endure and flourish. All it really means is that two people are strongly attracted to one another.

Stage II, Disappointment, begins when the rose-colored glasses come off. Conflicts and failure pile up and the couple begins to realize that perhaps their lives are not being transformed. The question now becomes one of how the couple works out their differences, how they learn to accept one another's short-comings, and how they handle the resentments that arise as they find that their partners are real live human beings rather than the idealized images with which they fell in love. The troubles people experience in Stage II do not necessarily mean that they have chosen the wrong partner, that they are no longer in love, that their relationship must be ended. There will always be ups and downs in a relationship and with persistence and goodwill a couple can move on into the third stage.

Stage III, Acceptance, finds the couple bringing their relationship into some kind of balance. Frustrations and anxieties don't stop, but they no longer trigger doubts about the goodness of the mate or their relationship. They have confidence in each other, they know that they can work differences out, they trust each other and share a deep intimacy, not of illusion, but of earned knowledge.

Romantic Love

Romantic love
Love at first sight, based on the ideas that there is only one true love and that love is the most important criterion for marriage

For many Americans the idea of **romantic love** most influences their thoughts about attraction and intimacy. This concept of love encompasses such ideas as "love at first sight," "the one and only love," "lifelong commitment," "I can't live without him/her," "the perfect mate," and so forth.

In essence the concept of romantic love supplies a set of idealized images by which we can judge the object of our love as well as the quality of the relationship. Unfortunately, such romanticized images usually bear little relationship to the real world. Often we project our beliefs onto another person, exaggerating the char-

acteristics that match the qualities we are looking for and masking those that do not. That is, we transform the other person into an unreal hero or heroine to fit our personal concept of a romantic marital partner. Thus we often fall in love with our own romantic ideas rather than with a real human being.

For example, the traditional romantic ideals dictate a strong, confident, protective role for a man and a charming, loving, dependent role for a woman. A woman accepting this stereotype will tend to overlook and deny dependent needs of her mate. She will tend to repress independent qualities in herself. Love for her means each correctly fulfilling the proper role. The same holds true for a man who has traditional romantic ideals.

Those who "fall in love with love" in this way will suffer disappointment when their partner's "real person" begins to emerge. Rather than meet this emerging person with joy and enthusiasm, partners who hold romanticized ideals may reject reality in favor of their stereotypical images. They may begin to search again for a love object, rejecting the real-life partner as unworthy or changed (see Chapter 5 for a more complete discussion of the problems of idealized expectations). Dating and broad premarital experience with the opposite sex can help correct much of this romantic idealism.

When people fall in love with their romanticized expectations rather than with their partner, they may either reject the partner or attempt to change the partner into the romantic ideal. John Robert Clark (1961, p. 18) has a pithy description of the first action:

> In learning how to love a plain human being today, as during the romantic movement, what we usually want unconsciously is a fancy human being with no flaws. When the mental picture we have of someone we love is colored by wishes of childhood, we may love the picture rather than the real person behind it. Naturally, we are disappointed in the person we love if he does not conform to our picture. Since this kind of disappointment has no doubt happened to us before, one might suppose we would tear up the picture and start all over. On the contrary, we keep the picture and tear up the person. Small wonder that divorce courts are full of couples who never gave themselves a chance to know the real person behind the pictures in their lives.

The second action, attempting to change one's spouse, also leads to trouble. Making changes is difficult, and the person being asked to do so may resent the demand or may not wish to change.

Generally, romantic love's rose-colored glasses tend to distort the real world, especially the mate, thereby creating a barrier to happiness. This is not to deny that romantic love can add to an intimate relationship. Romance will bring excitement, emotional highs, and color to one's relationship. From there one can move toward a more mature love relationship. As emotional, intellectual, social, and physical intimacy develops romance takes its place as one of several aspects of the relationship, not the only one.

Infatuation

Q. What is the difference between love and infatuation?

A. Infatuation is when you think that he is as sexy as Robert Redford, as smart as Henry Kissinger, as noble as Ralph Nader, as funny as Woody Allen, and as athletic as John McEnroe.

Love is when you realize that he's as sexy as Woody Allen, as smart as John McEnroe, as funny as Ralph Nader, as athletic as Henry Kissinger, and nothing like Robert Redford—but you'll take him anyway.

Romantic love and infatuation are often confused. Some (Hatfield & Walster, 1978) say that they are actually the same thing. Lovers use the term *romantic love* to describe an ongoing love relationship. The couple's feelings, bodily reactions, and interactions when they are romantically in love are the same as with infatuation. The difference may be only semantic. The term *infatuation* is used to negate one's past feelings of love that have now changed. Love is supposed to last forever, so falling out of love means that the feeling for the other person was not really love; it must have been something less, namely, infatuation (Udry, 1974). According to this line of thinking, perhaps it is only possible to tell infatuation from romantic love in retrospect.

Still others suggest that infatuation may be the first step toward love. The feelings of physical attraction, the "chemical" arousal, the intense preoccupation with the partner, all characteristics of infatuation, are also the precursors of "real" love. From the many ways the terms are used, it is apparent that we probably cannot agree completely on the difference between romantic love and infatuation.

Ann Landers periodically reprints a suggested list of differences between the two terms:

Love or Infatuation?

Infatuation is instant desire. It is one set of glands calling to another.

Love is friendship that has caught fire. It takes root and grows—one day at a time.

Infatuation is marked by a feeling of insecurity. You are excited and eager, but not genuinely happy. There are nagging doubts, unanswered questions, little bits and pieces about your beloved that you would just as soon not examine too closely. It might spoil the dream.

Love is the quiet understanding and mature acceptance of imperfection. It is real. It gives you strength and grows beyond you—to bolster your beloved. You are warmed by their presence, even when they are far away.

Infatuation says "We must get married right away. I can't risk losing you."

Love says, "Be patient. Don't panic. Plan your future with confidence."

Infatuation has an element of sexual excitement. If you are honest, you will admit it is difficult to be in one another's company unless you are sure it will end in intimacy.

Love is the maturation of friendship. You must be friends before you can be lovers.

Infatuation lacks confidence. When they are away you wonder if they are being true.

Love means trust. You are calm, secure, and unthreatened. Your partner feels that trust and it makes him/her even more trustworthy.

Infatuation might lead you to do things you'll regret later, but love never will.

Love lifts you up. It makes you look up. It makes you think up. It makes you a better person than you were before.

Such a list makes love sound grown-up and infatuation childish. Yet playfulness and childishness are acceptable and important parts of any intimate relationship.

How can we avoid the pitfalls of romantic love and infatuation? How can we be sure that we love someone just as they are and are not dazzled by our own romantic image of them? Perhaps we can't. Love is learned and part of learning to move toward a mature, realistic love may simply be trial and error.

Furthermore, the most important prerequisite for true love may be knowing and accepting ourselves, complete with faults and virtues. If we cannot deal with our own imperfections, how can we be tolerant of someone else's? As Erich Fromm puts it (1956, p. 59):

Love of others and love of ourselves are not alternatives. On the contrary, an attitude of love toward themselves will be found in all those who are capable of loving others. Love, in principle, is indivisible as far as the connection between "objects" and one's own self is concerned. Genuine love is an expression of productiveness and implies care, respect, responsibility, and knowledge.

Loving and Liking

In the play *Who's Afraid of Virginia Woolf?*, Edward Albee depicts a couple who are in love but who also dislike and at times hate one another. Can you really be in love with someone whom you dislike? The answer is that you can be passionately in love with someone you don't like, but your love probably will not evolve into companionate love over time. Rather, it will diminish as the dislike grows and ultimately will lead to the breakup of the relationship. In *Virginia Woolf* the dislike leads to hate and horrendous fighting rather than breakup.

Elaine Hatfield and William Walster (1978, p. 9) suggest that

> liking and companionate love have much in common. Liking is simply the affection we feel for a casual acquaintance. Companionate love is the affection we feel for those with whom our lives are deeply intertwined. The only real difference between liking and loving is the depth of our feelings and the degree of our involvement with the other person.

It is probably more important to like someone than it is to love them if you are to live together over an extended period of time. Roommate situations clearly demonstrate this. To live closely together on a day-to-day basis is difficult. Sharing cooking, eating, cleaning, and the many mundane chores that make daily living successful is next to impossible if you dislike your roommate. On the other hand, you don't have to love your roommate to live together successfully.

Positive reinforcement and positive associations are important to the maintenance of a liking relationship. It is obvious that someone you enjoy being with is easier to like than someone with whom you feel rotten. It is also important that the liked person be associated with positive experiences.

> You must associate your mate with pleasure if you're going to keep on loving [and liking]. Romantic dinners, trips to the theater, evenings at home together, and vacations never stop being important. It's critical that you don't come to associate your partner with wet towels thoughtlessly dropped on the floor, barked out orders, crying and nagging, or guilt ("You never say you love me"). If your relationship is to survive, it's important that you both continue to associate your partner with good things. And this requires some thought and effort. (Hatfield and Walster, 1978, p. 12)

In addition to liking the person we love, it is equally important to a long-lasting love relationship that the person you love be your friend as well as your lover. *Scenes from Marriage* at the end of the chapter discusses the relationship between love and friendship.

Love Is What You Make It

The more one investigates the idea of love, the harder it becomes to pin down. Everyone is quick to describe it, most have experienced it, and all know the mythology of the romantic ideal even though many disclaim their belief in it. Although there does seem to be some agreement on at least a few of the aspects of love, much of what love is appears to be unique to each person. That is to say, we each define love for ourselves. This may lead to problems for a couple if each member defines love somewhat differently from the other. It is important to examine your concept of love in order to understand it and thereby recognize differences between what you and your partner mean by love. For example, A. Lynn Scoresby (1977, p. 168) suggests that

> since love is the word symbol we are accustomed to use in explaining great varieties of marital events, if actual feelings of love are not determinant of happy marriages, then mutual agreement about what love means is. Love is, after all, the most often given reason for getting married, and loss of love is the most often given reason for dissolving a marriage.

So, if a couple can agree on what love and loving acts are and can act on this agreement at least most of the time, their chances are great of maintaining love in their relationship.

Let us begin by examining the aspects of love where there seems to be at least some agreement. Most people agree that there is a strong physical attraction between lovers at least during the early stages of their relationship. This attraction is often accompanied by a variety of physiological reactions such as more rapid breathing, increased pulse rate, and muscular tension. In other words, the person "in love" experiences general emotional arousal when thinking of the loved one or when in his or her presence.

Of course, such a reaction could be just sexual attraction and infatuation rather than love. But if the physical attraction is accompanied by a strong and growing emotional attachment, and if there is a marked tendency to idealize and be preoccupied with the person, then the reactions are more indicative of love.

Generally there is a feeling of openness between lovers. Both feel they can confide in the other. Both believe the other likes them as they really are, so they can be more open, more honest, more communicative—in a word, more intimate—than in nonlove relationships. One way of viewing love may be as "intimate self-disclosure" (Schultz & Rodgers, 1975, p. 2).

Such open sharing of your true feelings can be risky. A person in love is easily hurt, as all lovers, past and present, will attest. Thus to love is always an adventure because danger is involved. *Indifference is the opposite of love.* A lover cares, a lover reveals more of himself or herself and a lover is therefore vulnerable to being hurt. When hurt occurs, a lover may react to the pain with hostility and anger, and, at times, with hate. Indifference is the reaction of someone who doesn't care, who isn't hurt, who isn't in love. It is interesting to note that the indifferent person, the person who cares least in a relationship, exercises more control over the relationship. The caring person, the most loving person in the relationship, is more vulnerable to being hurt. Therefore caring persons often go out of their way to placate and please their mates. The fact that the mate who cares least in a relationship has more power and control over the relationship is called "**the principle of least interest.**"

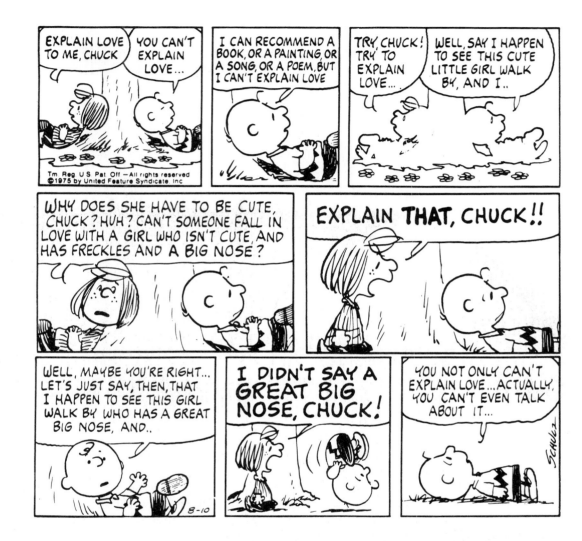

Another way of thinking of love is to ask whether the love experience is leading to personal growth. Most people in love experience an expansion of self. Being loved by another leads to feelings of confidence and security. Many people are encouraged to venture into new and perhaps unknown areas of themselves. "I feel more emotions than I've ever felt before." "I used to feel awkward meeting new people, but when I'm with Mary, I have no trouble at all." "Bill makes me feel like I can do anything I want."

Probably most Americans will agree on the characteristics of love thus far discussed: physical attraction, emotional attachment, self-disclosure and openness, and feelings of personal growth. Yet how these characteristics are expressed by individuals will vary greatly, and such variance can lead to communication breakdowns. To say and mean "I love you" is one thing. We all recognize the word, but it has become so worn by indiscriminate use through time that we can no longer identify it with certainty or clearly tell what it represents (Lasswell & Lobsenz, 1980, p. xii).

Two people very much "in love" may have quite different ideas about what this means and how to express it. For example, it is not uncommon for one partner to feel loving toward the other while at the same time the other feels unloved. It is as if they are on different emotional wavelengths. "But you never tell me that you love me," she may say. "I shouldn't have to tell you. I do loving things for you," he replies. Those "loving things" may include such actions as bringing home the paycheck, fixing broken appliances, and avoiding arguments. In her eyes they are merely things any good husband routinely does. She defines evidence of love as words of endearment, gifts, touching, tenderness: the kinds of behavior that may make him uncomfortable. He knows he loves her, but she is not getting the message. In other words love is more than emotion. Love is also an intellectual concept. It is what you think it is. It is how you define it, which will probably differ to some extent from how your partner defines it (Lasswell & Lobsenz, 1980).

Because we usually assume that our meaning of love is the same as our partner's, we may often feel unloved when, in fact, our partner's expression of love is simply unrecognized. The emotional script in this case is:

> I, like every man and woman, want to be loved. But I have my own idea, grounded in my personality and attitudes and experience, of what loving and being loved means. Moreover, locked in the prison of my own ways of thinking and feeling, I assume that my definition of love is the only correct one. As a result, I want and expect to be loved in the same way that I love others, with the same responses that I interpret as the evidence of lovingness.
>
> But I am not loved in that way. Instead (and quite logically, if one could be logical about love), I am loved the way my partner thinks and feels about love, the way he or she understands and expresses it. In my own distress, I do not recognize that my partner is experiencing the same incongruity in reverse. Puzzled, hurt, unable to communicate our confusion to each other, we both unreasonably feel unloved. (Lasswell & Lobsenz, 1980, p. 15)

In a truly loving relationship, each partner tries to learn the meaning of love as defined by the other person and to incorporate the differences into his or her own concept of love. Ideally, in a successful love relationship, each partner's concept of love grows to include the other's concept. As our personal definitions of love move closer together, our chances of feeling loved increase.

Jill and Bob are much in love. When Bob is alone with her and feeling particularly loving, he often grabs her and wrestles her down to the floor or couch. She hates this behavior and tells him, "If you really loved me, you wouldn't act like this. People who love one another don't wrestle." His feelings are hurt by her rejection of his wrestling. Jill feels most loved when Bob approaches her slowly and gently; she feels unloved when he is rough with her. He feels that she doesn't love him because she never enthusiastically physically attacks him.

In Jill and Bob's case it is clear that each person demonstrates love of the other in a different way. Bob's physical wrestling with Jill is perhaps his most comfortable way of touching her. Certainly it is the way American men are taught to display affection toward other men, as one can easily observe during a football game. On the other hand Jill has been taught that the more you love someone or something, the gentler you are. Both Jill and Bob are expressing their love, yet their differences of expression cause each to think that they are loved less than they really are. Love, it seems, is what you make it through your attitudes and behaviors.

Styles of Loving

Marcia Lasswell and Norman Lobsenz (1980) agree with our thesis that each person defines love in a unique manner based on life experiences. They believe that one's definition of and attitude toward love, although individual, can be classified into six general styles: best friends, game playing, logical, possessive, romantic, and unselfish. Most people will include a mixture of styles in their definition, with one or two predominating. To understand various styles of loving is valuable because they are basic to all of us and will characterize our intimate loving relationships.

Best Friends Love

> When Jennifer and Gary told their families they were going to be married, the news was a pleasant surprise to everyone. "We knew they were close," said Jennifer's mother. "After all, our families have lived on the same block for years, and the children went through school together. But we never dreamed they would fall in love." Neither did Jennifer and Gary. "Actually it's not as if we fell in love at all. It's more that we're comfortable with each other. We have a really warm and easy relationship, so why bother to search for anyone else?"

In this case a comfortable intimacy has developed out of close association over a substantial period of time. For persons in whom this style predominates, love grows through companionship, rapport, mutual sharing and dependency, and gradual self-revelation. There is seldom any assumption at the outset of the relationship that it will flower into love or marriage. Friendly lovers find it hard to conceive of becoming emotionally involved with someone they do not know well. They rarely fantasize about other potential lovers. Even if this thought should occur to them, they would probably want to share it with their partners. After all, isn't that what a best friend is for? Such persons tend to speak of their love as "mature" compared with other styles of love, which they are likely to see as infatuation.

Typically, a person with the best-friends love style is the product of an emotionally secure and close-knit family. He or she has usually been able to count on parents and siblings for companionship, warmth, and support. In many respects this style of love resembles a good sibling relationship. The divorce rate is low for best-friend couples, but if such a relationship does break up, the partners will most likely want to remain close. After all, two people who had once loved one another could not become enemies simply because they ceased to be lovers.

Game-Playing Love

To the game-playing lover an emotional relationship is a challenge to be enjoyed, a contest to be won. The more experienced one grows at the game, the more skilled one's moves can be, and often a wide range of strategies is developed to keep the game interesting. Commitment is anathema to this style of lover. The object of the game is to play amiably at love, to encourage intimacy, yet to hold it at arm's length. The other person is usually kept emotionally off balance, and the game player's affections are never to be taken for granted.

Game-playing lovers have many artifices. For example, they avoid making long-range plans with partners. Dates are usually arranged on a spur-of-the-moment basis. Game players are careful not to go out with the same person too often; this might lead him or her to believe in some prospect of stability. Much of this kind of love style is found before marriage when a one-to-one commitment is not required or expected. Obviously, men and women who play at love have both charming and infuriating qualities. They are usually self-sufficient, make few demands on the other person, and prefer not to have demands made on them. They tend to be amusing, quick-witted, self-confident. On the other hand, they tend to be self-centered. The charge is often made that game-playing love is not truly love at all, that it is hedonism at best and promiscuity at worst. But the true game player believes in playing fair and tries not to hurt the other person.

Logical Love

Logical love concentrates on the practical values that may be found in a relationship. This style has been called "love with a shopping list." "I could never love anyone who didn't meet my requirements for a husband and father (or wife and mother)." Moreover, logical lovers are quite realistic. They usually know exactly what kind of partner they want and are willing to wait for the person who comes closest to meeting their specifications.

It is not uncommon for a lover of this pragmatic bent to avoid any relationship that he or she does not think has a good chance of becoming permanent. "Why should I waste my time?" In one sense logical love is an updated version of the traditional "arranged" matchmaking of earlier times. The modern logical lover may think that romance does have some place in love, but he or she believes more strongly that love should be an outgrowth of a couple's practical compatibility.

Pragmatic lovers consider themselves in love as long as the relationship is perceived as a fair exchange. If matters turn out not to be what they seemed, logical love calls for a two-step response. First, an effort is made to help the partner fulfill his or her original potential. If such efforts fail, then the relationship is ended. Not surprisingly, logical love requires patience: to find the proper partner; to work out problems; and if the relationship should break up, to wait to end it until a reasonable and logical time.

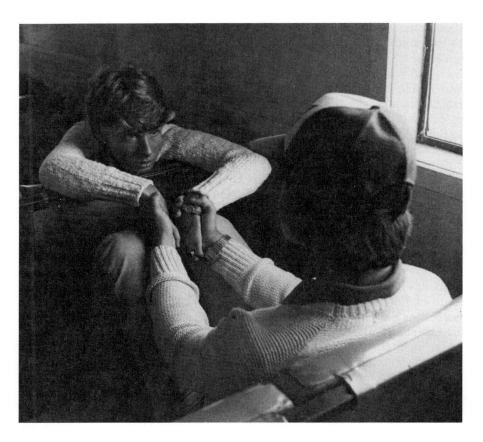

Possessive Love

Possessive love is perhaps the most unfulfilling and disturbing love style. Alternating between peaks of excitement and depths of despair, capable of shifting instantly from intense devotion to intense jealousy, this style of lover is consumed by the need to possess the beloved totally and simultaneously to be possessed by the other person. The fear of loss or rejection is omnipresent. Despite this bleak picture, the pattern is considered one of the most common definitions of being in love.

At the root of possessive love are two seemingly contradictory emotional factors. On the one hand, such lovers are enormously dependent. At the outset of the love affair they may be too excited to sleep, eat, or think clearly. Unable to control their intense reactions, they often feel at the mercy of the beloved. Yet at the same time such lovers are demanding, often placing great emotional burdens on the other person. Supersensitive, the possessive lover is constantly on the alert for the slightest sign that the partner's affection may be slackening. If such a sign is detected, or even imagined, the anxiety-ridden lover demands immediate reassurance.

When possessive love affairs break up, the ending is usually bitter and angry. The possessive lover finds it almost impossible to see the former partner again or to retain any concern or affection for him or her. It is easy to scorn possessive love and concentrate on its unpleasant characteristics, but many perfectly adequate and emotionally healthy people evidence this style of love to some degree. They prefer intense togetherness. They see jealousy as a natural part of being in love.

Romantic Love

Cupid's arrow piercing the heart and instantaneously awakening passionate devotion is the definitive image of romantic love. The romantic lover is often as much in love with love itself as with the beloved. Love at first sight is not only possible but almost a necessity. The typical romantic lover seeks a total emotional relationship with the partner. Moreover, he or she expects it to provide a constant series of emotional peaks. The fires of this love style are fueled in large part by a powerful sense of physical attraction.

Once they have found each other, the romantic lovers are likely to be in each other's arms quickly. There is a great urgency to merge physically as well as emotionally. Obviously the intensity of this initial attraction and passion cannot be maintained indefinitely at the same high level. When it begins to taper off, the romantic lover must either substitute fantasies for realities or learn to cope with growing evidence that the other person is not perfect.

One must be willing and able to reveal oneself completely, commit oneself totally, risk emotional lows as well as highs, and survive without despair if one's love is rejected. A romantic does not demand love but is confidently ready to grasp it when it appears.

Unselfish Love

Unselfish love (agape) is unconditionally caring and nurturing, giving and forgiving, and at its highest level, self-sacrificing. A characteristic of this love style is that one has no sense of martyrdom, no feeling of being put upon. The style rests on the genuine belief that love is better expressed in giving than in receiving. In a sense men and women with this style of love never actually "fall in love." Instead, they seem to have a reservoir of loving kindness that is always available. They are ruled less by their own needs than by the needs of others. Unselfish love occurs less often in real life than is imagined. Not many people have the emotional fortitude to be so giving. And even if they have, their altruism is not necessarily complete. An unselfish lover experiences in return feelings of satisfaction, recognition, even gratitude.

Learning to Love

If there really are such styles of loving as set forth by Lasswell and Lobsenz, where do they come from and how do we learn them? Essentially we learn the meaning of love and how to demonstrate it from those around us—our parents, siblings, and peers—and from the general culture in which we are raised. For example, such a simple thing as birth order will influence our definition of love. An only child becomes accustomed to a great deal of adult attention. Such a child may later feel unloved if the spouse (who is the third of four children and received relatively little adult attention) does not attend to him or her all of the time.

Our personal experiences mold our attitudes and behaviors. Thus the way we express love and what we define as love are the results of our past experiences.

Actions and Attitudes

The attitudes a person brings to love, to dating, and later to marriage have developed over many years. Because no two people experience the same upbringing, it is not surprising to find great attitudinal differences between people, even when they are "in love." Many of the difficulties we experience in our interpersonal relationships stem from conflicting attitudes and unrealistic expectations rather than from specific behavior. For example, a few socks on the floor are not as upsetting to a new wife as her husband's general attitude toward neatness. Does he expect her to wait on him? Often it is necessary to change underlying attitudes if behavior is to change, but this is difficult to do. We take our attitudes for granted without being aware of them. For example, a young man roundly criticized the double standard. But a day later, when discussing spouses' freedom to be apart occasionally, he stated that he certainly deserved time out with "the boys," but women probably shouldn't go out with their girlfriends after marriage because this might be misunderstood as an attempt to meet other men.

Attitudes generally consist of three components: affective, cognitive, and behavioral. The **affective** aspect is one's emotional response resulting from an attitude, such as "I like blondes." The **cognitive** component consists of a person's beliefs and/or factual knowledge supporting the particular attitude, such as "blondes have more fun." The **behavioral** component involves the person's overt behavior resulting from the attitude, "I date blondes."

Unfortunately, these components are not necessarily consistent. For example, my attitudes may not be founded on fact; I may not act on my attitudes; or I may voice attitudes that are not really a part of me. The young man above is an example of someone who voices one attitude—against the double standard—but favors another—for the double standard. Where do such attitudes come from? We are not born with them. We learn our most basic attitudes as we grow up, generally from our parents, siblings, and peers. The values of a society are passed on to new members, beginning at birth. This is why we must trace our attitudes toward sex, love, and marriage from early childhood in order to understand adult behavior.

Developmental Stages in Learning to Love

As we shall see in Chapter 13, children pass through varying stages of development as they grow to adulthood. Such stages are actually arbitrary classifications set up by theorists in their effort to understand development, yet the stages are useful to that understanding. Sigmund Freud delineated four psychosexual stages leading to adult sexual and love expression. Erik Erikson expanded on these to suggest eight general stages of development across a person's life span (see pp. 454–461). The following overview of Freud's four psychosexual stages will help us understand how we learn to love.

Self-love Stage: Infancy and Early Childhood During early years young children are so busy learning about their environment that almost all of their energy is focused on themselves and exploring the environment. Many believe that this early period of self-involvement sets the foundation for subsequent attitudes toward the self. It is important during these early years for the child to receive stimulation, including physical fondling. "By being stroked, and caressed, and carried, and cuddled, and cooed to, by being loved, the child learns to stroke, and caress, and cuddle, and coo to, and love others" (Montagu, 1972, p. 194). Ashley Montagu concludes that involvement, concern, tenderness, and awareness of others' needs are communicated to the infant through physical contact in the early months of life. It is here that the child begins to learn the meaning of love and to develop attitudes about intimacy, although the infant cannot intellectually understand these concepts. Thus the child deprived of early physical contact may later be unable to make relationships based on love and caring because he or she has not experienced loving relationships. Breastfeeding is one way to assure the infant of adequate holding, cuddling, and fondling. Feeding becomes a time of psychological as well as physical nourishment for the child (see p. 426, Chapter 12).

If children are given love and security and are generally successful in learning to master the environment during this first stage, the chances are that their attitude toward themselves will be accepting and positive. These positive self-attitudes are necessary for us to relate lovingly to others: "The affirmation of one's own life, happiness, growth, and freedom is rooted in one's capacity to love, i.e., in care, respect, responsibility, and knowledge. If an individual is able to love productively, he loves himself too; if he can only love others, he cannot love at all" (Fromm, 1956, pp. 59–60).

By loving oneself Fromm means coming to terms with oneself, realistically accepting both shortcomings and assets, and feeling at ease with oneself. People who hate or despise themselves have great difficulty loving others. People who lack the early love in their lives often try to compensate for their lack of self-love by demonstrating selfishness and high interest in personal gain.

Fromm (1970, p. 115) points out that while the selfish people are always self-concerned, they are never satisfied; always restless; always driven by a fear of not getting enough, missing something, or being deprived of something. Closer observation finds that this person is basically not fond of him- or herself, but deeply dislikes him- or herself.

In order to love, we must be loved. Thus even as small children, we learn about love from the way in which we are loved.

Parental Identification Stage: Early and Middle Childhood During this stage children learn the masculine or feminine role that goes with their biological gender. In many respects children act in a neuter way until they are about five or six years old, even though they start learning their gender roles much earlier. Many parents start guiding their children toward the appropriate gender role at birth. However, children are usually five or six before they make a commitment to their gender role by identifying with the like-sexed parent.

Although the parental identification stage is quite short, usually lasting a few months to a year, it is a crucial period since the child makes the basic identification with the proper gender role at this time. In a culture where the gender roles are moving closer together, it is more difficult for children to pass through this stage since the gender roles are more overlapping and not as clear-cut.

During this stage it is important for children to have close contact with an adult of their own sex. Under normal circumstances this is the father or mother. However, with the increasing number of single-parent families, the person may be a grandfather, grandmother, or a male or female companion of the parent. One can usually recognize when children have made this transition because they become more certain of their gender. A boy will probably not want to do "girl" things and vice versa. Children usually talk a lot during this time about what is proper for girls and boys. The importance of this stage to the child's development suggests that parents who can maintain a comfortable relationship even if apart and who can work together to help the child make the proper identification will make the child's transition smoother. If identification does not occur during this stage, it may occur later, but it will be more difficult for the child to achieve.

Masculine and feminine roles affect the way in which an individual demonstrates love. If it is unmasculine for a male to show tenderness, tenderness may not be a part of his style of love. The sex role that we learn will be an important determinant of our definition of love and an even more important influence on how we display love.

Gang Stage: Late Childhood and Preadolescence   This stage coincides fairly well with the usual elementary school years in our society. It is called the gang stage because of the tendency of each gender to avoid the other, preferring to spend time with groups of friends of the same sex. Freud called this the "latency" period because it appeared to be a relatively calm time sexually. Recent research has indicated that there is more sexual experimentation during this period than Freud thought. There is some sex play, such as "I'll show you mine if I can see yours."

The main tasks of this stage are consolidation of the socially appropriate gender role and adjustment to cooperative endeavor and formal learning. The gang, or peer group, helps the child to learn cooperative behavior and the give and take of social organization. In addition masculine and feminine roles are strengthened by the gang members' approval and disapproval, as well as by adult models the gang admires.

During this period the average boy or girl is often openly hostile toward the opposite sex. But the onset of puberty usually signals the end of this stage. The age that puberty begins is so varied in our culture that each child in a gang will probably enter it at a slightly different time. Thus the primary importance of the gang only gradually diminishes as one by one the members begin to turn their attention toward the opposite sex. Girls' groups dissolve first, because on the average they reach puberty two years ahead of boys. They have been ahead biologically all along, but the distance is greatest at the onset of puberty.

Heterosexual Adult Stage   Children who arrive at puberty earlier or later than average have additional problems during the transition into the fourth stage, adult heterosexuality. Those who are early often face ridicule and disdain from the gang when they begin showing interest in the opposite sex. The first boy in the gang who finds himself attracted to one of his sixth-grade female classmates will have to be careful to keep the gang from finding out, or he will be teased and perhaps ostracized. An early developing girl faces different problems. She may want to date and do things she sees older girls doing, but her family will most likely set limits, which causes arguments and conflict. Her peer group, on the other hand, may be titillated by her daring and she may "show off" to keep their approval. This may involve her seeing older, more-sophisticated boys, who may try to take advantage of her and may succeed inasmuch as she is entering a game whose rules she does not yet understand.

"I DON'T PLAY WITH GIRLS, MARGARET...."

"...WHERE PEOPLE CAN *SEE* ME!"

Children, especially males, who develop late usually suffer through a period of exclusion. They are deserted by friends who are no longer interested in their old activities, and they do not share the new interest in the opposite sex. Late developers often feel rejected and inferior, and they may turn to the company of younger children. For a boy this solution may be reasonably satisfying, as his age may bring him a position of leadership in the younger group, thus helping to offset his feelings of inferiority. Some boys may not have to go through a period of exclusion because male gangs usually retain their interest in sports and cars, which the late developing boy can still share with them. He can also pretend an interest in girls to go along with his friends and thereby avoid ridicule.

The late developing girl finds herself left out more completely, for girls become almost exclusively interested in boys during the transition to early puberty. With her confidence undermined, and lacking compensating support from the group, she faces a difficult time. She may withdraw from social activities and suffer from depression, which she may mask by future plans to enter a self-sacrificing vocation. If she remains biologically behind the group for an extended period, say, more than a year or two, she can develop such a strong inferiority complex that she may need additional help and guidance when at last she does catch up biologically.

Young people who enter adulthood at the same time as most of their peers avoid these problems. They begin to turn their attention toward the opposite sex and soon begin dating.

Each stage of development becomes the foundation for the next stage. And we must assimilate the lessons of all stages to become mature, loving individuals.

People who have passed successfully through the first three stages of development reach the heterosexual stage with a positive attitude toward themselves, a fairly clear idea of their roles as men or women, and a heightened interest in the opposite sex. They have learned several different kinds of love in their relationships with their parents and their peers. Their definitions of and attitudes about love are fairly well set and so is their own personal style of loving.

Love Over Time: From Passionate to Companionate Love

Many of the characteristics of love described so far can be labeled passionate love and are most apparent early in a love relationship. With time the wild emotional excitement of passionate love tends to fade into a lower-key emotional state of friendly affection and deep attachment. Being in love at age twenty with your new mate will probably be quite different from the love experienced with your mate after twenty years of marriage.

David Orlinsky (1972) postulates various kinds of love relationships over the life cycle, starting in infancy and moving through eight stages into parenthood. Let us briefly examine his ideas about love and then consider what further changes in love might occur in the later years of a love relationship.

Orlinsky suggests that each stage of the life cycle is marked by the emergence of a new form of love experience that is not only exciting but also necessary to the full development of the person. Each love relationship is a medium or vehicle of personal growth.

> One grows as a person through loving, though not only in this way. As one becomes a new and different self through this experience, one also becomes ready to engage in a new and different mode of relatedness to others. Love relationships are not merely pleasant or edifying but essential experiences in life, "growthful" in the same generous sense in which travel is "broadening." They are in fact necessary links in the process of personal growth. (p. 144)

What Orlinsky is saying, as many others have also noted, is that children become loving adults through interacting in loving relationships as they grow up. This preparation is necessary to experience mature love relationships. Orlinsky's first four stages are *infancy*, and *early*, *middle*, and *late childhood*, which are comparable to the early stages that we discussed in the last section. Each of these stages involves dependence on others. For example, infants must be nursed and children taught. If they are nursed and taught in a loving environment, the chances are good that they will have positive self-images, a prerequisite for mature adult love. By the fifth stage, *preadolescence*, relations with peers are becoming more important, and the love experience changes to one between equals rather than unequals. In the sixth stage, *youth*, the exciting, passionate, romantic love we have discussed is dominant. If a partnership is formed during the seventh stage, *adulthood*, the couple will grow together and find the emotional attachment

becoming stronger, and some of the passion may give way to a more enduring, caring, and comfortable relationship. The last stage, *parenthood*, is when a couple's love broadens to include children. There will then be a greater proportion of selfless love. This selfless love is seen by many philosophers and prophets as a more-mature, higher-order love than romantic love alone.

Where might love go from here? Hopefully, it will become more and more a mixture of romantic, selfless, and companionate love. Rollo May (1970) calls this mixture "authentic love." Erich Fromm (1956) uses the phrase "mature love" to describe healthy adult love. Mature love preserves the integrity and individuality of both persons. It is an action, not just a passive emotion. Giving takes precedence over taking, yet the giving is not felt as deprivation but as a positive experience (Miller & Siegel, 1972).

One must be able to accept as well as give love if a relationship is to remain loving. Loving is a reciprocal relationship. By the act of accepting your partner's love, you affirm that person as an accepted and valued companion (Scoresby, 1977).

It is hoped that a couple can maintain an interplay of all three kinds of love throughout most of their relationship. Stated another way, there are social, physical, intellectual, and emotional sides to love expression. Different periods in one's life may find one or another of these aspects dominant, and thus the way in which love is shown will vary from time to time. Such changes do not necessarily mean an end of love but may only signal a changing interplay of all of its factors.

So the route love might take in a relationship that lasts a lifetime is basically the pattern of dependency, mutuality, passion, caring, and respect, and then perhaps dependency again in old age. Of course, there are other courses that love can take when couples find their love has diminished or died.

American culture presents some obstacles to an enduring love relationship. Our culture, especially through mass media, exalts passionate love, which is usually linked closely to sexual expression. For those who equate passionate love with true love, intimate relationships are doomed to end in disappointment. It is impossible to maintain a constant state of highly passionate love with its concomitant elation and pain, anxiety and relief, altruism and jealousy, and constant sexual preoccupation. Certainly no one newly in love wants to hear that the flame will burn lower in time. Who, newly in love and preoccupied from morning till night with thoughts of their love, can think, much less believe, that the feelings they are experiencing so strongly will ever fade? On the other hand, who could tolerate being in this highly charged emotional state forever? The fact that love changes over time makes it no less important, no less intimate, no less meaningful when some of the passion is replaced by a warm, deeply abiding and caring, quieter love.

Mass media's exaltation of passionate love and sex has led many Americans to equate sex with love. Unfortunately this concentration on the sexual element of love causes us to neglect other important personal and interpersonal capacities and may diminish the overall quality of love in a relationship. Luther Baker (1983, p. 299) points out "that sex is not the 'pièce de résistance' of the good life, and our present concentration upon it often prevents people from developing other aspects of personal functioning which will produce a good life." The best sex, he says, flows

> spontaneously out of a life and a relationship filled with love, joy, struggle, growth and intimacy. Good sex is a by-product and, like happiness, is most likely to occur when one is not worried about having it. We may find that when we come to know one another better in nonsexual ways, the expression of sexual intimacy will take on a new and more fulfilling dimension.

Following Baker's suggestion to deemphasize the sex-is-love philosophy would make it easier for two people passionately in love to accept the changes that slowly bring their love feelings toward a subtler, more-relaxed, companionate love style.

Another obstacle to an enduring love relationship is our culture's emphasis on the individual, which leads to a preoccupation with oneself: self-improvement, self-actualization, and so forth. As Amitai Etzioni (1983) suggests, in this age of the individual ego, marriage (love) is often less an emotional bonding than a breakable alliance between two self-seeking individuals. Love must involve a strong feeling of community: the caring and loving of mate, children, and other intimates within one's environment. Passionate love tends to preclude all but oneself and the object of one's love. Indeed, if all Americans remained passionately in love, there would never be a sense of community. Passionate love ultimately is selfish love. As it transforms into companionate love, the selfish element is reduced, and one once again has time for other aspects of the loving relationship than just the passionate and sexual. As the preoccupation with the loved one subsides, one can again attend to the broader community.

It should be remembered that companionate love does not preclude passionate love. Ideally there will always be times of high passion in a loving relationship, no matter how long the relationship has lasted. These times are to be savored and enjoyed. Even though such times will become less frequent with the passage of time in a successfully loving relationship, one must not value the "loving" less.

From our discussions it is clear that it takes little effort to fall passionately in love even if we don't exactly understand what such love is or just why we fall into it. It is equally clear that thought and work are required to remain in love. Love neglected will not survive in most cases. To fall passionately in love is not the end. It must be a beginning that when nurtured and cared for will endure, albeit in a changed form to some degree. To love lastingly and well, to like and care for another over a long period of time is a unique gift that humans can give one another. To believe that enduring love will simply occur because one is passionately "in love" is a false belief that may destroy a relationship. Enduring love, if it is to evolve from passionate love, must be worked at and tended so that it will not wilt and die with the passage of time.

Love's Oft-Found Companion: Jealousy

Jealousy, the green-eyed monster, is an unwelcome acquaintance of nearly everyone who has ever been in love. Because it is a personal acquaintance, it is described in almost as many ways as love.

Jealousy relates to one's own feelings of confidence and security as much as if not more than to the actions of the loved one. As Margaret Mead (1968) has said: "Jealousy is not a barometer by which the depth of love can be read. It merely records the degree of the lover's insecurity. . . . It is a negative miserable state of feeling having its origin in the sense of insecurity and inferiority." Further, jealousy usually involves feelings of lost pride and threat to self-esteem or feelings that one's property rights have been violated. The threat or violation may be real, potential, or entirely imaginary, yet the jealous feelings aroused are real and strong.

Jealousy is also related to what one's culture teaches about love and possession inasmuch as the culture prescribes the cues that trigger jealousy (Hatfield & Walster, 1978).

> On her return trip from the local watering well, a married woman is asked for a cup of water by a male resident of the village. Her husband, resting on the porch of their dwelling, observes his wife giving the man a cup of water. Subsequently, they approach the husband and the three of them enjoy a lively and friendly conversation into the late evening hours. Eventually the husband puts out the lamp, and the guest has sexual intercourse with the wife. The next morning the husband leaves the house early in order to catch fishes for breakfast. Upon his return he finds his wife having sex again with the guest. The husband becomes violently enraged and mortally stabs the guest. (Hupka, 1977, p. 8)

This story seems unintelligible to an American. How can the husband condone his wife's having sexual intercourse with another man on one occasion and be enraged by it a short time later? The answer lies in the cultural ways of the Ammassalik Eskimo. In this culture the husband would be considered inconsiderate if he did not share his wife sexually with his overnight guest. "Putting out the lamp" is a culturally sanctioned game that acts as an invitation for the guest to have sex with the host's wife. Yet it is not unusual for an Ammassalik Eskimo husband to become so enraged as to try to kill a man who has sex with his wife outside the prescribed game rules.

Jealousy
The state of being resentfully suspicious of a loved one's behavior toward a suspected rival

So too in American society we are taught the rules of love. In the past love has meant exclusivity, monogamy, and lifelong devotion and faithfulness. Lovers were possessions of one another. Historically, adultery was grounds for divorce in every state. Thus jealousy was usually nearby when a young American fell in love.

For most who experience it, what an unpleasant experience jealousy is. Suspicious feelings that seem to manufacture their own evidence to support the jealousy at every turn; compulsive preoccupation with the perceived infidelity; anger, sorrow, self-pity, and depression all wrapped into one continual emotional upheaval; eating and sleeping problems and an assortment of physical ills evolving out of the continual emotional turmoil—all of these seem to characterize the jealous person.

Recent research has begun to shed some light on the manifestation of jealousy among Americans. The following characteristics have emerged from various studies (Adams, 1980):

- Jealousy goes with feelings of insecurity and an unflattering self-image.
- People who feel jealous because of a mate's real or imagined infidelity are often faithless themselves.
- People who report the greatest overall dissatisfaction with their lives are those who feel jealous most often.
- Happy or not, jealous people feel strongly bound to their mates.
- Younger people report jealousy more often than older people.
- It is difficult to conceal jealousy from others.
- Jealousy seems to cause women greater suffering than men.
- Women tend more often to try and repair the damaged relationship, whereas men more often try to repair their damaged self-esteem.
- Men are more apt to give up a relationship in which jealousy is triggered by the woman's infidelity than are women in the reverse situation.

■ Women are more apt to induce jealousy in their partner to test the relationship, bolster their self-esteem, gain attention, get revenge, or punish the mate for some perceived offense.

One last point: To the degree that one's culture teaches the cues that trigger jealousy, changes in the culture may change the characteristics and incidence of jealousy. As American sexual mores have loosened, as long-lived monogamy has eroded through increased divorce, and as cohabitation and premarital sexual intimacy become more acceptable, the need for jealousy has changed. Although it is unclear at this time, greater sexual freedom may be leading to decreased sexual jealousy for some people. Gary Hansen (1982) found that nontraditional sex role subjects were less jealous in their reactions to hypothetical jealousy-producing events than were traditional sex role subjects.

Is there anything that one can do to manage and control irrational jealous feelings? Naturally, anything we can do toward becoming confident, secure individuals will help us cope with our own jealousy. We can try to learn what is making us jealous. What exactly are we feeling and why are we feeling that way? We can try to keep our jealous feelings in perspective. We can also negotiate with our partners to change certain behaviors that seem to trigger our jealousy. Negotiation assumes that we too are working to reduce our own unwarranted jealousy. Choosing partners who are reassuring and loving will also help reduce our irrational jealousies. Unfortunately, following such advice is difficult because jealousy is so often irrational and, for the jealous partner at the moment of jealousy, all too often uncontrollable. It remains one of the puzzling components of love relationships.

Summary

American youths are given relative freedom to choose a mate. Unlike other societies where mate choice is directed by rigid prescriptions and parental and social guidance, ours permits young people to seek their own mates with a minimum of social interference or parental participation. American mate choice is usually based on the nebulous concept of romantic love: "I will marry the person I fall in love with."

Love is a difficult word to define. One helpful approach is the view of the ancient Greeks who classified three possible kinds of love: *eros*, or sexual love; *agape*, or spiritual love; and *philos*, or friendly love. Mature love includes all three aspects.

Our attitudes about and personal definitions of love guide mate selection and lead each of us to form a set of idealized expectations about the kind of mate we desire. These expectations, if highly unrealistic, often cause disappointment because the partner cannot live up to them. Overromanticized expectations of what a mate and a marriage should be almost ensure disappointment in, and subsequent failure of, a relationship.

Attitudes about love and marriage develop through a number of stages as one grows from infancy to adulthood. Each stage presents problems that the developing person must successfully overcome if the adult is to sustain mature love relationships. The first stage is the self-love stage. During this early period children begin to come to terms with themselves, establishing security, trust, and self-respect. In the parental identification stage, children identify with the like-sexed parent and begin to incorporate the masculine or feminine roles of their culture. In the gang stage children further consolidate their appropriate roles and learn interpersonal relations and communication skills. Finally, the heterosexual adult stage is reached, which is the stage of adult sexuality and eventual marital fulfillment.

Such stages, of course, are only theoretical and will vary with cultures and individuals. Yet the idea that we develop our attitudes toward love and marriage as we grow up is important. Childrearing practices, the immediate family, and the general subcultures in which we are reared will all influence our attitudes toward intimacy. Conflicting experiences during childhood may lead to confusion as an individual strives for intimacy. And differing childhood experiences may later lead to conflicts between lovers as they try to relate to one another. Awareness of these differences and concern for the other individual will help us make the transition to mature love. Finally, knowing and accepting ourselves is a necessary first step on the path to a successful love relationship.

It is important that we like as well as love our mates if the relationship is to endure. Passionate love can withstand dislike of the loved one for a short time, but unless the dislike can be changed into liking, passionate love can never evolve into a more permanent companionate love.

Jealousy is an oft-found, unwanted companion of love. The reasons for it are many; it is closely related to one's security and self-confidence. Although we are starting to understand some of its characteristics, thus far we have had little success in helping people control and manage jealousy. There is some evidence that sexual jealousy may be declining as sexual freedom has increased in the United States.

Love and Friendship

We have discussed many kinds of love and love in many contexts in this chapter. Recently Keith E. Davis (1985) published the results of some fascinating research he did in an effort to describe how love and friendship, two essential ingredients to a fulfilled and happy life, differ.

The researchers suggest that friendship includes the following essential characteristics:

- *Enjoyment*: Friends enjoy one another's company most of the time even though there may be temporary states of anger or disappointment.
- *Acceptance*: Friends accept one another as they are, without trying to make changes in one another.
- *Trust*: Friends share basic trust, and each assumes that the other will act in the friend's best interest.
- *Respect*: Friends respect each other in the sense of assuming that each exercises good judgment in making life choices.
- *Mutual Assistance*: Friends are inclined to assist and support one another. They can count on each other in a time of need.
- *Confiding*: Friends share experiences and feelings with one another.
- *Understanding*: Friends have a sense of what is important to each other and tend to understand the actions of each other.
- *Spontaneity*: Friends feel free to be themselves in the relationship.

The researchers felt that romantic relationships would share all of the characteristics of friendship but would also have additional characteristics, over and beyond friendship. They identified two broad categories unique to love relationships. The first they

termed the passion cluster characteristics, including:

- *Fascination*: Lovers tend to be preoccupied with one another, obsessed with one another, desirous of spending all their time together.
- *Exclusiveness*: Lovers are so intensely occupied with one another that it precludes having a similar relationship with another. Romantic love is given priority over all other relationships.
- *Sexual Desire*: Lovers desire physical intimacy with their partners.

The second cluster of characteristics related to romantic relations the researchers termed the *caring cluster*, including:

- *Giving the Utmost*: Lovers care enough to give the utmost, even to the point of self-sacrifice, when their partner is in need.
- *Being a Champion/Advocate*: Lovers actively champion one another's interests and make positive attempts to ensure that the partner succeeds.

The accompanying figure shows the way in which friendship and love were theoretically related for the research. In general, the reports of the researchers' subjects supported this love-friendship model. However, there were some interesting results that were different from the model.

The caring cluster did not show as strong a difference between lovers and friends as had been expected. In fact, the "being a champion/advocate scale" did not show any difference. Friends championed each other as much as lovers.

Another unanticipated finding was that best friendships were seen as more stable than spouse/lover relationships. Perhaps tied in with this was the finding that the level of acceptance was significantly lower among spouses and lovers than among friends. In other words, lovers tend to be more critical and less tolerant of each other than friends.

The researchers concluded that typical love relationships will differ even from very good friendships in having higher levels of fascination, exclusiveness, and sexual desire (the passion cluster); a greater depth of caring about the other person; and a greater potential for enjoyment and other positive emotions. Love relationships will also have, however, a greater potential for distress, ambivalence, conflict, and mutual criticism.

One clear implication of these differences is that love relationships tend to have a greater impact on both the satisfaction and frustration of the person's basic needs.

What Do You Think?

1. Why might lovers be more critical of one another than good friends.
2. How important is it that one's lover also be a friend?
3. Can men and women be friends and lovers at the same time?
4. Are there other aspects of friendship that you feel are important but not listed by the researchers?
5. For a long-lasting relationship, do you feel that the friendship factors or the lover factors are more important?
6. Why do love relationships have a greater potential for distress and conflict?

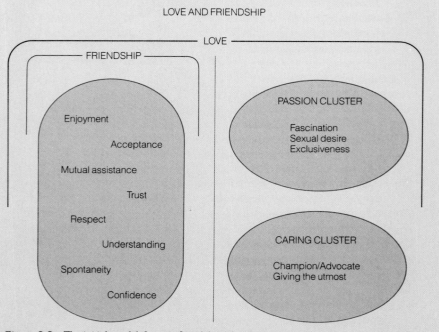

Figure 3-2 The initial model. Love is friendship plus the "passion cluster" and the "caring cluster."

Dating, Sexual Mores, and Mate Selection

Contents

Perhaps the most unique characteristic of mate selection in America as compared to the rest of the world, is that it is run and operated by the participants themselves. There are no arranged marriages, no marriage brokers, no chaperones, no childhood betrothals, no family alliance marriages, even few marriages of convenience. One Asian female exchange student recently mentioned, "I want my parents to choose my marriage partner. It is far too important a decision for me to make alone." In America this important decision is made by youth themselves, for better and for worse.

Every society has a system, formal or informal, by which mates are selected and new families are started. In the United States mate selection is carried out by relatively unrestricted dating among young persons. That is, the selection process is fairly informal. However, once the couple decides that each is indeed his or her choice for a future mate, the system becomes more structured and engagement and marriage usually follow.

Puberty and Sexual Stress

Puberty signals the beginning of adult sexuality. Children become biologically able to reproduce, and the male/female relationship takes on an overtly sexual nature. Adolescent years in most Western cultures are a time of sexual stress because although biology has prepared the individual for sexual intercourse and reproduction, Western society has traditionally denied and tried to restrain these biological impulses by placing restrictive rules and taboos on adolescent sexual behavior. For most, sexual stress lasts until the individual marries, for it is primarily in marriage that our culture allows its members to engage freely in sexual activities. If puberty begins for males at age fourteen and they marry at age twenty-five on the average, there is an eleven-year period of stress after biology prepares the male for adult sexuality before society condones sexual intercourse (that is, in marriage). There is a comparable eleven-year period for females, assuming that puberty begins at approximately age twelve and that females marry at about age twenty-three.

There are instances when the stress period is less lengthy, such as when the average age of marriage is low. For example, in 1950 the average American male married at 22.5 years of age and the female at 20.5 years of age. Some societies practice child marriage, which eliminates the period of sexual stress altogether. Other cultures, such as the Polynesian, are also highly permissive in allowing sexual activities among the young before marriage. In fact, an anthropological study by George Murdock (1950) found that of 250 societies throughout the world 70 percent permitted nonincestuous sexual relations before marriage. In the last twenty-five years American society has become much more permissive about sex. The sexual revolution has led to more permissive premarital sexual behavior as well as to more acceptance of young couples cohabiting before marriage.

Our society is not only more permissive than in the past but now actually encourages early contact between the sexes. Even elementary schools promote coeducational dances and parties. Some parents, worried that their children will not become popular, pressure them into developing an early interest in the opposite sex. Makeup, adult fashions, and bras for preteens are advertised as ways of increasing popularity. The teenage market is large, and business creates and caters to the tastes of adolescents. Much advertising is based on sex appeal, thus heightening the tensions of this period. Popular music is an especially strong influence in the lives of teenagers. Two major themes in popular music tend to be drugs and sex. In *Thunder Road*, Bruce Springsteen sings about Mary who is a romantic vision as she dances across the porch, listening to the songs of Roy Orbison on the radio. Sexual overtones are clearly stated when the young man indicates to Mary that she knows just what he is there for. He exorts her not to go back inside the house but to remain on the porch with him.

Certainly Bruce Springsteen's reputation is positive, and he is very concerned about society's problems. Yet, as we have seen, even his lyrics in this song are sexually suggestive.

Many other rock songs are far more graphic in their description of sexual behavior. For example, Prince and the Revolution include the song "Darling Nikki" in their album *Purple Rain* (Warner Bros. Records, 1984). Although the lyrics cannot be quoted directly, they describe Nikki as a sex fiend who is found masturbating with a magazine in an hotel lobby.

The stress of emerging sexuality is compounded by the extended opportunities a young American couple have to be alone together. The automobile has not only revolutionized transportation and contributed to the highly mobile American way of life, but has also facilitated early sexual experimentation. A boy and girl can be alone at almost any time in almost any place. The feeling of anonymity and distance from social control is increased, group control and influence is lessened, and there is no one who might comment or report on their behavior.

Thus what we find in America is a society that supposedly prohibits premarital sexual relations, yet through the mass media and the support of early boy/girl relations actually encourages them. In essence young people are often thrown completely on their own resources to determine what their sexual behavior will be. In the end they will make the decision about the extent of their sexual relationships based on their attitudes, peer influences, and the pressures of the moment.

American Dating

Dating
Social interaction and activity with a person of the opposite sex

Mate selection through **dating** is an American invention and is relatively new, having developed largely after World War I, mainly because of the emancipation of women and the new mobility afforded by the car. Also the population moved from the countryside into the cities where there were many more opportunities for youth to meet one another. In place of the church meeting, the application to the girl's father, and chaperoned evenings at home, modern youth meet at parties, make dates via telephone, and go off alone to spend evenings together on the town. Note that American dating is participant run. In other words, the American system of mate selection is close to being *open choice* for the participants as compared to the closed choice that participants have in an *arranged marriage* society. With open choice marital mate selection and the ensuing marriage are totally subservient to individual needs and desires (Adams, 1986, p. 178). Individual attraction is the main guide. There is no pure example of open choice but America probably comes the closest to it of any country. As we saw in Chapter 2, romantic love has been institutionalized as the basis for individual choice of a mate (Lee & Stone, 1980).

Open choice of mate does not mean that the parents of young adults have no influence at all on choice of mate. Parents often try to influence their children's dating choices and children, in turn, try to predispose their parents favorably toward their dating partners. In general parents try harder to influence daughter's choices, and daughters in turn attempt to influence their parents, especially mothers, to look favorably on their dating partners. The more serious the relationship, the more parents and children try to influence one another. However, such influencing attempts appear relatively unimportant to the process of movement toward marriage by young persons (Leslie et al., 1986).

Modern youth are so accustomed to having almost free access to one another that it is difficult to appreciate just how hard it was for a young man to meet a young woman at the turn of the century. Secondary schools were not coeducational then, so that after elementary school boys and girls were not surrounded by students of the opposite sex. An introduction of the young man to the young woman's parents had to be arranged, and this was not always easy. If the parents approved of the young man, there was little leisure time that the couple could spend together as most young people's time was occupied with work in addition to studies. What little time they had together was usually spent doing things with other family members.

Why Do We Date?

We date for many reasons:

1. Dating fills time between puberty and marriage. It is often simple *recreation*, fun, an end in itself.
2. Dating is a way to gain *social status* based on whom and how often one dates (Winch, 1971, pp. 530–531). The status function is performed by the family in arranged marriage societies. The American dating system makes it possible for certain persons to be rated highly desirable and in this way to raise their status within the peer group (Adams, 1986, p. 181). Thus dating can change one's status in an open choice system. The classic example for a young man would be marrying the boss's daughter.
3. Dating is an opportunity for the sexes to interact and learn about one another (to become *socialized*). Because Americans live in small nuclear families, they may have had little opportunity to learn about the opposite sex if they had no opposite-sex siblings near their own age. Dating is also an avenue to self-knowledge. Interacting with others gives one a chance to learn about one's own personality as well as the personalities of others. Dating allows one to try out a succession of relationships. And one learns something about marital and familial roles by relating with the opposite sex.

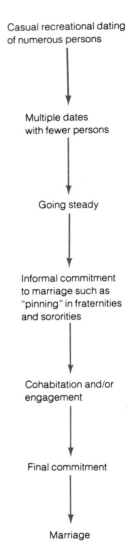

Casual recreational dating
of numerous persons

Multiple dates
with fewer persons

Going steady

Informal commitment
to marriage such as
"pinning" in fraternities
and sororities

Cohabitation and/or
engagement

Final commitment

Marriage

Figure 4-1   A continuum of dating.

4. Dating meets *ego needs* (Adams, 1986, p. 181). The young person needs understanding and to be considered important. Being asked for a date yields importance and a successful date usually involves understanding to some extent.
5. Dating leads to *mate selection* for most individuals. Most young people do not begin each date by asking, Would I marry this person? Yet somewhere in the course of their dating experience they will ask this question and answer it affirmatively (Adams, 1986, p. 182).

In early adolescence dating is mostly considered fun and recreation and learning about oneself. But the older one gets the more serious dating becomes, and the more concerned one becomes with mate selection. Thus dating patterns can be placed on a continuum leading from casual dating to marriage (see Figure 4-1).

In the past mate selection in America was viewed as movement down two paths. One was the path of commitment and the other was the path of physical intimacy. At first commitments are superficial: Let's get together for an evening. Finally at the end of the path there is the deep-seated commitment: Let's spend our lives together. The intimacy road runs from casual hand holding to a full and continuing sexual relationship.

As a result of the sexual revolution, in recent years the physical intimacy road has been traveled much faster than the commitment road. In fact today's youth, especially women, often complain that those in whom they are romantically interested are unable to make a commitment. Knox and Wilson (1983) found that the most often expressed dating problem among university women was "unwanted pressure to engage in sexual behavior." In fact, in the past few years the incidence of "date rape" has been widely recognized (Bernard et al., 1985; Barrett, 1982). For some the emphasis in America today on sexual intimacy seems to lead to the neglect of other important aspects of a relationship that promote commitment. For example, university men report that communication is their biggest problem on a date (Knox & Wilson, 1983). Social compatibility, development of shared interests, and increased knowledge of one another as well as of oneself are all important, especially if the relationship is to become permanent.

Dating Patterns

Adolescent boy/girl interactions have become increasingly more individualized in the past few years. This great variation makes it difficult to describe a common American dating pattern. Adams stresses that dating is a twentieth century phenomenon and has been in flux ever since it appeared. With the fluidity of the adolesent period and the fact that dating is, by and large, participant run, each new generation redefines the dating codes and norms (1986, p. 185). In general, formal dating, where a boy approaches a girl beforehand and arranges a meeting time, place, and activity for them, has declined (Murstein, 1980), especially in the larger urban areas such as Los Angeles and New York. Formal "going steady," where class rings and lettermen's jackets are given by the boy to the girl, has also declined in these areas. However, one still finds more traditional, formalized dating in small cities and towns and among those past college age. In small towns Main Street is cruised on Friday and Saturday nights, dates are prearranged, and afterward everyone meets at a drive-in restaurant or couples head into the countryside to neck, pet, and, increasingly, have sexual relations. Many still go steady for a good portion of their high school years.

There is another generalization we can make. The first date used to be the first time a couple would become acquainted. It usually involved a function or activity, such as going to the movies. By concentrating on the activity, some of the difficulties and embarrassments of getting to know one another were avoided. Today young people generally know one another better before actually dating. They have chatted with each other and perhaps done things together in the context of a larger group. Their first date comes more casually; they may decide on the spur of the moment to go to the beach together. Couples still go steady, but again, the relationship seems less formal, more relaxed and casual. Also, once they are past a period of almost total preoccupation with one another, there seems to be more group activity, going out with other couples or with friends. It is interesting that group dating behavior has regained favor even among college-age youth. It might be that group dating acts as a barrier to sexual relations which on an individual date would be hard to refuse because of the sexual revolution.

So while dates of the 1950s seemed more task-oriented (what will we do on our date), dates today have become more person/relationship oriented (what will the relationship be on our date). David Knox and Kenneth Wilson (1981) report that "our relationship" is the most frequent topic of conversation for their university student sample. The largest percentage of students meet their dates through a friend. Although we have stressed how free young Americans are to choose dating partners and activities, Knox reports that 60 percent of the women and 40 percent of the men in his sample indicated that some parental influence was involved in their dating patterns. Women are much more likely than men to say that it is important to date the "kind of people their parents would approve of" (Knox and Wilson, 1981; Leslie et al., 1986).

Because there is a diversity of dating patterns, it is impossible to discuss all dating variations. We can, however, describe the traditional, more formal dating game since there are still some rules by which it is played. Note that traditional dating occurs mainly in smaller towns and rural areas. The following description also applies to a first date or dates among the very young.

Traditional Dating and Going Steady   Let's start when our hypothetical couple is first beginning to date. Age at first dating varies greatly with each family and with social class, but in general people are dating earlier so that dating at twelve and thirteen, especially for a girl, is not unusual. Let us further assume that the boy has just reached the legal driving age (fifteen or sixteen).

The two will probably have known each other superficially for some time. They attend the same school and have met at various school functions. Although it requires courage, the young man asked the young woman to a movie on the coming Saturday night. A movie is usually a safe first date for a young adolescent because it requires little interaction. Neither has to worry about being boring or having nothing to say because the movie will occupy them. At the appointed time he arrives (hopefully driving dad's car or his own) to pick her up. Although she has been ready for some time, she is discreetly "not ready." This serves a twofold purpose: She does not appear overeager and it gives her parents a few moments to look him over and discuss the evening's rules with him, mainly what time to return. If the girl is particularly independent, she may make a special effort to be

ready when her date arrives so she can leave quickly to avoid interaction between her parents and her date.

In the darkened theater he often strongly feels the pressure of his friends and the anonymous larger group of peers loosely defined as "the guys" to approach her physically. He is also under pressure from himself, wanting to prove to himself that the girl likes him, thus boosting his self-esteem. The intimacy road leading to sexual contact often enters dating immediately. He generally pays for the date, and this pressures the girl into paying him back, usually with some kind of physical response. The double standard, where sexual advances are expected of him but are inappropriate for her, still operates in traditional dating. To feel masculine and proud among his peers, he wants at least to try to have some type of physical contact with his date. Thus as he sits watching the movie, the first of many conflicts concerning sexuality arises. He notices that her hands are lying one inch in his direction on her lap. Perhaps this is a cue. Should he attempt to hold her hand? If she vigorously rejects this advance, someone in the row might notice and he'll be embarrassed. If, however, she accepts, how will he be able to withdraw his hand when it becomes sweaty and begins to cramp? Will she take it personally as some kind of rejection if he withdraws it?

The fascinating characteristic of traditional American dating is what one may call "escalation." In other words, resolution of this first minor intimacy conflict does not end the problem. If the girl accepts his first advance, then the pressure he feels to prove his masculinity will actually increase because the whole procedure is designed to test just how far he can go with her toward overt sexuality. Granted, much of this pressure may be unconscious for the boy, yet he feels the need to prove himself. Naturally, the further he moves, the more pride he will feel when bragging to his friends of his success. Thus once he has taken her hand, he must now look to the slightly greater problem of attempting to place his arm around her. The reward of increased intimacy is obviously greater, but so are the risks. If she vigorously rejects his attempt, the whole audience will notice (at least it will seem this way to him). If she accepts, there is always the cramped shoulder to look forward to as well as the necessity of facing the new escalation level with its ensuing conflicts and insecurities.

She is having conflicts too because she does not want to lose her good reputation and yet she does not want him to think her a prude and not ask for another date. Of course, she may just have gone out with him to have a date and doesn't really want to date him again. In that case total rejection of his physical advances will let him know further dates are not desired. If she does like him, she wants to encourage him but not too much. How much physical contact can she allow without leading him to think she will eventually go all the way?

If the relationship continues, the couple will gradually limit their dating to each other. They enjoy the security of knowing they have a date. They find being together comfortable, and it's a relief to them not to have to face the insecurity of a new date. Going together requires a higher degree of commitment than casual dating; this ability to commit oneself becomes the foundation of later marriage. Going together helps the couple understand what kind of commitments are necessary to marriage.

Going together, though, does create problems. It tends to add pressure to the sexual conflicts experienced by the young couple. They see each other more frequently, and it becomes increasingly difficult to avoid sexual intimacy. The

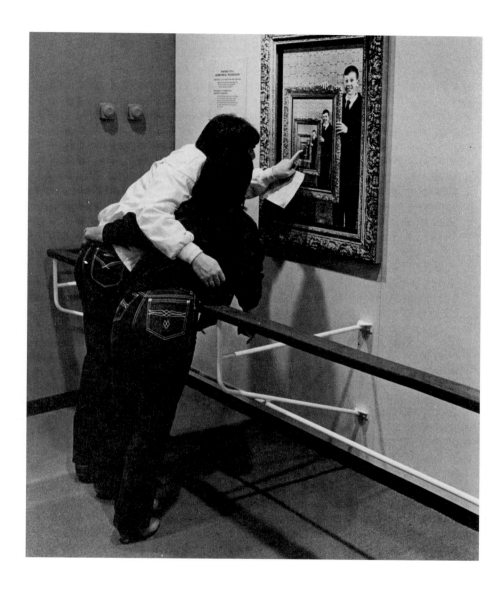

American young man also tends to be possessive. He tends to regard any attention or compliments paid to his girlfriend as insulting, and he tries to restrict her social interaction to himself. She may resent this, and fights may result.

On the whole, starting early and remaining in a steady relationship throughout adolescence is probably disadvantageous to later adult relations. The young person who has always gone steady is unlikely to have had enough experience with a broad cross-section of the opposite sex to have developed his or her interpersonal abilities to the fullest. Going steady early usually leads to earlier marriage, which tends to be less stable than later marriage. If dating is to work as a method of mate selection, it is important to date enough to ensure a good mate choice.

On the other hand, dating so many people that only brief relationships are formed during the dating period is also dysfunctional. The young person never gets any practice in the give and take of long-term relationships. Ideally, then, one must date enough people to understand the many individual differences that are to be found and at the same time experience some longer-term relationships in order to gain knowledge of the commitments and compromises necessary to maintain a relationship over time.

Getting Together   At the other end of the spectrum from traditional dating is "getting together" or "hanging out" together. Even the term *date* seems too old-fashioned to describe this more casual interaction. In "getting together" there is no orderly progression from the first parent-approved date to going steady to eventual marriage. Here meetings and even dates "just happen," a spur-of-the-moment affair. A couple may end one of these casual "dates" by having sex, or they may never even think of sex. Much of this more casual dating involves group activities.

For example, a young man may notice a group of young women at a local snack bar or other neighborhood hangout. When he comes back with a fresh cup of coffee, he joins them. He is particularly drawn to one of the young women. He notices that she laughs at some of his jokes and seems attentive to him. A day or two later he bumps into her on the street and asks if she wants to go along to the beach. She agrees and on the way they find they both like the same rock groups and that both were hitchhiking in Europe last summer. She joins him and his friends for dinner that evening. Perhaps a relationship begins to form, perhaps not.

The problems of this type of casual dating are, as you might expect, almost the opposite of those connected with going steady. Rather than too limited experience with the opposite sex, there tends to be too much superficial experience and too little commitment. Neither partner is likely to feel chosen or special when he or she knows the partner is likely to have many such casual dates with others. Both may have learned to avoid conflicts or "scenes" by keeping their dating behavior at a superficial level and moving on if the relationship seems to be getting serious. If this be true, then neither learns to work things through or to compromise. Because marriage involves commitment and compromise, such persons are poor marriage prospects if this type of dating is their only experience.

Probably most personal dating experiences will fall somewhere between traditional dating and "getting together," depending on location, upbringing and values, and what peers are doing. Regardless of dating style, everyone has the problems of finding dating partners, coping with "bad" dates, and avoiding exploitation. The fact that American dating today is so informal and without rules compared with mate selection processes historically and in other countries means that each young person has to make his or her own decisions about what is best. Of course, when we say "make his or her own decisions" we realize that there will be many social and cultural pressures guiding such decisions, but these pressures are not always clear-cut and there are more than one set of pressures.

These descriptions of American dating probably don't describe many American young people accurately. Most persons have dating experiences that fall between the two extremes. Sometimes a couple may just "hang around" together; at other times they may date more formally. Much will depend on the couple's circle of friends. Even within a small high school there will be different dating patterns. The important thing to remember is that any dating pattern, if it is to contribute to the courtship process, must give each person sufficient experience with the opposite sex to make good decisions about intimate relationships. Knowledge about the opposite sex comes largely through interacting with the opposite sex. Knowledge about intimate relationships in general comes through being in such relationships. The courting process, whatever its exact pattern, should give people these kinds of experiences.

Dating and Extended Singleness

Our discussion so far has examined the dating patterns of young Americans with the implicit assumption that dating is, in part, a form of courtship that leads to marriage. Not all dating Americans want to marry, though, and not all dating Americans are young. The period of singleness before marriage is longer today than it has been in the recent past. The greatly increased divorce rate has also increased the number of older single persons. These two factors have combined to cause a dramatic increase over the past fifteen years in the number of people living alone. Such households have jumped 90 percent since 1970, compared with a 37 percent increase in households overall (U.S. Bureau of the Census, October 1985, p. 3).

The major factor increasing the number of young singles and the length of the dating period before marriage is the trend to postpone marriage. The median age at first marriage has increased to 23.3 years for women and 25.5 years for men. This represents an increase in the median since 1970 of 2.3 years for men and

2.5 years for women. For women, this is the highest median age of marriage ever reported (U.S. Bureau of the Census, November 1986, p. 3). Note that the increase is age specific and does not imply fewer marriages. Indeed if we look at the single rate for those over forty years of age, in 1981 there are 21 percent fewer single women and 27 percent fewer single men than in 1970. The large increases in singleness occur mainly from ages twenty to twenty-nine for both men and women. As a group, the never-married represent almost 25 percent of the population.

During this same period (1970–1985), the divorce ratio (number of divorced persons per 1000 persons who are married and living with their spouse) more than doubled. The divorced represent about 6 percent of our population. Another group that tends to be forgotten when dating is discussed are the widowed singles who make up another 2.5 percent of the population. Overall then, single persons who find themselves in the dating pool make up about 34 percent of the population (U.S. Bureau of the Census, 1984).

Postponing marriage means that the dating period of one's life will be longer. And for those who divorce, there may be a return to dating later in life. Despite this increase in singleness, it is still a transitory state for most Americans and usually ends with marriage or remarriage. Dating then is more than just the young learning about and courting one another. Dating will vary greatly in its purposes and patterns according to the kind of single person: young and starting to date, divorced, or widowed.

Encouragement to marry undoubtedly will remain strong in America, yet several factors are acting to make prolonged single life more acceptable. The increasing emphasis on self-fulfillment as a major life goal and society's greater tolerance of differing lifestyles both reduce the pressure to marry. Personal growth and change have become popular goals, and they conflict directly with the traditional goals of long-range commitment to stability that marriage requires. The women's movement has also contributed to singleness in that it says to all women, "There are other roles you can fulfill that do not necessarily include being a wife and mother." Greater educational opportunity also acts, in some cases, to postpone marriage because going to school usually postpones economic independence (Stein, 1981).

What effect will remaining single longer have on marriage? Obviously, both partners will be older. Older persons, used to a long period of singleness, may well become more set in their ways and thus find the compromises of the marriage relationship more difficult. Couples will also be older when they have children, thus increasing the age difference between themselves and their children. Risks during pregnancy and childbirth are greater for older women. And older couples will probably have fewer children, with the resultant effect on schools, the baby food and clothing industries, and so on.

On the other hand, later marriages should mean better economic circumstances for the couple. The maturity of older couples may also make them more willing to work toward making marriage a positive experience. Data suggests that the older one is at marriage, the greater the chances of marital success.

But what of the single life itself? What are the advantages? Freedom is probably the major advantage. You need only worry about yourself. Obligations are made by voluntary decision rather than dictated by tradition, role, or law. You have time to do what you want when you want. Expenses are lower than for a family, and you can change jobs or even cities more easily. Independence can be maintained, and the conflicts about activities and lifestyle that arise in marriage don't occur.

Possible loneliness, failure to relate intimately, and a sense of meaninglessness are potential disadvantages of singleness. It is interesting and contrary to popular belief, but research shows that old people are less prone to loneliness than young people. Loneliness is particularly prevalent and intense during adolescence (Rubin, 1979).

Single people have a higher incidence of mental illness (National Institute of Mental Health, 1973). It is difficult to say just why the incidence of mental illness is higher for single than for married people. Perhaps those with a proclivity toward mental illness are bypassed by those seeking mates and are thus forced to remain single. Living closely with another person does serve a corrective function because the other person validates or invalidates many of one's thoughts and actions, thus keeping one closer to reality. General health is also not as good in single persons as in married persons (Verbrugge, 1979).

Cohabitation: Unmarried Couple Households

Cohabitation

A man and woman living together in an intimate relationship without being legally married

The increasing incidence of heterosexual **cohabitation** is, in part, directly related to the increase in the single lifestyle. The number of cohabiting couples has grown from 523,000 in 1970 to 2,000,000 in 1985, an increase of 300 percent (U.S. Bureau of Census, November 1985). Although the increase is dramatic, such households make up only 4 percent of all households in the United States. For the first time since 1970, the number of cohabiting couples did not increase between 1984 and 1985. Whether this is indicative of a changing trend remains to be seen. In addition, not all such households involve sexually intimate relationships. Although seldom reported in the mass media, these figures include a variety of living arrangements, such as that of an elderly woman who rents a room to a male college student or that of an elderly man who employs a live-in female nurse or housekeeper. Another change in this statistic is noteworthy. In 1970 a sizable majority (73 percent) of the cohabiting couples without children were over 45 years of age. By 1985 the number had dropped to 18 percent. Persons under 25 years of age now account for 21.4 percent of unmarried households, while those 25 to 34 years of age account for 44.3 percent. This probably reflects the later age of marriage that we discussed earlier plus more acceptance by society of cohabitation by young and never-married people (never-married people account for 51 percent of cohabiting couples).

Paul Glick and Graham Spanier (1980) characterize this data by stating: "Rarely does social change occur with such rapidity. Indeed there have been few developments relating to marriage and family life which have been as dramatic as the rapid increase in unmarried cohabitation." This statement is perhaps misleading in that it overlooks the fact that historically (nineteenth century) many young couples lived together without being married. There was a difference, however, in that most of these couples expected to marry their live-in partners, and even if they did not marry, most states legally recognized them as married after a set number of years (seven in most states). This legal change of status from cohabiting to married was called **common law marriage**.

It is possible that some of the increase in unmarried cohabitation is accounted for by a greater willingness to reveal the fact of living together outside of marriage.

Common law marriage

Legal recognition of a cohabiting couple as being married after a given number of years (usually seven) of cohabitation

On the other hand, there are an unknown number of couples living together who pass themselves off as married or, at least, do not divulge their living arrangements. They would not be included in the total figures, but enough couples are openly living together in intimate relationships that some theorists now consider living together to be an ongoing part of the mate selection process for a growing minority of couples (Macklin, 1983).

The Nature of Cohabiting Relationships

People choose to live together for many reasons, some of which may not be true for every cohabiting couple. First, it is clear that many consider these experiences to be no more than *short-lived sexual flings* and only gradually drift into a cohabitation relationship. Early research reported that 82 percent of those twenty years old or younger who reported cohabiting indicated that the relationship lasted three months or less (Peterman et al., 1974).

Second, some couples live together for practical reasons. They are essentially no more than *opposite-sex roommates*. In this case the couple live together without necessarily having a deep or intimate relationship. Having a member of the opposite sex as a roommate affords certain advantages. A woman may feel safer living with a man if she lives in a high-crime area. They can learn to share skills; for example, she might teach him to cook while he teaches her automobile maintenance. Generally, the couple simply lives together as would two same-sex roommates. They each date others, generally keep their love lives out of their living quarters, and react to one another as friends, each gaining something from living together in partnership rather than separately. The reason most often given for such an arrangement is "to save money." This is especially true of elderly cohabitants.

Third, there are couples who see cohabiting as a *true trial marriage*. As one young woman explained, "We are thinking of marriage in the future, and we want to find out if we really are what each other wants. If everything works out, we will get married." Some of these couples go so far as to set a specific time period.

Fourth, there are couples who view cohabiting as a *permanent alternative to marriage*. They often express philosophical rejection of the marital institution as being unfavorable to healthy and growing relationships. They are especially critical of the constraints imposed by laws on partners' rights in marriage. Many couples who see consensual union as a permanent alternative to legal marriage write their own contracts in an effort to form a more egalitarian union even though such contracts cannot invalidate state marriage laws. Many couples live together to avoid what they perceive to be the constraining, love-draining formalities associated with legal marriage. They say, "If I stay with my mate out of my own free desire rather than because I legally must remain, our relationship will be more honest and caring. The stability of our relationship is its very instability."

Fifth, some couples, especially where one or both have been divorced, live together out of fear of making the same mistake again. In 1985 the divorced made up 34 percent of cohabiting households (U.S. Bureau of the Census, October 1985, p. 9). These couples also account for the vast majority of children in such relationships. About 30 percent of cohabiting couples report children under fifteen years of age to be present (U.S. Bureau of the Census, November 1986, p. 14).

Is the Woman Exploited in Cohabitation?

Obviously the answer to this question will depend on the individual relationship. However, some interesting statistics bear on this question in a general way. A number of studies indicated that males seem less committed than their female partners to live-together relationships (Budd, 1976; Johnson, 1973; Kieffer, 1972; Lewis et al., 1975; Lyness et al., 1972; Risman, 1981; Macklin, 1983).

In the Lyness study couples living together were compared with couples going together. No significant differences were found between the groups in level of trust and reported happiness, both of which were high. A difference was found, however, in the reported degree of commitment to marriage. The couples who were going together, both males and females, were committed to future marriage. But males in the living-together couples were the least committed, far less so than the women with whom they were living. The researchers' tentative conclusions were, in part:

> To a striking degree, living-together couples did not reciprocate the kinds of feelings (of need, respect, involvement, or commitment to marriage) that one would expect to be the basis of a good heterosexual relationship. The question of whether such a lack of reciprocity is typical of such relationships and thus reflects the difficulties of bringing off a successful nonnormative relationship or whether it is merely typical of those who volunteered for our research cannot be answered. (Lyness et al., 1972, p. 309)

Many cohabitation relationships are short-lived and seem to revolve around the sexual part of the relationship. If the man tends to be less committed than the woman, it appears to be a reasonable assumption that he is often the one to end the relationship, if not directly then indirectly by refusing equal commitment.

Glick and Spanier (1980) also point out that cohabiting men are much less likely to be employed than married men, but cohabiting women were much more likely to be employed than married women. This might suggest that men are using women economically to help themselves get through school or pursue their own interests, which at the time may not produce much, if any, monetary return. Blumstein and Schwartz (1983, p. 126) report: "We notice that as a rule male cohabitors reject the economic responsibilities they would have as husbands. They do not want to become the sole supporter or breadwinner."

It is interesting to note that although cohabitation appears to be avant-garde, suggesting that those who are involved are liberated, the division of labor in the household tends to be traditional (Macklin, 1983; Whitehurst, 1974; Risman, 1981). That is, the woman does the cooking, cleaning, and household work. This, combined with the findings that she is much more apt to be in the workforce than her married counterpart, makes it clear that she is often overburdened in the cohabitation relationship.

Perhaps the woman considering cohabitation should examine carefully the nature of the intended relationship before entering it. One way that she can do this is to answer the questions posed in Inset 4-1.

The Relationship between Cohabitation and Marriage

Many young people argue persuasively that living together provides a good test for future marriage. Living together, they say, is like a trial marriage without the legal framework required to end the relationship if it doesn't work. Cohabitors espouse a variety of other arguments in support of cohabitation:

1. It provides an opportunity to try to establish a meaningful relationship.
2. It can be a source of financial, social, and emotional security.
3. It provides a steady sexual partner and companionship, thus providing some of the central pleasures of marriage without commitment and as much responsibility.
4. It provides a chance for personal growth, a chance to increase self-understanding while relating to another person on an intimate basis.
5. Cohabitors would have a more realistic notion of their partner and should generally have less-romanticized ideas about the relationship.
6. Cohabitors have a chance to get beyond typical courtship game-playing.
7. Long periods of intimate contact provide an opportunity for self-disclosure and concomitant modification and/or realization of personal goals. (Jacques & Chason, 1979, p. 37)

Although these arguments are logical and reasonable, research to date on the quality of marriage after cohabitation experiences finds little if any relationship between cohabitation and the degree of satisfaction, conflict, emotional closeness, or egalitarianism in later marriage (Macklin, 1983; Jacques & Chason, 1979; Markowski & Johnson, 1980). Clatworthy and Scheid (1977) report that while all couples in their sample who had premaritally cohabited considered the experience to be beneficial to their marriage, there was no evidence that they actually had better marriages or that they had selected more compatible mates than noncohabiting couples. Bentler and Newcomb (1978) found no significant differences

---

Inset 4-1

Questions for Couples Contemplating Living Together

1. How did you make the decision to live together?

Good signs: Each partner has given considerable thought to the decision, including the advantages and disadvantages of living together.

Concern signs: One or both partners have given little thought to the advantages and disadvantages of living together.

2. What do you think you will get out of the relationship?

Good signs: Each individual is concerned about learning more about self and partner through intimate daily living. Both wish to obtain further information about each other's commitment to the relationship.

Concern signs: One or both partners desire to live together for convenience only. They want to live together to show independence from parents or peers.

3. What is your role and your partner's role in the relationship?

Good signs: Each individual's expectations of self and partner are compatible with those of partner.

Concern signs: One or both individuals have given little thought to the roles or expectations of self and/or partner. Individuals disagree in terms of their expectations.

4. Identify your partner's primary physical and emotional needs and the degree to which you think you can fulfill them.

Good signs: Each individual has a clear understanding of partner's needs and is motivated and able to meet most of them.

Concern signs: One or both individuals are not fully aware of partner's needs. Individuals are not motivated or able to meet needs of partner.

5. Identify your own physical and emotional needs and the degree to which you think your partner will be able to satisfy them.

Good signs: Each partner clearly understands his or her needs? Most of these needs are presently being met and are likely to continue to be met in a cohabiting relationship.

Concern signs: One or both partners are not fully aware of their needs. Needs are not being met in the present relationship and/or are not likely to be met if the individuals live together.

6. Explore briefly your earlier dating experiences and what you have learned from them.

Good signs: Both individuals have had a rich dating history. Individuals have positive perceptions of self and opposite sex and are aware of what they learned from previous relationships.

Concern signs: One or both partners have had minimal dating experience. Individuals have negative perceptions of self and/or of the opposite sex and do not seem aware of having learned from their prior relationships.

7. How will your family and friends react to your living together?

Good signs: Each individual is aware of the potential repercussions of family and friends should they learn of the cohabiting relationship. Family and friends are supportive of the cohabiting relationship, or couple has considered how they will deal with opposition.

Concern signs: One or both individuals are not fully aware of possible family and friends' reaction to their living together. Family and friends are not supportive of the cohabiting relationship.

8. To what degree can you and your partner honestly share feelings?

Good signs: Each individual is usually able to express feelings to partner without difficulty.

Concern signs: One or both individuals have difficulty expressing feelings to partner or do not believe expressing feelings is important.

9. What are your partner's strengths and weaknesses? To what extent would you like to change your partner?

Good signs: Each individual is usually able to accept feelings of partner. Individuals are able to accept partner's strengths and weaknesses.

Concern signs: One or both individuals are not able to understand and accept partner. Individuals have difficulty in accepting partner's strengths and weaknesses.

10. How do each of you handle problems when they arise?

Good signs: Both individuals express feelings openly and are able to understand and accept partner's point of view. Individuals are able to mutually solve problems.

Concern signs: One or both partners have difficulty expressing feelings openly or in accepting partner's point of view. Couple frequently avoids problems or fails to solve them mutually.

Source: Adapted from Ridley, Peterman & Avery, 1978, pp. 135–136.

in divorce rates between couples who had cohabited before their marriage and couples who had not.

Several more recent studies report that couples who lived together before marriage actually report lower marital satisfaction than those couples who did not live together before marriage. Watson (1983) found that it was mainly the women in his sample who reported greater marital dissatisfaction. DeMaris and Leslie (1984) found lower marital satisfaction in their previously cohabiting couples. Feeling that such a result might be merely the duration of time the cohabiting couple had been together (marital satisfaction tends to fall with length of relationship) they correlated length of cohabitation with marital satisfaction but found no relationship. They did find that cohabitors were significantly lower in their feelings of permanent commitment to their marriage. They finally concluded that:

> Rather than acting as a filter that effectively screens out the less-compatible couples, cohabitation appears to select couples from the outset who are somewhat less likely to report high satisfaction once they are married. This may be due to the fact that these individuals expect more out of marriage from the beginning. Alternatively, these may be individuals who adapt less readily to the role expectations of conventional marriage. In either case it is most probably the difference between the kinds of people who do and do not choose to cohabit before marriage, rather than the experience itself, that accounts for our findings.

Studies done on those cohabitors who remarry after divorce or being widowed find slightly different results. DeMaris (1984) found that cohabitation did not seem to have a negative effect on marital satisfaction of remarried couples. Another study done on remarried families, found that cohabitation before marriage was positively related to marital quality (Hanna & Knaub, 1981). Remarried couples who lived together before marriage reported significantly higher degrees of happiness, closeness, concern for partner's welfare, and positive communication, and they perceived more environmental support than remarried couples who had not cohabited. In general, the remarried are older and more experienced than the never married. They have also gone through a marriage, not just a cohabitation experience.

Perhaps the dissimilarities between cohabitation and marriage negate the apparent advantages of cohabitation as far as future marriage success is concerned. Gerald Leslie (1979) lists the following dissimilarities between cohabitation and marriage:

1. In marriage one partner doesn't keep an address elsewhere to which he or she can retreat when the going gets rough.
2. Couples who live together know that they are not legally bound to one another. They can get out of the relationship with few sanctions.
3. Most living-together couples retain a degree of financial independence uncommon in most marriages.
4. Unwed couples have to worry about possible contraceptive failure, but they don't have to plan for children.
5. Cohabiting couples don't necessarily have to make plans for the future.

In discussing the high breakup rate of cohabiting couples, Leslie finds that cohabitors may unknowingly be creating a self-fulfilling prophecy. They enter a relationship partly to see if it will last, and, by keeping the possibility of discontinuing the relationship in mind, they actually help cause the breakup. In other words, while cohabiting they withhold total commitment to the relationship. It is possible that some relationships might turn out differently if the partners enter them with an unshakable determination to succeed, but the cohabiting experience teaches them to withhold this kind of total commitment. Leslie suggests that living together can be a way for young people to avoid responsibility. It is easier to play house than to be married. Such an attitude might be carried into a subsequent marriage and contribute to marital dissatisfaction.

Many cohabiting couples who subsequently marry report disappointment after the marriage. "Nothing changed when we married." "I expected our relationship to improve after we married, but it didn't." "Somehow I don't feel any different now that we are married." Couples who come to marriage without cohabitation experience a real change in their life situation when they marry. They are suddenly independent of their parents, in a relationship where sex is condoned, responsible for themselves economically, setting up their own living quarters, planning their activities without interference, etc. It is a new and exciting world. For the cohabiting couple, nothing really changes. What does a couple who has lived together for three years do on their honeymoon? What's new? What's exciting? Yet unconsciously this couple shares the social idea that marriage is a new and exciting happening in one's life. When they don't find this, they express disappointment: Something is missing.

Despite such criticisms, cohabitation, especially among college students, seems to be finding more acceptance in our society. However, deciding to cohabit is not a decision to be taken lightly. One needs to consider carefully the ramifications of such a decision. Legal ramifications, which we will discuss in a coming section, must also be considered, now more than ever.

Breaking Up

Society, including the cohabiting couples themselves, has largely ignored one of the philosophical foundations of cohabitation: that it is easy to break up if the relationship fails. Yet for partners who are highly committed to a relationship, a breakup can be as emotionally uncomfortable as a divorce. Society has support systems for divorced people (see Chapter 15), but no such support systems exist for the person leaving a cohabitation relationship. The breakup rate among cohabiting couples is high, and thus the number of people who must cope with the trauma of breakup by themselves or perhaps with only a friend's shoulder to cry on will increase as the number of cohabiting couples increases.

Living Together and the Law

Many readers may be surprised to know that as of July 1980 cohabitation was still a crime in fifteen states: Alabama, Arizona, Florida, Georgia, Idaho, Illinois, Kansas, Michigan, Mississippi, North Carolina, Rhode Island, South Carolina, Utah, Virginia, and Wisconsin (Weitzman, 1981). Indeed, sexual intercourse between unmarried persons is still a crime in sixteen states and the District of Columbia. Such laws are seldom enforced, but when they are, the penalties are stringent. Many states set a maximum fine of $500 and six months in jail. Macklin (1978a) suggests that such laws may be unconstitutional and may violate one's right to privacy.

In the states where such laws are in effect, there are numerous ramifications for the cohabiting couple. For example, living together can be grounds for losing one's job. Because membership in professional associations and licensing may be conditional on demonstration of moral fitness, such privileges could be denied to someone cohabiting outside of marriage (Macklin, 1978a). For those couples in which one is receiving alimony, cohabiting will cause loss of alimony in thirteen states. Also a divorced woman and her children who have been given the right by the court to remain in the family home until the children are eighteen years old (at which time the home is to be sold and proceeds divided) may lose that right if the woman cohabits (Weitzman, 1985, pp. 44, 88).

Laws making cohabitation a crime, however, are so seldom enforced that they are not nearly as meaningful to the cohabiting couple as several recent court decisions concerning property distribution and the obligation of support. Perhaps the best-known case involved actor Lee Marvin and his live-in friend, Michelle Triola. Out of this case came the term *palimony*, coined to describe settlements made to a nonmarried live-in partner. The term has no legal significance but is descriptive of what Michelle Triola was at first awarded.

Michelle Triola and Lee Marvin lived together for seven years. During this period she acted as a companion and homemaker. There was no pooling of earnings, no property was purchased in joint names, and no joint income tax returns were filed. They often spoke proudly of their freedom as unmarried cohabitors and went to some length to keep property separate. Eventually, Lee Marvin asked Michelle Triola to leave the household. He continued to support her for two years after the separation and then refused further support. Michelle Triola then brought suit and asked the court to determine her contract and property rights and to award her half of the property acquired during the period of their relationship.

The trial court dismissed the action as inappropriate; it was then appealed to the California Supreme Court, which ruled:

> The fact that a man and woman live together without marriage and engage in a sexual relationship, does not in itself invalidate agreements between them relating to their earnings, property, or expenses. . . . Agreements between nonmarital partners fail only to the extent that they rest upon a consideration of meretricious sexual services. (*Marvin* v. *Marvin*, 1976, as reported in Myricks, 1980, p. 210)

A *meretricious relationship* is essentially that of a prostitute to her customer; that is, sexual services are being paid for. This ruling enabled Michelle Triola to pursue her claim for support payments and established a precedent for unwed couples in that it granted such persons the right to sue for property settlements. Michelle Triola became the first unmarried person to win compensation from a former lover in a U.S. court (*Marvin* v. *Marvin*, 1979). She was awarded $104,000 for

> rehabilitation purposes so that she may have economic means to reeducate herself and to learn new, employable skills or to refurbish those utilized . . . during her most recent employment, and so that she may return from her status as companion of a motion picture star to a separate, independent but perhaps more prosaic existence (*Marvin* v. *Marvin*, 1979, as reported in Myricks, 1980, p. 211).

The award was primarily for retraining, yet some of the funds could be used for living expenses. Such equitable relief is similar to rehabilitative alimony, hence the term *palimony*. In effect the judge gave her disguised alimony. However, this award was later thrown out by the California appellate court, and the California Supreme Court has refused to reinstate it (*Marvin* v. *Marvin*, 1981).

Numerous other cases have been litigated both before and after the Marvin case. In those cases where the courts see the union as meretricious, any implied contracts are illegal.

The bottom line is that a given court will have the final word about a cohabiting couple's obligations to one another if they break up. After a review of many palimony cases, Noel Myricks (1980) draws the following conclusions:

1. Distribution of property acquired during cohabitation remains subject solely to judicial decision.
2. Courts should enforce express contracts between cohabitors except where the contract is explicitly founded on payment for sexual services.
3. Without an express contract courts should inquire into the nature of the relationship to determine if there is an implied contract.
4. Courts may compensate a person for the reasonable value of services regardless of any agreement about the value of such services.
5. Generally sexual services must be separated from other domestic services to make a valid argument. However, the state of Oregon has ruled more liberally and is willing to disregard the lifestyle of the parties (*Latham* v. *Latham*, 1976).
6. An implied contract may be inferred entitling a cohabitant to one half of the accumulated property where parties have held themselves out as husband and wife (*Carlson* v. *Olson*, 1977).
7. Palimony may be provided to a cohabitant for rehabilitation purposes.
8. Lawsuits may be kept to a minimum if cohabitants have written agreements concerning the nature of their relationship, although the court may change or invalidate such agreements.

Despite the fact that courts are slowly giving unwed cohabitants some legal rights, cohabitation still has few legal safeguards for either partner. As Lenore Weitzman summarizes (1981), a sanctioned marriage has legal rules and forums that provide otherwise unprepared married couples with an efficient system for dealing with the unexpected; the married couple is thus helped to minimize hardships resulting from unforeseen events. For example, if a spouse is killed, the state has rules for allocating that person's property in the absence of a will and for guaranteeing a share of it to the surviving spouse. By contrast, if one member of a cohabiting relationship dies without a will, the surviving partner has no legal rights at all. Legally, cohabiting couples are at a distinct disadvantage compared with married couples. This is especially true for the woman and is yet another reason for an affirmative answer to the earlier question: Is the woman exploited in the cohabitation relationship?

Nonmarital Sexuality

As we have seen, movement down the path of intimacy is a part of American dating. For most, it has been a gradual movement characterized by escalating sexual intimacy. Traditional American dating often evolves into a sexual game of offense versus defense. With each step the couple moves closer to sexual intercourse. In traditional dating, because it is the male who pressures the female for greater physical intimacy, it is she who is on the defensive. Because her value

---

Inset 4-2
Couple Wed So They Know What to Call Each Other

This piece will use names of two people, Pietro and Tess.

For three years Pietro and Tess lived together without marrying. Such an arrangement had ceased to be scandalous when they took it up, had even become fashionable. It expressed the partners' reevaluation of the culture, or their liberation from tired old values, or something. It doesn't matter what. Pietro and Tess did it.

They were married a few weeks ago.

The canker in the love nest was the English language. Though English is the world's most commodious tongue, it provided no words to define their relationship satisfactorily to strangers. When Tess took Pietro to meet her parents the problem became troublesome. Presenting Pietro, she said, "Mommy and daddy, this is my lover, Pietro."

Pietro was not amused. "It made me sound like a sex object," he said.

A few weeks later they were invited to meet the president. Entering the reception line, Pietro was asked by the protocol officer for their names. "Pietro," he said. "And this is my mate."

As they came abreast of the president, the officer turned to Mr. Reagan and said, "Pietro and his mate."

"I felt like the supporting actress in a Tarzan movie," said Tess. It took Pietro three nights of sleeping at the YMCA to repair the relationship.

Back to the drawing board, on which they kept the dictionary.

For a while they tried "my friend." One night at a glamorous party Pietro introduced Tess to a marrying millionaire with the words, "This is my friend, Tess." To which the marrying millionaire replied, "Let's jet down to the Caribbean, Tess, and tie the knot."

"You don't understand," said Pietro. "Tess is my *friend*."

"So don't you like seeing your friends

headed for big alimony?" asked the marrying millionaire.

"She's not that kind of friend," said Pietro.

"I'm his *friend*," said Tess.

"Ah," said the matrimonialist, upon whom the dawn was slowly breaking, "Ah—your—*friend*."

As Tess explained at the wedding, they couldn't spend the rest of their lives rolling their eyeballs suggestively every time they said "friend." There was only one way out. "The simple thing," Pietro suggested, "would be for me to introduce you as 'my wife.' "

"And for me," said Tess, "to say, 'This is my husband, Pietro.' "

And so they were wed, victims of a failure in language.

Russell Baker
New York Times

---

system may be vague or may become confused by the swiftly changing and pragmatic character of American society, the continuing pressure for more intimacy will often cause her confusion and insecurity.

For the young, continuing escalation of physical intimacy moves from the first cautious hand holding to necking, petting, and increasingly to intercourse. How rapidly the couple proceeds depends on the inner security of each member, the length of time and exclusiveness with which they date each other, and the dating patterns of their friends. The more insecure the persons are, the more they will seek security in conforming to what they believe the peer group is doing. Time is an important factor, too. To place vigorous young adults who like one another together for long periods of time without supervision in a culture that promotes sexuality is likely to lead to sexual activity.

But it is up to the individual couple to decide how far they will go. This strategy can be called "sex—nonsex," and it is usually the female who makes the rules. Because she must control how sexual the male becomes, she must have a personal definition of what sexual behavior is. She knows that intercourse is sex, but she may be unsure how to categorize other behavior: kissing, necking, and

various degrees of petting. If she can categorize necking as "nonsex," she can neck as much as she likes and feel no guilt. If on the other hand she categorizes necking as "sex," she will feel guilty when she engages in such behavior. For many American young persons, premarital sex is largely a matter of learning how to handle guilt.

When one asks a cross-section of young American women what they define as sexual behavior, there is no single answer. One may become upset at any action beyond kissing. Another may participate in mutual masturbation with little if any conflict because she has defined as "nonsex" all but actual intercourse. In the broadest sense, intimate physical contact of any kind between male and female is sexual behavior.

A man may not be able to judge where a woman will draw the line, and he will be insecure with a new woman until he knows the rules by which the game will be played. He also may be timid and afraid of overt sexuality, although he is obliged to hide any fears by the masculine stereotype that demands he be a sexual initiator.

The escalation toward physical intimacy may cause young people to become centered on sex to the exclusion of most other things. And of course the final "solution" to escalation problems, sexual intercourse, does not end the preoccupation with sex. Instead, it often exaggerates it.

The Sexual Revolution

The preceding description of movement down the path of intimacy will seem old-fashioned to many young Americans. The sexual revolution of the past twenty-five years has greatly affected the mores surrounding premarital sexual interaction. Essentially the sexual revolution has been a revolution for women. The double

Table 4-1

Percentage of College Students Having Premarital Intercourse

	Males	Females
1965	65.1	28.7
1970	65.0	37.3
1975	73.9	57.1
1980	77.4	63.5

standard that tacitly allowed males premarital sexual relations but forbade them to females is gradually disappearing since it was first studied by Alfred Kinsey and coresearchers around 1950. A look at the results of just one or two of the many studies of the incidence of premarital sexual experience makes it clear that young women have become more like young men in their sexual behavior. (See Clayton & Bakemeier, 1980, for an overview of the many studies done on premarital sexual behavior during the 1970s.)

Robinson and Jedlicka (1982) compared the percentage of college students having premarital intercourse in 1965, 1970, 1975, and 1980 (Table 4-1) and found little increase for college men (12.3 percent) but a large increase for college women (34.8 percent). In addition they found that college students' rejection of premarital sexual intercourse as immoral had dropped dramatically. The number of students strongly agreeing with the statement, "I feel that premarital intercourse is immoral," showed a continual decline over the fifteen years studied except for a reversal of the decline for women in 1980, the last year studied (Table 4-2).

Robinson and Jedlicka did find, however, that there was a similar reversal in 1980 for both men and women on the question of whether it is immoral to have sexual intercourse with many partners. More men and women agreed in 1980 that this was immoral than had agreed in 1975. Robinson and Jedlicka suggest that there may be a "sexual contradiction" in today's college students: Sexual intercourse is reported at higher levels than earlier while at the same time there is increasing disapproval.

DeLamater and MacCorquodale (1979) found a similar incidence of premarital sexual relations in both college student and nonstudent samples. This similarity seems to indicate that the sexual revolution encompasses all youth, not just college students. These researchers also discovered that the average age of onset of various sexual behaviors is lower for nonstudent men but higher for nonstudent women. For example, the age of first intercourse for male nonstudents was 17.2 years, whereas it was 17.5 years for male students. For female students it was 17.9 years, whereas for female nonstudents it was 18.3 years. Bell and Coughey (1980) found that the increase in premarital intercourse among women cut across all religions (see Table 4-3).

Although it is now clear that American sexual mores have become increasingly more liberal, there are some who suggest that a counterrevolution is setting in. This is being fueled by the increased incidence of sexually transmitted diseases (AIDS and herpes for example); growing social concern about unwed pregnancy and the single, never-wed, woman-headed family; growing female dissatisfaction with what they feel to be sexual exploitation by men; and the general movement toward a more conservative philosophy in America. (See pp. 338–341, A New Sexual Revolution?, for a more complete discussion.)

Although the sexual mores of American youth are becoming more permissive, middle-aged adults tend to react negatively to these changes. Most adults still support a position against premarital intercourse. The most common reasons they list for this position are:

1. Religious attitudes prohibit such behavior.
2. My own upbringing and personal moral code prohibit such behavior.
3. Sexual relations before marriage lead to serious problems: illegitimate children, damaged reputation, psychological problems, and so on.
4. Premarital sex contributes to the breakdown of morals in this country.

Table 4-2

Percentage of Students Strongly Agreeing with the Statement, "I feel that premarital sexual intercourse is immoral."

	Males	Females
1965	33.0	70.0
1970	14.0	34.0
1975	19.5	20.7
1980	17.4	25.3

Table 4-3
Percentage of Females Having Intercourse

	Jew			Protestant			Catholic			Total		
	1958	1968	1978	1958	1968	1978	1958	1968	1978	1958	1968	1978
Dating	11	20	45	10	35	56	8	15	46	10	23	50
Going steady	14	26	64	20	41	79	14	17	63	15	28	67
Engaged	20	40	69	38	67	88	18	56	69	31	39	76

Source: Bell & Coughey, 1980.

5. Sex is sacred and belongs only in marriage.
6. Premarital sex leads to extramarital sex and casual marital commitment.

It is easy for middle-aged individuals to urge young people to suppress their sex drives, but the fact remains that sexual needs are among the most basic human needs. It is extremely difficult for young adults to accept admonitions against premarital sex. Parents need to discuss openly and honestly the sexual problems youth face. Any ultimate decision about premarital intercourse will be made by the young couples themselves. Rather than giving lectures about morality, it is surely better to supply young people with as much good information as possible so that their decision will be based on a firm foundation of knowledge rather than ignorance. In a nutshell: "Knowledge breeds responsible behavior, ignorance just breeds" (Canfield, 1979).

Deciding for Yourself

There are four major areas for the couple contemplating premarital sexual intercourse to consider: (1) personal principles, (2) social principles, (3) religious principles, and (4) psychological principles.

Every person has a set of personal principles by which to guide his or her life. The following are some personal questions you should ask yourself if you are contemplating premarital intercourse:

1. Is my behavior going to harm the other person or myself, either physically or psychologically? Will I still like myself? What problems might arise? Am I protecting my partner and myself against sexually transmitted diseases and pregnancy?
2. Will my behavior help me become a good future spouse or parent? Do I believe sex belongs only in marriage?
3. Is my sexual behavior acceptable to my principles and upbringing? If not, what conflicts might arise?

Of course, there are no general answers to questions such as these. Each individual will have different answers, but the fact remains that most young adults should answer such questions if they engage in premarital sexual experimentation.

Other questions arise when one considers general social principles. Our society has long supported certain rules about premarital sex. If enough people break these rules, pressure is placed on the society to change them. Thus each person who decides to act against the established code adds his or her weight to the pressure for change. Before you make such a decision, you should ask yourself:

1. What kind of behavior do I wish to have prevail in my society? Is premarital sex immoral? Will premarital sex contribute to a breakdown of morals? Is this desirable?
2. What kind of sexual behavior do I believe would make the best kind of society? Would I want my friends to follow in my footsteps?
3. Am I willing to support the social rules? What will happen if I don't?

Questions concerning religious principles also need answering. Most of us have had religious training, and we have learned attitudes toward sexual behavior from that training. In a study of several hundred junior college students' attitudes toward premarital sex (Cox, 1978), 90 percent of those who were against it gave religion as their primary reason. In a comparison of cohabiting and noncohabiting couples, Watson (1983) found that 75 percent of the cohabiting couples never attended church, but only 25 percent of the noncohabiting couples never attended church. The following are some questions you should ask yourself:

1. What does my religion say about sexual conduct? Do I agree?
2. Am I willing or able to follow the principles of my religion?
3. Do I believe there is a conflict between the sexual attitudes of my church and society? My church and my friends?

Psychological principles may be the hardest to uncover. Because the socialization process begins at birth and continues throughout one's lifetime, it is difficult, if not impossible, to remain completely unaffected by society and family. Many of our attitudes are so deeply ingrained that we are unaware of them. When our behavior is in conflict with these attitudes, there will usually be stress and guilt. Some of the psychological questions you must grapple with are:

1. Can I handle the guilt feelings that may arise when I engage in premarital sex?
2. How will premarital sex influence my attitudes and the quality of sex after marriage?
3. What will I do if I (or my partner) get pregnant? Can I handle an abortion? A child? Marriage?

Freedom of Choice and Sexual Health

Freedom of sexual choice for the young unmarried individual can be much more threatening than for the married person. The sexual mores in many parts of American society have changed from supporting postponement of sexual intercourse until marriage to pressuring young people to engage in premarital sex. "Don't be old-fashioned." "Get with it." "Everyone does it." Especially for young women, it now seems harder to say, "No, I don't want to have sex." Or, "No, I don't want to have sex at this time." This is quite a change from the old fear of losing one's virginity. A young woman now often feels guilty and inadequate if she doesn't participate in sex. Virginity is maligned because it represents past traditions and morality and, of course, it is supported by all the wrong people: parents, grandparents, ministers, and others who aren't "liberated."

Yet part of a healthy model of sexual behavior is the freedom to choose whether to participate in sexual relations. Being coerced into sexual relations, either physically or psychologically, seldom leads to a healthy experience.

Healthy sexual expression is a primary part of human intimacy. As we try to make good decisions about our sexual intimacy, it is helpful to think about what we mean by healthy sex. There is much debate over this topic. For some no sexual involvement before marriage is healthy. Others argue that complete sexual freedom is healthy. In between these two opposing positions are a variety of less extreme viewpoints. The following questions may help you discover foundations to promote healthy sex.

Does My Sexual Expression Enhance My Self-Esteem?   If my behavior adds to me, increases my self-respect and my positive feelings about myself, and helps me like myself better, then the behavior is most apt to be healthy. Behavior that creates negative self-feelings and causes loss of self-esteem is better avoided. Low self-esteem, as we will see in Chapter 5, creates many problems, especially in intimate relationships. Thus for any behavior, not just sexual behavior, each of us can ask: Does my behavior increase my self-esteem?

Is My Sexual Expression Voluntary (Freely Chosen)?   Obviously rape is not voluntary sexual expression and not health enhancing. Other situations, however, are not always so clear-cut. Is my behavior voluntary when I have sex out of fear of losing my boyfriend if I don't? Perhaps it is, yet the element of fear raises a doubt. Does the fear make me think I must do it? Does the fear rob me of voluntary choice? Does the fear cause me to overlook the broader question: If I will lose him only because I will not have sex at this time, is he really someone with whom I want to have an intimate relationship? If my decision is really mine, independent of peer and social pressure, then the chances increase that my chosen behavior will be healthy.

Is My Sexual Expression Enjoyable and Gratifying?   This may sound like a strange question to ask. Isn't all sex fun and enjoyable? It generally will be if it is healthy, but we often find that it is not. Many people report disappointment with their early sexual encounters. A few people report that they seldom derive much joy from sex. For most, however, positive answers to the first two questions will help answer this question positively. In general enjoyable and gratifying sexual expression tends to occur most often within intimate relationships. This not to deny that at times sex for its own sake is gratifying. However, intimate relationships that involve one intellectually, emotionally, socially, and physically tend to promote healthy sexual relations.

Will My Sexual Expression Lead to an Unwanted Pregnancy?   Sexual activity leading to wanted children is healthy. Sexual relations using birth control methods and thereby avoiding unwanted children can also be healthy. Some people disagree with the latter statement for religious reasons. For them healthy sex might mean abstinence if children are not desired at a given time. For most people, though, sex leading to unwanted pregnancy is not sexually healthy. Taking steps to prevent unwanted pregnancy is an important element in healthy sexual expression.

Will My Sexual Expression Pass a Sexually Transmitted Disease to My Partner?   It is obvious in the medical sense that healthy sex does not promote sexually transmitted diseases (STDs). Thus knowledge of STDs and taking precautions against them must be a part of healthy sexual expression. (See pp. 347–355.)

Possible Problems Associated with Premarital Sexual Relations

As American mores have relaxed, the differentiation between premarital and marital sex activities has lessened. However, a number of problems are clearly more closely related to premarital sex than to marital sex.

Sexually transmitted disease is more prevalent among unmarried participants in sexual activities, whose chances of having more than one sexual partner are greater than married people's. The chances are also greater of having short-duration sexual encounters where communication is less open. Such encounters may lead, especially for women, to later discovery of sexually transmitted disease. (STD is discussed fully in Chapter 10.)

Unwanted pregnancies are also a problem. Despite improved birth control methods, especially birth control pills, nonmarital pregnancies have continued to increase. It is estimated that the number of illegitimate births per 1000 unmarried women ages fifteen to forty-four has increased from 14.1 in 1950 to 32 in 1984 (U.S. National Center for Health Statistics, 1982; Bureau of the Census, November 1985). Table 4-4 gives an overview of these statistics. Illegitimacy rates do not give the complete picture, though, because many babies conceived outside of marriage are legitimized by subsequent marriage. Perhaps as many as one-third of all first-born babies are conceived outside of marriage. A segment of *CBS Reports* (Reasoner, 1980) noted that over half of all teenage births resulted from pregnancies outside marriage.

Recent increases in the number of births to unmarried women have been due to a combination of two factors: a higher rate of childbearing by unmarried women and the growth in the number of unmarried women of childbearing age. It is difficult to determine precisely the weight of each factor because each varies substantially by race and age. It is clear, however, that the growth in the number of unmarried women age twenty-five and over continues to be a significant factor in the recent large increases in births to these women. By contrast the number of unmarried teenagers has leveled off and begun to decline in recent years. However, the increased birthrate among unmarried teens tends to offset their declining numbers.

Table 4-4

Live Births by Unmarried Mothers

Race and Age	1950	1960	1965	1970	1974	1981	1984
Total numbers (1000s)	141,600	224,300	291,200	398,700	418,100	665,747	624,410
Percent of all births	3.9	5.3	7.7	10.7	13.2	17.8	17.0
Rate per 1000 unmarried women	14.1	21.6	23.5	26.4	24.1	29.4	32.0
White women	6.1	9.2	11.6	13.8	11.8	17.9	20.1
Black and other women	71.2	98.3	97.6	89.9	81.5	67.2	78.7

The rate of pregnancy among teenage girls is such that, if present trends continue, 40 percent of today's fourteen-year-old girls will be pregnant at least once before they reach twenty. Of such pregnancies 45 percent are aborted (Wallis, 1985). It should be noted that the actual birthrate among teenage mothers was as high in the 1950s, but that reflected the lower age of marriage. The great majority of those pregnancies were within marriage. (See Scenes from Marriage, pp. 395–397 for a complete discussion of teenage pregnancies.)

An unmarried pregnant woman has limited alternatives. She may marry; seek an abortion, give birth to the baby and give it up for adoption, desert the infant, keep the child and go on welfare, or let her parents care for the child while she works or continues with school. Regardless of how one handles a premarital pregnancy, the problems are many and stay with one for years.

It should be noted that some women who are uninterested in marriage and/ or nearing the end of their childbearing years are now making a conscious decision to have a child out of wedlock. They become pregnant through artificial insemination or by having sexual relations with a man who has agreed not to assert his rights as father. Many of these women are economically successful and do not face the same kinds of problems that a teenage mother usually faces (Moore, 1983).

Early commitment and isolation are frequent partners of premarital sexual involvement. Sex is such a powerful force in young people's lives that it often overrides other aspects of a relationship. Sexual involvement often excludes growth in social, intellectual, or other areas. Also, sexual relationships can promote exclusivity in a relationship, thus narrowing a young person's interpersonal experiences. Such relationships may lead to sexual commitment alone rather than to a total relationship. An early commitment based on only one aspect of a relationship (sexual) is usually an unstable basis for any long-term relationship.

The *quality of sex may be impaired* by premarital sexual experience. Masters and Johnson (1966) point out that fear, hostility, and conflict are the three mental states that most often cripple the sex life of both men and women. Through education, Masters and Johnson assert, these three can be defeated. In their treatment conferences with couples they examine the couple's past sexual history and slowly guide them toward overcoming the negative emotional reactions that may be attached to early unhappy sexual experiences. Assuming that the couple's sexual problems are mental rather than physiological in nature, they help the couple through actual practice and desensitization to become more satisfactory sexual partners. They find that early unsatisfactory sexual experiences often have negatively influenced an individual's whole attitude toward sexuality. As long as society holds taboos against early sexual experience, indulging in premarital intercourse may be, for some, a factor working against later sexual fulfillment.

Because premarital sexual intercourse is becoming more prevalent, an increasing number of American youth may be initiated into sexual intercourse under the often adverse circumstances that surround much premarital sexual activity. Premarital sex in our culture is often of relatively poor quality for two major reasons: a negative environment and the sexual ignorance of the young couple.

The environment of early sexual experiences is usually negative and seldom conducive to relaxed, uninhibited sexual activities. Many of these activities take place in a car; having to duck each time another car passes doesn't help the couple relax and feel secure. Both relaxation and security are important psycho-

Dawn and Jim: But I Want to Keep the Baby Even If We Aren't Married

Dawn is twenty years old and a college junior, majoring in business administration. She has gone with Jim for two years. He is a senior in premed and has been accepted for medical school. She has recently discovered that she is pregnant. In the past both she and Jim have agreed to postpone marriage until they are finished with school and Jim has established himself.

Jim is angry with her for becoming pregnant. "How stupid of you to forget to take your pill, especially in the middle of the cycle when you knew your chances of pregnancy were higher. Are you sure you didn't do it on purpose? You could have told me and I could have used something although I don't like to. It isn't natural. It is really up to the girl to protect herself, and you were plain dumb to forget after all this time."

Dawn doesn't quite agree. "You're having sex with me, too. I don't see why birth control is always just my responsibility. You know as well as I do that I didn't want to get pregnant. It wasn't my fault that I forgot. After all, you didn't have to make love to me. You were the one that was hard up and pushing, not me. But now that I'm pregnant, I'm going to keep the baby. A lot of my friends are doing it. Having a baby before you are married isn't half as bad as it used to be. I really don't care what you or our folks think; it's the modern thing to do."

Jim objects strongly. "Well, I'm not going to marry you under these conditions. We agreed to wait until I was finished with medical school and you blew it. The only thing you can do is get an abortion. They're easy to get now. There is nothing to them physically, and I'm willing to pay for it. Keeping the baby will just foul up our lives and tie us down. We'll have plenty of time to have children after we're finished with school."

"No abortion for me," replies Dawn. "I don't think they're right. Besides, I don't expect you to marry me. I wouldn't want you to feel forced into anything. I've only a year of school left and I'm sure my folks would watch out for the baby until I'm working and independent. Then, with child care, I'll be able to take care of it just fine, without you."

"Well, if you're that stupid, I'm glad to find out now," retorts Jim. "I won't be a part of such a dumb plan. Unless you do the smart thing and get an abortion, I'm through with you, pregnant or not."

What Do You Think?

1. How will they resolve their conflict? What would you advise?

2. What would you do if you were Jim? Dawn?

3. What kind of attitudes show through Jim's statements? Dawn's?

4. How would your parents react to such a situation?

5. What are the alternatives open to the couple?

6. How do you feel about illegitimacy? How do you think society feels today?

7. Whose responsibility is birth control? Why?

logical prerequisites for satisfying sex. The general environment is especially important to a woman's ability to find satisfaction. A man's response is much more direct; he can feel satisfied, through ejaculation, almost regardless of the environment. A woman's response is more diffuse psychologically and depends more on her state of mind. A woman who is afraid of being caught, suffering from intense guilt, and possibly feeling used and manipulated by the man will seldom find great satisfaction in sexual intercourse. For example, the young woman's family home is now reported to be the place where first intercourse most often occurs. This environment can heighten her guilt, especially if her parents do not approve of premarital sex.

Indeed, most young women report that their first sexual intercourse experience was not very enjoyable. Only 18 percent in a large study reported their first experience to be "thrilling," and only 10 percent reported having had an orgasm (Wolfe, 1980). This is not to deny that first intercourse can be pleasurable and exciting. In light of what it could be, though, the girl may find herself disappointed. Such disappointment may breed later problems in her attitude toward sex. Because much modern literature, as well as movies and television, depict sexual satisfaction for the female as a wild and violent complete climax, she may interpret her lack of enjoyment as a personal shortcoming. She may begin to think that something is wrong with her sexually, a belief that will in turn increase her anxiety and make her less capable of finding satisfaction. Thus an early negative sexual experience may start a vicious circle of behavior.

In most cases there is nothing wrong with young women. If the environment is one of security and romance, if the man appeals to her on a total basis—that is, psychologically as well as physically, offering her intellectual rapport, warmth, and a feeling of self-respect—and if her conception of the experience is realistic, in all likelihood she will experience a great deal of satisfaction. Although we have mainly discussed the problems of the disappointed woman, it should be noted that if she shows disappointment, this threatens the man, who may react with his own inferiority feelings because he appears unable to satisfy her. His ability to satisfy is one of his chief masculine ego defenses, and he is highly vulnerable to insecurity in this area.

As implied earlier, it is important that the man be aware of the woman's psychological state as well as of her physical state. Candlelight, music, sweet nothings whispered in the ear—in a word, romance—are important ingredients to successful sexual experience for the woman. Yet the American male often lacks understanding of these dimensions. If he does understand them, he may be too preoccupied with himself or too embarrassed to do anything about them. In addition he can't admit to others, and occasionally even to himself, that he does not know all there is to know about sex. Indeed the man who is the biggest braggart about sex often knows the least. In addition most young men reach orgasm very quickly compared with young women. Often the male has ejaculated before the female has become much aroused. As we shall see in Chapter 10, premature ejaculation is the major problem of the young male while failure to achieve orgasm is the major problem of the young female. The two problems are complementary and therefore contribute greatly to dissatisfaction with early sexual experiences, especially for the woman.

The problems described above, although prevalent, do not appear in every case. Some couples can experience the joys of adult sexuality before marriage, but in all cases it is hard to predict just what effects premarital sexual relations will have on marital sexuality.

Although sexual intercourse is the end result of the physical intimacy path, it no longer signifies total commitment. Current research does not support the popular idea that "sexual relations and psychological commitment are related."

Peplau, Rubin, and Hill (1977) found that sexual intercourse was not significantly related to pair continuance as it had been in the past, when sexual intercourse was more closely restricted to marriage or at least to a strong commitment to marriage. The shotgun wedding used to be a common end for the couple caught having premarital sexual relations, especially if a pregnancy resulted. Today sexual relations are not necessarily a precursor to a long-term commitment.

Finding the One and Only: Mate Selection

Chapter 3 pointed out that "love" is the major reason Americans give for marriage. Yet is love really the magic wand that directs our mate selection? Certainly we fall in love, or we think we do at the time. Yet who we are attracted to and why is a complicated, not totally understood process. Critics who argue against using love as a basis for marriage believe that Americans are seduced by the romantic ideal into ignoring practical considerations that help ensure a successful marriage, such as compatible social and economic levels, education, age, religion, and so forth. Yet this is not really true. Our social system does take these factors into consideration, and a close inspection of love finds that it does indeed incorporate some of these factors. You don't fall in love with just anybody; on the other hand, there are a great number of "one and onlys."

First of all, there is a field of "desirables," or people to whom you are attracted. Within this field is a smaller group of "availables," those who are free to return your interest: You can meet them, they are not in love with another, they are unmarried, and so forth.

Availability is closely related to how we live. Our communities are organized into neighborhoods according to social class, and in America this generally means by economic level. So the people who live nearby will be socially and economically like us. Thus middle-class whites tend to marry middle-class whites; lower-class whites tend to marry lower-class whites; Catholics tend to marry Catholics; blacks tend to marry blacks; and so on. This idea that like marries like, or more specifically that we tend to marry within our own group, is called **endogamy**.

Endogamy
The inclination or the necessity to marry within a particular group

There are exceptions to the rule of endogamy, but generally society aims us toward loving and marrying someone similar to ourselves. If you don't marry the girl or boy next door, you are likely to marry someone you meet at school. The American system of neighborhood schools and selective college attendance makes education one of the strongest endogamic factors directing mate selection. Or you may find your future mate through your family's social circle, your job, or your church. All of the groups you join tend to some degree to limit their membership to people who are similar in socioeconomic status as well as in their more obvious reasons for being part of the group.

Strange are the ways of love, but even so it seldom happens that a banker's college-educated daughter falls in love with the uneducated son of a factory worker.

Kerckhoff and Davis (1962) suggest that we select a mate by passing him or her through a series of successive filters (see Figure 4-2). Orientation to marriage is the first filter. A person must start dating with an eye to marriage rather than just for fun and recreation. Proximity and "suitability" of background act as the next filter. Two people are likely to meet if they live or work close to one another, and they will be interested in further exploration if each seems, at first appearance, suitable to the other. Suitability is determined by one's values, most of which are

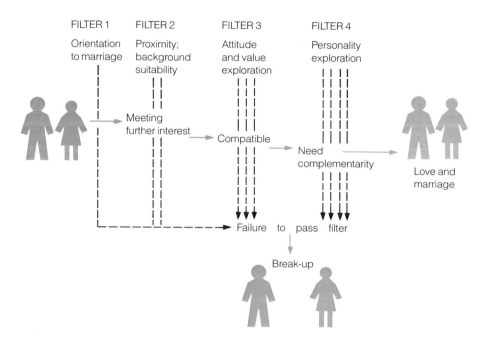

FILTER 1   FILTER 2   FILTER 3   FILTER 4

Orientation to marriage   Proximity; background suitability   Attitude and value exploration   Personality exploration

Meeting further interest

Compatible

Need complementarity

Love and marriage

Failure to pass filter

Break-up

Figure 4-2 Mate selection as successive filters.

learned and internalized from one's parents and peers. The third filter is a more thorough exploration of attitudes and values. For example, the two persons question each other about mutual friends, activities, and interests: "Where do you go to school?" "I know some people who go there, do you know Jim Black and Sally Brown?" "What classes are you taking?" "Really, I'm taking French next semester." "Do you ski? I'm going next week." If the couple's attitudes and interests prove compatible, they will progress toward more subtle personality exploration, finding out whether their needs for affection, independence, security, and so on are also compatible.

This kind of model is useful in understanding that mate selection is an evolving process. However, such an exact fixed set of filters or processes has yet to be proved.

Theoretically, two principles guide mate selection: endogamy and exogamy. Endogamy, as we have seen, is marriage within a certain group. Racial, religious, ethnic (nationality), and social class are the four major types of groups. The mores and taboos against crossing groups vary in strength. For example, only about 2 percent of Americans cross the racial black-white line when marrying. However, 20 to 25 percent of them cross religious lines. (For research purposes, the only listed religions are Protestant, Catholic, and Jewish. See Adams (1986) for a more thorough discussion of these factors.

Until recently most states had prohibitions that enforced endogamy. These prohibitions were generally termed **miscegenation** laws because they prohibited interracial marriages. Most of these laws were originally aimed at preventing white-Indian marriages, but they were also used to prevent white-black and white-Asian marriages. As recently as the end of World War II, thirty of the forty-eight states had such laws. Gradually, though, some states declared them void; and in 1967 the U.S. Supreme Court finally declared all such laws unconstitutional. By

Miscegenation
Marriage or interbreeding between members of different races

Exogamy

The inclination or the necessity to marry outside a particular group

chance the defendant's surname was Loving, so the name of the case, *Loving* v. *Virginia*, fits in well with the American romantic ideal.

Exogamy, on the other hand, is a requirement that people marry outside their group. In our culture requirements to marry outside your group are limited to incest and sex; that is, you may not marry a near relative or someone of your own sex. All states forbid marriage between parents and children, siblings (brothers and sisters), grandparents and grandchildren, and children and their uncles and aunts. Most states forbid marriage to first cousins and half-siblings, although some states do not. About half the states forbid marriage between stepparents and stepchildren, and about the same number prohibit marriage between a man and his father's former wife or his son's former wife.

The other rule of exogamy, which until quite recently has been taken for granted, is the requirement that we marry someone of the opposite sex. This helps ensure reproduction and continuance of the species. In the past few years attempts by homosexuals to obtain more rights have led to some "marriage" ceremonies for homosexuals. So far, though, such marriages have no legal value.

First Impressions to Engagement

Let us look more specifically at the mate-selection process for you, the individual. First impressions are usually belittled as superficial and unimportant. Yet without them the process cannot begin. A favorable first impression must be made or no further interaction will take place.

Physical attractiveness, although subjective, tends to create the first appeal (Hatfield & Walster, 1978). This seems true for people of all ages, from children to the elderly. Fair or not, good-looking individuals are given preferential treatment. They are seen as more responsible for good deeds and less responsible for bad ones (Seligman, Paschall & Takata, 1974); their evaluations of others have more potent impact (Sigall & Aronson, 1969); others are more socially responsive to them (Barocas & Karoly, 1972) and more willing to work hard to please them. Physical attractiveness is more important to male evaluations of females than vice versa (Miller & Revinbark, 1970).

Halo effect

The tendency for a first impression to influence subsequent judgments

It is interesting, too, that there is a **halo effect** operating in regard to physical attractiveness. The halo effect is the tendency for first impressions to influence succeeding evaluations. Physically attractive persons are imbued with other positive qualities that might not actually be present. Dion, Berscheid, and Walster (1972) found that both males and females rated pictures of attractive individuals of both sexes as more sexually warm and responding, interesting, poised, sociable, kind, strong, and outgoing than less-attractive people (Cash & Janda, 1984, p. 47). Attractive persons are also seen to be more competent as husbands and wives and to have happier marriages. Thus to be physically attractive is usually an advantage at the first-impression stage of a relationship. This is not always true, however. Some persons are known to avoid highly attractive persons in order to enhance their own chances of acceptance.

The importance of attractiveness is no doubt the reason that so many Americans express dissatisfaction with their body images. *Psychology Today* recently completed a body image survey. Table 4-5 shows the results.

Your impressions of *cognitive compatibility* (how the other thinks, what their interests are, and so forth) are also important in first impressions. In general

Table 4-5
Percent of Persons Dissatisfied with Body Areas or Dimensions

	Men	Women
Height	20%	17%
Weight	41	55
Muscle tone	32	45
Face	20	20
Upper torso	28	32
Middle torso	50	57
Lower torso	21	50
"Looks as they are"	34	38

Source: Adapted from Cash, Winstead, & Janda, 1986, p. 33.

similarity seems to go with attraction because (1) another's similarity itself is directly reinforcing, (2) another's similar responses support the perceiver's sense of self-esteem and comfort, and (3) such responses indicate the other's future compatibility (Huston & Levinger, 1978).

After the first impression has aroused interest, you must consider two factors in choosing a partner. First, you must believe that the potential partner's attributes will be found desirable. Second, there must be a degree of anticipation that the potential partner will react favorably to your invitation of further interaction. Except for traditional females who don't take the initiative in pursuing a relationship because they think it is improper to do so, most people will pursue if the potential partner is in the field of "eligibles" and the two factors mentioned are favorable.

We usually try to further a relationship by various attraction-seeking strategies. In order to draw a potential partner's attention, we may attempt to buoy the other's esteem by conveying that we think highly of them. We will probably try to do things for them. We will tend to agree with the other person, and we will attempt to ascribe attractive characteristics to ourselves (Jones & Wortman, 1973).

Attraction tends to lead to self-disclosure. Intermediate degrees of disclosure may in turn lead to greater attraction, but this depends on the desirability of the information disclosed. Self-disclosure tends to lead to reciprocity. This phase occurs early in a relationship when a lot of exciting mutual sharing takes place. "Is that the way you feel about it? That's great, because I feel the same way." As more is disclosed, excitement increases because the potential for a meaningful relationship seems to be rapidly increasing. However, the speed with which one discloses personal aspects is also important. Disclosure that seems overly quick may arouse suspicion rather than trust (Rubin & Levinger, 1975).

Using retrospective reports of courtship provided by newlyweds, Stambul and Kelly (1978) identified four relationship dimensions that interacted during courtship and finally led to marriage. The four dimensions are: (1) love, (2) conflict and negativity, (3) ambivalence (mixed feelings), and (4) maintenance (problem-solving efforts and attempts to change behavior). Love and maintenance activities were reported to increase as a couple moved from casual dating through serious dating to engagement. Conflict and negativity increased from casual to serious dating and then leveled off, presumably as a consequence of the couple's working out the terms of their relationship. Particularly interesting was the way the dimensions were interrelated at various stages. Early in the cycle, love was associated with efforts to maintain the relationship. Later on, however, love had little to do with maintenance activities. Instead, such activities were associated with conflict. Ambivalence was tied to conflict early in the relationship. Later it had more to do with concerns about love than conflict (Huston & Levinger, 1978).

Although much research has been done on interpersonal attraction, our efforts to predict the evolution of a given individual relationship based on the personal characteristics of the partners have been primitive at best and rather unsuccessful (Huston & Levinger, 1978). In fact, it is still almost impossible to determine in advance whom one should marry to ensure a successful relationship.

As an example of this complexity, let us look at two marriages, one built on similar needs and one on complementary needs. In a marriage of similar needs, the partners begin with similar interests, energy levels, religion, socioeconomic background, age, and so on. They share many characteristics and hence seem well selected for each other. Ideally their relationship can lead to mutual satisfaction, but this is not always so. If, for example, the partners are competitive, the result can be disastrous. Consider the case of Bruce and Gail:

> *Bruce and Gail are alike in most respects, including being computer programmers, but Gail has advanced more rapidly. Bruce, being competitive, feels like a loser and begins to resent his wife. He subtly puts her down and gradually becomes more critical of women in general. The more success Gail has, the poorer their relationship becomes because Bruce cannot accept, let alone find joy in, her success. To him it only points up his weaknesses.*

By contrast, a marriage of complementary needs is one in which each partner supplies something that the other lacks. For example, an extrovert may help an introvert become more social; an organized partner may help bring structure to the life of a disorganized partner; a relaxed partner may create an environment that helps ease the stress of a tense partner. Such complementarity can be most beneficial, but it cannot be counted on to happen reliably because such differences often polarize the partners rather than drawing them together. For example, consider Carol and Greg:

> *Carol is so organized that Greg counts on her to pay the bills, make social arrangements, find the nail clippers, and so on. The more Greg depends on her for these things, the more organized Carol feels she needs to be, and she begins to try to organize Greg. On his part Greg resents this pressure and becomes passively resistant (procrastinates and becomes forgetful and careless). Polarization has occurred.*

Unfortunately there are no fully satisfying techniques for selecting marriage partners for lasting satisfaction. As we saw, even cohabitation trial marriages have proved relatively ineffective.

Engagement

Marriage is the culmination of courtship. Traditionally, the final courtship stage has been engagement. Until recently this has been a fairly formal stage. But with the increased age for first marriage, higher number of remarriages, and greater cohabitation among nonmarried couples engagement has become much less formal for some. In a typical engagement the couple makes a public announcement of their intention to marry and begins active marriage preparation. Once the engagement is announced, the couple usually begins to make concrete plans for the wedding date, type of wedding, who will be invited, where they will live after marriage, at what level they can afford to live, and so forth.

During the engagement the couple often spend more time with each other's families and begin to be treated as kin. The families may also arrange to meet. Marriage is, after all, the union of two families as well as two individuals. Above all the two persons begin to experience themselves as a social unit. Families and friends as well as the public in general react to them as a pair rather than as separate individuals.

Types of Engagements

The short, romantic engagement lasts from two to six months. Time is typically taken up with marriage plans, parties, and intense physical contact. Normally such a short engagement period fails to give the couple much insight into one another's personalities. Indeed, so much time is taken up with marriage preparation that the couple may not have enough time for mutual exploration of their relationship.

The long, separated engagement, such as when one partner is away at college, also presents problems. There are two distinct philosophies of separation: "Absence makes the heart grow fonder" and "Out of sight, out of mind." In reality the latter tends to prevail. Prolonged separation tends to defeat the purposes of the engagement and raises the question of exclusivity in the relationship. Does one date others during the separation? Dating others may cause feelings of insecurity and jealousy, whereas separation without dating is lonely and may cause hostility and dissatisfaction. In general the separated engagement is usually unsatisfactory to both members of the couple.

Another possibility is the long but inconclusive engagement. Here the couple puts off marriage because of economic considerations, deference to parental

©1977 Universal Press Syndicate

"If you keep bugging me about getting married, I'm gonna break off our engagement."

demands, or just plain indecisiveness. When a couple is engaged for years but the engagement never culminates in marriage, it is probably a sign that all is not well between them.

About one in four engaged couples break up temporarily while some couples break their engagement permanently. The causes of breakups appear to be simple loss of interest, recognition of an incompatible relationship, or the desire to reform the prospective mate. The major areas of disagreement tend to be matters of conventionality, families, and friends. Broken engagements can be considered successful in the sense that the couple had the time during this formal commitment period to look more closely at one another and to realize that marriage would not succeed.

Functions of Engagement

What should an engagement do? How can engagement help the couple achieve a better marriage? Basically, the couple should come to agree on fundamental life arrangements. Where will they live? How will they live? Do they want children? When? Will they both work?

The couple also needs to examine long-range goals in depth. Do they want similar things from life? Are their methods of obtaining these things compatible? Do their likes and dislikes blend? What role will religion play in their lives? How will each relate to the other's family? Friends? Work associates? They may not be able to answer such questions completely, but they should at least agree on some tentative answers. In fact the most important premarital agreement may be an agreement about how answers to such questions will be worked out in the future. A couple with a workable, problem-solving approach to life is in a good position to find marital success.

An important part of the engagement is the premarital medical examination, which serves several useful functions. For instance, one of the partners may have a general health problem that will require special care by the other partner. Marrying a diabetic, for example, means that diet will have to be carefully controlled and insulin administered periodically. Both persons need to be checked and cured of any possible sexually transmitted disease. The Rh factor in each partner's blood needs to be determined, as this factor is of major importance in future pregnancy. Information on mutually acceptable methods of birth control can be given at this time if the couple has not already chosen such methods. And each partner will have the opportunity to talk over with the physician questions about the coming marriage.

Premarital counseling is good because often there is a blindness that comes with "being in love." It can be helpful to discuss ideas and plans with an objective third person such as a minister, marriage counselor, or mutual friend. A truly successful engagement period leads either to a successful marriage or to a broken engagement. An unsuccessful engagement in all likelihood will lead to marital failure.

Summary

The onset of puberty signals the beginning of adult sexuality. The age of sexual maturity, however, does not coincide in America with social acceptance of overt sexual behavior, especially sexual intercourse. Marriage is the socially accepted vehicle for sexual intercourse. Because marriage for most Americans does not occur until they are in their late teens or early twenties, there is a period of several years during which there is conflict between the dictates of biology and of society. This is called the "sexual stress period."

American dating has been a unique form of courtship and mate selection historically. In a sense it has been America's contribution to the world's various mate-selection systems. American dating has become increasingly less formal, especially in the last twenty years when it can perhaps better be termed "getting together" or "hanging around."

Cohabitation has increased in the past twenty years to such an extent that some theorists now consider it to be a stage in the courtship system. Cohabitation has drawbacks, both legal and psychological, compared with marriage. It would appear that the cohabiting woman is at more of a disadvantage than the cohabiting man. The law is becoming increasingly interested in the cohabitation relationship, but the relationship remains precarious legally.

Although much of our society does not consider premarital intercourse a legitimate outlet of sexual energies, a great deal of premarital intercourse is taking place. There appears to be increasing acceptance of premarital intercourse among American youth despite societal pressures against it. However, because there are social mores against premarital intercourse, those engaging in it often face conflict within themselves. Questions about social, personal, religious, and psychological principles should be answered by anyone contemplating premarital intercourse.

Mate selection and sexuality for the young are handled mainly through the American invention of dating. Although dating varies greatly from person to person and place to place, there is some recognizable pattern to traditional dating, especially outside of large metropolitan areas. American dating is controlled by the youth themselves and involves relative freedom for the young man and woman to be alone together. This intensifies the pressure for the pair to move toward premarital intercourse as a means of handling their sexual drives.

Mate selection is an involved process that is not yet fully understood. However, it is fairly clear that similarities of socioeconomic backgrounds, energy levels, and degrees of restraint help to increase the chances of marital success.

Mate selection usually leads to engagement, a formal expression of marital intentions. The engagement period is used to make wedding plans, make philosophical decisions about the relationship, make practical decisions about where and how to live, etc. A successful engagement leads to marriage or to the breakup of the couple.

Is Living Together a Bad Idea?

Judith Krantz, novelist and commentator about modern American women, wrote a popular article entitled "Living Together Is a Rotten Idea." Her general thesis is that from the woman's standpoint cohabitation is a losing proposition. The cohabiting woman loses her independence, her freedom to make choices, her privacy, all of her mystery, any practical bargaining position in the power structure of love, an opportunity to make a meaningful change in her life by taking a genuine step toward full adult status, the prospect of having a child other than an illegitimate one, and the protection of the law. This is a disturbing list of losses to say the least.

She has given up all these extraordinarily important elements of her life in return for what is fundamentally little more than a half-assed living arrangement.

Living together is not a true commitment. It is only a commitment that says, "I can leave anytime I wish." As Krantz says, "[It is] not the sink or swim of marriage, but a mere dog paddle at the shallow end of the pool." In essence the lack of commitment makes the relationship at best only "playing house."

Krantz suggests that living together without marriage has become a bourgeois cliché and has developed into the biggest rip-off of women's rights since the invention of the chastity belt. Women are making a series of compromises with themselves that rest on a number of falsehoods that they must devise to rationalize their behavior.

Falsehood number one is, "He is not yet ready to make a total commitment but once we are living together

I know it's only a matter of time until we marry." Unfortunately, as we pointed out earlier in this chapter, most cohabiting men do not share this assumption. In fact, moving in with a man gives **him many reasons not to marry.** Looking at the data on division of housework and the proportion of cohabiting women working to support the relationship monetarily compared to their married sisters, it is clear that the man has a gold mine. He has a built-in housekeeper whom he not only doesn't have to pay, but who herself pays him for doing the work. Marriage means moral and financial obliga-

tions. Why marry when one can have a bedmate-companion-housekeeper for free?

[This is the] only time in recorded history when women who are not literally slaves have made themselves totally available to men without expecting something concrete in return. Who can blame men for taking advantage of such sappy, soft-minded, pseudoidealistic stupidity?

Also there remains deep in many men, the remnants of the "double standard" which said, "It's great to have sex with this woman, but I wouldn't want to marry her." As unfair as it is, many men still assume that if you are willing and eager to have a sexual relationship with him, you will have been or will be that way with other men. The "double standard" says, "You don't marry a promiscuous woman."

Falsehood number two says, "How can you really get to know a person unless you live with them?" This is a very popular belief among cohabitors who equate their relationship with a "test marriage." The idea seems rational and makes good sense in light of the high divorce rate among married couples. Unfortunately cohabiting seems to be just as prone to error as marriage. To date research on the relation of cohabitation with spouse prior to marriage and the permanence of the marriage seems to show no difference between the cohabitors and the noncohabitors. It is also interesting to note that many who live together feel that their problems with their partner will go away after they marry. Yet as we shall see in Chapter 5, expectations that a person will change in marriage are usually disappointed. The fact that a cohabiting couple is only "playing house" means that it is possible that one's behavior will not be the same in marriage as it is in the cohabiting relationship. That marriage asks of both partners a strong, true, lasting commitment changes the basic relationship greatly from the dating, cohabiting relationship. The two relationships simply aren't usually similar enough to assume that what is true of one will automatically be true of the other.

Falsehood number three says, "We're in love, and I trust him completely. Why bring marriage into it? It's just a piece of paper." But what a piece of paper it is. The legalities of marriage provide protection to both partners. Protection that, no matter how much we are "in love," may be needed if the great love evaporates as America's high divorce rate indicates it often does. Of course, both in cohabitation and marriage one assumes that the legalities will never be needed. How could this loving couple do anything to hurt one another? Yet experience tells us that loving couples more often than casual couples do hurt one another. The bitterness of many divorced spouses towards one another years after the divorce attest forcefully to this fact. As we saw in the "Living Together and the Law" section of this chapter, cohabiting couples are still open to legal entanglements. However, at this time these entanglements are unpredictable, open to the whim of a given state or a given judge. At least in marriage, the rules of breaking up are spelled out, giving each spouse fair consideration and protection.

One story may clarify the impact of the lack of that piece of paper (marriage certificate) in cohabitation. The couple in question were mature, in love, yet reasonable about their relation-

ship. He was divorced and in the settlement had retained ownership of the family home. She lived in a small apartment: when they decided to live together, it seemed only sensible that she move into his home. This she did, and over the next seven years she worked hard to make his house into their home. She had a good job and earned as much as he did, and much of the home improvement was done with her money because she felt it only fair since he made the house payments. However, she did in fact occasionally make the house payment when for some reason he was a little short on cash in a given month.

She wallpapered, painted, and gardened over the years, and the home took on much of her personality and became her home as well as his in every way but legally. In the seventh year of their relationship she began to feel increasing distance between them. Finally she confronted him with her feelings. With some reluctance he told her that he had fallen in love with one of his colleagues whom he now wished to marry. Naturally, since the house belonged to him, she would have to move out to make room for his soon-to-be new bride. It was true that she was free to take the furniture she had bought and all of the things that she had brought with her into the relationship. But how do you take hung wallpaper, wall-to-wall carpeting, and an attractive garden? Had these things been put into her own home, they would remain even if he didn't. At least with marriage, there would have been some division of property, some possible reimbursement for her years of work. As it was, she had to move out and return to a small apartment, because she had not bothered to save during

the seven-year relationship. After all, why should she? She had a home with her beloved partner.

Falsehood number four is, "I'm simply not ready to get married yet, but I don't like being alone and need someone to give my love to." For the young woman who hasn't been away from her family this is particularly dangerous. As we have seen, in the past many young women left their parental homes only to enter marriage. Later in their lives when the marriage failed and they were on their own for the first time, they were helpless and afraid. The young woman who is robbed, by entrance into a cohabitation relationship, of her early years of independence, living alone and learning about her own individuality, is also robbed of experiences that she may never again be able to recapture. To be learning about independence and one's own strengths and weaknesses at age forty after a marriage failure is difficult. The best time to learn about oneself is before one takes on the responsibility of marriage. It is a precious short time and should never be given away lightly. Young adulthood is an exciting time of testing one's wings, reaching for the sky, looking for the limits. To hide from this time in an early marriage is bad enough, but to hide from it in a possibly meaningless cohabitation experience is even worse.

How sad to forfeit the freshest years of life—a time of unbounded freedom and opportunity that will never be repeated—for the lukewarm comforts of premature domesticity.

It is true that some of these things we have been discussing could also apply to men. But it is the man who marries approximately two years later than the woman; it is the man who is most apt to adventure with a friend on a trip to far off places; it is the man who is most likely to enter the military and be forced to test himself and find out who he is; it is the man who in his work world is most likely to have a career as opposed to only a job. The cards, unfortunately, are still stacked in his favor as we shall see in Chapter 7. For him to live with a free companion-housekeeper who also shares her body with him is much less dangerous for him than for her. If she wants to give these things to him for little in return why should he not accept?

In the past, it has been the woman who has controlled sex because it was the woman who had the most to lose. Today it is the woman who must control cohabitation and not enter into it lightly, because it is she who has the most to lose.

Inescapably, a woman who lives with a man without a total commitment on his part risks becoming boring and familiar to him, but without having literally become a part of his family, with all that implies. Her position is more fragile in every way than that of a married woman. She has abandoned her own precious apartness, surrendered her claim to the life of a separate individual— too soon. Much *too soon. . . .*

What Do You Think?

1. Do many of your friends cohabitate? What kinds of problems do they have in the cohabitation relationship?
2. Does the man or the woman usually seem most committed to the relationship?
3. In cohabitation relationships that have broken up, has the man or the woman initiated the breakup?
4. Who benefits more from cohabitation, the man or the woman? Why? What are the benefits?
5. Would you cohabitate? If so, why? If not, why not?

Marriage, Intimacy, Expectations, and the Fully Functioning Person

Contents

Marriage is the most intimate of all human interactions. At its heart marriage is an interpersonal relationship between two persons, a man and a woman. Most adults try to fulfill their psychological, material, and sexual needs within marriage. To the degree that they are successful the marriage is successful. We know, however, that success in meeting these needs is difficult to achieve. This is reflected in America's high divorce rate.

You may remember that one of the primary functions of the contemporary American family is to provide emotional gratification to members, help them deal with emotional crises, and grow in the most fulfilling manner possible. In other words marriage and the family ideally act as a haven from which individual members can draw support and security when facing the challenges of our rapidly changing, technological society. A fully functioning family helps its members grow, mature, and become self-actualized individuals. Ideally a good marriage acts as a buffer against mental health problems: alienation, loneliness, unhappiness, and emotional depression. In a word marriage can be therapeutic, a curative to the problems of its members.

In this chapter and the next we will explore marriage as an interaction between two individuals. We will examine techniques and case histories to help us create marriages that are nurturing and that support self-fulfillment and growth for all family members. Although we will be discussing interpersonal relations in the context of marriage, the insights are applicable to any kind of human relationship: boyfriend-girlfriend, employer-employee, parent-child, and so forth.

Reasons for Marriage That Tend to Reduce or Increase the Chances of Success

As we examined dating and mate selection in the last chapter, it became clear that many factors affect both. The reasons one finally chooses a mate are varied and not always clear. What is clear is that some of the reasons we choose to marry work to enhance our chances of success, while others work against success. It is worthwhile to examine some of the more common positive and negative reasons for marriage.

Reasons for Marriage That Tend to Reduce Success

1. *Love at first sight*: It is easy to understand falling in love at first sight but hard to justify selecting a marriage partner on this basis alone. Generally this reason leads to marriage after a very short acquaintance and with little knowledge of one another.
2. *Escape from home*: Rather than dealing with a current relationship, many people run away, hoping a new person or a new environment will be better. Any alternative seems better than remaining in the current unpleasant situation. A marriage so conceived is often the first of a series of failures because the person is driven by the negative present situation and often fails to assess correctly the results of changing the situation. It may be hard for such a person in an unpleasant relationship to believe that a new relationship could be worse.
3. *Avoiding loneliness*: Loneliness can sometimes drive a person into a hasty marriage. To seek companionship in marriage is a proper goal. However, if overcoming loneliness is one's only motivation for marriage, chances are high that this reason alone will not sustain a long-lasting relationship. This particular reason is most prevalent among the divorced and widowed.
4. *Sexual attraction*: Unfulfilled sexual attraction, or guilt over sexual involvement, is a popular but weak reason for marriage. An unusually fulfilling sexual

relationship alone is not reason enough to marry. Chemical attraction is certainly a part of romantic love and of mate selection, yet as we saw in the last chapter, the strong sexual aspects of a relationship can blind the partners to other important relational aspects.

Reasons for Marriage That Tend to Increase Success

1. *Similar socioeconomic backgrounds*: Social research has clearly demonstrated that a similar socioeconomic status improves the chances of success in marriage.
2. *Similar energy levels*: Similar or dissimilar activity levels are fundamental to every aspect of the relationship. For example, consider a marriage where the energy levels are dissimilar:

Bill is a quiet person who needs eight to nine hours of sleep to function well the next day. His tempo is slow and deliberate but he finishes everything he starts. His slowness causes him to be habitually late. Joyce, his wife, needs little sleep and appears to be a bundle of energy. She does many things, finishing most of them quickly. She is always ready earlier than Bill if they are going out and seems always to be waiting for him and nagging him to hurry. She likes companionship in the evening and dislikes going to bed before midnight. Bill usually wants to go to bed around 10 P.M. and is annoyed if she doesn't accompany him. Over several years, the conflicts engendered by their differing energy levels have grown. They wonder if they should look for new partners better suited to their activity levels.

3. *Openness to growth or desire for stability*: A good relationship can occur between two partners who want stability or between two partners who want growth or change, but differences between partners in these respects are extremely difficult to overcome. For example, consider this marriage where the partners differ:

Mary is comfortable with routine and stability. It makes her feel safe and secure to know exactly what is going to happen today, tomorrow, and next week. On the other hand, her husband, Jack, is spontaneous and dislikes committing himself too far in advance to any plan of action. He says that this allows him freedom and flexibility, which he feels is necessary if a person is to grow and avoid stagnation. Their differing philosophies about growth and stability cause them to disagree continually.

Although finding "the one and only" might seem ideal, our chances of doing this are slim. In fact any number of persons can become satisfactory and long-lasting partners, for the key to a successful relationship is more in the building and maintenance of the relationship than in the selection of the imaginary perfect mate. The marriage ceremony is really a beginning, not a culmination. The key to successful relationships is not the initial mate-selection process so much as it is the couple's learning to compromise and communicate with one another.

You and the State: Legal Aspects of Marriage

Every society has some kind of ceremony in which permanent relationships between the sexes are recognized and given status. The society (or the state) sets minimum standards for marriage in the interests of order and stability. In Western societies the state is interested in supporting a monogamous marriage; assuring the "legitimacy of issue"; protecting property and inheritance rights; and preventing marriages considered unacceptable, such as those between close relatives.

In the United States marriage laws are determined by individual states. Although there are differences in requirements, all states recognize marriages contracted in all other states. California law is typical of many state laws relating to marriage:

> Marriage is a personal relation arising out of a civil contract, to which the consent of the parties capable of making that contract is necessary. Consent alone will not constitute marriage; it must be followed by the issuance of a license and solemnized as authorized. (Section 4100, West's Annotated California Codes, 1986)

Marriage in the United States is a contract with obligations set by the state. Like all contracts, the marriage contract must be entered into by mutual consent, the parties must be competent and eligible to enter into the contract, and there is a prescribed form for the contract. All states set minimum age requirements, and most require a medical examination and a waiting period between the examination and license issuance (see Appendix A). However, unlike most contracts, which are between two parties, the marriage contract involves three parties: the man, the woman, and the state. The state prescribes certain duties, privileges, and restrictions. In addition the contract cannot be dissolved by the mutual consent of the man and woman but must be dissolved by state action.

In a few instances a couple may be exempt from the marriage license law. For example, section 4213 of the California Civil Code allows couples living together to marry without applying for a license, provided they are eighteen or older. A certificate of such marriage must be made by a clergyman, delivered to the parties, and recorded in the records of the clergyman's church. Thirteen states (Alabama, Colorado, Georgia, Idaho, Iowa, Kansas, Montana, Ohio, Oklahoma, Pennsylvania, Rhode Island, South Carolina, Texas) and the District of Columbia recognize common law marriage if a couple can prove they have lived as husband and wife for seven or more years (Clark, 1980).

The state also sets a number of other standards. It limits how closely within family relationships one may marry. It considers a marriage invalid if consent to marry is obtained by fraud or under duress, if there is mental incapacity, if there is physical inability to perform sexually, or if either party is already married.

No particular marriage ceremony is required, but the parties must declare, in the presence of the person solemnizing the marriage, that they take each other as husband and wife, and the marriage must be witnessed, usually by two

persons. Although some states are quite specific, there is a general trend away from uniform marriage vows. Traditional vows reflect the permanence expected of marriage by society: ". . . . to have and to hold from this day forward, for better or worse, for richer, for poorer, in sickness and in health, to love and to cherish, till death do us part."

Up to this point we have discussed the legal aspects of marriage set up by the state. However, it must be remembered that marriage is regarded by most faiths as a sacrament. About 75 percent of all marriages in the United States take place in a church. The state vests the clergy with the legal right to perform the marriage ceremony. God is called on to witness and bless the marriage: "Those whom God hath joined together let no man put asunder." Some religions feel so strongly that marriage is a divine institution and not to be tampered with by humans that they do not recognize civil divorce. (The Roman Catholic church is the best-known example.)

The marriage ceremony commits the couple to a new status. It sets minimum limits of marital satisfaction. Typical of these directives are those found in Title 8, Husband and Wife, of California's Senate Bill 252:

> Husband and wife contract toward each other obligations of mutual respect, fidelity, and support.

> The husband is the head of the family. He may choose any reasonable place or mode of living, and the wife must conform thereto.

> Neither husband or wife has any interest in the property of the other, but neither can be excluded from the other's dwelling (except under certain circumstances recognized by the court).

> The respective interests of the husband and wife in community property during the continuance of marriage relations are present, existing, and equal interests under the management and control of the husband.

Note that these directives give authority to the man in a number of areas. The feminist movement is working to change such laws so that marriage can truly be an arrangement between equals.

Marriage, then, is much more than "just a piece of paper." It commits the couple to a new set of obligations and responsibilities. In essence the couple in many ways marries the state, and it is the state to whom they must answer if the prescribed responsibilities are not met.

Writing Your Own Marriage Contract

As we have seen, marriage is a formal contract between the couple and the state and has a set form in each state. Not every couple's needs can best be met by the standard state contract, however; hence an increasing number of couples are writing their own **marriage contracts**. Such a personal contract cannot take the place of the state marriage contract, nor can it reject legally any of the state contract obligations. However, as a supplement to the state contract, it can afford a couple the freedom and privacy to order their personal relationship as they wish. It can also permit them to escape to some degree from the sex-based legacy of legal marriage and move toward a more egalitarian relationship. The couple can formulate an agreement that conforms to contemporary social reality. Personal contracts can also be written by couples who wish to have a relationship but not one of marriage (for example, a cohabiting couple or a couple barred from marriage, such as a homosexual couple) (Weitzman, 1981).

As Lenore Weitzman suggests, in addition to its legal advantages, a personal contract facilitates open and honest communication and helps prospective partners clarify their expectations. Once the contract agreement has been reached, it serves as a guide for future behavior. Contracts also increase predictability and security by helping couples identify and resolve potential conflicts in advance.

Personal contracts need to be constructed carefully if they are to be legal. For example, when one partner brings to marriage a great deal of wealth that has been accumulated before the marriage, the couple may want to sign a contract that keeps this property separate from the property that may accumulate during the marriage. This is particularly difficult to do in community property states. Such a contract needs to be drawn by an attorney with a thorough knowledge of the state laws governing community property. Any topic can be handled in a personal contract, but such contracts generally cover the following:

Marriage contract
A written agreement between married partners outlining the responsibilities and obligations of each partner

- Aims and expectations of the couple
- Duration of the relationship
- Work and career roles
- Income and expense handling and control
- Property owned before the contract and that acquired after
- Disposition of prior debts
- Living arrangements
- Responsibility for household tasks
- Surname
- Sexual relations
- Relations with family, friends, and others
- Decisions regarding children (number, rearing, etc.)
- Religion

- Inheritance and wills
- Resolving disagreements
- Changing and amending the contract
- Dissolution of the relationship

The list of what could be covered is endless. As unromantic as it seems to sit down before marriage with your intended partner and work out some of the details of your future relationship, it is a worthwhile task even if you don't plan to have a written legal contract. As we shall see in this chapter, people's expectations about one another and their relationship are important determinants of behavior. If one partner's expectations differ greatly from the other's and are left unexpressed and unexamined, the relationship is probably doomed to conflict and disappointment. By going through the steps of working out a personal contract, the couple bring into the open their attitudes and expectations; they can make appropriate compromises and changes before major problems arise.

The Transition from Single to Married Life

Married life is indeed different from single life. Marriage suddenly brings duties and obligations. You are no longer responsible only for yourself but now share responsibility for two people and perhaps more if children arrive.

Furthermore, your identity is changed with marriage. No longer are you simply you, you are now Mark's wife, or Tanya's husband, or Randy's father or mother. You become interdependent with the others in your family and lose the independence you had when single. You enter a two-person pattern of life: Planning together, working together, and playing together become more important than what you do as an individual. Decisions now involve the desires of two people, involve discussion or debate, and end in compromise.

The transition from dating to establishing a home and family is a large step for both partners. The couple may have cooked some meals together during courtship, but preparing 1095 meals a year for two on an often tight budget is a far greater challenge. Planning a month's finances is certainly more difficult than raising money for a weekend of skiing. In fact living within some kind of a family budget is a difficult transition for many newly marrieds. Before marriage they were used to spending their incomes as they wished. Now another person must be consulted, and what they earn must be shared.

Leisure activities, which are often spontaneous and unplanned when you are single, now must be planned with another person, and often compromises must be worked out. As we shall see with Mark and Tanya, conflicts over leisure time pursuits can be difficult to resolve.

New relationships must be developed with both sets of parents after marriage. Your primary relationship is now with your spouse rather than with your parents. Also, you must learn to relate to your in-laws. Before marriage there usually isn't much interaction with the parents of your partner. But after marriage interaction will be more frequent and more important. Failure to build a satisfactory in-law relationship makes married life more difficult inasmuch as the relationship with parents is important to each spouse.

The sexual relationship may also involve a transition. Premarital sexuality may have been restrained, covert, and only partially satisfying. Ideally, the marital sexual relationship will become fully expressive and satisfying to both partners. However, this may not occur if one or both partners have been taught excessive control and repression of sexual impulses. The many sexual technique manuals, the lack of sexual enjoyment, and the increasing interest in sex therapy attest to the great problems in this area of the relationship and to the need for greater openness about sex.

There are many other transitions that must be made if a marriage is to be successful. Basically, all the transitions are from the self-centeredness of childhood to the other-centeredness of adulthood. To consider the likes and dislikes of your partner, to compromise your desires at times in favor of your partner, to become a team that pulls together rather than in opposing directions, to become a pair that has more going than the sum total of the two individuals making up the pair are a few of the things that indicate a successful marriage. If the majority of transitions cannot be made by one or both partners, the chances for a successful marriage are slim.

Mark and Tanya: Married Singles

Both Mark and Tanya were active singles until they met, fell in love, and married in their midtwenties. Mark's single-life pattern had involved a great deal of time for sports, especially trips to the desert to ride his motorcycle with other dirt bike enthusiasts.

Tanya had spent a great deal of time with her office colleagues, going to picnics, bowling on the office team, and window shopping on Saturdays. Sunday was reserved for church. Although she had dated a great deal, her religious background had restricted her sexual activities. She had spent much of her time on dates defending herself. Although she was no prude about her sexuality, she did not feel it necessary to sleep with every date.

As the newness of marriage begins to wear off, both Mark and Tanya find themselves somewhat bored and uncomfortable with the other's activities. Tanya did go to the desert twice when Mark went motorcycling, but she found it dirty, boring, and lonely because she didn't know the other women and the men were away from camp riding all day.

Mark doesn't like bowling although he tried once or twice. He doesn't like being alone at night either, and so he pressures Tanya to give up the bowling team. "After all, why am I married if I have to be alone in the evening?" he complains.

Tanya also has difficulty relaxing and enjoying sex with Mark. For so long her impulses, when she was approached sexually, had been to back away and defend herself that she finds it difficult to change. Mark, feeling this tension, takes it as a rejection of himself rather than as a transition stage that Tanya has to pass through.

He begins flirting with other women because it makes him feel good when they respond. He even entertains the idea of going out with other women behind Tanya's back. "It's her hang-up that our sex life isn't very good," he often says.

Gradually, each falls back into old single-life patterns, and they spend less and less time together. Although they are still married, they do almost nothing together. Mark spends more time on motorcycle trips, and Tanya has joined a second bowling team. Their friends wonder if they ever see one another.

The transition from single to married status does not end the need for change. As time passes the marriage will also change and require further transitions of both partners. The coming of children, for example, places a whole new set of demands on the married couple.

In general the couple contemplating marriage seldom realizes the extent of the changes necessary to make a successful marriage. After all, "love" should take care of all of the transitions from single to married life. "We get along now; of course we'll get along after we marry." Not necessarily so.

Marriage: A Myriad of Interactions

Each day we interact with numerous people. On the job we talk with colleagues, receive instructions from superiors, and give orders to those who work for us. At stores we talk with salespeople. On the way home we interact with other drivers or with people on the bus. All of these interactions are relatively simple. For example, when buying things at a store, I simply want to make my purchases. I don't need to know how the salespeople are feeling, how their children are doing in school, how their sex lives are, or how they feel about their jobs. I need only relate to them as a customer. The interaction begins and ends at a superficial level.

Not so with marriage. The family, perhaps more than any other institution, is an arena of intimate and complex interaction. Not only are there literally hundreds of interactions within a family each day, but also they vary in infinite ways. We can think of these interactions as ranging from purely intellectual, with no emotional involvement, to strongly emotional. Note in the following conversations how the interactions move from superficial and distant to caring, committed, and emotionally involved:

"Good morning. How are you feeling?"
"Morning. Fine. How're you?"

"Good morning. How are you feeling? Did you sleep well?"
"Morning. I slept fine. Hope you did, too."

"Good morning. I'm really glad to see you looking so well this morning! I'm glad the headache went away."
"Morning. It's great not to be in pain. Thanks so much for reminding me to take those aspirins—they really did the trick! Don't know what I'd do without you!"

"Good morning! You know, it's always wonderful to wake up in the morning with you!"
"It makes me feel so good when you say that! I'm so happy with you!"

The first interaction is superficial, a general morning greeting. The next, while still superficial, demonstrates more concern and awareness of the other person. The concern deepens in the next interaction: The first speaker remembers the other's headache of the previous day and is happy that the partner is out of pain. The partner expresses gratitude for the concern and for the aid. And the last interaction demonstrates a deep emotional level of sharing between the partners.

Let's also look at some of the role interactions that go on in a marriage:

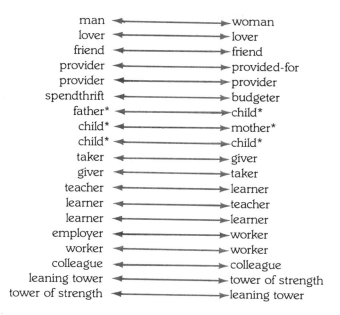

What Do You Think?

1. What kind of marital role expectations do you think you have learned?
2. Are they similar to the roles your parents fulfilled in their marriage?
3. What do you think are the two most important roles your spouse should fulfill?
4. What would you do if your spouse disagreed with you and didn't wish to fulfill one of these two roles you consider important?

Obviously, the list of possibilities is endless! And think of the complications that can arise when children enter the picture. Remember also that cross-interactions can occur, such as between lover and friend or lover and teacher. For example, the friend can interact with the woman, the lover, and so on down the list. Thus when I wake up in the morning and say to my wife "How do you feel?" it means far more than saying the same thing to a passing acquaintance. It could mean, "I am concerned about you" as a friend; "I'd like to have sex with you" as a lover; "Will you be able to work today?" as an employer; and so forth. To further complicate matters, the spouses may not agree on what the meaning is. The wife may take the husband's question to mean he'd like to make love before getting up, whereas he really meant to inquire how she was feeling because she had been sick the day before. Complicated, isn't it?

To manage successfully the hundreds of interactions that occur daily in marriage would be a miracle indeed. But to manage them better each day is a worthy and attainable goal. If people can be successful in marriage, the chances are they will also be successful in most other interpersonal relations because other relationships will almost certainly be simpler than the marital relationship.

Fulfilling Needs in Marriage

Marriage can supply love and affection, emotional support and loyalty, stability and security, romantic and sexual fulfillment, companionship and friendship, and material well-being. This is a big order to expect of any relationship and explains in part why there is a high rate of marital disruption in the American society. Americans ask a great deal more of marriage than they have in the past and a

*These are not interactions between real children and real parents, but interactions that involve one partner acting like an authority or parent and the other partner reacting as a dependent child. The child-child interaction involves the partners acting like children with each other.

great deal more than do many other peoples in the world. Such high expectations must certainly lead to disappointments.

Society recognizes that fulfilling three areas of needs—sexual, material, and psychological—is a valid responsibility of the marriage institution. In fact, so important is the meeting of these needs for individuals that failure to do so is recognized by all states as a legitimate reason for divorce.

Sexual Needs   Marriage is the only legitimate outlet for sexual energies recognized by American society. Indeed, sexual intercourse is a state-mandated part of marriage. If sexual needs are not fulfilled in a marriage, the marriage can be dissolved. Thus American spouses must function as lovers to their mates (see Chapter 10).

Material Needs   "Room and board" is a part of every marriage. Breadwinning and homemaking are essential to survival. Material needs also affect how successfully psychological and sexual needs are met. Marital disruption is considerably higher among families in economic trouble than among families satisfactorily meeting material needs (see Chapters 8 and 9).

Psychological Needs   As you may remember from Chapter 2, one of the basic assumptions of this book is that the family becomes increasingly important to its members as social stability decreases and/or people feel more isolated and alienated.

Mobility, increased anonymity, ever larger and more bureaucratic institutions, and lack of social relatedness all contribute to feelings of loneliness and helplessness. Because of these feelings, our psychological need for intimacy has increased greatly. It is in marriage that most people hope to find intimacy.

What men and women seek from love today is no longer romantic luxury: it is an essential of emotional survival. More and more they hope to find in intimate love something of personal validity personal relevance, a confirmation of one's existence. For in today's world, when men and women are made to feel as faceless as numbers on a list, they want intimate love to provide the feelings of worth and identity that preserve meaning and sanity. (Bach & Deutsch, 1970, pp. 14–15)

Need Relationships It is obvious that psychological needs are closely related to both sexual and material needs. As was pointed out, marital disruption tends to be highest among the materially least well-off.

The relationship between sexual and psychological needs tends to be more complicated than the relationship between material and psychological needs. A satisfying sexual relationship certainly fulfills many of one's psychological needs. However, a satisfying sexual relationship often reflects the general success of need meeting within a relationship, not just sexual success. For example, Lauer and Lauer (1985) found in their study of successful marriages that agreement about and satisfaction with one's sex life was far down the lists of top reasons for a good marriage given by the respondents. Fewer than 10 percent of the respondents felt that a good sexual relationship kept their marriage together. However, unhappy couples or those from broken marriages often list sexual relations as one of their major problems. When other psychological needs are not being met, the sexual relationship is often the first place in which trouble appears. A couple's sexual relationship often acts as a sensitive indicator of the goodness of the rest of their relationship. A couple having serious marital problems seldom find that their sex life is unaffected. Problems in a couple's sex life may indeed result from unmet sexual needs, but such sexual problems may also arise when psychological needs of any kind are left unmet. Thus, although we list meeting sexual needs as one of the three need areas that marriage must serve to be successful, it is clear that a couple's sexual relations relate to the totality of their relationship, not just the sexual aspect.

Factors Influencing Marital Success

Marital success is difficult to define, partly because it is often confused with *marital adjustment* and *marital happiness* and these three concepts are not necessarily the same. For example, Bohannan (1984) points out that a neurotic relationship of mutual misery (as found in the play *Who's Afraid of Virginia Wolf?*) may be just as binding as a healthy relationship of mutual support, esteem, and love. Thus a couple may be said to have marital adjustment although the adjustment has not led to happiness or marital success in the broadest sense. On the other hand, if marital success is defined as permanence only, it might be said that this miserable couple has marital success as long as their misery does not lead to destruction of the marriage.

Over the years, many factors, such as socioeconomic level, years of schooling, presence of children, length of premarital acquaintance, role congruence, and communication patterns, have been studied and related to marital success. Yet the results of such research remain vague and inconclusive. In fact, Lewis and Spanier (1979) list more than 150 references on the subject covering 87 probable propositions about factors that possibly relate to marital success.

For our purposes, marital success will be defined broadly to include adjustment, happiness, and permanence. Thus a successful marriage is one in which the partners adjust to the relationship; are in relative agreement on most issues of importance; are comfortable in the roles that they assume; and are able to work together to solve most of the problems that confront them over time. Each partner expresses satisfaction and happiness with the relationship.

Unfortunately and despite all of the research, it remains impossible to give a definitive list of factors that influence a couple's ability to attain marital success. Couples probably vary so from one another (just as individuals do) that what is an important factor for one couple may be unimportant to another. This is especially true in a society such as ours where there is not only great freedom in mate selection but also great freedom to build the kind of relationship that one desires. Of course this freedom is accompanied as always by responsibility. If you are free to build the marriage you want and it does not work, you alone are responsible for the failure.

Because there are no longer any hard-and-fast rules about what a marriage should be, about the roles that each sex will play in marriage, or even about the primariness of the relationship (for some couples), the expectations that one brings to the marital relationship play an important and perhaps primary role in the success of the relationship. Each individual has expectations, both conscious and unconscious, about what marriage will be. Because we are all brought up differently and have different life experiences, it is nearly impossible for a couple's expectations of marriage to be exactly the same. Thus an examination of the role that personal expectations play in marital success is perhaps more important than an examination of a long list of factors that may or may not affect a particular couple's marital success.

Marital Expectations

In a very real sense, humans create their own world. The wonderful complexity of the human brain allows us to plan, organize, and concern ourselves with what we think should be, as well as with what is. We predict our future and have expectations about ourselves, our world, our marriage, our spouse, and our children. In a way expectations are also our *hopes* about the future, and hope is an important element to our well-being. We often hear about the person who has given up hope, and we know that this can be dangerous to both physical and psychological well-being. The average American certainly enters marriage (the first marriage at least) full of high hopes for success and happiness. Who can be any more hopeful than the couple newly married, in love, and off on their honeymoon?

In our earlier discussion of love, we noted that love often acts like the proverbial rose-colored glasses in that we don't see the people we love as they really are, but as we wish (expect) them to be. It is the spouse's failure to meet these expectations that so often leads to disappointment in marriage.

In essence the world is as we perceive it, and our perceptions are based in part on the input of our senses as well as what we personally do to put our own meaning on that input: accept it, reject it, interpret it, change it, or color it. The study of how people experience their world is called **phenomenology**. It is important to realize that most people react to their perceptions of the world rather than to what the world may really be. A simple example may clarify this point. If we place a straight metal rod halfway into a pool of clear water, the rod appears bent or broken because of the refraction of the light waves by the water. How would

Phenomenology
The study of how people subjectively experience their environment

we react if we knew nothing about light refraction and had never before seen a partially submerged object? We would see that the rod was bent and would act on that perception. But we have measured and examined the rod, and we know it is straight. Moreover, most of us have learned that light waves will be refracted by the water and appear bent, so we assume that the rod is straight even though our eyes tell us it is bent. In other words, we know that our perceptions do not always reflect the objective world. We have learned that appearances can be deceptive.

How does this relate to marriage? In our interactions with other people, we often forget that our perceptions may not reflect "reality" or that our spouse may have different perceptions. Consider the following situation:

> *Jim asks his steady out for Friday night. She says she's sorry, but she has to go out of town to visit her grandparents.(She is actually going to do this.) Jim becomes jealous and angry and accuses her of having a date with someone else. No matter how she reassures him that she is indeed visiting her grandparents, he remains unconvinced. When she returns from her visit, he is even more angry and upset because of her refusal to tell him the truth as he believes it to be.*

Jealousy can be a difficult emotion with which to cope. We can see that Jim's behavior is being dictated by his own subjective view of the world, not reality. Yet even though both we and his girl know that his view is incorrect, the difficulty is just as real as if he were correct. Because he is angry, they may fight and not speak to each other for a week. If Jim finds out from others that she was indeed visiting her grandparents, he will be apologetic and sorry that he acted that way. Remember, we act on our perceptions, and they are not necessarily the same as objective reality.

The Honeymoon Is Over: Too High Expectations

> *One morning, after Jim and Sue have been married for about a year, Sue awakens and "realizes" that Jim is no longer the same man she married. She accuses him of changing for the worse: "You used to think of great things to do in the evenings, and you enjoyed going out all the time. Now you just seem to want to stay home." Jim insists, of course, that he has not changed; he is the same person he has always been, and that, indeed, he always said he looked forward to quiet evenings alone with her.*

This interaction may be signaling that "the honeymoon is over" for Jim and Sue. This stage is very important in most marriages. It usually means that the unrealistic, overly high expectations about marriage and one's mate created by "love" are being reexamined. In a successful relationship it means that subjective perceptions are becoming more objective, more realistic. It means also that we are at last coming to know our mate as a real human being rather than as a projection of our own expectations.

Unfortunately, some people throw away the real person in favor of their own idealizations. In essence they are in love with their own dreams and ideals not with the person they married. Originally their mate became the object of their love because the mate met enough of their expectations that they were able to project their total set of expectations onto the mate. But living together day in and day out makes it only a matter of time until the partners are forced to compare their ideals with the flesh-and-blood spouse. Seldom, if ever, will the two coincide exactly.

Romantic ideals and expectations lead us to expect so much from our mates and from marriage that disappointment is almost inevitable. How we cope with this disappointment determines, in part, the direction our marriage will take when the honeymoon is over. If we refuse to reexamine our ideals and expectations and instead blame our mates for the discrepancy, trouble lies ahead. On the other hand, if we realize that the disappointment is caused by our own unrealistic expectations, we can look forward to getting to know our mates as real human beings. Further reflection also makes it clear that recognition of our mates as real human beings with frailties and problems rather than as perfect, godlike creatures greatly eases the strain on our marriages and ourselves. Realizing the humanness of our partners allows us to relax and be human as well. But consider what can happen if we are unwilling to give up our expectations of an ideal mate:

Carol, the Perpetual Seeker

Carol's father died when she was eight years old. Her mother never re-married because she felt no other man could live up to her dead husband. Through the years Carol was told how wonderful and perfect her father had been, both as a man and as a husband.

As a teenager Carol fell in love often and quickly, but the romances also ended quickly, usually, she said, because the boy would disappoint her in some way. The only romance that lasted was when she met a young man while on a summer vacation to California. Even though they knew one another for only a month, they continued their romance via mail during the following year. They met again the next summer. Carol was now nineteen. Three months after they parted, after school had resumed, and after many letters declaring their love and loneliness, Carol's friend asked her to come to California and marry him. Carol assured her mother that he was the right man: strong, responsible, and loving, just as her father had been.

They married and everything seemed to go well. However, by the end of the first year Carol was writing her mother letters telling how her husband was changing for the worse, how he wasn't nearly the man Carol had thought him to be. She was questioning whether he would ever be a good father, and she noted that he didn't have the drive for success that her dad had at his age.

Two years after marrying, Carol divorced her husband. She had met an exciting, wonderful man who had given a talk to her women's sensitivity group. He was all of the things her husband wasn't and, incidentally, all of the things her father had been. She married him not long after her divorce was final.

Carol is now thirty years old and married to her third husband, about whom she complains a great deal.

What Do You Think?

1. Why does Carol seem to find so little satisfaction with her husbands?
2. Why did Carol's romance persist so long with her first husband before marriage while all of her earlier relationships dissolved quickly?
3. What are the qualities of your dream spouse?
4. How does your relationship with your parents influence your marriage ideals?
5. How can Carol find satisfaction in marriage?

It is clear that Carol is in love with her idealized image of her father. Since she never was or will be able to know her father, she has no way to correct her idealized images of him. A real live husband has no chance to live up to her expectations because they are based on someone who can't make mistakes. The chances of Carol ever being happy with a spouse are low unless she can stop comparing her spouse with her romanticized images of her father.

Love or Marriage?

We can see why disappointment with marriage is almost inevitable if we consider that our prevailing cultural view of marriage as expressed in the mass media is one of everlasting romance. One of the greatest disappointments newly married couples face is the fading of romantic love. Romantic love depends on an incomplete sexual and emotional consummation of the relationship. Physical longing is a tension between desire and fulfillment. When sexual desire is fulfilled, romantic love changes to a feeling of affection that is more durable, though less intense and frenzied, than romantic love. Because we have been flooded with romantic hyperbole by the media, we are often unprepared for this natural change in the emotional quality of the relationship. For example, let's look at a typical couple:

Allison fell in love with Mike when she was sixteen and he was seventeen. Neither of them had ever been in love before. After two years they are still deeply in love, and Mike persuades Allison to marry him because he is tired of dealing with their guilt about premarital sex, worrying about pregnancies, and hiding their intimacy from parents. After two years of marriage, Allison finds herself not nearly as excited by Mike as she had been earlier. The couple is struggling to make a living, and she feels that "the bloom is going from the rose." One day, as she listens to a lecture from her art history teacher, she feels a lump in her throat, a thumping in her heart, and a weakness in her knees. This was the way she felt about Mike two years ago, and she suddenly realizes that she doesn't have these feelings for Mike any more. She can't tell Mike, and she is afraid of her feelings for the teacher, so she drops the class and tells Mike it's time for them to have a baby.

It's clear that Allison confuses feelings of sexual attraction with love. Since American folklore says you can't love more than one person at a time, she must either suppress these feelings of tension and longing, as she does, or decide that she is no longer in love with Mike and perhaps consider a divorce. Narrowly defining love as only "the great turn-on" means that all marriages will eventually fail because that intense feeling usually fades with time.

Mixed Expectations

Even if expectations about marriage are realistic, spouses may have different expectations about marital roles. This is especially true about roles that each expects the other to play in marriage. Traditional gender roles are no longer clear-cut. For example, the husband is no longer the sole breadwinner and the wife only a homemaker. However, many of our expectations about role behavior come from our experience with our parents' marriage, and often we are unaware of these expectations. For example, consider the possibilities for conflict in the following marriage:

Randy and Susan: Who Handles the Money?	*In Randy's traditional midwestern family his father played the dominant role. His mother was given an allowance with which to run the house. His father made all of the major money decisions.*
	In Susan's sophisticated New York family both her mother and her father worked hard at their individual careers. Because they both worked, they decided that each would control his or her own money. While both contributed to a joint checking account used to run the household, individual desires were fulfilled from personal funds. There was seldom any discussion about money decisions because each was free to spend his or her own money.
	Randy and Susan marry after Susan has been teaching school for a year and Randy gets a good position with a New York bank. Randy believes that because he has a good job, it is no longer necessary for Susan to work; he can support them both, which he believes is the proper male marriage role. He sees no reason for Susan to have her own bank account. After all, if she wants something, all she has to do is ask him for it.

The increasing diversity of acceptable relationships found in modern America means that children in the future may be raised differently from the way we were. Their expectations about marital roles will also be different from ours. And their marriages may well involve a flexible interchange of roles.

When roles are not clear-cut and accepted by everyone, the chances of conflicting role expectations increase greatly. A man and a woman from a culture in which roles are clearly specified find it easy to define what a good spouse is. If the spouse is fulfilling the assigned roles well, ergo they are automatically a "good" spouse. Where role specification is not socially assigned but left up to the individual couple, confusion may occur. For example, each spouse might want

to fulfill a specific role and compete with the other to do so. Or each may automatically think the other is fulfilling a role and come to realize later that neither is.

80 Percent I Love You—20 Percent I Hate You

Many people hold the expectation that their partner will meet all of their needs, indeed that it is the partner's duty to do this. To the extent that partners fail to live up to this expectation, they are "bad" spouses. However, human beings are complex. It is probably impossible for any two people to meet one another's needs completely. If a couple could mutually satisfy even 80 percent of each other's needs, it would be a minor miracle.

The expectation of total need fulfillment within marriage ruins many marital relationships. As time passes, the spouse with the unmet needs will long to have them satisfied and will accuse the partner of failure and indifference. Conflict will grow because the accused spouse feels unfairly accused, defensive, and inferior. Life will revolve more and more around the unfulfilled 20 percent rather than the fulfilled 80 percent. This is especially true if the partners are possessive and block each other from any outside need gratification. Unless such a pattern of interaction is broken, a spouse may suddenly fall out of love and leave the mate for someone else. These sudden departures are catastrophic to all the parties. And the ensuing relationship often fails because of the same dynamics. For example, the dissatisfied spouse finds a person who meets some of the unfulfilled needs and, because these needs have become so exaggerated, concludes that at last he or she has met the "right" person. In all the excitement, the person often overlooks the fact that the new love does not fulfill other needs that have long been met by the discarded spouse. In a few years the conflicts will reappear over different unmet needs, and the process of disenchantment will recur.

Carl and Jane: A Good Spouse Will Meet All My Needs

> *They are very much in love. Their friends are amazed at how compatible and well suited they are to one another. Each expects total fulfillment within the marriage. Jane enjoys staying up late and insists that Carl, who likes to go to bed early to be fresh for work, stay up with her as she hates to be alone. At first Carl obliges, but he gradually returns to his habitual bedtime. But, of course, he can't sleep well because he feels guilty leaving Jane alone, which, she reminds him, demonstrates his lack of love and uncaring attitude. She tries going to bed earlier but also can't sleep well because she isn't sleepy, and so she simply lies there resenting Carl. She begins to tell him how he has failed her, and he responds by listing all the good things he does in the marriage. Jane acknowledges these good things but dismisses them as the wrong things. He doesn't really do the important things that show real love, such as trying to stay up later. Naturally, sex and resentment are incompatible bed partners, and Jane and Carl's sex life slowly disintegrates. Each begins to hate the other for not fulfilling their needs, for making them lose their identity in part, and for making their sex life so unsatisfactory. Then Carl, working overtime one Saturday, spontaneously has intercourse with a coworker and is soon "in love." Sex is good, reaffirming his manhood, and the woman loves to go to bed early. He divorces Jane and marries his new "right" woman. Unfortunately, they also divorce three years later because Carl can't stand her indifference to housekeeping and cooking. He reminds her periodically during their marriage that Jane kept a neat house and prepared excellent meals.*

Such dynamics are prevalent in "love" marriages. This is true because "love" blinds, reducing the chances of realistic appraisal and alternative seeking. To the person who believes in love as the only basis of marriage, the need to seek realistic alternatives is a signal that love has gone. But:

> The happy, workable, productive marriage does not require love or even the practice of the Golden Rule. To maintain continuously a union based on love is not feasible for most people. Nor is it possible to live in a permanent state of romance. Normal people should not be frustrated or disappointed if they are not in a constant state of love. If they experience the joy of love for ten percent of the time they are married, attempt to treat each other with as much courtesy as they do distinguished strangers, and attempt to make the marriage a workable affair—one where there are some practical advantages and satisfaction for each—the chances are the marriage will endure longer and with more strength than so-called love matches. (Lederer & Jackson, 1968, p. 59)

Lack of Commitment: Too Low Expectations

We have looked at the problem of too high expectations because these are most common in a society that believes in romantic love as a basis for marriage. However, it is also possible to have expectations of marriage that are too low.

The expectation of *permanence* is important to making a marriage last. Even though it is clear from divorce statistics that American marriages do not necessarily last forever, it is important that the couple bring to the marriage the expectation that *their* marriage will last "until death do us part."

All of the studies done on successful marriage find that the couple's expression of commitment to the permanence of the relationship is high on the list of reasons for marital success (Stinnett, 1979; Curran, 1983; Lauer & Lauer, 1985). Some of Lauer and Lauer's (pp. 24–25) respondents expressed their commitment to the relationship as follows:

"I'll tell you why we stayed together, I'm just too damned stubborn to give up."

"You can't run home to mother when the first trouble appears."

"Commitment means a willingness to be unhappy for awhile. You're not going to be happy with each other all the time. That's when commitment is really important."

This kind of total commitment is often withheld in the cohabitation relationship. Since one of the purposes of cohabitation is to be in a relationship that is easy to get out of, it is clear that total commitment cannot be offered. It may be this element of cohabitation that makes it less than good training for marriage.

The Expectation of Primariness: Extramarital Relations

In large part because American marriage is rooted in Judeo-Christian principles, one's sexual and emotional outlet is limited to one's spouse. The ideal of *monogamy* is an important part of American marriage. It is interesting to note that in Murdock's (1949) study of 148 societies, 81 percent of them maintained taboos against adultery, so America is not alone in the expectation of primariness in marriage.

Despite the strongly stated expectation of primariness in sexual relations, many do not live up to this expectation. Kinsey's research (1948, 1953) indicated that about one-half of American husbands and about one-quarter of American wives had engaged in at least one extramarital sexual relationship. More recent data indicate that these percentages have risen at least for certain groups. Younger wives (under age twenty-five) now engage in extramarital relations about as often as their husbands. This may relate to the greater numbers of women entering the workforce. Research indicates that working wives of all ages have an incidence of extramarital relations about twice as high as that of housewives (Tavris & Sadd, 1977; Hunt, 1974). Since most married people have the expectation of primariness, it is difficult to get accurate figures on extramarital sexual experiences because study participants tend to conceal such experiences. There is little doubt, however, that this expectation is being disappointed more and more often.

In the 1970s the media reported a great deal of consensual adultery, that is, adultery that was accepted by the couples involved. Estimates range up to 5 percent of married couples under thirty have practiced consensual adultery at some time (Johnson, 1974). Again research is difficult to do in this area since the general society does not accept the practice. Recent polls seem to indicate an increasing rejection of such activity. For example, Wallenberg (1984) found that 86 percent of his sample welcomed more emphasis on traditional family ties and only 23 percent favored more sexual freedom.

Generally speaking, men tend to take their extramarital affairs more lightly than women. They tend to associate their affairs with an increase in marital satisfaction and a decrease in boredom and tension within their marriages. Older women tend to have affairs that last longer, tend to be more emotionally involved and tend to associate their affairs with decreasing marital satisfaction.

The reasons for extramarital sexual affairs are many and varied. For some, it is simple curiosity and the desire for some variation of sexual experience. For others, it might be a yearning for the romance that has been lost in their marriages or a search for the emotional satisfaction they feel is missing in their lives. Some simply fall into an affair out of friendship for someone of the opposite sex. An adulterous affair can also be a rebellion or retaliation against the spouse. Of course, most threatening to a marriage is an affair that stems from falling in love with the new partner.

Extramarital affairs are often difficult for a spouse to combat. Early in the affair, the couple is very aroused and can usually manage only a very limited time together. The partners are on their best behavior and make special efforts to be attractive and appealing. There is high expectation and excitement because of the clandestine nature of the affair. This kind of excitement is hard to bring back into a long-standing marriage.

Although the expectation of primariness is often broken, it remains an important expectation. Breaking it for whatever reason often causes the spouse to become very upset and even to end the marriage. At the least, it spoils the mutual trust in the marital relationship, and creates feelings of inadequacy in the spouse who discovers the other's extramarital affair.

The Self-Fulfilling Prophecy

There is evidence suggesting that the expectations you hold about another person tend to influence that person in the direction of the expectations (for a more extensive discussion see Rosenthal & Jacobson, 1968). Thus, to hold *slightly* high expectations about another person is not totally unproductive as long as the expectations are close enough to reality that the other person can fulfill them. Remember, though, that to expect something different of a person implies that you don't approve of the person at the present time. Also, expectations that are clearly out of another's reach tell that person that he or she is doomed to failure because the expectations can't be met. This often happens to children. Sometimes children feel so frustrated by their inability to meet their parents' expectations that they deliberately do the opposite of what their parents desire in an effort to free themselves from impossible expectations. "All right, if you are never satisfied with my schoolwork, no matter how hard I try, I'll stop trying."

Such dynamics are also often found in marriage. If your mate constantly expects something of you that you can't fulfill, you may begin to feel incompetent, unloved, and unwanted. On the other hand, positive and realistic expectations about the spouse, or anyone else for that matter, may be fulfilled because they make the other person feel wanted and valuable and the person then acts on this positive feeling.

It is clear that the closer we can come in our expectations and perceptions to objective reality, the more efficient our behavior will generally be. If we expect impossible or difficult behavior from our mates, we doom both our mates and ourselves to perpetual failure and frustration. If, on the other hand, we accept ourselves and our mates as we are, then we have the makings for an open, communicative, and growing relationship.

How can we be realistic in our expectations of others and of marriage? Perhaps we can never be totally realistic, but if we can accept ourselves basically for what we are, can feel respect and genuine liking of ourselves, can admit error and failure and start again, can accept criticism, and can be self-supportive rather than self-destructive, then we will be on the right road. Of course, if these were easy steps, we would all be living happily ever after. Although much is known about helping people live more satisfying lives, a great deal remains to be learned. Individuals are complex and vary greatly; no single answer will suffice for everyone. Thus we need many paths by which people can travel to self-actualization. In this chapter and the next we will map some of these directions by examining common marital conflicts and possible solutions to these conflicts. Our first step will be to set up ideal yet realistic goals toward which we may move in our quest for maturity and **mental health**.

Characteristics of Mental Health

The National Association for Mental Health has described mentally healthy people as generally (1) feeling comfortable about themselves, (2) feeling good about other people, and (3) being able to meet the demands of life.

Feeling Comfortable about Oneself   Mature people are not bowled over by their own fears, anger, love, jealousy, guilt, or worries. They take life's disappointments in their stride. They have a tolerant, easygoing attitude toward themselves as well as others, and they can laugh at themselves. They neither underestimate nor overestimate their abilities. They can accept their own shortcomings. They respect themselves and feel able to deal with most situations that come their way. They get satisfaction from simple everyday pleasures.

Notice that this description recognizes that people's lives have negative aspects: fear, anger, guilt, worries, and disappointments. Mentally healthy people can cope with such negative aspects. They can accept failures without becoming angry or considering themselves failures because of temporary setbacks. Moreover, they can laugh at themselves, which is something maladjusted people can seldom do.

Feeling Good about Other People   Mature people are able to give love and consider the interests of others. They have personal relationships that are satisfying and lasting. They expect to like and trust others, and they take it for granted that others will like and trust them. They respect the many differences they find in people. They do not push people around or allow themselves to be pushed around. They can feel part of a group. They feel a sense of responsibility to their neighbors and country.

As you have probably noticed, this description includes a great deal of common sense. Certainly we would expect people who are considerate of other people's interests to have lasting relationships. Furthermore, as we noted before in our discussion of self-fulfilling expectations, if we approach people in an open, friendly manner, expecting to like them, they will feel warmed by our friendliness and will probably feel friendly toward us. If, on the other hand, we approach people as if we expect them to cheat us, the chances are that they will be suspicious of us and keep their distance.

The Self-Actualized Person in the Fully Functioning Family

Mental health
A mode of being in which a person is free of mental problems and/or disease

Another aspect of this description is that it recognizes that we are gregarious, or, as the song says, "People who need people." Mature people recognize this need and are also aware of the responsibilities that people have toward one another.

Feeling Competent to Meet the Demands of Life   Mature people do something about problems as they arise. They accept responsibilities. They plan ahead and do not fear the future. They welcome new experiences and new ideas and can adjust to changed circumstances. They use their natural capacities. They set realistic goals for themselves. They are able to think for themselves and make their own decisions. They put their best effort into what they do and get satisfaction out of doing it.

Self-Actualization

Abraham Maslow spent a lifetime studying people, especially those he called self-actualized people. These were people he believed had reached the highest levels of growth, people who seemed to be realizing their full potential. They are people at the top of the mental health ladder. Let's take a look at some of the characteristics they share:

1. A more adequate perception of reality and a more comfortable relationship with reality than occur in average people. Self-actualized people prefer to cope with even unpleasant reality rather than retreat to pleasant fantasies.
2. A high degree of acceptance of themselves, of others, and of the realities of human nature. Self-actualized people are not ashamed of being what they are, and they are not shocked or dismayed to find foibles and shortcomings in themselves or in others.
3. A high degree of spontaneity. Self-actualized people are able to act freely without undue personal restrictions and unnecessary inhibitions.
4. A focus on problem centeredness. Self-actualized people seem to focus on problems outside themselves. They are not overly self-conscious; they are not problems to themselves. Hence they devote their attention to a task, duty, or mission that seems peculiarly cut out for them.
5. A need for privacy. Self-actualized people feel comfortable alone with their thoughts and feelings. Aloneness does not frighten them.
6. A high degree of autonomy. Self-actualized people, as the name implies, for the most part are independent people capable of making their own decisions. They motivate themselves.
7. A continued freshness of appreciation. Self-actualized people show the capacity to appreciate life with the freshness and delight of a child. They can see the unique in many apparently commonplace experiences.

Sidney Jourard (1963) lists such traits as a democratic character structure; a strong ethical sense; an unhostile sense of humor; creativeness; a feeling of belonging to all humanity, including occasional mystical experiences about this sense of connection; and a resistance to **enculturation** (being overly influenced by one's culture).

Jourard sums up the qualities of the fully healthy person:

Enculturation
The process of learning the mores, rules, ways, and manners of a given culture

Healthy personality is manifested by the individual who has been able to gratify his basic needs through acceptable behavior such that his own personality is no longer a problem to him. He can take himself more or less for granted and devote his energies and thoughts to socially meaningful interests and problems beyond security, or lovability, or status. (p. 7)

Living in the Now

Marriages are constantly troubled because one or both spouses cannot live in the present. Are the following remarks familiar? "I'm upset because Christmas now reminds me of how terrible you were last Christmas." "This is a nice dinner but it doesn't compare with the one I want to fix next week." "In my last marriage this never happened."

All phases of time—past, present, and future—are essential for fully functioning people. To retain what has been learned in the past and use it to cope with the present is an important attribute of maturity. To project into the future and thereby modify the present is another important and perhaps unique characteristic of humans. Past and future are used by the healthy person to live a fuller, more creative life in the present.

But while retention and projection of time can help us cope with the present, they can also hamper present behavior. In the preceding comments the present Christmas is being ruined because of the past Christmas. Probably the spouse is now being perfectly pleasant, yet the other is unhappy because he or she is dwelling on the past rather than enjoying the present. People who do not learn from the past are doomed to repeat mistakes, yet people must develop the capacity to learn from the past without becoming entrapped by it. Much the same can be said of the future. To plan for the future is an important function. Yet people may also hamper their behavior by projecting consequences into the future that keep them from acting in the present. For example, look how a husband's performance fears can create a lonely night for himself and his wife:

> *James knows his wife is in a loving mood, but he is tired and fears that if they make love he will fail to satisfy her. When she approaches him, he says he doesn't feel good and goes to the guest room to sleep.*

James may have been correct, but, on the other hand, he may not have been. By avoiding the situation, he ensured his wife's dissatisfaction. Of course, he could have been honest and simply said, "Let's just cuddle for a while and then go to sleep. I'm really bushed."

As we saw, some people live frustrated lives because their expectations of the future are unrealistic. Remember Carol and her three husbands? Carol projects idealized expectations onto her husbands. Rather than letting them be the persons they are, she expects them to act in a certain manner (as she imagines her father did). She is so preoccupied with expecting her husband to behave as she thinks he should that she derives no satisfaction from his actual behavior.

People who can let go of past animosities and hurts and who can plan intelligently for the future without belittling the present find a great deal of happiness in the present.

The Goals of Intimacy

It seems clear that building a satisfying intimate relationship is a difficult and complex task. Many factors will influence the success of such relationships. Certainly if we prepare ourselves to meet the problems so often found in intimate relationships of all kinds and learn the skills of open communication and problem solving before hostilities and inability to communicate make problem solving more difficult, we stand a better chance of maintaining and fulfilling intimate relationships.

What we are proposing is that marriage be treated as a complex vehicle to personal happiness and that, like any vehicle, preventive maintenance and regular care will minimize faulty operation.

Marriage counselors see many couples whose marriages are so damaged that little if anything can be done to help them. But most American couples begin their marriages "in love." They do not deliberately set out to destroy their love, each other, or their marriage. Yet it is often hard to believe that the couples in the marriage counselor's office or the divorce court ever felt love and affection toward each other. Too often they are bitter, resentful, and spiteful. Their wonderful "love" marriage has become a despised trap, a hated responsibility, an intolerable life situation.

Why? Marriages often become unhappy because we are not taught the arts of "getting along" intimately with others or the skills necessary to create a growing and meaningful existence in the face of the pressures and problems of a complex world. According to Paul Popenoe (1974, p. 3): "Far more could be done to handle marital difficulties more intelligently and successfully, and failure to teach how this can be done, both before and after marriage, is a notorious deficiency of contemporary treatment of the subject of marriage."

To get along intimately with another person, to create a fully functioning family, we need to be clear about the basic goals of intimacy. In their most general terms they are identical to some of the functions of the family that we discussed in Chapter 2. In particular they are (1) providing emotional gratification to family members, (2) helping members deal with crises and problems, and (3) helping members grow in the most fulfilling manner possible. The following examples show how a marriage can fulfill these functions.

Emotional Gratification

Pete loves to tinker with things, and he feels important and emotionally gratified if he can fix something in the house for Gail. Gail loves to knit and Pete loves sweaters, so she feels worthwhile and appreciated when she knits him a sweater. Gail knows she can sound off when she gets angry, because Pete understands and doesn't put her down. Pete feels emotionally supported by Gail because she backs him when he wants to try something new. Both partners are having emotional needs met as well as meeting many of the needs of the other.

> *When Pete has a crisis in the office, he tells Gail about it, and she listens, offers support, asks questions, and, very occasionally, offers advice. When he is through telling her about it, Pete often understands the situation better and feels more ready either to accept or change it.*

Dealing with Crises

> *Gail wants to be less shy, and Pete encourages her to be more assertive with him and to role play assertiveness with others. Gradually, she finds she can overcome her shyness, in large part because Pete encourages and supports her.*

Growing in a Fulfilling Manner

Certainly it does not seem to be asking too much of a marriage to supply emotional gratification to the partners, to help them deal with crises that arise, and to encourage each to grow in a personally fulfilling manner. Yet marriage often fails this assignment or, to put it more accurately, marriage partners often fail to create a marriage in which these positive elements thrive.

Summary

Marriage is the socially accepted relationship through which sexual drives are fulfilled. It is also much more than this—it is the generally accepted mode of life for most Americans. Legally, marriage is a three-way relationship that involves the man, the woman, and the state. The state sets certain eligibility requirements that must be met in order for a couple to marry. The state also prescribes certain obligations that each partner must fulfill in marriage. The marriage ceremony commits a couple to a new status, with certain privileges, obligations, and restrictions. In addition to state-mandated marital obligations, some couples are writing their own marriage contracts, stating goals, obligations, and responsibilities that they wish to be a part of their marriage. Such contracts, if properly written, are considered legal as long as they do not disregard state-mandated duties and obligations.

Marriage is many things, but more than anything else it is constant interaction between family members and fulfillment of many roles within the family relationship. How does one interact with another person at the intimate level of marriage? Basically, how we interact will be determined by our attitudes and expectations about marriage and our partner. We assimilate these attitudes and expectations of the larger culture from our parents. When our expectations and attitudes differ from our spouse's, there will usually be conflict in the marriage.

The basic goals of intimacy in a marriage are emotional gratification of each partner, helping each deal with crises, and helping each grow in a fulfilling manner. The ideal goal of a family is to provide an environment in which each family member is encouraged and free to become the most actualized person that he or she is capable of becoming. Each family member will have to work toward maintaining his or her own balance and growth while at the same time contributing to the well-being of all the other family members. This is a large order and requires self-understanding and common sense of all family members.

Self-actualizing people essentially are people who feel comfortable about themselves and others. They are able to meet most of the demands of life in a realistic fashion. They tend to use their past experiences and ideas about their future to enhance the present rather than to escape from it. They are not prisoners of their past but are free to use it to improve the present. Intimacy includes the commitment to help each other realize to the fullest possible degree all of the human potential inherent in each individual family member. Granted this is a difficult and at times impossible task, yet it is a worthy goal toward which to strive.

Finding What's Good in Marriage

Because Americans tend to have such high expectations for their marriages, disappointment in marriage and a preoccupation with a mate's failures tend to overinfluence many relationships. The passage of time with attendent day-to-day responsibilities tends to bury the spark of romance. Concentration on the unmet 20 percent of one's needs tends to make one forget the good job one's spouse is doing in meeting 80 percent of one's needs.

Ayala Pines, a psychologist in private practice, suggests that one way to combat this kind of negative change in a couple's relationship is to ask a couple, "Why were you attracted to your mate in the first place?" In other words, rather than concentrating on the often long list of things that the couple feels is wrong with their relationship, get the couple to thinking and talking about those characteristics that brought them together in the first place. "You feel a change in the atmosphere when they start reminiscing about the good times they had at the beginning of their relationships," Pines says (1985).

Comparing that idyllic beginning to their current situation, couples often criticize each other with the accusation, "You used to do this. You don't anymore." What a person found attractive about their partner in the beginning is often what is causing stress today. If a woman tells you she fell in love because he was the tall, dark, handsome, and silent type, then what's causing her problems is that he doesn't communicate. At first the silence was mysterious and attractive. As time passes, it becomes frustrating and irritating.

And he was attracted to her energy. Now he says she is manipulative,

hysterical, and bossy. Pines suggests that when you show the couple that the same thing that is causing the trouble in the relationship is what they found attractive at the beginning, it takes away the feeling of helplessness. They recognize that although they feel changes have taken place in their

partner, the characteristics that drew them together still exist.

Although Pines suggests focusing on the positive, it is not always easy. Most couples come in with a laundry list of complaints. What they ever found attractive or interesting about each other is submerged beneath a tidal wave of negative feelings.

Couples come in with examples cast in concrete. "She's bossy." "She's demanding." "He's so cold and uncommunicative." Pines asks such couples, "Was there ever a situation in which he was warm and communicative?" Always, no matter how awful the relationship has gotten, there is at least one example that is positive. And it is much more exciting to figure out what in a situation made him warm and communicative, rather than listing all the situations in which he isn't. It also starts the couple looking at what has been good in the marriage rather than dwelling only on what is now bad.

Pines feels that concentrating on what has been and may still be right about a relationship helps a couple to realize that much of their trouble may stem from unrealistically high expectations. It may also help a couple to be more tolerant of each other's faults when they are asked to remember what has been positive about their mate.

To find out why a couple came together and why they have stayed together as long as they have focuses on the couple's strengths. To concentrate on their problems only adds emphasis to the negative aspects of their relationship and in fact lends the authority of the counselor or therapist to the fact that they do indeed have terrible problems.

An old song from the 1940s suggests "accentuate the positive, eliminate the negative." Since few of us can be a 100 percent perfect spouse to our mate, expecting perfection can only lead to disappointment. Perhaps an attitude of accentuating the positive is best found in a comment made by one of the persons interviewed in the Lauer (1985, p. 24) study of successful marriages. A husband of twenty-four years said, "She isn't perfect but I don't worry about her weak points, which are very few. Her strong points overcome them too much."

To take periodic inventories of what's good in one's marriage is a helpful step to counteract the all-too-natural tendency for people to dwell on what seems wrong in one's relationship. To remember what drew you together, why you fell in love, what excited you about your mate in the first place will help you rekindle the spark of romance that too often is buried under unrealistic expectations of perfection and the mundane chores and stresses of everyday living.

Communication in Intimate Relationships

Contents

I see communication as a huge umbrella that covers and affects all that goes on between human beings. Once a human being arrives on earth, communication is the largest single factor determining what kinds of relationships he/she makes with others and what happens to him/her in the world.

Virginia Satir

Communication is basic to every human relationship. Without it, there could be no relationship. The more intimate the relationship, the more important communication becomes. Good communication skills are always found within strong families. In a study by Curran (1983, p. 34), communicating and listening were chosen as the primary trait of healthy families. This is echoed throughout the research on strong, healthy, and successful families.

Although most Americans are now well aware of the importance of communication to successful relationships, this awareness is quite new. David Mace (1980) indicates that before 1970, we really had little understanding of how communication processes affected family relationships.

I once made a survey of what I considered to be the twenty-six best books on marriage published between 1930 and 1970, in order to find out how they treated the subject of communication. Most of them scarcely mentioned it at all. Of those that did, only a few had any real perception of its importance.

By contrast Olson and Markoff (1985) list 123 articles in 1984 alone under the general heading "Communication in the Family." (This heading includes the subheadings, "Conflict Resolution," "Power in the Family," and "Decision Making.")

You might wonder why the importance of communication skills was overlooked for so long. Probably, it was because families of the past were built on gender roles (Chapter 7). The definition of a good wife was clear. She cleaned, cooked, bore and cared for the children, and supported her husband emotionally. A good husband was strong and protected his family, supported them economically, did the heavy work around the home or farm and assumed full responsibility for the family's well-being. A "good" wife, a "successful" husband, a "strong" family resulted when all family members fulfilled their clearly specified roles.

Today, gender roles are no longer clear-cut. The family's major function has become relational rather than role fulfilling. The meeting of emotional needs has become more important in families than the meeting of physical needs. Because emotional needs are so individual, they are much harder to define and understand than physical needs. A proper role for a family member cannot be easily prescribed when it is judged by the nebulous standard of "meeting emotional needs."

Stating that meeting emotional needs is more important than the meeting of physical needs in the modern American family assumes that the family is affluent enough to meet those physical needs. For families in real poverty, the meeting of day-to-day physical needs is still more important than the meeting of emotional needs. It is difficult to be happy with my partner and my children if my stomach is empty. Traditional gender roles have not changed nearly as much in the lower economic class families as they have for economically better off families. In essence, communication skills become more necessary as the individual seeks emotional and psychological intimacy, happiness, and fulfillment in marriage rather than simply successful fulfillment of socially prescribed family roles.

Building and maintaining a marriage that supplies emotional gratification to each partner and helps each to deal with crises and grow in a fulfilling manner can only be achieved by an active process of interaction between partners. Talking, listening, negotiating, and problem solving are necessary skills for building a strong relationship.

In a successful marriage, communication produces mutual understanding, a *knowing* of one another, so that pleasure is maximized and pain minimized for both partners. A possible complication is that pleasure for one may cause pain for the other, or that avoidance of pain for one may add to the pain of the other. Thus successful marital communication leads to pain reduction or pleasure enhancement for one partner, with regard to the impact on the other partner. It requires appreciation of the partner's viewpoint and the ability to compromise.

Successful communication is the cornerstone of any relationship. Such communication must be open, realistic, tactful, caring, and valued. Maintaining this kind of communication is not always easy unless all family members are committed to the belief that good communication is important to life satisfaction. This sounds simple, yet couples in marital trouble almost always list failure to communicate as one of their major problems.

Good communication is especially important and especially difficult in marriage because of the intensity of emotions in an intimate relationship. High emotional levels tend to interfere with rationality and logic, and thus with clear communication. If you have ever had trouble communicating when you are calm and collected, imagine the potential problems when you are excited and emotionally aroused. Yet only through clear communication can each partner know the needs of the other. When conflicts arise, the only chance to resolve them is if each partner is able to communicate fairly about the problem, define it clearly, and be open to alternative solutions. Good communication also helps minimize hostilities. For example, unexpressed dissatisfactions tend to create hostility, but fairly expressed dissatisfaction allows the other partner to understand the problem and act to reduce the partner's dissatisfaction and deflate the hostility.

Conflict management is essential to all intimate relationships. This is true because conflict is bound to occur in any long-lasting relationship. When one considers that two people marry after many years of growing up and learning multiple attitudes, it is surprising that the two can get along at all on an intimate day-to-day basis because what each individual has learned about handling interpersonal relationships will be to a large extent peculiar to that person. For example, one partner may learn that you do not talk about problems until everyone is calm and collected. Sometimes this has meant that a problem is not discussed for several days. The other partner has learned that you always speak your mind immediately. She or he has been taught that waiting only makes things worse. You can see that these differing beliefs about when to communicate will cause difficulty.

Communication is also affected by the general society. For example, American men are taught to be less communicative, less self-disclosing about their feelings than American women. The traditional American masculine role is one of strength and silence. To be expressive, sensitive, and tender is considered feminine. But obviously the latter three traits are important in good communication even if the traditional masculine role denies them to males. Thus marital communication is certainly affected by general social values about masculinity and femininity as well as by the individual communicative skills of the partners.

It is important to emphasize the influence of the general society and its institutions. Most people encountering marital problems tend to believe that the problems are personal. That is, they believe that the problems are unique to their partner, their family, themselves, or the immediate circumstances. Placing the source of problems solely within the couple and their marriage reinforces the myth that marriage to the "right" person will solve all problems and result in a happy family life. Certainly many problems are unique to a given family, but it is equally true that many family problems arise because of social expectations. For example, stereotypical sex roles may lock a family into rigid patterns of behavior that cause problems for individual family members and therefore stress for the family.

The myth of the "right" partner sometimes leads a troubled couple to end their problems by changing partners when, in fact, it is their relational skills that need changing. A person whose lack of communication skills finally leads to the demise of his or her marriage will soon find that any new relationship is also in trouble.

Part of good communication is the ability of a couple to relate to one another in a manner relatively free from cultural or sociological influences, such as sex role stereotypes (Montgomery, 1981). In other words, partners should attribute meaning to each other's communications based on personal knowledge of one another, rather than on traditionally accepted interpretations.

Jane calls her husband Jim "pigheaded," but instead of becoming angry at a traditionally accepted put-down, he laughs and hugs her. Calling him pigheaded is her special way of complimenting him for being properly assertive.

The example also makes it obvious that good communication depends on high levels of agreement between partners on the unique meanings of each other's communications. Jim needed to know his wife's positive meaning in the traditionally negative label in order to react with a hug rather than anger. This means that successful communication takes time to develop. It requires a learning process between two people and develops gradually over time. The ultimate goal of successful communication is the achievement of interpersonal understanding.

Such understanding between people in close relationships also implies a certain "richness" in their communication. This means that they have many ways of communicating with one another, even many ways of conveying the same thing (Galvin & Brommel, 1982). Research indicates that marital happiness increases the number of communication styles of the couples, whereas less happily married spouses tend to have fewer communication styles (Honeycutt, Wilson & Parker, 1982).

Failure to communicate is not usually an accident. The failure is usually intentional, though not overtly or consciously so. *People choose not to communicate.*

Often when a marriage is disintegrating, the partners say "We just can't communicate" or "We just don't talk to each other any more." They identify a deficiency of communication as the cause, when actually it is not a deficiency but a surplus

**What Causes
Communication Failure?**

of negative or aversive communication that causes the disintegration. Of course, a deficiency of talk may eventually replace the unproductive aversive talk, but the deficiency is not the same as no communication. Silence can be communication. The "silent treatment" is just about as aversive as communication can become.

Failure to communicate with others usually begins with a breakdown of internal communication. Anger, emotional maladjustment, stress and strain, and faulty perceptions can all lead to blind spots and overly strong defenses. If we become rigid and inflexible, we may be threatened by new experiences and change. Our self-images may become unrealistic, causing us to filter all communications to fit the faulty self-picture. When this happens, it is hard to have good communication.

Aversive Communication

One basic principle of human behavior is that people seek pleasure and avoid pain. Actually, people first avoid pain and then seek pleasure, because in the hierarchy of human needs pain avoidance is basic for survival. This point is crucial in our understanding of communication failure because motivation to communicate will be most urgent when avoiding pain. Unfortunately the quickest means of changing the spouse who is giving us pain is by threatening him or her. That is, by combating pain with an aversive communication, we get the spouse "off our back." But this causes pain to the spouse and is counterproductive because the threatened partner will most likely respond on the same level, creating a "vicious circle," and we both become losers. This kind of communication is a power struggle in which the winner is the one who generates the most aversion. The loser feels resentful and may engage in typical loser's behavior such as deceit, procrastination, deliberate inadequacy, sarcasm, sullenness, and so forth. Any verbal input by the loser is likely to be an emotional discharge of the resulting resentment and hostility. Generally the loser stops talking because communication

I know you believe you understand what you think I said, but I am not sure you realize that what you heard is not what I meant.

has become so painful. Often the loser will begin to seek fulfillment outside the marriage, at which point communication failure will become an intentional goal. The loser stops talking or becomes deliberately misleading because he or she knows that his or her behavior is unacceptable to the winner.

An example of aversive communication is one that starts out to deal with one conflict but instead brings up a confusing kaleidoscope of other marginally related disagreements connected only by the pain each partner causes the other:

"Where did you put my socks?"

"You mean the socks I have to crawl under the bed to find every time I do the laundry?"

"Yes, every time you do the laundry—the second Tuesday of every month."

"With the machine that's always broken, that nobody fixes."

"Because I'm so busy working to pay for tennis lessons and ladies' luncheons."

"And losses at Tuesday night poker bashes."

"I'm sick of this argument."

"Well, you started it."

"How?"

"Well, I can't remember, but you did."

It is important to remember that negative things must be communicated, but there are positive ways by which to communicate them (see Table 6-1, p. 174).

Note that in Table 6-1, most of the positive responses are ways of saying to the partner, "Yes, I'm listening." More explicit listening invitations are "I see," "Tell me about it," "This seems important to you," and "Okay, let's work on it together." As you become aware of negative responses in your interaction with your partner, substitute more positive responses that show your care and concern for him or her.

Note also that praising and reassuring may be negative responses when the other person has a problem because such responses tend to prevent that person from sharing feelings that are more threatening or painful. Don't be too quick to reassure. Later, when the partner has sufficiently explored all of the feelings that are associated with the problem, expressing appreciation and confidence in the partner will be positive.

There is a sense of order in successful communication where communications flow smoothly back and forth between sender and receiver. Three general conditions must be met for successful communication to occur:

Developing a Flow of Communication

1. *Commitment*: The partners must be motivated to work on their relationship.
2. *Growth orientation*: The partners must accept the fact that their relationship is dynamic and changing rather than static.
3. *Noncoercive atmosphere*: The partners must feel free to be themselves, to be open, and to be honest.

These three conditions represent the foundation blocks of successful communication, but they are difficult to attain. We shall look at each in more detail later.

Table 6-1

Negative and Positive Responses in Communication

Negative		Positive	
1. Ordering, directing, commanding	"Stop ordering me around." "You can't buy that." "Don't talk to me like that."	1. Providing self-direction and choice	"You appear very disappointed." "Let's discuss whether that would be a good purchase." "When you talk like that, I feel frightened."
2. Warning, admonishing, threatening	"Listen to me or else." "If you won't, then I'll find someone who will."	2. Seeking causes for differences	"What did I say that turned you off?" "Help me understand why you don't want to . . ."
3. Exhorting, moralizing, preaching	"You should tell your boss you want that raise."	3. Choosing one of several alternatives	"Which do you think would be best for you, . . . for us, . . . for all involved?"
4. Advising, giving solutions or suggestions	"Why don't you try . . ." "You ought to stay home more."	4. Exploring possibilities	"What could you try?" "Would it help you if . . ."
5. Lecturing, teaching, giving logical arguments	"It makes more sense to do it this way." "The Browns are happy and they don't have a new car."	5. Considering consequences	"Which way seems to get better results for you?" "Let's think about what would result from each decision."
6. Judging, criticizing, blaming	"You are wrong." "It's all your fault." "What a stupid idea!"	6. Sharing responsibility	"Those two statements seem to conflict." "Let's do what we can to solve it." "Let's see if that idea will work."
7. Praising, agreeing, evaluating	"I think you are absolutely correct." "You do so many good things."	7. Expanding openness	"This seems like a difficult decision for you to make." "You sound discouraged. I'll listen."
8. Name calling, ridiculing, shaming, categorizing	"You're no good." "You're just like all the other men/women." "You're a liar."	8. Enhancing self-esteem and uniqueness	"I love you." "I appreciate your understanding." "Your interpretation is different from mine."
9. Interpreting, analyzing, diagnosing	"If you weren't so tired, you could see my point." "You don't care what I think."	9. Increasing sensitivity	"If you prefer, we can discuss this at another time." "Right now, I'm feeling so alone and left out."
10. Reassuring, sympathizing, consoling	"Don't worry about it." "All men/women go through that at some time."	10. Expressing care and concern	"What worries you about that?" "This is an especially difficult time for you."
11. Probing, questioning, interrogating	"Where have you been?" "Now, tell me the real reason you feel that way."	11. Giving freedom and privacy	"I've missed you a lot." "You don't need to explain if you would rather not."
12. Withdrawing, distracting, humoring, diverting	"You're funny when you're mad." "Why don't you tell me something new!"	12. Accepting, giving attention to the other person	"I understand that you are feeling mad because . . ." "That point is something you haven't mentioned before."

Source: From Richard Hunt and Edward Rydman, *Creative Marriage* (Boston: Holbrook, 1976), pp. 50–51.

The first step in communicating is to "encode" the message and send it to the partner via some communication channel, for example, verbal or written. The receiver must "decode" that message and, to ensure that it has been correctly received, must feed back what has been decoded to the sender. The source either

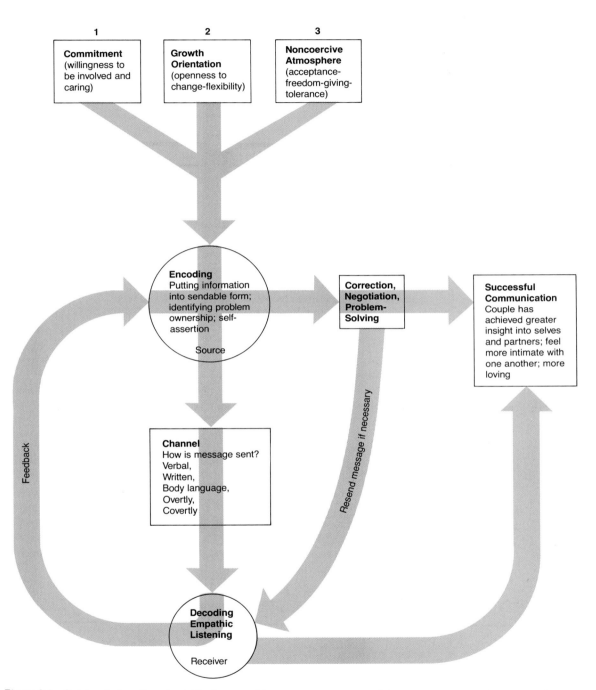

Figure 6-1 Communications flow chart. The three conditions necessary to successful communication are shown at the top.

verifies the message or—through correction, negotiation, and problem solving—resends the message, and the process is repeated. This circular pattern may have to be repeated several times before successful communication is achieved (see Figure 6-1).

Inset 6-1

Is Honesty Always the Best Policy?

It is a popular notion that the more open, the more honest the self-disclosure, the better the communication and thus the better the relationship. Yet research is mixed about this idea. Certainly there is a correlation between openness and satisfaction (Jorgensen & Gaudy, 1980), but some researchers suggest that both too much and too little self-disclosure can reduce satisfaction with a relationship (Cozby, 1973; Galvin & Brommel, 1982).

As time passes in a relationship restraints tend to be released, so that manners are sometimes forgotten, frankness may override tact, and hostility can result. If the hostility and frankness become too overwhelming, the couple tends to limit their self-expression and to withdraw from each other because communication becomes so aversive.

Eckman (1985) asks his reader to:

Consider what life would be like if everyone could lie perfectly or no one could lie at all . . . If we could never know how someone really felt, and if we knew we couldn't know, life would be more tenuous. Certain in the knowledge that every show of emotion might be a mere display put on to please, manipulate, or mislead, individuals would be more adrift, attachments less firm.

And if we could never lie, if a smile was always reliable, never absent when pleasure was felt, and never present without pleasure, life would be rougher than it is, many relationships harder to maintain. Politeness, attempts to smooth matters over, to conceal feelings one wished one didn't feel—all would be gone.

Cutler and Dyer (1966) found that nearly half of the "nonadjustive responses" for both husbands and wives come as a result of open sharing of feelings about violated expectations. Contrary to popular belief about the

benefits of such sharing, this open communication did not lead to improved relations.

What is being suggested is that there exist pros and cons of openness and that previous research does not suggest the existence of an unequivocal relationship between self-disclosure and satisfaction in human relationships (Gilbert, 1976). Schuman and his colleagues (1986) suggest that the quality of the self-disclosure is an important variable that has been overlooked. They found that when there was high regard for the partner and this was part of the self-disclosure, then the more disclosure the better. Where low regard of the partner is what is being disclosed, then greater openness seems to create less marital satisfaction.

The real question is how to disclose rather than whether to disclose. What is said (the content), how positive or

---

In addition to the three foundation blocks of good communication, and the communication channel, communication requires that five additional communication skills be mastered (Gordon, 1970):

1. Identifying ownership of a problem
2. Self-assertion by the owner of the problem
3. Empathic listening by the other partner
4. Negotiating
5. Problem solving

We will first discuss the three foundation blocks to good communication.

Commitment

Simply stated, commitment means making a pledge or binding oneself to the idea of working to build and maintain the relationship as well as to the partner as

negative it is, and the levels on which it is said (superficial to deeply meaningful, intellectual to emotional) all have to be taken into account. For example, M. J. Bienvenu (1970) has found a number of elements that differentiate between good and poor communication for couples. These elements include the handling of anger and of differences, tone of voice, understanding, good listening habits, and self-disclosure. The elements that contribute to poor communication are nagging, conversational discourtesies, and uncommunicativeness.

Certainly both partners must share a willingness to communicate. But equally important is that they learn how to communicate successfully and that they remain aware of each other's weak and sensitive points. For example, people who are insecure, and feel inferior and worthless, tend to be self-deprecating. They also tend to be fearful of open communication and usually react with hostility to what they perceive to be unfair criticisms. On the other hand, people with a high level of self-esteem tend to be comfortable with open communication and are willing to disclose their own feelings and to accept their partner's feelings.

So, how one discloses thoughts and feelings, especially negative ones, strongly influences how the communication will be accepted. Those who believe it is important to keep everything out in the open, to express themselves always to the fullest, must also concern themselves with how this is done and the feelings of their partner or they may find such openness backfiring and actually destroying communication rather than enhancing it.

There is a fine line between inviting disclosure or encouraging openness in one's partner and invading his or her privacy. Respect of each other's privacy is an important element of a successful relationship. Each couple has to work out just what the balance will be in their relationship between openness and privacy. To go beyond this line unilaterally will usually be offensive to one's partner. Rather than becoming more open, the offended partner may withdraw, becoming cool and distant, or attack, becoming sarcastic and resistant to ideas (Strong, 1983, p. 240). In this case openness reduces rather than enhances the chances for successful problem solving.

Generally, however, the more openness a couple can tolerate and agree upon between themselves, the better their chance of success.

a person. Couples often fail to seek marriage counseling until so much pain and suffering has occurred that the commitment of one or both marital partners has ceased. At that point there is little hope of resolution. Often one partner is still committed enough to want counseling, while the other has covertly given up hope and commitment and resists counseling for fear of being drawn back into a painful trap. Sometimes an uncommitted partner will seek therapy only in the hope that a dependent spouse will become strong enough to survive without the marriage. This situation leads to an added complexity if the dependent partner, sensing abandonment, avoids getting stronger in the hope that the noncommitted partner will stay in the marriage. As we saw in Chapter 1, overt commitment of both partners is essential to building and maintaining a strong marriage.

Many uncommitted partners allow the other spouse to plan activities, anticipate problems, make necessary adjustments, and so on. Sometimes this kind of relationship works. More often than not, the partner with the greater commitment feels resentment. Paradoxically, the one who cares the least controls the relationship. This is termed the principle of "least interest."

> *Alice is more committed to their marriage than Roger. For their summer vacation she wants to go to San Francisco, whereas he wants to go backpacking. Because he is not as committed to the relationship, it is easy for him to say, "Go to San Francisco if you want, but I'm going backpacking and you can come along if you like." Alice can plead with Roger to consider her desire but, more likely, she will resign herself to going backpacking.*

Although commitment is a precondition to effective communication, each partner's commitment to the relationship can be increased through use of the five communication skills, to be discussed later.

Growth Orientation

Individuals change over time. The needs of a forty-year-old person are somewhat different from the needs of a twenty-year-old (see Chapter 14). Marriage must also change if individual needs are to be continually met within the marriage framework. Yet change is often threatening. It upsets comfortable routine and is therefore often resisted. Such resistance will be futile since time does not stand still, so it is wise to accept and plan for change. An individual oriented to growth is someone who incorporates the inevitability of change into his or her lifestyle. This implies not only accepting change but also creating intentional and orderly change in a chosen direction.

> *Going to a large social gathering was something Helen anticipated with pleasure but that her husband Art dreaded. However, they were both oriented to growth and Art wanted to be more comfortable in social situations. So they decided to work actively on helping Art change his dread to an enjoyment of social interaction. At Art's suggestion Helen began to invite one or two couples over to their house, because Art felt more comfortable at home. He soon began to enjoy these small get-togethers, which Helen then gradually expanded. Although Art is still not perfectly at ease away from home in large groups, he is much more comfortable than before and accompanies Helen most of the time.*

Had Helen and Art not been growth-oriented, they might have grown apart or become resentful of one another. Helen might have chastised Art for his social inabilities and gone out without him, leaving him home to brood and resent her. On the other hand, Art might have been dictatorial and forbidden Helen to go to large social gatherings, which would probably have made her feel entrapped and rebellious. Because neither was afraid of change and each thought that change in Art would be beneficial, they set out deliberately to encourage this process. Notice that both were committed to the change. If only one partner desires change, particularly in the other partner, and the other disagrees, conflict and diminished communication can result. Successful communication requires noncoercion and a positive regard for each other.

Noncoercive Atmosphere

The goals of marriage will usually be lost if either partner is subjugated by the other. Free and open communication cannot exist in a one-sided totalitarian relationship. When any two people share a common goal, the issues of responsibility and authority arise. The situation in marriage is not unlike that in government. A marriage can be laissez-faire, if both partners have freedom of choice and action; democratic, if responsibility is shared and authority is delegated by equitable agreement; or autocratic, if authority is assigned to a single leader.

Most Americans say they desire to establish a democratic marriage. In reality this pattern is the most difficult to maintain, although it is ultimately the most satisfying.

When power is invested in an authority, a coercive relationship usually results. At least one partner and often both feel a loss of freedom because there are ways the subjugated person can manipulate the authority and vice versa. Free and open communication usually cannot coexist with coercion.

Mike and Daphne have been married six months. She pleads with him to give up his weekly poker game because she is afraid to be alone. He feels unfairly restricted and calls her a child. She in turn calls him an immature "jock" who can't give up the boys. One thing leads to another, and he walks out of the room and slams the door. She tearfully runs to the bedroom and locks herself in, leaving him to nurse his guilt. Although he apologizes profusely, she won't come out. So Mike stays home, having had his physical coercion (walking out and slamming the door) overpowered by her emotional coercion. He is resentful, and she is resentful and frightened. The intimacy that they experienced in their courtship is being dissolved by the acid of resentment created by coercive acts committed by both of them.

It is clear that successful communication will not survive long in such an environment. Sharing responsibilities, giving control voluntarily, and feeling relatively free in a relationship greatly facilitate communication.

Instead of the foregoing sequence, Mike and Daphne might have worked out a compromise that would have satisfied both of them. For example, knowing how much Mike enjoys his weekly poker session, Daphne might have supported him in this desire, in the hope of leading him to respond to her fear of being alone. He might reduce the number of times he plays poker; she might suggest holding the games at their house or plan to visit her parents or a friend that evening. If each saw the other as noncoercive and supportive, compromise solutions would then be far easier to work out.

Communication Skills

When all is going well with a couple, they usually don't think about communication. Yet this is the best time to build communication skills, as disruptive forces are minimal. If problems arise later, the skills will be there. It is apparently irreconcilable conflicts that destroy relationships. In most cases conflicts become irreconcilable because the partners have failed to develop communication skills.

Identifying Problem Ownership

Clarifying responsibility or problem ownership is an important first step in communication. This is not always easy. A problem can belong to either partner, or it can be jointly shared. The key question is, "Who feels tangibly affected?" That is, to own or share ownership of a problem, we must know and openly admit that we are personally disturbed by it. For example, let's look at the following situation:

> *Jane thinks that her husband Ray is losing friends because he drinks heavily and becomes belligerent. But he isn't concerned about his behavior. He thinks people exaggerate his drinking; so he refuses ownership of the problem. Because he doesn't have a problem, no change on his part is necessary.*

In addition to accepting ownership of a problem, one must be tangibly affected by it. In the preceding situation if Ray's behavior does not interfere with Jane's friendships, it does not affect her, and she does not own or share ownership of the problem. The fact that she might be concerned for him does not make it her problem. However, if Jane is tangibly affected by Ray's behavior, she then shares ownership of the problem. For example, if their friends stop calling, her needs are being tangibly affected. If she communicates this to Ray and he refuses to admit to it, as paradoxical as it may seem, only Jane owns the problem. If, however, Ray acknowledges that his behavior is affecting Jane, then the problem is jointly owned.

Assuming ownership of a problem is extremely important, yet we often shun responsibility. Some people think that if they don't pay attention to problems, the problems will disappear. However, the reverse is generally true. In the long run unattended problems usually become worse. Denial effectively cuts off communication and prevents change.

Modern American society has, unfortunately, too often encouraged individuals to "cop out" of problems by supplying many scapegoats on which responsibility can be placed:

"My parents made me this way because they rejected me as a child."

"My father beat my mother when he drank, so I can't relate to men because of my deep hostility at his behavior."

"The establishment controls everything, so why bother to change?"

"American society is racist, I am black (or Jewish or Hispanic) and therefore all my problems are caused by society."

The list could go on and on, but these examples give an idea of what must be avoided if we are to solve personal problems. For instance, it may be true that you have problems because your parents rejected you, but they are still your problems. Rejecting parents are not going to suddenly become loving parents in order to solve your problems. Obviously your parents have problems of their own, but you can't make them solve their problems; you can only work to solve your own. The first step toward solution is assuming responsibility for a problem if it is yours.

We must add an important caution to the discussion of problem ownership. Forcing problem ownership on your partner can also be "blaming," which is highly destructive. Some people use this aspect of good communication in a negative manner, that is, to show the other person that he or she is wrong and to blame for the trouble because "it is your problem." We can make the same kind of comment about the next skill we will discuss, self-assertion. One partner can, in essence, attack the other under the guise of being self-assertive, thus perverting a positive communication skill into a disguise for harmful communication.

If the problem is mine, then I will use skill 2, *self-assertion*. If my partner owns the problem, then I will try to use skill 3, *empathic listening*. If we both own the problem, we will alternate these two communication skills.

Self-Assertion

Self-assertion is the process of recognizing and expressing one's feelings, opinions, and attitudes while at the same time being aware of the feelings and needs of others.

Some people are nonassertive. They fail to make their feelings and thoughts known to others. This makes communication almost impossible.

> *Mary sees Jim as becoming less affectionate. He doesn't seem to hug her and touch her as much as he used to. Mary always liked the close physical contact and misses it. But it is hard for her to talk about her physical desires with anyone, much less a man, and so she says nothing. Her anxiety and discomfort grow. She believes that if Jim really loved her, he would recognize how miserable she feels and give her more physical contact. She becomes increasingly hostile to him until one day he asks, "What's the matter?" She replies, "You ought to know, it's your fault."*

Jim is completely in the dark. Mary's nonassertive behavior has precluded successful communication and thus has foreclosed solving the problem.

Some of the personal reasons for nonassertive behavior are fear, feelings of inferiority, lack of confidence, shyness, and embarrassment. Society and its traditional role expectations may also influence nonassertive behavior. For example, in Mary's case she may have incorporated the traditional American feminine role of being passive and nonassertive, of expecting the male to solve her problems. Whatever the reasons, if we can't express our needs, we cannot expect others magically to recognize and fill them for us.

In contrast to nonassertive individuals, aggressive individuals completely by-pass tact and recognition of others' needs in expressing their feelings. They demand attention, support, and whatever they want at the moment, often over-riding the rights and feelings of others. In fact, they often seem unaware that other people have rights and feelings, and they can hurt other people without being aware of what they are doing. However, not all aggression is destructive. Used in a constructive manner, aggression offers emotional release, lets a partner know how intensely the other partner is feeling, and helps both partners learn how to cope with all kinds of aggressive and emotional behavior.

Self-assertive people, on the other hand, feel free to express themselves but at the same time are aware of the feelings and needs of others. Self-assertive people's communications are also about themselves rather than critical of other persons. For example, contrast the statement, "This kind of behavior is hard for me to handle and makes me angry even though I don't want to be" with "You make me mad." The second statement is almost useless to successful commu-nication. It judges and places blame on the other person. It will usually only provoke a defensive comment on the part of the person to whom it is said.

It may seem surprising that special help with self-assertion should be required in building a relationship. Many people believe that what is needed is less self-assertion. They see self-seeking assertions and selfishness as the basis of marital difficulty. Remember, though, that our definition of self-assertion includes aware-ness of others' feelings and needs. We certainly need to be less destructively aggressive in our relations, but we must not confuse that with being nonassertive.

It is important to be aware that recognition and expression of needs do not necessarily lead to their fulfillment. For example, I may recognize and express my desire to smoke, which is self-assertive. If, however, other people in the room find cigarette smoke unpleasant and tell me so, they are also being assertive. This conflict can be successfully resolved in a couple of ways. I may go outside to smoke, thus satisfying my needs without interfering with the needs of other people. Or I can recognize that smoking would be more unpleasant to them than pleasant to me and forgo smoking in their presence. In either case I have been assertive: I have recognized and expressed my need, though I may not have fulfilled my desire. Self-assertion does not mean getting one's way all the time.

Note that the definition of self-assertion includes recognizing needs and inner feelings. This is not always easy, as the following example shows:

Alice has to conduct a PTA meeting tomorrow morning, and she is both anxious and resentful about it. She has put off planning the meeting until there is almost no time left. Harry comes home and says, "How about going to the movies tonight?" Alice blows up and says irritatedly, "I still have dinner to cook and dishes to do—as the old saying goes, 'Man works from sun to sun, but woman's work is never done.' " Harry re-sponds, "If women have it so tough, why do men get all the ulcers and heart attacks?"

Inset 6-2

"Psyching-Out" the American Male

The traditional sex roles of a strong, silent male and a submissive, emotional female lead to stereotyped behavior and to communication difficulties. Carol Pierce and Janice Sanfaco have studied and outlined some of this traditional conditioning; they point to the following results (1977, pp. 97–98):

■ Women are encouraged from childhood to feel it is better to have a man's approval than a woman's approval.
■ Women are set in competition with other women for male approval.
■ Women experience lines of power as going from women to men.
■ Women are taught to be reactive rather than proactive.
■ Women learn to live for and through others and to define themselves in terms of others.
■ Women are expected to be selfless helpers and not to have needs for a lot of space, both territorial and psychological.

On the other hand, men are taught: to be self-sufficient, intact, a closed system; they are not expected to acknowledge their dependence needs.

. . . Eventually men begin to deny to themselves that they even have such needs. They lose touch with their feelings, become task-oriented, compartmentalized, mechanical, totally rational and therefore totally dependent on women to fill their needs for nurturing and caring of their own personal relationships and interaction with others (women playing the role of facilitator between father and child, adult son and father, man and friends). Men are now ripe for women's "psyching-out."

For women this necessitates the development of mental processes and styles characterized by continual forethought as to how to "use" another person. Hence, women learn to be schemers. Women often learn to gear their thoughts to what will make a man feel comfortable; the best way to make a man appear pleasing and smart to others; what problems a man needs to talk about; and how to make a man feel fascinating and powerful.

The cost to women in this process is that they learn to deny their own wants and needs and, hence, do not gain a sense of self-esteem, integrity as an individual, and autonomy. They have little feeling of being powerful enough to shape their environment. Women frequently "psych-out" to get male approval, to compete with other women, to manipulate, because these are the modes familiar to them. Whereas, in those interactions characterized by the sharing of straight, factual knowledge, giving orders or advice, and the initiating of sexual encounters, one sees the preponderant type of communication behavior of men in a male-dominated world. Many men are now experiencing a revolution to learn those behaviors and expressions necessary to grow emotionally and to relate in a more personal way.

"Psyching-out" then is a mode of behavior where a person constantly takes on the responsibility of figuring out what is most helpful and pleasing to another person, hoping the result will be that in return he/she will be liked, appreciated, and will receive attention. The problem is that because of role-stereotyping, the same kind of attention is seldom initiated or returned to women, and the giver is frequently neither noticed nor appreciated.

And so the argument rages on without chance of solution because Alice has not recognized the real source of her irritation; namely, her anxiety about the PTA meeting. But, why doesn't she?

Perhaps she doesn't want to admit to herself that she is afraid of conducting the meeting. She avoids thinking about the meeting and thereby avoids the fear that arises when she does. Or maybe she knows she is afraid but doesn't want Harry to see this weakness, so she covers it by starting an irrelevant argument.

Self-assertion requires self-knowledge. That is, successful communication depends in large part on knowing oneself. In any relationship there will be known and unknown dimensions. One way of diagramming and discovering these dimensions is called the Johari window. This is shown in Figure 6-2.

Figure 6-2   The Johari window.

Things about myself that I . . .

		do know	don't know
Things about myself that the other . . .	does know	**common knowledge**	**my blind spots** (such as an irritating mannerism I'm unaware of)
	does not know	**my secrets** (things I've never shared about myself)	**my unknown self** (things neither you nor I know about myself)

Let's see how to use the Johari window. As you begin a new relationship with another person, one where you both are committed to helping each other grow, you can both draw Johari windows. The easiest window to fill in is that of common knowledge. At the beginning of the relationship, common knowledge will probably only include such things as height, hair color, weight, food preferences. As the relationship continues, you will be able to fill in some of the other's blind spots, perhaps such things as insensitivity, selfishness, nervous laughter, bad breath, snoring. Then, as you continue to develop trust in each other, you can begin to fill in your secrets, perhaps feelings of inferiority, fears of homosexuality, being afraid to be alone at night. By now you may be discovering aspects of each other's unknown self; these may be hidden potentials, talents, or weaknesses that are uncovered by the relationship itself, by the interaction between the two of you and your friends. As you get to know each other better, the blind spots and secret areas will become smaller as more information is moved into the common knowledge window.

Of course you don't have to have a new relationship to use the Johari window: It can also illuminate behavior and knowledge in ongoing relationships. In fact, the process of exploring new dimensions of the self and the other person is exciting and never ending. Unfortunately many couples share little common knowledge because each has little self-knowledge. People who are afraid to learn about themselves usually block communication that might lead to self-knowledge. Aversive reactions, as we saw earlier, are excellent ways to stifle communication. For example, consider the following interaction:

> *Jim thinks his wife Jane looks unusually good one evening and says, "I really feel proud when men look at you admiringly."*
>
> *Jane replies angrily, "When you say that, I feel like a showpiece in the marketplace."*
>
> *"Why don't you get off that feminist trip?" he retorts.*

Her aversive reply to his statement will probably make him more reluctant to express his feelings the next time. In essence her aversive response punished him for expressing his feelings. But why did she respond aversively? Of course she may simply have been in a bad mood. Or perhaps she has always felt negative about her appearance and thus needs to deny Jim's statement because it is inconsistent with her self-image. Her appearance might be a blind spot in her Johari window. Regardless of how objectively attractive Jane may be, if her view of herself is negative, that is what she will believe. However, if we really think about Jim's statement Jane's reaction becomes more understandable. Her objection may be to his implied feelings of ownership, as if she were a shiny new sports car, the envy of all his friends.

So we can define the communication skill of self-assertion as learning to express oneself without making the other person defensive. Neither Jim nor Jane is particularly good at this aspect of self-assertion.

Empathic Listening

Of all the skills we have been discussing, none is probably more underrated and overlooked than that of being a good listener. We are all very ready to give our opinions but not so ready to listen to others' opinions. Often we are so preoccupied with our own thoughts or replies that we simply don't hear what is being said. To be a good listener is an art in itself and much appreciated by most people. To be a good listener may be one of the most therapeutic things we can do for our intimate relationships. The research on strong and healthy families (Chapter 1) finds that family members feel as if they are listened to by other family members. They feel understood because family members not only listen but also recognize nonverbal messages. Good listening implies a real empathy for the speaker.

Real listening keeps the focus on the person who is talking. By focusing on the speaker, the listener actively tries to reduce any personal filters that distort the speaker's messages. Usually we as listeners are actively adding to, subtracting from, and in other ways changing the speaker's message. For example, someone says, "I wrapped my car around a tree coming home from a party last night." You might be thinking, "Well, you probably were drinking (inference) and one should not drive when drinking (value judgment)." Although you have no evidence of drinking, you have immediately put your own meaning on the statement. If the speaker recognizes your negative implications, he or she might react with anger or cease talking.

Empathic listening, on the other hand, is nonjudgmental and accepting. To the degree that we are secure, we can listen to others without filtering their message. Because really listening to and understanding another means that we allow our own self to be open to new self-knowledge and change, it can be frightening to the insecure.

George is very unsure of Gloria's love for him and fears she may one day leave him. At dinner she comments, "I really like tall men with beards." George feels his clean-shaven chin and begins to feel insecure. He doesn't hear much of the ensuing conversation because he is busy trying to decide whether she would like him to grow a beard or if she has a crush on another man. He has completely filtered out the part about tall men because he is tall and therefore not threatened by that.

George has put his own inferences on Gloria's comment and becomes increasingly upset as he ponders, not what she actually said, but what he thinks she meant by what she said.

It is interesting to note that it is easier to listen empathically to a stranger than to someone close. Married people often state that some friend or acquaintance understands them better than their spouses. This may well be true because emotions often get in the way of hearing. For example, when George's coworker says she likes tall men with beards, George doesn't even think about it, he simply says, "That's nice." Also, when a couple has spent years together, each partner often assumes that "of course we understand one another," and there is no reason to listen.

When we listen empathically the speaker feels that the listener hears and cares. In essence the speaker feels nonthreatened, noncoerced, and free to speak—some of our preconditions for successful communication.

Empathic listening has several components. Obviously the listener must feel capable of paying close attention to the speaker. If we are consumed by our own thoughts and problems, we cannot listen to another. But when we know that we cannot listen well, we should point that out (self-assertion) and perhaps arrange to have the discussion at another time. For instance, family members often bring up problems at the end of the day when everyone is tired and hungry or at other inopportune times and then become upset because no one is willing to listen. We all need time, a quiet environment, and a peaceful mind to be good empathic listeners.

We may also need practice to become good listeners. As children we receive plenty of training to enhance our verbal skills, but we seldom receive training for our listening skills. Just as our verbal skills can be improved through training, so can our listening skills (Garland, 1981; Strong, 1983).

Part of our attention needs to be directed to the *nonverbal communications* of the speaker known as *body language*. Emotions are reflected throughout the body. Although bodily communication generally is more idiosyncratic than verbal communication, it is also often more descriptive of the person's feelings. For example, Mary habitually uses her hands in an erasing motion to wipe away unpleasant thoughts. Ralph pulls at his ear and rubs the back of his neck when being criticized. The nonverbal message usually represents the emotional message and therefore may yield a more accurate picture of how a person is feeling than verbal communications. Strong (1983, p. 65) suggests that we process the emotional messages first since we cannot reach agreement on content unless we know each other's feelings about the content. It takes time to learn what a person's nonverbal communication patterns are, but such patterns are perceived by the empathic listener.

Feedback is another key component of empathic listening. The listener must periodically check perceptions with the speaker. This is best done by rephrasing the speaker's words. This allows the speaker to have reassurance that she or he is being listened to and heard accurately, to have the opportunity to correct the listener's perceptions, and to hear his/her ideas from the listener's perspective. Some examples of feedback are:

Speaker: I'm not getting out of bed today.

Listener: Is there a problem?

Speaker: You're always working.

Listener: I know. Is it interrupting something we need to do?

Speaker: Why don't we get out of this town?

Listener: I don't understand why. I guess you don't like it here.

Speaker: Nobody does any work around here but me.

Listener: It sounds like you feel tired of all the work you have to do.

Note that empathic listening involves an effort on the listener's part to pick up feelings as well as content. Feeding back feelings is, however, more difficult than feeding back content.

The desire we have to give advice is one of the major deterrents to empathic listening. Advice always has a negative side. It says to your partner, "You don't know what to do," which could be interpreted as, "Boy, are you stupid." There is no better way to turn off the speaker's listening skills than to make him or her defensive. It is better to offer alternatives as this increases the speaker's number of options but also leaves the speaker with the responsibility of making the decision while, simultaneously, respecting the speaker's intelligence (Strong, 1983, p. 137).

Remember, though, that we are discussing enhancing good problem-solving communication. Much communication is for play and fun, to establish contact, or to impart information. To use problem-solving skills in inappropriate situations can cause problems. For example, if someone asks you to "Please pass the butter," it would not be appropriate to reply, "Oh, you feel like having some butter on your bread." Such a remark will probably invoke the muttered comment, "There you go using that dumb psychology again." Knowing how to listen is an invaluable skill, but it can be misused. Knowing when to listen is just as important.

Inset 6-3

Exercises for Sending and Receiving Feeling Messages

People often intermix sending and receiving messages. For example, the speaker may be overconcerned with the effect the message might have on the listener and may thus modify and change the message so that it is not quite what was originally meant. In other words, the sender fails to send a true message because of fear about how it will be received. And the listener may put a personal interpretation on the message or may be thinking about how to reply and thus not concentrate on getting the entire message.

When feelings are involved, as in conflicts between family members, messages are even more likely to get changed. Practice in sending—self-assertion—and receiving—empathic listening—will help keep the two separate and enhance clear, good communication.

The following exercise should give you and your family and/or friends the opportunity to improve both your ability to assert yourself clearly and your ability to listen effectively. Begin by choosing a speaker and a listener. The speaker should send a brief, personally relevant communication in which he/she recognizes and owns some feeling. The listener then repeats, to the best of his or her ability, the speaker's statement. The others listen attentively and, after the listener has responded, share with the speaker any other feelings they think were involved in the communication but which the speaker did not express. When the message is clearly understood by both speaker and listener, they should change places. All members of the group should have a chance to practice as senders and receivers. The exercise serves two purposes:

1. The speaker does not receive a critical reaction and therefore does not have to defend the statement. This frees the speaker to deal more honestly with feelings and also to hear the message she or he has communicated.

2. The listener gets practice in effective listening without having to react, interpret, or evaluate. This frees the listener from feeling he or she has to resolve or somehow deal responsibly with the feelings the speaker has expressed, so the listener can concentrate on what is actually being said.

In the practice situation the burden of reaction is lifted from the listener. Thereby he or she may concentrate on receiving the message accurately and clearly. The listener will feel a strong connection with the speaker. On page 174 are examples of poor sending and receiving as well as examples of clear communication where listening and speaking are well separated.

Negotiating

If a problem is jointly owned, the situation calls for negotiation. In this case the partners alternate between self-assertion and empathic listening. Usually the most distressed partner starts with self-assertion. But because the problem is jointly owned, the listener's feelings are also involved, so it is imperative to switch roles relatively often to be sure that each person's communications are understood by the other. Set a time period, say, five to ten minutes, for each partner to speak. Remember that listening will take extra effort to avoid the temptation of thinking about your side of the problem while the other is speaking, which, of course, interferes with empathic listening.

When roles are exchanged, the partner who was listening should first restate the assertive partner's position (feedback) so that any necessary corrections can be made before going on to his or her own assertions. The very fact of knowing that the speaker's position must be restated to his or her satisfaction before your own position can be presented works wonders to improve listening ability.

This simple procedure of reversing roles and restating the other's position before presenting your own is also amazingly effective in defusing potential

---

Inset 6-4

Fighting Fairly in Love and Marriage

Many couples state that their basic problem is that they fight all the time. Yet fighting is a normal part of any intimate relationship. The problem is not whether one fights, but how one fights. Fighting is simply a form of communication and all of our principles apply. George Bach is a therapist who gives fight training to help increase intimacy. The following dialogue is an example of pointless fighting. It is followed by the same fight done in a constructive manner. Within the parentheses are Bach and Wyden's analysis of the interactions.

Ralph: I don't like the way the kids handle money.
Betsy: What's the matter with it? They're good kids.
Ralph: Yes, but they haven't learned the value of money.
Betsy: They're just kids. Why not let them have their fun? They'll learn soon enough.
Ralph: No, I think you're spoiling them.
Betsy: How in the world am I doing that?
Ralph: By giving them the idea that money grows on trees.
Betsy: Well, why don't you set a better example? You might start by spending less on your pipe collection.
Ralph: What's that got to do with it?
Betsy: Plenty. When the kids see you waste money on nonessentials, they feel they have the same rights.
Ralph: I shop for my pipes. They're very carefully selected.
Betsy: Maybe, but whenever I send you to the market, you always spend more than I would. You're always

dragging in stuff we don't really need.
Ralph: OK, OK. I know you're a better shopper at the market, but that's your job, you know, not mine.
Betsy: Well, then, don't blame me for the kids.

After several training sessions, we asked the Snyders to refight the same fight before one of our training groups. Here is how it went the second time around:

Ralph (*starting with a specific objective, not a general observation*): I want you to stop slipping the kids extra money beyond the allowances I give them.
Betsy (*showing Ralph why his idea may be difficult to accomplish*): But you're not around. You don't know their needs.
Ralph (*spelling out his objective further*): I want to know their needs. I want them to come to me with their money needs.
Betsy (*justifying her past practices*): Well, you know what goes on. I tell you everything. You know where the money goes.
Ralph (*specifying the real issue that this fight is all about*): That's fine, but it's not the point. I believe the children should learn more about responsibility—having to justify getting the money from me and spending it wisely.
Betsy (*making sure he's serious*): You really want to supervise all this piffle?
Ralph (*reconfirming the stakes as he sees them*): Don't you see the im-

portance of teaching them early responsibility for money matters?
Betsy (*specifying the reasons for her opposition*): Frankly, no. They are good kids and they're having a good time. I like to give them a little extra now and then. I enjoy it when they have fun. They'll learn responsibility soon enough.
Ralph (*sizing up the results of the fight thus far and rechecking his wife for more feedback*): I can see we really differ on this issue. Do you understand my position?
Betsy (*reconfirming her understanding of Ralph's real objective*): Yes, you want us to teach the kids responsibility.
Ralph (*seeking a meeting ground, at least in principle*): Yes, don't you?
Betsy (*agreeing to his principle but dissenting from his method*): Yes, but your method would deprive me of something I enjoy doing, and I don't believe I am overdoing it. You know I'm careful with my money.
Ralph (*hardening his stand*): Yes, you're a careful shopper and all that—I have no complaints about that—but I must ask you to stop slipping the kids extra money. That's the only way to control careless spending.
Betsy (*realizing that she'll probably have to give some ground*): I see you really are concerned with this specific issue.
Ralph (*elaborating on the reasons for his firm stand*): I love the children as much as you do, and I don't want to see them develop into careless adults.
Betsy (*offering a proposal for a compromise*): I don't think they will, but

since this seems to mean so much to you, let me suggest something. Why don't you tell me how much you think would be reasonable to give them "extra" and for what occasions, and I'll stick to it.

Ralph *(checking out that Betsy isn't likely to compromise further):* You still want to keep giving them extra money?

Betsy *(reconfirming her stand):* Yes, I do. I enjoy it, as I told you.

Ralph *(accepting Betsy's compromise, proposing details on how to make it work, and offering another compromise as a conciliatory gesture):* Well, let's sit down and bud-get how much money they should get from us altogether, for everything every week, how much for extras, and so on. It's not so terribly important to me who gives them the money, as how much and what for.

Betsy *(confirming Ralph's acceptance and offering a further implementing proposal showing that she too is now trying to accomplish his objective):* OK. Let's figure it out; then every weekend you can sit down with the kids and me and see that we didn't go over the limit.

Ralph *(confirming that he understands and approves her latest idea):* Yes, I could vary the regular pocket money, depending on how much you've slipped them.

Betsy *(offering another suggestion to make sure their new plan will work and maybe show Ralph that she was right about the kids' sense of responsibility after all):* Certainly, you can also ask them how much they've spent and what for. Then you would find out all about their needs and learn how responsible they can be.

Ralph *(nails down the deal and specifies the date it goes into effect):* OK. Let's try it this Saturday.

Source: Bach & Wyden, 1968, pp. 65–68.

emotional outbursts. Frustration usually builds up because partners do not listen to one another and therefore often feel misunderstood. But with this process even if your partner strongly disagrees with your position, at least you both have the satisfaction of knowing your position will be heard and understood by the other.

Problem Solving

When ownership of the problem has been established, clarification of the problem started, and some of the emotion surrounding the problem discharged, you are ready to solve the problem. Of course, by now the problem will have been greatly diminished and may even have disappeared. However, if you and your partner still think you have a problem, you can now apply the scientific method to solving it. There are seven steps to scientific problem solving:

1. Recognizing and defining the problem
2. Setting up conditions supportive to problem solving
3. Brainstorming for possible alternatives (establishing hypotheses)
4. Selecting the best solution
5. Implementing the solution
6. Evaluating the solution
7. Modifying the solution if necessary

The first two steps have already been accomplished if you have used the skills discussed. Step 3, *brainstorming*, helps to broaden the range of possible solutions. Brainstorming is producing as many ideas as possible in a given time period. That is, if you select a half hour to brainstorm the problem, you both call out any ideas you have as fast as possible without pausing to evaluate. That is, all ideas

---

Inset 6-5

Additional Suggestions for Constructive Conflict

1. Be specific when you introduce a gripe.

2. Don't just complain, no matter how specifically; ask for a reasonable change that will relieve the gripe.

3. Confine yourself to one issue at a time. Otherwise, without professional guidance, you may skip back and forth, evading the hard ones.

4. Always consider compromise. Remember, your partner's view of reality may be just as valid as yours, even though you may differ. There are not many totally objective realities.

5. Do not allow counterdemands to enter the picture until the original demands are clearly understood, and there has been a clear-cut response to them.

6. Never assume that you know what your partner is thinking until you have checked out the assumption in plain language; never assume or predict how your partner will react, what he or she will accept or reject.

7. Never put labels on a partner. Don't call your partner a coward, a neurotic, or a child. If you really believed your partner was incompetent or suffered from some basic flaw, you probably would not be with him or her. Do not make sweeping labeling judgments about your partner's feelings, especially about whether or not they are real or important.

8. Don't use sarcasm. Sarcasm is dirty fighting.

9. Forget the past and stay with the here-and-now. What either of you did last year, last month, or this morning is not as important as what you are doing and feeling now. And the changes you ask cannot possibly be retroactive. Hurts, grievances, and irritations should be brought up at the very earliest moment; if they are not the partner has the right to suspect that they may have been saved carefully as weapons.

10. Meditate. Take time to consult your real thoughts and feelings before speaking. Your surface reactions may mask something deeper and more important. Don't be afraid to close your eyes and think.

11. Remember that there is never a single winner in an honest intimate fight. Both either win more intimacy or lose it.

Source: Adapted from George R. Bach and Ronald M. Deutsch, 1974, *Pairing.* Copyright, David McKay, Inc. Reprinted by permission of the publisher.

---

are put out regardless of whether they are ridiculous or possible. All too often negative judgments stifle creative thinking, so it is important to suspend any evaluating until both of you have run out of ideas or reached the end of the time period. Just jot down ideas as they occur, don't think about them.

Once you have run out of ideas, or time, you can begin to select the best solution. Be sure to consider all ideas. Then use the skills of self-assertion and of empathic listening to evaluate the likely ideas. It is good to decide on an amount of time to spend defending and judging each idea.

Once you agree on the best idea, you must implement it. If the problem has been a serious one, it is a good idea to schedule discussions of how the solution is working. If the solution works well, you will not need to use Step 7. If, however, you are still experiencing difficulties, you may have to modify the solution in light of your evaluation sessions. Or you may have to go back to the possible alternatives generated during the brainstorming session and select another solution to test.

Every intimate relationship will have periods of conflict. Research suggests that conflicts are equally present in happy and unhappy marriages (Vines, 1979). The difference is that in successful marriages the partners have learned how to handle their conflicts and use them to improve their relationship. Murray Straus (1979)

Communication and Family Conflict

suggests that if conflict is suppressed, it can cause stagnation and failure to adapt to changed circumstances and can erode the couple's relationship because of an accumulation of hostility.

Conflict occurs when two or more family members believe that what they desire is incompatible with what other (one or more) family members want (Galvin & Brommel, 1982). Realistic conflicts result from frustration of specific needs, whereas nonrealistic conflicts are characterized by the need for tension release by at least one of the partners. By exploring the process of conflict and how it can be used constructively, we can better manage it. Successful management of conflict solves problems and helps a good relationship evolve into an even better one. Recognition of and successful coping with nonrealistic conflict helps reduce tensions and change nonrealistic conflict into realistic conflict, which is usually easier to cope with.

Conflict becomes damaging to a relationship when it is covert or hidden. If we can't confront and work with real conflict, it is nearly impossible to resolve the problem. Generally, hidden conflict relies on one of the following communication strategies: denial, disqualification, displacement, disengagement, and pseudo-mutuality (Galvin & Brommel, 1982).

Using denial, one partner simply says, "No, I'm not upset. There is no problem," when in fact he or she is upset and there is a problem. Often, however, the person's body language contradicts the words.

In disqualification a person expresses anger and then discounts it. "I'm sorry I was angry, but I am not feeling well today." Of course, this could be true. It only becomes disqualification when the person intends to cover the emotion and deny that there is a real conflict.

In displacement emotional reactions are placed elsewhere than on the real conflict source. For example, John is really angry at his wife, but he yells at the children. Thus the source of the conflict is kept hidden.

Disengaged family members avoid conflict simply by avoiding one another. This keeps the conflict from surfacing. Unfortunately, the conflict remains below the surface and creates anger that can't be vented, which increases the tension in the relationship.

Pseudomutuality is the other side of the disengagement coin. It characterizes families whose members appear to be perfect and to be delighted with each other. In this style of anger no hint of discord is ever allowed to spoil the image of perfection. Only when one member develops ulcers or a nervous disorder or acts in a bizarre manner does the family reveal a crack in its armor of perfection. Anger remains so far below the surface that the family members lose all ability to deal with it directly. Pretense remains the only possibility (Galvin & Brommel, 1982).

We also need to note the relationship of sexual behavior to these covert strategies. For many couples sex becomes a weapon in guerrilla warfare. Demands for, or avoidance of, sexual activity may be the most effective way of expressing covert hostility.

Overt conflict can also be destructive to a relationship even though the chances of dealing with it are greater than with covert conflict. This chapter doesn't allow space enough to discuss the many destructive overt patterns of conflict. In general, however, attacking one's partner, either verbally or physically, is almost always counterproductive.

There is an old saying, "Sticks and stones may break my bones, but words can never hurt me." Unfortunately verbal abuse often does hurt. Emotional verbal attacks, such as "You idiot," "Liar," "I hate you," and other attacks on a person's self-respect and integrity do real damage if continued for an extended period. Most people can forgive an occasional verbal attack during an outburst of anger, but if the attacks come often or become the norm for handling conflict, the partner and the relationship can become damaged.

Whenever Jane becomes frustrated with her husband, she heaps verbal abuse on him: He has no drive; he is too dumb to get ahead in his job; he is a lousy lover; and so forth. The name calling greatly affects his self-esteem, and he slowly loses self-confidence. He begins to doubt himself, which in turn causes him to act in ways that are self-defeating. What began as name calling and negative labeling has become his reality over time.

Physical violence seldom solves a conflict; it tends to lead to more violence (Steinmetz & Straus, 1974). Generally, physical violence occurs in families lacking communication skills. One member may be increasingly frustrated in his or her relationship and unable to communicate with the partner or the children about the conflict. Finally, the frustration becomes so great that the family member loses control and strikes out physically. Anything that lowers one's inhibitions and/or frustration tolerance, such as alcohol, will also increase the possibility of physical violence.

Inset 6-6

Topics of Conflict over Time

Edward Bader and his colleagues (1981) gathered data about topics of conflict over a period of five years. They first interviewed sample couples just before marriage. They then reinterviewed them after six months of marriage, after one year, and again after five years. The table shows the ranking of conflict topics for the couples at each interview time.

Before marriage the man's job and time and attention were the two topics (tied for first) that aroused the most conflict. Six months after marriage, household tasks had become number one, with handling of money second, while time and attention had fallen to third place. At the end of one year of marriage, household tasks were still the number one topic of conflict. Time and attention was second, and handling money was third. At the end of five years, household tasks and time and attention were tied for first, while

sex had moved all the way from thirteenth to third. The table makes it clear that the basic job of living together (how we divide the household tasks,

how and how much time and attention we give one another, how we handle our money, and so forth) creates the most conflict for couples.

Percentage of Couples Where One or Both Partners Indicated Any Disagreement in Fourteen Specified Areas

Disagreement Areas	Premarriage (N63) %	Rank	Six Months (N63) %	Rank	One Year (N63) %	Rank	Five Years (N56) %	Rank
1. Husband's job	74	1	75	4	68	6	76	4
2. Wife's job	56	8	63	6	62	10	53	10
3. Household tasks	66	3	87	1	91	1	88	1
4. Handling money	62	6	79	2	76	3	72	6
5. Husband's relatives	49	11	52	10	67	7	72	6
6. Wife's relatives	64	5	56	9	71	4	72	6
7. Husband's friends	61	7	63	6	51	12	52	11
8. Wife's friends	54	10	50	12	46	13	42	12
9. Affection	56	8	65	5	67	7	76	4
10. Children	44	12	48	13	54	11	42	12
11. Religion	25	14	21	14	19	14	28	14
12. Social activities	66	3	51	11	71	4	65	9
13. Time and attention	74	1	76	3	86	2	88	1
14. Sex	41	13	62	8	64	9	78	3

A good review of the communication principles discussed in this chapter is provided by Galvin and Brommel (1982) and Strong (1983). They characterize successful conflict management as follows:

1. Communication exchange is sequential; each participant has equal time to express his or her view.
2. Feelings are brought out, not suppressed.
3. People listen to one another with empathy and without constant interruption.
4. The conflict remains focused on the issue and doesn't get sidetracked into other previously unresolved conflict.
5. Family members respect differences in the opinions, values, and wishes of one another.
6. Members believe that solutions are possible and that growth and development will take place.
7. Some semblance of rules has evolved from prior conflicts.
8. Little power or control is exercised by one or more family members over the actions of others.

Curran (1983, p. 62) suggests family control over television as another communication principle. We have mentioned the powerful role that television now plays in people's lives (Chapter 1). The television-dominated family will not have good communication skills. Interaction time is necessary to develop such skills, and television can be a major deterrent to family interaction.

Summary

Nowhere are communication skills more important than in the marriage relationship. Couples having marital trouble almost always report communication failure as a major problem. Communication failures occur because one or both partners choose not to communicate or lack the skills of communication.

Although communication problems are often the result of personal problems and inadequacies of the partners, society can also facilitate or hinder good communication. Society's support of stereotypical sex roles, especially that of the strong, silent male, restricts good communication.

When most people talk about failure in communication, what they mean is that communication has become so aversive that it causes discomfort. In other words, there is too much negative and hurtful communication rather than no communication. If the aversive communication continues too long, however, the couple may indeed stop communicating.

Three basic conditions must be met before good communication can be assured. First, there must be a commitment to communicate. Both parties must want to communicate with one another. Second, the partners must be oriented to growth and to improving the relationship. Each must be willing to accept the possibility of change. Third, neither partner must try to coerce the other with communications. Communication should not be so aversive and attacking as to cause a partner to be defensive or to withdraw.

When these basic conditions are met, problem-solving skills can be called into play. Basically, five skills are involved in successful communication. The ownership of the problem must be identified; each partner must be willing to speak up and state his or her position and feelings (self-assertion); each must be a good listener (empathic listening); each must be willing to negotiate; and each must be willing to use problem-solving methods if needed.

Fighting fairly and using problem-solving skills will enhance any relationship and keep it alive and growing. Failure to communicate clearly and fight fairly will usually cause disruption and the ultimate failure of intimate relationships.

Communication Failure and Family Violence

We include a Scene from Marriage on family violence in this chapter because physical violence is most apt to erupt in the family lacking communication skills. Such families cannot talk to one another, don't listen to one another, and simply lack enough communication skills to make themselves understood. Children are often physically violent because they haven't learned how to communicate. In a way, adults who cannot communicate remain like children and too often express themselves physically rather than verbally.

In earlier chapters the importance of the family as a source of love, caring, and emotional support has been emphasized. Yet it is also true that the possibility of violence and abuse within the poorly functioning family exists. The family is an emotional hothouse. While it is true that the finest of emotions, love, can be fully expressed in the strong, healthy family, it is also true that the emotions of hate and anger can lead to violence in the poorly functioning family.

Family violence is difficult to measure and document because most of it occurs in the privacy of the home away from public view. The late 1970s and 1980s might reasonably be described as the decade in which the social sciences "discovered" domestic violence (Bernard, 1985, p. 573). We saw many newspaper and magazine articles as well as television presentations on the battered wife and abused child. Studies report high percentages of violence between husbands and wives (one in six of a sample of 2143) American households (Straus et al., 1980), between courting couples (Makepeace, 1981; Bernard &

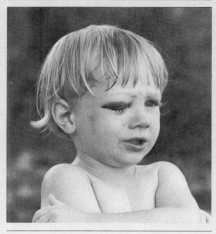

Bernard, 1983), and between parents and children (Berger, 1986, p. 242).

Violence between Spouses

The most life-threatening situation that a police officer can enter is a family dispute. Emotions run high and family members usually see their problems as a private matter and the police officer as an unwanted intruder. Homicide rates between husbands and wives are high with about equal numbers of wives killing husbands as husbands killing wives. Other physical violence usually involves the husband hurting his wife, although the reverse happens too.

In general physical violence flares between spouses who do not have good communication skills. Because of this, frustration and hostility build and finally something (a conflict, alcohol or drug use, etc.) triggers an emotional outburst resulting in violent behavior.

Most major cities now have battered women's shelters with programs available to intervene in violent family situations (Giles-Sims, 1985). However, for many women, entry into the criminal justice system is difficult and often unpredictable (Ford, 1983). Also, most battered women return to the abusive relationship even after eliciting justice system support or after staying in a shelter (Strube & Barbour, 1983, 1984).

It is interesting that family violence tends to follow a domino pattern. That is, those who experience courtship violence tend to experience spousal violence, those experiencing spousal violence tend to abuse their children, and abused children tend to abuse one another and become abusive adults.

Child Abuse

Mistreatment of children by parents hardly seems compatible with mom, apple pie, and Sunday family outings. Yet there are many parents who emotionally and physically abuse their children. In 1984 about 1.5 million cases of child abuse were reported to authorities—a tenfold increase since 1963—although 65 percent were found to be unsubstantiated (Johnson, 1985, B-11).

Increasing interest in child abuse has also revealed more sexual abuse and incest than heretofore uncovered. Although numbers are hard to verify, studies report that anywhere from 9 to 28 percent of female children are sexually abused with smaller percentages for male children (Finkelhor, 1984).

As child abuse became more recognized, the law moved to protect children from abuse. States began to make it legally mandatory to report suspected abuse. As an example of this legislation, the following are paraphrased excerpts from Section I, Section 1161.5, of the California Penal Code, effective January 1, 1975:

Any person who willfully causes or permits a child to suffer, or inflicts thereon unjustifiable physical pain or mental suffering, or willfully permits a child to be placed in a situation dangerous to its person or health, is punishable by imprisonment in the county jail for a period not exceeding one year, or in the state prison for not less than one year nor more than ten years.

Any person who, under circumstances other than those likely to produce great bodily harm or death, willfully causes or permits any child to suffer unjustifiably or permits the child to be injured, or places the child in a dangerous situation is guilty of a misdemeanor.

In any case in which a minor is brought to a physician, dentist [there follows a long list of persons, including teachers, social workers, and so forth], and they determine from observation of the minor that the minor has physical injury or injuries which appear to have been inflicted by other than accidental means by any person, that the minor has been sexually molested, or that any injury prohibited by the terms of Section 273a has been inflicted upon the minor, shall report such fact by telephone and in writing, within thirty-six hours to both the local police authority having jurisdiction and to the juvenile probation department; or either to the county welfare department or to the county health department. The report shall state, if known, the name of the minor, the minor's whereabouts, and the character and extent of the injuries or molestation.

Reports and other pertinent information received shall be made available to any licensed physician and surgeon, dentist, resident, intern, podiatrist, chiropractor, or religious practitioner with regard to the patient or client; any director of a county welfare department, school superintendent, supervisor of child welfare and attendance, certified pupil personnel employee, or school principal having a direct interest in the welfare of the minor, and to any probation department, juvenile probation department, or agency offering child protective services.

The most important thing about this law is that it becomes mandatory for those in contact with children to report cases of suspected abuse. This provision helps greatly in uncovering cases that remained hidden in the past. This also accounts for the greatly increased numbers of reported child abuse incidents. Child abuse has probably not increased in recent years, it has simply become more recognizable due to such laws.

The flood of publicity about child abuse has had one undesirable effect. So many cases are now being reported that parents and school workers are becoming fearful of physical contact of any kind with children. Certainly with young children, physical contact with adults in the form of holding and hugs is important to development (Chapter 13). If in our zeal to protect children from abuse, we make parents and child-care workers afraid of any and all physical contact with children, we may be losing more than we have gained. Unfortunately, too, the flood of reporting brought on by changes in the law have greatly increased the number of unfounded reports. In 1984, 65 percent of all reported child abuse cases were closed after initial investigation because there was no evidence of abuse, whereas only 35 percent were so closed in 1975 (Johnson, 1985, B-11).

On the other hand, laws and publicity seem to have combined to reduce both spousal and child abuse. Using a large nationally representative sample. Straus and Geller (1986) found a 47 percent lower child-abuse rate and a 27 percent lower wife-abuse rate in 1985 than in 1975. They hasten to add that the rates remain unacceptably high, however; thus, the problem is far from disappearing.

Three elements must usually be present in a family for child abuse to occur. First, the parent must be a person to whom physical punishment is acceptable. It is often found that the abusive parent was abused as a child. The abusive parent has also often been found to be self-righteous and moralistic and to have unrealistic expectations for the child. The parent often expects things of the child that are impossible for the child's level of development. Second, the child is usually difficult and trying. Third, there is usually a crisis event of some kind. The parent has lost a job or is having marital conflict, or something else that has reduced the parent's tolerance level is occurring (Helfer & Kempe, 1974; Starr, 1979).

Some cities have created telephone hot lines that a parent can use to receive immediate help if he or she feels unable to cope with the child or children. One program to help abusive parents was started in 1970 in Santa Barbara, California. Claire W. Miles became so concerned about child abuse that she installed an extra phone in her home and advertised in the personal column of the local newspaper asking anyone who knew of an abused child to call the number. Within the next month she received twenty-eight calls, many from parents who abused their children. From this simple beginning the Child Abuse Listening Mediation (CALM) program grew. In the first year CALM was involved in 213 cases. Since that time the program has grown to include educational presentations throughout the country and visits to parents by volunteers, as well as the immediate help offered by telephone.

Help for the Abusive Parent from CALM (Child Abuse Listening Mediation)

A good example of the effectiveness and dedication of CALM volunteers is demonstrated in the following case of a young mother:

The mother has a son three years old. About two years ago, she had a nervous breakdown and was confined for some time in the psychiatric ward of a hospital. Her baby

was cared for by grandparents during her confinement. When she was able to take her baby back, she remarked how fat and healthy he was. The improvement in his physical condition seemed to accentuate her feelings of inadequacy as a mother, and gave her a feeling of even greater insecurity in her relationship with her son. Her child is hyperactive, and her energy is not often a match for his. She has been trying to toilet train him without much success. When she tries to feed him, he throws food all over and refuses to eat. Then later he cries and is cross because he is hungry. Generally she feels that he does nothing right and everything wrong. She is fearful that he is abnormal in some way.

She would like to take him to a nursery school one or two days a week, so she could just be alone and rest, but she can't afford the private nurseries, which are the only ones who will take a child under three or one in diapers. She said, "I don't know what to do—I can't stand it much longer. Can you help me?"

She was told about the volunteer program, and she agreed to have someone come over the next day. A volunteer was selected who lives near her, and who has seven children of her own, ranging in age from ten to one, including a set of twins three years old.

The volunteer found that the girl has no friends here, since she has recently come from the east. She is lonely and overanxious and tense from being a twenty-four-hour-a-day mother every day. On the initial visit, she didn't want the volunteer to leave, so the volunteer stayed as long as possible, then took the client and child home with her. For two or three weeks, the volunteer invited her over three mornings a week. She encouraged the girl to use her sewing machine to make kitchen curtains. The client gained assurance that there was nothing abnormal about her child, and through association with the volunteer's twins of the same age, the boy began to eat normally without throwing his food

around. The mother observed many traits in the volunteer's children similar to those she had worried about in her son, and in a relatively short time has already expressed a relieved sense of relaxation in her relationship with her son. She is being more realistic in her expectations of him, and is gaining self-confidence in her feelings of being able to care for him more adequately.

Sibling Abuse

Probably the most physical abuse occurs between siblings. Young children have fewer ways to express themselves than do adults. They also have less self-control, and thus their frustrations are often expressed aggressively via physical means. Almost 5 percent of surveyed families reported a sibling's having used a knife or gun at some time. If this statistic is correct, it is estimated that 2.3 million children have been attacked by a sibling or at least threatened with such a weapon (Steinmetz, 1977b).

Parental Abuse by Children

Although abuse against parents sounds improbable, there are cases where children physically attack and even kill their parents. Such violence tends to occur most often with troubled teenagers. Although physical abuse of parents by their children is limited, verbal and psychological abuse is common. Children place heavy demands on their parents and seldom fail to react at least verbally when they are frustrated. Verbal abuse heaped on parents by teenage children seems to be the norm during that stage of development.

Factors Associated with Family Violence

1. *The cycle of violence*: One of the consistent conclusions of domestic violence research is that individuals who have experienced violent and abusive childhoods are likely to grow into violent adults (Geller, 1980; Geller & Straus, 1979; Straus, 1980; Straus, Geller & Steinmetz, 1980). In other words, violence begets violence.

2. *Socioeconomic status*: There is an inverse relation between parental income and parental violence: Those with incomes below the poverty line have the highest rates of violence (Straus, Geller & Steinmetz, 1980). Parental violence is also related to the father's occupation. The rate of severe violence is higher when the father is a blue-collar worker than when he is a white-collar worker. This conclusion, however, does not mean that domestic violence is confined to lower-class households.

3. *Stress*: A third consistent finding is that family violence rates are directly related to social stress in families. Unemployment, financial problems, pregnancy, single-parenthood, and alcohol abuse all relate to violence in the family.

4. *Social isolation*: Social isolation increases the risk that severe violence will be directed at children or between spouses. Families who have religious affiliations or a large circle of intimate friends or who participate in community and social activities report less familial violence.

5. *Traditional male role orientation*: Participants in violent relationships tend to hold a traditional view of the social roles of men and women. The abusive male is described as dominant, controlling, and "macho" in his outlook on women (Bernard et al., 1985, pp. 573–574).

People Liberation: Changing Masculine and Feminine Roles

Contents

My wife and I have been married 41 years. We think of ourselves as being happily married. But the dominance is there. It means that in my relationship with my wife, I am totally the boss. When we have a discussion, more often than not it is I who declare when the end of it arrives. If we make a plan together and she does most of the work on the plan, it is given to me for approval. If I do most of the work on the plan, I submit it to her for her information. If she agrees to the plan, she'll say, "Good, should we do it?" If I agree to the plan, I'll say, "Good, let's go." That doesn't mean that I make all the decisions, control all the funds, make all the choices, talk louder than she does. I don't have to. It simply means that I do not have to ask my wife for permission to do anything. Whether she does or says something about it or not, everything my wife does is to a large extent qualified by what I think or will think. In effect, she must ask my permission. What's more, as husband, I seem—no matter how hard I try to avoid it—to assign all the jobs in our family. In effect, I win all the arguments—even the ones we don't have. That's emotional dominance—and it means that everything that occurs between us, everything we do together, is monitored by me.

Sey Chassler (1984)

Male and female, man and woman, boy and girl—this duality is easily recognized in the human species. Almost everyone's first thought upon meeting another human is "he or she." Radical feminists of the 1970s chided us for automatically making this differentiation. Others said, "Vive la difference."

We all recognize this duality, but where did it come from? Are men and women really different biologically? Psychologically? Intellectually? Socially? If so, are such differences inborn (based on a different biological foundation) or learned? Are men the stronger sex because on the average they are physically stronger? Are women the stronger sex because they generally live longer than men? Can a woman really be like a man? Can a man really be like a woman? Why have men traditionally been breadwinners and women homemakers? Is the relationship between men and women one of equality? One of dominance and submission (as Mr. Chassler suggests)? One of independence and dependence? Complimentarity? What would happen if a society did away with gender role differentiation (if it could) and we all became "unisex"?

Such questions have been increasingly asked over the past three decades. Controversy about the answers swirls around us all. Regardless of how we answer such questions, it seems clear that the meanings assigned to *man* and *woman* and the relationships between the sexes are undergoing change.

When men and women are free to choose gender roles for themselves, especially within intimate relationships like marriage, their chances for success and fulfillment seem to increase. If intimate partners can share the decisions and responsibilities of their relationship in ways that feel right for them, their satisfaction will be greater than if each is forced into stereotyped behaviors that may not fit. Free choice should help reduce the feelings of oppression and dissatisfaction that so often appear over time in intimate relationships. To do away with gender role rigidity and stereotyping and move toward freedom to choose a personally and socially fulfilling lifestyle is a proper goal of a free society.

Role Equity

Instead of new roles for the sexes we need an acceptance of the concept of role equity. This means that the roles one fulfills are built on individual strengths and weaknesses rather than preordained stereotypical differences between the sexes (granted that there are some differences between the sexes that are biologically influenced). *Equity* implies the "fair" distribution of opportunities and restrictions without regard to gender. *Equity* does not necessarily mean "the same." For example, one spouse may have more interest or better skills in arithmetic and bookkeeping, and so he or she manages the family finances. If such an arrangement is freely chosen and believed to be fair by the individuals concerned, it is an equitable arrangement.

Equity between the sexes in family life embraces variation, many relationship models, not just one. True equity between the sexes implies freedom to establish roles within the relationship that accent the unique personalities of each partner and allow each to fulfill his or her own capabilities to the greatest possible degree. "Constructive liberation" takes into account the fact that people vary; a relationship that is good for one person may be restrictive for another. Rhona and Robert Rapaport (1975) suggest that those who rigidly extol the virtues of a "liberated" relationship are really only suggesting that we move from one prison (traditional prescribed roles) to another (any and all roles acceptable).

If roles are tightly prescribed by society and few if any deviate from them, people tend to feel safe and secure; they may feel threatened by many alternatives. American society encompasses a great deal of diversity, however. People may find that their neighbors have a different lifestyle. Children may point to imperfections in their parents' marital life and question whether people need to get married. Couples may find the mass media criticizing a relationship they have never seriously questioned. They may read articles praising alternative living arrangements that they were taught were immoral. Such experiences often cause confusion, insecurity, anxiety, resentment, and an even firmer commitment to the status quo. Indeed, the extreme attacks on the "traditional American marriage" mounted by radical feminists, gay liberationists, sexual freedom leagues, and others may have undercut a thoughtful and constructive approach to change within the family structure and certainly contributed to the failure of the Equal Rights Amendment in 1982. It is our belief that flexible gender roles are valuable although most people will continue to choose, at least partially, the traditional roles for some time to come.

Male = Masculine and Female = Feminine: Not Necessarily So

Simply stated, whether one is male or female is biologically determined. The behaviors or roles that go along with being male or female, however, are largely learned from one's society. For example, French males may cry in public over a sad event; American males generally repress tears in public. The social behavior assigned to their sex differs. We call this socially assigned behavior in a given society "masculine" for the male and "feminine" for the female.

One's sex is determined by the different chromosomal and hormonal influences that lead to the anatomical differences between the sexes. One's "gender" includes not only one's sex but all of the attitudes and behaviors (masculine and feminine) that are expected of one's sex by a given society. Thus sexual identity includes both physiologically prescribed sex and socially prescribed **gender** behaviors.

Gender
Attitudes and behavior associated with each of the two sexes

Norms and Roles

Before we discuss gender development, it is important to define the terms *norm* and *role*.

Norms are accepted and expected patterns of behavior and beliefs established either formally or informally by a group. Usually the group rewards those who adhere to the norms and punishes those who do not. Note that the sanctions against cross-gender behavior are greater for boys than for girls (Archer, 1984; Archer & Lloyd, 1985, p. 277). These sanctions operate through the influence of parents, peers, and others in the child's environment and start at an early age.

Roles involve people doing the activities demanded by the norms. That is, a husband working to support his family is fulfilling his role as husband and thereby fulfilling the social norm of husband as supporter of the family. Because there are many norms in a society, a person plays many roles. For example, a married woman may fulfill the roles of sexual partner, cook, mother, homemaker, financial manager, psychologist, and so on. If she works outside the marriage, she also fulfills career roles. A married man may fulfill the roles of breadwinner, sexual partner, father, general repairman, and so on. The point is that all people play a number of roles at any given time in their lives. Conflict between roles often occurs because of the many roles necessary to live successfully in a complex society. For example, in our society a woman's mother and wife role may interfere with her career role (see Chapter 9).

The expectation that people will fulfill their roles, and thus meet social norms, is strong. Because roles are so taken for granted, most of us are probably not aware of the pressure to conform. In fact, the expectation that people behave in prescribed ways probably makes much of life simpler for us. But what happens when people behave in unexpected ways? To find out how unconscious expected role behavior is, try stepping out of an expected role and observe the reactions of those around you!

Norm
Accepted social rules for behavior

Role
Particular type of behavior one is expected to exhibit when occupying a certain place in a group

Norms and roles obviously play important parts in marriage, too. That is, each of us brings to a marriage, or to any intimate relationship, a great number of expectations about what our roles and those of our partners should be. Many disappointments in marriage stem from frustration of the role expectations we hold either for ourselves or our spouses (see Chapter 5). For example a man may assume that the role of wife is restricted to caring for him, the house, and the children. His wife, however, may believe that the role of wife can also include a career and that the role of husband can include household duties and care of children. Such conflicting role expectations will undoubtedly cause conflict for this couple.

Norms and roles, when accepted, tend to smooth family functioning. Problems occur when roles and norms are not accepted or when they are unclear. In many societies there are very definite goals for marriage, such as increasing the family's land holdings, adding new workers (children) to the family, or even bringing new wealth into the family in the form of the wife's dowry. But our society does not set definite goals other than the vague "living happily ever after" we see in movies and romantic fiction.

In societies where roles and norms are stable, people enter marriage with clear ideas of each partner's rights and obligations. In our society, though, almost all norms and roles are being questioned and none more so than those associated with masculinity, femininity, and sexuality. Because the classification of behavior by gender is so central to human society, and to the concept of marriage as we have known it, this chapter will take a closer look at division according to gender and at the expectations, roles, and norms that arise from such division.

How Sex and Gender Identity Develops

Three factors determine sex identity. First, sex is genetically determined at conception. Second, hormones secreted by glands directed by the genetic configuration produce physical differences. Third, society defines, prescribes, and reinforces the gender aspect of sex identity. Problems with any of these factors can cause faulty sex identity.

Biological Contribution

Every normal person has two sex chromosomes, one inherited from each parent, which determine biological sex. Women have two X chromosomes (XX), men an X and a Y (XY). Thus if the man's X chromosome combines with the woman's X, the child will be female (XX). If, on the other hand, the man's Y chromosome combines with the woman's X, the child will be male (XY).

Although the Y chromosome has few functional genes, the X chromosome has a number of them, including some responsible for such unwelcome conditions as color blindness and hemophilia. Most of the harmful genes are recessive, which means that when they pair with another gene that is dominant, the negative characteristic will not appear. In the female, the possession of two X chromosomes usually results in the harmful gene in one chromosome being overridden by the dominant gene in the other chromosome. In the male, however, the harmful condition will usually appear because the Y chromosome is ineffective in counteracting the harmful sex-linked gene on the X chromosome (Archer & Lloyd, 1985, p. 30). Hence, a problem like hemophilia is found exclusively in men.

At first all embryos have the potential to become either sex. That is, the already existing tissues of the embryo can become male or female (see p. 209). In order for a male to be produced, the primitive undifferentiated gonad must develop into testes rather than ovaries. The male hormone (a chemical substance) testosterone spurs the development of testes, while another chemical (Müllerian-inhibiting substance) simultaneously causes the regression of those embryonic tissues that would become the female reproductive system. In the absence of male hormones, the female organs develop. The hormones have already started working by the time the embryo is six millimeters long, at about two weeks. By the end of the eighth to twelfth week, the child's sex can be determined by observation of the external genitalia (see Chapter 12, pp. 404–405, for a further description of embryonic development).

Note that the male appears to develop only by the addition of the male hormones, which are stimulated by the Y chromosome. Without that stimulation a female develops. This occurrence has led some researchers to conclude that the human embryo is innately female (Sherfey, 1972; Kimura, 1985).

By puberty hormonal activity has increased sharply. In girls estrogen (one of the female hormones) affects such female characteristics as breast size, pubic hair, and the filling out of the hips. Estrogen and progesterone (another female hormone) also begin the complicated process that leads to changes in the uterine lining and subsequently to the first menstruation, followed about a year later (or sometimes immediately) by ovulation (the cycle, mediated by these hormones, that causes an egg to mature each month; see the section in Chapter 10 on female sex organs for a fuller discussion of the menstruation and ovulation processes).

In boys the active hormone is testosterone. At puberty it brings about the secretory activity of the seminal vesicles and the prostate and the regular production of sperm in the testes (see the section in Chapter 10 on male sex organs for a fuller discussion of this process). Testosterone also affects such male characteristics as larger body size, more powerful muscles, and the ability of blood to carry more oxygen. Castration (removal of the testicles) generally leads to obesity, softer tissues, and a more placid temperament in the male because of the reduction in the quantity of testosterone.

It is interesting to note that both sexes produce male and female hormones. It is the relative balance of these hormones that directs development in one direction or the other.

In lower animals these hormones have been found to cause other differences between the sexes besides just sexual differences. In rats and mice, the hormones seem to influence brain development, which in turn influences such activities as fighting, exploration, and play (Goy & McEwan, 1980; Blizard, 1983; Archer & Lloyd, 1985). This has led to some suggestions that these hormonal differences also cause personality differences between human males and females.

Because every human starts with the potential of becoming either male or female, each as a fully differentiated adult still carries the biological rudiments of the opposite sex. For example, the male has undeveloped nipples on his chest and the female has a penislike clitoris. In a few rare individuals, even though gene determinants have set the sexual direction, the hormones fail to carry out the process. Such persons have characteristics of both sexes, though neither are fully developed, and are called **hermaphrodites**. Hermaphrodites are rare and should

Hermaphrodite
A person who has both male and female sexual organs, or organs that are indeterminant, such as a clitoris that resembles a penis

Inset 7-1

Transsexualism: A Confusion in Sexual Identity

Dr. Richard Raskind, a successful physician, was an avid tennis player (well over six feet tall) who was ranked thirteenth nationally in the amateur men's thirty-five-and-over division. In 1977, after undergoing sex-change therapy, Dr. Renee Richards was ranked tenth among professional women players in the United States, an unbelievable accomplishment for a forty-two-year-old woman who had never played tennis professionally. For several years she was the coach to the tennis star Martina Navratilova. Such quick success may also speak to physical differences between men and women.

Another transsexual example may be found in Jan Morris's autobiography Conundrum:

> I was three or perhaps four years old when I realized that I had been born into the wrong body, and should really be a girl. I remember the moment well, and it is the earliest memory of my life.
>
> I was sitting beneath my mother's piano, and her music was falling around me like cataracts, enclosing me as in a cave. . . .
>
> What triggered so bizarre a thought I have long forgotten, but the conviction was unfaltering from the start (Morris, 1974, p. 3).

Morris attended Oxford which led to a glamorous position as correspondent for *The Times* (London). He scored one of the world's historic journalistic coups by climbing 22,000 feet up Mt. Everest with Edmund Hillary and Tenzing Norgay, and flashing the first word of their conquest of the peak. The lean, stubble-chinned Morris, whose "manly" stamina made such a feat possible, became a Fleet Street legend. By this time, in spite of his inner contradictions, he had married, and he and his wife, the daughter of a Ceylonese tea planter, had five children. Eventually he resigned from *The Times* to write books, and in this endeavor, too, he distinguished himself.

However, for all of his outward appearance of normalcy, his inner anguish remained. He consulted physicians, and was advised either to wear gayer clothes or to "soldier on" as a male. His quest for help led him to New York City where he was counseled by Dr. Harry Benjamin, an endocrinologist who has specialized in the study of gender confusion. Dr. Benjamin prescribed female hormone treatments to prepare the way for Morris's sexual changeover. For men, such treatments involve estrogen and progestin to soften the skin and enlarge the breasts. Morris underwent the treatment for eight years and estimates that he swallowed 12,000 pills.

In July, 1972, James Morris took the final, irreversible step. He checked into a Casablanca clinic that specializes in transsexual operations and submitted to the surgery. The male-to-female procedure is carried out by amputation of the penis and castration, after which an artificial vagina is created, using scrotal or penile tissue or skin grafts from the hip or thigh. Because the penile tissue is still sensitive, male-to-female transsexuals may experience orgasm, though, of course, pregnancy is impossible.

Today the former James Morris is in virtually every respect a woman, with a new name, the properly androgynous Jan since it is used by both male and females; a new relationship with her former wife (divorced, they regard each other as unofficial "sisters-in-law"); and with her children, who now call their father "Aunt Jan."

James Morris was a very conventional male, who did all of the things that a man was supposed to do. He has turned into a very conventional female, doing the things that a woman is traditionally supposed to do. The new Jan Morris enjoys having men open doors for her, flirt with her, and kiss her. She says, "Women who like to feel cherished by a stronger man have every right to their feelings."

Such cases are extremely rare. It is estimated that about 5,000 individuals in the United States have altered their sex by surgery. For them, biology and the environment had failed to work together to produce a stable sex identity.

When it was active in the sex-change field, Johns Hopkins Medical Center received about 1,500 applications for sex-change operations per year but only performed about six operations per year. Researchers there found that the vast majority of persons who think they are transsexual are not and can be helped with psychotherapy. It is interesting to note that Johns Hopkins Medical Center ceased doing sex-change operations in 1979. The follow-up studies of sex-changed persons indicated that the psychological and other gains were minimal and not worth the problems risked with the extensive surgery necessary to accomplish a sex change.

not be confused with transsexuals or transvestites. A **transsexual** is a person who believes that he or she is actually of the opposite gender and who may have undergone a sex-change operation as discussed in Inset 7-1. A **transvestite** is a person who enjoys and gains sexual pleasure from dressing like the opposite sex.

The strength of the sex hormones can be seen when pregnant rhesus monkeys are injected with testosterone for twenty-five to fifty days. The genetically female offspring of the injected mothers have malformed external genital structures, which include a scrotum, a small penis, and no external vaginal orifice. In addition, the behavior of such pseudohermaphroditic females is altered in the direction of normal male behavior.

The early adaptability of the tissues that grow into mature sexual organs is also quite amazing. Ovaries and vaginas transplanted into castrated male rats within the first twenty-four hours after birth will grow and function exactly like normal female organs. This plasticity of the sex tissues quickly vanishes as the hormones cause further differentiation. Transplants of female organs into male rats more than three days old are unsuccessful.

Environmental Contribution

Once a baby is born, society begins to teach the infant its proper gender role and reinforce its sexual identity. In the United States we name our children according to their gender; we give girls pink blankets and boys blue blankets; and at Christmas and birthdays boys receive "masculine" toys and girls "feminine" toys.

In keeping with cultural prescriptions, we show different attitudes toward children of different sexes, and we expect and reward their different behaviors. For example, we encourage boys to engage in rough and tumble activities and discourage girls from engaging in such activities. (This may explain, in part, why men tend to be more interested in contact sports than women are.) Parents provide guidance to help the child assimilate the proper role. Nothing inherent within the child will give rise to the socially sex-appropriate behaviors. Each child must learn—from parents, relatives, teachers, and friends—the appropriate behaviors for the culture. (See also p. 460 on accepting the new body image at puberty.)

Feminists take the position that because gender roles are learned, it is possible for a society to change masculine and feminine behavior (see Inset 7-2). One interesting piece of evidence they offer is those few babies whose ascribed sex differs from their biological sex. Some of these babies have been studied over a twenty-year period, and one researcher (Weitzman, 1975, p. 108) concludes:

> In virtually all cases, the sex of assignment (and thus of rearing) proved dominant. Thus, babies assigned as males at birth and brought up as boys by their parents (who were unaware of the child's female genetic and hormonal makeup) thereafter thought of themselves as boys, played with boys' toys, developed boys' sports, preferred boys' clothing, developed male sex fantasies, and in due course fell in love with girls. And the reverse was true for babies who were biologically male but were reared as girls; they followed the typical feminine pattern of development.

In one case one of two identical twins was reassigned as a female following a surgical mishap. At seven months the twin boys were to be circumcised by electrocautery. Because of an electrical malfunction, the penis of one twin was

Transsexual
A person who has a compulsion or obsession to become a member of the opposite sex through surgical changes

Transvestite
A person who prefers to dress as the opposite sex.

Inset 7-2

The Xanith of Oman

The Xanith are biologically men. They sell themselves in passive homosexual relationships, but they also work as skilled domestic servants and are in great demand earning a good wage. Their dress is distinctive, cut like the long tunic worn by men but of pastel-colored cloth. Although they retain men's names, they violate all of the rules that control female seclusion. They may speak intimately with women in the street without bringing the women's reputation into question. They sit with the segregated women at a wedding, and they may see the bride's unveiled face. They may neither sit nor eat with men in public. Their manners, perfumed bodies, and high-pitched voices make them appear effeminate even though they have undergone no medical changes to their bodies as did Jan Morris (Inset 7-1).

Since their feminine gender is socially selected, they have several possibilities open to them. Should they wish to become men again, they need only marry and prove themselves able to perform heterosexual intercourse with their brides. Some Xanith never choose this path and remain women until they grow old, at which time their anatomical sex places them in the category of "old men." Some actually become women, then men, then women again until old age places them back into the "old man" role.

Since Omani women are off limits to all men but their husbands, the Xanith offer a sexual outlet for the single men in the society. Since Xanith are socially women, to have intercourse with them (so long as the man purchasing their services penetrates) in no way casts a man in an unfavorable light. His manhood remains unquestioned.

The ease with which these transformations can be made clearly points out the strength of the society in determining gender roles.

Source: Adapted from Archer & Lloyd, 1985.

---

totally destroyed. Following the recommendations of the doctors, the parents of this little boy elected to have his sex reassigned. At seventeen months the boy came to the Johns Hopkins clinic for the necessary surgical corrections to give him female external genitals. John Money and Anke Ehrhardt reported that since surgery, the parents have made every effort to raise the twins in accord with their assigned sex— one male and one female. According to the reports of the parents, the two children are developing to fit the role expectations of their assigned sex. The mother described her "daughter's" behavior this way (Money & Ehrhardt, 1972, p. 119):

> She likes for me to wipe her face. She doesn't like to be dirty, and yet my son is quite different. I can't wash his face for anything. . . . She seems to be daintier. Maybe it's because I encourage it.

Occasionally, children fail to learn the role that traditionally accompanies their biological sex. This failure can lead to the unusual circumstance of a person being one sex biologically but the opposite sex psychologically, thus resulting in sexual identity confusion (see Insets 7-1 and 7-2).

A Theory of Gender Role Development

The old argument about whether environment and learning or genetics and biology determine sex role behavior should not be stated in this either/or form. In truth, of course, it is the interaction of these two great molders of behavior that determines one's actual behavior. The following theory tries to take both into consideration (Ullian, 1976). In the early years (Stage 1) biological influence is most clearly seen. Children ten through thirteen (Stage 2) demonstrate much more socially influenced behavior. Finally, during adolescence (Stage 3), a more personal psychological orientation seems to direct sex role behaviors.

Stage 1: Biological Orientation

Level One (six years): Differences between masculine and feminine are expressed primarily in terms of external bodily differences, such as size, strength, length of hair, etc. Social and psychological differences are recognized but are assumed to be the consequence of these external physical differences. Conformity to sex differences is viewed as necessary in order to maintain gender identity and to allow for the expression of innate gender differences.

Level Two (eight years): There is a growing awareness that masculine and feminine traits can exist independently from biological and physical features. Emphasis is placed on the ability of the individual to act according to choice, since he or she is no longer limited by physical or biological constraints. Also the role of training and social conditions begins to be recognized. Finally, since children no longer see sex differences as biological necessities, they do not demand the conformity to sex roles characteristic of the younger children.

Stage 2: Societal Orientation

Level Three (ten years): Masculine and feminine traits are seen as inherent in the requirements of a system of social roles and are viewed as fixed and unchangeable. The traits associated with certain adult social roles are assumed to be characteristic of the members of the sex expected to fill those roles. Conformity to masculine and feminine standards is based on the need to satisfy external demands of the social system.

Level Four: (twelve years): There is a growing awareness that the system of social roles is arbitrary and variable, and may function independently of sex of individual. Stress is put on the individual's freedom to act according to individual self-interest. Conformity is no longer expected.

Stage 3: Psychological Orientation

Level Five (fourteen to sixteen years): Masculine and feminine traits are based on the adoption of an appropriate psychological identity by males and females. Adolescents admit that sex differences are not biologically based and may not be the result of social necessity, but they see traits as central to men's and women's identities. They view deviation as "sick" or "abnormal" and conformity to external standards as required for maintenance of marriage and the family.

Level Six (eighteen years): There is an awareness that masculinity and femininity may exist independently from conformity to traditional standards, roles, and behaviors. Sex-stereotyped traits are not assumed to be crucial aspects of personal identity. Principles of equality and freedom are proposed as standards for behavior, and are used to define an ideal model of personal and interpersonal functioning.

Recent studies of the human brain indicate that there may be gender-related differences in how certain mental processes are controlled and the location of the control area (Goleman, 1978; Kimura, 1985). There are no commonly accepted, observable differences in the physical size, structure, and biochemical components of brains, however, and the degree to which gender-related differences influence behavioral differences is difficult to determine. Table 7-1 shows some of the stereotypical differences between the sexes and compares them to scientific findings. There seems to be little support for the belief that there are many strong and consistent differences between males and females. The studies that have been done on the subject of sex differences do support some mild differences. In every case, however, the differences between persons of the same sex on a given characteristic can be greater than the average differences between the sexes.

Reduction in the use of gender role stereotypes—or any behavioral stereotypes—is a worthy goal. Furthermore, to argue endlessly over the relative influence of biology as opposed to environment is a waste of energy. Because we know that culture does influence gender roles to a great extent, it is certainly possible to modify them.

Sweden has moved in the direction of reducing gender role differences. Boys and girls are now required to take identical subjects in school. All jobs are open to both sexes. Laws are applied equally. Perhaps gender roles in the future will become flexible enough so that individuals will be able to choose roles that maximize their own unique capabilities. Yet such flexibility will not destroy the basic duality of the sexes.

The Androgynous Person

Androgynous
The quality of having both masculine and feminine characteristics

The concept of the **androgynous** person who exhibits both male (andro) and female (gyno) behavioral characteristics now associated with one or the other sex has become popular among many who are in favor of reducing gender role differences. Abraham Maslow's (1968) self-actualized person (see pp. 160–161 for a fuller discussion of Maslow's ideas) comes close to being such a person, open to both masculine and feminine sides of his or her personality. The self-actualized person has no need to assert dominance or play the coquette. He or she is free to build an individualized role.

To create such adults, society would have to train children for competence in many areas without regard to sex. Whether this is an ideal that most Americans want to strive for remains to be seen.

> In an androgynous society children strive for competence in many areas without regard to sex. They develop motor skills through running and jumping, and hand-eye coordination through needle work, art work, and handling of tools. They learn the skills necessary to take care of themselves, such as cooking, sewing, and household repairs. They play with friends of both sexes, in school as well as out. They engage freely in games of competition as well as games of cooperation with friends of the other sex and friends of the same sex. They learn to respect (or to dislike) each other on the basis of individual differences, not according to sexual category.
>
> Children learn not only self-confidence and a sense of mastery but also attitudes of caring and concern for others. Both sexes are held and touched often as infants and after. They learn to understand and express their own feelings and to recognize the needs and feelings of those around them. Verbal and physical displays of emotion are encouraged as long as they are not harmful to other people. (Lindemann, 1976, pp. 185–186)

Table 7-1	
Stereotypic Sex Role Differences Compared with Research Findings	
Stereotype	**Findings**
Perceptual Differences	
Men have: better daylight vision	Mild but in direction of stereotype.
less sensitivity to extreme heat	"
more sensitivity to extreme cold	"
faster reaction times	"
better depth perception	"
better spatial skills	"
Women have: better night vision	"
more sensitivity to touch in all parts of the body	"
better hearing, especially in higher ranges	"
less tolerance of loud sound	"
better manual dexterity and fine coordination	"
Aggression	
Males are more aggressive.	Strong consistent differences in physical aggression.
Females are less aggressive.	
Dependency	
Females are more submissive and dependent.	Weak differences that are more consistent for adults than for children.
Males are more assertive and independent.	
Emotionality	
Females are more emotional and excitable.	Moderate differences on some measures; overall findings inconclusive.
Males are more controlled and less expressive.	
Health	
Females suffer more depression and phobic reactions.	Moderate differences.
Males have more heart disease.	Strong differences.
Verbal Skills	
Females excel in all verbal areas including reading.	Moderate differences, especially for children.
Males are less verbal and have more problems learning to read.	
Math Skills	
Males are better in mathematical skills.	Moderate differences on problem-solving tests, especially after adolescence.
Females are less interested and do less well in mathematics.	

Source: This table has been constructed using several sources:

1. Maccoby, E., Jacklin, C. *The Psychology of Sex Differences* . Palo Alto, Calif.: Stanford University Press, 1974.
2. Goleman, D. "Special Abilities of the Sexes: Do They Begin in the Brain?" *Psychology Today*, November, 1978.
3. Frieze, I. et al. *Women and Sex Roles*. New York: W. W. Norton, 1978.
4. McGuiness, D., Pribram, K. "The Origins of Sensory Bias in the Development of Gender Differences in Perception and Cognition." In *Cognitive Growth and Development*, edited by M. Bortner. New York: Brunner-Mazel, 1979.
5. Kimura, D. "Male Brain, Female Brain: The Hidden Difference." *Psychology Today*, November, 1985.
6. Archer, J., & Lloyd, B. *Sex and Gender*. Cambridge, England: Cambridge University Press, 1985.
7. Durden-Smith, J., & DeSimone, D. "Is There a Superior Sex?" *Playboy*, May, 1982.

The relaxation of gender stereotypes may already be having some effect on American children. Beeson and Williams (1983) studied the play habits of children aged three to five and found that boys sometimes chose stereotypical feminine play activity. However, the girls play choices did not yet show gender crossover.

Traditional Gender Roles

The depth of most people's belief in gender role stereotypes is often overlooked and is sometimes hard to believe. Most people simply take the various traditional gender role behaviors for granted. See how you react when reading Inset 7-3 which substitutes male terms for female in an imaginary article of advice for a young man about to wed. Reversing the genders often quickly reveals our stereotypes.

To the degree that our behaviors are dictated by stereotypical thinking about gender roles, we close ourselves to potential growth and broader expression. A husband may have a need to express his emotions, yet the masculine stereotype forbids him to do so. A wife may be a natural leader, yet she may suppress leadership behavior because the stereotype says it is not feminine.

Traditional roles historically reflected the woman's childbearing functions and the man's greater physical strength and need to defend his family from attack. A male's status today is still partially determined by his physical prowess, especially during the school years. The traditional role stressed masculine dominance in most areas of life, in the society as well as within the family. The traditional role also allowed men sexual freedom while severely limiting women's sexuality — the **double standard**.

The traditional feminine role was essentially the complement of the masculine role. Man was active, so woman was passive and submissive. Wives helped their husbands, took much of their personal identity from their husbands, ran the home and family, and worked outside the home only if necessary. Women were the source of stability, strength, and most of the love and affection within the home.

In sociological terms the traditional masculine character traits are those labeled "instrumental." Such traits enable one to accomplish tasks and goals. Aggressiveness, self-confidence, adventurousness, activity, and dominance are examples. "Expressive" character traits—gentleness, expressiveness, lovingness, and supportiveness—tend to be used in describing feminine behavior. Notice how the traits often complement one another. For example, the man exhibits aggressiveness, and the woman is the opposite, gentle.

It is interesting to note that we find relative agreement between American men and women when they assess the advantages and disadvantages of their gender roles. Essentially, the perceived advantages of one sex are the disadvantages of the other:

Double standard

Role orientation in which males are allowed more freedom than are females

Inset 7-3

How to Hold a Wife: A Bridegroom's Guide

Oh, lucky you! You are finally bridegroom to the woman of your dreams!

But don't think for a minute that you can now relax and be assured automatically of marital happiness forever. You will have to *work at it*. While she may have eyes only for you *now*, remember that she is surrounded every day by attractive young men who are all too willing to tempt her away from you. It will be up to you to make your physical relationship so exciting, so totally satisfying to her, that she won't be tempted to stray!

Here is what you need to know and do to succeed in your marriage, your greatest challenge in life—and the one that will be utterly essential to your wife's future happiness and thus your own.

1. Let's start in with the essentials. You should always be available to your wife whenever she wants you. It is, of course, your husbandly prerogative to say no, but you will be wise to never do so unless you are really ill, for that may tempt her to turn to other men to fulfill her essential needs. She cannot do without sex, so you as a smart husband should always be ready to provide it.

2. That means that you should never let yourself get too tired to perform. The cardinal sin for a husband—and

a good way to lose the wife you love—is to fail at your duty to achieve a good erection and to sustain it until your wife is fully satisfied. So never let your work or anything else get in the way of plenty of rest each day, regular but moderate exercise, and plenty of protein in your diet—and stay away from excessive alcohol.

Remember that women's sexual needs vary. Some need it more often than others, and some (lucky you if you are married to a real woman like that!) can achieve multiple orgasms in a single night of love if you can do your part!

3. "But how about me?" you may ask. "How about my sexual needs and satisfactions?"

Now man's passion, of course, often does not equal that of woman. But you have a wonderful surprise in store for you, if you concentrate your efforts on your wife's pleasure and don't worry selfishly about your own. For sooner or later you will discover the ecstasy of truly mature male coital orgasm that can be induced only by total surrender to the exquisite sensations of a woman's orgasmic contractions.

4. Remember that your first duty is to your wife: So if you fail to satisfy her (and yourself, too) in the above-described natural way, you should talk to a good psychiatrist who specializes in

this kind of problem. She will help you if, for instance, you have not fully accepted the natural masculine role that will bring you the joy of selfless service to others instead of the futile envy of woman's natural leadership role. . . .

5. Now for a subject that may seem trivial: your appearance and dress. Don't overlook it—it is a vital ingredient in marital happiness.

Every woman likes to be proud of how attractive her husband is, so dress to please her. If she likes you to show off your youthful figure, by all means do so! Broad shoulders can be accentuated by turtleneck jerseys (with shoulder pads if needed), as can the well-tapered waist. Small, firm, well-shaped buttocks (very much in fashion this year) can be set off by well-cut . . . pants. . . .

If you do your job well—for husbandhood is the true career for all manly men, worthy of all your talents—you will keep your wife happy and hold her for the rest of her days. Remember that marriage for a man should be *life's Great Adventure, so relax—relax—relax—and enjoy.*

Source: Macleod, *The Village Voice* (February 11, 1971).

Masculine disadvantages consist overwhelmingly of obligations with a few prohibitions while the disadvantages of the female role arise primarily from prohibitions, with a few obligations. Thus females complain about what they can't do, males about what they must do. Females complain that they cannot be athletic, aggressive, sexually free, or successful in the worlds of work and education; in short, they complain of their passivity. Males complain that they must be aggressive and must succeed; in short, of their activity. The (sanctioned) requirement that males may be active and females passive in a variety of ways is clearly unpleasant to both. (Chafetz, 1974, p. 58)

When people are polled, however, and asked to describe their ideal man and woman, their descriptions do not follow the stereotypes just described (Tavris, 1984). Both men and women generally agree on similar lists of ideal characteristics for both sexes, which leads to the belief that androgyny is something both sexes would like to seek even though it is difficult to achieve.

	Ideal Woman
As Men Describe Her	**As Women Describe Her**
1. Able to love	1. Able to love
2. Warm	2. Stands up for beliefs
3. Stands up for beliefs	3. Warm
4. Gentle	4. Self-confident
5. Self-confident	5. Gentle

	Ideal Man
As Women Describe Him	**As Men Describe Him**
1. Able to love	1. Able to love
2. Stands up for beliefs	2. Stands up for beliefs
3. Warm	3. Self-confident
4. Self-confident	4. Fights to protect family
5. Gentle	5. Intelligent

If you examine the first five highest-rated traits for the ideal woman and ideal man as seen by each sex, there is a striking similarity. And all of the lists contain some of the positive traits of each sex as seen traditionally (see Table 7-2).

Unfortunately, the attempt to free each gender from stereotypical role behaviors is, at best, limited. Gender roles are so deeply embedded within society that they are probably impossible to escape completely. A man who is taught to be competitive and dominant may easily stand up for his beliefs yet have a difficult time being warm and gentle. On the other hand, a woman who is taught to be warm and gentle may have trouble standing up for her beliefs. A man who is only warm and gentle and not aggressive will probably have difficulty being successful in our highly competitive work culture. Successful men in our culture must still be aggressive and often make their work their first priority, leaving the family in second place in their lives. Women, although probably freer than men in their selection of gender role behaviors still bear children and, by and large, retain the day-to-day responsibility for the children's upbringing.

The conflict between the idea of androgyny, the ideal masculine and feminine traits, and the real world of our culture causes each of us to feel confusion, ambiguity, and frustration as we attempt to mold our lives. For example, women are told to expand themselves by seeking careers outside the home, but they are made to feel guilty if they do not devote themselves to their families. Unfortunately, they are also made to feel guilty by some feminists if they choose to devote themselves to their families. Thus women often find themselves in a "catch 22" or "no win" situation.

Table 7-2
Positive and Negative Ascribed Character Traits
as Seen by a Cross Section of Americans

Positive	Negative
Women	
Gentle	Passive
Tactful	Nonassertive
Loving	Cunning
Social	Talkative
Sensitive	Moody
Caring	Subjective
Warm	Dependent
Communicative	Illogical
Sympathetic	Insecure
Socially aware	Submissive
Modest	Shy
Men	
Strong	Tactless
Aggressive	Rough
Brave	Egotistical
Objective	Unemotional
Logical	Socially unaware
Adventurous	Inconsiderate
Self-confident	Domineering
Decisive	Insensitive
Independent	Loud
Cool under stress	Lacking empathy
Self-reliant	Uncaring

Gender Roles and the Female Liberation Movement

If people do become freer from past gender role stereotypes, much credit must be given to the women of America. As Betty Friedan puts it in her recent critique of the feminist movement:

> At the moment, I feel like women are ahead of men, and it's a lonely thing. We still have to deal with men who want to control us in the old way. . . . Is the new man going to come soon enough for us? . . . It's not women versus men any more—the anger's gone. But there can't be that flow between us until men stop playing games, too. Women have made the big leap; men are still stuck. Men have to break out of the mold next. (1981, p. 122)

The women's movement has contributed much toward focusing our attention on gender inequalities and thereby has energized our desire to change these inequalities and ourselves. It has brought about profound changes in the relationships between men and women and within the American family.

As women have made changes in their roles, changes in the masculine role have also taken place. Women's liberation, to the extent that it has succeeded, has also meant men's liberation. For example, as more and more women have entered the workforce, more families have become two-paycheck families (Chapter 9). No longer is the husband alone responsible for fulfilling the role of breadwinner for the family. Shared economic responsibility means more freedom for men. Economic participation by women also means that they have become more independent.

There are some who feel that a male revolt against the economic burdens of being the sole source of family support actually predated the feminist movement (Ehrenreich, 1983). Postponement of marriage, increasing divorce, fewer children, a decreasing percentage of men in the workforce (see p. 292), and failure to pay child support after divorce are all cited as evidence of this revolt against the breadwinner role. As men became less willing to assume the economic burdens of family, and less committed to the total support of their families, women were forced onto the labor market to survive. Even if this view is accurate, it was the women's movement that focused public attention on stereotypical gender roles and the harm that such stereotypes could do to both men and women.

All of the changes fostered by the women's movement and its allies have not been readily accepted. Failure of the ERA (Equal Rights Amendment) to win ratification, the strength of the prolife attack on abortion, and the antifeminist movement all bear witness to the conflicts that are stirred up when traditional gender roles are challenged.

Women and the Economy

The major restraint to freer role choice is women's inferior economic position in our society. (See Chapter 9 for a complete discussion of women in the workforce.) In general a man can earn more than a woman regardless of their individual skills. This economic differential in earning power locks each sex into many traditional roles. For example, a father who would prefer to spend more time at home caring for the family usually cannot afford to do so. In most cases this means giving up a portion of his income that his wife generally cannot completely replace.

Although more and better job opportunities for women are now available, the male/female earnings gap has remained. In 1956 women's earnings averaged 63.3 percent of men's. In 1965 this figure dropped slightly, to 59.9 percent; in 1975 it dropped further, to 58.8 percent; and by 1985 the figure had risen to approximaately 65 percent.

The real stumbling block to freer role choice for both men and women is comparable pay for comparable work. For most of the time since women entered the workforce in large numbers, they have been America's best source of cheap labor. Often they have done work comparable to men's but have been paid less for it. Ehrenreich (1983, p. 7) shows that the stereotypical social idea of the man as sole breadwinner (that is, earning enough to support a family) is also used in reverse to say that a woman does not need to earn enough to support herself (a man will do it for her).

The pay differential between men and women is so great that there is a serious question about whether the economy can afford comparable pay. To follow society's years-long struggle against inflation with an overall increase in women's pay to the level of men's would be an inflationary shock not easily absorbed. The potential shock is considered by the courts to be so great, in fact, that so far they have refused to rule in favor of comparable worth legislation (Ms., 1985, p. 19). See pp. 290–291 for further discussion of comparable worth ideas.

The Equal Pay Act of 1963 and the creation of the Equal Opportunity Commission (EOC) under Title VII of the Civil Rights Act of 1964 have greatly helped

---

Inset 7-4

"Firsts" for Women in the ERA Decade

In 1977 Alice Peurala was elected the first woman president of a major steel workers' local, the USW's then 5,500 strong Local 65 in Chicago. Peurala entered union politics after she saw men getting promoted ahead of her ("I was wild; I couldn't believe it"), but was defeated for re-election in 1982 and returned to her $19,000 factory job.

In 1972 Sally Priesand was ordained the first woman rabbi. Since then there have been sixty others. Priesand is now installed at Monmouth Reform Temple in Tinton Falls, N.J.

In 1977 Dr. Olga Jonasson was named the first woman head of a major surgical department, at Chicago's Cook County Hospital. "There aren't nearly enough women who strive for the kind of position I have," she says. "And we need a lot more of them."

Lauded for her eloquence during the 1974 Watergate impeachment hearings, Texas Congresswoman Barbara Jordan appeared at the Democratic National Convention two years later and became the first woman ever to deliver the keynote address. She decided not to seek a fourth term in 1978 and now teaches at the Lyndon B. Johnson School of Public Affairs in Austin.

Janet Guthrie is the first woman to have driven in the Indianapolis 500. Guthrie took part in the 1977, 1978 and 1979 Memorial Day classics and had her best race in 1978 when she finished in ninth place. She is now automotive editor for *Working Woman* and races rarely.

Sandra Day O'Connor became the first woman justice on the U.S. Supreme Court. Said O'Connor, "Women have a great deal of stamina and strength. It is possible to plan both a family and a career and to enjoy success at both."

In 1985 Sally K. Ride became the first American woman astronaut in space. "I was not an active participant in women's liberation," Ride once said, "but my career at Stanford [where she earned a Ph.D. in physics] and my selection as an astronaut would not have happened without the women's movement."

In 1984 Congresswoman Geraldine Ferraro became the first vice-presidential candidate when she was picked as running mate to Walter Mondale, the Democratic candidate.

In 1983 U.S. Air Force women pilots flew troop and cargo-carrying missions to Grenada during the initial phases of the invasion while fighting was taking place. [In 1948 only 2 percent of Aiir Force personnel were women. In 1985 that had increased to 11.6 percent (Dean, 1986).]

---

women to move in the direction of equal pay for equal work, but there is still a long way to go. Barrett (1979, p. 57) concludes:

> The rapid evolution of the law from sanctioning sex discrimination in the guise of protecting the weaker sex, to establishing the principle of equal employment opportunity, and finally to mandating the eradication of discrimination through affirmative action is one of the most significant legislative developments of the post–World War II era. . . .

It is interesting to remember that women's rights advocates fought hard during the earlier part of the century for protective legislation to help women avoid exploitation in the workplace. Today those protective laws are considered to be discriminatory.

Although women's earning power and choice of jobs are still more limited than men's, this century has witnessed dramatic changes in women's participation as workers outside the home. In 1985 women comprised 44 percent of the labor force up from 31 percent in 1950 (see Chapter 9 for complete figures on women's participation in the workforce).

What changes can be made in the economic system to make better and fairer use of women in the workforce? Equal pay for equal work is certainly one necessary change (see Chapter 9). Next, a number of societal rearrangements could help the working mother. First, the quality of care provided for children of working mothers is a matter of public, as well as private, concern. Traditionally children have been cared for by their own mothers. When the mother works outside the home, other arrangements must be made. Children must be left with otherwise unemployed women, with relatives, or at child-care centers. Although professionally run child-care centers seem to offer the most advantageous help to working mothers, most women cannot afford even the modest cost of $10 to $15 per day ($200 to $300 per month) that good private centers currently charge. Consequently, in recent years feminists have argued and worked for government funding of day-care centers. They have had some limited success on the state level but little on the federal level.

One objection to government funding of child care is that it gives the government too much control over childrearing practices. Granted that minimal standards for day-care centers should be established for such things as fire and health precautions, general funding usually provides for much more detailed control. Those who pay the bill usually decide what sort of service will be provided. It is possible that legislation for child-care funding would provide for parental control over governing boards of child-care facilities. The trend, however, in other segments of public education has been in the opposite direction, toward loosening of local community control and greater regulation from the federal bureaucracy.

A second objection to governmental funding, especially from a feminist viewpoint, is that it provides a substitute for adequate pay for women workers. In effect the government is giving a subsidy to employers. Because the government is paying for the child care that employees cannot afford, employers can keep wages low and still find workers. Such government funding does benefit the worker but at the same time limits options. If parents do not like the kind of care provided in the government-funded centers, they have little recourse. They often cannot afford to send their children elsewhere, and they would have little influence on the center's policies.

A third objection to government funding is that the quality of child care may be poor. Consistency and predictability are crucial to the development of young children. In the past this guidance has been provided by parents. Profamily groups argue that the chances for good care are best with the child's own parents. Parents know the child best; they are ego-involved with the child. In day-care centers the quality of care, the philosophy of child care, and the sort of person interacting with the children is often unknown to the parents. If a working mother were paid an adequate wage, parents would be more likely to have a choice of private or public child care and could choose the type of care that best meets their and the child's needs. If women were paid adequate wages, the resulting demand for quality child care would make it profitable to establish child-care centers, and a variety would then be opened with differing educational policies. Even if parents had little direct influence over the programs offered, they would have some indirect control because they would not have to patronize the centers whose practices were inconsistent with their own values.

In spite of the merits of these arguments, for the immediate future government help for early child care would be an improvement over the present situation in which children of working mothers often receive only minimal care. In the long

---

Inset 7-5

The Case for a Parent Staying Home

As more and more mothers with small children enter the workforce, there has been an increasing call for child-care centers to help them cope with their children. Certainly, from the adult perspective day care is the most obvious answer to the child-care quandry. But is it an answer that works for the child?

A great deal of research and theory supports the idea that the young child needs meaningful adult attention for proper development (see pp. 450–451). Although such attention need not come from a parent, it is clear that the adult who gives it must be around the child enough for a meaningful relationship to develop. What is "enough" is not yet clear. However, it seems obvious that the two-year-old who is placed in a day-care center at 7:30 A.M. and picked up at 5:30 P.M. by a tired, overworked parent will have less chance to form a meaningful intimate relationship than a child not so treated. Even in an excellent facility, the child-care workers will have to divide their time among many children, rather than devoting it to just one or two children as a nonemployed parent can. At least in a child-care center there are adults to interact with the children. Older children are often "latchkey" children (children who have no supervision except perhaps at school and must await the return of their working parents alone).

In the recent book *The Day Care Decision*, the authors, who for several years ran a day-care facility, describe their progressive disenchantment with the system. "The problem was not with our facility," they wrote of their decision to close down their center. "The amount of toys and educational materials far exceeded the supplies of most centers. The problem was not our well-trained, credentialed staff; all staff members were qualified people who really liked and cared about young children. After two years of doing child day care, it was obvious that there was a problem inherent in day care itself, a problem that hung like a dark storm over 'good' and 'bad' day-care centers alike. The children were too young to be spending so much time away from their parents. They were like young birds being forced out of the nest and abandoned before they could fly, their wings undeveloped, unready to carry them into the world."

Although there are numerous studies that indicate good day-care centers do not harm the children, Dr. Burton White, author of the classic, *The First Three Years of Life*, suggests that such studies ask the wrong question—"Is there any damage involved?"—rather than asking the right question—"What is the best way to raise a child?"

Perhaps most fearful is the possibility that many American children simply are not getting enough parenting to become socialized, to internalize the ethics, values and mores that make it possible for a society to operate smoothly. The high level of violence among some segments of American youth, the drug and alcohol use, and the sometimes frightening lack of conscience and empathy for their neighbors makes one wonder if perhaps a segment of our youth is becoming sociopathic from lack of parenting? Has neglect perhaps become the worst child abuse of all?

It is the view of us alarmed by the trend toward full-time day care that parents, quite simply, have an obligation to their children to find other ways of coping. Often it involves making sacrifices and more than occasionally it involves innovation. For example, it is reported that an estimated 5 million Americans now earn their living working at home and this is expected to increase as computer-linked communication possibilities increase. No one ever claimed that having a child was convenient.

Source: Stein, 1984.

---

run wage scales for women's jobs must be raised to levels comparable to those for men's jobs. That is the best way to help families choose quality child care that will meet their needs.

In addition to better child care, more part-time jobs at good pay could be created. For example, two women could share one job. They could alternate days, or one could work a morning shift and the other an afternoon shift. Some companies offer mothers shortened shifts within school hours. These shifts allow mothers time to be with their children and maintain their home and yet contribute economically to the family. In addition, such mothers can participate in the world outside the home and maintain a career without working themselves into exhaustion as so often happens when a woman works all day and then returns to her homemaking job at night. Flexible time schedules can also help working parents cope with the demands of the home while at the same time maintaining high productivity on the job (Fisher, 1985).

Maternity leaves should be a normal fringe benefit of all jobs. The man who desires it should also be allowed such a leave to participate with his wife in the birth of their child. More than one hundred countries have laws that protect pregnant workers and allow new mothers a job-protected leave and full or partial wages at the time of childbirth. At this time, only about 40 percent of American working women are entitled to such leaves (Mall, 1986).

Business should reconsider age limitations in its hiring practices. The woman whose children have left home is often a reliable and conscientious employee. She may need some training if she has been away from the working world for a long time, but given that training she is far freer to devote herself to the job than is her counterpart with children at home, and she is often more stable and experienced in dealing with people than a younger man or woman.

Employers also need to reconsider their position on maintaining child-care facilities at the workplace. An employer supplying child-care facilities provides a number of advantages for working mothers. No extra time must be taken to deliver and pick up the child because the child is at or close to the workplace. Also, because the child is close by, the parent(s) may be able to visit, perhaps have lunch with, the child during the day, thus maintaining a higher level of parent/child contact. The company also gains a number of benefits (McCadam and Meadows, 1985). It has been found that companies that supply good child care for their employees also dramatically reduce worker turnover and absenteeism (often a parent must miss work if his or her children cannot be taken care of for some reason). Recruitment problems diminish because the selection of employees is increased.

With these suggested changes women would have more alternatives and would derive more satisfaction from their work. Business would have better workers, because the person who feels worthwhile and productive in all areas of life does a better job and is less prone to quit. Fair pay and a humane work system that supports rather than hinders home life are worthwhile social goals.

Credit and the Single Woman

Obviously, the lower pay scale for women makes it more difficult for them to obtain credit. For example, for house purchases lending institutions require that the monthly payment be no more than a certain percentage of the borrower's monthly income (see p. 269). The lower the income, the lower the possible loan.

The single, never-married, working woman usually has some credit standing, but the divorced or widowed woman may find herself without credit. Until recently credit standing has been based almost entirely on the husband's income. Even a working wife's income has often been discounted in the belief that she is only a temporary worker.

Susan and Larry Stevens both worked and earned well above the national average. Both had and used many credit cards. After Larry was killed in an automobile accident, Susan decided to move to the city where her parents were living. Although she and Larry had never had any problems obtaining credit, she now finds herself turned down because she has no credit history. Although she contributed to their joint income during their entire marriage, her past jobs and savings are not considered assets. She is lucky in only one way. If Larry's credit had been bad, she would have a negative credit history.

The 1975 Equal Credit Opportunity Act has curbed such unfair practices to a degree. The act requires that credit rights be spelled out. Credit may not be refused solely on the grounds of sex or marital status. A woman who qualifies for credit does not need a cosigner. Everyone has the right to know on what grounds credit was refused. Everyone has the right to examine the information used in making the credit decision (this must be done within sixty days). A woman's income or savings must be counted as equal to a man's. The credit history of "family accounts" must be considered in extending credit to either spouse, and credit ratings must be established for each partner.

Just how much these regulations will help women remains to be seen, but they are a step in the right direction. Of course, both males and females must be good credit risks if credit is to be obtained. Prompt and consistent payments on loans and accounts is the best way to build a good credit rating.

Women and the Law

Another restraint on freer gender roles has been the legal structure. Our laws are extremely complicated and have often worked to the detriment of both sexes. (It is important to remember that most of the laws governing marriage and gender roles are state laws and hence do not apply throughout the country.) In the past laws have considered females to be weaker and less responsible than men and therefore in need of protection. For example, in California a married woman had to use her husband's home as her legal address, and until a recent change in the law she could not buy or sell stocks or property without her husband's consent and thereby his acceptance of responsibility for her actions. The current Georgia code (written in 1856) states: "The husband is head of the family and the wife is subject to him; her legal and civil existence is merged in the husband . . . either for her own protection, or for her benefit or for the preservation of public order." This may sound archaic, but recent attempts to change this wording were defeated in the Georgia state legislature.

Although many laws remain in effect that are unfair to one or the other sex, the 1970s and 1980s have seen much change. These changes have been precipitated mainly by women challenging the laws they believed discriminated against them. Changes in laws on living together, divorce, child custody and support, on crimes such as rape and sexual harassment, and on benefits such as social security have resulted.

A change in a law to make the sexes more equal sounds like a worthy goal. Yet some critics see new inequities resulting. For example, divorce laws that require equal division of property may leave older women who have little work experience much worse off than their former husbands (Weitzman, 1985). Indeed the growing numbers of women-headed, single-parent families falling beneath the poverty level has resulted in what many researchers are now calling the "feminization of poverty" (see p. 511). The divorced woman may get her half of the property and still be unable to support herself. "Rehabilitative alimony" is one legal response to this new problem created by changing laws. The idea is that the former husband should provide financial help to the former wife so that she can retrain herself to become self-supporting.

Many law changes are making work and economic participation fairer to women. One example is the California statute enacted in 1978 making it an unfair employment practice to discriminate on the basis of pregnancy, childbirth, or medically related conditions. This law also requires employers who provide disability insurance programs for their employees to include disability for normal pregnancy as a benefit (AB 1960, Berman, Chapter 1308, Statutes of 1978).

In the criminal courts women have successfully strengthened rape laws. Punishments for rapists have been made stronger. For example, California now prohibits the granting of probation to any person who has been convicted of rape by force or violence (SB 1479, Deukmejian, Chapter 1308, Statutes of 1978). More important, many states have eliminated the humiliating defense tactic of cross-examining the victim about her previous sexual conduct. In 1977 Oregon passed a statute that made it a criminal offense for a husband to rape his wife. This stance is a complete departure from marital law of the past where there was no such thing as rape within a marriage.

Sexual harassment is another area in which the law is slowly beginning to help women (and even some men). Women have won numerous cases against employers who used the woman's need for work to pressure them for sexual favors. A few men have also won such cases.

Gender Role Stereotypes

Intimate relationships built on stereotypical gender roles tend to limit freedom and impair growth for both the individuals and the relationship. Although it is true that many married couples function well fulfilling traditional gender roles (i.e. husband-provider, wife-homemaker), such roles if adhered to rigidly and without flexibility might limit a couple. A female who has truly internalized the traditional wifely role, may too often limit herself to a child-centered, home-centered, husband-centered life. She may feel isolated and restricted. She may have to repress other aspects of herself as Mary did to conform to her role as she sees it. Such repression may lead to dissatisfaction and unhappiness. Her husband may find himself married to someone who is virtually dependent on him for the fulfillment of all her needs, for making all decisions, and so on. What begins as an ego trip (the helpless idolizing wife and the strong responsible husband) quickly becomes a heavy burden. Few honest males today would deny that such overwhelming responsibility is difficult and unpleasant, as well as constricting to their own lives.

A stereotypical relationship that locks the husband into a set of roles may limit his growth as well. He may be locked into the role of provider, which tends to give him many commitments other than his wife and family. In our competitive society, where success is measured by individual productivity and achievement, the husband often must manage two marriages: the first to his career and the second to his wife and family. When conflict arises between the two, he may place his job first. He has become "career-oriented." This situation may be difficult for the traditional wife, who is "family-oriented," to accept. She may feel cheated and rebuffed by her husband because he concentrates so much energy outside the family. She wants him to be successful, but by encouraging and supporting his efforts outside the family, she also loses some of his interest and presence in the family. Many older men locked into the traditional provider role complain that they have missed their family life, missed the children growing up, and lost out on the benefits of close emotional family ties because of their emphasis on the provider function.

As long as the economic system is partial to men, it will be difficult for them to escape the provider role. In the middle classes the unfortunate antagonism between male economic success and marital life is difficult to resolve. One step that can be taken to limit this conflict is for the wife to participate as much as she can in the husband's life outside the family. He can encourage this by sharing his career experiences and encouraging her interest in his work world. This is especially important if the man's work demands almost total commitment, as in medicine or the ministry. In such cases, if the wife does not participate, she may risk sharing little with her husband. Here important factors in marital satisfaction will be the wife's acceptance of and respect for her husband's commitment, as well as comfortableness with her own role. On the other hand, efforts must be made by the man to find free time to spend with his family.

A similar conflict exists for the married career woman. To succeed, she may have to put even more energy into her career than her husband puts into his. She must overcome prejudice about career females. Her husband may become jealous of the attention she gives her career, or he may resent her encroaching on his domain. Unemployed men who are dependent on their wife's earnings are likely to suffer feelings of failure and guilt. Some may respond to these feelings with hostility.

Most of our discussion has focused on the middle-class family. The traditional working-class family in many ways has even more rigidly stereotyped marital roles. The wife is expected to be in the home most of the time unless she is working. The man, on the other hand, fulfills much of his social life in his relations with his male friends. Thus sharing activities and joint participation in family matters seem much less important than in middle-class families. However, while shared conjugal roles may have greater potential for mutual satisfaction, they may also lead to conflict. Segregated roles may leave husband and wife with little to say to one another and yet give each a sense of competence and independence.

Lillian Rubin (1983) suggests that the lower-economic-class male may be threatened when his wife works because she will contribute a much higher proportion of the family income than would her middle-class counterpart. By maintaining rigid traditional roles in marriage, he is better able to maintain control and a sense of pride and importance. Working wives in these families express satisfaction with their jobs; often their husbands do not. The wife's working broadens her world and opens choices for her. Her husband may feel trapped and oppressed by his work. His choices may be limited by low pay and low prestige. Often his own lack of skills entraps him, and he is unable to think about moving ahead economically. He feels as though he is in a dead-end situation and often blames his family responsibilities for his unfavorable circumstances.

On the surface marriage based on stereotypical gender types may give a couple security and reduce conflict, yet in the long run such a marriage will probably create resentments on the part of both partners. The rigidity of the marriage also tends to make the marriage fragile and unable to adjust to new strains and pressures.

A traditional marriage that is based on stereotypical, but understood and accepted, gender roles may work perfectly well for a couple. It need not be restrictive, equity of roles can apply and flexibility can remain a part of such a relationship. The key is that the traditional roles are understood and freely accepted by the partners. Traditional marriage has long been criticized, but any relational pattern will have both positive and negative aspects. If suddenly all marriages were of some new form, it would not be long before new criticisms would arise. Traditional marriages in which the husband was the primary breadwinner and the wife had primary responsibility for the home and family worked well for many years. Who knows exactly what problems will arise with other marital relational forms? Perhaps one day we will return to the traditional marriage if we find that problems generated by new marital designs are, in fact, greater than the problems we were trying to escape.

A relationship based on equity (see p. 204) is one in which both members are freer to create their marital roles. By becoming aware of the roles society now expects us to fill and by understanding the role expectations that we have learned, we can begin to choose roles for which we are best suited and that will yield the most satisfactions. Such freedom of choice in itself can cause problems. Certain tasks must be accomplished to make marriage viable. Who will do the necessary tasks that neither partner wants to do? For example, neither partner may want to be tied to a nine-to-five job, yet in most families someone must earn money. The bills must be paid, the children raised, the car fixed, the house cleaned, the in-laws telephoned, and so forth.

For a relationship to foster growth each mate must be committed to the idea of seeking equity in the relationship and to communicating openly any feelings of inequity. This philosophy requires that the couple be willing to experiment and to change if first solutions fail.

Sally and Jim find, after several years of marriage, that their dissatisfactions with themselves, their marriage, and each other are growing dangerously large. They decide together to take an adult education class called Creative Marriage. The class examines many facets of marriage and family living, first analyzing common marital problem areas and then suggesting creative ways of approaching problems.

Sally and Jim decide that they will rearrange family responsibilities so that each can have more time to do the things he or she wants to do as an individual. They hope that by being freer as individuals, they will also find more joy in doing things together. Because both Sally and Jim work, each felt put upon by the children and the household chores. Sally did most of the chores, but was angry at Jim for doing so little. Even when he did help, he did not do it happily and then Sally felt guilty for not properly fulfilling her role as housewife. Now they make a list of all the things that have to be done each month to keep the family running smoothly. They each pick out the four things they think they are best at. In one case they picked the same thing. Jim thinks he is good at handling money and Sally thinks she is. They decided that each will handle the money on alternate months. The chores neither wants, they divide between them. They agree to try the new arrangement for two months and then reevaluate.

At the end of the two months, they decide to change how they did the chores neither had wanted to do. Both had felt burdened by the chores even though they did not feel unfairly put upon. They decide that rather than dividing the unwanted chores, each will assume responsibility for all of the chores on alternate weeks. In this way each is completely free of the chores for one week and then totally responsible for them the next week.

To date, this arrangement is working well for Jim and Sally. Each feels freer and less resentful toward the other; at the same time the family is running efficiently.

This kind of exploring can lead to a great deal more satisfaction than limiting oneself to prescribed roles that may or may not fit. However, seeking equity in marriage means that the partners be willing to explore and compromise. Each couple will have to sort responsibilities in order to yield the greatest freedom while maintaining love and intimacy. This is no small task, but the rewards can be large. The Couple's Inventory (see Inset 7-6) can help you explore your own and your partner's gender role attitudes.

Even with such equity a couple may still be encumbered by the stereotypical gender roles held by society. For example, Sally and Jim may agree that she is to handle the investments but find that the banker or stockbroker always asks for

---

Inset 7-6

Couple's Inventory

Personal goal   To look at how sex role behavior influences decision making, autonomy, and intimacy in your relationship with your partner.

Directions   Both partners fill out separate inventories and then compare statements.

1. I am important to our couple because _____

_____

2. What I contribute to your success is _____

_____

3. I feel central to our relationship when _____

_____

4. I feel peripheral to our relationship when _____

_____

5. The ways I show concern for you are _____

_____

6. The ways I encourage your growth are _____

_____

7. The ways I deal with conflict are _____

_____

8. The ways I have fun with you are _____

_____

9. I get angry when you _____

_____

10. I am elated when you _____

_____

11. The way I get space for myself in our relationship is _____

_____

12. The ways I am intimate with you are _____

_____

13. The ways I am jealous of you are _____

_____

14. I have difficulty being assertive when you _____

_____

15. You have difficulty being assertive when I _____

_____

him. Be that as it may, each couple can work to realize more freedom within marriage. As one student of changing gender roles suggests:

> A society that has gone beyond narrow ideas of femininity and masculinity to the ideal of the self-actualized person offers the widest possible range of choices to its members. It is a society that has reached a level of material comfort that allows it to put resources

16. The strengths of our relationship are _____

_____

17. The weaknesses of our relationship are _____

_____

18. Our relationship would be more effective if you _____

_____

19. I feel most masculine in our relationship when I _____

_____

20. I feel most feminine in our relationship when I _____

_____

21. I trust you to do/be _____

_____

22. I do not trust you to do/be _____

_____

23. I deal with stress by _____

_____

24. You deal with stress by _____

_____

25. The division of labor in household tasks is decided by _____

_____

26. Our finances are controlled by _____

_____

27. The amount of time we spend with our relatives is determined by _____

_____

28. Our vacation plans are made by _____

_____

29. Our social life is planned by _____

_____

30. Taking stock of our relationship is done by _____

_____

31. I am lonely when _____

_____

32. I need you to _____

_____

Source: Alice G. Sargent. *Beyond Sex Roles*. St. Paul, Minn.: West, 1977, p. 87.

into human rather than only material development. The real issue is not the liberation of women so much as the liberation of humanity, the establishment of a society where men and women have equal opportunity to fulfill their hopes and dreams unhampered by oppressive and irrelevant sexual stereotypes. (Lindemann, personal communication, 1986)

The idea described here seems at last to be more acceptable to many Americans.

The Movement Toward Gender Equality: Some Losses

On the death of the Equal Rights Amendment ("Equality of rights under the law shall not be denied or abridged by any state on account of sex. The Congress shall have the power to enforce, by appropriate legislation, the provisions of this article.") in 1982, *Time* magazine devoted a cover story to the women's liberation movement ("How Long till Equality," 1982). The story began "And yet." Its overriding message was that American women had made large gains in their efforts to achieve equal opportunities with men, "and yet" they hadn't reached equality, there had been some losses as well as gains, and in some areas men may have gained more from the women's movement than women have. The haunting feeling that the women's movement has been successful and yet has failed permeated the story.

- More job opportunities are available to women than ever before *and yet* the pay differential between men and women remains large (see Chapter 9).
- The number of women-headed, single-parent families has increased greatly *and yet* the largest percentage of these families falls below the poverty line (see Chapter 15).
- Women are freer sexually than they were when there was a strong double standard *and yet* the number of children born out of wedlock has increased greatly (see Chapter 10).
- Women have become more economically independent and have increased their economic responsibility for the family *and yet* men have reduced their economic support of the family.

Other writers echo this mixed evaluation of the movement toward gender role equality. Among them is Betty Friedan, whose book *The Feminine Mystique* (1963) helped set the women's movement in motion. In 1981, much to the dismay of ardent feminists, Friedan wrote *The Second Stage*, a critique of the movement that pointed out both failures and successes but emphasized the need to move in new directions and to abandon some of the dead ends of the first twenty years of women's struggle for equality.

Though the women's movement has changed all our lives and surpassed our dreams in its magnitude, and our daughters take their own personhood and equality for granted, they—and we [the founders of the movement]—are finding that it is not so easy to live, with or without men and children, solely on the basis of the first feminist agenda. I think, in fact, that the women's movement has come about as far as it can in terms of women alone. (pp. 26–27)

Friedan points to the strident militancy of the women's movement that turned off many American housewives who also yearned for greater fulfillment but who loved and cherished their families as well. What did the hue and cry about lesbian rights mean to these women, to their families? How would bra burning make them equal partners with their husbands in the world of work?

"The men still have the power," "ERA has lost so we must fight even harder," "We haven't won yet," suggest some of the feminist leaders. But perhaps winning isn't the point. Perhaps the first stage of the women's movement was cast too much in "win or lose" terms. Polarization was the result rather than cooperation. Gain for me, loss for you, instead of gain for both. Friedan suggests that we have to begin talking about a second stage, a new stage that unlocks us from obsolete power games and irrelevant sexual battles that we may *lose by winning*. Personal liberty and equality cannot be won by one sex at the cost of the other. They can be won for each sex only by both sexes working in partnership. The women's movement must now become the "women's and men's movement" if a full measure of liberty and equality of sexes is to be realized.

We must make sure that the feminist image does not harden into a confining and defensive radical *feminist mystique* where personal truths are denied and questions unasked because they do not fit the new image of woman.

> "I'm suffering from feminist fatigue," writes Lynda Hurst. . . . "After the last dazzle of the [feminist] fireworks, there was deeper darkness. [Women] are perhaps *more enslaved now than [they] have ever been*." . . .
>
> Don't get me wrong. It's not the women's movement I'm fed up with. . . . It's the "feminist" label—and its paranoid associations—that I've started to resent. I'm developing an urge to run around telling people that I still like raindrops on roses and whiskers on kittens, and that being the local easy-to-bait feminist is getting to be a bore.
>
> I'm tired of having other people (women as well as men) predict my opinion on everything from wedding showers to coed hockey. . . .
>
> I don't want to be stuck today with a feminist label any more than I would have wanted to be known as a "dumb blonde" in the fifties. The libber label limits and shortchanges those who are tagged with it. And the irony is that it emerged from a philosophy that set out to destroy the whole notion of female tagging. (Friedan, 1981, p. 33, italics added)

In discussing the second stage of the movement, Friedan suggests:

> The second stage cannot be seen in terms of women alone, our separate personhood or equality with men.
>
> The second stage involves coming to new terms with the family—new terms with love and with work.
>
> The second stage may not even be a women's movement. Men may be at the cutting edge of the second stage.
>
> The second stage has to transcend the battle for equal power in institutions. The second stage will restructure institutions and transform the nature of power itself. (p. 28)

Perhaps the questions of the second stage that must be asked today are more difficult than earlier questions. Perhaps women fear to ask them because the very act of asking spotlights the failures of the women's movement. Yet the new questions are eminently more important to the successful quest for personal equality and liberty. The very success of the movement is now forcing other questions on women and indirectly on men.

- Has my increased equality really made me freer? Or have men simply let me take on more responsibility while they have reduced their own?
- How can I have the career I want, and the kind of marriage I want, and be a good mother?
- Can I make it in a man's world, doing it the man's way? What other way is there? But what is it doing to me? Do I want to be like men?
- Will the jobs open to me now still be there if I stop to have children?
- Does it really work, this business of "quality, not quantity" of time with my children? How much time is enough?
- Do men really want an equal woman? Do I really want an equal man?
- If I put off having a baby till I'm thirty-eight, and can call my own shots on the job, will I ever have kids?
- Am I really freer sexually, or have I gained the right to say "yes" only to have lost the right to say "no"?
- Am I really freer if I have to work to pay my own way?
- How can I remain free while at the same time my partner and I make loving, caring, responsible commitments to one another and to our children?
(Some of these questions are from Friedan, 1981, pp. 34–35.)

These and many other questions must be answered by women seeking broader and more fulfilling roles in American society. Yet, after twenty-five years of concern with self-actualization, self-improvement, and self-awareness, can American men and women make the compromises necessary to build a successful and happy intimate relationship with a person of the opposite sex?

Trying to answer all of the questions above would be presumptuous. Yet the answers to such questions will determine the future of intimate relationships between the sexes and therefore will direct the kind of families Americans develop in the future. The answers are complex at best. Each change in the feminine role brings about changes in the masculine role and brings some gains and some losses. In some cases losses may outweigh the gains, especially during the transitional period. Certainly to some extent the questions raised by the women's movement have contributed to feelings of discontent and dissatisfaction among women and thereby have caused problems in intimate relationships. Moreover, as their increasing economic freedom has decreased their dependence on men, women have been freer to leave unsatisfying relationships.

The gains of equality for women are well discussed, but the losses engendered by these gains are seldom mentioned. What are some of women's losses? The most important losses seem to revolve around sexuality, childbearing, and childrearing.

Hand in hand with the women's movement came the sexual revolution. Only the latter moved at a faster pace than the former. "The pill" brought reliable contraception to women and allowed couples to separate sexual intercourse from procreation. The gains for women were significant. A woman could reliably plan pregnancies and thereby participate in the working world on different terms. She found new sexual pleasures as the fear of unwanted pregnancy was reduced. She became sexually more equal with men as the double standard broke down. Above all, she gained the freedom to say "yes" to her own sexuality.

Her sexual freedom came so fast that within a few years, young women were as embarrassed to admit to virginity as they had formerly been to admit to premarital sexual relations. And men loved the change! No more lengthy coaxing, cajoling, necking, and petting. No more need to promise love and commitment to get sex. The female who refused sex wasn't "liberated," "free," or "with it." To say no to sex was to say no to the sexual revolution, to the women's movement, to modern society. To say no was to be old-fashioned. Hence many young women, having won the right to say yes to sex, found that they had lost the right to say no. And the sex they were saying yes to was often sex without love and commitment.

The practical result of the combination of sexual revolution and women's movement was to *liberate men, not women*. It was as if men encouraged women's liberation so that they could gain unhindered access to women's bodies without making any kind of commitment. Today's young women complain not about the double standard, or being unfree sexually, or being nonorgasmic. They complain about finding men who care, who will make commitments, who will respect them, who will share responsibility for birth control and pregnancy.

And what of unwanted premarital pregnancy? Men had long been morally obligated to provide for children they helped to conceive. The shotgun wedding had traditionally forced the man to provide if he tried to dodge his obligation. Today the term *shotgun wedding* sounds prehistoric. The enlightened parents of a premaritally pregnant girl wouldn't think of such a thing. "They made a mistake. Let's help them get out of it." **Statutory rape** (sexual intercourse with an underage female) is seldom prosecuted and seems as out of date in today's society as the shotgun wedding. As Deidre English (1981, p. 28) says: "If a woman gets pregnant, the man who twenty years ago might have married her may feel today that he is gallant if he splits the cost of an abortion." Legally he is obligated to support the child, yet if he will not acknowledge the child as his, a woman can do little aside from a paternity suit, which is costly, painful, and often unsuccessful.

Even the expectations for child support are far from the legal norm that support of children must be assumed by both parents. Over 53 percent of women who are legally entitled to child support do not receive it (U.S. Bureau of the Census, 1983).

Thus a combination of the pill, free-choice abortion, the sexual revolution, the women 's movement, and unenforced child support laws has freed (liberated?) American men from responsibility for their sexual behavior. Of course, failure to assume responsibility may leave a man isolated and alienated from what could have been a loving family.

And what have these liberating changes brought the American woman? She has been freed to say yes to her own sexuality. She no longer bargains with her sexuality, offering it in return for commitment. She now assumes full responsibility for her sexual behavior, and she is often solely responsible for birth control, for any pregnancy that may occur, and for the support of her children. "We have to at least consider the possibility that . . . feminists have been duped into futile competition with men in exchange for the companionship of children" (Greer, 1984, p. 29) and, it might be added, the companionship and commitment of a caring man.

In *Sex and Destiny* (1984) Germaine Greer goes so far as to write a chapter entitled "Chastity as a Form of Birth Control," in which among other things she suggests:

Statutory rape
Sexual intercourse with an underage female.

> Chastity endows sexual activity with added importance by limiting its enjoyment to special persons and special times . . . Chastity may actually serve to stabilize marriage unions by maintaining a constant level of sexual interest in a wife who is often unavailable . . . It may sustain sexual interest over a long time period rather than allowing interest to burn out through unbridled indulgence. (Greer, 1984, p. 114)

Surprising words from an ardent and often radical feminist.

The family type that has grown the most rapidly over the past twenty-five years is the single-parent family, of which 88 percent are headed by women. Between 1970 and 1984 all families with children under 18 increased 8 percent, and single-parent families increased by 100 percent. Overall, single-parent families now account for 21 percent of all families with children, up from 11 percent in 1970 (Norton & Glick, 1986).

It is true that most single-parent families are transitional; that is, most of them ultimately become married-couple families. However, the greatly increased numbers of such families (even if only temporary) relate directly to the economy, inasmuch as it is the woman-headed, single-parent families that have the most difficult economic struggle. These are the families that disproportionately fall below the poverty line and cost society a disproportionate share of public monies via various welfare programs that help them survive. Poverty is being feminized as the responsibility for children has shifted more and more to women. The number of poor people in families headed by women jumped by 25 percent between 1981 and 1985 and accounts for about 12 million mothers and children (Penner & Menvosh, 1985, p. 84). Most of these single-parent families are headed by divorced mothers (50 percent plus). Another 18 percent are headed by unwed mothers, while the remainder are headed by separated mothers (U.S. Congress, 1983). In today's economy a mother alone with her child or children generally has a difficult time economically.

Examined in these terms, the movement toward sexual equality for women appears to have freed the American man, not the American woman. When we look at the American woman today in terms of sexuality, childbearing, and child rearing, a good case can be made that she has never been worse off, never more manipulated by men. It is little wonder that the ERA failed, that the feminist movement seems in disarray, that some women yearn for the days of the housewife happy in her kitchen. But to go back is to give up the real gains. Yet to go blindly forward might mean even greater losses.

It seems that it is now time to take stock. We need to reevaluate past gender roles so that we can keep those parts that were positive (rather than simply throwing out all traditional roles as bad), and we need to evaluate honestly some of the changes already made in order to keep the beneficial ones and rectify those that have proved damaging.

It is now time for "people liberation." Only when men and women work together to gain equality will it happen. Only when men and women work together in mutual respect and with love and care and commitment to one another will the American family again be strong. This does not mean the American family of old or some rigidly idealized new family form of the future. It means any family form in which men and women can realize their individual abilities and work together to rear children who become responsible adults willing to make commitments and assume the responsibilities that make a society great.

Equity between the sexes, not sameness, is the goal to seek. Yet gaining such a goal is not easy. First, one is born male or female, though this is not always as clear as it may at first seem. Second, one learns from society the roles (masculinity and femininity) that go with one's gender. If a society holds hard-and-fast stereotypes of gender roles, individuals will find it difficult to achieve equitable roles because variation will be discouraged. For change to occur, individual couples must strive to create equitable roles in their own marriages and at the same time join with others to fight cultural stereotypes. One group working to change stereotypes has been the women's movement. The movement has worked toward the passage of the Equal Rights Amendment (ERA) to end discrimination by sex. Women have also been moving slowly into what have traditionally been male fields, and more women than ever are now working.

Two important stumbling blocks to people's liberation caused by stereotypical gender roles are the economic deprivation of women and laws that discriminate between the sexes. Until women are able to earn the same wages as men for the same work, it will be difficult for couples to change the traditional roles of "man the provider" and "woman the homemaker." In addition, many kinds of discrimination are built into our system of laws. For example, women in the past have not been able to establish their own credit if married, though this law has recently been changed. Men are discriminated against by our criminal laws and by the armed forces drafting system.

Ridding the society of gender role stereotypes means that a couple is free to establish the most satisfying relationship they can. It means that they can establish the gender roles that best fit them. It also means freedom of choice within the marriage. Some may choose older, traditional roles. In such traditional marriages the roles may be rigid, yet tasks necessary to maintain the marriage are clearly spelled out and each partner knows his or her responsibilities. A specific role assignment may be more comfortable for some inasmuch as it yields efficiency and security. Some may choose a radical alteration of traditional roles into new but equally rigid roles. Others may opt periodically to change roles and to maintain a flexible system. The concept of reduced gender role stereotyping does not dictate the kind of relationship a couple will have. What it does is free couples to explore and feel encouraged to make their own choices. One of the basic suppositions on which this book is based, as you'll remember from Chapter 2, is: A free and creative society is one that offers many structural forms by which family functions can be fulfilled. The best marital roles are those that best fit you.

As positive as the movement toward gender equality has been, it has also caused some losses especially among women. For women these losses center around sexuality, pregnancy, and childrearing. For both sexes there have been losses of commitment, security, and stability within intimate relationships. It is hoped that such losses are transitional. As female liberation moves on to a second stage, such losses may disappear as the sexes cooperate and work together to improve and enhance commitment, caring, and loving within the man/woman relationship.

Too Many Women??

Guttentag and Secord (1983) hypothesized that the feminine liberation movement, the changes in sexual mores, the changes in marital interaction, the postponement of marriage, the reduced birth rate—that is, all the current social changes taking place in American family life—have their roots in the sex ratio of men to women. The sex ratio is reported in terms of the number of men per 100 women. If the ratio were 110, there would be 110 men for every 100 women. If the ratio were 90, there would only be 90 men for every 100 women.

Figure 7-1 shows the sex ratios in the United States from 1790 to 1975. A mere glance reveals that the last few decades have been unique to our history. Only then has there been a shortage of men in the country. Before World War II there was always an excess of men. *Is it possible that contemporary attitudes toward sexual behavior, toward relationships between men and women, and toward marriage and divorce are in part a consequence of this reversal in the sex ratio?*

Without going into detail about how the sex ratio differs for age groups, minority groups, or the pool of marriage eligibles, suffice it to say that there have been large groups of American women who have found a shortage of available men. Under these circumstances, many of the women would not be able to find a man to marry and would have difficulty finding casual partners. How would this affect the birth rate? How would this make women feel? What kinds of actions might they take? Would their attitudes and behaviors toward men change? Would they begin to relate differently to other women? Would

women get together in protest? Would they want to become less dependent on men?

And what about men? With an unusual number of women available, what would they do? Would they be more promiscuous? What about men that were already married? Would the presence of available single women lead to more affairs? A higher divorce rate? Less commitment to the family?

Guttentag and Secord suggest that under these circumstances the follow-

ing demographic changes would occur:

1. People would enter first marriage at a later age.
2. There would be an increase in the proportion of women who remain single.
3. There would be a large pool of divorced women.
4. More divorced and widowed women would not remarry.

They then go on to show that all these things are true in the United States today.

In addition, Guttentag and Secord predict that men would be less committed to one woman and to a family; rates of illegitimacy would increase; the number of women supporting themselves would increase; the number of single-parent, women-headed families would increase; and women would band together to try and better their situation. Again as we have seen and will see throughout this book, all of these predictions seem to have been fulfilled over the past few decades.

Guttentag and Secord suggest that when the sex ratio is low, women will take one of two courses of action:

1. They will work on such intangible aspects of themselves as their beauty, making themselves attractive to men as reflected in extreme form today in such magazines as *Cosmopolitan*, or in books like *Total Woman*. They will also emphasize "doing" for men as in the homemaking and childrearing roles. This direction includes doing things to please a man such as dressing according to his tastes, participating in activities he enjoys, and catering to his needs.

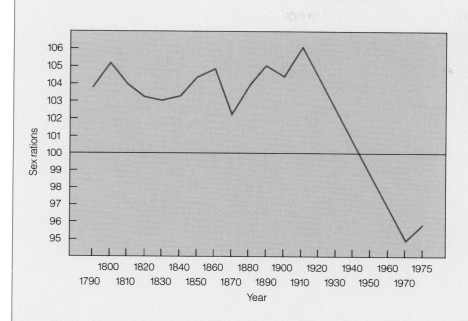

Figure 7-1 Sex ratios in the United States from 1790 to 1975.
(*Source*: U.S. Bureau of the Census, *Historical Statistics of the United States, Colonial Times to 1970*, Bicentennial ed., part 1. Washington, DC: Government Printing Office.)

2. They will work to lessen their dependence on men by increasing their independence and power socially, economically, and politically as reflected in the current feminist movement. The direction taken here emphasizes being oneself, instead of being what some man wants one to be, giving attention to one's own needs, and developing an independent identity as a person.

Certainly we have seen these two possible reactions to a low sex ratio in the feminist movement and the reaction against it. Remember that the antifeminist movement was fueled by women more than by men. Thus, for Guttentag and Secord, many of the profound changes taking place in American family life and in the relations between men and women occur because of a shortage of men rather than because of some deep philosophical or sociological set of reasons.

What Do You Think?

■ What changes would you predict in our society if women outnumbered men?

■ Do you see any other relational patterns that might occur if there was a shortage of one sex?

■ Do men or women have a wider choice of mates when considering age only? If one sex has an advantage, why is this so?

■ What effect on "power" does an imbalanced sex ratio have?

■ If men are in short supply, what kinds of legislative ends would you predict that women would seek?

■ What changes would you predict if there were more men than women?

The Family as an Economic System

Contents

As a computer analyst earning more than $32,000 a year, 31-year-old Bill Mitchell could be your typical affluent baby boom professional. But, rather than enjoying the glow of his career success, he is increasingly frustrated.

After paying rent on his apartment and other expenses, he, his wife, and two young children have little money left over to enjoy the good life. They can afford to eat out only about once a week. And he has little left over to save or invest in stocks or bonds or what he really wants—a house.

"I'm making more money than my dad ever did in his life, but I can't afford the home he could." Noting that his car payments of $260 a month were more than his dad's house payments he said, "It's frustrating. I've got a good and stable job with potential for upward mobility, but yet with just one income, to get a nice home would be difficult." (Sing, 1986)

Work, money, and intimacy are closely intertwined for most families. So closely are they related that trouble in one area almost guarantees trouble in the other two. The spouse who works two jobs in order to earn enough money to make ends meet almost certainly comes home overtired and disinterested in the more intimate functions of his or her relationship. Time for togetherness, sharing, play, enjoying the children, making love, and other intimate family activities is limited for the family in which both partners work full-time. On the other hand, unemployment within a family brings worry and stress as bills accumulate and money dwindles. Worry and stress are two particularly troublesome enemies of successful intimate relationships.

Most couples today pay almost no attention *at first* to each other's financial values. Money is often a more taboo subject than sex. Courting couples may discuss their prior sex lives but never raise the question of economic histories. After all, it is not very romantic or interesting to talk about one's potential income, or the use of credit cards, or one's feelings about indebtedness. Yet as pointed out in one widely read study of American families (Blumstein & Schwartz, 1983, p. 52), money matters are the topics most commonly discussed by married couples. Indeed their study focuses on just three areas of couples' lives—money, work, and sex—because these areas are so crucial to a successful, enduring relationship.

What should we buy? When should we buy? Who should buy? Who should make the spending decisions? Who will pay the bills? Shall we pool our money or maintain separate accounts? Such questions become particularly troublesome if the partners have divergent attitudes about money. For example, consider a person who comes from a background of thrift and practicality and takes pleasure in making a good buy. Such a person will be excited about buying a used car at wholesale rather than retail prices and will probably brag about the purchase. Any minor problems with the car will not be upsetting because of the value of the "good buy." Suppose this person's partner comes from a luxurious environment that places value on achieving precisely what one wants. Success is often measured by an economic standard. The partner sees a new car, of the appropriate model, as the proper vehicle to buy. A used car, especially a "steal," will be considered a mark of poor taste and economic failure. The married life of such a pair may be filled with conflict over money matters because of their differing monetary attitudes. Moreover, conflict over money matters usually leads to other problems.

Money and work are involved in everything we do, both as individuals and as family members. We are involved with work and money on a daily basis. Even the retired or sufficiently wealthy who do not work formally on a nine-to-five job must attend to money matters on a daily basis. (How are my investments doing? Will my retirement check arrive today? Can we afford a new car or should we repair the old car?) Successful work and efficient money management are the foundations for family success. Whether one is poor or rich, work and monetary decisions play all-important roles in people's lives.

As we think about the characteristics of strong healthy families (Chapter 1), it is clear that economic stability is necessary for the development of family strength. Economic stability and security enable families to turn their attention from issues of basic survival to enhancing the quality of life. Family strengths can evolve only if economic survival is possible. Given the complexity and uncertainty of the economic climate in which families must make decisions, it is clear that families need to learn all that they can about the economic system in which they exist if they are to be successful (Hefferan, 1984, p. 383).

Work also provides by-products beyond money. Personal as well as family status are derived from occupation. A medical doctor and his or her family enjoy high status (at least in America; the status of occupations varies among cultures) and this, in turn, will influence the lifestyle of the family members. One's sense of self-esteem relates closely to one's work. Self-esteem is one of the first things threatened by unemployment. Also one's sense of identity is based largely on what is done in the workplace. Often the first question asked of a new acquaintance is "What do you do?" A person's (family's) circle of friends is often partially drawn from the work world. Thus we see that the world of work and the family world are intimately related, and each influences the other in many ways.

Americans have more money per person than most people on earth. Yet the fact that Americans are comparatively rich does not lessen the importance of work and money in their lives. Per capita income—the gross national product (GNP) divided by the total population of men, women, and children—gives each American more than $15,000 per year (GNP figures based on the year 1984). Although there are a few nations with a higher per capita income (Switzerland and Sweden for example), in many nations it is much lower. For example, countries like Bangladesh, India, and Nepal, have per capita incomes of less than $200.

Despite American families' apparent wealth, dissatisfaction with money matters remains high. Almost all families, regardless of their actual income, feel that if they could earn $5000 to $10,000 more per year everything would be fine. In fact, as income increases most families find their needs and desires increasing even faster than their income (see "The Seductive Society," p. 251). Thus monetary dissatisfaction may be as high for families earning $50,000 per year as it is for families earning $25,000 per year.

Americans may earn more money than others, but they also spend more than any other people. Most money is spent by family units to support family members, so family income is an important measure of family function. Real median family income was $26,433 in 1984, up over 100 percent from 1969 and up 1.6 percent from 1982. This, however, followed a decline in family income from 1978 to 1982. Part of this decline was due to the increased number of single-parent families (most headed by women with lower earning power) and part of it was due to the economic recession of 1981–1982. The family in modern America is the basic economic unit of the society in that it is the major consumption unit. In the early years of our country the family was also the major production unit. Then

---

Inset 8-1

Comparison of Attitudes toward Money

Answer the following questions without discussing them with your partner. Then have your partner answer them. If you answer the questions differently, it may indicate points of attitudinal difference and possible conflict. You should each discuss the reasoning behind your answer and how your two positions can be reconciled.

1. Are you comfortable living without a steady income?

2. Did your parents have a steady income?

3. Do you consider yourself to come from an economically poor, average, or wealthy background?

4. Do you think that saving is of value in America's inflationary economy?

5. Do you have a savings account? Do you contribute to it regularly?

6. In the past have you postponed buying things until you had saved the money for them, or did you buy immediately when you desired something?

7. In the past have you often bought on installment?

8. Do you have credit cards? How many? Do you use them regularly?

9. Do you have money left over at the end of your regular pay period?

10. Do you brag about making a really good buy or finding a real bargain?

11. If it were possible to save $100 a month, what would you do with the money?

12. Possible answers to question 11 are listed below. Rank them in order of importance using 1 for what you would most likely do with the $100 and 10 for what you are least likely to do:

a. Save it for a rainy day.

b. Save it to buy something for cash rather than on credit.

c. Invest it.

d. Use it for recreation.

e. Use it for payments for a new car.

f. Use it for travel and adventure.

g. Use it to buy a home or property.

h. Use it to improve your present living place.

i. Divide it in half and let each spouse spend it as he or she chooses.

j. Use it for an attractive wardrobe, eating out, and entertaining.

---

90 percent of the population worked in agriculture on family-owned farms. Over the years, however, most fram workers became factory workers. Thus today's average family is not directly involved in economic production.

As a consuming unit the family exerts great economic influence. A couple anticipating marriage and children is also anticipating separate housing from their parents. This means a refrigerator, stove, furniture, dishes, television, and so on. And how will this new family acquire all of these items? Probably by the use of credit, not an American invention perhaps but certainly an American way of life. How much do Americans owe in installment debt? Approximately $549 billion, or about $2070 per person for outstanding personal credit as of January 1986. This represents an increase of about 67 percent since 1982 (Rudolph, 1986, p. 50). About 38 percent of this is accounted for by automobile purchases.

"Buy now, pay later!" "Why wait? Only $5 per week." These and many more are the economic slogans of modern American society. The extension of credit to the general population has produced a material standard of living the likes of which the world has never seen. We may, on the promise of future payment, acquire and use almost anything we desire—material goods, travel, education, and services such as medical and dental care—all without immediate monetary payment. If the credit system were suddenly ended, the degree to which it supports the economy would become glaringly clear. Traffic congestion would end as the majority of autos would disappear from the roads. Many buildings, both business and residential, would become empty lots or smaller, shabbier versions. Thousands of televisions would disappear from living rooms. A vast amount of furniture would also vanish from our homes. If debtors' prisons were reestablished at the same time, practically the entire population would be incarcerated!

If we think back over the economic events of the past few years, it becomes clear that the economy goes through drastic changes, and we all must adjust to these changes. For example, in 1979 and 1980 inflation was rampant, running as high as 13 percent per year. Yet by 1982 and 1983 inflation had dropped to less than 5 percent per year in the face of higher unemployment rates and a growing recession. By 1984 the recession was past, inflation remained low, but the dollar was so strong against foreign currency that America's balance of trade suffered and steps had to be taken to lessen the value of the dollar. Family income has been rising rapidly since 1984 but the country's rapidly increasing deficit threatens each family with future economic instability.

Such economic uncertainties make it imperative that individuals carefully plan their economic destiny. Those who do not are doomed to lose control of their economic lives. Knowing how to budget, spend, save, borrow, and invest are important skills for personal and family happiness.

However, even in good economic times, married couples often quarrel over money. Essentially, quarrels over money revolve around allocation of resources and control of the allocation as we shall see later.

Credit and Loss of Freedom

Credit buying has allowed the average American a higher standard of living than was ever dreamed possible. It has given Americans the means for a healthier, more fulfilling life about which, in centuries past, one could only dream. Despite these positive results, the system can boomerang and place people in a slavery system that traps them subtly but with great psychological cost. This entrapment and loss of freedom usually comes from ignorance of the system and blind acceptance of persuasive and seductive advertising. A clear understanding of economics and the relationship of debt to personal freedom enables people to make the system work for instead of against them.

Credit and debt are directly opposed to personal freedom. To contract to pay for a new automobile over a period of sixty months, for example, involves gaining the use of the automobile but losing a degree of personal freedom. Regardless of circumstances or what you do with the car, you have promised and legally made yourself responsible to pay a certain amount each month for the next three years. If at the end of one year, you wish to take a lower-paying but more-satisfying job, or to return to school to improve your skills, you would be unable to do so unless you could make adequate arrangements to continue payments. If you decide to return the car, this does not cancel your debt. Even if the credit company's policies allow you credit for the money it receives when the car is sold, the chances are that you will still owe because during the first year or two the car depreciates in value faster than the debt is reduced. Although the remaining debt may be small, it still exists, and so does your obligation.

Any debt curtails a certain amount of personal freedom. If you cannot at least partially resist the temptations of credit buying, you can become so obligated as to lose almost all freedom. This modern economic slavery is far more seductive than historical slavery systems based on power. In real slavery a person knows who the enemy is and where to direct hostility engendered by loss of freedom. But in the American economic system one places oneself in the slavery of debt and thus has no one else to blame for the predicament. No one is forced to keep buying "goodies" on "easy" installments. Unfortunately too many small, easy payments can add up to heavy debts—often too heavy for the individual or family to bear.

Joe and Mary—Slowly Drowning in a Sea of Debt

Let's take a closer look at a hypothetical, newly married young couple and follow them through their first few years of confrontation with the American economic system. Let's see how they handle work decisions, allocate their economic resources, control the power that accrues to the major economic contributor, cope with increasing economic pressures as children arrive, and confront the realization that today's average family must now be a two-earner family if it is to enjoy some of the benefits of the American economic system.

This analysis will make clear the slow and often insidious nature of the loss of freedom and eventual economic entrapment suffered by so many families. For many young couples marriage actually means a drastic reduction in their standard of living. Accustomed to living at home, to sharing their parents' standard of living (usually created by twenty years of their parents' earnings), the newlyweds are now on their own economically. Beginning jobs may be scarce, and pay is low compared with their parents' earnings. If the newlyweds fail to understand this and attempt to maintain their parents' standard in their new marriage, they are likely to be trapped in the economic system to such a degree that they will never be able to regain their lost economic freedom.

When Does Joe's Entrapment Begin?   Joe's actual entrapment begins before his marriage. Joe finds he is not as popular with girls as some of his friends. Like many young men, he has always been interested in automobiles. He figures that if he had a good car, he would probably be more popular. He also notes that his parents often judge their friends by the cars they drive. Thus he believes that his car should be one of the better ones. He has a job as a stockboy at a local supermarket, and because he lives at home and doesn't have any living expenses, he can use his earnings to pay for the car. It seems so simple. His parents don't object to his buying a car but make it clear that they are in no financial position to help him. So he contracts to pay $200 a month for the next five years. Of course, in addition to the $200 he now has all the expenses of an automobile: tax, license, insurance, gas, upkeep, and, quite likely, modifications (lowering it, turbocharging it, adding mag wheels, a tape deck, or whatever else is popular at the time). Car ownership costs are much higher than many people realize. Hertz Corporation reports yearly on per mile costs of their fleet of rental vehicles. For example, in 1984, a typical compact car such as a Ford Tempo cost 45.67 cents per mile to operate or $4,567 every 10,000 miles. This included all costs such as insurance and depreciation.

The automobile is one of the few products in the American inflationary economy that usually loses money. But the practical reason for the automobile, transportation, is rarely considered by young people. For many the car is much more than this. It is an extension of the ego. (In general the relationship between the strength of ego and the cost of the car is inverse. That is, the weaker a person's ego, the more important the car.) It is a means to prestige and status. It gives one a feeling of power because one can make the car do whatever one wants. Many adolescents drive hundreds of aimless miles per week. Car theft statistics demonstrate dramatically the importance of the auto to the young American male. FBI national figures show a heavy preponderance of male youths involved in car theft.

Joe soon attracts a wonderful young woman with his new symbol. Although she first noticed him because of his new car, Mary finds him to be a nice person, and they are soon going steady. The pressures of the American dating game build up, and they consider themselves deeply in love. Joe is near the end of his senior year in high school and will soon be able to work full-time. If he stays at the supermarket and becomes a checker, he will be earning $1100 a month to start, with the possibility of increasing this to as much as $2000 a month over time. This seems like a fortune compared with the $400 a month he now receives as part-time help. Both Joe and Mary have always heard that two can live as cheaply as one: another of the great modern myths.

Setting Up Their Apartment   After graduation, Joe and Mary wed and set up housekeeping. At first they are the envy of their friends. They are now independent, free of parental domination, and can participate in many things that were previously taboo. Soon, however, Joe finds that his salary isn't going as far as he anticipated. Somehow rent, food, and basic necessities are eating huge chunks of his new, large salary. Before his marriage he thought he would have enough to update his car a bit, go on some trips, and model their apartment after those seen on television. But now Mary says they need a new washing machine; it is something all young married couples must have. When they look at washing machines, the salesperson convinces them that they should buy the deluxe model with five washing speeds and three water temperatures. Of course, it's $70 more than the ordinary machine, but according to the salesperson, it's far superior and the payments are the same, just stretched over a longer time period. Of course, the salesperson doesn't tell them that the motor and all the basic parts are the same in both models. But the salesperson does add that there's a special this week on the matching dryer, which they can get for $30 off, plus free installation. It's a great opportunity and would only add $2 per week to their existing payments. Joe is beginning to feel a little nervous about adding more payments to the $200 he is still paying on the car, but Mary does seem quite happy, and he supposes the machines will make life easier for both of them. He still wishes he had his car fixed up, though.

Gradually Joe will find that his salary is claimed before he receives it. The couple will reach the point where they no longer have the freedom of decision over their income. One problem is that they are starting off with large purchases, some of which they don't need. A washer and dryer, for example, are unnecessary items for a young couple without children.

Credit to Cover Credit   A year after their marriage, Joe and Mary's first child is born with concomitant hospital, doctor, and general care bills. A surprising number of salespeople come knocking at their door to help them get their youngster started off right. First there are disposable diapers, a must for the modern mother. Then there is a photographer who will take regular pictures of their child so they will have a permanent record of the child's growth. There are toys that will help increase their child's intellectual growth. And, of course, they now need a set of encyclopedias.

One month Joe discovers that his paycheck doesn't quite cover their monthly expenses. At first they panic, but then Mary remembers an ad she saw that said "Borrow enough money to get completely out of debt." At the time it didn't seem to make sense, but now it does. They can wipe out all of their small debts by combining them into one large package loan that reduces their total monthly payments. With a sigh of relief they go to the finance company and soon have things financially under control again. The discount interest rate is 15 percent, but they don't really care as long as they can meet the payments. Rather than continue Joe's story, suffice it to say that five years after his marriage, Joe is in bankruptcy court. No, he hasn't gambled on a big investment speculation; he has slowly drowned in a rising sea of debt.

Contrary to popular opinion, most personal bankrupts are not big speculative investors who get into financial trouble. Rather they are low- and middle-class families like Mary and Joe who slowly become overburdened with increasing debts. Moreover, going through bankruptcy procedures does not seem to help people become more prudent with their purchases. Of those who file for bankruptcy, 80 percent use credit and are in debt trouble again within five years (Miller, 1983, pp. 249–250). Hence it is especially important for all of us to know as much about credit and borrowing as we can so that we control it rather than it controlling us.

People borrow for two basic reasons: to buy consumer goods and services and to invest in tangible assets. Consumer debt is high-priced money because it is used for consumable goods, such as cars, furniture, and clothing, where value

Credit, Borrowing, and Installment Buying

Discount interest
Interest paid on the full amount initially borrowed even though some of the loan is repaid each month.

Simple interest
Interest paid only on the unpaid balance of a loan.

diminishes with time. **Discount interest** is usually charged for consumer debt. This kind of interest is charged on the total amount of the loan for the entire time period.

Investment debt, or real-property debt, is lower-priced money because it is used for tangible assets, such as real estate or businesses, where value is more permanent. If for some reason the debt is not paid, the creditor may assume ownership of the asset and sell it to regain the loaned money. **Simple interest** is charged for investment debt. This kind of interest is charged only on the unpaid balance of the loan. (See Table 8-1 for comparative costs of consumer credit.)

Examples of Actual Interest Costs

Discount Interest: Consumer Purchases   If you borrow $1000 for three years at 10 percent interest per year, you must pay $100 per year interest for the use of the money (0.10 × $1000 = $100). Each month you will pay $8.33 interest ($100 ÷ 12 months = $8.33). In addition, you will pay back the principal of $1000 in thirty-six equal monthly installments so that it is all paid off at the end of the three years. The monthly principal payment will be $27.77 ($1000 ÷ 36 = $27.77). Thus your total monthly payment is $36.10, or your interest plus your principal payment ($8.33 + $27.77 = $36.10).

Although you will pay $100 interest each year on your $1000 loan, the fact is that you do not actually have the use of the full $1000 for the entire three years. Each month you pay back $27.77 of the loan. As Table 8-2 shows, at the end of a month (after one payment), you only owe $972.23 ($1000 minus your principal payment of $27.77 = $972.23) on your loan. Each month what you actually owe (or retain) on the loan is reduced by your principal payment until at the end of the three years (thirty-six payments) your loan is paid off.

Table 8-1
Comparative Costs of Credit

Lenders	Type of Loan	Annual Percentage Rate[1]	Remarks
Banks	Personal loans (consumer goods) Real-property loans General loans	10–18[2]	60% of all car loans, 30% of other consumer-good loans; real-property loans have lower interest rates because property retains value, which may cover defaulted loans.
Credit cards	Personal loans Cash loans	17–21[2]	Used as convenience instead of cash; credit is approved for the card rather than individual purchase; no interest charged if bills are paid in full each month; cash in varying amounts, depending on individual's credit rating, may also be borrowed against.
Credit unions	Personal loans Real-property loans	8–15	Voluntary organizations in which members invest their own money and from which they may borrow.
Finance companies	Personal loans Real-property loans	12–40	Direct loans to consumers; also buy installment credit from retailers and collect rest of debt so that retailers can get cash when they need it.
Savings and loan companies	Real-property loans	9–15[2]	Low interest rates because real property has value that may cover defaulted loans.

[1]Interest rates vary because of pressures of inflation and recession.

[2]If the institution charges interest on the *face amount* of the loan over the entire period of the loan, double the listed interest rate to estimate the actual interest rate.

Table 8-2				
Simple Interest Payments				
Original Loan	Interest Payment	Payments Principal Payment	Total per Month	Balance
1st month $1000	$8.33	$27.77	$36.10	$972.23
2d month	8.33	27.77	36.10	944.56
3d month	8.33	27.77	36.10	916.79

Keep in mind that interest rates now vary so rapidly that the rates used in these examples may not accurately reflect the rates in effect when you are reading this text. The general principles hold, however.

With discount interest the stated interest (10 percent in this case) is paid each year of the loan even though with each payment a portion of the loan has been paid back. The actual interest rate in such a case can be estimated by doubling the stated interest rate (in this case it would be 20 percent). This is done because, on the average, you don't really have the full amount of the loan ($1000) to use (see Table 8-2). You actually have the full $1000 to use only before you make your first payment. After your first payment, you have only $972.23, as the table shows. After the second payment, you have only $944.56 left, and by the thirty-sixth or last payment you have only $27.77 left. By adding up the amount of loan you actually still have after each payment and dividing by the length of the loan (in this case thirty-six months), you will find that you only have an average of $500 to use. Yet you pay $100 per year interest. This means your actual interest on this loan is 20 percent ($100 interest ÷ $500 average cash available from loan = 20 percent).

Actually, all you have to remember is that on a discount interest loan, you pay interest on the full amount of the loan each year even though you have paid back part of the loan. Such interest is usually figured for the full term of the loan and is added to the face amount of the loan at the time you receive the loan. Thus in our example you would sign for a $1300 debt ($1000 principal + $300 interest = $1300) but only receive $1000. The rule of thumb to figure the actual interest rate on this type of loan is simply to double the stated interest rate. When figured accurately, however, the interest rate will slightly exceed the doubled figure.

Credit Card Use If you maintain a balance on your credit card rather than paying promptly at the end of each month, you are charged interest at a very high interest rate. As of December 15, 1985, the interest rates charged by the top ten credit card lenders varied from 17.8 to 21 percent. For example, Bank of America charged 19.8 percent and Sears charged 21 percent interest on unpaid credit card balances. Note, however, that no interest is charged if you pay for your credit card purchases within thirty days. Thus, if used properly, your credit card gives you thirty days of "open credit," that is, use of funds without having to pay interest.

To give you an idea of the actual monetary cost involved, consider what a $1000 loan for thirty-six months will cost you at 21 percent interest per year: .21 × 1000 = $210 per year or $630 for three years. Because the actual amount of interest charged in credit transactions was often difficult to determine, the Truth in Lending Law was passed in July 1969. Under the terms of this law, lenders must clearly explain the credit costs of a transaction.

Simple Interest: Home Loans   Since home loans are invested in a tangible asset, the interest charged is usually at a lower percentage rate in addition to being *simple interest* (that is, charged on only the outstanding balance).

If you decide to buy a $100,000 home (home prices vary greatly from area to area; see p. 270), you may receive a loan of $80,000 for thirty years at 13 percent simple interest (interest rates for home loans have varied dramatically in the past few years from lows of 9 percent to highs of 18 percent). For example, to pay off your $80,000 loan and interest in thirty years, your payments will be $885 per month. Actually, $867 of your first payment will be for interest and $18 will be credited against the principal. Thus for your second payment you will owe interest on a principal of $79,982. Of your second payment $866.50 will be for interest and $18.50 will apply to the principal. Each month you will pay less interest and more against principal. However, at the end of thirty years, while you have paid off the $80,000 loan, you will also have paid about $238,600 in interest! (At present you can deduct home mortgage interest charges from your taxable income, which somewhat reduces the actual amount of money that interest costs you.)

Table 8-3 shows what monthly payments would be at different rates of interest on a $100,000 house when $20,000 is put down ($80,000 owed) or $50,000 is put down ($50,000 owed).

Financial Problems and Marital Strain

But What about Joe and Mary?

Constant worry about overdue bills and whether there are enough savings to cover a medical emergency, constant disappointment about being unable to take a vacation or buy a new dining set, constant comparing of their marginal economic survival with the plush lifestyles seen on television, and constant discontent with work or the way in which their income is spent all combine to lower Joe and Mary's marital satisfaction and increase marital stress. It is clear that financial difficulties will also harm all the other areas of their relationship.

Under the court-supervised payment plan (remember that the couple declared bankruptcy), Joe and Mary are slowly paying off their debts, including those incurred by the birth of their second child. Both Joe and Mary resent not being able to buy new things, including a new car now that theirs is so "out of date," but it seems as if every cent of Joe's salary is earmarked for the old debts. Mary keeps asking him why he doesn't get a better job. At one time Joe investigated going back to school to qualify for a market manager position. But he would need to spend two years in school, and Mary cannot earn enough to support the family during those two years. Instead, he has taken a second job as a night watchman. He is so tired when he comes home that the least little noise is painful, and he finds himself constantly yelling at the children to be quiet or at Mary to make them be quiet. He also finds he is usually too tired to make love at night. At work he envies the younger, unmarried men who are driving new cars. Why, he wonders, did he get married in the first place? Mary sometimes wonders the same thing about herself.

Table 8-3		
Thirty-Year Mortgage on a $100,000 House		
	Example A	**Example B**
Down payment	$20,000	$50,000
Amount borrowed	80,000	50,000
Interest Rate	**Monthly Payments**	
9%	$ 644	$402
10	702	439
11	762	476
12	823	514
13	885	553
14	948	592
15	1012	632

It is obvious that financial pressures have put a great strain on this marriage. In fact, in view of this pressure and the fact that they married in their teens, it is quite likely that Joe and Mary's marriage will end in divorce.

Are Joe and Mary alone to blame for their predicament? Why didn't they make the system work for them? Why didn't they wait before making major purchases? Why didn't they postpone children for a year in order to get on their feet economically? What are the answers to such questions as these? In the wealthiest nation in the world, how could this couple have been economically strangled?

Certainly Joe and Mary must shoulder much of the responsibility for their economic predicament. However, American society in general puts great pressure on all Americans to BUY NOW!!! and pay later (if you can).

As so often occurs, the actual behavior found in our society bears little resemblance to the truisms we learn in the family or at school. Buying and spending have quietly taken the place of thrift and saving. Traditional values, though still preached, are often no longer practiced. And in a productive, inflationary economy such as ours, they are no longer even virtues. Spending is important in a credit, inflationary society. Goods must be kept moving. The failure of the consumer to buy can immediately produce dire consequences for the economy.

Commenting on a Department of Commerce report about consumer spending, analysts said:

> . . . the report dispelled fears that consumer spending was on the verge of a sharp decline and brightened the outlook for economic growth in the months ahead. Consumers are alive, well, kicking and spending said the chief economist for Shearson-Lehman Bros., a New York brokerage firm. (Santa Barbara News Press, 1986)

The report on which the analysts were commenting indicated that Americans' spending was up 2 percent during December 1985, the biggest monthly rise in a decade. Spending outpaced the accompanying gain in personal incomes (1.4 percent). The report showed that consumers were continuing to spend more than they make, thereby increasing their debt and drawing down their savings. The savings rate fell to 3.7 percent of family income.

A slowdown in consumer spending in any one of the basic industries affects the whole economy, not just the one industry. The auto industry is a good example

The Seductive Society: Credit and Advertising

of this effect. A slowdown in the sale of cars, as occurred between 1980 and 1983, affects literally hundreds of subsidiary industries, as well as many other major industries such as steel, rubber, and aluminum. If the consumer fails to buy, production must be cut back, which means laying off workers, thus compounding the problem by loss of these workers' buying power as consumers. In order to keep goods flowing, a new field of endeavor has opened, namely, stimulation and creation of wants and desires in the consumer.

In the classic work *The Affluent Society* (1958) John Kenneth Galbraith states that the theory of consumer demand in America is based on two broad propositions:

1. The urgency of wants does not diminish appreciably as more of them are satisfied.
2. Wants originate in the personality of the consumer and are capable of indefinite expansion.

These two propositions go a long way toward explaining why actual income bears little resemblance to a family's feeling of economic satisfaction and also why Mary and Joe got into financial difficulty. Although Americans command a better standard of living than has ever before been known, many Americans are dissatisfied with the amount of money they make. The most dissatisfied group is that of professionals, where income is generally high, but so are aspirations. Economic contentment appears to relate more to one's attitudes and values than to actual economic level.

Advertising and need stimulation have become essential parts of the American economic picture. A family or individual has to be made to want new material goods for more than rational, practical reasons. For example, though a well-made automobile can last ten years with care, such longevity for the average car would greatly upset automobile production. The auto industry has met this problem with the yearly model change and the concept of built-in obsolescence, often under the guise of improvement. In all fairness to the auto industry, it should be noted that many yearly model changes *are* improvements, but change has often been made simply so that older models will appear less desirable.

Today's youth are growing up in a different economic atmosphere from that of their grandparents. The society they know is an affluent society. Even the recent period of relative job scarcity, inflation, and recession has had little effect on spending habits. Restaurants, for example, felt little of the 1982 recession. Buying, spending, credit, and debt are now familiar accompaniments of marital life. The advantages of such a system cannot be denied. Yet youth must also be aware of the dangers of such a system in order to use it to their fullest advantage. Joe and Mary became trapped and lost their economic freedom because they never had a chance to stand apart from the system and analyze its negative aspects.

The power of advertising and the ability to satisfy one's needs or desires immediately are formidable and seductive forces for mature adults to cope with, much less youth. How well can a young couple resist the invitation to use a store's credit again when they have almost paid off their bill? An official-looking check arrives in the mail announcing that they can obtain an additional $500 worth of merchandise for nothing down and no increase in the monthly payments that were otherwise about to end. If they thoroughly understand what exercising their desires in this manner means, they can make use of some or all of the offer with no danger. On the other hand, another purchase could be the straw that breaks the camel's back when added to the rest of their financial debt.

A young couple must remember that personal freedom and indebtedness vary inversely. The more debt they take on, the less personal freedom they have. Most experts suggest to families that they control their debts so that they total no more than 20 percent of their spendable income (Miller, 1984, p. 233).

In *The Affluent Society* (1958, p. 155), Galbraith points out that a

> direct link between production and wants is provided by the institutions of modern advertising and salesmanship. These cannot be reconciled with the notion of independently determined desires, for their central function is to create desires—to bring into being wants that previously did not exist.

Vance Packard's well-known book *The Hidden Persuaders* (1958) exposed the extent to which advertising influences the public's attitudes, values, and behavior. He questioned the morality of some advertising techniques that manipulated the consumer into buying regardless of the consequences. In concluding his book, he asked a series of provocative questions that young married couples might well consider (p. 143):

1. What is the morality of the practice of encouraging housewives to be nonrational and impulsive in buying family food?
2. What is the morality of manipulating small children even before they reach the age where they are legally responsible for their actions?
3. What is the morality of playing upon hidden weaknesses and frailties—such as our anxieties, aggressive feelings, dread of nonconformity, and infantile hangovers—to sell products?
4. What is the morality of developing in the public an attitude of wastefulness toward national resources by encouraging the "psychological obsolescence" of products already in use?

Approximately $26.7 billion was spent on advertising in 1985 (see Table 8-4 for the top fifteen advertisers). This represents a 2.7 percent increase over 1984.

Table 8-4
Fifteen Leading National Advertisers, 1985*

Rank	Company	Advertising
1	Procter & Gamble	$1,600,000
2	Phillip Morris Inc.	1,400,000
3	R. J. Reynolds/Nabisco	1,093,000
4	Sears Roebuck & Co.	800,000
5	General Motors	799,000
6	Beatrice Companies	684,000
7	Ford Motor Co.	614,000
8	K Mart Corp.	567,000
9	McDonald's Corp.	550,000
10	Anheiser-Busch	522,900
11	AT&T	521,318
12	Ralston-Purina	508,365
13	Dart & Kraft	489,349
14	General Mills	484,146
15	J. C. Penney	478,892

*Based on measured media expenditures only; does not include local advertising coupons, direct mail, premiums, trade shows, product sampling.

Source: Advertising Age, 4 September 1986.

Note: Dollars in thousands.

The majority went toward creating wants and desires that will in turn add new frustrations to the already monetarily unhappy American family who live at one of the highest material levels in the world.

Effective Money Management

Effective money management is the first step toward the reduction of conflict over money within the family. The most important step in reducing marital financial conflict is to determine ahead of time how most money decisions will be made. There are at least six possible ways in which a family can handle monetary decisions: (1) the husband can make all the decisions, (2) the wife can make all the decisions, (3) all decisions can be made jointly, (4) one spouse can control the income but give the other a household allowance, (5) each spouse can have separate funds and share agreed-on financial obligations, and (6) the spouses can have a joint bank account on which each can draw as necessary. Once a couple reaches an agreement on the system by which they will handle family finances, most day-to-day monetary decisions can be handled automatically.

To Pool or Not to Pool Family Money?

There seems to be no *right* answer to this question. In *American Couples*, Blumstein and Schwartz found that couples who favor pooling their money were neither more nor less satisfied with their money management than those couples who insisted on keeping money separate, yet each kind of couple felt that their system was the right way to handle money (1983, p. 108).

Both systems have advantages and disadvantages. For the newly married couple, it is often difficult to avoid pooling. If one partner suggests separation of money, the other is very apt to interpret it as a lack of commitment to the relationship. The same kinds of suspicions may arise when one prospective marriage partner suggests a prenuptial economic agreement.

Pooling is simpler as there aren't as many accounts to balance. Also each spouse knows what the other spouse is doing monetarily. On the other hand, one's feeling of independence can be lost. Confusion can arise as in the case where each partner writes a check on a joint account unknown to the other and they overdraw the account. Despite how a couple may feel about pooling their funds when they first marry, however, pooling tends to become the method of choice as the relationship persists.

Pooling is more highly favored by married couples than cohabiting couples, probably because married couples feel more "permanent" than cohabiting couples. It is interesting to note that people who remarry after divorce are more apt to maintain separate funds. This is probably caused by two factors. First, they may feel less permanence in the new relationship due to the divorce trauma. Second, they are very apt to bring to the new marriage assets that were accumulated prior to the new relationship and therefore seem to belong not to the new relationship but to themselves as individuals (and perhaps to any children of the first marriage).

Allocation of Funds: Who Makes the Spending Decisions?

The decision about whether to pool funds influences the decision about who is responsible for spending those funds. If funds are separate, some kind of joint responsibility for family spending must be made. Does one partner assume monetary responsibility for rent or house payments while the other pays for food? Do they both contribute from the separate funds to a single household account that is used to make family payments? If so, who controls such an account? Are both partners free to spend their separate funds in any way they wish? If one partner has greater income or assets than the other, does that partner assume more of the responsibility for family expense?

Note that the answers to such questions are related to power control within a relationship. Generally the partner that supplies the primary monetary support also claims the majority of the power in a relationship. "After all, it is my money and I can spend it any way I please!" "Remember that I earn the money in this family, and you will spend it the way I want you to!" Power through monetary control is greatest in the single-earner family. Obviously in the past the power would most often accrue to the male partner since it was he who worked outside the home to supply the necessary funds. However, as women have entered the world of work outside the home, the number of two-earner families has increased. The rapidly growing contribution of wives to family finances has wrought a revolution in family power structure (see Chapter 9).

It is clear that the answers to the questions posed above will vary greatly between single-earner and two-earner families. It is also clear that the answers must be satisfactory to both partners if a family is to function smoothly and efficiently. No evidence suggests that a particular manner of monetary allocation is most desirable. What is important is that the partners agree and are comfortable with the manner of allocation chosen.

Budgeting: Enlightened Control of Spending

The next step in reducing monetary conflict is to agree on a budget. A budget is actually a plan of spending to assure attaining what is needed and wanted. For example, a family's income must cover such basic necessities as housing, food, clothing, and transportation and, ideally, leave some money for discretionary expenditures such as vacations and recreation. How Americans spend their money is shown in Table 8-5 and Figure 8-1.

Certainly to many people budgeting sounds like a boring and uninteresting task. Yet we all budget at least informally. If you want to buy a new stereo system but do not have the money to do so and choose not to buy it on credit, then you are budgeting. To budget formally, however, is to gain control over your life. If we look at the numbers of people who have monetary problems, it is clear that budget control is imperative for most of us. Without it, it is easy to lose monetary control and to slip into economic entrapment as Joe and Mary did.

The first step is to allot money for necessities. Whatever money is left over can be divided among the family's other wants. The inflation/recession/inflation economy we have been experiencing has made planned spending more important than ever. For example, it is estimated that the spontaneous food shopper spends

Table 8-5

Summary of Annual Expenditures for a Four-Person Family at an Intermediate Income Level, Urban United States, February 1986

Component	Dollars[1]	% Total Budget
Total budget	$30,487	
Total family consumption	21,888	
Food	7001	23%
Housing	6654	21
Transportation	2846	9
Clothing	1999	5
Personal care	608	2
Medical care	1731	6
Other consumption[2]	1434	5
Other items[3]	1225	5
Social Security and disability	2043	7
Personal income taxes	5331	17

Source: U.S. Department of Labor, 1982: updated to January 1986 by author by adding inflation factor.

[1]Because of rounding, sums of individual items may not equal totals.

[2]Other consumption includes average costs for reading materials, recreation, tobacco, alcohol, education, and miscellaneous.

[3]Other items include allowances for gifts and contributions, life insurance, and occupational expenses.

Figure 8-1 Annual expenditures for a four-person, medium-income family.

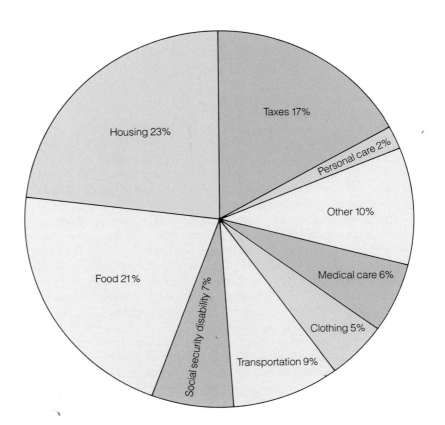

approximately 10 to 15 percent more for food than the shopper who has a planned food budget and a shopping list of needed items.

By living within a budget (see Table 8-6 and Inset 8-2), a family can avoid many of the problems that defeated Joe and Mary. In addition, by budgeting even a small amount to savings, they can make investment possible. Saving is really only deferred spending. If immediate spending is deferred, it becomes possible to use the money to earn additional income.

A budget should only be used for a specified time, and then it should be updated to reflect changing family circumstances. For example, the newly married couple may feel well off if both work. They have two incomes and minimal expenses. But danger lies ahead if they become accustomed to using up both incomes. For example, if they decide to have children, the wife may give up her income, at least for a while. Expenses also increase when children are added to the family. The combination of lower income and rising expenses can throw a family into an economic crisis unless they have planned economically for both eventualities.

Another eventuality that some families must plan for is college education for the children. This usually means a drastic rise in expenditures. The cost of putting a child through college will be between $30,000 to $60,000 including room and board.

After their children have become independent, the couple can usually enjoy a comfortable period of relative affluence. They must, however, plan carefully for their coming retirement. Without such planning they may spend their older years in a state of poverty, especially if inflationary pressures exist. Thus good budgeting remains important across the lifespan.

As dull and uninteresting as budget planning may seem, the family that does not put time into planning its finances may face increasing monetary strain, even destruction. This is especially true when there is a high rate of inflation.

Saving through Wise Spending

When many families think of saving, they think only of putting money into a savings account. Yet wise spending—that is, buying when an item is "on sale," seeking out bargains, buying used instead of new, being aware of consumer traps in marketing, studying seasonal price fluctuations to buy at the best time (see Table 8-7), and simply being an astute consumer—is another important way of saving.

Table 8-6
Suggested Budget for Necessities for a Family of Four

Item	Low Income Percentage Range	Median Income Percentage Range
Food	25–35	20–30
Housing	25–35	20–30
Transportation	16–20	12–18
Taxes	12–15	20–23
Clothing	10–15	10–15
Health and insurance	8–12	8–14
Recreation and savings	4–10	8–12

Inset 8-2
How to Budget Your Income

Once you decide to do some positive money management, you must figure out a budget and try to stick to it. The budget is a planning tool to help you reduce undirected spending.

Steps in Budget Making

Create a spending plan by following these four basic steps:

1. Analyze past spending by keeping records for a month or two.
2. Determine *fixed expenses* such as rent and any other contractual payments that must be made—even if they are infrequent, such as insurance and taxes.
3. Determine *flexible expenses*, such as food and clothing.
4. Balance your fixed plus flexible expenditures with your available income. If a surplus exists, you can apply it toward achieving your goals. If there is a deficit, then you must reexamine

your flexible expenditures. You can also reexamine fixed expenses with a view to reducing them in the future.

Note that so-called fixed expenses are only fixed in the short run. In the longer run everything is essentially flexible or variable. One can adjust one's fixed expenses by changing one's standard of living, if necessary.

The Importance of Keeping Records

Budget making, whether you are a college student, a single person living alone, or the head of a family, will be useless if you don't keep records. The only way to make sure that you are carrying out your budget is by keeping records of what you are actually spending. The ultimate way to maintain records is to write everything down, but that becomes time consuming and therefore costly. Another way to keep

records is to write checks for everything. Records are also important in case of problems with faulty products or services or the Internal Revenue Service.

General Budgeting

Figure 8-2 is a monthly general budget form that encompasses both estimated and actual cash available and fixed and variable payments.

You will note that the savings category is located under the *Fixed Payments* heading. This is because the money in your savings account may be used to pay such fixed annual expenses as auto, fire, and life insurance, and it is necessary to plan to save in advance for these expenses.

The key to making a budget work for you is to review your figures every month to see how your monthly estimates compare with your spending.

It is not as easy as one might imagine to be a wise shopper. Salespeople may be more interested in making a sale than they are in the exact needs of you or your family. Also since salespeople are not necessarily highly knowledgeable about the products they sell, they may not be able to help you decide whether the product is right for you. Naturally wise salespeople will learn about their merchandise and will take into consideration their customers' needs. By doing this they assure themselves of satisfied customers and repeat business.

You should do extensive research before purchasing "big ticket" items such as household appliances and automobiles. For example, you can find objective test reports on various household items (as well as other things) in the magazine *Consumer Reports*. The various automotive magazines describe car tests each month. To know exactly what you want before approaching a salesperson is an important basis for wise buying. You will not be sold an item that is inferior, fails to meet your needs, or is more than you want or need.

Avoiding consumer traps is important to wise shopping. Although not every trap can be discussed here, it is important to know about some of the more common ones:

CASH FORECAST MONTH OF _____	ESTIMATED	ACTUAL
Cash on hand and in checking account, end of previous period	_____	_____
Savings needed for planned expenses	_____	_____

RECEIPTS

	ESTIMATED	ACTUAL
Net pay	_____	_____
Borrowed	_____	_____
Interest/dividends	_____	_____
Other	_____	_____
Total cash available during period	_____	_____

FIXED PAYMENTS

	ESTIMATED	ACTUAL
Mortgage or rent	_____	_____
Life insurance	_____	_____
Fire insurance	_____	_____
Auto insurance	_____	_____
Medical insurance	_____	_____
Savings	_____	_____
Local taxes	_____	_____
Loan or other debt	_____	_____
Children's allowances	_____	_____
Other	_____	_____
Total fixed payments	_____	_____

FLEXIBLE PAYMENTS

	ESTIMATED	ACTUAL
Water	_____	_____
Fuel	_____	_____
Medical	_____	_____
Household supplies	_____	_____
Car	_____	_____
Food	_____	_____
Clothing	_____	_____
Nonrecurring large payments	_____	_____
Contributions, recreation, etc.	_____	_____
Other	_____	_____
Total flexible payments	_____	_____

TOTAL ALL PAYMENTS _____ _____

RECAPITULATION

	ESTIMATED	ACTUAL
Total cash available	_____	_____
Total payments	_____	_____
Cash balance, end of period	_____	_____

Figure 8-2 A general way to budget.

Table 8-7
When to Buy Selected Articles and Food Items

Sale Months	Consumer Articles	Food Items
January	Linens, baby things, men's and women's clothing, home furnishings, luggage, lingerie, furs, diamonds, cosmetics, and nonprescription drugs	Citrus fruit, cauliflower, potatoes, onions, and turkeys
February	Housewares, hosiery, and fabrics	Citrus fruit, potatoes, greens, celery, snap beans, apples, and canned fruit
March	Hardware, paint, gardening tools, made-to-order slipcovers and drapes, china, glass, women's shoes, and rain gear	Texas carrots, Florida lettuce, oranges, and green peas
April	Paint, wallpaper, building supplies, air conditioners, and tires	Asparagus, artichokes, snap beans, cabbage, carrots, onions, Maine potatoes, and fish items
May	Jewelry, candy, housewares, gardening tools, bed linens and towels, vacation gear, and cleaning supplies	Eggs, Florida corn, and onions
June	Gifts for brides, grads, and dads; men's clothing; sporting goods; and small appliances	Apricots, cantaloupes, cherries, and eggs
July	Furniture, bedding, bed linens and towels, and major appliances	Raspberries, blackberries, blueberries, limes, mangoes, peaches, beets, and okra
August	School supplies, summer clothing and equipment, and fall fashions	Corn, peaches, watermelon, cabbage, tomatoes, and seafood
September	Home improvements, sporting goods, china, glassware, major appliances, children's shoes, and auto batteries	Grapes, cucumbers, melons, squash, and lamb
October	Furniture, lamps, outerwear, and furnaces	Apples, cauliflower, grapes, pears, eggplant, and pumpkins
November	Rugs, men's clothing, furnishings, linoleum, liquors, toys, and games	Gourmet foods, avocados, cranberries, persimmons, sweet potatoes, turnips, raisins, and nuts
December	Post-Christmas cards, wrappings, lights, and decorations; toys; games; and housewares	Coconuts, flour, shortening, sugar, spices, and early citrus

1. Bait and switch. An ad describes a certain product, such as a washing machine, with a very low price. When you go to make the purchase, the salesperson claims that the product is inferior or the store is out of the advertised machine and guides you to a more expensive machine.

2. Low ball. This technique is often used in car sales. The salesperson offers you the car at a good price, you think you have a deal, but then a higher authority (sales manager) countermands the salesperson's offer. By now you may be psychologically committed to buy, and the few hundred extra dollars added to the price may seem acceptable.

3. High ball. Again this is mainly found in car sales. Here the salesperson offers you an inflated trade-in allowance on your old car. This is reduced by the manager once you are psychologically committed to buy.

4. "Borax" furniture stores. These stores advertise rooms of furniture or carpeting for very low prices, but then point out the inferiority of the merchandise, and "switch" you to presumably better, but more expensive, merchandise.

5. Contest winner. In this case you are told that you have won a contest that you didn't enter, but it turns out you must buy something in order to receive your prize.

6. Free goods. If you buy this carpeting, you will get free installation. Normally such free(??) extras are included in a higher price for the goods you are actually buying.

7. Off brand items. If you are knowledgeable about what you want to purchase, it may be perfectly all right to purchase a product that is new to the market or not a well-known brand. However, well-known brands, although usually higher priced, do offer certain advantages (especially to the ignorant buyer). There is usually less variance in quality; warranties are often better; you know that the company will be there to honor the warranty, and there is usually a wider repair network.

8. Hard sell. Beware of the salesperson that tells you you must buy this sales item today because it is the last one or that the price will go up tomorrow. There is always time to buy and an attempted rush act usually is a signal that all is not right.

9. "Boiler room" telephone sales. Telephone sales of services or products are usually to be avoided. If you accept such an offer and there is a problem, you generally have no recourse since "boiler room" operations are often "here today, gone tomorrow" businesses.

Inflation and Recession

Normally the economy alternates between relatively long periods of inflation and shorter periods of economic downturn or recession. Not many years ago economists thought that inflation and recession were opposites and could never occur together. Yet this combination has occurred at times during both the 1970s and the 1980s. Therefore, effective money management must take into consideration inflation, recession, and a mix of the two. In an **inflationary recession** economy every possible bad thing is happening at once. Production is falling, unemployment is rising, and inflation continues. Fortunately this state of the economy seldom lasts for long.

This book is not the place for a detailed economic discussion of inflation and recession, although you will need some understanding of it if you are to make the economy work for you rather than against you. Because inflation, recession, economic growth, and employment are all related, a change in one tends to produce changes in the others. Thus the successful money manager must understand these trends.

Inflation

Since World War II there have been many, often revolutionary social and economic changes. One of the most noticeable changes, especially in the 1970s and continuing into the 1980s, has been the constant inflation with which families have had to cope. Each day we have been surprised, dismayed, and angry at increased nominal costs (absolute price for an item) of almost everything we buy. Bread is more than $1 a loaf, yet it seems only yesterday that it was 50¢. A new car ten years ago cost about $5000, tax and license included. Today, the same model is priced closer to $10,000. "Buy now before the price increases," is an often-repeated advertisement that feeds our fears about inflation. Month by month those on fixed incomes slowly drop further into poverty. The demands for increased wages, just to stay even with inflation, become more insistent. Public opinion polls show that inflation is a constant major concern. Books on personal finance often begin with a discussion of inflation in the first chapter

Constantly rising prices and periods of real income (buying power) stagnation combine to bring more and more wives into the labor force. A thorough understanding of inflation can help today's family make better use of their resources.

Americans born after 1940 have only known an inflationary economy with constantly rising prices. Beginning with World War II, the rate of inflation has averaged 5 to 6 percent a year. The rate dropped at the beginning of the 1960s but then began to rise again until it reached a dramatic double-digit high of 12 percent in 1974. Thereafter it declined until 1978 when it went to 9 percent and 1979 when it reached a new post–World War II high of over 13 percent, the highest rate in 33 years (see Figure 8-3). By 1982, however, the inflation rate had dropped dramatically to less than 5 percent and has remained there through 1986.

Prices do not always rise, although younger people might not believe this. Figure 8-4 shows the Consumer Price Index (CPI) since 1910. Declines in the index indicate a recession or depression in the economy. The CPI has risen over 700 percent in the past 75 years. Goods costing $100 in 1967, the current base year for most goods, cost $327.90 in June 1986.

It is interesting to examine some of the specific components in the CPI. Take, for example, June 1986: Residential rents lagged behind other increases (279.4) while the cost of home ownership soared above gneral increases (358). Apparel lagged behind (204.5), while energy prices soared (380.6).

Inflation rates by themselves only tell half the story of the American economy. Inflation simply indicates that nominal prices have risen. However, income has also risen during this time. If income rises at the same rate as prices, buying

Figure 8-3   Inflation rates. The figures cover each full year. The highest gain was in 1979 when the Consumer Price Index soared to 13.3 percent.

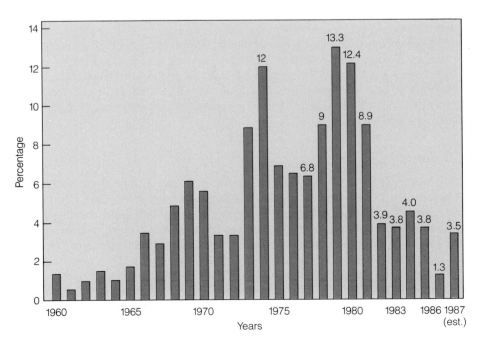

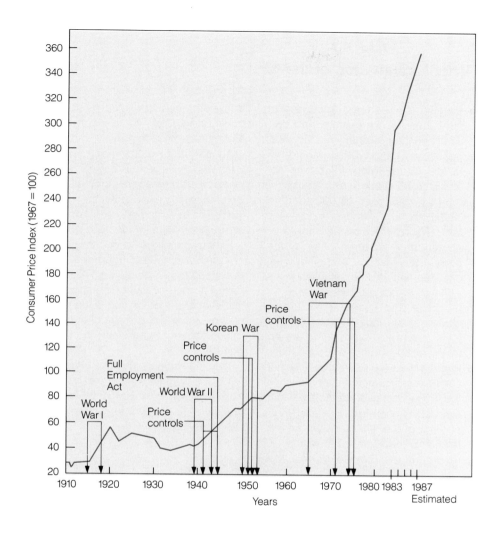

Figure 8-4 The Consumer Price Index has its ups and downs (mostly ups).

power remains the same. Thus a more important measure of the economy than the inflation rate is the *real per capita income*. This is computed by taking the per capita income increase and subtracting the inflation rate. If my income increases 10 percent in a year during which inflation is only 5 percent, my real income (buying power) has increased 5 percent. Most people have actually increased their real income (buying power) since World War II. However, there have been years (such as 1976–1977) when the real per capita income has declined. Fortunately family per capita income after several years of stagnation has been rising recently. Real personal income rose .5 percent in 1982, 3.5 percent in 1983, 6.8 percent in 1984, and 2.1 percent in 1985.

The CPI is the most common indicator used in popular media to measure price fluctuations. (See Inset 8-3 for an explanation of the CPI figures.) Because it is an average, it tends to mask actual price fluctuations for a specific item. Thus it is important for the consumer to look at the relative price of a product rather than just the nominal or absolute price. Although most goods have greatly increased in nominal price, some relative prices have actually decreased. For

---

Inset 8-3
Brief Explanation of the CPI

The Consumer Price Index (CPI) is a measure of the average change in prices over time in a fixed market basket of goods and services. Effective with the January 1978 index, the Bureau of Labor Statistics began publishing CPI's for two population groups: (1) a new CPI for All Urban Consumers (CPI-U), which covers approximately 80 percent of the total noninstitutional civilian population; and (2) a revised CPI for Urban Wage Earners and Clerical Workers (CPI-W), which represents about half the population covered by the CPI-U. The CPI-U includes, in addition to wage earners and clerical workers, groups that historically have been excluded from CPI coverage, such as professional, managerial, and technical workers, the self-employed, short-term workers, the unemployed, and retirees and others not in the labor force.

The CPI is based on prices of food, clothing, shelter, fuels, transportation fares, charges for doctors' and dentists' services, drugs, and the other goods and services that people buy for day-to-day living. Prices are collected in 85 urban areas across the country from over 18,000 tenants, 18,000 housing units for property taxes, and about 24,000 establishments—grocery and department stores, hospitals, filling stations, and other types of stores and service establishments. All taxes directly associated with the purchase and use of items are included in the index. Prices of food, fuels, and a few other items are obtained every month in all 85 locations. Prices of most other commodities and services are collected every month in the five largest geographic areas and every other month in other areas. Prices of most goods and services are obtained by personal visits of the Bureau's trained representatives. Mail questionnaires are used to obtain public utility rates, some fuel prices, and certain other items.

In calculating the index, price changes for the various items in each location are averaged together with weights, which represent their importance in the spending of the appropriate population group. Local data are then combined to obtain a U.S. city average. Separate indexes are also published for 28 local areas. Area indexes do not measure differences in the level of prices among cities; they only measure the average change in prices for each area since the base period.

The index measures price changes from a designated reference date—1967—which equals 100.0. An increase of 22 percent, for example, is shown as 122.0.

---

example, compared with 1967, the base year, when the CPI was set at 100, the index rose to 324.5 in September 1985, indicating that the CPI-measured average prices had more than tripled in the preceding eighteen years. But television sets dropped to only 86.5 on the index. In other words, television sets did not go up in absolute cost between 1967 and 1985 and, relative to other goods on the CPI, actually became much cheaper. So, although overall prices as measured by the CPI are going up, some goods go up more slowly than others and therefore become relatively better buys. Decreases in nominal price have also occurred because of technological breakthroughs that have lowered production costs in certain industries such as electronics.

Another way to see the relationship between inflation of prices and income is to compare the actual amount of income needed to remain at the same purchasing power level from 1950 to 1981. A family that earned $10,000 in 1950 needed $12,219 in 1960, $16,130 in 1970, $27,200 in 1981, and $32,640 as of December 1986 to retain their initial 1950 purchasing power of $10,000.

Compared with many other countries, the United States has had a relatively low rate of inflation since World War II. Many countries have experienced 40, 50, and even 100 percent inflation every year. As Table 8-8 shows, the government

Table 8-8
A 9.4 Percent Increase in All Prices and Salaries over a One-Year Period*

	Gross Income	Federal Income Tax	Effective Rate	After-Tax Income in Year 1 Dollars
Year 1	$14,000	$1,600	11.4%	$12,400
Year 2	15,316	1,890	12.3	12,164
Year 1	20,000	3,010	15.1	16,990
Year 2	21,880	3,506	16.0	16,646
Year 1	30,000	6,020	20.1	23,980
Year 2	32,820	7,035	21.4	23,361

*Because of graduated income tax rates, even families lucky enough to get raises matching the big increase in living costs wound up losing purchasing power. Here we show how a 9.4 percent inflation outruns a 9.4 percent pay raise. The 1986 tax reform and indexing of tax rates should correct this problem.

benefits from mild inflation, so government efforts to control inflation are often half-hearted.

High energy costs are one of the major causes of recent inflation, along with the inflationary mentality that has been created in the last few years. Hopefully the current extended period of low inflation, which started in 1982, and the recent decrease in energy costs due to an oversupply of oil will break the inflation mentality.

Living with Inflation

Even though severe inflation was controlled in 1982, it appears that some degree of inflation will influence the economy for the foreseeable future, and Americans must take it into consideration if they are to be successful economically. Even a 5 percent inflation rate each year means that in ten years a dollar has lost half its value. You can combat mild inflation in a number of ways:

1. *Minimize your cash holdings.* Cash obviously loses value at the rate of inflation. If I bury $1000 cash to protect it from theft for a year during which the inflation rate is 10 percent, inflation robs me of $100. At the end of the year I have only $900 in purchasing power.
2. *Select high-yield savings accounts whenever possible.* There are now many savings plans paying interest rates from 5 to 16 percent. In the longer term accounts there are often substantial penalties if you withdraw your funds before the end of the term. Hence one must spread one's savings over a number of different kinds of accounts. For instance, you will want to keep a small balance to cover unexpected expenses in a regular passbook account where you can withdraw at any time without penalty. You will probably only earn between 5 and 6½ percent interest on this money. You may want some money in a six-month to one-year term account on which you may earn higher interest, although the higher yields may require larger minimum deposits. If you have enough funds, you can place more money into longer-term, higher-paying savings certificates. (Recent banking deregulation is quickly changing the characteristics of savings accounts.)
3. *Try to have a cost-of-living clause tied to your employment contract.* Many unions have been successful in gaining this for their members. If inflation

increases the CPI by 10 percent, cost-of-living clauses take effect and the worker's income is automatically increased to match. This, of course, also maintains inflation.

4. *Try not to let inflation panic you into buying before you are ready.* We are constantly told to buy now before prices increase. Yet, as we pointed out, some prices may actually decline relative to the CPI even though they go up in absolute terms. Even with large items, such as automobiles, that have risen in cost as fast as the CPI, you might want to postpone buying. If your present auto has two more years of trouble-free life, drive it those two additional years and you will probably save money even though a new car in two years will cost you more in absolute terms.

   Example: Take a new-car cost of $10,000. If you bought the car outright (no payments), you'd lose 10 percent interest per year that the money could be earning in a savings account. In two years you'd lose $2100 of potential interest. (Remember you received additional interest during the second year on the interest you earned during the first year.) If the inflation rate was also 10 percent per year, the car would cost you $2100 more two years from now (10 percent × $10,000 = $1000 the first year, 10 percent × $11,000 = $1100 the second year; adding the two yields $2100 as the price increase of the car over two years). Thus the interest you earn on your money offsets the price increase of the car. If your income increases faster than inflation, as incomes have since 1982, the car will actually cost you relatively less if you buy it two years from now at the higher price. Of course, if you don't have the money and must buy the car on credit, these figures do not apply.

5. *Learn about investments.* Money earns money. The wise investor can stay ahead of inflation. For example, real estate has stayed ahead of inflation in many parts of the country. By this, we mean that it has gone up in price faster than the CPI has risen. Unfortunately, inflation brings with it a certain amount of irrationality. Thus we see speculation causing unusual and unpredictable surges in prices. The small, prudent investor would do well to avoid volatile investments in favor of more predictable ones. (See p. 276.)

6. *Understand that an inflationary period tends to favor the borrower.* Money borrowed today is paid back in cheaper dollars in the future.

   Example: I borrow $10,000 at 10 percent interest per year for a five-year period. During that period inflation is 10 percent per year. In essence I am paying nothing for the use of the money. I will have paid $1000 per year or $5000 in simple interest at the end of five years. However, at the end of five years, the $10,000 I pay back is worth only $5000 in buying power because of the accumulated 50 percent inflation, which has halved the value of my dollars.

7. *Try to buy wisely.* Watch for bargains such as year-end sales and seasonal price reductions (see p. 260).

8. *Have more members of the family work.* This suggestion is discussed in more detail in Chapter 9. Higher inflation rates are partially responsible for the increasing number of married women seeking employment.

9. *Conserve and save to accumulate investment funds.*

Periods of Reduced Inflation and Mild Recession

The recession of 1981–1983 demonstrated what happens when the government makes a strong effort to slow inflation. Unemployment goes up, productivity decreases, and government income falls, while social program (unemployment benefits and so forth) costs rise. Because such economic problems are much more obvious than the negative effects of creeping inflation, great pressure is brought on government to support at least a mild form of inflation despite the long-term negative effects. You may remember how quickly the hue and cry against inflation that brought President Reagan to office abated when he instituted monetary changes to reduce inflation. In the face of a recession, people quickly forgot about their problems with inflation.

The prudent money manager most likely will live with mild inflation most of the time, thus giving more weight to suggestions about living with inflation than to suggestions about how to deal with a recession. There will be times, however, when the economy slumps. In order to guard against such times, the prudent money manager will want to do the following:

1. Maintain enough liquidity to cover emergencies.
2. Beware of investments with a large balloon payment due in the short-term future. For example, in the late 1970s the inflation rate on well-located real estate was 20 percent or higher per year. Because interest rates were high, many people bought under so-called creative financing plans that included only short-term financing of the mortgages, with the total loan due in three to five years. Buyers assumed that the high rate of inflation would continue and that they could then refinance based on the increased value of the property. When inflation slowed, property values leveled out or fell slightly so that it became impossible to refinance such property, and many people were unable to meet loan due dates. In some of the most speculative real estate markets the number of foreclosures increased greatly during the early 1980s.
3. If you are able to foresee a slowing of inflation and resulting economic downturn, try to maintain a larger percentage of your assets in cash so that you can take advantage of good buys that may result. In the example just described, there were numerous good buys in real estate as short-term mortgages became due and could not be met by owners who had banked too strongly on inflation to bail them out of their debts.
4. Keep yourself in a financial position that has enough flexibility for you to ride out short-term economic downturns. Judging from the inflation history of the United States during the past 100 years (p. 263), we can probably safely assume that some amount of inflation will remain for the foreseeable future. And as always there will be periodic short-term economic downturns that must be planned for in advance.

A Word about Insurance

Proper use of insurance can protect a family from catastrophic financial setback. Every family must have medical insurance, automobile insurance if they own a car, and fire insurance if they own their own home.

Medical coverage is an absolute necessity. Medical costs have become so high that no average family can sustain the expense of a prolonged illness. For a young, healthy couple, coverage can be limited to catastrophic illness with a large deductible, perhaps as high as $500. This is the least expensive type of medical coverage. When children arrive, a policy that covers everyday medical problems and that has a lower deductible should be sought. A family of four may have to pay $100 to $400 per month for medical coverage depending on how comprehensive it is. In addition to insurance plans such as Mutual of Omaha and Blue Cross, there are also prepaid foundation plans such as the Kaiser Permanente plan where one may have full medical coverage at a certain facility, hospital, or clinic for a specified monthly fee.

Many employers offer group medical plans as part of their fringe benefits; this helps reduce health coverage costs for their employees. In such cases the family will not need to supply its own medical coverage.

The government is also entering the health field more strongly with Medicare plans of various kinds, Social Security disability, and Workers' Compensation insurance. Many analysts suggest that health services will one day be a branch of government, but for the time being unless you are very poor, you must cover for health emergencies or face potential financial ruin.

Automobile coverage is also essential. It is so important that many states make it illegal to be uninsured. Property damage and liability are the crucial elements. Covering one's own car for damage is less important unless, of course, it is being purchased through an installment loan, in which case the lender requires coverage for collision damage.

If you own your own home or other real property, you must have fire coverage. This is a mandatory condition of borrowing mortgage money. Because of inflation you should increase such coverage periodically to keep up with rising construction costs. Homeowner's package policies give much more protection than just fire coverage. Usually they include coverage for such things as theft, personal liability, wind and water damage, and personal belongings.

Even if you do not own your own home, it is a good idea to have a personal belongings insurance policy. Such things as stereo equipment, cameras, furniture, and clothing are surprisingly expensive to replace if they are stolen or lost in a fire. Insurance, on the other hand, is relatively inexpensive.

Life insurance is also important, although not an absolute necessity. There are many kinds of life insurance, and newly married couples are often pushed by insurance agents to overinsure or to choose an unnecessarily expensive policy. Remember that the purpose of life insurance is to protect one's estate and provide for the family until the children are independent. The best protection for the least money is term insurance. In term insurance a given amount of insurance is bought for a set period of years, usually five. As one becomes older, the premium becomes higher because the chance of death increases.

Savings life insurance policies are very expensive and should usually be avoided by young couples. For example, a young couple can buy about $16,000 worth of five-year term life insurance for $100 a year, whereas that amount will only pay for $6000 worth of coverage in an insurance plus savings policy. Insurance agents tend to push savings life insurance because both they and their company earn a great deal more on this type of policy. The savings aspect of the policy now yields only 3 to 6 percent, but returns are increasing as insurance companies try to remain competitive with other types of savings. By investing the usually substantial difference in cost between term and savings life insurance, a couple can have a great deal more insurance protection and at the same time accumulate savings at a much faster rate.

Basically, the amount of life insurance a couple needs will depend on the number and ages of their children, their standard of living, and their other investments. What life insurance must do is protect the family if the major monetary contributor should die. It should cover death costs, taxes, outstanding debts, and should supply enough money to allow the family to continue functioning. Just how much this will be depends on the individual family.

Home ownership has been a way of life for most Americans. More Americans (64 percent in 1985) own their own homes than any other people in the world. The percentage has dropped only slightly from the peak of 65.8 percent late in 1980 (Sternlieb & Hughes, 1986). As you will see in Chapter 14, their home is a major source of savings for many retired Americans. Depending on the state of the economy, arguments can be made that the costs of home ownership make the investment less attractive than is commonly believed. Assuming that the money spent on home ownership is saved and invested wisely, it is probably true that most of the time more money can be made than will accrue through appreciation of a home. This is especially true if rents continue to remain lower than the general inflation rate as they have in the past. A person's home, however, yields many personal satisfactions beyond the possibility of economic gain. The American dream of one day owning your own home is therefore more than merely an economic dream.

Unfortunately, for many young couples the dream may not come true. The costs of home ownership have risen so drastically in the past ten years as to place a home out of reach of many Americans. Home prices, mortgage interest rates, property taxes, and utilities costs have all risen at a much faster rate than the overall Consumer Price Index increase. As of June 1986 the overall CPI stood at 327.9. Housing was at 358. Residential rents, it is interesting to note, stood at 279.4. Rents historically have lagged behind general inflation rates by about two years. With the soaring costs of home ownership, rent is one of the consumer's better buys today. Although we hear much grumbling about increasing rents, in relation to the rest of the economy rents simply have not increased as rapidly as most goods and services.

Mortgage interest rates have risen from a low of 6 percent to as high as 18 to 20 percent over the past fifteen years. They are extremely volatile. For example, in the beginning of 1982 they were at record highs, but by the beginning of 1983, they had dropped back to the 12- to 14-percent range and by 1986 they had dropped into the 9- to 12-percent range. To give some idea of what these fluctuations mean to prospective home buyers, Table 8-9 shows the amount of pretax income necessary at various interest rates to qualify for a thirty-year, $50,000 mortgage.

Your Own Home: The End of an American Dream?

Table 8-9
Pretax Income Needed to Qualify for a Thirty-Year, $50,000 Mortgage

Interest Rate	Monthly Payments[1]	Monthly Income	Annual Income
10%	$439	$1,752	$21,024
12%	514	2,056	24,672
13%	553	2,212	26,544
14%	592	2,368	28,416

[1]Principal and interest payment.

Although housing prices have risen dramatically over the past fifteen years, the acceleration in prices seems to have leveled off. In many parts of the country, prices actually began to decline in 1982, although not dramatically. In 1978 the new-house median price was $61,900. By the middle of 1985 the median price had increased to $99,000. Local averages vary greatly from these national statistics. For example, during the second quarter of 1985, the median prices of a resale home in the following areas were:

Detroit	$ 51,000
Tulsa	$ 68,000
Chicago	$ 81,800
Los Angeles	$116,900

The rate of change of prices for resale homes (as well as new homes) also varies greatly. Comparing median prices between the second quarter of 1984 and the second quarter of 1985, prices went up 23 percent in metropolitan New York City but dropped 2 percent in Houston, Texas.

The economy has reacted in a number of ways to try to keep home ownership within reach of the American family. Smaller homes, modular homes, mobile homes, condominiums, and cooperatives have all increased in popularity. Government funding of lower-interest mortgages has also been made available. Shared ownership is another way to move into home ownership. Two families can pool their funds and buy a large home or better yet a duplex or perhaps a triplex. With a triplex, the families can rent out the extra apartment and the income from it can help with the monthly home owner expenses.

An Alternative: Investment

There is a popular belief that one 's chances of earning $1 million are much less than they were for one's grandfather. But the number of millionaires today actually far exceeds the number in grandfather's time. Granted, $1 million may be worth considerably less in buying power today, but it is still a healthy mark of affluence. A gradually inflationary economy is also an economy in which money can be made easily by a person who is intelligent and willing to work. Another important qualification is the ability to stay clear of early economic entrapment, as we have described. For most young people the necessity of gathering the first small amount of capital is particularly crucial because of the strong tendency of the system to work against them. In the early years they must stay alert to keep the system from entrapping them and thereby canceling their attempt to accumulate initial investment capital. If they can win this battle and start on the road to financial success, they will be using the system to their advantage rather than being used by it. When one compares costs of living in America with those in other countries (as in Table 8-10), it is clear that America offers a great deal economically to its citizens.

Thinking about investments on even a modest scale is important if newly married couples or individuals are to make the economic system work for instead of against them. Figure 8-5 shows the broad range of investment opportunities

Table 8-10
Comparative Standard of Living in Minutes, Hours, or Months of Work Needed to Buy the Item

Commodity	Washington	Moscow	London	Paris
Weekly food basket (family of four)	18.6 hrs.	53.5	24.7	22.2
Lipstick	30 mins.	69	60	76
T-shirt (cotton)	19 mins.	185	66	53
Panty hose	18 mins.	366	18	17
Levi jeans	3 hrs.	46	6	6
Color television	65 hrs.	701	132	106
Small car	5 mos.	53	11	8

Source: National Federation of Independent Business Research and Education Foundation.

Inset 8-4

You Can Still Make a Million Dollars

Debbi Fields has done very well indeed with chocolate chip cookies. Mrs. Fields, a native of Oakland, California, couldn't have started smaller: baking cookies for meetings held by her wealthy financial-consultant husband. She couldn't help but hear the munches as her homemade recipe was devoured. So she opened a little cookie shop in Palo Alto. "Not a single customer showed up," she says. "I began walking up and down the block with my cookies asking people to try them." Today, Mrs. Fields has more than 300 company-owned stores, with 1000 employees and annual sales of about $50 million.

"I never expected it to grow to these proportions," she says. She maintains a hands-on, people-oriented style of management (every worker got a handwritten Christmas card from the boss), stringent quality controls, and winning recipes. "I'm driven to perfection," she says, adding that she's still not through after her usual 12-hour day at her headquarters in Park City, Utah.

To the computer industry, Bill Gates was always seen as a young man in a hurry. The inventor of the operating system now built into every IBM home computer, Gates became a business legend *before* his twenty-first birthday. He founded his company, Microsoft, with money he earned as a teenage programming consultant and has never had to borrow from a bank. Last June the company's sales exceeded $140 million.

Gates has been the model entrepreneur. He has hired good professional managers and constantly adds innovative products to the company. "We wanted to be a leader in the goal of putting a computer onto every desk in America. It would be a great failure not to see that through."

Although there are only about 410,000 millionaires in the United States, such stories as Mrs. Fields's and Mr. Gates's are possible in america and that really is the beauty of the economic system. America's handful of young millionaires rely less on luck than on talent, tenacity, and creativity. They display enormous energy, patience, and resolve in getting what they want, which often is the personal satisfaction of having done something profitably and well.

Source: Adapted from David Rosenthal, "You Can Still Make a Million Dollars," *Parade*, 26 January 1986, p. 4.

Figure 8-5   The investment continuum. Note that the percentage return in successful investments increases as the risk increases. The chances of striking gold are slim, but if you do, the return is great. Percentages also change with economic conditions.

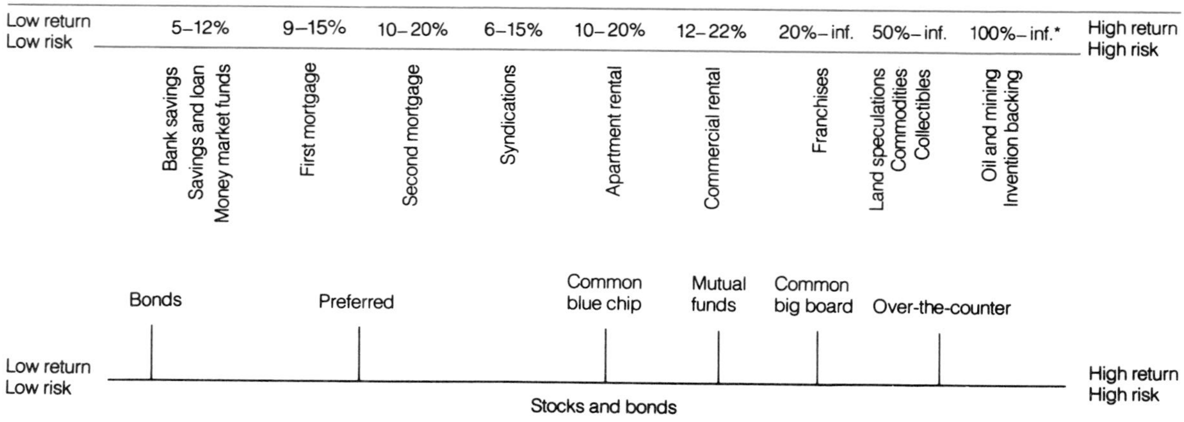

*"100%–"inf." means 100% upwards without limit (infinite).

_____ Table 8-11 _____
$100 per Month Invested at 6% and 12%

Years	Amount Invested	6%	12%	Difference
10	$12,000	$ 16,766	$ 23,586	$ 6,820
20	24,000	46,791	96,838	50,047
30	36,000	100,562	324,351	223,789
40	48,000	196,857	1,030,970	834,113

from which to choose. They range from the very conservative bank savings account to the highly speculative gambles for high return on such things as mining and oil exploration. You might ask: How can the average newly married couple even consider investments? It's all they can do to set up housekeeping. This is a legitimate question. However, the couple who plan investing into their life, even if only at a later date, have the greatest chance of economic prosperity and freedom. _A positive attitude toward investment is actually even more important than investment itself._ Such an attitude recognizes that "money makes money," that there is value in budgeting and staying free of consumer debt, that controlling one's desires in early years can lead to greater rewards later, and that the American economic system if used properly can free one from economic worries. Even if a couple can put aside only a few dollars a month toward future investments, they stand a chance of improving their economic position compared with their friends who have no interest or knowledge of investing. (See "Gaining Freedom through Investment," p. 276.)

For example, to put away $20 per month starting at age twenty-five is the same as putting away $200 per month starting at age forty-five with retirement at age sixty-five. Table 8-11 shows how money grows at 6 percent and at 12 percent compounded daily interest. The figures are predicated on putting aside $100 per month initially until you have $12,000.

It is also valuable to know that in recent years the government has added greatly to the incentive to save toward retirement by offering several different savings plans where the money placed into the savings plan as well as the interest earned by that money is tax-free until the money is withdrawn at a later age. The best known of these plans is the Individual Retirement Account, better known by its initials IRA. The 1986 income tax revisions made some changes in the IRA legislation.

In simple terms a young person and/or family can make investment a part of their planning by following these steps:

1. Use the credit system wisely to avoid economic entrapment.
   a. Avoid credit buying for consumer goods.
   b. Avoid running balances on credit card accounts.
   c. Pay bills promptly in order to maintain a good credit standing.
2. Get in the habit of regular saving even if at first you can only save a small amount.
3. Learn about the many types of investment open to the individual in America, some of which are described in "Gaining Freedom through Investment," p. 276. Such steps can lead to successful investments, which can in turn lead to economic freedom.

Summary

The family is the major unit of consumption in the United States. For a family to survive it must have the economic ability to provide food, shelter, and transportation and meet all the needs of its members. Ideally there will also be money to supply pleasurable and recreational activities as well. The family that is economically successful stands a much better chance of staying together than the family that fails economically. The poorest segment of the American society has the highest rate of divorce.

Credit use in the United States has allowed Americans to maintain the world's highest standard of living. Yet this easy availability of credit can also curtail individual and family freedom when it is abused or misunderstood. Agreeing to make future payments for present goods or services can lock a person into an inflexible life pattern. Money must be earned steadily to meet the payment schedule. For many families the debt burden is so large that almost all funds are allocated automatically to make the many payments due each month. The family has little or no monetary flexibility to meet unforeseen emergencies or to act quickly if a good investment opportunity arises.

On the other hand, a thorough understanding of credit, installment buying, interest costs, and budgeting can work to a family's benefit, allowing them to invest and perhaps to achieve not only economic security but also economic freedom.

The day-to-day handling of money can be a problem in a family if the partners have different values about money. Conflict can be minimized if the couple decides ahead of time how monetary decisions will be made. Their choices are: to let the husband make all decisions, to let the wife make all decisions, to make all decisions jointly, or to let both have separate funds and share agreed on obligations. Budgeting will also allow them to plan for necessities and to see how their income is spent. Deciding together how to use income left over after meeting necessities is another way to reduce monetary conflict.

Inflation is the primary economic enemy of the newly married couple. Inflation rates have risen in recent years, as have wages. However, at times wages do not keep up with inflation, and many people find that their real income actually goes down. It is important for families to understand inflation so that they can take steps to guard against it. Proper budgeting and good investments are two steps that a family can take to reduce the unwanted effects of inflation.

Insurance should be considered a necessity. A family with a car and a home needs medical, automobile, and fire insurance. Life insurance is also important, though not a necessity. Couples should start with a medical policy that protects them against catastrophic illness and then, as children arrive, change to broader coverage. This pattern should also be followed with life insurance. The couple should buy term insurance, increasing the amount of the coverage as needed to protect family members.

The American dream of home ownership for every family shows strong signs of fading in the face of drastically increased housing prices. Smaller homes, condominiums, and cooperatives will probably be the housing of the future.

Investments are a means of supplementing income and making money work to produce more money. The family able to save and invest even a small portion of their income is freer of possible economic entrapment and stands a better chance of survival than families who cannot control wants and desires and spend their entire income. Investments can be plotted along a continuum from low risk, low return to high risk, high return. Examples of low-risk, low-return investments are bank savings and savings and loan accounts. Risk and return increase with such investments as first and second mortgages, syndications, apartment houses, commercial property, and franchises. While the rate of return can be very high for such speculations as land, commodities, oil and mining, and invention backing, the risk is too high for young couples with limited funds. The stock market is another investment outlet. Here again there is a continuum from low risk, low return to high risk, high return.

Gaining Freedom through Investment

Note to reader: Many readers of this book have little experience with investments. Most students don't have the money or the time to invest. However, education is an investment in oneself and for most people this investment will pay monetary dividends over the years. If as you look at this section, you feel that the ideas are foreign to you, if you feel disinterested in investments, if you feel that investments only come later in life as you contemplate retirement, then this is definitely a section for you. The individual who thinks in investment terms early in life is the person who stands the best chance of monetary success. Over the years, many students who claimed disinterest in investing have learned about it and suddenly become enthusiastic. And a good number of these students went on to monetary success far beyond what they had envisioned. The next Bill Gates or Mrs. Fields (p. 272) is sitting right in your class. It could be you.

The world of investment has undergone drastic change in the past few years. Investment opportunities for the small investor have greatly expanded. Perhaps the best example is the revolution in banking that occurred with the passing of the Depository Institutions Deregulation Act of 1980. For years checking accounts earned no interest and bank savings accounts earned only minimal interest, 3 to 6 percent per year, which did not even offset inflation.

Savings Accounts

Starting in 1982, however, gradual deregulation allowed banking institutions to offer a greater variety of

investment and savings opportunities with much higher interest return to their customers. Because most investors must start by first saving some investment capital, the many new types of accounts allow those savings to start working immediately. Table 8-11 indicated the difference in interest earned over time between a 6 percent return and a 12 percent return. Using the new savings opportunities can thus pay the investor big dividends.

Banks and savings and loan associations are now offering a variety of money market accounts that pay between 6 and 15 percent depending on the market. Investors with a great deal of money, say $100,000 or more, have always been able to invest in a number of money instruments, such as certificates of deposit, that were not limited in interest by law. For the small investor money market funds pool the monies of a number of persons and invest them in high-yield certificates

as well as Treasury bills and so forth. Money market savings accounts are now offered by all savings institutions. Checking accounts also now earn interest on the average balance. A type of checking account, the SuperNow account, pays money market rates as long as some minimum balance, such as $2500, is maintained. If the balance drops below this amount, the institution may pay no interest or a maximum of 5.25 percent, depending on the institution's policies. Because of the partial deregulation of the banking industry, consumers must shop more carefully to maximize their savings and possible checking account returns because there are almost as many plans as institutions.

Once a person has instituted a savings program and has accumulated some capital, one can begin to investigate a broader range of investments. Space allows only a superficial discussion of a few of the many investment opportunities possible. Each person must make her or his own decisions about saving and investing. For example, a young family with small children should lean toward conservative investments that require little personal time because they probably have little free time at this stage in their lives. Each couple must consider their personal interests and their financial goals. For example, the family in which the husband or wife has flexible time (perhaps they own their own business, do free-lance work, teach and have considerable vacation time, and so on) can consider apartment ownership and management. Where time is rigidly structured, the family can investigate the stock market, real estate or business syndicates, mortgage purchase, house trading, and so on.

It is also important to review investment choices often. The economy has shifted so quickly during the past five years that what was an excellent investment one day may have been a poor investment the next. Table 8-12 examines the current value of $10,000 invested in different types of investments. Some interesting facts appear that point out clearly the necessity of continually reviewing investment choices. If you invested in coins five years ago, your $10,000 would be worth $37,500 today. However, if you invested in coins only one year ago, your $10,000 would be worth only $7140 today. In other words, coins were a great investment five years ago but a poor investment during the past year. Notice that stocks were not a particularly good investment five years ago, nor even one year ago (figured as of January 1, 1983). However, 1985 and 1986 found the stock market constantly reaching new highs.

First Mortgage

Money is loaned with real estate as security for the debt. If the debt is not paid, the land and/or building is taken over by the lender. First mortgages are quite safe as long as no more money is loaned than the property is worth. For example, most savings and loan institutions lend 80 percent or less of the selling or appraised price of a property, thus assuring themselves that their loan will be covered in case the property must be sold to recover the debt. Young couples usually cannot consider buying first mortgages because to do so requires a good deal of money. For example, 80 percent of an $80,000 house is $64,000. Also, the money is usually tied up for a long time, twenty to thirty years in most cases.

Second Mortgage

This kind of investment can be considered by a young couple because the amount of money required can be low. The loan is the same type as a first mortgage but more speculative because it is given after a first mortgage has already been placed against the property. (The first-mortgage holder has first claim on the property in case of default.) A second mortgage is often made when the buyer of a property doesn't have enough cash for the down payment or when money is needed to make up the difference between the price and the first mortgage. Take, for example, a house bought for $65,000, with a $55,000 first mortgage, by a buyer who has only $5000 for the down payment. The buyer is therefore $5000 short of the sales price. A short-term second mortgage of $5000 will make up the difference.

Second mortgages are usually for only a few years, seldom more than seven and more often for only two to three. They can be in any amount, which makes them investment possibilities for young couples. They may be purchased from real estate agencies and money brokers. Ads for both first and second mortgages may also be found in the classified newspaper sections. In general one should not invest more in a second mortgage than the buyer has put down on the property. One should also be sure that the property is worth the price paid, so that in the case of default, sale of the property will realize enough money to

---

Table 8-12
Current Value of $10,000 Invested*

5 Years Ago		1 Year Ago	
Coins	$37,500	Corporate bonds	$14,085
Gold	29,780	Treasury bonds	14,085
Gems	22,467	Money market funds	11,394
Growth funds	21,015	Growth funds	11,022
Platinum	18,663	Passbook savings account	10,572
Money market funds	17,575	NYSE stocks	10,170
Silver	17,400	Single-family existing home	10,149
Old masters painting	15,197	Old masters painting	10,000
Single-family existing home	15,148	Gold	9,250
Treasury bonds	14,896	Silver	8,912
NYSE stocks	14,470	Gems	7,956
Passbook savings account	12,927	Platinum	7,312
Corporate bonds	12,647	Coins	7,140

*Figured as of January 1, 1983.

cover both the first and second mortgages.

Although the standard interest rate for most second mortgages is 10 to 15 percent, one can often earn more by buying the second at a discount. Let's say that the previous owners of the $65,000 house took the second mortgage of $5000 from the new buyer. However, the previous owners find that they need cash before the mortgage is due. In order to make the second mortgage more attractive, they offer to sell the mortgage at a 10 percent discount. Perhaps $4000 is still due on the mortgage. The discount means that the new investor would get the mortgage of $4000 for $3600, thus effectively increasing the profit margin.

Syndicates

Money for investment is raised by a group of individuals who form a partnership and usually buy real estate or a business. It is often possible for a young couple to join such a venture in the position of limited partner. There will be a few general partners who actually put the deal together and run the investment on a day-to-day basis. They will also assume the risks beyond each limited partner's investment. All the limited partner does is contribute some minimum amount of money. For example, the limited partner shares might cost $1000 each. The limited partners have no responsibility in the management and no risk other than their initial investment. If the venture is profitable, they share in the profits. Such syndicates are often advertised in the financial pages, but more often one learns about them from other investors and professional money management persons. State laws control the syndicates so that the investor knows how the money will be used and what liabilities will be assumed, as well as what profit will be paid if the venture works well.

Apartment and Commercial Rentals

This kind of investment requires time as well as money because the rentals must be managed and maintained continually. However, apartment management for other owners is a good way for a young couple to get started. They not only make money but learn the fundamentals of property management before actually investing in apartments themselves. Commercial rentals are generally beyond the economic means of young couples, so they won't be discussed here.

If a couple has time and is handy at minor repairs, buying and living in a duplex or triplex is a good start toward property ownership. The rents help with the payments and maintenance, and in addition the value of a well-located property will follow the upward inflationary trend.

Franchises

This kind of investment involves buying a business such as McDonald's, Radio Shack, or Colonel Sanders' Kentucky Fried Chicken. The advantage is that one starts a business supported by a large company's reputation, experience, backing, and advertising. The new owner must use the parent company's products and maintain a given standard of service. The price for good franchises is high, but many of the larger companies have loan funds that can help the new owner get started.

Land Speculation and Commodities

These are really speculations rather than investments and should be avoided by the small investor because the risk of loss is high. Both involve gambling on the future desirability of land or the future price of commodities (commodities are farm products such as corn, wheat, cattle, or oats, or raw materials such as copper, silver, gold, or timber).

Let's look at one commodity speculation. Suppose a cattle raiser needs money or decides to avoid the risk of changing prices by entering into a futures' account. The calves are bought at today's prices and then are sold to the futures' account at the going rate for year-old steers. (The cattle raiser still has to feed the calves for the year but has been assured of a moderate profit.) The speculator who buys the account hopes, of course, that the price of beef will be higher when the steers are actually ready for market. Risks are high because such unpredictable things as weather, governmental policies, and the international situation affect commodity prices.

Oil and Mining and Invention Backing

These investments are even more speculative and should not be considered by a young family entering the investment market.

Stocks and Bonds

Another major form of investment is the stock market, or stocks and bonds. We will consider these investments in some detail, starting at the low-risk, low-return end of the continuum and continuing to those investments that involve more risk and also more return.

In general stocks, bonds, and notes of various kinds are bought through stock brokerage firms. These firms are members of various stock exchanges through which they buy and sell. The customer pays a small fee to the brokerage house to buy or sell.

Bonds

Bonds are a form of IOU or promissory note that companies issue when they need funds. Bonds are usually issued in thousand-dollar multiples. The issuing company promises to pay the bondholders a specified amount of interest for a specified amount of time at the end of which the bond will be redeemed for the face amount. Because of generally low risk, bonds usually offer low interest rates. There are several kinds of bonds: U.S. savings, corporation, and municipal bonds. U.S. savings bonds are the safest investment but are also long term and low interest. Because of inflation, an investor can actually lose money over the period of the bond. Corporation bonds are relatively safe because the company pledges properties it owns as collateral. Municipal bonds are similar except that a government unit offers the bonds, usually to complete a building or park project. They are relatively safe, but as city finances have become more strained in recent years, there is doubt that some municipal bonds will be repaid at the expiration date. Municipal bonds have the advantage of having their interest exempt from federal income taxes.

Stocks

A stock is a piece of paper (stock certificate) that gives the owner the right to a portion of the assets of the company issuing the stock. Like bonds, stocks are issued when companies need money, usually for expansion. Unlike bondholders, stockholders are part owners of the company they have invested in and can vote at stockholders' meetings. The stocks of large companies are usually listed on stock exchanges, either regional ones around the country or the two largest, the New York Stock Exchange and the American Stock Exchange. These organized exchanges set minimum requirements that must be met by a company to have its stock listed. For example, the New York Stock Exchange specifies that a company must have at least $10 million in tangible assets, at least $2 million in annual earnings, and at least 1 million shares divided among 2000 or more shareholders. Stocks are also sold over the counter in markets that are less organized than the exchanges. These stocks are usually not traded as often as those listed on the exchanges and are issued by smaller and less well known companies (over-the-counter stocks offer the highest risk and highest return).

1. *Preferred stocks.* These are called preferred because when earnings are distributed or when a company is liquidated or becomes bankrupt, holders of preferred stock are paid first.
2. *Common stocks.* Most stocks are common stocks. They are the last to earn and normally fluctuate more than bonds and preferred stock. Whereas common stocks usually pay dividends, most investors hope to buy the stock at a low price and sell it at a higher price after a rise in the stock market. Blue chip stocks are those of strong companies such as General Motors or IBM. The stronger the company, usually the safer the stock.

Mutual Funds

Mutual funds are companies that buy and sell large blocks of stocks. The investor can buy shares in such companies rather than shares in "real" companies. Each mutual fund stock represents a share of the large and diversified group of shares the fund owns. There are two kinds of mutual funds, closed end and open end. Closed-end funds usually do not issue stock after the initial issue. Many closed-end mutual funds are listed on the New York Stock Exchange, and their shares are readily transferable in the open market and can be bought and sold like other shares. Open-end funds, on the other hand, usually issue more shares as people want them and are not listed on the stock exchange.

The young family should consider diversified investment rather than placing all of their capital into one venture. For example, in the stock market the mutual fund is safer than the single stock because it represents a widely diversified holding of stocks. Before considering any investment, though, the family should be sure it has enough insurance for basic security (see "A Word about Insurance," pp. 267–269).

Chapter 9

The Dual-Worker Family: The Real American Revolution

Contents

The relationship of work and family in America has undergone a profound change since World War II. More and more women have entered the labor force (see Table 9-1). In the past, the women in America's labor force were generally single. Now married women, often with children under eighteen, are entering the labor force in unprecedented numbers. In 1985 54 percent of all American women over age sixteen were working. Of those women 56 percent were married with spouse present (see Table 9-2). Over 53 percent of all married women were working outside the home and 60 percent of all mothers with children under eighteen were in the labor force. Over 80 percent of young married women with no children were in the workforce (California Commission on the Status of Women, 1986). This has created what the U.S. Bureau of Census now describes as a "husband—primary earner, wife—secondary earner" family, more popularly known as the "two-career," "two-earner," or "dual-worker" family.

Because of this migration of women into the labor force, the relationship between work and family is now more complex. Work and family intersect more intimately. Partners grapple with more of the same problems. Sex roles are less clear, less distinct, more blurred, more overlapping. Power within the family is distributed differently as both partners contribute monetarily to their family's support. Family activities and time schedules are more restricted. The care of children is more variable, ranging from full-time parental supervision to none at all as represented by the "latchkey" child. Mothers try to become "supermoms" as they cope with both family responsibilities and an outside career. Fathers may become "house husbands" if their wives' careers blossom.

The many changes in family life so eagerly reported by the media really represent the reaction of society in general and families in particular to the revolutionary move of wife and mother into the world of work.

The wife entering the work world and sharing the breadwinner role has wrought a revolution in the family and in the overall relationship between the sexes. In years past, the working woman generally, and the working wife in particular, was an unusual phenomenon. Before 1900 the labor force included few women. Married women were full-time wives and mothers and were considered negligent in their duty if they worked outside the home. If we consider the strong past attitudes about the importance of the mother being at home when her children are young, the fact that 60 percent of mothers with children under eighteen are now in the labor force is an amazing change in behavior and social mores. The number of children at home is no longer strongly related to workforce participation by women (Ferber, 1982). Of the workers in the labor force in 1890, women accounted for only 17 percent of all workers and represented only 18 percent of the female population over fourteen years of age. Only 4.5 percent of married women were in the labor force (Smith, 1979).

It is clear that the role of the woman as homemaker and mother only is passing. Thus the traditional marriage in which the husband works to support the family while the wife remains home caring for the family has become a minority pattern. Labor department projections indicate that by 1990 this traditional description of the family will be accurate for only 25 percent of married women's families (Smith, 1979).

A number of factors have led to the increased numbers of married women working outside the home:

1. The inflationary pressures of the American economy and the rising expectations of living standards have combined to bring many women into the work-

Women in the Workforce

Table 9-1

Women as a Percentage of Employed Civilian Labor Force

Year	Percentage
1950	31.4
1960	33.3
1970	37.7
1980	43.5
1985	43.8

Source: U.S. Bureau of Census, *Statistical Abstract of the United States: 1984*, 104th ed., Washington, D.C.: U.S. Government Printing Office, 1983, no. 683, p. 413. U.S. Department. of Labor, *Monthly Labor Review*, December 1985. Washington, D.C.: Bureau of Labor Statistics, p. 58.

Table 9-2

Married Women, Spouse Present, in Labor Force as Percentage of All Women in Labor Force

Year	Percentage
1950	24.8
1960	31.7
1970	41.4
1980	50.7
1985	56.0

Source: U.S. Bureau of Census, *Statistical Abstract of the United States: 1984*, 104th ed., Washington, D.C.: U.S. Government Printing Office, 1983, no. 683, p. 413. U.S. Department of Labor, *Monthly Labor Review*, December 1985. Washington, D.C.: Bureau of Labor Statistics, p. 60.

force. The majority of working wives work to help make ends meet. Thus economic need is the major reason most women go to work.

2. Since World War II real wages have increased dramatically. (Real wages are those that have been adjusted to take inflation into consideration.) Because a woman can now earn much more than in the past (but still less than men), the relative cost of staying home with her family all day becomes too large, and more women are drawn into the labor force. One might think that the opposing effects of increased real income for a family—namely, less economic pressure to work and greater financial means to enjoy leisure pursuits—would work to keep women home. However, this has not been the case. One reason might be that desires for increasingly higher standards of living (see p. 252) have outpaced the increase in real income. Secondly, in recent years of high inflation, real income has not increased rapidly. Indeed, in some years it has actually declined. Thus despite generally increasing real income, women have not remained home to enjoy it but have entered the labor market to participate in the higher wages. Increased income also permits the reduction of unpaid labor in the home by the woman, because labor-saving devices and domestic help can be purchased.

3. There has been a tremendous increase in the kinds of jobs available to women. The importance of physical strength in many industrial jobs has diminished. Service jobs, such as clerical and sales work, have expanded greatly. The opportunity for part-time work has also increased. Equal opportunity legislation (see p. 218) has created demands for women in jobs previously unavailable. Because of the greatly increased demand for women workers, their wages have increased, although they remain below men's wages (see p. 288).

4. Declining birthrates have certainly contributed to women's working more. For example, over 80 percent of wives without children are in the labor force. Women with small children are still the least likely to work outside the home, however.

5. Increasing education has contributed to women's working outside the home. College attendance by women gradually increased until in 1980 the number of bachelor's degrees conferred on women equalled the number given to men (Blau & Ferber, 1985, p. 33). Better education certainly creates job opportunities. More importantly, the educated person's awareness tends to increase, and as a result, he or she will seek fulfillment as well as the chance to make a broader contribution to society. The role of wife and mother becomes only one of many roles for the educated woman as she becomes more aware of her potential. In fact increased education for both men and women has led to the creation of a "new breed" of worker who places high value on opportunities for self-expression (Nieva, 1985, p. 163).

6. Attitudes about the role of the woman in the family have changed greatly during this century. In 1930 only 18 percent of surveyed women believed married women should have a full-time job outside the home (Smith, 1979). Valerie Oppenheimer (1977) reports that in 1964, only 54 percent of the women surveyed agreed that a working mother could still establish a close relationship with her children. By 1970 that percentage had risen to 73 percent. Today most women also believe that working outside the home is important for personal satisfaction, rather than just for earning additional money. Acceptance of wives' working outside the home is not yet universal, however. Blum-

stein and Schwartz (1983, p. 118) discovered that 25 percent of the wives and 34 percent of the husbands in their sample still believed there should be only one breadwinner in a family.

Although the surge of women into the workforce seems to be slowing, the Bureau of Labor Statistics predicts that 59 to 63 percent of all women over sixteen years of age will be working in the 1990s (Fullerton, 1985). Even though the role of housewife and mother is back in good standing (after being much maligned by radical feminists in the late 1960s and early 1970s), few experts believe that women who have tasted the freedom, satisfaction, and added affluence of a paycheck will return to being full-time housewives in great numbers. Many white, employed wives appear to be working less because of financial need (although this has become increasingly important) than because of interest in their jobs. They simply enjoy their employment, deriving satisfaction and self-esteem from their work (Avioli, 1985, p. 744).

Joe and Mary Revisited

In the last chapter (p. 250), we left Joe and Mary trying to pay off their debts under a court-supervised bankruptcy payment plan. Mary was busy at home with her second baby. Another, more common scenario for this story is that Mary goes to work to help make ends meet. In this way Joe and Mary are able to avoid the drastic step of bankruptcy, at least for a while and probably indefinitely.

The Working Wife

The woman entering the work world is faced with more complicated and, often, more limited choices than her husband. Basically she must choose from four major work patterns:

Pattern A: Working for a few years before she marries or has children, and then settling into the homemaker job for the rest of her life. This was the predominant pattern for white, middle-class women until World War II. Although the numbers of such women are large, their proportion is declining. Today such women are most apt to be mothers of more than three children, wives of affluent men, and women who have meager opportunities in the job market because they do not have a high-school education.

Pattern B: Following the same career pattern as men, that is, she remains in the paid labor force continuously and full time through the years between school and retirement. Women most likely to be in this pattern are women without children, black women, and women in professional and managerial jobs.

Pattern C: Working until she has children, then staying home for a certain amount of time (perhaps five to ten years), and returning to the labor force on a basis that won't conflict with her remaining family responsibilities.

Pattern D: Remaining in the labor force continuously with short time-outs to have children. Family duties combine equally with work responsibilities.

Most men follow Pattern B, and more and more women are entering this pattern also. Patterns A and C are limited by the job opportunities available. Many employers hesitate to place young, unmarried or newly married women in jobs with long-term advancement potential or higher-level jobs that require extended training. They fear that such women will soon leave the job by choosing one of the other two patterns. Pattern C has special difficulties for the woman returning to work after a long absence. She often finds that her skills are outdated. Higher-level jobs may also demand too much of her attention, causing conflict with her second job as mother, homemaker, and wife. Pattern D is increasingly being chosen by women. Its major problem is the stress and strain of too much responsibility leading to overwork. The woman tries to be a superwoman, both running the family and home and doing a job outside the home.

Job Opportunities for Women

The jobs of the vast majority of working women are not the glamorous professions, the upper management levels of corporate America, or the government leadership roles depicted by mass media. No, the work world for women is much the same as it is for most men: eight-to-five days, two-week yearly vacations, and often mundane duties. Unlike her husband, though, the working wife must usually shoulder a second job, that of running her home and family.

Women have gained access to a greater variety of jobs as well as to higher-level employment in all areas. There are more women doctors, lawyers, corporate executives, and managers than ever before. But these are the exceptions just as they are among men, and women are still far less represented than men in these occupations. Although it is a worthy goal to open all types and levels of jobs to women, the reality is that most women and men will not achieve such lofty occupational ends. It is wonderful for the mass media to say, "Women executives are on the move and taking over top jobs in corporations" (*Time*, 1985, p. 64). But to the vast majority of women (and men) in the labor force general nondiscriminatory job availability and good pay is far more important.

Women's employment opportunities are broadening greatly as they successfully penetrate historically male-dominated fields. Between 1973 and 1983 women have made substantial gains in such fields as engineering (1.3 percent female in 1973, 5.8 percent female in 1983), law (5.8 percent to 15.3 percent), medical doctor (12.2 percent to 15.8 percent), and managers and administrators (18.4 percent to 32.4 percent) (Trafford et al., 1984).

The U.S. Department of Labor (1982) reported that in eight major job categories women had become the majority in the ten-year period from 1972 to 1982. These categories were insurance adjusters, examiners and investigators, bill collectors, real estate agents and brokers, photographic process workers, checkers, examiners and inspectors, and production line assemblers. Although one might be tempted to dismiss a list of jobs like this, these kinds of changes in the job market will have far more impact on the working woman than the acceptance of women into the glamorous jobs described in Inset 9-1. Even more important, the Labor Department reported that during the last decade the most significant change in distribution of the sexes among major occupational groups was the increase in female managers (U.S. Department of Labor, 1984, p. 16).

Despite such gains for women, most still work in jobs and occupations that have historically been open to them and that for the most part are low on the pay scale. As of 1983, the following occupations (partial listing) had more than 80 percent female workers (U.S. Labor Dept., January 1985, pp. 55–59):

	Percentage Women
Secretaries, stenographers, typists	98.5%
Receptionists	97.9
Licensed practical nurses	96.8
Teacher aides	94.6
Textile sewing machine operators	94.0
Bank tellers	92.9
Financial records processing	89.2
Dieticians	88.9
Information clerks	88.6
Librarians	84.6
Cashiers	80.9

Note that these occupational categories all tend to be associated historically with women. Note further that they tend to be at low or moderate pay levels compared to such occupations as engineering (94 percent men) and construction trades (98.5 percent men).

Despite these job concentrations of women, it is clear that the variety and levels of jobs opening to women are improving. Because level of education and employability go hand in hand, the fact that so many young women reach higher educational levels than in the past means that they will find a greater variety of

---

Inset 9-1

Women Executives on the Move

Women are now setting their corporation goals high, and more and more are achieving their ambitions. Between 1972 and 1983, the number of executive women in U.S. business more than doubled from 1.4 million to 3.5 million. Although only one woman, Katherine Graham, chairman of the Washington Post Co. (1984 sales $984 million), heads a *Fortune* 500 company, more women executives are climbing the corporate ladder. These executive women are now in middle management, and it is inevitable that after twenty years of work experience, some of these women will reach the top.

As the number of women managers grows, male views about them are changing. The *Harvard Business Review* (September 1985) published an update of a survey done in 1965 on opinions about women executives. While only 9 percent of the men questioned in 1965 said that they held "strongly favorable" attitudes toward women executives, 33 percent of those asked in 1985 were "strongly favorable." Perhaps more significant, 47 percent of male executives said they would feel comfortable working for a woman, compared to only 27 percent in 1965.

Still, while women have been making dramatic progress through the lower and middle ranks of U.S. companies, many say that there seems to be a remaining invisible line that blocks them out of the topmost positions. Some women, upon reaching this line, simply drop out of the corporation and start their own company. Says one woman company owner and president, "The best way for a woman to get to the top is to start there."

Another sign that women are not yet fully accepted is a persistent salary gap. Female MBAs (Masters in Business Administration) entering the workforce are paid the same salaries as men with the same qualifications. Yet after ten years the women have fallen behind in pay by about 20 percent, regardless of the company or of their specific jobs.

Now that women make up nearly half the labor force and are earning half the bachelor's degrees, tapping that pool of skills is nothing more than good business.

Source: adapted from *Time*, 1985.

---

higher-level jobs available. Remember that it was not until 1980 that women earned as many bachelor's degrees as men. In fact, examining the fields in which these college degrees were awarded gives reason to hope that the job market will continue to widen for women. For example, agriculture degrees awarded to women moved from 4.2 percent in 1970 to 29.6 percent in 1980, architecture degrees went from 12 to 27.8 percent, law degrees went from 5 to 45.5 percent, and business and management degrees moved from 9.3 to 33.8 percent. It is clear that these better-educated women will find the labor market friendlier and will help break down what job discrimination remains against women.

Pay Differentials between Men and Women

Table 9-3 clearly shows the earnings gap that exists between male and female full-time workers. It is also clear that, although the gap varies slightly from year to year, it has remained very consistent overall.

The data in Table 9-3 raise the question: Why does such an earnings gap exist and persist? The debate over the answer to this question is loud and often emotional. Some say it is discrimination against women, pure and simple. Others suggest that at least in the past men have been better trained (more schooling and experience) and are therefore more productive. Still others suggest that men are the primary breadwinners and therefore more committed to their work. Many

_____ **Table 9-3** _____
Median Annual and Usual Weekly Earnings of Full-time Women Workers as Percentage of Men's Earnings

Year	Annual	Weekly
1955	63.9%	
1960	60.8	
1965	60.0	
1970	59.4	62.4%
1975	58.8	62.0
1980	60.2	63.4
1981	59.2	64.6
1982	61.7	65.0
1983	63.6	65.6
1984		64.8

Source: 1955–1975 (U.S. Bureau of Labor Statistics, 1977); 1976–1983 (U.S. Bureau of the Census, various years); weekly earnings 1970–1983 (U.S. Department of Labor, March 1984, pp. 17–28); 1984 (U.S. Department of Labor, 30 January 1985).

have felt that long-term training and investment in women does not pay off for companies because they will get married and/or pregnant and quit work periodically.

Much research has been done to answer the question, but the findings are equivocal and mixed. Madden (1985, pp. 83–85) summarizes the results of most of the major earnings differential studies completed in the past fifteen years. Overall the studies account for less than half the observed differential based on real productivity differences between men and women. Hours worked, amount of past experience and/or length of job tenure, occupation and/or industry (all real productivity measures) account for 30 to 40 percent of the pay differential.

One might conclude from this that the remaining difference is indeed discrimination against women in the labor force. Again, however, such a conclusion can be disputed. Discrimination, in light of civil rights laws and general societal disapproval is not always easy to discover. If women freely make different choices about their work than men and these choices result in a pay differential, has there been discrimination?

One argument against the existence of job discrimination suggests that family and housekeeping duties frequently lead women to make different choices about work hours, type, and amount of work experience, and occupation or industry, than men. Because of their home responsibilities, women work fewer hours and thus accumulate less experience than men. Furthermore, because women anticipate lower levels of lifetime employment and lower returns, they devote less effort to acquiring skills and choose jobs that require less training, experience, and so on (Madden, 1985, p. 87).

An alternative argument suggests that as a result of labor market discrimination, women have more difficulty in finding jobs that are full-time, offer opportunities for training and advancement, or are in "male" occupations. Significantly more of the pay differential is accounted for by sex barriers to high-paying jobs than to differential pay between men and women for doing the same job. Thus women do not freely choose the less remunerative jobs, but are forced into such jobs because of discrimination.

Regardless of which argument one supports, and what the real reasons are for such a pay differential, it does exist, and it does influence family life. For

Debate the Issues

Comparable Worth (Pay Equity) Legislation: The Only Way to End Pay Discrimination against Women

It is clear from the data presented in Table 9-3 that women overall have consistently earned only between 55 percent and 65 percent of what men earn. The concept of "comparable worth" has been suggested as a remedy to this pay differential. Essentially it means "equal pay for equal worth." Although neither Title VII of the Civil Rights Act of 1964 nor the Equal Pay Act of 1963 specifically mention comparable worth, both acts do mention hiring and discharge, compensation and conditions of employment, and the limiting of opportunities for employment. Those proposing comparable worth as a solution to the pay differential problem suggest that the concept can be justified and is at least implied in these acts.

In order to make the concept work, it is necessary to evaluate jobs on some kind of a point system that takes into account training, skill, responsibility, and effort needed to do the job. Most companies have already done job evaluation studies in order to produce the "job specifications" used to assist in hiring and wage determination. Thus the basis for comparing jobs already exists. Based on this evaluation some traditionally female jobs, such as executive secretary, might be found to be equal to a traditionally male job, such as cross-country trucker, and thus each job should be paid at the same wage. Since women have tended to concentrate in historically low-paying jobs (clerical work, etc.), to find that a given job for a woman is actually comparable in skills needed (granted perhaps different skills) on a given job most often held by a man lays the basis for a fair pay comparison.

In the few cases where comparable worth has been tried, it seems to work without bringing undue hardship on employers. In Minnesota legislation approved in 1982 has led to pay equity wage hikes for 9000 out of 29,000 state employees. The state's commissioner of employee relations claims that this raised state payroll costs only about 3 percent and the total state budget less than 2 percent. Comparable worth legislation in Australia has helped to increase women's wages to 80 percent of men's from 65 percent a decade ago (*Business Week*, 1985, pp. 82–83). The fear that large wage increases for women would cause employers to stop hiring women has not been realized in Australia.

As noted earlier (p. 36), single-parent, women-headed families are overrepresented below the poverty level. Increased wages for women will help these families survive economically. Perhaps a savings in public money can be made as these families are able to get off welfare and on their own economically.

In addition, equal pay for women will free men of some of the financial burden they now bear for the family. For example, in Joe and Mary's case, Joe might have been able to return to school and make himself eligible for a better job had Mary been able to earn a good enough living to support the family at least temporarily.

Perhaps the major benefit will be the greatly increased buying power higher wages will give women. The overall economy as well as the very businesses resisting the idea of comparable worth may be the real winners as women exercise their new buying power.

example, when Mary goes out to work to help Joe with the expenses, her earnings will probably be small compared to his for whatever reason. Because of this, perhaps Joe and Mary would be better off if Joe took a second or third job since he could earn more. The ramifications of such a decision for their relationship are great. If society can narrow the pay differential between men and women, families will have more economic choices. With more choices comes greater freedom for the family to meet both family and individual needs successfully.

Recently the rallying cry against the pay differential has been for government intervention to mandate "equal pay for equal work," in the form of "comparable worth" legislation. Thus far (mid-1986) little such legislation has been passed and much of that has been negated by the courts. (See "Debate the Issues," p. 291.)

Debate the Issues

Comparable Worth (Pay Equity) Legislation: It Will Cost Women Jobs and Fuel Inflation

---

Economic theory can be used to predict the direction of market adjustments when there is a dramatic change in one segment of the market. Comparable worth legislation would substantially .increase women's wages (by at least 20 percent). Other things being equal, economic theory suggests that employers will hire fewer employees in these jobs in an effort to hold down costs. However, at the same time, the increase in relative pay will make these jobs more attractive, thereby encouraging more people, particularly women, to seek positions in these already women-crowded occupations. Also, such wage increases will deter some women from moving into nontraditional, male-dominated jobs thereby slowing the pace of occupational desegregation.

In addition to labor market effects, the potential for inflationary pressure generated by comparable worth wage increases could be great. If women's wages were suddenly increased by 20 percent, the cost would be enormous. Such costs would be passed on to the consumer.

In light of the highly complex reasons for poverty among women, those who advocate comparable worth legislation as means of improving the welfare of the poor offer a simplistic solution. It is not clear that raising wages would help many poor women for whom the constraints on employment would be unaffected. In other words, the uneducated, unskilled poor woman will be no better able to get a job just because wages for women increase. Perhaps more impor-

tantly, the advocates of comparable worth as a means of reducing poverty among women implicitly shift parental responsibility away from men to women. The case for equity surely requires that both parents support children, rather than that children be lifted out of poverty by changing their mothers' wage rates. A more equitable remedy for female poverty than comparable worth would be effective action in collecting financial support from absent fathers (Bell, 1985, p. 8).

Another outcome of comparable worth legislation might possibly be the lowering of all men's wages. The assumption implicit in such legislation is that a fair wage is a male wage. No one suggests lowering male wages as a way of reducing the pay differential between men and women, yet this is certainly a noninflationary alternative to raising women's wages. Although most unions support the idea of comparable worth, some male unions oppose it. For example, in Minnesota, police and firefighter unions began to lobby against comparable worth legislation when a librarian's job was classified at the same level of pay as a firefighter's job (*Wall Street Journal*, 1985). In some unions, the feeling is that if companies must give their women employees substantial pay raises there will be nothing left over for the male employees. In addition, raises for men would have to be limited or the pay differential would remain regardless of the increases in female wages.

Perhaps more promising than legislation are the signs of improving employment opportunities for women that we have already discussed. Better education, more training, higher percentages of women in historically male-dominated occupations, and more women in managerial positions all should help reduce the pay differential in the long run. Perhaps most important of all is the sheer magnitude of women now in the workforce (Table 9-1 and Inset 9-2). As these numbers grow even larger so will women's power and with power comes the ability to invoke change.

One very positive change is already occurring. If the pay differential is broken down according to age, as in Table 9-4, some significant changes emerge.

Note that women in the youngest age group (25–29) earn considerably more compared to men than the overall average for women. It appears as if the efforts

What Do You Think?
- Are women really discriminated against in the workplace?
- How is this done?
- Can one really compare jobs as diverse as librarian and firefighter?
- If women earn really high wages, will men further shirk their family responsibilities?
- What will be the inflationary effect of comparable worth legislation?
- Are there other ways that the pay differential could be reduced?

Inset 9-2

Men versus Women in the Labor Force

Commencing in 1960 the percentage of the total male population in the civilian workforce has dropped, while the percentage of total female population in the labor force has increased dramatically.

Several reasons may account for the lower number of men in the workforce. Length of schooling for both men and women has increased greatly thus holding people out of the workplace longer. Since most men have historically been in the labor force, longer education works to reduce men's numbers in the labor force while its

effect is overridden for women because of the great numbers of women entering the labor force compared to earlier times.

Another reason is the recent encouragement of early retirement. Since many women are newly employed, retirement has not yet affected them to the degree it has affected men.

A lesser reason and one not yet really demonstrated by objective data, might be that as women share more and more of the economic burden of the family, men can reduce their contribution. Be that as it may, it is clear

that women are quickly gaining employment relative to men and surely their increased numbers will bring change to America's employment practices.

Percent of Men and Percent of Women in the Workforce

Year	Men	Women
1960	83.3	34.5
1970	79.7	41.6
1980	77.4	51.5
1983	76.7	52.3
1984	76.7	54.0

Source: Diamond, 1984.

---

to achieve equal pay for women are beginning to pay off in starting wages for women. If these starting wage gains persist, then indeed a start has been made toward reducing the pay differentials.

Another positive change has occurred in the female-male unemployment differential. Females have historically suffered higher unemployment rates than males. This obviously contributes to lower overall earnings for women and thus to the pay differential. The unemployment gap between men and women started to narrow in 1978 and for the first time actually reversed in 1982 (9.9 percent male unemployment versus 9.4 percent for women). Due to projected employment patterns, the Department of Labor predicts that the female unemployment rate relative to the male rate might decrease as much as 2.4 percent over the 1982 to 1995 period (DeBoer & Seeborg, 1984).

Work Availability: A Double-Edged Sword for Married Women

Increasing work availability for women has also meant increasing independence. Not only does this mean increased freedom within marriage, but also it can mean increased freedom from marriage. There is little doubt that the working woman's ability to support herself has freed her to seek new roles. As Ralph Smith (1979, pp. 23–24) says:

> To the extent that employment provides a woman with a reason and the means to postpone marriage, with meaningful roles other than motherhood, and with the ability to support herself after divorce, women's employment has contributed to these changes in marriage formation and dissolution.

In the past a woman's inability to support herself trapped her in marriage. She had to have a husband to survive. But with wider economic opportunities, this has become increasingly untrue. A woman alone is now able to survive financially, even when she has children. She does not need to remain trapped in an unhappy, unfulfilling marriage.

Not only did a woman in the past have fewer economic alternatives than her husband, but also she had to derive her status from his success. As sociologists Hornung and McCullough (1981) put it, hers was only "relational property" status—that is, her status was derived from information about the substantive relationship between her and her husband: "Who are you?" "I'm the wife of a doctor." (See p. 491.) Work availability for women, then, frees them to have their own identity. Thus one edge of the work availability sword is the woman's increased economic and psychological independence from marriage.

The other edge of the sword is that work outside the home can improve and enhance a woman's family life. Her earnings can increase the family's standard of living and alleviate the family's monetary restraints. For example, when Mary goes to work, she reduces the pressure on Joe. This should help him feel happier and more satisfied with his family life. The family can take longer vacations together, afford better housing in a nicer neighborhood, and improve the children's education. Thus the wife's working can contribute greatly toward the family's well-being and the permanence of the marriage.

There are numerous other advantages in addition to the direct economic advantages of having another wage earner in the family. The working wife may derive great personal satisfaction from her work just as many men do. By interacting with other adults outside her family, she may feel more stimulated and fulfilled, especially if she has small children at home. Her self-esteem may increase, with the knowledge that she is a more equal partner in the marriage.

The results of the increased independence of the woman who enters the workforce are hard to predict. Each individual will react differently. The point is that this increased independence is now a fact of life. It may effectively end the marriages of some women and greatly enhance those of others.

Table 9-4	
Women's Earnings as Percentage of Men's Earnings Broken Down According to Age	
Age	**Women's Earnings as Percentage of Men's**
25–29	75.7%
30–34	69.5
35–39	61.6
40–44	56.7
45–49	54.8
50–54	56.5
55–59	58.3
60–64	58.0

Source: U.S. Bureau of Census, 1982.

The Effect of Female Employment on the Time of Marriage

A working woman is more likely to postpone marriage (Moore & Hofferth, 1979; Smith, 1979) because she is able to support herself. Although this seems to support the idea of employment as an alternative to marriage, overall marriage rates have not declined.

About 90 percent of contemporary American women will marry at some time in their lives (U.S. Bureau of the Census, July 1985). Presently approximately 62 percent of all women over age eighteen are married. The young woman who works tends to postpone marriage rather than reject it altogether. On the other hand, for older women employment seems to act as a "dowry," particularly for those who have children and are contemplating remarriage (Oppenheimer, 1977; Moore & Hofferth, 1979). Men are apparently more willing to marry a woman with children if she is able to help support them.

The age at first marriage has risen in the past few years, a fact that may be due both to the increasing education of women and to their greater participation in the workforce. The average age of marriage for women has moved from 20.8 in 1970 to 23.5 in 1984. For men, the average age of marriage has moved from 23.2 in 1970 to 25.4 in 1984 (U.S. Bureau of the Census, July 1985). Moore and

Hofferth (1979, p. 29) summarize the effect of women's working on time of marriage as follows:

> To the extent that increased employment of women raises occupational aspirations and educational attainment, age at marriage will continue to rise. Employment does not seem to lead many people to develop tastes or lifestyles that preclude eventual marriage, however. Nevertheless, there may be a slight increase in the proportion of never married among those who turned 20 during the 1970s to about 7 percent. Rather than indicating a rejection of marriage, this will probably reflect the inability among some of those who postpone marriage to find a suitable partner when ready for marriage and some increase in the frequency of cohabitation.

The Effect of Female Employment on Divorce and Separation

As with time of marriage, female employment seems to have differing effects on the possibility of marital disruption. A woman can support herself outside of marriage if necessary. On the other hand, by economically contributing to the marriage, she can improve the quality of her family's life and consequently the stability of her marriage.

Studies on this question yield mixed results. Nye and Hoffman (1974) reviewed the literature and concluded that families in which the wife is employed are no more likely to separate or divorce than those in which the wife is not employed. If the wife earns more than the husband, however, or if he is periodically unemployed, the probability of divorce or separation increases (Moore & Hofferth, 1979).

An interesting and controversial side question concerns the effect of welfare aid on marital disruption. Some research teams have reported that receipt of welfare or income maintenance decreases marital stability (Hoffman & Holmes, 1976; Hannan & Tuma, 1977). In addition, welfare recipiency severely depresses remarriage rates in the first two years after divorce. This negative effect seems to disappear after two years have passed.

Mary Decides to Go to Work

> *Joe manages to keep the family afloat financially until their second child is two and one-half years old. Mary and Joe realize that they simply aren't going to make it comfortably on his earnings alone. Mary has heard that a local company is expanding and needs new employees. She applies for a job, gets it, and suddenly finds herself a full-time working mother. Although her income is relatively small compared with Joe's, she believes her $900 per month will not only get them out of debt but will also allow them a few luxuries they have had to forgo. She and Joe hope it will also allow them to save money toward a down payment on a house.*

The Working Wife's Economic Contribution to the Family

Unfortunately, Joe and Mary learn that her $900 does not raise the family income by that amount. Before Mary can go to work, arrangements must be made for child care. There are several choices. Mrs. Smith, an older mother down the street, also needs some extra money and, for $10 a day, is willing to keep both children at her house during Mary's working hours. Joe's mother is willing to keep them one day a week for free. There is a public day-care center near Mary's workplace that will care for the children for $45 a week. What the center charges is based on a family's income, so that the weekly costs vary from family to family. Mary decides to leave the children with Mrs. Smith four days a week ($40 a week) and with Joe's mother for the remaining day (free). This way the children will be with people they know and will be staying in their own neighborhood as well. If this arrangement doesn't work out, Mary can put them in the day-care center. Thus Mary's monthly child-care costs are $160. This leaves $740 from her paycheck.

Transportation must also be considered. There is a bus that goes past Mary's workplace, but the route is circuitous and requires her to leave the house half an hour earlier than she would have to leave if she drove. Taking the bus both ways will take an hour a day and cost $22 a month ($1 a day). Riding the bus also means that Joe will have to take the children to the sitter's each morning. They decide that buying an older economy car is probably the best solution. With the car Mary can help deliver and pick up the children and can be more efficient generally. They borrow $1200 for twenty-four months at 15 percent interest and buy a used car from a friend. The car is in good shape and, other than needing a new set of tires, requires no work. There are additional insurance costs, however. They purchase only liability coverage, thinking that because the car is old, it isn't worth the cost of collision coverage. The total monthly cost for the car is $100, broken down as follows:

Payment	$ 65	Discount interest adds up to $360 for two years. This makes a total debt of $1560. Divide by 24 months to get monthly payment of $65.
Insurance	$ 10	
Gas and maintenance	$ 25	
Total	$100/month	

Subtracting $100 more from Mary's monthly paycheck leaves $640.

Taxes and social security are also deducted from Mary's paycheck. She takes no deductions for the children and finds that another large bite has been taken from her paycheck. They will receive a refund at the end of the year because of child-care costs and other deductions, but when all is said and done, the taxes and Social Security costs average about $150 per month. Thus, Mary's monthly check shrinks further, to $490.

There are other miscellaneous costs associated with Mary's going to work. She doesn't have as much time for food preparation and household work. She uses more partially prepared foods such as frozen dinners that tend to be more expensive. She sends more clothing to the laundry, and she has to buy some new clothes to wear to work. These costs add up to about $100 per month.

The bottom line is that Mary's $900 a month pay adds only about $390 to the family income. This amounts to about 43 percent of her gross pay. In fact, studies indicate that the working mother will spend between 25 and 50 percent of her income in order to work, depending on the age of her children, type of work, and other factors unique to her situation (Vickery, 1979).

Because women tend to hold lower-paying jobs, the actual amount of money they contribute to the family tends to be small. Yet for many families this contribution is increasingly important. In the past, when the working wife was the exception, her work was viewed as a family insurance policy, a buffer against hard times, or a source of "play" money, money used for recreation, luxuries, and extras. For many families today a working wife's income has become necessary for survival. This means that many families no longer have an economic buffer against hard times. They become accustomed to living on two incomes; if either is lost, family finances become precarious if not impossible.

Household Activities

It seems strange to hear a mother of two small children reply to the question "What do you do?" with "Oh, nothing, I'm just a housewife." Obviously, a mother with two small children does a great deal of work for her family inside the home. She certainly doesn't "do nothing." Therefore when she takes a job outside the home, something has to change inside the home. Mothers with children at home average about thirty-six hours a week working in the home. Generally, their time is divided into three major household activities: (1) meal preparation and cleanup, about 30 percent; (2) care of family members, 15 to 25 percent; and (3) clothing and regular house care, 15 percent.

What happens to all of this work when mother takes an outside job? Essentially nothing. It must still be done and mother still does it. She simply cuts down the amount of time she gives to each task and donates much of her leisure time (weekends and evenings) to household tasks.

Although seldom discussed, the "just housewife" role usually includes more than homemaking activities. It is the "just housewives" that often do much of the important volunteer work for society. They are the ones who attend the PTA meetings, organize the church rummage sale, help a neighbor, and raise extra money for the children's school by conducting a paper drive. As more and more wives enter the formal workforce, our society may experience a loss in the informal workforce of volunteers. Community service may diminish because the working wife simply won't have time, or if she makes the time, as many do, the energy drain may be too great.

Many people suggest that the husband and children of the working wife should increase the amount of housework they do. Husbands, in fact, are likely to agree that they should do more in the households when their wives work, but they rarely live up to their professed beliefs or their wives' expectations. Pollster Mervin Field (1986) reported that 89 percent of married men and women agreed that household cleaning should be shared when both work. But when asked to describe their personal situation, 41 percent of the full-time employed wives and only 8 percent of the husbands reported doing most of the housework. Often men report doing a large share of the housework and childcare, but when it comes down to actually doing it, they rarely take as much responsibility for it as their wives do. A husband, for example, may take out the garbage (2 minutes) while the wife does the dishes (15 minutes). Only 22 percent of husbands with wives working full-time report doing more than ten hours of housework per week. Even among unemployed husbands with full-time working wives only 31 percent report doing more than ten hours per week of housework (Blumstein & Schwartz, 1983, p. 144). Barnett and Baruch (Cunningham, 1983) reported that men increased their housekeeping chores by only one and one-half hours per week (from 4.3 to 5.8 hours per week) when their wives went to work. Clearly men have done little to offset the household pressures created by women's increased participation in the labor force (Coverman & Sheley, 1986).

Distribution of family work (housework and child care combined) is a critical issue for most dual-worker families (Yogev, 1983) yet husbands' low level of household labor compared with their wives' is not necessarily negatively perceived. In Berk's (1985) study, 90 percent of both husbands and wives felt the division of labor was fair. Apparently, then, the perception by the spouses of the willingness of the other to shoulder responsibility for family work is more important to marital satisfaction than the actual amount of work accomplished (Yogev & Brett, 1985). Thus the expressed change in men's attitudes toward family work (more willing to do it in attitude) even if not much acted on, is important to marital happiness.

Although husbands don't appreciably increase their share of household work when their wives go to work (Berk, 1985), overall they are sharing more household work than they have in the past, whether their wives work or not (Maret & Finlay, 1984). This change stems from shifting attitudes about sex roles and the increased emphasis on egalitarian marriage in the United States.

For many wives one result of going to work is "overload" and strain. They end up doing two jobs, one outside the home and one inside. Their leisure time is greatly reduced. The quality of their household work diminishes. Time becomes their most precious commodity.

It is this overload of the working wife, especially the working mother, that families most resent. In the General Mills report, "American Families at Work" (1981), 63 percent of the working mothers surveyed indicated that they did not have enough time for themselves. It is interesting to note that only 40 percent of the working fathers felt the same way. Both working parents listed lack of time with family and children and long hours on the job as the greatest strains placed on the family when both husband and wife work. Constant complaints were made about lack of time for recreation, picnics, vacation trips, children, love making, and plain old "doing nothing." Of the working women in the study, 41 percent indicated they would prefer to work part-time.

Despite the strains reported by working wives, the triple roles of spouse, mother, and employee are linked with good health. "Of the factors we examined, employment was by far the strongest and most consistent tie to women's good health. Marriage ranked second and parenthood third. The combination of no job and no spouse was linked strongly to poor health, especially for women aged 25 to 34" (Verbrugge & Madans, 1985). These differences may reflect the fact that unhealthy women stay out of the workforce, or that working outside the home is healthy. This data conflicts with the ideas suggested in Inset 9-3.

Mary Seeks Part-time Work

Mary works for seven months at her new full-time job. This helps get all their debts paid off. However, she finds that she is increasingly fatigued. She and Joe never seem to have fun together any more. If she does find some free time, all she wants to do is sleep. The house looks unkempt. She hasn't had fun cooking a meal in months. She feels guilty about the little time she is able to spend with the children. She finds herself grumpy and unhappy much of the time. Mary decides, now that they are out of debt, to see if she can find a part-time job. She finally does, and with a sigh of relief, quits her full-time job.

Inset 9-3

Working Women and Health

Sickness and death may seem like far-fetched consequences of female employment, but when one considers that women have, within the traditional role, made nurturing and home production their principal concern, the loss or diminution of these services might be feared to lead to poorer health among family members. Women, of course, as they opt for the working world, are exposing themselves to job tensions, commuting accidents, and occupational hazards; consequently, their mortality may rise. Especially given the picture of overwork and strain in households with two full-time earners plus children, it seems possible that less attention might be given to proper diet and rest. Parents cannot afford to take the time to relax or be ill, so their physical health may deteriorate. Two-job couples may consequently have shorter life spans.

On the other hand, the higher incomes of families with employed wives may provide the wherewithal for an adequate diet and preventive medical care. Husbands who are freed from the omnipresent concern of supporting their families might enjoy lower blood pressure and fewer heart attacks. Husbands may be able to turn down overtime or leave a job that is harmful to their long-term health. These benefits from women's rising labor force participation might lengthen the average life span, particularly among men.

At this time, no studies are known that have addressed this issue. If it is the case that increases in female employment affect longevity and the incidence of disease, however, the ramifications are enormous. The frequency and length of widowhood would be lessened. Fewer retired people might be unmarried. Pension systems and health care services would be affected. If the strains experienced by two-earner families are reflected even in the incidence of sickness and death, the importance of flexible and part-time employment becomes self-evident. Clearly, this is a topic that merits research attention.

Our speculation at this point is that the long-run effect of women's working will be to equalize the life span, lengthening men's lives but shortening women's. A shorter life span would be less likely, however, to the extent that both sexes reject the aggressive, competitive model of employment (Moore & Hofferth, 1979; Verbrugge & Madans, 1985).

Part-time Work

Approximately half of all women who work part-time give "taking care of the home" as their reason for preferring part-time work. The creation of more and better part-time jobs for mothers with young children would help alleviate the overload experienced by the full-time working mother. Unfortunately, part-time work reduces the economic contribution to the family, due not only to fewer hours worked but also to lower pay standards. On an hourly basis part-time work generally pays only 75 percent as much as full-time work.

Those who seek part-time employment are usually assumed to be intermittent workers without long-term career commitment. Therefore part-time work seldom gives fringe benefits, job protection, or advancement opportunities. Lack of fringe benefits, especially health insurance, combined with low pay in part-time jobs, may keep some people on welfare. Welfare recipients are eligible for free medical care under the Medicaid program, and welfare payments in some cases can be as much as can be earned in a part-time job.

The proportion of women working part-time has increased because of the larger proportion of mothers with young children who search for such jobs. As of

October 1985, over 13 million men and women (13 percent of the workforce) were employed part-time (U.S. Department of Labor, December 1985, p. 60).

Where are part-time jobs to be found? Usually in the occupations where women predominate, the so-called pink-collar occupations. Very few jobs are available for part-time managers, accountants, butchers, and machinists. At the same time, four out of five waitresses work less than full time. Department store saleswork is becoming increasingly part-time, and offices are turning more and more to temporary help. Beauty shops have always used part-time people. In the health field, where women make up 75 percent of the workforce (except in upper level positions), shift work and part-time arrangements are commonplace. Schools are turning increasingly to part-time substitute teachers in order to save money. In contrast, in the industries dominated by men, part-time and temporary work is seldom found.

What this means for most mothers is that they will be downwardly mobile at work rather than upwardly mobile like their husbands. More and better jobs are open to women before they have families, because they can work full-time. After a woman has a family, when she is available for work often determines the job

---

Inset 9-4

Job Sharing

Joan and Pamela, each recently divorced, share quite a bit: a job, a paycheck, a house, and their children.

The two friends persuaded a small company to hire both of them to split one secretarial job. One works while the other cares for the children. This arrangement has numerous advantages. Each woman has a job, which is necessary if she is to make ends meet because neither receives more than a minimum amount of child support. Each saves money that would go to baby-sitters. Each knows the other well so that the children are left with a friend rather than a stranger. The children also remain in their own home rather than being sent away for the day. In addition, each mother has time with her own children. Each has reduced her expenses by sharing the costs of the house.

Each woman works three days one week and two days the following week. This schedule gives the company a full-time secretary while each mother works only half time.

The company has also derived some extra advantages from the job sharing. Occasionally one of the women's children becomes sick. The other woman can cover for her at work. If only one mother were involved, the company would probably have to do without an employee for the day.

Both workers are also fresher and less tired because they are not coping with two full-time jobs every day, mother and employee.

---

she finds. In the face of demands on her time, the young mother is likely to find that the scheduling of her job is the most important single consideration. Her immediate job choice is dictated in large measure by the time constraints imposed in the short run, and this in turn directs her subsequent career development. However, as more and more mothers enter the workforce and prove to be good workers, part-time jobs may take on more of the advantages that come with full-time work.

There are some problems for an employer who hires two part-time people to do one full-time job. Social security contributions, for example, will be higher for two workers than for one full-time worker, even if the rates of pay are identical (see Inset 9-4). Generally record keeping and paperwork are increased. However, as the advantages of part-time work are recognized, such inequities may be removed.

Mary's New Part-Time Job

Mary's new half-time job pays her $350 per month. With her mother-in-law's help, she is able to do away with child-care costs. Transportation costs remain the same, $100 per month, leaving her $250. Taxes and social security are reduced to $70 per month, leaving $180. Miscellaneous costs are also reduced to $50 per month. In the end she contributes $130 extra dollars to the family compared with the $390 she contributed when working full-time. This is just enough to keep them out of debt. There is a great deal less strain on Mary, however, and hence on the family.

Mary moved from full-time employment to part-time and experienced a reduction in family conflict. However, women moving into part-time work from nonemployment (full-time housewife role) may actually experience more conflict than if they had moved into full-time employment. In a study by Blumstein and Schwartz (1983), 42 percent of the couples where the wife was working full-time reported fights about working. But 60 percent of the couples where the wife worked part-time reported such fights. Part-time wife employment may cause increased marital conflict because of the small amount of extra money that she brings into the family. "It's not worth having you work. We lose more than we gain." Couples where the wife is contemplating taking a full-time job are more apt to make a considered decision than are couples where the wife takes on a part-time job. Often a wife just slides into part-time work because it has become available. Little thought is given to the family ramifications of her doing part-time work.

Marital Satisfaction When the Wife Works

As with so many areas we have discussed, the question of marital satisfaction is double-edged. The family may gain satisfaction through the wife's economic contribution; the family may lose satisfaction because she is no longer able to supply all of the caring and services of a full-time wife and mother. Economic strain may be reduced when she works; psychological and physical strain may be increased.

Moore and Hofferth (1979) find that the research evidence on marital satisfaction when the wife works is mixed. After reviewing many studies, they conclude that wives who work from choice rather than economic necessity, those whose husbands are favorable toward their employment, and those who work part-time are happier with their marriages than full-time housewives. Smith (1985) reviewed twenty-seven research studies and, although the studies again showed mixed results, concluded that whether a wife works has little relation to marital satisfaction. How couples cope with the wife working seems individually determined by each couple. Once a couple works out the new routines and relationship changes, marital satisfaction seems to return to its normal level.

Although we have spoken mainly of the working wife's economic contribution to the family, it is clear that her participation in the world of work may also pay her psychological dividends. Work may allow her to use some of her skills that are unused in the homemaker role. She will meet and interact with a wider variety of adults. She will gain more power in relationship to her husband (Rank, 1982). Her feelings of integrity, self-respect, competency, self-determination, and accomplishment may increase if she has work she enjoys and has successfully solved the problems of working and caring for her family.

The evidence of husbands' marital satisfaction when their wives work is also mixed but tends to indicate that they are less satisfied than the wives (Mehren, 1986). As Moore and Hofferth report (1979, p. 121):

> Evidence from other studies suggests that many husbands accept their wives' work grudgingly; that men may have more trouble than women do adapting to nonstereotypical roles; and therefore that men experience greater difficulties resolving the resulting stress. Other researchers note that in going to work a woman is frequently expanding into a new role, one that is higher in status than that of homemaker, while a husband

who assumes homemaking functions is adopting a role of lower status—a role that may strain not only his sense of status and identity but his feeling of competence as well. Furthermore, a busy wife may not be able to provide the same level of physical and emotional support that a full-time homemaker can, so a husband may well come to feel he is losing out on all fronts.

On the other hand, a second income can provide the husband additional freedom. He can cut down on moonlighting or overtime work. He might be able to take a temporary reduction in pay to enter a new career or job he finds more satisfying. Increased free time may allow more family enjoyment and leisure time pursuits.

Because of the importance of expectations in human relations (p. 150), what one thinks or expects about something is often as important as what actually happens. Research on marital quality in families where the wife works indicates that happiness with the relationship is more related to the congruence between role expectations of one spouse and the role performance of the other spouse than to any particular pattern of roles. It is not simply a matter of whether a woman's working has an impact on marital adjustment but rather the extent to which that behavior violates role expectations, her own as well as her family's (Lewis & Spanier, 1979; Houseknecht & Macke, 1981). If a woman expected to be a housewife, if her husband expected her to stay home, and if significant others in her environment (parents, in-laws, children, and so forth) have negative attitudes about her working, the chances are great that both her and her family's satisfaction will drop when she goes to work. The General Mills study (1981) found that almost twice as many family members believed that the effect of both parents' working outside the home has been negative (52 percent) as believe it has been positive (28 percent).

On the other hand, as the working wife becomes the norm for the society, negative attitudes about her will diminish. Children of working mothers tend to be more supportive of the idea of wives working (Corder & Stephan, 1984). Dual-career families tend to produce children whose attitudes are more egalitarian and who prefer dual-career families themselves (Stephan & Corder, 1985, p. 928). This being the case, the incidence of families in which the wife works should continue to increase as should the level of marital satisfaction in such families.

Researchers have discovered an interesting social-class difference in marital satisfaction when the wife goes to work: Lower-class families seem to have more adjustment problems than middle-class families. For example, studies report that lower-class sons who have full-time working mothers were less admiring of their fathers (Hoffman, 1974; Gold & Andres, 1978). Lower-class working wives score lower on marital adjustment (Burk & Weir, 1976; Rallings & Nye, 1979). One possible explanation of this is that the lower-class woman usually must work in order for the family to survive. Her working is thus a direct statement about her husband's inability to provide for his family and may be seen by him as a threat to his status. In contrast with lower-class women, middle-class women are more likely to be in the labor force voluntarily. One must be careful interpreting social-class differences in marital satisfaction because there are many differing influences. For example, differing educational levels lead to differing attitudes about a mother's entering the work world.

Traditionally, only a small minority of mothers with children under age six have been employed. Two factors have worked to keep the mother of young children out of the labor force. First, the logistics of caring for the children are often unsolvable. Second, there has been a long-standing belief that a mother belongs with her children, especially when they are young. Because of earlier studies of the effects of prolonged separation of children from caring parents (orphanage and foster home placements, war orphans, and so forth), many people believe that the mother's absence during the early years will harm the child (see p. 221).

There is a large body of research on both animals and humans that suggests the importance of early maternal nurturing to proper maturing. In each case the research notes that the maternally deprived child has difficulty forming close relationships as an adult. Many researchers have noted that it is more important to the survival of humans than to any other mammals to provide prolonged care through intense attachment of mother and infant. Alice Rossi (1978) indicates that throughout most of human history infants had extremely close physical contact with their mothers for 70 percent of the day during infancy and for about 30 percent of the day until the middle of the second year. Today most infants have body contact with others less than 25 percent of the day soon after birth, and that time shortly falls off to 5 percent. J. W. Prescott (1970, 1975, 1976) has demonstrated neurostructural, neuroelectrical, and neurochemical abnormalities of sensory system functioning and development as well as related behavioral deficits associated with sensory deprivation. Others (Schwartz, Money & Robinson, 1981) conclude from such research that absence of fondling, stroking, touching, and playing during the early years may make a person particularly susceptible to attachment and intimacy difficulties later in life.

Yet effective child care by other than the true biological mother does not necessarily lead to severe problems in children. Actual effects of substitute child care are just as difficult to uncover as are the effects of natural parenting. The effects depend on (1) the quality of the substitute care, (2) the characteristics of the child, (3) the mother's reasons for working and the quality and quantity of the time both parents spend with the child, and (4) the general social acceptance of substitute child care.

The quality of substitute child care can be excellent. It can provide for the child both physically and psychologically. A loving, caring baby-sitter is often an important and happy influence on a child. Most working mothers (48 percent) leave their children with other family members. Only about 19 percent leave their children in day-care centers (General Mills, 1981). It seems that other family members would be more likely than strangers to give the child adequate love and attention. Substitute child care cannot be wholly praised or condemned but must be judged on its specific merits. It can be good or bad for a child, just as the child's biological parents can be.

Individual children will react differently to the partial loss of their mother and the substitution of another manner of care. Their reaction can be positive or negative. A hyperactive, disruptive child may experience much negative feedback in a large day-care center. The same child may thrive with an attentive baby-sitter. If the mother is an unhappy, frustrated homemaker and prefers the work world, her child would probably be better off with a substitute. It is perhaps not the quantity of time parents spend with their children but the quality of time that counts. A working mother may spend less time with her children, but if she makes it high-quality time, her relationship with her children may be improved. Note, however, that a generous quantity of time must be spent with children if there is to be quality. Note also that the overworked mother trying to do both her job and family work may lack the energy to offer her children quality time.

Mary Tries to Improve the Time She Spends with Her Children

When she was a full-time homemaker, Mary found that her two children were always underfoot. She never seemed to have a minute's peace. They were calling "Mommy, Mommy, Mommy" so often that she almost never paid attention to it. In fact, sometimes when she heard them, she'd deliberately hide from the children to escape their constant pressure. Now that she works, she finds she enjoys spending time with them. She looks forward to the weekends so she can do projects with them and give them her undivided attention. She spends much less time with them now that she works, but she enjoys that time more than she ever has.

It is interesting to note that daughters of working mothers as compared with the daughters of nonworking mothers view women as more competent (Broverman et al., 1972) and view female employment as less threatening to marriage. This seems to indicate that their mothers provided adequate nurturance even though they worked. Obviously, a working mother may shortchange her children. On the other hand, she may also be better able to provide for them.

Work and Family: Sources of Conflict

Ideally work and family should complement and support one another. Yet in reality these two arenas of life often conflict. The conflicts tend to differ for husbands and wives in large part because of the historical division of labor between the sexes. The work world tends to intrude on a husband's family life. If he is asked to work overtime, for example, he must usually do it to keep his job, regardless of what plans he may have made with the family. It is more likely that the family will intrude into a wife's work world. For example, if a child is sick traditionally it is her responsibility to tend the child. A husband's family usually must bend to his work demands; a wife's work must usually bend to her family demands. Note also that sanctions against a man for poor performance have traditionally been greater on the job, while sanctions against a woman for poor performance have traditionally been stronger in the family.

Essentially work and family conflicts are of three types: (1) time-based conflict, (2) strain-based conflict, and (3) behavior-based conflict (Greenhaus & Beutell, 1985).

Time-based Conflict

As we have already noted, time becomes a very valuable commodity to both partners in the dual-worker family, but especially to the wife and especially if there are children present in the home. Since the husband in the dual-worker family does not usually shoulder his fair share of household tasks (pp. 296–297), it is clear that time is more of a constraint to the working woman. This is also true of the single-parent family. Returning home from a long day's work to face preparing dinner, housecleaning, and other family chores is hardly an inviting prospect. If children are present, how does one find any time for them, much less summon up enough energy to make it quality time? The increased pressure on home time due to long hours at work and inflexible work schedules means that much less of a couple's time can be devoted to their children, one another, recreation, play, and self-renewal activities.

When both husband and wife work, it doesn't necessarily mean that they will have less time together. What it means is that the time they have together is consumed by daily necessities. Too often it is the important time for self-improvement and the time of intimate caring and working on their relationship that is lost. When a couple work exactly the same hours, there is no lost "togetherness" time. If, however, there is some "off-scheduling" (Nock & Kingston, 1984, p. 335)— that is, if one mate starts work an hour earlier than the other—then the couple loses an hour of togetherness time.

It should also be noted that time at home is not necessarily family time. A spouse might well bring work home, either concretely or psychologically. A career-oriented partner is much more apt to do this than a family-oriented partner. A career-oriented partner puts his or her career ahead of the family, and this usually causes family resentments because of the perceived lack of commitment to the family. "You're married to your job," is a criticism often made by other family members.

Strain-based Conflict

In this case, strain on the job causes difficulty at home or vice versa. "Don't ask your father to borrow the car the minute he gets home. Give him time to relax." This is an example of work strain causing family difficulty. Obviously the stresses and strains of the work world take their toll emotionally on the working family member and will be felt at home as well.

Much less often discussed is the effect of family strain on the job. "Jack is not very efficient today. Its probably because he and his wife are fighting again." Many companies considering a person for promotion consider both job performance and family life. One might object to this as an invasion of privacy, but the worker undergoing severe family strain (illness, divorce, etc.) will be hampered in his or her job performance.

Behavior-based Conflict

Specific patterns of role behavior may be incompatible with expectations regarding behavior in another role. For example, the male managerial role tends to emphasize self-reliance, emotional stability, aggressiveness, and objectivity. Family members, on the other hand, may expect a person to be warm, nurturing, emotional, and vulnerable in his or her interactions with them. If a person is unable to adjust behavior to comply with the expectations of different roles, he or she is likely to experience role conflict (Greenhaus & Beutell, 1985).

Such role disparities are especially difficult to cope with when the home-oriented spouse does not share in the spouse's work world. In the traditional husband working—wife homemaking family, failure to know and understand each other's domains causes conflict. In fact, in the extreme, the husband lives in a work world totally unknown by his wife, and he has little understanding or empathy for her problems with the family. A husband and perhaps father is legally in the family but for all practical purposes is not a functioning member of the family other than supplying economic support.

If a dual-worker family is really a two person—single career family, then work-family conflicts may be reduced. Such a family shares the same career and works together in the work world. Obviously the husband who comes home tired and upset after a day at the office is better understood and supported by the wife who comes home from the same office, and vice versa.

Jobs, Occupations, and Careers

Up to this point, we have been discussing women taking jobs in the labor market. However, a short- or even long-term job is not the same as a long-term career. Essentially we can place work on an attitudinal continuum according to the degree of commitment (Kahn & Wiener, 1973, p. 153):

Basic Attitude Toward Work	Basic Additional Value
1. Interruption	Short-run income
2. Job	Long-term income; some work-oriented values (working to live)
3. Occupation	Exercise and mastery of gratifying skills; some satisfaction of achievement-oriented values
4. Career	Participating in an important activity; much satisfaction of work-oriented, achievement-oriented, advancement-oriented values
5. Vocation (calling)	Self-identification and self-fulfillment
6. Mission	Near fanatic or single-minded focus on achievement or advancement (living to work)

Most women in the labor force occupy one of the first three levels. Although many men also occupy one of these levels, there is a far higher percentage of men than women in the latter three categories. This is true because the man traditionally has been the family breadwinner while the woman has been the homemaker. However, as women have increasingly entered the workforce, and as attitudes about sex roles have changed, more and more career opportunities are opening to them. The two-career family will become a more visible reality in the future. A career may be denoted by (1) a long-time commitment including a period of formal training, (2) continuity in that one moves to higher and higher levels if successful, (3) mobility in order to follow career demands.

In the families of most career men, the man's career dictates much of the couple's life. Where and how they live often depends on his career demands. These demands are met relatively easily if the wife is a homemaker or works at one of the first three levels. A dual-career family, however, can have possible conflict between the partners over career demands as well as the other kinds of problems that occur in any family when both partners work. Suppose, for example, that the dean in a local community college is married to a woman who is also a high-level school administrator in that district. When he wins a new position as president in another district, it means moving several hundred miles to a new college. After much discussion the couple decide that each should continue his and her own career. They are now a "weekend family." Each spends the week at the job, and they take turns visiting each other on the weekends.

Such a lifestyle is of course not suitable for families with small children. Research indicates that families that choose this lifestyle tend to be those free of childrearing responsibilities; older couples; those married longer; those with established careers (Gross, 1980); and those having high educational levels, high-ranking occupations, and high income levels (Kirschner & Wallum, 1983).

An overwhelming proportion of the literature on the dual-career family reports that the impact of dual-career stress is felt most by women. This is true not only in the woman's family life but also in her work. She takes more career risks, sacrifices more, and compromises career ambitions in attempting to make the dual-career pattern work. The stress is reduced if she has a supportive husband who is willing to leave his job and relocate to advance his wife's career. Strain is also greatly reduced if she is free of childrearing responsibilities (Houseknecht & Macke, 1981).

> *Marjorie Smith, a trust officer at Chase Manhattan Bank, is up every morning at 6 o'clock. After making breakfast and laying out clothes for her five-year-old daughter Suzy, she leaves for work. At that point, her husband, Lee, takes over—getting Suzy dressed and walking her to school. At 5 o'clock, after her day at the office, Marjorie picks up their daughter at a day-care center. Once home, the Smiths continue their hectic schedule, doing the laundry, dashing through a supper of soup and sandwiches, and dividing up the other household tasks: grocery shopping by Marjorie, vacuuming by Lee. The only trouble is that the routine rarely works. "The norm is frantic phone calls and schedule changes," says Lee with a laugh.*

The Smiths are one of a growing number of couples whose daily life is fraught with the hassle of keeping two careers and a family afloat. This short description of Marjorie Smith's day may help give some feeling of the frenetic pace found in many dual-career families, especially those with children still living at home.

If both partners are successful in their careers, it usually means that major career decisions will have to be made periodically throughout the relationship. Each new decision may upset the balance that has been worked out by the couple. For example, what happens when one spouse is offered an important promotion, but this means moving to another location? Will harm be done to the partner's career? If the new location is not too far away, should one spouse commute? Should they take up two residences? What will this living arrangement do to their relationship? Each time one partner has a major career change, a series of such questions will have to be answered. In most cases, where the couple strives for career equality, the answers will not be easy.

Summary

Many consider the number of women entering the workforce to be the major revolution affecting the American family in this century. In the past the woman's, and especially the mother's, place was in the home. This is no longer true. In most families today the woman is an active participant in the economic support of her family.

Although now a permanent and large part of the American labor force, women still earn a disproportionately lower income than their male counterparts. In addition, career opportunities are still narrower for women than for men. Many steps have been taken to change these inequities, and although change is slow there are many hopeful signs that the future work world will be as advantageous for women as for men.

The working mother is often overburdened, carrying out her job as well as being the major worker in the home. This is because husbands of working wives do not yet shoulder their fair share of family work.

Increasing job availability has made women more independent than they have been in the past. This has brought pressure on many husbands, because women now have a realistic alternative to a bad marriage: moving out and supporting their families themselves. But a woman's increasing independence can also reap rewards for the family. Her additional earnings may help the family invest and start the economy working for them; ease the pressure on the husband to be the only breadwinner; and generally lead to a more egalitarian relationship within the marriage.

Unfortunately, the lower incomes often received by women tend to blunt some of the possible advantages of working. The costs of working, including clothes, transportation, increased taxes, and child care, often make the woman's real economic contribution small and even "not worth it" at times. However, as women improve their skills and become a more indispensable part of the workforce, gain political power, and become more career-oriented, the pay differential between the male and female worker should decline.

Employers, Pregnant Employees, and Working Mothers

Many employers feel that women with children are not as likely to make the same commitments to their careers as are men. Yet with women soon to make up almost half of America's workforce and with 60 percent of mothers with children under eighteen years of age already in the workforce, it is clear that women are an integral and necessary part of America's labor supply. It is true that mothers bear the major responsibility for child care and thus are more torn between their families and their work than men. Yet by taking this into account rather than only complaining about it, business can improve workers' performance while at the same time supporting family stability.

More than one hundred countries have laws that protect pregnant workers and allow new mothers a job-protected leave and full or partial wages at the time of childbirth (Mall, 1986). The recent "Report on a National Study of Parental Leave" (Mehren, 1986) found that 46.8 percent of women with children under one year of age are working outside the home, yet only 40 percent of American working mothers get even six weeks of postpartum leave with any income or job guarantee. Of the companies surveyed, 42.6 per-

cent offered a comparable job while only 38 percent offered the same job back after a maternity leave. Only 39 percent offered full payment during the disability leave.

A bill in Congress proposes that we grant new parents a minimum of 18 weeks of unpaid leave with job protection. A Yale study recommends child-care leaves of six months with 75 percent pay for half of that time. Yet Goodman (1986) suggests that leaves *only* for infancy miss the point. She asks, "Will the focus on those with newborns allow employers and legislators to pretend that the conflicts between work and family are temporary, limited to the earliest months of life?" What about parents who must stay home with a seriously ill child? What about the "latchkey" child without supervision? What about allowing fathers to enjoy their new infant or to stay home once in awhile with a sick child?

If the family is to survive both parents working outside the home and if business is to have satisfied productive workers, the obligations of family will have to be integrated with the obligations of work. Instead of setting family and work in opposition and conflict, Americans are going to need

to figure out a way to make them allies, cooperative partners in the business of life. Better leave policies, more flexible working hours, job sharing, on-site child-care facilities, and, with the advent of computer networking, increased use of the home as a workplace are all actions that could improve the relationship between family and work.

When women ran their homes and reared their children and men supported their families via working outside the home, employers did not need to concern themselves with these types of accommodations to keep their workers satisfied and productive. However, the days of such separation between family and work are probably gone forever. It is interesting that 100 years ago work and family were integrated on the American farm. The Industrial Revolution separated the two and now as women have become essential to the American workforce, the family and work will have to become integrated and supportive of each other again. Once employers team up with the family instead of conflicting with it, American productivity will be stimulated to reach new heights.

Human Sexuality

Contents

Friend: *What is sex?*

Student: *Everyone knows what sex is! Sex is for having babies—you know, reproduction.*

Friend: *I know, but if sex is only for reproduction, why don't humans mate like other animals, once a year or so? Why don't human females go into "heat" to attract males?*

Student: *Well, human females are more sexually receptive at certain times during their monthly cycle, aren't they?*

Friend: *The evidence on that is mixed, but even if it were true, why are humans interested in sex all the time? Why do they spend so much time talking about, reading about, thinking about, and having sex?*

Student: *Perhaps sex is for human pleasure.*

Friend: *But if sex is for fun, why are there so many restrictions on sexual behavior? Why does society try so often to regulate sexual expression? Why are there so many sexually transmitted diseases? STDs certainly aren't fun. Why does religion try to focus sexual behavior toward some higher purpose?*

Student: *Well, then, perhaps sex is for love, and love will limit the number of sexual partners.*

Friend: *But, what is love exactly? Does sex always mean love? If masturbation is sex, does it mean I love myself if I do it? Can I love more than one person at the same time?*

Student: *Love is emotional closeness that allows you to communicate at an intimate level. Love also makes you feel good about yourself—it enhances your ego. So if sex is love, it does all these things too.*

Friend: *Certainly sex can be for all of the things you mention. But isn't sex sometimes just for biological release such as when a man has a wet dream during which semen is released? This doesn't sound much like love or ego enhancement, does it?*

Student: *No, but sex can and should be an expression of love.*

Friend: *Ah, yes, but what it sometimes is and what it should be are often two different things.*

Student: *What do you mean?*

Friend: *Well, is sex an expression of love when it is used to possess another person, such as when a woman is considered to be a man's property? Or when it is used to gain status, such as when a king marries the daughter of another king to increase his holdings and thereby his prestige? Or when it is a part of violence, such as in rape? Or when it is a business, as in prostitution? Or when it is used indirectly, as in advertising where appeals based on sex are made to sell many different products?*

Student: *Now I'm really confused. Just what is sex?*

From this short discussion it is obvious that sex is many things, and, at times, something of a riddle. If sex were only for reproduction, or only an expression of love, or only for fun, there would be little controversy about it and no need to control it. Sex isn't for one purpose, though, but for many. It is this fact that causes people to be so concerned and, at times, so confused about the place of sex in their lives.

Inset 10-1

Sex Knowledge Inventory

Sex is a subject that most people think they know a lot about. Let's see if we do. Mark the following statements true or false. Answers can be found on page 317.

1. Women generally reach the peak of their sex drive later than men.

2. It is possible to ejaculate without having a total erection.

3. Sperm from one testicle produce males and from the other, females.

4. A person is likely to contract STD when using a toilet seat recently used by an infected person.

5. If a person has gonorrhea once and is cured, he or she is immune and will never get it again.

6. Certain foods increase the sex drive.

7. Premature ejaculation is an unusual problem for young men.

8. The penis inserted into the vagina (sexual intercourse) is the only normal method of sex.

9. It is potentially harmful for a woman to take part in sports during menstruation.

10. A woman who has had her uterus removed can still have an orgasm.

11. During sexual intercourse a woman may suffer from vaginal spasms that can trap the male's penis and prevent him from withdrawing it.

12. The cause of impotence is almost always psychological.

13. For a certain time period after orgasm, the woman cannot respond to further sexual stimulation.

14. For a certain time period after orgasm, the man cannot respond to further sexual stimulation.

15. Taking birth control pills will delay a woman's menopause.

16. The size of the penis is fixed by hereditary factors and little can be done by way of exercise, drugs, and so on to increase its size.

17. If a woman doesn't have a hymen, this is proof that she is not a virgin.

18. As soon as a female starts to menstruate, she can become pregnant.

19. About 80 percent of women infected with gonorrhea show no symptoms.

20. The penis of the male and the clitoris of the female are analogous organs.

21. A woman can't get pregnant the first time she has intercourse.

22. A good lover can bring a woman to orgasm even when she doesn't want to have an orgasm.

23. Herpes is easily curable with antibiotics.

24. Thus far slightly over one-half of AIDS victims have died.

25. One can become infected with herpes simply by kissing an infected person.

Marriage is society's sanctioned arrangement for sexual relations. A happy, satisfying sex life is a characteristic of the healthy family. Sex is one of the foundations of most human intimate relationships. Sex is the basis of the family—procreation—and the survival of the species. Sex is communication and closeness. It can be pleasuring in its most exciting and satisfying form. Certainly it is proper to study marriage by viewing humans as the sexual creatures they are. And though thoughts and attitudes toward sex are the most important part of human sexuality, we must start with the biological foundations if we are fully to understand sexuality and the male-female bond.

Because of the sexual revolution, all Americans are supposed to know everything about sexuality. See if you do by taking the Sex Knowledge Inventory in Inset 10-1 before you continue to read the chapter.

Human Sexual Anatomy

When describing human anatomy, we think in terms of two descriptions, male and female. Yet the development of male and female anatomical structures rests on a common tissue foundation. As described in Chapter 7, hormonal action triggered by chromosomal makeup differentiates the tissues into male and female organs. Figures 10-1 and 10-2 show this differentiation, as well as the homologues

Undifferentiated

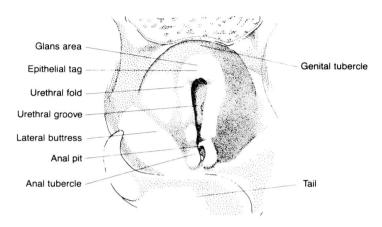

Glans area

Epithelial tag

Urethral fold

Urethral groove

Lateral buttress

Anal pit

Anal tubercle

Genital tubercle

Tail

Figure 10-1   External male and female genitals: development from undifferentiated to differentiated stage.

Male   **Embryo**   **Female**

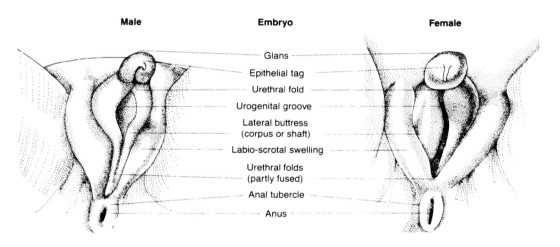

Glans

Epithelial tag

Urethral fold

Urogenital groove

Lateral buttress
(corpus or shaft)

Labio-scrotal swelling

Urethral folds
(partly fused)

Anal tubercle

Anus

Fully Developed

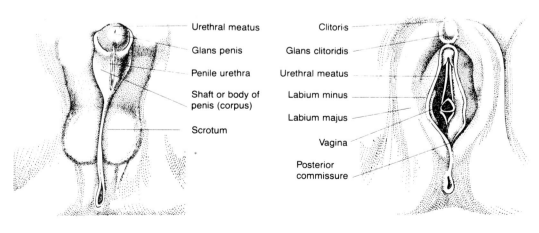

Urethral meatus

Glans penis

Penile urethra

Shaft or body of
penis (corpus)

Scrotum

Clitoris

Glans clitoridis

Urethral meatus

Labium minus

Labium majus

Vagina

Posterior
commissure

UNDIFFERENTIATED

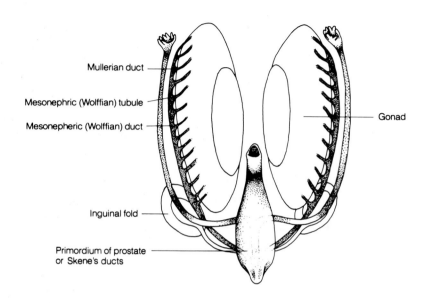

Mullerian duct

Mesonephric (Wolffian) tubule

Mesonepheric (Wolffian) duct

Gonad

Inguinal fold

Primordium of prostate
or Skene's ducts

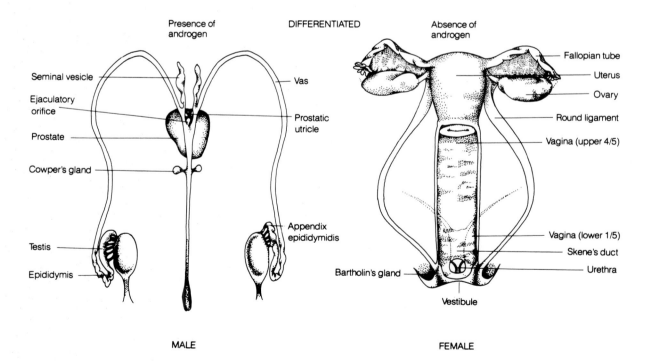

DIFFERENTIATED

Presence of
androgen

Absence of
androgen

Seminal vesicle

Ejaculatory
orifice

Prostate

Cowper's gland

Testis

Epididymis

Vas

Prostatic
utricle

Appendix
epididymidis

Fallopian tube

Uterus

Ovary

Round ligament

Vagina (upper 4/5)

Vagina (lower 1/5)

Skene's duct

Urethra

Bartholin's gland

Vestibule

MALE

FEMALE

Figure 10-2   Internal male and female genitals: development from undifferentiated to differentiated stage.

(similar in origin and structure but not necessarily in function) of external and internal male and female genitals. The contrast between the sexes begins around the fifth or sixth week after conception.

It is interesting that human sex organs have always been of more interest to people than other organs. Many past societies have glorified the genitals in their arts. But the advent of Christianity brought a more negative attitude toward sexuality, generally limiting it to reproduction. The interest in sexuality as pleasure went underground, so to speak, and graphic display of sexual activities became known as pornography.

The **genitals** have long been studied medically in modern America, but only recently have they been studied as organs of sexuality. Masters and Johnson in their classic study, *Human Sexual Response* (1966) pioneered the study of the genitals as pleasure organs. Today every aspect of human sexuality—whether physical, psychological, or social—is a legitimate area of study. For example, the following papers were presented at a recent regional meeting of the Society for the Scientific Study of Sex: "Feminine Sexual Hygiene," "Penile Sensitivity, Aging and Degree of Sexual Activity," "Clitoral Adhesions: Myth or Reality," and "The Vaginal Clasp."

Male Sex Organs

Although most people's interest focuses on the external organs because of their obvious sexual connotations, the internal ones are regarded as the primary organs of procreation (see Figures 10-3, 10-4).

The testes in the male produce *spermatozoa* (or sperm for short). If the coiled tubules within the testes that produce and store the sperm were straightened out, they would be several hundred feet long. Other special cells within the testes produce the important hormone **testosterone**. This hormone directs the developing tissue toward maleness and, at adolescence, causes the maturing of the sexual organs and the appearance of secondary sexual characteristics, such as deepening voice and facial and body hair. Figure 10-5 shows the course taken by the sperm in ejaculation. Sperm are matured and stored in the *epididymis*. With ejaculation they travel up the *vas deferens* where it joins the duct of the *seminal vesicle* in the lower abdomen. The two seminal vesicles produce the secretion **semen**, to increase the volume of the ejaculatory fluid, which empties into the ejaculatory ducts. These ducts empty into the *urethra*, which is the canal extending through the penis. (The urethra is also the canal through which urine is discharged, but urine and semen can never pass through at the same time. Sexual arousal and ejaculation inhibit the ability to urinate.) The *prostate gland* surrounds the first part of the urethra as it leaves the bladder. This gland secretes a thin fluid that helps alkalize the seminal fluid. In addition the muscle part of the prostate helps propel the ejaculatory fluid out of the penis. The last contribution to the seminal fluid comes from the *Cowper's glands*, two pea-sized structures flanking the urethra. During sexual arousal they secrete an alkaline fluid that further neutralizes the acidic environment of the urethra and provides penile lubrication to facilitate intercourse.

The process of **ejaculation** begins with contractions of the ducts leading from the seminiferous tubules in the testes and simply continues on through the system. The actual amount of ejaculate varies according to the male's physical condition

Genitals
The external reproductive organs

Testosterone
An important component of the male sex hormone androgen; responsible for inducing and maintaining the male secondary sexual characteristics

Semen
The secretion of the male reproductive organs that is ejaculated from the penis during orgasm and contains the sperm cells

Ejaculation
The expulsion of semen by the male during orgasm

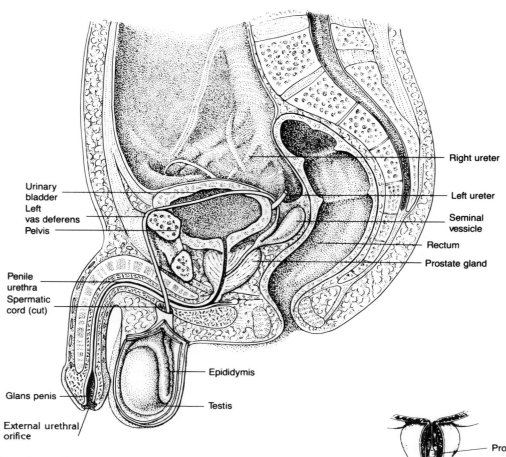

Right ureter

Urinary
bladder
Left
vas deferens
Pelvis

Left ureter

Seminal
vessicle

Rectum

Prostate gland

Penile
urethra
Spermatic
cord (cut)

Epididymis

Glans penis

Testis

External urethral
orifice

Figure 10-3   The male reproductive
system.

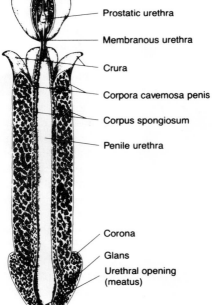

Prostatic urethra

Membranous urethra

Crura

Corpora cavernosa penis

Corpus spongiosum

Penile urethra

Corona

Glans

Urethral opening
(meatus)

Figure 10-4   A longitudinal section of the
penis.

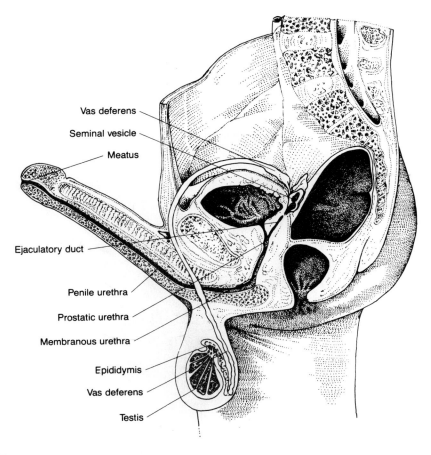

Figure 10-5 The passage of sperm.

Vas deferens

Seminal vesicle

Meatus

Ejaculatory duct

Penile urethra

Prostatic urethra

Membranous urethra

Epididymis

Vas deferens

Testis

and age and the time elapsed between ejaculations. Usually about a teaspoon of fluid is ejaculated; it contains about 300 million sperm. To be considered of normal fertility, the ejaculate must contain a minimum of 60 to 100 million sperm per cubic centimeter of semen. The ejaculatory amount is reestablished in the healthy male within twenty-four hours.

The strength of the ejaculatory response also varies: The semen may simply ooze out of the urethra or may be discharged as far as several feet beyond the penis. Figure 10-6 diagrams the route taken by the sperm for fertilization to take place.

Ejaculation is accompanied by a highly pleasurable sensation known as *orgasm*. This will be discussed more fully later.

The testes are particularly sensitive to temperature and must remain slightly cooler than the body to produce viable sperm. Hence when the temperature is hot, the sac containing them will hang down farther. When the temperature is cold, the testicles will be pulled up close to the body. Since high temperature of the testes reduces sperm count, it is unwise for a man to spend long periods of time in a hot tub or sauna if his mate is trying to get pregnant. Occasionally, the testicles don't descend into the scrotum properly and sterility results. Surgery and hormone treatment usually can correct this (McCary & McCary, 1982). Sometimes only one testicle descends, but one is usually enough to ensure fertility.

Figure 10-6   The route of a sperm during ejaculation from its origin to its fertilization of an egg.

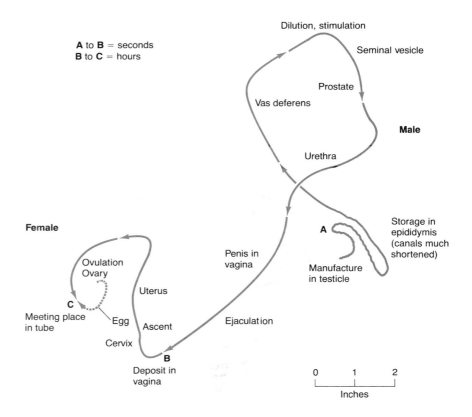

A to **B** = seconds
B to **C** = hours

Dilution, stimulation

Seminal vesicle

Prostate

Vas deferens

Male

Urethra

Storage in epididymis (canals much shortened)

Female

Penis in vagina

A

Ovulation
Ovary

Manufacture in testicle

Uterus

C

Meeting place in tube

Egg   Ascent

Ejaculation

Cervix

B

Deposit in vagina

0   1   2
Inches

In order to have intercourse, it is necessary for the male to have an erection. Both erection and ejaculation can occur without physical stimulation, such as with a nocturnal emission that usually is accompanied by an erotic dream.

Figure 10-4 shows the three cylindrical bodies of spongy erectile tissue that run the length of the penis. Sexual arousal causes the dilation of blood vessels within the penis, and small valvelike structures (polsters) emit blood into the vascular spaces of the erectile tissue. Because the rate of blood inflow is greater than the rate of outflow, the volume of blood in the penis increases. As the erectile tissue becomes engorged with blood, the penis stiffens into an erection. The average penis is three to four inches long in a flaccid state and six to seven inches long when erect. Size variations are less in the erect state than they are in the flaccid state and are not related to virility. Men do not have voluntary control of erection and cannot always be sure that they will be capable of intercourse. This fact sometimes leads to sexual insecurity in males. Failure to achieve and hold an erection long enough for sexual intercourse is called **impotence**.

Modern technology has succeeded in duplicating the erection's mechanism and the device has been successfully implanted to aid men who cannot become erect. The device consists of two silicone rubber cylinders implanted into the penis, a bulb in the scrotum, and a liquid containing reservoir in the pelvic region. Repeated pumping of the bulb causes the liquid to flow into the cylinders, creating an erection. The penis remains erect until a release valve is squeezed to evacuate the fluid back to the reservoir (see Figure 10-7).

Impotence
Usually temporary inability of a man to experience erection; may be caused by either physical or psychological factors

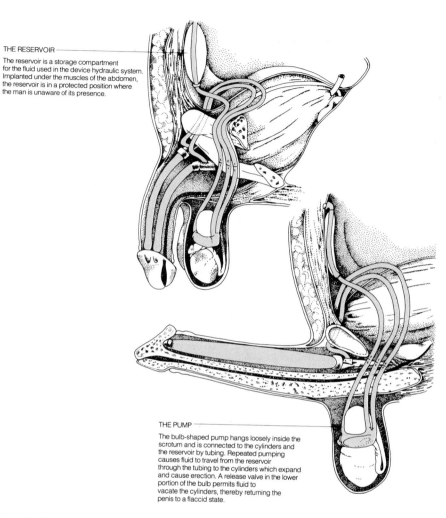

THE RESERVOIR

The reservoir is a storage compartment for the fluid used in the device hydraulic system. Implanted under the muscles of the abdomen, the reservoir is in a protected position where the man is unaware of its presence.

THE PUMP

The bulb-shaped pump hangs loosely inside the scrotum and is connected to the cylinders and the reservoir by tubing. Repeated pumping causes fluid to travel from the reservoir through the tubing to the cylinders which expand and cause erection. A release valve in the lower portion of the bulb permits fluid to vacate the cylinders, thereby returning the penis to a flaccid state.

Figure 10-7 The inflatable penile prosthesis. The operation of the inflatable penile prosthesis mimics the natural action of the erection process. A miniature hydraulic system transfers fluid to implanted cylinders, which causes the cylinders to fill and expand, creating an erection. When an erection is no longer desired, the man activates a deflation mechanism to return the penis to a normal flaccid state.

Female Sex Organs

To focus our discussion of the female reproductive system (see Figure 10-8), let us trace the course of development and ultimate fertilization of the female egg (**ovum**). Eggs are released from the female gonads or **ovaries**. Each ovary contains an estimated 50,000 to 200,000 tiny sacs or *follicles*, but only 250 to 400 will become active during a woman's lifetime and produce eggs (see Figure 10-9). Each woman is born with a lifetime supply of eggs and does not actually produce them as the male produces sperm. After puberty normally once every twenty-eight days one egg will ripen and burst from a follicle and will enter the **Fallopian tube**, where fertilization may occur.

Each month the ripe egg travels through the Fallopian tubes to the uterus where, if fertilized, it will implant in the blood-rich uterine lining that has built up during the month to receive it. This cycle is known as the menstrual cycle, and release of the ripe egg from the follicle is called **ovulation**. If the egg is not fertilized, it will be shed, along with the thickened uterine lining, as menstrual flow. The easiest way to describe this process is to label the first day of menstrual flow as

Ovum

The female reproductive cell (egg) that when fertilized develops into a new member of the same species

Ovaries

The female sex glands in which the ova (eggs) are formed

Fallopian tubes

The two tubes in the female reproductive system that link the ovaries to the uterus; passageway for eggs

Ovulation

The regular monthly process in the fertile woman whereby an ovarian follicle ruptures and releases a mature ovum (egg)

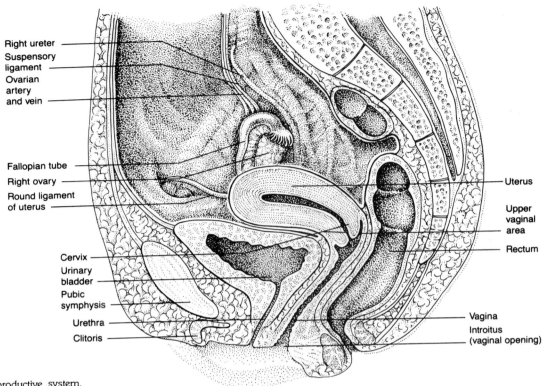

Right ureter

Suspensory ligament

Ovarian artery and vein

Fallopian tube

Right ovary

Round ligament of uterus

Cervix

Urinary bladder

Pubic symphysis

Urethra

Clitoris

Uterus

Upper vaginal area

Rectum

Vagina

Introitus (vaginal opening)

Figure 10-8   The female reproductive system.

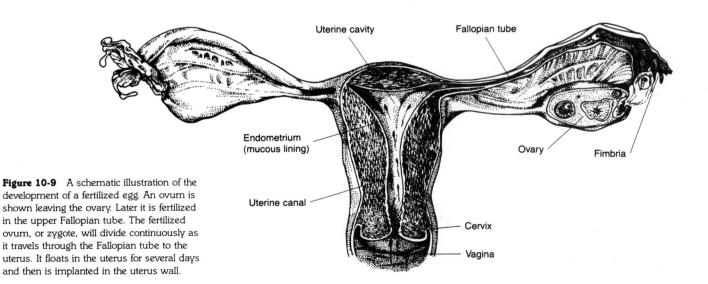

Uterine cavity

Fallopian tube

Endometrium (mucous lining)

Uterine canal

Ovary

Fimbria

Cervix

Vagina

Figure 10-9   A schematic illustration of the development of a fertilized egg. An ovum is shown leaving the ovary. Later it is fertilized in the upper Fallopian tube. The fertilized ovum, or zygote, will divide continuously as it travels through the Fallopian tube to the uterus. It floats in the uterus for several days and then is implanted in the uterus wall.

day 1 because it is easy to observe. On the average the cycle lasts twenty-eight days, with menstruation lasting five days. Individuals may vary considerably from these averages.

Follicle-stimulating hormones (FSH) are released from the anterior lobe of the pituitary gland, which is a pealike gland suspended from the base of the brain. The follicle-stimulating hormone activates the ovarian follicles, and two to thirty-two eggs begin to ripen. The follicles mature at different rates of speed. By the tenth day the most mature follicles look like rounded, fluid-filled sacs. The maturing follicles begin to produce **estrogen**, which prepares the uterus for implantation of the fertilized egg. At this time one of the follicles speeds its growth. The others, developed to various extents, regress, and die. Occasionally a woman may produce more than one ripe egg per cycle and thus be prone to multiple births. Many women taking certain chemicals designed to increase their fertility have had multiple births, indicating that the chemicals stimulate numerous follicles to continue ripening.

By about day 13, the egg is ready to be released. This is accomplished by the *luteinizing hormone (LH)*, also produced by the pituitary gland. The luteinizing hormone causes the follicle to rupture, which is ovulation.

The egg survives for about twenty-four hours. Sperm, on the other hand, can normally survive from one to three days after being deposited in the vagina. If ovulation occurs between the twelfth and sixteenth days of the cycle, intercourse any time between the ninth and the eighteenth days may cause pregnancy (see Figure 10-10).

As the egg has been developing, estrogen has also worked to enrich and thicken the uterine lining, or *endometrium* (see Figure 10-11). Blood engorges the tissue to provide a nourishing environment for the fertilized egg. If fertilization does occur, the fertilized egg will be implanted in the thickened uterine wall, and the menstrual cycle will be suspended for the duration of the pregnancy (see Chapter 12). Usually, however, fertilization does not take place, and the menstrual cycle is completed. Without fertilization the estrogen level falls and the thickened uterine lining, as well as the remnants of the unfertilized egg, are shed as **menstruation** through the cervix and vagina. About two ounces of blood are lost in an average menstrual period. There may be some cramps in the pelvic region as well as general discomfort at this time. Many women also report some fatigue, irritability, depression, and psychic distress just before menstruation. This premenstrual tension is probably the result of the shifts in hormonal levels. (See Inset 10-2.)

Estrogen
Often called the "female hormone"; directs the differentiation of embryonic tissue into female genitals and of prenatal brain tissue that governs female physiological functions; responsible for the development of female secondary sexual characteristics

Menstruation
The discharge of blood from the uterus through the vagina; normally occurs every twenty-eight days in women from puberty to menopause

Figure 10-10 Timing of the menstrual cycle.

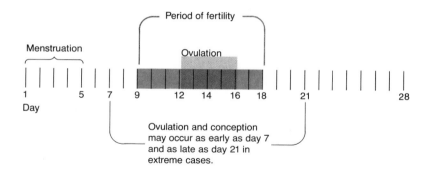

Period of fertility

Menstruation

Ovulation

| | | | | | | | | | | | | | | | | | | | | | | | | | | |
1   5   7   9   12   14   16   18   21   28
Day

Ovulation and conception may occur as early as day 7 and as late as day 21 in extreme cases.

Inset 10-2
Premenstrual Syndrome

Premenstrual syndrome (PMS) is the name given to a number of symptoms, both physical and psychological, that may accompany a woman's period. Although the numbers vary according to the studies, probably 70 percent of menstruating women notice at least one emotional, physical, or behavioral change in the week before menstruation. For most of these women the symptoms are negative, but for about 12 percent they may be positive (such feelings as increased energy and a general feeling of well-being). For another 5 to 10 percent of menstruating women the symptoms are numerous and so severe that their lives are disrupted for a week or so each month (Hopson & Rosenfeld, 1984).

Although physical problems such as breast tenderness and water retention are troublesome, it is the changes in mood, depression, feelings of worthlessness, irritability, despair, un-reasonableness, and lack of emotional control that trouble women most. Generally such symptoms start to occur about seven to ten days before menstruation. The symptoms usually abate and disappear shortly after the onset of menstruation.

Doctors at first felt that such symptoms occurred due to a drop in progesterone level (Dalton, 1979) and so prescribed daily doses of the hormone to treat the symptoms. However, research has found that placebos (pills thought to be the hormone but actually containing no medication) also alleviated the symptoms. Progesterone treatment has lost some popularity due to these studies and other studies that suggest progesterone might increase the risk of breast tumors.

Unfortunately because researchers cannot agree on a definition of just what constitutes PMS, there is little agreement on its treatment. Some go so far as to say it doesn't really exist, but there are thousands of women who strongly contest that point of view. Since most women can predict the time of their menstruation fairly accurately, they can also predict the onset of PMS. The ability to predict just when the symptoms might arise help women to plan ahead and prepare to cope with the symptoms.

Today's treatment uncertainties are bound to frustrate PMS sufferers in search of a quick, safe, effective cure. While there are many treatments, both behavioral and biological, none has been proven safe and effective. Yet, ironically, since PMS sufferers seem to respond to almost any treatment, the chances of an individual finding relief are quite good.

Source: Adapted from Hopson & Rosenfeld, 1984.

Toxic shock syndrome (TSS) is a new problem that has recently come to public attention via well-publicized lawsuits against some tampon manufacturing firms. The cause of TSS is unknown, but a bacterium, *Staphylococcus aureus*, is suspected. The continuous use of tampons during menstruation may favor the growth of this bacterium. In actuality the problem is rare (6 to 15 per 100,000 menstruating women (Crowe, 1984, p. 546) but dangerous. It is characterized by sudden onset of symptoms such as vomiting, diarrhea, fever, skin rash, and a drop in blood pressure. If you get such symptoms, remove the tampon immediately and contact your doctor. TSS can develop within a matter of hours. There is also some evidence that TSS might also be caused by use of a diaphragm or contraceptive sponge (Radetsky, 1985).

The remaining organs of the female reproductive system, the *vagina, clitoris,* and other external genitals (Figure 10-12) are important to sexual behavior. The vagina is about three and a half inches long when it is relaxed and can stretch considerably during intercourse and childbirth (see Chapter 12). The clitoris is important to female sexuality, being highly erogenous. It is located just under the upper part of the labia minora.

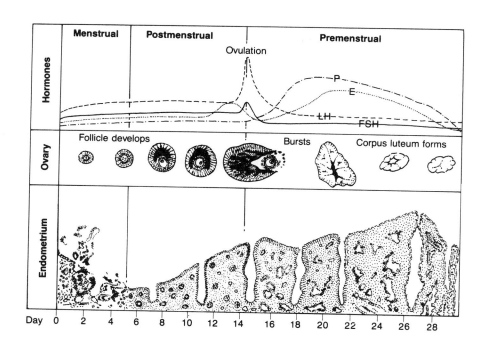

Figure 10-11   Lining buildup.

The cessation of the menstrual cycle in women is termed **menopause** or the climacteric. Menopause generally occurs between the ages of forty-six and fifty-one. Menstruation does not stop suddenly but usually phases out over a period of time not exceeding two years. As long as a woman has any menstrual periods, no matter how irregular, the possibility of ovulation and therefore conception remains.

Because of the changing hormonal balances during menopause, a woman may experience some unpleasant symptoms such as "hot flashes," excessive fatigue, dizziness, muscular aches and pains, and emotional upset. These symp-

Menopause

Menopause
The cessation of ovulation, menstruation, and fertility in the woman; usually occurs between ages forty-six and fifty-one

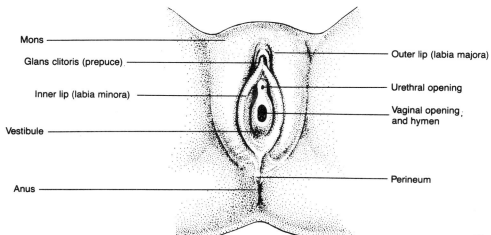

Figure 10-12   External female genitals.

toms may last considerably longer than two years. Some women also worry that menopausal changes will bring decreased or changed sexual interest and desire. In actuality menopause does not seem to decrease sexual desire. In fact, many women report increased sexual desire because they no longer worry about pregnancy.

Estrogen therapy may be prescribed to help reduce negative symptoms. Because of this use, estrogen gained a reputation during the 1960s for slowing down the general aging process. However, several studies done during the 1970s appeared to link it to the development of uterine cancer (Smith et al., 1975; Ziel & Finkle, 1975). It is now suggested that estrogen therapy be limited to the control of serious negative menopausal reactions and not be prescribed over extended time periods inasmuch as it does not appear to have any real value in retarding the aging process (Wallis, 1981; MacDonald, 1981; Doress, 1984, p. 448). Also, research indicates that far fewer women suffer serious negative symptoms from menopause than was once believed (Bruck, 1979), thus reducing even further the need for estrogen therapy.

The Physiology of the Sexual Response

Only recently have we begun to understand the physiology of the human sexual response. In a series of controversial studies, Masters and Johnson (1966) pioneered research using human subjects engaged in sexual activities. Before these studies most of our knowledge was derived from animal research. Among other techniques Masters and Johnson photographed the inside of the vagina during sexual arousal and orgasm. As controversial as this research was, it opened a new field of study, gave us a new understanding of the human sexual response, and paved the way for programs to help people with sexual difficulties. Recently Masters and Johnson's work has been criticized for methodological errors and careless reporting (Zilbergeld & Evans, 1980), yet it was their pioneering efforts that finally brought scientific research to bear on human sexuality.

Masters and Johnson divide the sexual response of both men and women into four phases: *excitement, plateau, orgasm,* and *resolution.* A partial description of these phases follows. The responses in all the stages for both females and males are usually independent of the type of stimulation that produces them. In other words the basic physiological reactions are the same regardless of whether they are produced through manual manipulation, penile insertion, or in some other manner.

The Female Sexual Response

Sexual response begins with the excitement phase, which may last anywhere from a few minutes to several hours. The breasts swell with blood. The skin may also be flushed; the nipples may become erect; and there may be general muscle contractions in the thighs, back, abdomen, and throughout the body. The **clitoris** becomes engorged with blood (tumescent); the vagina walls begin to sweat a lubricating fluid that facilitates the entrance of the penis. The inner portion of the vagina balloons, and the uterus may have irregular contractions. The labia minora (inner vaginal lips) increase in size. Blood pressure, heart rate, and breathing rates all increase.

Clitoris
A small organ situated at the upper end of the female genitals that becomes erect with sexual arousal; homologous with the penis

swelling

The next phase, the plateau phase, lasts from only a few seconds to about three minutes. Tumescence and the sex flush reach their peak. Muscle tension is high and the woman experiences a complete physical and emotional absorption with the impending climax. The clitoris withdraws beneath its hood and can only be stimulated indirectly. (The idea that direct stimulation of the clitoris is necessary for female orgasm is untrue. Indirect stimulation is effective, and, in fact, the heightened clitoral sensitivity during this phase may make direct stimulation uncomfortable.) Muscle rigidity reaches a peak as shown by the facial grimace, rigid neck, arched back, and tense thighs and buttocks. The labia minora change color dramatically. (In women who have not borne a child, the color will be pink to bright red; in women who have had children, the color will be pink to deep wine.) Blood accumulates in the arteries and veins around the vagina, uterus, and other pelvic organs. This pelvic congestion is relieved by the orgasmic phase.

The third phase, **orgasm**, is the most intense. During orgasm, most of the built-up neuromuscular tension is discharged in three to ten seconds. Orgasm is so all absorbing that most sensory awareness of the external environment is lost. The whole body responds, although the sensation of orgasm is centered in the pelvis.

Orgasm
The climax of excitement in sexual activity

Of all the widespread muscle responses, the muscles that surround the lower third of the vagina cause the most unique phenomenon. These muscles contract against the engorged veins that surround that part of the vagina and force the blood out of them. These contractions also cause the lower third of the vagina and the nearby upper labia minora to contract a number of times.

Although it is generally recognized that women do not ejaculate as men do, a few researchers (Addiego et al., 1980) report isolated cases in which women have experienced an ejaculatory-type phenomenon. The researchers claim to have evidence that "some women ejaculate a fluid which contains the product of the 'female prostate,' . . . which is homologous to the male prostate" (p. 100). Their evidence suggests that such responses occur most frequently from stimulation of the so-called Gräfenberg spot (G spot), an area located on the front wall of the vagina halfway between the top of the pubic bone and the cervix. It lies along the urethra, just below the neck of the bladder. The G spot ranges from the size of a dime to that of a quarter. This research remains suspect because even the existence of the Gräfenberg spot is questionable at this time. Researchers Perry and Whipple (1981) report finding the G spot in 400 of the women in their sample. Masters and Johnson (1982), however, were unable to replicate this finding. Because areas of the body can be eroticized psychologically, Masters and Johnson suggest that some women may have located a psychological pleasure spot within a certain area of the vagina and that there is no physiological basis for the increased sensation. Masters and Johnson also note that the few women in their studies who show considerable fluid discharge with orgasm secrete fluid that has essentially the chemical makeup of urine, although some claim the fluid is similar to prostatic fluid (Maloney, 1982). The fluid bears no chemical similarity to male semen.

In the last phase, resolution, the body returns to its prestimulated condition, usually within ten to fifteen minutes. If orgasm does not take place, the resolution phase may last twelve hours or more. Women have the capacity of repeating the four-phase cycle immediately after resolution and can experience multiple orgasms if stimulation is continued.

The Male Sexual Response

The four stages of the sexual response cycle cause the same changes in the male as in the female, with a few differences. For example, during excitement the penis (as well as the breasts and nipples) becomes engorged with blood until it erects. Also, the sperm begin their journey from the epididymis to the penis.

The next and major difference occurs during the orgasmic phase. Orgasm for the male is reached by the ejaculation of the semen and sperm through the penis. Once the male ejaculates, penile detumescence (loss of erection) usually follows quickly in the resolution phase, though complete detumescence takes longer. Unlike the female, who can reach repeated orgasms, the male usually experiences a refractory (recovery) period during which he cannot become sexually aroused. This period may last only a few minutes or up to several hours depending on such factors as age, health, and desire. Recent research has found that not all men have an immediate, complete refractory stage (Griffitt & Hatfield, 1985, p. 143). Some men are able to keep an erection or partial erection after they ejaculate and continue to enjoy sex for a while (Nass & Libby, 1984). Because in our society the male has usually been taught that it takes time to become sexually aroused again after ejaculation, the refractory period may be psychological as well as physiological. Although orgasm and ejaculation occur simultaneously in the male, it is possible for the male to learn to withhold ejaculation even though orgasm occurs. Such an ability is claimed by certain eastern yogis and others although exactly how this ability is learned is vague.

The male who is sexually aroused for a length of time without ejaculating may experience aching in his testicles and a general tension. These sensations can last for an hour or two. Such tension can be relieved by masturbation if a sexual partner is unavailable.

Variations in Sexual Response

Although Masters and Johnson's early work suggested that all persons follow the four-phase pattern of sexual response, more recent research indicates that there may be more individual variation than first thought (Hartman & Fithian, 1972, 1979; Nass & Libby, 1984). This research suggests four variations on the basic pattern of sexual response described by Masters and Johnson. Some people appear to experience orgasm as they're approaching the peak of heartbeat and breathing, some as they hit the peak, and some on their way down; a few people have orgasms that are so gradual the researchers can't tell when they start, although it is obvious when they end.

Masters and Johnson believed that the woman's orgasm was identified by vaginal contractions and that without these the woman's sexual response was not an orgasm. They concluded that women experience only one kind of orgasm, although earlier researchers had described two kinds of female orgasms, clitoral and vaginal. At first it appeared that the Masters and Johnson research had settled the question of one type or two types, but the question has been reopened. Shere Hite (1976), for example, found that during intercourse many women experience a peak of tension followed by total relaxation without any sensation of involuntary contractions in the vaginal area. Some researchers think that such women are having mild vaginal contractions but aren't aware of them because muscles all over their bodies are contracted (Kerr, 1977). Many of the women in Hite's survey also believe that there is a subjective difference between intercourse orgasms and those brought on by masturbation or oral sex where there is little or no penetration. These women describe the intercourse orgasms as more "diffuse" and whole-body involving, whereas the nonintercourse orgasms are more intense and localized. Some women found the former more satisfying, and some found the latter more satisfying.

Other researchers (Singer & Singer, 1972) suggest that there may be three kinds of female orgasms. The first is the vulval or clitoral orgasm described by Masters and Johnson. The second is a uterine or upper orgasm during which breathing changes lead to involuntary breath holding (because of a strong contraction in the muscle at the back of the throat) and then to explosive exhalation. This orgasm is not accompanied by vaginal contractions. The researchers suggest that the third type is a blending of these two.

Although much research has been done on the female orgasm, we still do not have a definitive answer about its nature. What is clear is that females have a greater diversity of sensation and reaction to sexual stimulation than males do. Therefore when a woman reads a popular description of what she "should" be feeling and how she "should" be reacting to sexual stimulation, she must be aware that the description may or may not fit her. If the description does not fit her, she need not necessarily label her sexual responses inadequate.

For both the male and female hormonal balances play a large role in sexual interest and arousal. Hales and Hales (1982) point out that a drop in a man's testosterone levels will lead him to gradually lose interest in sex. Many believe that the same will be true of a woman if her estrogen level drops. However, although estrogens influence a woman's attractiveness by keeping her skin soft, hair full and shiny, and breasts round and firm and help sex to be pleasurable by stimulating vaginal lubrication, they seem to have little to do with desire. Interestingly, it seems to be testosterone that influences women's level of desire just as it is in men. Long after estrogen levels drop with menopause, women remain interested in sex. But if her testosterone level drops, a woman loses interest just as a man does. Conversely, women treated for medical disorders with synthetic testosterone typically experience a surge in sexual desire that may come as quite a surprise.

Some Myths Unmasked

Masters and Johnson's research put to rest a number of myths about human sexuality. First, it established beyond question that women can have multiple orgasms. It also established that, within normal ranges, the size of the penis and vagina have little to do with the experience of orgasm. For example, the back two-thirds of the vagina is practically without nerve endings and plays little part in orgasm. Most of the stimulation occurs in the front third of the vagina, the labia minora, and the clitoris. A larger penile circumference may increase a woman's sexual sensation by placing pressure on the vaginal ring muscles thus causing pleasurable tugging of the labia minora. Further, a longer penis may heighten sensations by thrusting against the cervix (Keller, 1976; McCary & McCary, 1982). On the other hand, too large or too long a penis may be uncomfortable for the woman, detracting from her sensual enjoyment.

Masters and Johnson also revealed that it is not essential to stimulate the clitoris

---

Inset 10-3

On the Trail of the Big O

Ralph: Quiz time, dearest. What moves around more often than Elizabeth Taylor, the *QE2* and the wandering albatross?

Wanda: I give up, Ralph. What?

Ralph: The female orgasm. In the old days, it used to be in the vagina. Then they moved it to the clitoris, where it remained stationary for a decade. Now it seems to be on the move again. Just restless, I guess.

Wanda: Ralph, what on earth are you talking about?

Ralph: The Great Traveling Orgasm, my pet. Under the majestic scepter of science, not to mention the cattle prod of sexual politics, the Big O is thrashing about once again. It's gone from vagina to clitoris and now seems headed for the brain and back to the vagina. Before you know it, it will come to rest on the elbow or the pancreas. Ralph's *Guide to Sex*, as yet unpublished, will advise all ardent males to rub everything once. One never knows where tomorrow's sexual climaxes will be located.

Wanda: I am about to have an out-of-body experience, Ralph. But I suppose I could remain here with you and your monologue if a fact or two happened to intrude.

Ralph: Facts are the backbone of good argument, my beloved. I hold here in my hand the current winter issue of the *Journal of Sex & Marital Therapy*. I quote: "From recent empirical studies it can be concluded that most (and probably all) women possess vaginal zones whose tactile stimulation can lead to orgasm." Apparently the long tyranny of the clitoris is coming to an end, dearest. At least until the next dramatic breakthrough of sexual science or the next wave of feminism.

Wanda: You argue like a rogue elephant runs, Ralph. Look, Masters and Johnson showed that the clitoral-vaginal debate was irrelevant. There is only one kind of orgasm, and it almost always involves stimulation of the clitoris. It's just that orgasms without that stimulation are rarer and milder than those with it.

Ralph: Manfully argued, my pet.

But let us cast a practiced eye at the politics of orgasm. Freud thought that truly mature women always shift their focus from the clitoris to the vagina, so women who needed clitoral stimulation were made to feel like retards or perverts. The feminists just reversed that. It was a much-loved way of downgrading penis-vagina sex and upgrading masturbation. Soon pro-vagina women had to take to the hills like guerrillas. Clitoral enforcers like Shere Hite were sent out to mop up any remaining opposition: the poor deluded women who said they had vaginal orgasms and thought they were enjoying them. Hite called this "emotional" orgasm, as opposed to "real" orgasm. The clitoro-feminists also managed to clear out the compromisers, who believed in "blended" vaginal-clitoral orgasms. What the heck. It worked for Scotch, why not for climaxes? But no, the clitoral-pride movement got so strong it became somewhat embarrassing to admit that you owned a vagina or a penis. For all we know, women who used to fake

---

directly for orgasm to occur, though such stimulation produces the quickest orgasm for most women. And they found that the myth that the female responds more slowly is not necessarily true. When she regulates the rhythm and intensity of her own sexual stimuli, the time required for her to reach orgasm is about the same as for the male. The female's much-discussed slowness in arousal is probably due to cultural repression rather than to some physiological difference.

Partners often believe that to achieve complete sexual satisfaction they should try to experience orgasm simultaneously. As pleasant as this may be, there is no reason why partners must always reach orgasm at the same time. In fact, doing so may hinder spontaneity and may deprive each of being fully aware of the other's pleasure. They may find it equally satisfying for them to reach orgasm at different times in the lovemaking sequence.

In addition to these specific findings, Masters and Johnson's work changed our ideas about other general aspects of sexuality. For example, masturbation is now

vaginal orgasms for their hubbies began to fake clitoral ones for the women's movement. I guess you could call this progress of a sort. But do women really have to limit themselves to politically correct orgasms? Wanda, I stand before you as that rarest of males, a true feminist, calling for relief from the dogmas of Freudians and clitorists alike!

Wanda: I liked you better as a chauvinist pig, husband of mine. Your argument has only one minor flaw, Ralph: it's totally wrong. There is no clitoral party line, though easily threatened males may think so. The clitoris is the normal center of women's sexuality, and it is not our fault that it happens to be located in a spot that men find inconvenient. I bet that the article in the *Journal of Sex & Marital Therapy* is just more woolgathering about the G spot.

Ralph: Wrong, beloved helpmate. In fact, the author of the journal's piece, a sexologist named Heli Alzate, says that his own studies show no evidence of any such sexually sensitive tissue in the vaginal wall where the G spot is alleged to be. These are dark days for G spotologists, my dear. Ernst Gräfenberg discovered his spot in the late '40s. But after many exhausting years in the lab stimulating all those hired prostitutes and cutting up all those cadavers, there's still no convincing evidence. But then, sexology is not an exact science. Who says sexologists should be able to locate a major sexual organ after only 40 years of searching? Anyway, the G spot people say the sensitive spot is usually found between 11 o'clock and 1 o'clock on the vaginal barrel. Alzate thinks there may be two other hot spots, at 4 o'clock and 8 o'clock.

Wanda: Why do I find all this so tacky? All these white-coated males poking around the female body, checking the wiring and looking for new buttons to push. Why are you all so obsessed with the technology of women's bodies?

Ralph: Easy, Wanda. It's just that males found out where their orgasms were located a million years ago, and women are still working on it. They'll probably figure it out any day now. No offense. It's just that if men's bodies were constructed like that, we'd still be looking for our knees.

Wanda: Let me tell you a little secret, Ralph. I married a lout. Who cares about the technology of orgasm? Sex is supposed to be part of a relationship, not a high school biology course. Some women have orgasms without contractions, and the white coats smile down and say, "Sorry, we can't count those because we can't measure them." Same old stuff of males using science to define and control women.

Ralph: Mellow out, dearest. Surely an acknowledged feminist such as myself is not the enemy . . .

Wanda: I'm developing a blinding headache in my R spot. That's the tiny part of my brain that thinks you're rational, Ralph. This headache is fully located between 9 p.m. and 6 a.m. on both my clock and my cranial barrel. Thank you and good night.

Source: John Leo.

---

considered by many sexologists to be an important and necessary part of sexual expression rather than a taboo behavior. Some women who have never experienced orgasm can learn how by first learning the techniques of masturbation. Once they have learned how to reach orgasm, they can transfer the learning to sex with their partners. The rationale behind this is that so many emotions surround sex (for example, shame and guilt about the failure to achieve orgasm, disappointment, and perhaps insecurity on the part of the partner) that it becomes almost impossible for some women to enjoy sex or change their behavior. The direct stimulation of masturbation encourages orgasm, and being alone may ease the emotional tension associated with sex.

Americans' attitudes toward sexual expression have generally become more open as they have learned more about their sexuality. Rather than ignoring or hiding sexuality, it is important to understand it so that you can use it to enhance your life and bring greater joy and pleasure to your intimate relationships.

Inset 10-4
Sex and Physical Disability

The physically disabled (more than 11 million people) are sometimes thought of as uninterested in or unable to engage in sexual behavior. Generally, however, the disabled are every bit as interested in sexual behavior as anyone else. It is true that because of their disability they may not be able to engage in certain kinds of sexual behavior, but this does not mean that they are less interested in sex than they might otherwise be. The love and intimacy that can be expressed in various forms of sexual interaction are as important to the disabled person as to anyone else. In fact, sexual expression might be even more important to

the disabled as it verifies their acceptability to others.

> "People in wheelchairs have to stop thinking that their sex life is over," said one spinal-cord injured patient. "While your genitals may or may not be dead, your emotions are very much alive. And you can still express your emotions without your genitals—your eyes, hands, fingers, lips, and tongue still work." (Knox, 1984, p. 394)

Various diseases also can interfere with one's sexual expression. For example, the person with rheumatoid arthritis, swollen and painful joints and muscular atrophy, may have pain when

interacting sexually with a partner depending on the positions used. They may have to select sexual positions carefully and choose times when the arthritis is quiescent. If their arthritis responds to heat, they may need to plan sex after a warm bath.

What is clear is that sexuality is important to all people and important to the building of intimate relationships. If a person is injured or has a disease that interferes with normal sexual expression, the person and his or her partner must be creative and learn different ways of expressing sexuality.

Differences between Male and Female Sexuality

There are a number of basic differences between male and female sexuality that are well documented yet controversial. These differences stem from both biological and cultural sources (see Chapter 7 for a discussion of the biological and cultural background of male-female differences).

Figure 10-13 diagrams some general differences in sexual drive between men and women across their adult life span. There is considerable debate over the source of these differences. Some researchers, such as sociobiologist Edward Wilson (1978), suggest that these dissimilarities stem from inborn differences in biological makeup between males and females. Most sociologists and psychologists believe that the differences stem from the socialization processes that teach men and women their sex roles and the place of sexual behavior in their lives. The truth probably lies somewhere between these two views, with both nature (biology) and nurture (culture) combining in some manner to create the differences between the sexes.

Because puberty begins on the average about two years earlier in females than in males, young girls develop an interest in sexuality earlier than boys do (area A of Figure 10-13). This interest is usually described as "boy craziness." During this period most boys remain essentially uninterested in girls. When puberty does arrive in young men, their sexual interests and desires soar above those of similar age girls. From age fifteen through age twenty-five, males are at the height of their sexual drive. Most similar age females perceive their male counterparts as "preoccupied with sex" during this period (area B on Figure 10-13), whereas the male's major thought is "I don't get enough sex." (See Inset

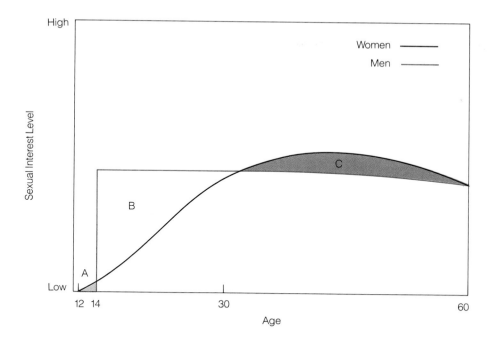

Figure 10-13   Intensity of sex drive across the adult life span.

10-5 on page 334.) During this time periodic **masturbation** is common among young men.

Various studies indicate an 86- to 96-percent incidence of masturbation among men, while the same studies indicate only a 47- to 69-percent rate among women (Nass & Libby, 1984). These studies are misleading to some degree because they look at the incidence of masturbation over the entire life span. Most men have masturbated in their early youth, whereas relatively few women have. Women's masturbation rates climb slowly over the life span to reach the levels reported, whereas the men's rates are reached early in their lives. The male during his teens and twenties (area B in Figure 10-13) is simply a much more sexual creature than the female. The female's sexual drive gradually increases, reaching its peak when the woman is between thirty and forty years of age. Because of some females' multiorgasmic capability, their sexual drive may become even stronger than the males in later years (area C in Figure 10-13).

Figure 10-13 indicates that males and females are somewhat incompatible across their sexual lives. If we consider only sexual drive, older men and younger women and older women and younger men make the most compatible partners sexually. Margaret Mead, in fact, suggested that a sexually compatible culture would be one in which older men married very young women, who on the death of their first husbands would be left economically secure. These women in turn could marry young sexually compatible men whom they could help to a good economic start. Although such an idea might solve the problem of differing sex-drive strength between men and women at different ages, it is not apt to find wide acceptance in our culture. Thus men and women will have to work out compromises as their sex drives vary over time and clash periodically.

In the early teens males are far more genitally oriented than females, who are more socially oriented. When young males are sexually stimulated, there is an

Masturbation

Stimulation of the genital organs, usually to orgasm, by means other than intercourse

---

Inset 10-5

What Are Your Biggest Problems and Complaints about Sex?

See if you can identify which of the following comments have been made by a male and which by a female. The answers will be found on p. 336. These comments have been gathered from students in my marriage and family classes when they respond anonymously to the following question: "What are your problems or complaints in the area of sex?" It is interesting to note that females write much more and describe many more problems than the males. The fact that females are more expressive in answering this question might indicate that they are more troubled by their sexuality. On the other hand, perhaps they are simply more open about it than males. Or maybe they just write more and better.

1. Many people just want to jump right into bed and "do it." The preliminaries are totally skipped. All it seems my partners want is a piece of the action. Is all romance dead?

2. My problems in the area of sex are the moral questions: Is it right to have sex before marriage? I will, probably, but not until I am in a lasting relationship, and some love is there. I find myself sexually attracted to the opposite sex before I know them emo-

tionally. This is difficult because I'm not sure if there is any emotion in it too.

3. Many of the times that I have had opportunities to have sex, anxiety seems to set in and I back out. Too much pressure on being "good."

4. I really hate it when the opposite sex expect us to start and do everything. They want equality but want us to start all of the seduction games.

5. After dating steadily for awhile, I start to feel this pressure to go farther than just necking and petting. I have broken off a lot of relationships because of this pressure. I am amazed at how many of the opposite sex expect you to do it, like it isn't any big deal.

6. My biggest complaint about sex is that, to me, it's such a definite step toward total commitment to a person. When I do have intercourse, I want it to be with the person I marry. I want this part of me to belong to only one person. Sometimes this bothers me, because it's such a hard thing for my dates to accept.

7. Basically the problem of the still-existing double standard. Men are allowed to enjoy casual sex without acquiring a negative label, whereas a

woman enjoying sex for the sake of sex can risk her "good reputation" unless she is very discreet in her choice of sexual partners.

8. My biggest complaint is pressure from friends. "Hey, we're doing it, why aren't you?" I'm not out for a quickie.

9. I can't get enough, can't last all night, am afraid of VD and possible pregnancy.

10. Not enough responsibility taken for birth control by my partner. Not enough communication between partners. There should be more sex education for younger men and women.

11. The hang-ups people have about sex. If both partners want it, then what's wrong? I never get enough.

12. After having sex my partners want a commitment that I don't feel is necessary to give just because you sleep with someone.

13. I never get enough holding, cuddling, and talking before or after sexual intercourse.

14. My partner never seems interested in sex, he/she never starts anything sexual. He/she seems more interested in talking about our relationship.

---

increased flow of seminal fluid. This buildup causes a preoccupation with the genital area and the need to ejaculate.

Males generally are aroused more easily and directly than women by visual stimuli or mental imagery caused by pictures of nude women and pornography (Barclay, 1971). Women are also aroused but at times don't recognize their arousal (Heiman, 1975). Their reactions to various sexually provocative materials are more complex, with much depending on the type of material. In addition they are more apt than men to react negatively to sexually explicit material (Nass & Libby, 1984).

Sexual fantasies play an important part in both men's and women's sex lives. Such fantasies can be important to sexual arousal. Gathering information on people's sexual fantasies is difficult because they are regarded as private and intimate. Fantasies are influenced by personal experiences as well as by societal mores regarding sex. Although the details of people's fantasies vary greatly, certain general themes have been found in both sexes. Masters and Johnson (1982) report the top five fantasy contents for heterosexual men and women as follows:

Heterosexual Male	Heterosexual Female
1. Replacement of established partner	1. Replacement of established partner
2. Forced sexual encounter	2. Forced sexual encounter
3. Observation of sexual activity	3. Observation of sexual activity
4. Cross-sex encounters	4. Idyllic encounters with unknown men
5. Group sex experiences	5. Cross-sex encounters

Probably the most outstanding thing about these lists is their similarity. Their general similarity masks more specific gender differences, however. For example, women tend to surround sexual fantasies with more romantic images than do men (Wilson & Lang, 1981; Friday, 1974). Masters and Johnson point out that fantasy content will change with time, personal experience, and one's culture. They also note that analysis of fantasy content for diagnostic purposes is usually nonproductive. For example, it is sometimes said that a person who fantasizes about same-sex experiences may be a "latent homosexual." Yet both heterosexual men and women report such fantasies, and both homosexual men and women report fantasizing about heterosexual relations. We do not label homosexuals who fantasize about heterosexual relations as "latent heterosexuals."

Women have to learn how to reach orgasm but men do not. This is probably where the idea comes from that a woman must be awakened to her sexuality. Researchers have found that about one-half of married women experience orgasm with regularity (Hunt, 1974; Wilcox and Hager, 1980).

Another important difference is that the degree of sexual response variation is far wider in women than in men. Some women never achieve orgasm and some only when they are thirty to forty years of age. At the other extreme some women have frequent multiple orgasms. Neither of these extremes is true for males (Masters & Johnson, 1966). There is also an interesting difference in the reported subjective feelings of pleasure with repeated orgasm. Women who experience multiple orgasms usually find their second and third orgasmic episodes the most pleasurable. But most men report greater pleasure from the first ejaculation rather than from a repeated orgasmic experience (Masters & Johnson, 1966). This might be explained in part by the relatively greater volume of seminal fluid in the first ejaculation, especially following a period of continence.

Another difference is that females tend to have a cyclical increase in sexual desire related to the menstrual cycle. Most women report increased sexual desire just before menstruation and a few report increased sexual desire right afterward. Evidence also indicates increased female sexual arousal close to ovulation (Adams, Gold, & Burt, 1978). There is no counterpart of this cyclically heightened desire in the male. It is also interesting to note that sterilized women report an increase in sexual enjoyment because they are free of fear of pregnancy. Such differences should be understood so that they do not cause misunderstanding or conflict.

What Do You Think?

1. What differences between male and female sexuality have you found troublesome?
2. There has always been a double standard of sexual conduct for the sexes in America. How does this affect sexual differences between the sexes?
3. Must sex and love always go together? Why or why not?

Human Sexuality Compared with Other Species'

No society has ever been found where sexual behavior was unregulated. True, regulations vary greatly: one spouse, multiple spouses; free selection of sexual partners, rigidly controlled selection; and so forth. Actually, the specific regulations include almost any arrangements imaginable if one takes a cross-cultural view of sexuality. Within a given culture, however, the regulations are usually strictly enforced through taboos, mores, laws, and religious edicts. To transgress may bring swift and sometimes severe punishment, as in some Middle Eastern cultures where an adulterous woman may be stoned to death.

Why do humans surround sex with regulations? Certainly among lower animals sex is controlled, but the controls are usually identical throughout the species, dictated by built-in biological mechanisms. Humans have regulated sex precisely because their biology has granted them sexual freedom of choice. Sexual behavior can occur at any time in humans. Among animals sexual behavior occurs only periodically, depending on the estrous cycle of the female in all mammals below primates. For mammals sexual behavior is for reproduction. Thus, sexual responsiveness is tied directly to the period of maximum fertility in the female. The female gives clues, such as odor change and genital swelling, to which the male responds.

In lower animals sexual behavior is controlled by lower brain centers and spinal reflexes activated by hormonal changes. In general the larger the brain cortex, the higher the species and the more control the animal has over its own responses. So we come to humans with their large cortex and what do we find? Earth's sexiest animal, an animal with few built-in restraints and hence many variations in sexual behavior. Without built-in guidelines, human sexuality is dependent on learning, and because different societies and groups teach different things about sexuality, there are many variations in sexual attitudes and behavior. Sexual compatibility, in part, depends on finding another person who shares your attitudes about sex. Sex for human beings is less tied to reproduction, thus sexual expression seems to serve other purposes as well. For example, Desmond Morris notes:

> The vast bulk of copulation in our species is obviously concerned, not with producing offspring, but with cementing the pair-bond by producing mutual rewards for sexual partners. The repeated attainment of sexual consummation for a mated pair is clearly, then, not some kind of sophisticated, decadent outgrowth of modern civilization, but a deep-rooted, biologically based, and evolutionarily sound tendency in our species. (1971, pp. 65–66)

Human sexuality differs significantly from that of other animals in several other important ways besides the greater freedom from instinctive direction. It appears that human females are the only females capable of intense orgasmic response. The sexual behavior of the human male, however, still resembles the sexual behavior of male primates; it depends largely on outside perceptual stimuli and is under partial control of the female in that she usually triggers it. Of course, with the human this trigger can be indirect, as in fantasies.

Another important difference is that human females are not necessarily more sexually responsive during ovulation as are most other animals. There seems to be no particular time during the menstrual cycle when all women experience heightened sexual desire (McCary & McCary, 1982). A few women seem to become more sexually aroused at midcycle when they are most fertile (Adams,

1. F,   2. F,   3. M,   4. M,   5. F,   6. F,
7. F,   8. M,   9. M,   10. F,   11. M,
12. M,   13. F,   14. M,

Gold & Burt, 1978). However, of twenty-eight studies on this subject, thirteen revealed that women's sexual desire peaks just after the menstrual flow begins. It is possible that this relates to her reduced fear of pregnancy. Nine studies showed the peak to be just before the menstrual flow, and six located it midway in the menstrual cycle (Cavanagh, 1969). According to A. M. Barclay, "This difference, coupled with the development of the orgasm in females, might tentatively be interpreted to mean that humans are the only species to derive pleasure out of sexual behavior without becoming involved in its reproductory aspects" (1971, p. 61).

The major difference between humans and animals is that *much of human sexuality depends on what the individual thinks rather than on biology.* Compared with other species', human sexuality is:

1. Pervasive, involving humans psychologically as well as physiologically
2. Under conscious control rather than instinctual biological control
3. Affected by learning and social factors and thus more variable within the species
4. Largely directed by an individual's beliefs and attitudes
5. Less directly attached to reproduction
6. Able to serve other purposes in addition to reproduction such as pair bonding and communication
7. More of a source of pleasure

It is these differences that have led humans to create such a variety of sexual standards and practices. Because human sexuality is not tied totally to biological control, in a free society there will also be changes in sexual attitudes and behaviors. Such changes have been occurring rapidly during the past several decades in the United States.

What Do You Think?

1. What do you think is the major purpose of human sexuality? Why?
2. Do we need any controls on human sexuality? Why or why not?
3. What controls would you have if you believe they are needed?
4. If there were no controls, how would the institution of marriage be affected?

Human Sexuality in the United States

For better or worse sexual attitudes and behavior in American society have changed rapidly over the past twenty-five years. Generally, sexual expression has become freer, more diverse, and more open to public view. The infamous double standard, which promoted sexual expression for men while limiting it for women, has broken down for many Americans. Alternatives to traditional sexual relationships and practices have become more acceptable. Better understanding of one's own sexuality has become an important goal in many people's lives.

In fact, better understanding and acceptance by women of their sexuality may be one of the revolutionary changes affecting the family and all intimate relationships during the 1980s. As noted in Chapter 4, the sexual revolution has really been a revolution for women in that their sexual behaviors have become more like men's.

As women have become freer to initiate sexual activity and to express their desires, they have been able to set the stage for sexual expression or at least to share in the decision. Thus women too can pick times for sexual activity when they feel interested, ready, and capable. And if they can pick these times, their chances of sexual satisfaction are increased.

Women are now able to channel sexuality into their lives in their own way and at their own pace. Sexual equality should reduce sexual dysfunction in both men and women. If each person is free to express him- or herself sexually with a partner and respects that same freedom for the partner, the chances of sexual exploitation of one partner by the other are reduced. Without exploitation and manipulation, the chances for sexual fulfillment and enjoyment are greatly increased. Freedom of sexual expression also includes the freedom to say "no."

In a sense greater sexual diversity and freedom create as well as solve problems. Freedom means responsibility. I must assume personal responsibility for my actions if I am free to choose those actions. In the past when sexual expression was surrounded by mores, taboos, and traditions, responsibility was removed from the individual. One could always blame the rules for lack of satisfaction, for failures, for unhappiness. But the America of the past few years has rapidly removed the rules from sexual expression. The decisions are now more than ever up to each individual, and this can be frightening.

A New Sexual Revolution?

As we have seen and will continue to see throughout this book, American sexual attitudes and practices have been considerably liberalized. However, a number of factors appear to be combining during the 1980s to modify some of the changes brought about by the sexual revolution.

The most important factor has been the epidemic return of sexually transmitted diseases that has accompanied freer sexual life (see pp. 347–355). Several years ago with the emergence of herpes simplex virus, Type II and a resurgence of all of the historical diseases, Americans began to curb their sexual experiences and question just how far sexual liberation could go. The appearance of the deadly acquired immune deficiency syndrome (AIDS) has had an even greater impact on American sexual behavior. A few researchers go so far as to suggest that some people seem actually relieved by the threat of herpes or AIDS. It's a good excuse for them to give up a sexual lifestyle that has become increasingly unsatisfying (Leo, 1984, p. 77).

A second factor may be that recreational sex alone becomes dull and boring. Boy meets girl; boy and girl have sex; they part. The excitement of the chase, the enjoyments of sex placed within the wider relational context, the bonding that sex can create (see Marital Sex, p. 342), sex as an expression of care and intimacy and many of the other roles that sex can play in an intimate relationship are never discovered. One young woman declared, "I have sex with a new date as soon as I can to get the hassle out of the way." Such a person has not yet discovered some of the many pleasures and relational enhancements sex can provide. Many young women report that they are getting tired of dating only to have sex and express interest in doing other things on a date as well as going to bed. More and more they complain that their dates seem interested only in the bedroom aspect of a date. If they say no, the date doesn't call back. If they say yes, he leaves after the sex, although he may call back. Many young women seem to be asking of young men, "Aren't you interested in anything else besides my body?"

As noted in Chapter 7 (pp. 230–234), many of those women who were early supporters of the women's movement and had more liberal sexual attitudes are starting to criticize some of the practical outcomes (Coveney et al., 1984). They feel that they have gained the right to say yes to their sexuality but lost the right to say no. They feel men have come out the big winners in that they can now have sex whenever they want (since the liberated women can't say no) without

the necessity of commitment to a more meaningful relationship or even the responsibility for birth control or ensuing pregnancies. Numerous young women who find themselves pregnant and approach the author for counseling indicate that the father-to-be doesn't know of their problem. When asked why, they say that they don't want to bother him with it. This attitude is leading many older women to think that they may have been conned by the sexual revolution.

> Some female veterans of the sexual revolution think they have been tricked into playing the male's game of easy sex. Men compartmentalize their feelings. They can be casual about their sex lives. For women it is more of a bonding experience. Men use intimacy to get sex. Women use sex to get intimacy (Leo, 1984, p. 77).

Freedom to have uncommitted sex, freedom to become pregnant, and freedom to be a single parent were not exactly what women had in mind when they voiced support for the sexual revolution and women's rights. In a way it has been the men that have been freed of the responsibilities that, in the past, went with an intimate sexual relationship. And it is the newly liberated women who now must bear the responsibilities. Women who have been unable to make a long-lasting intimate relationship with a man despite their liberated ways are beginning to express much bitterness. "I feel used and manipulated by the men I meet." "I really am getting tired of wondering whose bed I'm in and whether he cares who I am." "I'd like someone to at least offer to share in birth control responsibilities." "Isn't there someone who cares about my head, my thoughts, my interests, who cares about me and not just my body?"

Women's magazines are beginning to echo some of the feeling expressed by these women. A *Cosmopolitan* survey found that "so many readers wrote negatively about the sexual revolution, expressing longings for vanished intimacy and the now elusive joys of romance and commitment that we began to sense there might be a counterrevolution underway in America," says editor Helen Gurley Brown. "Sex with commitment is absolutely delicious," says another author. "Sex with your date for the evening is not so marvelous—too casual—too meaningless" (Leo, 1984, pp. 74–75). Ann Landers found similar sentiments when she asked her readers what they preferred, sex or tenderness. She was overwhelmed by responses from women who said that the latter was what they wanted. For some people, then, sexual liberation has become as much of a trap as the old Victorian constraints on sexuality.

> The subtle acid of requirement (sexual) curdles desire and clouds relationships. To say no when you want to say yes, because you think you shouldn't, is sometimes heroic. But to say yes when you want to say no, because you think you should, is merely grotesque. If anything in human life should be voluntary and spontaneous, erotic behavior should. And yet, over the past two decades millions of Americans have forced themselves, perhaps with sinking hearts, to try anal sex, use mechanical sex aids, attempt multiple orgasms, to engage in premarital sex, group sex, spouse swapping, open marriage—not because they wanted to, but because they thought they should. (Leonard, 1984, p. 142)

Another factor modifying America's liberalized sexual behaviors may be that despite all of the sex education efforts, the practical outcome of more sex is more children. Often unwanted, often born to a young unwed woman who is forced to be a single parent with all the attendant drawbacks (see pp. 463–467), these children too often are neglected and/or abused (see pp. 196–199) and ultimately become unsocialized and troubled adults who cost the society rather than contributing to it. In most cases, it is the society as a whole that has to pick up the monetary costs as well as the social costs of "sex is fun" for the young woman and her child.

In a way, the very emphasis on sex and liberation brought about by the sexual revolution has made sex education more difficult. Everyone is now supposed to know all there is to know about sex. Not to know is not to be "in," "with it," "liberated," and what young person doesn't want to fit in? Better not to ask and feign knowledge rather than show ignorance by asking. Dr. Ruth Westheimer, the popular TV hostess of *Sexually Speaking* says that no subject is as rife with misunderstanding and misinformation as human sexuality (1983). This is the same statement that experts have been making since before the sexual revolution. How our youth can remain so ignorant in such a sexually enlightened society is a question our society has yet to answer despite the sexual revolution.

Such factors will not cause a return to earlier mores. However, there is no doubt that they are moderating the sexual revolution. There is no doubt that many Americans are beginning to ask more of their intimate relationships than recreational sex alone. It is interesting to note that much of this reaction against the sexual revolution is coming from the young, whom one would guess would most favor liberalized sexuality as they have in the past. In a 1969 *Psychology Today* reader survey, some 17 percent of the men and 29 percent of the women believed that sex without love was either unenjoyable or unacceptable. In a repeat study fourteen years later 29 percent of the men and 44 percent of the women felt this

---

Inset 10-6

A Precoital Contract

The following letter in a student newspaper was obviously written by a coed with her tongue in her cheek (a little bit).

Editor:

Recently, a mere acquaintance presumed I'd be thrilled to have casual sex with him. I told him to buzz off. Next time I am going to be prepared. I don't know about you, but as a woman, I am forced to be exceedingly responsible about my reproductive capacities. What is casual sex for some is a headache for me. How can sex be casual when I run the risk of getting pregnant or contracting any of a variety of ghastly diseases?

Being a diehard romantic, I've got to temper my idealism with a good dose of realism. So I've devised a

PRECOITAL CONTRACT to stifle any attempt by my pheromones to sabotage my good intentions:

1. All prospective lovers must submit a signed medical report that proves they are free from sexually transmitted diseases.

2. All prospective lovers must submit proof of attending a sex education and contraception class, and must be fully prepared to participate in preventing pregnancy.

3. All prospective lovers must post a bail of $300 in case of an accidental pregnancy because no method of birth control, no matter how diligently used, is 100 percent effective.

Presenting this PRECOITAL CONTRACT is going to be a problem. Do I

slip it under the door and demand signature when a prospective lover arrives to pick me up for our first date? Do I pick him up and drive to La Cumbre Peak and demand his signature and bond before I'll give him a lift back to town? Do I wait for a lull in the conversation somewhere between the peas and the prune danish to spring the contract on him? What would happen if I procrastinated until after our first embrace—would my prospective lover be so overcome by desire that he would sign anything—would I want him to be?!

Sex in the eighties demands a PRECOITAL CONTRACT—I just haven't worked out the logistics—YET.

---

way. Of those under age twenty-two, half felt this way (Rubenstein, July 1983). In the past sexual intimacy was usually accompanied by commitment to a broader relationship. As sex became more and more an end in itself, commitment, caring, and the broader aspects of a meaningful intimate relationship became lost. The new revolution (if there is one) seems, in part, to be searching for these lost relational elements. Perhaps *Time* magazine summed it up best in their article, "The Revolution Is Over":

> The new conservatism is no victory for puritans. No sexual counterrevolution is under way. The sexual revolution has not been rebuffed, merely absorbed into the culture. America is more relaxed and open about sex, but also blessedly a bit tired of the subject. A sexual revolutionary at a party, chattering earnestly about sex as a natural function, etc. would quickly end up standing alone. Many sexual techniques and practices that were shocking a generation ago—oral sex or living together for example—have been widely accepted. . . . Other practices such as group sex and open marriage have been firmly rejected. Though many values are still to be sorted out, most Americans seem stubbornly committed to family, marriage, and the traditional idea that sex is tied to affection or justified by it. "Cool sex" cut off from the emotions and the rest of life, seems empty, unacceptable, or immoral. There is a return to the understanding that the main function of sex is the bodily expression of intimacy. (Leo, 1984, p. 83)

What Do You Think?

1. Do you feel that there is a sexual counterrevolution going on?

2. If you do, what do you see as evidence of it?

3. Have you made any changes in your own sexual behavior because of fear of STDs?

4. Do you think that men and women have benefited equally from the sexual revolution?

5. Do you think that there are negative aspects to the sexual revolution? For men? For women?

Marital Sex: Can I Keep the Excitement Alive?

The sexuality question most often asked by married couples is: How can we maintain the excitement and interest that we had in our sexual interactions through years of marriage?

Certainly there are many factors in married life that act to reduce sexual interaction and excitement. Monetary concerns, job demands, household chores, and children all conspire to rob a couple's sexual life of spontaneity and time. Both quantity and quality of the average couple's sex life is diminished by the daily chores of maintaining a family. Many studies indicate a reduction in the quantity of sexual relations as time passes (Kinsey, 1948, 1953; Blumstein & Schwartz, 1983; Greenblat, 1983). However, reduction in quantity seems less important to most couples than the reduction in quality. Quality sex takes time and concentration, both of which are lacking in a busy family, especially now since more than ever both partners are often employed.

Children make it especially hard to find time alone together, and even when the couple is alone concern about the children is very disruptive. "We don't make love until the kids are in bed and asleep. Then it's 'Be quiet,' or 'Don't make so much noise.' " Postponing sexual relations until the children are asleep often means that both parents are tired and sleepy themselves. Who wants to be romantic, build a fire, listen to music by candlelight, and spend three hours making love and attending to one another starting at 11 P.M. when you both must get up at 6:30 A.M. the next day to get the children off to school and get to work on time?

Research indicates that husbands complain the most about their children interfering with their sex lives. Wives tend to dismiss the impact of childrearing as a temporary inconvenience or attribute their sexual problems to other factors such as fatigue. "Jennifer has taken a lot of time away from us. It seems like maybe on the weekend when we would normally like to sleep in, or just have lazy sex, Jennifer wakes up and needs to be fed. But I'm sure that will pass as soon as she gets a little older. We're just going through a phase," says one young mother.

> It may be that for mothers the rewards of having children are so great that the costs are not recognized. Or mothers may find it so threatening to think that children disrupt their sex lives that they will not consider it. However, we do not believe that motherhood is blinding women to the truth about their sex lives. Mothers accept disruptions caused by children more readily than fathers do. Women do not feel less satisfied sexually when they have children. This makes them very different from their husbands who often feel deprived. (Blumstein & Schwartz, 1983, p. 205)

Rather than continuing to discuss the various difficulties (jobs, housework, etc.) that plague married couple's sex lives, let's examine a more ideal role that sex can come to play in a long-term healthy and growing relationship. In one husband's words:

I find that after fifteen years of marriage the quality of our sex life has increased immensely even as the quantity has decreased. Sex between us seems to serve as a bonding agent. Sexual relations are embedded in our total relationship now rather than existing in and of itself as it did at first. Perhaps I can best explain this by telling you what turns me on sexually now as compared to when my wife and I first met. You may be surprised.

Like most young men I was at first attracted to her physical attractiveness, her smile, her body (wow!) her walk, etc. and these attributes still attract me. However, today I can take a shower with her and not necessarily become sexually aroused. I couldn't even imagine such a thing at the start of our relationship. A tiny glimpse of her nude and I was turned on. If seeing her nude does not necessarily turn me on today, what does?

We take a ski trip with the children. I watch both of them happily skiing down the hill with grace and skill. Suddenly I feel sexually aroused towards my wife. I'd like nothing better than to throw her down in the snow and make mad, passionate love to her. Why? Because she is the mother of these wonderful children. She bore them and cared for them and helped (along with me, I hope) to make them what they are. I admire and respect her and love her and want to tell her this. What better way to communicate this than to physically get close to her, feel her, share our love together?

We have a fight and she makes the first efforts to resolve the conflict. I love her for still making the effort after fifteen years. For wanting to make the effort. For caring to make the effort. How lucky I am. How sexually attracted I am.

She is sound asleep. She looks peaceful and contented. She looks like an angel. I think back over the ups and downs of our relationship. I think of the things she really doesn't like about me but tolerates and accepts. I think about her encouragement when I tried something new or difficult. And suddenly I am sexually attracted to her and want to hold and cuddle her and tell her, "thank you."

Down inside I've been lusting for an expensive new car, which I know we can't afford and which I really won't buy. The new model that I have been reading about for three years finally is produced and she suggests we go look at it. It is beautiful but out of reach monetarily. She says, "You've worked hard, honey. Buy it, you deserve it. I'll help make ends meet." Whether I really buy it or not is immaterial. I want to take it for a drive to the hills and make love to her in the back seat because of her thought.

Of course we have "quickie" sex. Of course, we have sex for sex. Of course, we have sex when there is no time, when we can't concentrate. But then there are times when our souls meet, when sex becomes the ultimate communication, when it stands for all the things she means to me, when it transcends all our differences, all our problems, when it becomes the ultimate expression of our love. Once you experience sex in this way, avant-garde discussions of number of orgasms, love-making techniques, sex as an end in itself, multiple partners, etc. pale in comparison.

Of course, I'm titillated at times by such thoughts. Of course, I'm attracted to other women at times. Of course, the sexual excitement is sometimes missing, but I wouldn't trade in our sex lives. After all it took years to build it into a meeting of our souls. Would I really trade that in on a one-night stand because I was horny? No way!

One of the dangers of the more liberal sexual practices brought on by the sexual revolution might be that when sex becomes too casual, too taken for granted, or too available, the bonding qualities described by this husband might be lost. Many people who have participated to a great extent in liberalized sexual behavior, but especially women, now talk about the meaninglessness of sex in their lives (Leo, 1984, p. 78). In the *Psychology Today* follow-up sexuality study, the leading sexual problem expressed by both men and women was "lack of desire." A full 28 percent of the men and a whopping 40 percent of the women felt lack of interest (Rubinstein, 1982). As one sex therapist reports, "Being part of the meat market is appalling in terms of self-esteem" (Leo, 1984, p. 78). Many of my sexually active students report increasing dissatisfaction with their sexual relationships. Few seem to have deeply meaningful sexual relationships. It might be that when one knows a relationship is only transitory or fears that it may be, that one guards oneself against the impending loss by reserving total commitment, by holding back from too much closeness. If such reservations are a constant part of one's premarital sexual life, it may be hard to escape them in one's married sexual life. If this is true, then premarital sexual activity may work against fulfilling, broadly meaningful marital sex.

Married couples must work to maintain a fulfilling sex life. First of all it is imperative to find time alone together to concentrate on one another without distraction. When there are children present, baby-sitting money is a couple's best expenditure in helping to maintain sexual happiness. One technique that some couples have found helpful is to start dating one another again, with the partners alternating responsibility for the dates. To add interest some of the dates may be surprises. One partner asks the other out for a coming night but doesn't say what the date will be, indicating perhaps only the appropriate dress. In general, the couple that makes working to improve their overall relationship a part of their everyday lives will stand the best chance of maintaining a satisfying sexual life.

Sex and Drugs

Aphrodisiac

A chemical or other substance used to induce erotic arousal or to relieve impotence or infertility

People have long sought the ideal **aphrodisiac**, a substance that would arouse sexual desire. Thus far the search has failed, although folklore is extensive about the use of such things as powdered rhinoceros horn and "Spanish fly," or cantharis. Alcohol is the most widely used sexual stimulant in America, but in reality it is a depressant and inhibits the sexual response in males if ingested in large amounts (Wilson & Lawson, 1978; Wilson & Abrams, 1978). Long-term alcohol consumption increases the production of a liver enzyme that destroys testosterone, thereby reducing sexual desire (Rubin et al., 1976; Malatesta et al., 1979). Sexual-response times for erection and ejaculation are also increased as alcohol ingestion increases (Kolodny, 1982). In women the effects of alcohol are somewhat more mixed than in men. Researchers (Malatesta, 1982) found that women have a more difficult time achieving orgasm and experience less orgasmic intensity. Despite this, women believed (self-reports) that they experienced increased sexual arousal and increased pleasure. Alcohol's reputation as an aphrodisiac apparently stems from its psychological effects: It loosens controls and inhibitions, thereby indirectly stimulating sexual behavior. Perhaps Shakespeare's phrase about "much drink" best sums up the effect of alcohol on sex, "It provokes the desire, but it takes away the performance."

Marijuana has mixed effects on sexuality. There is no evidence of heightened physical reactions, but there is some sense distortion that probably heightens sexual sensitivity with a compatible partner (Kogan, 1973). As a true aphrodisiac, however, it is a failure, as it appears to have neither a positive nor a negative effect on sexual desire (Mendelson, 1976). There is some evidence that those who use marijuana heavily for prolonged periods have a higher incidence of impotence than nonusers, probably because testosterone levels drop (Maugh, 1975; Jones & Jones, 1977; Kolodny et al., 1974). Feelings of increased sexuality probably stem from reduced inhibitions and the relaxing of tensions as in the case of alcohol.

Robert Kolodny (1982) reported research in which five groups using different amounts of marijuana were studied for sexual dysfunction. Table 10-1 catalogs the results. Infrequent marijuana use showed no effects on either secondary impotence or premature ejaculation (see Chapter 12). Chronic marijuana use, however, was clearly related to secondary impotence but apparently unrelated to premature ejaculation. Those using marijuana every day showed almost two and a half times more secondary impotence than those using it fewer than three times a week.

LSD, by distorting time, may seem to prolong the sexual experience. However, a bad "trip" (frightening hallucinations and so forth) can have disastrous effects on one's sexuality (Jones & Jones, 1977).

Amphetamines (speed) act as stimulants, in that the male can maintain a prolonged erection, but their long-term use destroys general health as well as sex drive and ultimately leads to impotence. Cocaine has similar effects. For the female, because these drugs have a drying effect on vaginal secretions, prolonged intercourse may be uncomfortable unless extra lubrication is supplied. Direct injection of cocaine seems to prolong a man's erection (Rubenstein, 1982). Some cocaine users believe that placing the substance directly on the end of the penis or on the clitoris heightens sensitivity. The opposite is true. Cocaine is a local anesthetic and so acts to deaden the area to which it is applied. It is interesting to note also that because of the high expense of cocaine, offering it to a person of the opposite sex is almost always secondarily an invitation to have sexual interaction as well.

The Roman philosopher Seneca knew the best aphrodisiac: "I show you a philtre [potion], without medicaments, without herbs, without witch's incantations. It is this: If you want to be loved, love." Masters and Johnson echo this when they say that intimacy—being close to another in all ways—is the best stimulant to eroticism.

Anaphrodisiacs are drugs that decrease sexual desire and activity. Perhaps the best known is saltpeter (potassium nitrate). Saltpeter acts as a diuretic, and

Anaphrodisiac
A drug or medicine that reduces sexual desire

_____ **Table 10-1** _____

Male Sexual Dysfunction and Chronic Marijuana Use

	N	Secondary Impotence	Premature Ejaculation
Control group (no use)	225	8.4%	14.2%
Group A (less than once a week)	272	8.5%	13.2%
Group B (1 to 2 times a week)	342	7.3%	14.0%
Group C (3, 4, and 5 times a week)	117	13.7%	12.8%
Group D (daily use)	94	19.2%	16.0%

frequent urination may act to deter sexual activity. However, saltpeter has no known direct physiological effect on sexual behavior.

There are four groups of drugs that impair sexual functioning. *Sedatives* such as barbiturates and narcotics can suppress sexual interest and response. *Antiandrogens* are drugs that counter the effect of androgen on the brain and thus diminish sexual responsiveness. *Anticholenergic* and *antiadrenergic* drugs work to diminish sexual response by blocking the blood vessels and nerves connected to the genitals. These drugs are used to treat diseases of the eye, high blood pressure, and circulatory problems. Two drugs commonly used to treat hypertension, reserpine and methyldopa, cause loss of sexual interest and erectile incompetence (Gotwald & Golden, 1981). *Psychotropic drugs* such as tranquilizers and muscle relaxants may cause ejaculatory and erectile difficulties. Some of the psychiatric drugs reported to cause erectile dysfunction include Tofranil, Vivactil, Pertofrane, and Nardil. Those reported to impair or delay ejaculation include Librium, Haldol, and Elavil (Knox, 1984, p. 174).

As the discussion shows, there are a number of drugs with known anaphrodisiac qualities. On the other hand, drugs with aphrodisiac qualities are less understood and many times are surrounded by unsubstantiated "old wives'" tales.

Sex and the Aging Process

For some inexplicable reason the myth has grown up that for older persons sex is a thing of the past. Yet we find that the natural function of sex remains as we age, just as the other natural functions do, albeit in changing forms. We don't expect at age seventy to run as fast or to have the physical strength we had at age twenty. Yet we accept these changes and don't give up jogging or exercise. Likewise, changes in our sexual functioning don't mean that we shouldn't still use it.

Masters and Johnson (1981) indicate that there are three criteria for continuing sexual activity regardless of age. First, one must have good general health. Second, one needs an interesting and interested sexual partner. Third, past fifty years of age, the sexual organs must be used. "Use it or lose it," is their advice to aging people, especially males.

As a man moves past his midfifties, he may notice four changes in his basic sexual physiology:

1. It may take him longer to achieve a full erection even with overt sexual stimulation, and he may experience fewer spontaneous erections. What has been a pattern of rapid erective response to real or imagined sexual opportunity becomes slowed and more dependent on his partner's direct physical approach.
2. He may notice a reduction in expulsive pressure.
3. He may have a reduction in the volume of seminal fluid during ejaculation.
4. He may notice an occasional reduction or loss of ejaculatory demand. Aging men continue to have a high level of interest in the sensual pleasure specific to sex, but subjectively their felt need to ejaculate may be reduced. Perhaps one out of three or four times that aging men have intercourse they may not experience the need to ejaculate. It's not that they can't if they force the issue; they just don't feel the need to ejaculate.

Knowledge of such changes is important to both the man and to his partner. If a man does not anticipate and understand the changes associated with aging, he may develop fears about his sexual performance that may rob him of his sexual desire. If his partner does not understand these changes, she may question her own sexuality when confronted by them. For example, his slower erective response may be interpreted as loss of interest in her. If he doesn't ejaculate regularly, she may be concerned that he doesn't desire her.

The aging process also brings a number of changes in the woman's sexual facility. The older woman produces less lubricating fluid at a slower rate. The vaginal walls lose some of their elasticity, which can lead to the creation of small fissures in the lining of the vagina with sudden penile penetration or long-continued coital thrusting. Just as with the aging male, more time should be allocated for precoital stimulation. If neither partner evidences a sense of urgency in sexual interaction, erections and lubrication usually develop satisfactorily. Even with the physiological changes mentioned, it is important to remember that the psychologically appreciated levels of sensual pleasure derived from sex continue unabated (Masters & Johnson, 1981).

Older men and women are losing their sexual involvement far earlier than necessary because there has been little effort to educate them to the physiologic facts of aging sexual function. Older people are and should continue to be sexually responsive human beings.

Unfortunately, no discussion of human sexuality is complete without mention of the most social of human diseases, an oft-found bedmate, sexually transmitted disease (STD) (Table 10-2). In the past, the incidence of such disease in the United States has been drastically reduced by the use of antibiotics such as

Sexually Transmitted Disease (STD)

Table 10-2
Sexually Transmitted Disease (STD)

Disease	Cause	Incubation Period[1]	Characteristics	Treatment[2]
Primary syphilis	Bacteria	7–90 days (usually 3 weeks)	Small, painless sore or chancre, usually on genitals but also on other parts of the body	Penicillin and broad spectrum antibiotics
Secondary syphilis	Untreated primary		Skin rashes or completely latent, enlarged lymph glands	Same
Tertiary syphilis	Untreated primary		Possible invasion of central nervous system, causing various paralyses; heart trouble; insanity	Same
Gonorrhea	Bacteria	3–5 days	Discharge, burning, pain, swelling of genitals and glands; possible loss of erectile ability in males who delay treatment, with chance of permanent sterility; 80% of infected females asymptomatic	Same
Chancroid	Bacteria	2–6 days	Shallow, painful ulcers, swollen lymph glands in groin	Sulfa drugs, broad spectrum antibiotics
Lymphogranuloma venereum	Virus	5–30 days	First, small blisters, then swollen lymph glands; may affect kidneys	Broad spectrum antibiotics
Genital herpes	Virus	Unknown	Blisters in genital area; very persistent	Pain-relieving ointments
Chlamydia	Bacteria	10–20 days	Men: early morning watery discharge, hot or itchy feeling within penis. Women: may be similar to men or symptom free. Untreated causes pelvic inflammatory disease leading to infertility.	Tetracycline
Venereal warts	Virus	Unknown	Observable in genital areas	Removed by freezing or ointment
AIDS	Virus	1–5 years	Many symptoms	Treat symptoms

Note: As soon as you suspect any sexually transmitted disease, or notice any symptoms, consult your doctor, local health clinic, or local or state health department. Both syphilis and gonorrhea, in particular, can be easily treated if detected early; if not, both can become recurrent, with dire results.

[1] If sexually transmitted disease is diagnosed, all sexual partners during the infected person's incubation period and up to discovery of the disease should be examined medically.

[2] Local health clinics or local and state health departments will have more detailed information on current treatment and follow-up.

penicillin. Recently, however, there has been an epidemic of some kinds of STD. In fact, next to the common cold, gonorrhea is the most common infectious disease in the United States. Over 75 percent of all reported STDs occur in young adults age fifteen to thirty (Zaidi et al., 1983).

Of the various kinds of STD, AIDS and genital herpes are the ones people are discussing the most. Genital herpes appears to be infecting Americans at an epidemic rate (500,000 per year), yet the disease was practically unknown to the public just a few years ago. Of the five types of human herpes, Types I and II are those at the center of the current epidemic. Type I is most familiar as the cause of cold sores; Type II causes genital lesions. The two types are similar, with Type I also able to cause genital problems.

The first symptom of genital herpes is usually an itching or tingling sensation. Blisters appear within two to fifteen days after infection. The moist blisters ooze a fluid that is extremely infectious. After one to three weeks they gradually dry up and disappear. The infected area is extremely sensitive and sore to the touch. For this reason genital herpes precludes sexual activity when it is in an active state. Also, the friction of sexual activity can reactivate the herpes sores unless they are completely healed.

Because the herpes virus remains in the body once it has been contracted, it can be activated at any time. The exact causes of reactivation are not known, but stress, sunshine, and nutritional, and environmental changes are clearly involved (McKean, 1981; Knox, 1984). Indeed herpes is so related to a person's moods and emotions that learning to remain calm and under emotional control is one of the most effective preventives against its reactivation.

At this time there is no cure for genital herpes, only treatment for its symptoms. Acyclovir (trade name Zovirax), a creamy salve, alleviates symptoms and speeds healing. Unfortunately, it is less effective on subsequent episodes and does nothing to reduce the frequency of outbreak. There is some evidence that taken in oral form it reduces both the severity and frequency of outbreak.

Because no cure exists, many herpes sufferers have sought help from one another. A national group that encourages this self-help is the Herpes Resource Center in Palo Alto, California. There are forty-five chapters known as "help groups." The chapters offer group therapy sessions, letting newcomers talk about their problems and assuring those with herpes that they are not alone.

Although herpes is not as physically threatening as syphilis, its incurability is so discomforting and its incidence so widespread that it is beginning to put a damper on indiscriminate sexual contacts. A recent *Time* magazine article concluded:

> For now, herpes cannot be defeated, only cozened into an uneasy, lifelong truce. It is a melancholy fact that it has rekindled old fears. But perhaps not so unhappily, it may be a prime mover in helping to bring to a close an era of mindless promiscuity. The monogamous now have one more reason to remain so. For all the distress it has brought, the troublesome little bug may inadvertently be ushering in a period in which sex is linked more firmly to commitment and trust. ("The New Scarlet Letter," 1982, p. 66)

Another sexually related disease that is making headlines is acquired immune deficiency syndrome (AIDS). Although AIDS affects very few people compared to other STDs, the fact that it often leads to death makes it frightening. AIDS was first observed in the male homosexual population (72 percent of all cases) and in intravenous drug users (17 percent). First fully described in 1981, the disease destroys the immune system, leaving victims prey to all manner of viruses and bacteria. As of January 1, 1987, approximately 35,000 people in the United States had the disease and 18,000 others had already died. (See Scenes from Marriage, p. 351 for a complete discussion.)

At least three factors play a role in the resurgence of STDs. First, because the pill has become the major method of birth control, the condom, with its built-in protective barrier against STD infection, is no longer so widely used. Second, the antibiotics themselves have lulled people into apathy. "Who cares about VD, it's easy to cure," appears to be a common attitude. (Although this is partly true, cure depends on prompt treatment; furthermore, new forms of antibiotic-resistant strains of the infecting organisms are appearing.) Third, the increased sexual activity among the young, especially the increased number of sexual partners, has contributed to the widespread outbreak of STDs.

If you, your spouse, or a sexual partner suspect an STD, have a medical examination as soon as possible. In most cases the disease does not "go away," even though some of its symptoms may change or even disappear. Begun early, treatment is effective; delayed, the disease may recur or become more dangerous. Also, anyone seeking treatment will be treated with confidentiality. If an STD is diagnosed, all persons who have had recent sexual contact with the carrier should be notified and should also be examined. With increased public awareness of STD, it is hoped that the incidence can be cut back to earlier low levels, although that has not yet started to happen.

Summary

Sexuality pervades the life of humans. This is mainly because human sex is to a great extent free from instinctual control. Although sexuality is a biological necessity, much of the way in which sex is manifested is learned. For this reason there is far greater variation in sexual behavior among humans than among other animals. All human societies try to control sexual expression, but the controls vary from one society to another. Because of the variability of sexual expression and the often conflicting teachings about sexuality, there is confusion both within societies and within individuals about sexuality. In all societies, human sexuality serves purposes other than procreation, such as communication, strengthening the male-female bond, increasing intimacy, pleasuring, having fun, and generally reducing tension.

Our understanding of sexual physiology has increased greatly as science and medicine have learned more about the functioning of the body. It is clear that males and females are physiologically similar, having developed their sexual organs from common structures. There are timing differences in function, however. Another major difference is the cyclical preparation for pregnancy that the female goes through each month.

Basically, both males and females share the same physical responses during sexual activity. These are called the excitement, plateau, orgasmic, and resolution stages. It is during the orgasmic stage that the major difference between the sexes takes place: the ejaculation of the male. Also, the male usually goes through a refractory period after the resolution stage before he can have another erection.

Unfortunately, sexually transmitted disease too often accompanies sexual activity. All STDs seem on the increase and many new STDs have appeared in recent years. This increase is attributed to use of the pill rather the condom, people believing that modern drugs have eliminated the diseases, and, most of all, to youth's increased sexual activity and variety of sexual partners. Genital herpes has increased to epidemic proportions and may slow the sexual revolution by encouraging more careful choices of sexual partners.

Occurrence of AIDS

As of January 1, 1987 there were 35,000 reported cases of AIDS in the United States. The number of cases is doubling approximately each year so that the Centers for Disease Control (CDC) predicts approximately 300,000 cases in 1990. At this time it is estimated that there are one million exposed persons. It remains to be seen just what percentage of those infected will actually contract clinical AIDS.

The three leading cities for AIDS cases are New York (285.7 cases per million population), San Francisco (254.1 per million), and Los Angeles (97.6 per million). At this time AIDS is most widespread in Africa (estimated 50,000 cases) but has now been found in fourteen other countries.

However, many of these cases are reported in citizens that have been to or had contact with those in the United States.

AIDS cases fall into the following categories:

Homosexual men	73%
Intravenous drug users	17%
Hemophilia patient	2%
Transfusion recipients	2%
Other/unknown	6%

It is interesting to note that these percentages have remained very consistent since the first AIDS cases reports in June–July 1981.

At this time, 50 percent of all reported AIDS victims have died and 80 percent of all patients diagnosed before July 1982 are dead. No one who has contracted AIDS has yet been known to recover, thus mortality is thought to be 100 percent amongst those contracting AIDS. The majority die within two years of being diagnosed.

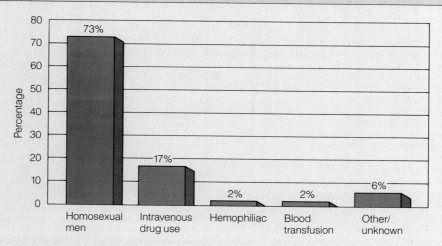

Figure 10-14 AIDS population by categories.

Figure 10-15 Total AIDS cases.

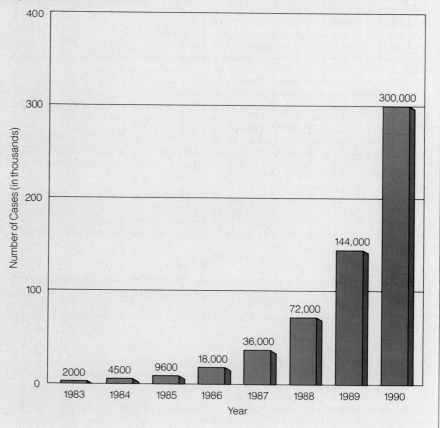

In addition, another 200,000 to 300,000 persons are infected with AIDS-related complex (ARC). They seem to have some of the symptoms of AIDS but do not develop the entire AIDS syndrome.

What Is AIDS?

In April of 1984 the discovery of a causative virus was announced simultaneously by research groups in the United States and in France. The virus is called HTLV III by the Americans and is a T-lymphotropic retrovirus that was isolated from the lymphocytes of AIDS patients. The French group termed the virus LAV (lymphadenopathy-associated virus) and it was isolated from the lymph nodes of an AIDS patient. These two are thought at this time to be the same (Morbidity and Mortality Weekly Report, August 1984, pp. 442–444).

The virus apparently affects the T-4 cell in the immune system leading to a gradual cessation of immune system functions. As the immune system fails, the infected individual loses protection against opportunistic diseases. Mortality stems not from AIDS itself but from one of the numerous diseases that attack the individual, such as Kaposi's sarcoma (cancer) and Pneumocystis pneumonia.

Early Symptoms

1. Weight loss of more than 10 pounds in two months or less with no known reason.
2. Swollen glands (lymph nodes) in the neck, armpit, or groin that persist for three months or more.
3. Severe tiredness (not related to exercise or drug use) or hypertension.
4. Unexplained persistent and recurrent fevers or night sweats.
5. Dry cough (not from smoking) that cannot be explained by a cold or flu.
6. Unexplained persistent diarrhea.
7. Persistent whitish coating or spots inside mouth or throat (thrush) that may be accompanied by soreness and difficulty in swallowing.
8. Newly appearing lumps or spots on the skin, usually appearing purplish like small bruises in whites. In blacks, they appear darker than the surrounding skin.

Note that any of these symptoms can be related to other problems than AIDS.

Protecting the Blood Supply

Persistent reports of infection from blood transfusion led to the fear that blood donations by AIDS carriers may serve as one bridge by which the disease might be transmitted to the general population.

It appears that all blood products—packed red cells, frozen plasma, platelets, and whole blood—may be capable of transmitting the virus. In March of 1983 the FDA, upon recommendation of the Public Health Department, issued the following three recommendations to blood-collecting agencies:

1. Provide educational materials to all donors.
2. Take a donor history.
3. Ask for voluntary self-exclusion from high-risk populations.

Testing of the blood supply and potential donors began in April of 1985. Many localities set up separate testing centers for those in the high-risk groups so that they would not be drawn to the blood banks to see if they had been exposed to the virus. Note that the blood test screens for antibodies to the virus, meaning only that a person has been exposed to the virus, not that they will necessarily get AIDS. With the long incubation period (probably 2 to 5 years) we cannot at this time say what percentage of those testng positive will develop clinical AIDS.

AIDS in the Male Homosexual Population

Most of the concern about AIDS focuses on the male homosexual population because it accounts directly for the great bulk of cases (70 to 75 percent) and contributes to a large number of the remaining cases indirectly.

Just how AIDS entered this population is still unknown, although it is speculated that it entered from some one of the African countries where it is thought to originate. At this time Zaire and the Congo account for most African AIDS cases.

In San Francisco, testing for exposure to the virus has found that about 50 percent of the gay male population tested positive. If such a percentage holds true throughout the country, it means that a very high proportion of gay men have been exposed to the virus already. Given the long incubation period and our lack of knowledge about the percent of exposed persons who actually contract clinical AIDS, it is possible that we could have a catastrophe in this population within the next five years that would resemble some of the pandemics that swept across Europe in the Middle Ages.

It is important that gay men recognize those sex practices that relate highly to the transmission of the virus. Reducing the incidence of those practices may slow the spread of the virus. It is clear that there have been substantial changes in the sexual practices of gay men, but sadly, such changes have thus far done little to reduce exposure chances. The number of men carrying the virus has already increased so drastically that it has offset the reduction of risk brought about by the sexual practice changes. Three years ago, if a man had sexual relations with thirteen other men, his chance of being infected was just two in thirteen. Today, if a man has sexual relations with just two other men, he has a chance of one in two of being infected. Hence, even though he has cut down drastically on the number of sex partners he has, his chances of infection have increased.

It is clear that the following factors relate highly to HTLV III/LAV viral infection: number of sex partners, especially anonymous partners; anal receptive intercourse; and rimming, fisting, and fellatio receptive relations. However, recognition of the danger of these activities has led to a general reduction in them within the male homosexual population over the past several years.

Numerous sexual partners tends to be one of the characteristics of this population. From several studies, it appears that only about 15 to 20 percent of male homosexuals live in a closed monogamous relationship (only one sexual partner). Approximately another 50 percent of gay males report being in a primary relationship that allows other casual sexual relationships. About 35 percent of gay males report no primary relationship. It is interesting that those males reporting to be in a primary but open relationship, actually have more sexual relations with anonymous partners than do those males who report no

primary relationship. This might occur because both partners in the primary relationship are soliciting other sexual relationships, which are then shared. The man without a primary relationship has only himself to depend on in seeking out sexual partners.

The risk factor for contracting AIDS is related directly to the number of sexual partners.

Number of Sexual Partners	Risk Factor
24–40	7.4
41–100	11.0
over 100	25.3

The risk factor means that chances of contracting the virus increase by 7.4 times if one has twenty-four to forty sexual partners as compared to having just one partner. In general the risk factor increases two- to threefold for each additional twenty sexual partners.

As noted, the number of sexual partners in the male homosexual group tends to be very high. A study of male homosexuals in Southern California with a mean age of twenty-eight years found that their lifetime sexual partners numbered 350 plus or minus 55. Their mean number of partners in the past six months numbered twenty-one plus or minus three.

Another study reported that of 733 gay men in the sample, 690 reported having sex with anonymous partners at least sometimes. Yet another study reported that 94 percent of their sample of gay men reported the same behavior. It is not unusual for the gay men who have contracted clinical AIDS to report 1000 or more lifetime sexual partners. It is easy to see why AIDS has spread quickly in the gay male population. The combination of many sexual partners and the fact that many of them are anonymous makes rapid

spread of the disease inevitable. However, it should be noted that from November 1982 to November 1984 the percent of gay men reporting no anonymous sexual contacts had risen from 6.6 percent to 14.9 percent, while the number reporting six or more contacts per month had declined from 25.8 percent in November 1982 to 10.4 percent in November 1984. A *Los Angeles Times* poll (1986) found widespread reduction in unsafe sex practices among gay men.

Numerous sexual activities involving the rectum also relate highly to infection. Receptive anal intercourse, rimming or analingus (applying the mouth, tongue, and lips to a partner's anus and rectum) and fisting (placing one's hand into a partner's rectum) all relate highly to contracting the virus and disease. The virus is carried in the semen and apparently must make contact with the partner's bloodstream for infection of the partner to occur. The anus and rectum are rich in blood vessels and are also easily torn. Thus it is a simple matter for semen to come into contact with the blood of the partner when rectal sexual activities are employed. Again high percentages of homosexual men engage in such activities. The study of 733 gay men reported above indicated that 710 had engaged sometimes in anal intercourse and 638 engaged sometimes in rimming. However, 80 percent of the men sampled report at least some reduction in such activities in light of the AIDS fear. Fellatio receptive relations also relate to infection but on a lesser scale. Refraining from ejaculating in the partner's mouth and the use of a condom during anal intercourse might well serve to reduce one's risk to infection.

With the long incubation period and

the lack of an effective medical countermeasure to AIDS, the male homosexual population is currently at great risk. The fact that we do not know at this time exactly what proportion of those infected with HTLV III/LAV virus will actually contract clinical AIDS, makes the situation especially dangerous. If only a small proportion of those infected with the virus actually go on to develop AIDS, the problem will probably remain manageable.

Intravenous Drug Users

Intravenous drug users constitute the second largest group of AIDS victims, representing approximately 17 percent of the cases. It is an important group however, since it represents a major bridge by which AIDS enters the heterosexual population. AIDS probably entered this group via the 7 percent of the bisexual males who are intravenous drug users. Adding this group into the statistics, we find that drugs are involved in approximately 24 percent of the AIDS cases.

Eighty percent of the I.V. drug user AIDS cases come out of three states, New York, New Jersey, and Connecticut. For example, in New Jersey this population accounts for 58 percent of the AIDS cases while in San Francisco, they account for less than 1 percent of the cases.

This group serves as a bridge to the heterosexual population in two ways:

1. Infecting the opposite sex partner
2. Infecting babies born of infected mothers

As of March 1985 of the seventy-three opposite-sex partners infected with AIDS by their AIDS victim partner, fifty-three were in the drug user population. Fifty-five of the pediatric cases (approximately 108) were babies born of drug-using mothers who had picked up the AIDS virus. In the drug centers, men and women intravenous drug users have about the same percentage with infected blood.

Variables in this group related to AIDS risk are:

1. Number of times the user shoots up (the higher the number of times, the higher the risk)
2. Number of times he shoots up in a shooting gallery (the higher the number of times, the higher the risk)
3. Use of shared cookers (lower relationship)
4. For women, number of sexual partners (the greater the number, the higher the risk)

As we shall see later, fear of AIDS has produced some behavior changes among the homosexual male population in an effort to reduce individual exposure. Unfortunately, the same cannot be said about the intravenous drug users. This is probably true because knowledge of danger is something that they have constantly faced in their lives as drug users. Their mortality rate is 1.5 percent per year. Thus, one-third with this habit are dead at the end of twenty years regardless of the AIDS incidence of death.

Apparently, female partners of intravenous drug users contract the AIDS virus either through sharing their drug habit (sharing needles, cookers, etc.) or through sexual relations with the infected partner. Infants infected with AIDS by their mothers are probably infected in utero, as they show the symptoms very early.

Casual Transmission

The question is often asked, "What are my chances of contracting the infec-tion by being in contact with an infected person?" To date it appears as if casual contact with an AIDS victim does not lead to infection. At this time, there have been no positive reactions to the blood test and no cases of AIDS, for example, among health workers who have come into contact with AIDS victims except for those who were themselves in the high-risk groups.

Other studies of casual contact within the families of AIDS victims have failed to find positive blood tests and/ or cases of AIDS, except for those having sexual relations with the infected person. There have been repeated reports of casual contact leading to AIDS, but such reports have largely been individual cases where little is known about the background of the person supposedly contracting AIDS only through casual contact.

Perhaps the best evidence against casual contact spread of AIDS is the fact that the distribution of AIDS throughout the different populations has not changed since 1981. AIDS is found in the same percentage distribution within the groups where it was first found.

Prevention of AIDS

At this time the major prevention technique is educational. If people understand the danger of the disease and the major methods of transmission, they can take steps to guard themselves against possible infection. Similar work is needed within the general population before the disease becomes prevalent. The following are suggestions to guard against the transmission of AIDS.

1. Reduce your number of sexual partners and limit them to people that you know and trust.

2. Reduce your contact with unknown members of the high-risk groups. For example avoid shooting galleries, gay bath houses, and tea houses.

3. Avoid sexual practices that may lead to the tearing or rupture of tissue.

4. Avoid rectal sexual practices.

5. Avoid the exchange of fluid with sexual partners.

6. Do not share needles and cookers.

7. Avoid accidental wounds from sharp instruments contaminated with potentially infectious materials and contact of open skin lesions with material from AIDS patients.

8. Wash hands before and after direct patient contact.

9. Wear gloves when handling fluids or fluid-soiled clothing from the AIDS patient.

10. Bend or reinsert into original sheaths and place in puncture-proof containers all needles used in medical procedures with AIDS patients.

11. If possible, avoid transfusion with blood products and/or have friends whom you trust donate the blood to be used. (Now that we are able to check the blood supply, this is less important than previously.)

12. Share substantiated knowledge about AIDS with your friends and avoid spreading hearsay rumors about the disease.

Possible Legal Ramifications

Several interesting legal questions arise when the newly developed blood test for discovery of antibodies to the HTLV III/LAV virus is used on individuals. If an individual reacts positively to the test (meaning that he has been exposed to the virus) it indicates that he is a carrier of the virus and thus has a potential of infecting other persons. If a person, knowing that he is a carrier of the virus, has sexual relations with another, and this partner develops AIDS in the future, can the carrier be held liable by the infected partner? Some precedent has been established with herpes infection. A woman who became infected with herpes after having relations with a man who knew that he was infected with the virus sued the man for damages and won a substantial verdict. Rock Hudson's estate has been sued by his last lover because Mr. Hudson exposed him to possible AIDS infection.

To take this a step farther, what if the partner infected with AIDS by a known carrier dies? Is the known carrier then vulnerable to criminal charges such as manslaughter?

Source: The material for this report was derived from the INTERNATIONAL CONFERENCE ON ACQUIRED IMMUNODEFICIENCY SYNDROME (AIDS) held at the Georgia World Congress Center in Atlanta, Georgia, April 14–17, 1985. A copy of the official program with abstracts of the presentations may be obtained from the Department of Health and Human Services, Centers for Disease Control, Atlanta, Georgia 30333. In addition, material was obtained from reports on AIDS published in the MORBIDITY AND MORTALITY WEEKLY REPORT June 1981 through January 1987.

Family Planning

Contents

Having Babies   *Karen, 16, and James, 19, are spending this Saturday night watching television in Cottage Hospital with their two-day-old infant, Susan Marie. "When I get out we'll celebrate," says the new mother. "We're too young to go to a bar, so I guess we'll hang out at the mall." "Yesterday we were talking about how we would pay the baby's wedding," says James who has offered to marry Karen although she has refused his offer.*

With an estimated 11.6 million teenagers now sexually active, a few schools have begun dispensing birth control devices and establishing day-care facilities on the premises. Karen's solution is more common: Her mother will look after the baby until the high school junior graduates. "I think Karen will think twice about having sex now," says her mother, who like many parents thinks that birth control measures give teens too much license. "A single girl Karen's age shouldn't need contraception. I don't want her on birth control—she's only a teenager." (Life, 1986, p. 33)

A paradox has arisen in America during the past twenty years. Condoms and vaginal spermicides are no longer hidden behind the drugstore counter so that an embarrassed young person must ask an adult for them. Prescription devices such as the pill and IUD (see p. 364) are easily obtained from such organizations as Planned Parenthood. *Yet despite greatly increased availability of contraceptive devices, the number of unwanted pregnancies seems higher than ever.* Pregnancies among unwed teenagers appear to be reaching epidemic proportions. If present trends continue, researcher's estimate, fully forty percent of today's fourteen-year-old girls will be pregnant at least once before the age of twenty (Wallis, 1985). We know that the "sexual revolution" has had a lot to do with increasing pregnancies. Obviously more sexual activity will lead to more pregnancies. Yet society has worked hard to get the family planning message across. What has gone wrong is a matter of growing debate (see Inset 11-1).

Family planning means just that, intelligently planning one's family. It means controlling one's sexuality to avoid unwanted pregnancies and to create, when desired, an ideal family in which children can grow up in the healthiest possible manner. Family planning means, in part, responsible sex. Family planning means avoiding pregnancy through intelligent use of contaceptive methods including abstinence. Family planning means becoming pregnant and giving birth only when one wants and is ready to have children. *Thus family planning deals with both the avoidance of pregnancy and the creation of pregnancy.* It means learning about birth control, and it means working to solve infertility problems.

The place and function of children within the family and the culture varies from culture to culture and over time. In countries with high infant mortality, women have to bear many children to ensure that at least a few will reach adulthood. Pregnancy for women living in such a country may be nearly a perpetual state. In this case family planning emphasizes fertility and pregnancy rather than contraception.

Years ago when the United States was still an agricultural nation, it was important to have many children to help work the land; children were major economic contributors to the family. In today's urban America, however, the costs of rearing children far outweigh their economic contributions to the family. Thus from a strictly economic viewpoint, children have changed from assets into liabilities. The Department of Agriculture estimates an average family spends $60,000 to $100,000 rearing a child to age eighteen. In urban America then, contraception is often the major focus of family planning.

Inset 11-1

Why More Unwanted Pregnancies Despite More Availability of Contraceptives???
A Woman's Point of View

The increased availability and effectiveness of birth control methods can encourage friends, husbands, and lovers to pressure us to have intercourse whenever they want. We need to be assertive about our desires: Being protected does not always mean we want intercourse. Many of us have found that we ourselves resist using birth control. What may appear to be personal reasons are actually due to social and political factors.

■ We are embarrassed by, ashamed of, or confused about our own sexuality.
■ We cannot admit we might have or

are having intercourse, because we feel it is wrong.
■ We are unrealistically romantic about sex: Sex has to be passionate and spontaneous, birth control seems too premeditated, too clinical, and often too messy.
■ We hesitate to "inconvenience" our partner. This fear of displeasing him is a measure of the inequality in our relationship.
■ We feel, "It can't happen to me. I won't get pregnant."
■ We hesitate to find a practitioner and face the hurried, impersonal care or, if we are young or unmarried, the mor-

alizing and disapproval that we feel likely to receive. We are afraid the practitioner will tell our parents.
■ We don't recognize our deep dissatisfaction with the method we are using and begin to use it haphazardly.
■ We feel tempted to become pregnant just to prove to ourselves that we are fertile or to try to improve a shaky relationship, or we want a baby so that we will have someone to care for.

Source: Adapted from Bell, 1984, p. 222.

Modern contraceptive techniques give couples free choice about the number and timing of children. These same techniques also have population control ramifications. Countries, such as India, that chronically suffer from overpopulation can initiate programs to reduce birthrates and gain some control over burgeoning populations. In addition, efficient birth control has brought a revolution in our standards of sexual conduct, the effects of which are still to be understood.

Family Planning in America Today

As noted above, the ideal family is one that allows children to grow up in the healthiest possible manner. Aside from environmental considerations, this requires that: (1) the children are wanted by both partners, (2) the partners are healthy enough physically and psychologically to supply love and security to children, (3) family economics are such that children can be properly nourished and kept physically healthy, and (4) the family can supply the children with sufficient educational opportunity to learn the skills necessary to survive and enjoy success within the culture.

Are We Ready for Children?

Proper family planning leads to the first question a couple should answer when thinking about raising a family: Do we really want children? The answer requires a resolution of the questions raised above in the definition of a healthy family. More specifically: How much time do we want for just each other and establishing

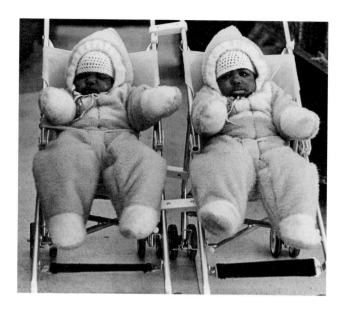

a home? How much more education do we want or need for the jobs and income we want? Are we ready to give a baby the attention and love it needs? Can we afford to provide it with the food, clothing, and education we want for it? Can a child successfully fit into the style of life we feel is best for ourselves?

Most family planning experts advise young couples to wait awhile before having their first child. Waiting gives them time to make important adjustments to each other, to enjoy one another's individual attention, and to build some economic stability before adding the responsibility of a child. Yet we know that couples like Karen and James can't wait. For them, it is already too late for good family planning.

The decision to have children is one of the most important family decisions, and yet it is often made haphazardly. Karen and James hadn't even made a decision about their relationship, much less about becoming parents. "It just happened."

Having children generally means assuming long-term responsibilities, usually for eighteen to twenty years or more. There is almost no time when children do not make heavy demands on their parents, sometimes even long after they have become adults. True, having children also brings many rewards. There is joy in watching a child grow and become competent and assume a responsible role in society. There is joy in learning to know another person intimately. There is just plain fun in doing things together as a family. Responsible family planning makes it easier to gain these joys and to create the healthy family.

The chances of Karen and James creating a healthy family for Susan are certainly less than if they had planned for the pregnancy and for parenthood. Responsible family planning avoids "It just happened."

Remaining Childless

Reliable contraception allows couples who so desire to remain childless. Although the mass media has in the recent past played up reports of large numbers of

American women choosing to remain childless, government population reports tend to show otherwise. What is clear is that women are having fewer children. In addition, they are postponing both marriage and childbirth. For example, the median age at first marriage remained between 20.2 and 20.4 years for women who first married between 1950 and 1969. However, delayed marriages have increased the median age to 23.3 years for women marrying in 1985 (U.S. Bureau of the Census, 1985). The highest proportion of childless women since records have been maintained occurs among women born in 1880 (22 percent). In this century the highest proportion (15 percent) occurred among women born during the 1920–1924 period (U.S. Bureau of the Census, 1980). The best current estimates of childlessness and parenthood in the United States among currently married women aged fifteen to forty-four are: 2 percent are voluntarily childless, 2 percent are involuntarily childless, 15 percent are temporarily childless (they indicate they will have children in the future), and 81 percent are parents (Bachrach & Mosher, 1982). If we look at all women of childbearing age (eighteen to forty-four years) rather than just married women, we find that 38 percent were childless as of June 1984 (U.S. Bureau of the Census, 1985, p. 1).

Remaining childless after marriage is more acceptable in the 1980s than it was in the recent past. During the 1950s and early 1960s, to marry and postpone having children (or worse yet, decide not to have any children) brought a great deal of social criticism. Parents of the newly married couple dropped hints about how nice it would be to become grandparents. Friends who already had children wondered if perhaps something was wrong with one of the partner's reproductive capabilities. Others saw the couple as selfish and preoccupied with themselves. Fortunately, such pressures on the newly married couple have lessened. It is interesting to note that men today are significantly more likely than women to regard childlessness as disadvantageous (Blake, 1979).

Although the kinds of pressures described above are easing, a new pressure has appeared. With the postponement of marriage and parenthood, age becomes a factor in pregnancy. The only group that has experienced an increase in pregnancies between 1980 and 1984 is women thirty to thirty-four years old. Of the women having children between July 1983 and June 1984 28 percent were thirty to forty years old (U.S. Bureau of the Census, 1985, p. 1). It is clear that many women who decided when they were young to remain childless, either temporarily or permanently, are now feeling the pressures of advancing age and are deciding to have children before it is too late.

Childlessness offers numerous advantages to the couple. The major advantage is increased freedom. The couple does not have the responsibilities of children, and they are less encumbered economically. Their time and money are their own to devote to their careers, each other, hobbies, travels, and adult life in general. Often the childless couple is a two-career family. Although the differences are not great, research does lend support to the idea that childlessness is related to enhanced marital adjustment and satisfaction (Houseknecht, 1979).

Birth Control

Modern techniques of birth control, though far from perfect, have made better family planning possible. The idea of birth control has long been a part of human life. The oldest written records mentioning birth control date back to the reign of

Amenemhet III in Egypt around 1850 B.C. Women were advised to put a pastelike substance in the vagina to block male sperm from reaching the egg. Pliny's *Natural History*, written in the first century A.D., lists many methods of birth control, including potions to be taken orally, magical objects, primitive suppositories and tampons, and physical actions such as jumping to expel the semen. These early birth control methods were generally unsuccessful.

Two ancient birth control methods did evolve into the first effective contraceptive techniques. First, the ancient attempts to block the cervix so that sperm could not penetrate to the egg evolved into the vaginal diaphragm and cervical cap when vulcanized rubber was invented. The most sophisticated historical prototype of the modern cervical cap was the use of half a lemon, emptied of its contents and inserted over the cervix; the residual citric acid, which is mildly spermicidal (causing the death of sperm), provided additional protection. Second, early attempts to cover the penis evolved into the modern condom. Starting in the sixteenth century, the penis was covered to protect it from venereal infection. Manufacturers began to make condoms of inexpensive rubber in the 1840s and later switched to latex.

Despite the long history of birth control, modern birth control and family planning have had a difficult and eventful development. Englishman Francis Place, the father of fifteen children, was the founder of the birth control movement. In the 1820s he posted handbills advising contraception to counteract the effects of the growing industrialization and urbanization that he believed were creating poverty. His handbills recommended that women place a piece of sponge tied with a string into the vagina before intercourse and remove it afterward by pulling the string. (Note that one of the newest birth control devices is a spermicidal sponge.)

In the United States Margaret Sanger and others waged a long hard battle for birth control that lasted well into this century. The Puritan morality in the United States opposed birth control. Although contraceptives were recommended for the highest ethical reasons—that is, to avoid poverty, disease, misery, and marital discord—their promoters were accused of immorality and were often brought to trial and fined. In 1873 Congress passed the Comstock Law, which prohibited the distribution of contraceptive information through the mail. Numerous states also passed repressive laws. For example, the right of physicians to prescribe contraceptives was a legal issue in Connecticut until 1965 when the state law banning prescription of contraceptive devices was overthrown by the U.S. Supreme Court in *Griswold and Duxton v. Connecticut*.

Of course, family planning is possible without the aid of mechanical contraceptive devices. **Infanticide** was practiced historically in many cultures. Postponing marriage acts as an effective birth deterrent, providing illegitimacy is controlled. In China today, for example, marriage is discouraged until the woman is twenty-four and the man is twenty-seven. Rigid peer group control has reduced illegitimacy to a low level.

Withdrawal and abstinence also reduce fertility rates. France, for example, has long had a relatively stable population of about 50 million. Inasmuch as contraception is prohibited by the Roman Catholic church, population stability has been achieved mainly by withdrawal (coitus interruptus), even though it is only 50 percent effective. Other methods of sexual outlet, such as masturbation, oral sex, and homosexuality, also serve a contraceptive purpose.

Infanticide
The deliberate killing of infants as a population control measure or for some other purpose

Table 11-1
Contraceptives

Popular Name	Description	Effectiveness (Pregnancies Per 100 Women Using Method for 1 Year)[1]
The pill (oral contraceptive; consultation with physician required)	Contains synthetic hormones (estrogens and progestin) to inhibit ovulation. The body reacts as if pregnancy has occurred and so does not release an egg. No egg—no conception. The pills are usually taken for 20 or 21 consecutive days; menstruation begins shortly thereafter.	Combined pills, 2[3]
IUD (intrauterine device; consultation with physician required)	Metal or plastic object that comes in various shapes and is placed within the uterus and left there. Exactly how it works is not known. Hypotheses are that endocrine changes occur, that the fertilized egg cannot implant in the uterine wall because of irritation, that spontaneous abortion is caused.	3–6
Contraceptive sponge	A soft, round polyurethane sponge saturated with spermicide.	10
Diaphragm and jelly (consultation with physician required)	Flexible hemispherical rubber dome inserted into the vagina to block entrance to the cervix, thus providing a barrier to sperm. Usually used with spermicidal cream or jelly.	10–16
Chemical methods	Numerous products to be inserted into the vagina to block sperm from the uterus and/or to act as a spermicide. Vaginal foams are creams packed under pressure (like foam shaving cream) and inserted with an applicator. Vaginal suppositories are small cone-shaped objects that melt in the vagina; vaginal tablets also melt in the vagina.	13–17 (More effective when used in conjunction with another method, such as the diaphragm.)
Condom	Thin, strong sheath or cover, usually of latex, worn over the penis to prevent sperm from entering the vagina.	7–14
Withdrawal (coitus interruptus)	Man withdraws penis from vagina before ejaculation of semen.	16–18
Rhythm	Abstinence from intercourse during fertile period each month.	10–29
Abstinence	Avoid sexual intercourse.	0

[1]Without some method of birth control, between 80 and 90 out of 100 sexually active women would get pregnant in the course of one year.

[2]Individuals vary in their reaction to contraceptive devices. Advantages and disadvantages listed are general ones.

[3]If taken regularly, pregnancy will not occur. If one or more pills are missed, there is a chance of pregnancy.

Although various chemical and mechanical means of birth control are widely used in the United States (by about 68 percent of married couples), approval of such methods is by no means universal. The Roman Catholic and Mormon churches both have official doctrines banning "artificial" methods of birth control, although Catholic women use the pill at about the same rate as other women (U.S. Department of Health and Human Services, 1982; Mosher & Hendershot, 1984). Some minority group members also discourage birth control in an effort

Table 11-1
continued

Advantages[2]	Disadvantages	Cost
Simple to take, removed from sexual act, highly reliable, reversible. Useful side effects: relief of premenstrual tension, reduction in menstrual flow, regularization of menstruation, relief of acne.	Weight gain (5 to 50% of users), breast enlargement and sensitivity; some users have increased headaches, nausea, and spotting. Increased possibility of vein thrombosis (blood clotting) and slight increase in blood pressure. Must be taken regularly. A causal relationship to cancer can neither be established nor refuted.	$9–$13 per month
Once inserted, user need do nothing more about birth control. Highly reliable, reversible, relatively inexpensive. Must be checked periodically to see if still in place.	Insertion procedure requires specialist and may be uncomfortable and painful. Uterine cramping, increased menstrual bleeding. Between 4% and 30% are expelled in first year after insertion. Occasional perforation of the uterine wall. Occasional pregnancy that is complicated by the presence of the IUD. Associated with pelvic inflammatory disease. Availability limited.	$50–$100 for insertion
Does not have to be fitted. Simple to use. Allows repeated intercourse.	Disliked by some women because insertion requires manipulation of genitals, 2% of users report allergic reaction.	$1 each
Can be left in place up to 24 hours. Reliable, harmless, reversible. Can be inserted up to 2 hours before intercourse.	Disliked by many women because it requires self-manipulation of genitals to insert and is messy because of the cream. If improperly fitted, it will fail. Must be refitted periodically, especially after pregnancy. Psychological aversion may make its use inconsistent.	$40–$75 for fitting
Foams appear to be most effective, followed by creams, jellies, suppositories, tablets. Harmless, simple, reversible, easily available.	Minor irritations and temporary burning sensation. Messy. Must be used just before intercourse and reapplied for each act of intercourse.	$7–$9 for month's supply
Simple to obtain and use; free of objectionable side effects. Quality control has improved with government regulation. Protection against various sexually transmitted diseases.	Must be applied just before intercourse. Can slip off, especially after ejaculation when penis returns to flaccid state. May rupture (rare). Interferes with sensation and spontaneity.	50¢ each and up
Simple, free, requires no other devices.	Requires great control by the male. Possible semen leakage before ejaculation. Possible psychological reaction against necessary control and ejaculation outside the vagina. May severely limit sexual gratification of both partners.	
Approved by the Roman Catholic church. Free, requires no other devices.	Woman's menstrual period must be regular. Demands accurate date keeping and strong self-control. Difficult to determine fertile period exactly.	
Simple, free, reversible. Reduces chance of contracting a sexually transmitted disease.	May have adverse psychological effects.	0

to increase their proportion of the population. Still other groups have different reasons for shunning certain birth control methods. However, the vast majority of Americans practice birth control at times, using many of the specific methods we will describe in the next section.

Contraceptive Methods

Although family planning in itself is generally healthful, methods of implementing it may have mixed results as far as health is concerned. Table 11-1 summarizes the various contraceptive devices, indicating their effectiveness, advantages, and disadvantages (including possible side effects).

Figure 11-1 Types of contraception.

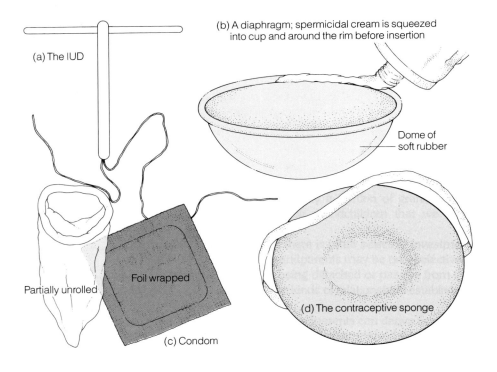

(a) The IUD

(b) A diaphragm; spermicidal cream is squeezed into cup and around the rim before insertion

Dome of soft rubber

Partially unrolled

Foil wrapped

(c) Condom

(d) The contraceptive sponge

and how far apart they should be. They must also answer questions about birth control, including "Who will be responsible for using a birth control method? What method will be used? How will the method chosen affect our sex lives? What will be the cost?"

An *ideal* **contraceptive**—which does not exist yet, though research continues—would be harmless, reliable, free of objectionable side effects, inexpensive, simple, reversible in effect, and removed from the sexual act, and it would also protect against venereal disease (Guttmacher, 1969, 1984). Although the contraceptives shown in Figure 11-1 do not fulfill all of these requirements, they do meet many of them.

The Condom The **condom** is a sheath of very thin latex or animal gut that fits over the penis and stops sperm from entering the vagina when ejaculation occurs. The condom should be placed on the penis as soon as it is erect, to ensure that none of the preejaculatory fluid (which contains sperm) gets into the vagina. Either the man or the woman can put the rolled-up condom over the head of the penis and unroll it to the base of the penis, leaving a small space at the tip to collect the semen.

Both partners must be careful not to puncture the condom. After ejaculation either partner should hold the condom tightly around the base of the penis as the man withdraws so that no semen will spill from the now loose condom, enabling sperm to find their way to the uterus.

The condom has always been a popular method of contraception in the United

Contraceptive
Any agent used to prevent conception

Condom
A sheath, usually made of thin rubber, designed to cover the penis during intercourse; used for contraceptive purposes and to control sexually transmitted disease

Planning a family requires couples to decide how many children they want States and though briefly eclipsed by the pill and the IUD, it is now coming back into widespread use because of the possible dangerous side effects of other birth control methods and increased worry about sexually transmitted disease (STD). Condoms are openly displayed and sold and thus are easily acquired.

Condoms afford protection against sexually transmitted disease. In fact, they were first used for this reason rather than for protection against pregnancy. The sudden rise of herpes and AIDS has increased condom use greatly by both heterosexual and homosexual men. Condoms are now freely distributed to homosexual men by groups trying to halt the spread of AIDS.

The risk of pregnancy with condom use is quite low. At least some of the pregnancies occur because of careless removal of the condom. Some may occur because of a puncture in the condom. Both risks can be reduced by using a vaginal spermicide in addition to the condom. The main disadvantages of condoms are that they diminish sensation and interfere with spontaneity.

The Diaphragm   The **diaphragm** is a dome-shaped cup of thin latex stretched over a metal spring. It is available on prescription from a doctor. Because of differences in the sizes of vaginal openings, the diaphragm has to be carefully fitted to ensure that it adequately covers the mouth of the cervix and is comfortable. The fitting should be checked every two years, as well as after childbirth, abortion, or a weight loss of more than ten pounds.

Diaphragm
A contraceptive device consisting of a hemispherical thin rubber that is placed within the vagina covering the cervix

Once she has been fitted properly, the woman can insert the diaphragm with the dome up or down, whichever feels more comfortable. Before insertion, she should spread a spermicidal jelly or cream over the surface of the dome that will lie against the cervix. Then she squeezes the diaphragm flat with one hand, and pushes the diaphragm up along the back of the vagina as far as it will go. Then she tucks the front rim behind the pubic bone. It helps if she squats, lies down, or stands with one foot raised while inserting the diaphragm. After it is inserted, she should feel the cervix through the dome to make sure that it is completely covered.

A woman can insert a diaphragm just before intercourse or several hours ahead of time. If she inserts it more than two hours before intercourse, however, she should insert additional spermicide into the vagina before intercourse or take the diaphragm out and reapply spermicide. Spermicide should also be added before any further acts of intercourse. The diaphragm must stay in place for six hours after the last intercourse to give the spermicide enough time to kill all sperm.

A woman removes a diaphragm by unhooking the front rim from behind the pubic bone with a finger and pulling it out. She should then wash the diaphragm with mild soap and water, rinse it, and gently pat it dry. Before putting the diaphragm away, she should examine it in front of a bright light for holes or cracks, and she may dust it with cornstarch.

The diaphragm is highly effective when used with a spermicide and has no physical side effects. However, it dampens spontaneity, and loses effectiveness when fresh spermicide is not used for additional intercourse. It is avoided by some women who do not like to touch their genitals.

The main causes of pregnancy with diaphragm use are inaccurate fitting and incorrect insertion. Sometimes, too, the vaginal walls expand during sexual stimulation and dislodge the diaphragm.

Similar to the diaphragm in that it blocks entrance to the cervix is the *cervical cap*. It is much smaller and made of flexible rubber. It looks something like an elongated thimble and fits over the cervix much as the thimble fits over one's thumb. Unlike the diaphragm, the cap may be left in place for up to three days. After intercourse, it should not be removed for eight to twelve hours. Also like the diaphragm it should be used with a spermicide. Although it has been in use for years, especially in Europe, it is still little known and used in the United States.

The Contraceptive Sponge   A variation on the diaphragm is the Vorhauer sponge (trade name Today). It is a soft, round polyurethane sponge permeated with spermicide. It has numerous advantages over the standard diaphragm. It does not have to be fitted by a doctor because it automatically conforms to the woman's shape and size. It is easier to insert than the diaphragm, and it remains effective for twenty-four hours regardless of how often the woman has intercourse. It is not messy or awkward. A small polyester loop attached to the sponge makes removal easy although it should be left in place at least six hours after intercourse. Each sponge costs about $1. About 2 percent of the women using it report an allergic reaction.

Intrauterine device
A small object inserted into a woman's uterus to prevent conception

The Intrauterine Device (IUD)   The **intrauterine device** is a stainless steel or plastic loop, ring, or spiral that is inserted into the uterus. A doctor uses a sterile applicator to insert the IUD into the cervical canal and presses a plunger to push the device into the uterus. The protruding threads are trimmed so that only an inch or an inch and a half remain in the upper vagina. Usually they can't be felt during intercourse. The best time for insertion (and removal) is during menstruation because the cervical canal is most open then and there is no possibility of an unsuspected pregnancy.

Just how or why the IUD works is still unknown. Theories include production of biochemical changes, interference with the implantation of eggs or the movement of eggs or sperm, and spontaneous abortion. The IUD is quite effective, second only to the pill in overall effectiveness. Once inserted it can be used indefinitely without additional contraceptive measures; it doesn't interrupt sexual activity; it is fully reversible; and it has a low long-term cost.

However, the IUD has numerous disadvantages. The most common is abnormal menstrual bleeding. Bleeding starts sooner, lasts longer, and is heavier after IUD insertion. Bleeding and spotting between periods are also fairly common. Women who have never been pregnant often experience uterine cramps and backache. The uterine cramps usually disappear in a few days, although they often recur with each period and may be severe enough to require removal of the IUD.

Intrauterine devices are spontaneously expelled in about 10 percent of women who try them, and if the woman does not notice the expulsion, an unwanted pregnancy may result. Most expulsions occur during menstruation, so it is a good idea to check sanitary pads or tampons for the device. The threads can also be checked periodically to make sure the device is still in place.

A more serious complication that may occur is pelvic inflammatory disease (salingitis). About 2 to 3 percent of women using the device may develop the disease, usually in the first two weeks after insertion. Most of these inflammations are mild and can be treated with antibiotics. In rare cases the IUD may puncture the wall of the uterus and migrate into the abdominal cavity, requiring surgery. Pelvic infection, usually caused by bacteria, also seems to be more common among IUD users (*Time*, 1980; Piatrow, Rinehart & Schmidt, 1979; Bell, 1984, pp. 249–255).

Most of the risk of pregnancy occurs during the first few months of IUD use; therefore an additional method of contraception should be used for that period. The failure rate tends to decline rapidly after the first year of use. Pregnancy may occur with the device in place, but the rate of spontaneous abortion for such pregnancies is 40 percent (compared with 15 percent for all pregnancies). There is little additional risk of birth defects for babies born of such pregnancies. The device usually remains in place during the pregnancy and is expelled during the delivery.

The Dalkon Shield was taken off the market because there was an unusually high pregnancy rate among its users, and its users developed uterine infections at a much higher rate than nonusers (Bell, 1984, p. 249). Also IUDs appear in general to be related to infertility in a small percentage (2 to 3 percent) of women (Haney, 1985).

From the various research done on the IUD a safe conclusion would be:

> for the woman who has never had a child and is attempting to choose a contraceptive, it should be emphasized that use of an IUD may double her risk of tubal infertility over the use of other methods. It should be noted that copper IUDs seem to expose her to less risk. (Cramer, 1985, p. 947)

Unfortunately for those women who can successfully use an IUD, all but one have now been withdrawn from the market because of the manufacturers' fear of lawsuits. The only one left on the market as of August 1986 was a T-shaped device that secretes a hormone and must be replaced annually (trade name is Progestasert) (O'Hara, 1986). It is rumored that this IUD also will soon be removed from the market, thereby eliminating the IUD as a contraceptive choice in America (*Population Today*, 1986, p. 8).

The Pill   The **pill**, or **oral contraceptive**, is a combination of the hormones estrogen and progesterone, and must be prescribed by a doctor. The daily ingestion of these hormones bluffs the body into thinking it is pregnant, and it stops further ovulation. Because no mature eggs are released, pregnancy cannot take place. In addition, the hormones thicken the mucus covering the cervix, thus inhibiting sperm entry.

Oral contraceptive
Hormonal material in pill form suspends ovulation and prevents conception

The combination pill is a monthly supply of twenty or twenty-one tablets. The woman takes pill 1 on day 5 of her menstrual cycle, counting the first day of the cycle as day 1. She takes another pill each day until all the pills have been taken. Menstruation usually begins two to four days after the last pill.

The pill should be taken at about the same time each day. If a pill is forgotten, it should be taken as soon as possible, and the next pill should be taken at the scheduled time. If two pills have been forgotten, an additional form of contraception should be used for the rest of the cycle. If three pills are forgotten, withdrawal bleeding will probably start. In this case, the woman should stop taking the pills and start using another method of birth control. She should then start a new cycle of pills when the bleeding stops but continue to use an additional method of birth control for the first new cycle.

If menstruation does not occur when expected, a new series of pills should be started a week after the end of the last series. If a period doesn't begin after this series, the woman should consult a doctor.

During the first month of the first pill cycle, an additional method of contraception should be used to ensure complete protection.

Taken properly the pill is the most effective method of contraception today. It is relatively simple to use, does not affect spontaneity, and is inexpensive and reversible. However, irregular use does not afford protection.

The pill was once the most widely used method of contraception in this country. In 1975 as many as 8 million American women, or about 40 percent of all women using birth control, used the pill. However, use of the pill began to drop rapidly thereafter due to fear of a link between the pill and breast cancer. Such a fear, however, is presently unsupported. Studies have not found a link between oral contraceptives and breast cancer—regardless of type of pill or duration of use (up to 15 years). However, the relation needs to be studied further to determine whether use has very late effects (Sattin et al., 1986). Although the link was not proved, other negative effects as well as reaction by women against the idea of chemically changing their bodies reduced pill popularity greatly. By 1985, only about 20 percent of women using birth control chose the pill (Welles, 1985).

The pill's side effects range from relatively minor disturbances to serious ones. Among the former are symptoms of early pregnancy (morning sickness, weight gain, and swollen breasts, for example), which may occur during the first few months of pill use. Such symptoms usually disappear by the fourth month. Other problems include depression, nervousness, alteration in sex drive, dizziness, headaches, bleeding between periods, and vaginal discharge. Yeast fungus infections are also more common in women taking the pill. The more serious side effects include blood clot problems and a possibe increase in the risk of uterine cancer. Although the incidence of fatal blood clots is low (about thirteen deaths among 1 million pill users in one year), women with any history of unusual blood clotting, strokes, heart disease or defects, or any form of cancer should not use the pill (for a more complete discussion of oral contraceptives, see Hatcher et al., 1984; McCary & McCary, 1982; Bell, 1984).

The arguments over the relationship of pill use and cancer continue and may only be resolved at some time in the future when large numbers of women have been using the pill for many years. If there is a relationship, it appears to be minimal; the chance of death from cancer caused by pill use is far less than the chance of death in childbirth.

Another form of the pill, the minipill, is taken throughout the month, even during menstruation, thus eliminating the necessity of counting pills and stopping and restarting a series. The minipill eliminates many of the negative side effects related to the estrogen component of the regular pill. Minipills contain only progestin. They do not stop ovulation or interfere with menstruation. Instead, they make the reproductive system resistant to sperm or ovum transport. Should fertilization take place, they also impede implantation. Their effectiveness is slightly less than the regular pill (Hatcher et al., 1984; McCary & McCary, 1982).

Rhythm   The **rhythm** method of contraception is based on the fact that usually only one egg per month is produced. Because the egg lives for only twenty-four to forty-eight hours if it is not fertilized, and because sperm released into the uterus live only forty-eight to seventy-two hours, theoretically conception can occur only during four days of any cycle. Predicting this four-day period is what is so difficult. If each woman had an absolutely regular monthly cycle, rhythm would be much more reliable than it is. Unfortunately, not all women have regular cycles. In fact, about 15 percent have such irregular periods that the rhythm method cannot be used at all.

To use the rhythm method, a woman keeps track of her menstrual periods for a full year. Counting the day menstruation begins as day 1, she notes the length of the shortest time before menstruation starts again and also the longest time. If her cycle is always the same length, she subtracts 18 from the number of days in the cycle, which gives the first unsafe day. Subtracting 11 gives the last unsafe day. For example, a woman with a regular twenty-eight-day cycle would find that the first unsafe day is the tenth day of her cycle and the last is the seventeenth day. Thus she should not engage in intercourse from the tenth to the eighteenth day. Figure 11-2 shows the twenty-eight-day cycle.

If a woman's cycle is slightly irregular, she can still determine unsafe days by using the formula. In this case she subtracts 18 from her shortest cycle to determine the first unsafe day, and 11 from her longest cycle to find the last unsafe day. Table 11-2 gives the unsafe days for periods of varying duration.

A breath and saliva test may soon allow women to predict their optimum fertile days more accurately. Scientists have found a correlation between levels of mouth odor and saliva chemicals and fluctuations in basic body temperature during the menstrual cycle. By using simple tests on saliva samples, a woman will be able to recognize when she is ovulating and thus know exactly when to avoid intercourse if she does not want to become pregnant (Kosteic & Preti, 1982).

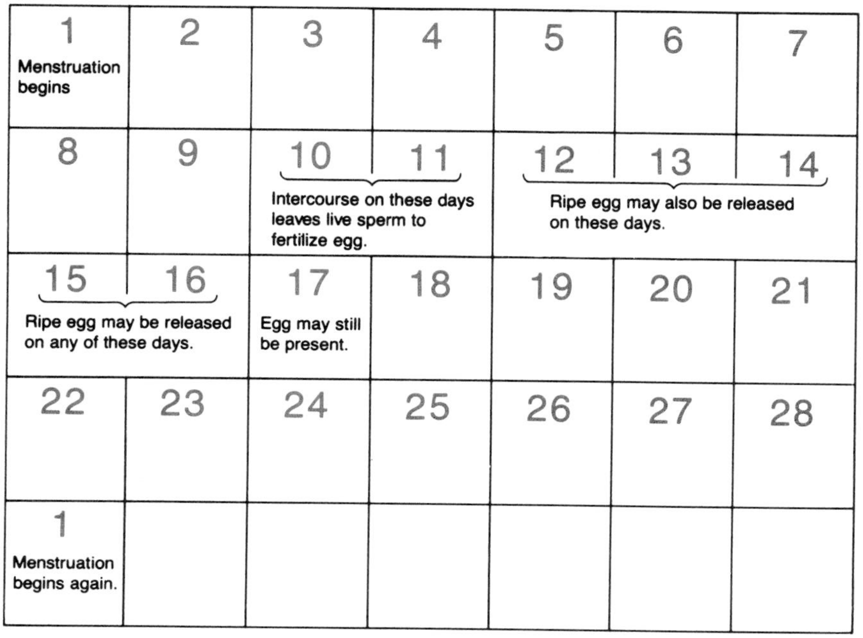

Figure 11-2 The 28-day cycle.

_____ Table 11-2 _____

How to Figure Safe and Unsafe Days

Length of Shortest Period	First Unsafe Day after Start of Any Period	Length of Longest Period	Last Unsafe Day after Start of Any Period
21 days	3d day	21 days	10th day
22 days	4th day	22 days	11th day
23 days	5th day	23 days	12th day
24 days	6th day	24 days	13th day
25 days	7th day	25 days	14th day
26 days	8th day	26 days	15th day
27 days	9th day	27 days	16th day
28 days	10th day	28 days	17th day
29 days	11th day	29 days	18th day
30 days	12th day	30 days	19th day
31 days	13th day	31 days	20th day
32 days	14th day	32 days	21st day
33 days	15th day	33 days	22d day
34 days	16th day	34 days	23d day
35 days	17th day	35 days	24th day
36 days	18th day	36 days	25th day
37 days	19th day	37 days	26th day
38 days	20th day	38 days	27th day

Spermicides
Chemical substances that destroy or immobilize sperm

Vaginal Spermicides (Chemical Methods)   Spermicides (sperm-killing agents) come as foams, creams, jellies, foaming tablets, and suppositories. Foams are the most effective because they form the densest, most evenly distributed barrier to the cervical opening. Tablets and suppositories, which melt in the vagina, are the least effective.

Foams are packed under pressure (like shaving cream) and have an applicator attached to the nozzle. Creams and jellies come in tubes with an applicator. A short time before intercourse, the woman (or the man) places the applicator into the vagina (like a sanitary tampon) and pushes the plunger. Vaginal spermicides remain effective for only about half an hour, so another application is necessary before each act of intercourse.

Vaginal spermicides are generally harmless, relatively easy to use, and readily available in most drugstores without a prescription. However, they are not very effective, though their effectiveness can be increased by using them with a diaphragm. Other disadvantages are that they are messy, may interrupt the sexual mood, must be reapplied for each act of intercourse, and sometimes cause a burning sensation or irritation. If this occurs, usually changing to another brand will solve the problem. If irritation persists, a doctor should be consulted.

Withdrawal (Coitus Interruptus)   Withdrawal is simply what the name implies; just before ejaculation the male withdraws his penis from the vagina. Withdrawal is probably the oldest known form of contraception. It is free, requires no preparation, and is always available. However, it has a high failure rate. It requires tremendous control by the man, and the fear that withdrawal may not be in time can destroy sexual pleasure for both partners. The woman also may be denied satisfaction if the man must withdraw before she reaches orgasm. Also semen leakage before withdrawal can cause pregnancy.

Douche A **douche** is a stream of water applied to a body part to cleanse or treat it. As a contraceptive method, douching involves forcing water through the vagina by use of a douche syringe. *Used as contraception, douching is probably useless and may in fact wash sperm into the uterus, thus increasing the chances of pregnancy.* A number of commercial douches are available, but their use should be limited. Using a substance other than water can cause a bacterial imbalance in the vagina, leading to yeast and other infections.

Douche
The process of flushing the vagina with water or spermicides

Sterilization

Sterilization is the most effective and permanent means of birth control. Despite the fact that in many cases it is irreversible, more and more Americans are choosing sterilization as a means of contraception. The Association for Voluntary Sterilization estimates that 10 to 12 million people in the United States have been voluntarily sterilized and about 1 million more are being sterilized each year. The association further estimates that about 90 million people in the world are now sterilized. In 1985 about 40 to 45 percent of couples using birth control were choosing sterilization (Welles, 1985).

Sterilization
Any procedure (usually surgical) by which an individual is made incapable of reproduction

Vasectomy **Vasectomy** is the surgical sterilization of the male. It is done in a doctor's office under local anesthetic and takes about thirty minutes. Small incisions are made in the scrotum, and the vasa deferentia, which carry the sperm from the testes, are cut and tied (see Figure 11-3).

The man may feel a dull ache in the surgical area and in the lower abdomen after a vasectomy. Aspirin and an ice bag help relieve these feelings. Usually the man can return to work in two days and can have sex again as soon as he doesn't feel any discomfort, usually in about a week.

An additional method of contraception must be used for several weeks after the operation because live sperm are still in parts of the reproductive system. After about one to two months and a number of ejaculations the man must return to have his semen examined for the presence of live sperm. If none are found, other birth control methods can be dropped.

Although the man will continue to produce sperm after the operation, the sperm will now be absorbed into his body. His seminal fluid will be reduced only slightly. Hormone output will be normal, and he will not experience any physical changes in his sex drive. Some males do experience negative psychological side effects. For example, some equate the vasectomy with castration and feel less sexual (Kogan, 1973). Such feelings may interfere with sexual ability. Postvasectomy psychological problems occur in perhaps 3 to 15 percent of men (Lear, 1969; Wolfers, 1970). On the other hand, many men report they feel freer and more satisfied with sex after a vasectomy (Kogan, 1973).

In about 1 percent of vasectomies, a severed vas deferens rejoins itself so that sperm can again travel through the duct and be ejaculated (Insel & Roth, 1976). Because of this possibility, a yearly visit to a doctor to check for sperm in the semen is a good safety precaution.

A promising new nonsurgical alternative to vasectomy is a process called vas sclerosing. In this procedure the wall of the vas deferens is injected with small quantities of material that produces scarring, thus blocking the passageway. The technique greatly reduces the risks inherent in any surgical process, as well as

Vasectomy
A sterilization procedure for males involving the surgical cutting of the vas deferens

Figure 11-3 Male reproductive system, showing effects of vasectomy. Note that in actual sterilization, surgery is performed on both sides of body.

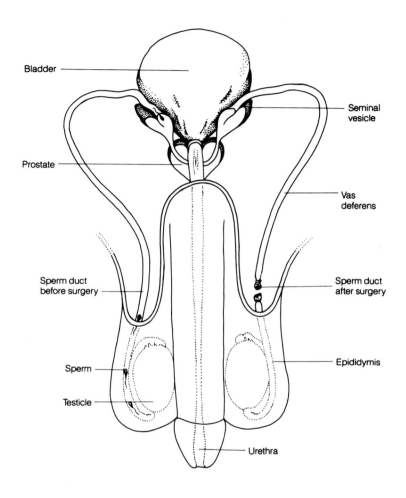

overcoming the psychological objections that some men have to cutting in the genital area (McCary & McCary, 1982).

One of the major drawbacks of vasectomy (or any other method of sterilization) is that in many cases it is irreversible. Thus the husband and wife should be sure to discuss the matter thoroughly before deciding on this method of contraception.

If reversal is desired, the tubes can be reconnected in some cases. Doctors at the University of California Medical Center in San Francisco have recently reported much higher success with reversal operations than in the past. In one study up to 50 percent of the men who underwent microsurgical vasovasotomy (reconnecting the vas) subsequently ejaculated sperm, and three-quarters of those men were able to impregnate their wives (Brody, 1979; Willscher, 1980). However, some vasectomized men develop antibodies to their sperm, which may persist after the reversal and counteract fertilization (Insel & Roth, 1976).

Earlier concerns about later health problems, especially heart disease, seem unfounded (Siegel, 1984). The only health problem seen significantly more often in vasectomized men is inflammation of a sperm-collecting duct near the testicles, and this minor problem is seen in only about 1 percent of the vasectomies.

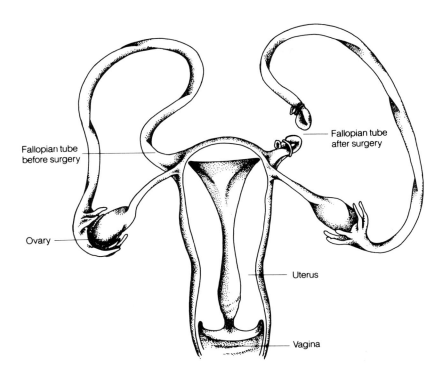

Fallopian tube
before surgery

Ovary

Fallopian tube
after surgery

Uterus

Vagina

Figure 11-4 Female reproductive system, showing effects of tubal ligation. Note that in actual sterilization, surgery is performed on both sides of body.

Tubal Ligation **Tubal ligation** is the surgical sterilization of the female. Until recently it has been a much more difficult operation than vasectomy because the Fallopian tubes lie more deeply within the body than the vasa deferentia. The operation, done in a hospital rather than a doctor's office, requires a general anesthetic and a hospital stay of about three to four days. One or two small incisions are made in the abdominal wall, the Fallopian tubes are located and each is severed, a small section of each is removed, and then the two ends of each tube are tied (see Figure 11-4). Incisions can also be made through the vaginal wall, which will not leave a scar and requires shorter hospitalization (however, recent pregnancy or obesity make this approach more difficult or impossible). Both procedures take about thirty minutes.

Besides being more difficult than vasectomies, tubal ligation is also riskier. About 7 percent of women experience problems after the operation, mainly from infections (Insel & Roth, 1976). Some women also experience abdominal discomfort and menstrual irregularity. Most women, however, have no aftereffects.

A more recent and now more widely used procedure is called **laparoscopy**. This too is a hospital procedure that requires a general anesthetic. However, the operation takes only fifteen minutes and does not require overnight hospitalization. A tiny incision is made in the abdomen and a small light-containing tube (laparoscope) is inserted to illuminate the Fallopian tubes. The surgeon then inserts another small tube carrying high-intensity radio waves that burn out sections of the Fallopian tubes. The incision is so small that only a stitch or two is needed; hence the procedure is often referred to as "Band-Aid" surgery. Most women leave the hospital two to four hours after surgery.

Tubal ligation
A sterilization procedure for females in which the Fallopian tubes are cut or tied

Laparoscopy
A sterilization procedure for females involving the use of a telescope instrument (laparoscope) to locate the Fallopian tubes, which are then cauterized

Both forms of tubal ligation have a failure rate of about 3 in every 1000 cases (Insel & Roth, 1976). Attempts to reverse the sterilization have been about 70 percent successful (Hatcher et al., 1984). However, the reversal procedure is a major operation lasting several hours and as such is very costly ($10,000 to $15,000).

Women who have been sterilized tend to report an increase in sexual enjoyment because they are now free of the fear of pregnancy. A few women report reduced sexual enjoyment because of the loss of fertility that they may equate with femininity (Easley, 1972).

Hysterectomy, which is the surgical removal of the uterus, also ends fertility. But it is an extreme procedure and should be used only when a woman has uterine cancer or other problems of the uterus and not just for birth control reasons.

Hysterectomy
Surgical removal of a female's uterus;
results in sterilization

Tomorrow's Contraceptives

As probably became obvious in the discussion of the different contraceptive methods, the ideal method is still to be discovered. Researchers hope to find a safe, simple, and reversible contraceptive. They also want to find one that does not need to be taken every day or require a doctor's prescription. The following lists will give you a better idea of some of the research in contraception.

Possible Future Female Methods

1. *One-time implant*: A plastic capsule filled with synthetic progestin would be inserted into an arm or leg where it would remain in the fatty layer just under the skin. The progestin would be released at a regulated rate to block ovulation. If a woman wished to become pregnant, the capsule could be easily removed.
2. *Continuous low-dosage progestin*: Again, the constant presence of progestin would stop eggs from being released. Possible sources of the progestin would be: implanted capsule as just described, removable vaginal insert, pill, long-term injection, IUD, or perhaps skin contact with a progestin-impregnated ring or cosmetic.
3. *Immunization against eggs or sperm*: Theoretically a woman could be sensitized against her own egg cells (or against sperm) so that she would produce antibodies that would inactivate the eggs or sperm as if they were a foreign disease.
4. *Once-a-month pill*: A combination estrogen/progestin pill that has to be taken only once a month would eliminate the accidents that now occur among pill takers who forget to take a pill or two during the monthly cycle.
5. *Postcoital estrogen pill (morning-after pill)*: A form of morning-after pill is already in use. It contains large doses of artificial estrogen and is taken for five days after unprotected intercourse. However, the large doses have caused nausea, vomiting, and other undesirable changes in metabolism.
6. *Long-term injection*: Long-term (every ninety days) injections of progestin have been found to be almost completely effective in preventing pregnancy. Researchers are trying to discover a safe combination of estrogen and progestin that will also be effective, perhaps for periods of up to six months.
7. *Once-a-month injection*: A lower dosage of estrogen and progestin that

would only have to be injected once a month might be safe. It might be possible to package the hypodermic needles already loaded, much as insulin is now packaged for diabetics.

8. *Reversible tubal occlusion*: Instead of cutting and tying the Fallopian tubes, they would be plugged by injecting liquid silicone. Because the plug could be removed, the woman could later decide to become pregnant.

9. *Improved ovulation-detecting devices*: If ovulation could be pinpointed accurately, rhythm would be a reliable method of birth control. A small, battery-run device called an Ovulometer has come on the market. The device registers changes in body temperature and voltage that occur during ovulation. By touching her body with electrodes, a woman can tell if ovulation has taken place (*San Francisco Chronicle*, 1976). By using a small hand-held computer dubbed "bioself" a woman can accurately find her unsafe days (*Los Angeles Times*, 1982). Another method, "First Response," is a simple urine test that takes about 20 minutes. An obvious color change tells when ovulation will occur within the next 12 to 24 hours. Unlike methods based on temperature, a woman will know ahead of time rather than after ovulation occurs. A test that analyzes a woman's breath and saliva can also reveal time of ovulation (Kosteic & Preti, 1982).

10. *Contraceptive nasal spray*: Hormones contained in the spray would go directly to the area of the brain that regulates ovulation and stop ovulation. So far, five inhalations a month have kept rhesus monkeys from becoming pregnant.

11. *Tissue-adhesive injection*: A tissue-adhesive substance—somewhat like a quick-acting glue—could be injected into the Fallopian tubes to block them.

Possible Future Male Methods

Devising a male chemical contraceptive is more difficult than devising one for females. Simply put, the difference is between stopping the release of one egg once a month and stopping the production of millions of sperm every day (Berger & Wenger, 1985).

1. *One-time implant*: This would be an as-yet-undiscovered chemical that would prevent sperm from being produced. The chemical would be placed in a plastic capsule that would be implanted in an arm or leg and would slowly release the chemical into the body. If a man decided to have children, the capsule could be easily removed.

2. *Immunization against sperm*: The man would be sensitized to his own sperm so that he would produce antibodies that would attack them as if they were a foreign disease.

3. *Once-a-month or daily pill*: Some combinations of hormones or chemicals would prevent maturation of sperm when taken orally. So far a safe combination has not yet been discovered.

4. *Long-term injection*: A sperm suppressor would be injected every three to six months. Again, no safe suppressor has been discovered to date.

5. *Reversible vasectomy*: Instead of cutting and tying the vasa deferentia, they would be plugged with some substance. Experimenters have tried blocking the flow of sperm with removable clips and plugs, but so far these have damaged the vasa and have interfered with full restoration of fertility. In some

cases the sperm have made a new path around the plug, so that birth control was not achieved. Another technique has involved implanting small mechanical valves. In the closed position the valves prevent sperm from reaching the penis. If fertility is desired, another operation is performed to change the valves to the open position.

Abortion

Abortion
Induced or spontaneous termination of a pregnancy before the fetus is capable of surviving on its own

In the United States the 1960s witnessed mounting interest in induced **abortion** as a method of birth control. Although each state had restrictive legislation against abortion, many illegal abortions were performed. Expectant mothers were sometimes killed and often harmed because of nonsterile or otherwise inadequate procedures.

Other countries successfully use abortion to control population, and to help women avoid unwanted pregnancies. Japan, for example, was plagued by overpopulation for years, until in 1948 it enacted the Eugenic Protection Act that, in essence, allowed any woman to obtain a legal abortion. Consequently, and in conjunction with a massive educational campaign to make the populace aware of the need to reduce family size, the birth rate fell from 34.3 to 17 per thousand by 1956 and has remained at this lower level ever since.

After a number of states liberalized their abortion laws, the U.S. Supreme Court on January 22, 1973, in *Roe* v. *Wade* and *Doe* v. *Bolton*, made abortion on request a possibility for the entire country. Essentially, the court ruled that the fetus is not a person as defined by the Constitution and therefore does not possess constitutional rights. "We do not resolve the difficult question of when life begins. When those trained in the respective disciplines of medicine, philosophy, and theology are unable to arrive at any consensus, the judiciary . . . is not in a position to speculate as to the answer."

More specifically, the court said that in the first trimester (twelve weeks) of pregnancy no state may interfere in any way with a woman's decision to have an abortion as long as it is performed by a physician. In the second trimester (thirteen to twenty-five weeks) a state may lay down medical guidelines to protect the woman's health. Most states that do permit abortion permit it by choice only through the twentieth week. After that there must be clear medical evidence that the mother's health is endangered or that the baby will be irreparably defective. Only in the last trimester may states ban abortion, and even then an abortion may be performed if continued pregnancy endangers the life or health of the mother.

The proponents of abortion on request believed they had won a final victory, yet this conclusion has proved premature. Abortion has become one of the most emotional issues that the nation now faces. On one side are the crusaders "for life," otherwise known as "right-to-lifers," who argue on religious and moral grounds that abortion is murder and thus should be outlawed. On the other side are the "pro-choice" crusaders who contend that abortion is a right that any woman has to the control of her own body and thereby of her life (see Issues, p. 380).

One reason why the conflict continues is that the American public is fairly evenly divided on the question. A 1977 national poll by Yankelovich indicated that 48 percent approved abortion while 44 percent did not (*Time*, 1977). Ten years after the Supreme Court decision, a Gallup Poll (1983) still found 50 percent of Americans favoring the 1973 Court ruling while 43 percent were opposed.

The rapidly increasing number of abortions after the 1973 Court decision also fueled the conflict. Although it is difficult to guess the number of illegal abortions performed before 1973, the number of legal abortions had at least doubled to around 1.5 million by 1978. This figure has remained relatively constant since then. It is estimated that one in eight women of reproductive age has had an abortion. About 25 percent of these women are married. About 65 percent of the

---

Debate the Issues
Abortion on Demand Is Everyone's Right

The proabortionists believe a woman's body belongs to her, and she should have the right to determine whether to pursue pregnancy to completion. They believe that laws governing abortion are an unconstitutional invasion of privacy.

When we women approach abortion from the point of view of our own experience, it does not seem to us that we are arriving at a radical conclusion when we suggest that *choice* is the answer. On the contrary it seems sweet reason. Surely, at least, we have the ability to control our own physical selves, surely we can make decisions from the skin in if not from the skin out. What could be more reasonable than to ask that we be allowed to make choices for our own bodies? Nothing is more reasonable than that. (Steinem, 1982)

They also argue that overpopulation is a major threat to civilization and humanity. Thus to fail to use every acceptable method to reduce population growth is immoral and shortsighted and will ultimately lead to world disaster.

They further argue that it is more immoral to have unwanted children than it is to seek abortion. The unwanted child suffers and becomes the source of many of society's problems. Problems are created both for and by unwanted children.

The American Friends Service Committee makes the following statement:

We believe that every child should be wanted by and born into a family that is able to feed, clothe, educate, and, above all, love him; that the family is the basic unit of our society and that the married life of the parents should encompass sexual activity whether or not for purposes of procreation; that an appropriate contraception, which spaces children and eliminates the fear of unwanted pregnancies, strengthens family ties and establishes a sense of responsible parenthood; that in view of the problem of overpopulation, every couple has a responsibility to society as well as to their own family not to overburden the world with more lives than it can sustain.

We believe that responsible parenthood demands consideration not only of the number of children individual parents want but also of the effect of that number on society as a whole. (American Friends Service Committee, 1970)

Abortion is not as dangerous to the mother as childbirth. The maternal death rate in New York, for example, is 29 per 100,000 births, whereas the death rate from legal abortions is only 3.5 per 100,000 abortions. Deaths from pregnancy and birth in England are about 20 per 100,000 deliveries and the death rate is about 4 per 100,000 from abortions. There appears to be little or no risk in first trimester abortions done by vacuum aspiration (p. 382) (Hogue, 1977; Hogue et al., 1983).

Women have always sought abortions and always will. By making abortion illegal, society fosters a black market in abortions and increases the woman's chances of injury and death.

---

women having abortions are under 25 years of age. Approximately 58 percent of the women have no other children. About 90 percent of the abortions take place in the first trimester (12 weeks) of pregnancy (Henshaw, 1985; *World Almanac*, 1986).

The prolife movement's ultimate goal is to add a "human life amendment" to the Constitution that would reverse the Supreme Court's decision. A congressional bill amendment (Human Life Statute) has been introduced several times to do what the Supreme Court said it could not do; namely, define "life." The bill simply says, "For the purpose of enforcing the obligation of the States under the 14th amendment not to deprive persons of life without due process of law, human life shall be deemed to exist from conception" (*Time*, 1981, p. 22). The bill would allow states to pass laws defining abortion as murder. To date the bill has not been passed.

Congress has passed bills cutting off most federal funds for abortions, and such restrictions have been upheld by the Supreme Court. Federally financed

Debate the Issues
Abortion Is Murder

"Prolife" groups believe that abortion is murder and that inasmuch as murder is not condoned in our society, we should not condone abortion.

Social utility is not a viable criterion in matters that involve life and death and essential liberties. Although a huge proportion of unhappy lives and a whole network of social ills can be traced to the unwanted child, no one can predict with certainty how a child will turn out. No one can say that an unwanted child won't later be wanted and loved. How many people, even unhappy ones or ones in trouble from time to time, seriously wish they had never been born? The social utility argument reduces human life to the value of a machine—how well does it work (Lessard, 1972)?

Prolife groups believe that easy availability of abortions will lead to promiscuity. The Christian heritage in the United States not only bans abortion but also has a great deal to say about sexual mores. Making abortion freely available encourages promiscuous behavior because the consequences of the act are removed. The possibility of pregnancy means that one needs to contemplate sexual intercourse in a responsible manner inasmuch as it is possible that the act will involve a child for whom responsibility must be taken. Free abortion leads to irresponsible sexual activity because one need not be responsible for a child even if pregnancy does occur.

Abortion can lead to severe psychological trauma. The feelings of guilt, the frustrated desire to have the child, and the feelings of responsibility for the death of the child—all these and many more psychological reactions can and do occur and are as much a threat to the mother's health as the continued pregnancy.

Research suggests that multiple abortions or second trimester abortions may involve future risks. There may be a greater risk in future pregnancies of low-birth-weight babies, premature deliveries, or spontaneous abortions (Harlap et al., 1979; Levin et al., 1978).

abortions have dropped from a high of 300,000 to essentially zero. Many states had passed restrictions controlling second trimester abortions as allowed by the Supreme Court decision. However, in June of 1983 the Supreme Court reacted negatively to such state laws, and reaffirmed their original decision much to the disappointment of prolife groups, which had made considerable headway in restricting abortions during the second trimester (Press & Camper, 1983). Again in June 1986 the Supreme Court struck down restrictive state controls on abortion. In this case Pennsylvania required pre-abortion counseling that pointed out the dangers involved. The court claimed that to "require" the counseling was illegal.

Another part of the debate concerns the right of the father to participate in the abortion decision. Current laws exclude him from the decision, on the ground that it is the mother-to-be's body and therefore under her control. This remains a controversial aspect of the abortion law. Should a man who is the father of an unborn child be totally banned from participating in the abortion decision? What happens if the mother-to-be and father cannot agree on an abortion?

Improving medical technology also influences the abortion debate. In 1973 the earliest that a fetus could survive outside of the womb was about 28 weeks. Now that threshold has dropped to 24 weeks and many doctors predict that it will soon be 22 weeks. What does this mean for the woman contemplating

What Do You Think?

■ Do you believe that a fetus is an alive person with all of his or her individual rights under the Constitution?

■ Under what circumstances would you personally have an abortion?

■ What do you think about underage women having the right to an abortion without parental knowledge?

■ Should we think of abortion as simply another birth control method?

■ What role in an abortion decision should the father/husband have?

■ Do you think abortion, giving up the child for adoption, or raising an unwanted child is harder psychologically on the mother?

abortion later than 22 weeks? What happens when a saline abortion is done late in pregnancy, but the fetus, although damaged, can survive with the new technology? Twenty-six states hold physicians to the same standard of care for fetuses born live from induced abortions as for any other premature infant (Hager, 1985). This occasionally results in the strange paradox of a doctor performing an abortion and then fighting to keep the infant alive.

Where the continuing debate will go is anybody's guess, but one thing is sure: The question of abortion will remain a controversial one for some time.

The debate over induced abortion tends to cloud the physical act of abortion itself. First of all, spontaneous abortion occurs in 10 percent or more of all diagnosed first pregnancies by the end of the tenth week. If undiagnosed first pregnancies are taken into account, the figure is probably closer to 25 percent. Interestingly, a high percentage of spontaneously aborted embryos are abnormal. There is also evidence that emotional shock plays a role in spontaneous abortions as well as abnormalities of the reproductive process.

Abortion is a fairly simple procedure, though it can be more unpleasant than abortion advocates claim. One major method of legal abortion is **dilatation and curettage (D and C)**. In this method the cervix is dilated by the insertion of increasingly larger metal dilators until its opening is about as big around as a fountain pen. At this point a curette (a surgical instrument) is used to scrape out the contents of the uterus. An ovum forceps (a long, grasping surgical instrument) may also be used. The woman is instructed not to have sexual intercourse for several weeks, and she may take from ten days to two weeks to recover fully from the procedure.

Vacuum aspiration is now the preferred method of abortion because it takes less time, involves less loss of blood, and has a shorter recovery period than a D and C. In this method the cervix is dilated by a speculum (an expanding instrument), and a vacuum-suction tube is inserted into the uterus. A curette and electric pump are attached to the tubing, and suction is applied to the uterine cavity. The uterus is emptied in about twenty to thirty seconds. The doctor sometimes also scrapes the uterine lining with a metal curette. The procedure takes five to ten minutes. The woman may return home after a rest of a few hours in a recovery area. She is usually instructed not to have sexual intercourse and not to use tampons for a week or two after the abortion (see Figure 11-5).

After the fourteenth week, a different method, called the **saline abortion**, must be used because the fetus is now too large to be removed by suction, and a D and C performed now may cause complications. The uterus is stimulated to push the fetus out; in other words, a miscarriage is caused. When a fetus dies, the uterus naturally begins to contract and expel the dead fetus. In order to kill the fetus, a local anesthetic is given the mother and a long needle is inserted through her abdominal wall into the uterine cavity. The amniotic sac (see Chapter 12) is punctured and some of its fluid is removed. An equal amount of 20-percent salt solution is then injected into the sac. The injection must be done slowly and carefully to avoid introducing the salt solution into the woman's circulatory system. She must be awake so that she can report any pain or other symptoms. Once the fetus is dead, the uterus begins to contract in about six to forty-eight hours. Eventually the amniotic sac breaks and the fetus is expelled. In up to 50 percent of cases, the placenta does not come out automatically and a gentle pull on the umbilical cord is necessary to remove it. In about 10 percent of cases, a D and

Dilatation and curettage (D and C)
An abortion-inducing procedure that involves dilating the cervix and scraping out the contents of the uterus with a metal instrument (curette)

Vacuum aspiration
An abortion-inducing procedure in which the contents of the uterus are removed by suction

Saline abortion
An abortion-inducing procedure in which a salt solution is injected into the amniotic sac to kill the fetus, which is then expelled via uterine contractions

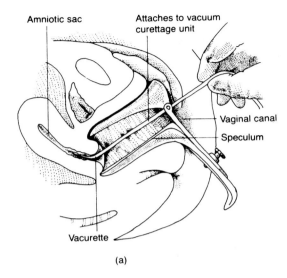

Amniotic sac
Attaches to vacuum curettage unit
Vaginal canal
Speculum
Vacurette

(a)

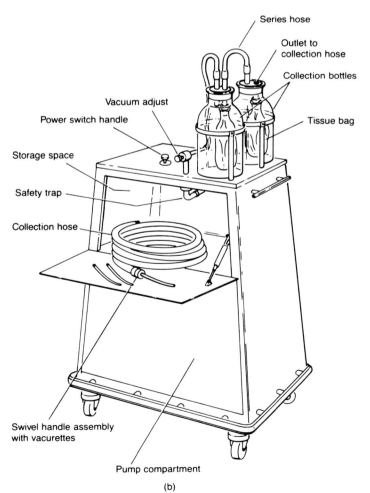

Series hose
Outlet to collection hose
Collection bottles
Tissue bag
Vacuum adjust
Power switch handle
Storage space
Safety trap
Collection hose
Swivel handle assembly with vacurettes
Pump compartment

(b)

Figure 11-5 Vacuum aspiration, an abortion method, takes only five to ten minutes; it can be performed up to the twelfth week of pregnancy. (a) The vacuum aspiration process. (b) An operating unit for vacuum aspiration.

C must be performed to remove any remaining pieces of the placenta. The saline procedure should be carried out in a hospital, and the woman should remain there until the abortion process is complete. The recovery period is longer than for other forms of abortion, and complications are more frequent.

A **dilatation and evacuation (D & E)** is another method used after the first trimester. It is quicker than inducing labor and delivery and safer for the woman. It is simply a combination of dilatation and vacuum curettage. Since the fetus is larger, the cervix must be dilated to a larger opening and the surgeon may need to crush the fetus so that it can pass out through the larger bore vacuum (Hatcher et al., 1984).

A new chemical abortion procedure that may make the preceding methods obsolete is being used in Sweden. A synthetic prostaglandin is the chemical used in a suppository that is placed in the vagina. The chemical causes muscle contractions within one to five hours after a "missed period." The uterine contractions lead to abortion.

The decision to have an abortion may not be easy and should not be made lightly. Whenever possible, it is wise for the woman considering an abortion to discuss the decision with the prospective father, parents, physicians, counselors, and/or knowledgeable and concerned friends. Although abortion should be a considered decision, the decision to have an abortion should be reached as quickly as possible since the later in the pregnancy the abortion, the greater the risks of complications.

Professional abortion counseling can be obtained at local Planned Parenthood chapters and in most states with the Clergy Consultation Service on Abortion. Both agencies are listed in local telephone directories. Many prolife groups also run consultation facilities. Abortion is not recommended as a means of birth control and should be used only as a last resort. A woman who is well informed about sex and contraceptive devices usually will not be faced with having to make an abortion decision.

Infertility

Although many people think only of contraception when hearing the phrase "family planning," problems of infertility are also important aspects of family planning. The U.S. Public Health Service estimates that 25 percent of married couples cannot have any children or as many as they want because they are infertile or subfertile (Mosher, 1980). Infertile for a man means that he is not producing viable sperm and for a woman that she is either not producing viable eggs or has some other condition that makes it impossible to maintain a pregnancy. It is estimated that about one-third of all married couples do conceive the first month they try and that about 60 percent conceive within the first three months. Thus 40 percent of couples seeking pregnancy must try for longer than three months.

There are three phases in the treatment of infertility: education, detection, and therapy. Young couples should persist in trying to conceive for at least one year. If they are not successful, they should seek help from a physician. Often if the couple learns more about how conception occurs and the possible reasons for failure to conceive, they will feel less tense and anxious and thus increase the chances of conception.

Prerequisites of Fertility

There are at least nine biological prerequisites for achieving conception (Gutt-macher, 1969, 1984). Four pertain to the male:

1. Healthy live sperm must be produced in sufficient numbers. Ordinarily a single normal testicle is all that is required, though usually both assume an equal role in producing sperm. To function properly, a testicle must be in the scrotal sac. In the male embryo each testicle is formed in the abdomen and descends into the scrotum during the seventh month of intrauterine life. Infrequently, one or both testicles fail to descend. If they have not descended by five or six years of age, the boy is usually treated with a hormone to stimulate testicular growth. This makes the testicle heavier, which in some instances brings about descent. If hormone treatment fails, surgery is performed, usually when the boy is about eight.
2. Seminal fluid (the whitish, sticky material ejaculated at orgasm) must be secreted in the proper amount and composition to transport the sperm.
3. An unobstructed seminal passage must exist from the testicle to the end of the penis.
4. The ability to achieve and sustain an erection and to ejaculate within the vagina must be present.

The other five biological requirements for reproduction pertain to the female:

1. At least one ovary must function normally enough to produce a mature egg.
2. A normal-sized uterus must be properly prepared to receive the developing fetus by chemicals (hormones) fed into the bloodstream by the ovary.
3. An unobstructed genital tract must exist from the vagina up through the Fallopian tubes to the ovary to enable the egg to pass down and the sperm to pass up.
4. The uterine environment must adequately nourish and protect the unborn child until it is able to live in the outside world.
5. Miscarriage must be avoided, and the infant must be delivered safely.

It is not uncommon for couples seeking fertility help to conceive before treatment begins and for adoptive parents to conceive shortly after they decide on adoption. Clearly, emotional and psychological factors are tremendously important to the process of conception. Psychological factors account for approximately one-quarter of subfertility cases (Guttmacher, 1969, 1984).

Causes of Infertility

Males account for about 40 percent of infertility problems. Problems with both members of a marriage account for another 20 percent of infertility problems (Wallis, 1984, p. 50). With men, for example, impotence, the inability to gain or maintain an erection, precludes sexual intercourse and thus conception. Often impotence is psychological in nature, though it can be caused by alcohol, general fatigue, or a debilitating disease. Low sperm count is another possible reason for infertility. An ejaculation that contains fewer than 100 to 150 million sperm limits the possibility of conception. Infectious diseases such as mumps can damage sperm production. Sterility can also occur if the testes have not descended into the scrotum, because the higher temperature of the body reduces production of healthy sperm. Testes often do not descend because they are abnormal in some way, and this also affects production of healthy sperm. A prolonged and untreated sexually transmitted disease (STD) can cause permanent sterility in both men and women.

If a couple consults a physician, as they should, about their apparent infertility, it is easier to test the man first because fertility tests for the male are quite simple compared with those for the female. Basically, the tests involve collecting a sample of ejaculate and analyzing it for the number and activity level of sperm and for abnormal sperm.

Unfortunately, some men tie fertility and manhood closely together. They consider an examination for possible fertility problems an attack on their manhood and may be unwilling to cooperate. Both partners, however, must share in the search for a solution to infertility.

A woman must ovulate if she is to conceive. Almost all mature women menstruate, but in about 15 percent of a normal woman's cycles an egg is not released. In a few women, even though they menstruate, ovulation seldom occurs, making them almost infertile.

A woman may have a problem conceiving if the tract from the vagina through the uterus and Fallopian tubes to the ovary is blocked. This is the most common reason for infertility in women. If the egg and sperm cannot meet, conception cannot occur. It is possible to determine if the Fallopian tubes are open by filling them with an opaque fluid and X-raying them.

In a woman both vaginal infections and ovarian abnormalities can cause infertility. Infection probably accounts for the dramatic jump of infertility problems among young women aged twenty to twenty-four. Such problems increased 177 percent between 1965 and 1982. Doctors place some of the blame for this increase on more liberalized sexual attitudes. Increased sexual activity and numbers of sexual partners have led to increasing occurrences of genital infections, especially pelvic inflammatory disease. Such infections scar the delicate tissue of the Fallopian tubes, ovaries, and uterus. About half of these cases result from chlamydia, currently the most common STD. It is estimated that there are 5 million new cases each year. Unfortunately, many infected persons display no symptoms; thus, the disease often goes untreated. For men, the symptoms are painful urination and watery discharge from the penis. For women, the symptoms are genital itching, burning, and vaginal discharge. Another 25 percent of pelvic inflammatory infections are accounted for by gonorrhea. Also the trend to postpone childbirth until a later age increases fertility problems for women (Wallis, 1984, p. 50).

Another possible problem can arise from the chemical environment of the woman's reproductive organs. Too acid an environment quickly kills sperm. Also, the chemical environment may make implantation of the fertilized egg into the uterine wall difficult or impossible. In the latter case the woman may conceive and then spontaneously abort (miscarry) the embryo.

Methods of Treatment

Recent advances in the understanding of reproduction have led to a whole new technology that can be used to battle infertility (see Table 11-3). Artificial insemination, in vitro fertilization, and the use of surrogate mothers are all used to help infertile couples. Combinations of these methods produce a dozen different patterns of parenting (see Figure 11-6).

Artificial Insemination   When the cause of infertility rests with the husband **artificial insemination** is sometimes used to induce conception. This consists of injecting sperm—from the husband, if possible, or from an anonymous donor—into the wife's vagina during her fertile period. Even if the husband's sperm count is low, his ejaculate can be collected and the concentration of sperm increased to bring it within the normal range necessary for fertilization. It is interesting to note that, for reasons unknown, artificial insemination results in conception of a marked preponderance of males.

Sperm banks have been established where sperm is frozen and stored for

Artificial insemination
Induction of semen into the vagina or uterus by artificial means

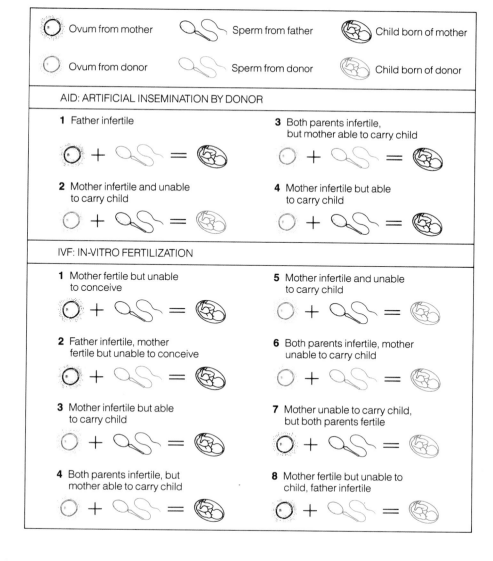

Figure 11-6   New ways of creating babies.

Table 11-3
New Reproductive Alternatives

Method	Advantages	Risks	Cost*
Fertility pump	Physiologic, mimics what naturally occurs No known side effects Works when Clomid (fertility pill) doesn't Much less costly than in vitro fertilization No surgery Normal incidence of multiple births	Inflammation of vein	$330 pump rental plus cost of synthetic GnRH
In vitro fertilization	Best, if not only way for a couple to have their own baby if woman's tubes are irreparably blocked Potential for correcting genetic defects in embryo	Surgery and anesthetic Multiple births Potential for genetic manipulation to malevolent as well as benevolent ends	$5000
Embryo transfer	No surgery or anesthetic Avoids genetic disorders carried by mother Pregnancy possible for women who have no ovaries or ovaries that don't function	Not being able to retrieve fertilized egg from donor	$4000–$6000
Cryopreservation (freezing embryos for later implantation)	A second chance without surgery for a woman whose first attempt at in vitro fertilization fails Banks of fertilized ova available for transfer to infertile women who are willing to bear another woman's child Potential for correction of genetic defects	Slight increase in risk of abnormalities Potential for genetic manipulation to malevolent as well as benevolent ends	Not known yet

later use; it seems to remain viable for long periods. Sperm that has been frozen for up to three years has been used for successful human fertilization. Japanese researchers recently reported successfully inseminating a cow with frozen bull sperm eighteen years old (*Santa Barbara News Press*, 1982).

There are numerous controversies surrounding artificial insemination, especially when the sperm comes from someone other than the husband. Questions of legitimacy and parental responsibility have arisen. For example, after a divorce can a sterile husband deny financial responsibility for a child conceived with sperm from another man? Conversely can such a husband be denied visitation rights because he is not the biological father of the child? It is estimated that some 250,000 children have been born in America by AID pregnancies (artificial insemination by donor) (Friedrich, 1984, p. 54). Biologically it is a perfectly acceptable manner of overcoming a man's infertility.

	Table 11-3 continued		
Method	**Advantages**	**Risks**	**Cost***
Microsurgery	Very effective in reversing female sterilization	Surgery and anesthetic	$8000
	Very effective in removing scar tissue around Fallopian tubes		
	Effective on tubes blocked at end near uterus		
Surrogate mothering	Women whose infertility is not correctable can rear a child fathered by their husband	Wife must adopt baby	$10,000–$20,000
		Legal questions of legitimacy, inheritance, adultery, financial responsibility and rights of the biological mother	
Artificial insemination	Best sperm can be used	Cramping	$100
	Sperm is deposited directly into uterus	Slight risk of infection	
		When sperm is donor's, not husband's, legal questions of legitimacy, inheritance, financial responsibility, adultery and rights of biological father	
Clomiphene citrate (Clomid) (fertility pill)	Very effective in women with normal or high estrogen level	Multiple births	$40 per menstrual cycle
		Effective only 50 percent of time	
Pergonal (fertility injections)	Very effective for low estrogen levels	Multiple births	$500–$800 per menstrual cycle

*Costs are estimated.

Fertility Drugs When the cause of infertility is the woman's failure to ovulate, fertility drugs such as clomiphene citrate (Clomid) and menotropins (Pergonal) have been used to stimulate ovulation. However, the drugs often overstimulate ovulation and cause multiple births.

In Vitro Fertilization For the woman who cannot become pregnant, it is now possible for a human egg to be fertilized outside her body and then implanted within her uterus. Louise Brown, born in July 1978 in England, was the first such "test-tube baby." The first baby in the United States conceived by the in vitro fertilization (IVF) technique was born in December 1981. By the beginning of 1985, approximately 1000 babies had been born as a result of IVF.

The first step in IVF is the retrieval of a mature female egg. The egg is extracted using a laparoscope inserted through a small incision so that the doctor can see the follicle inside the ovary where the egg is being produced. Then a long hollow needle is inserted through a second incision and the egg and surrounding fluid is gently suctioned up. The ovum is carefully washed and placed in a petri dish containing nutrients, and the dish is placed in an incubator for four to eight hours. The second step is to gather sperm from the husband and add them to the dish containing the egg. If all goes well, the egg is fertilized and starts to divide. When the embryo is about eight cells in size it is placed in the woman's uterus.

Inset 11-2

A Surrogate's Story

Valerie is a New Jersey mother of two boys, ages two and three, whom she describes as "little monsters full of mischief." Her husband works as a truck driver, and money is tight. The family of four is living with her mother while they save for an apartment of their own. One day last March, Valerie, 23, who prefers to remain anonymous, saw the following advertisement in a local New Jersey paper: *Surrogate mother wanted. Couple unable to have child willing to pay $10,000 fee and expenses to woman to carry husband's child. Conception by artificial insemination. All replies strictly confidential.*

The advertisement made Valerie stop and think. "I had very easy pregnancies," she says, "and I didn't think it would be a problem for me to carry another child. I figured maybe I could help someone." And then there was the lure of the $10,000 fee. "The money could help pay for my children's education," she says, "or just generally to make their lives better."

The next day Valerie went for an interview at the Infertility Center of New York, a profit-making agency owned by Michigan Attorney Noel Keane, a pioneer in the controversial business of matching surrogate mothers with infertile parents. She was asked to fill out a five-page application, detailing her medical history and reasons for applying. Most applicants are "genuine, sincere, family-oriented women," says agency Administrator Donna Spiselman. The motives they list range from "I enjoy being pregnant" and an urge to "share maternal joy" to a need to alleviate guilt about a past abortion by bearing someone else's child. Valerie's application and her color photograph were added to 300 others kept in scrapbooks for prospective parents to peruse. Valerie was amazed when only a week later her application was selected, and she was asked to return to the agency to meet the couple.

Like most people who find their way to surrogate agencies, "Aaron" and "Mandy" (not their real names) had

undergone years of treatment for infertility. Aaron, 36, a Yale-educated lawyer, and his advertising-executive wife, 30, had planned to have children soon after marrying in 1980. They bought a two-bedroom town house in Hoboken, N.J., in a neighborhood that Aaron describes as being "full of babies." But after three years of tests, it became painfully clear that there was little hope of having the child they longed for. They considered adoption, but were discouraged by the long waiting lists at American agencies and the expense and complexity of foreign adoptions. Then, to Aaron's surprise, Mandy suggested that they try a surrogate.

Their first choice from the Manhattan agency failed her mandatory psychological test, which found her to be too emotionally unstable. Valerie, who was Aaron and Mandy's second choice, passed without a hitch. A vivacious woman who is an avid reader, she more than met the couple's demands for a surrogate who was "rea-

---

It takes two to three weeks to know whether the pregnancy will be viable, and the chance of success is only about 20 percent. Even when pregnancy is progressing about one-third of the women will miscarry within the first three months. The cost of this procedure is approximately $5000 (Wallis, 1984, pp. 48–49).

In 1983, the first successful transfer of human embryos was achieved. Women who were carrying fetuses had them transferred into nonfertile women at an early stage (around the fifth to sixth weeks) (Jacobs, 1983).

Another interesting method of achieving conception was developed in 1985. In this case the woman's mature egg is removed and then reimplanted in her Fallopian tube with sperm from her husband. In this procedure the egg is only out of the woman's body for a few minutes and sperm are assured of reaching it (Harper, 1986).

sonably pretty," did not smoke or drink heavily and had no family history of genetic disease. Says Aaron: "We were particularly pleased that she asked us questions to find out whether we really want this child."

At first, Valerie's husband had some reservations about the arrangement, but, she says, he ultimately supported it "100%." Valerie is not concerned about what her neighbors might think because the family is planning to move after the birth. Nor does she believe that her children will be troubled by the arrangement because, she says, they are too young to understand. And although her parents are being deprived of another grandchild, they have raised no objections.

For their part, Aaron and Mandy have agreed to pay Valerie $10,000 to be kept in an escrow account until the child is in their legal custody. In ad-

dition, they have paid an agency fee of $7,500 and are responsible for up to $4,000 in doctors' fees, lab tests, legal costs, maternity clothes and other expenses. In April, Valerie became pregnant after just one insemination with Aaron's sperm. Mandy says she was speechless with joy when she heard the news.

Relationships between surrogate mothers and their employers vary widely. At the National Center for Surrogate Parenting, an agency in Chevy Chase, Md., the two parties never meet. At the opposite extreme is the case of Marilyn Johnston, 31, of Detroit. Johnston and the couple who hired her became so close during her pregnancy that they named their daughter after her. She continues to make occasional visits to see the child she bore and says, "I feel like a loving aunt to her."

Not all surrogate arrangements work so well. Some women have refused to give up the child they carried for nine months. As a lawyer, Aaron is aware that the contract he signed with Valerie would not hold up in court, should she decide to back out of it. "But I'm a romantic," he says. "I have always felt that the real binding force was not paper but human commitment." Valerie, whose pregnancy is just beginning to show, says she is "conditioning" herself not to become too attached to the baby. "It is not my husband's child," she says, "so I don't have the feeling behind it as if it were ours." She does not plan to see the infant after it is born, but, she admits, "I might like to see a picture once in a while."

Source: Wallis, 1984, p. 53.

Surrogate Mothers   When it is impossible to correct a woman's infertility, another woman may be hired to bear a child for the couple. Such a woman is termed a **surrogate mother** (see Inset 11-2) and is usually paid between $10,000 and $20,000. Normally she is fertilized via artificial insemination using the husband's sperm. Once the baby is born, it is legally adopted by the infertile couple. There are a number of organizations throughout the United States that bring infertile couples together with potential surrogate mothers. The organizations screen and match the parties and handle the complex legal problems of adoption and payment. Because it is illegal in every state to buy or sell a child, payment must be made to compensate the surrogate mother, not for the child, but for such things as taking the risk of pregnancy and childbirth and for the loss of work because of pregnancy. The contract in each situation is unique and may specify such things

Surrogate mother
A woman who becomes pregnant and gives birth to a child for another woman who is incapable of giving birth

as no drinking or smoking during pregnancy. Generally all contracts stipulate the following:

On the Part of the Surrogate

1. The surrogate agrees to terminate maternal rights and allow adoption by the couple.
2. The surrogate must not seek the identity of the adoptive parents unless this is mutually agreeable.
3. Should the surrogate breach the contract and decide to keep the child, she must reimburse the adoptive couple for all payment, expenses, and legal fees.
4. The surrogate agrees to abort the fetus if an abnormality is discovered during pregnancy.

On the Part of the Adoptive Couple

1. The couple is required to take out an insurance policy on the surrogate mother and on the biological father (husband), with the child named as beneficiary.
2. The couple agrees to compensate the surrogate at a reduced rate if she should miscarry.
3. The couple agrees not to seek the surrogate's identity unless this is mutually agreeable.
4. The couple agrees to accept all babies should multiple births occur.
5. The couple agrees to accept the child should it be born abnormal.
6. The couple must show proof of marriage and wife's infertility.

The potential legal problems are complex. Even though a contract is signed, what actually happens when a surrogate mother decides to keep the child (*Santa Barbara News Press*, 1981)? Or what happens when the parents-to-be decide they don't want the child, if, for example, a surrogate mother gives birth to a mentally defective child? If a surrogate mother contracts with another couple to bear their child, does she have the right to smoke or drink in defiance of their wishes? Does she still have a right to an abortion? Does a child born of such methods have a right to know its biological mother? To solve such questions, surrogate mother bills defining the rights of the parties have been introduced in a number of state legislatures but none has yet been passed.

The use of a surrogate mother is a method of last resort. However, the procedure informally is as old as history. In days past it was not unusual for a woman to have a child and give it to another couple, infertile or not. This often happened with an illegitimate birth that was hidden from public view. For example, a daughter might have an illegitimate child that was then passed off as her parent's child, her new brother or sister.

One seldom-discussed problem common to all these methods is the potential reaction of the person who finds that he or she was born of one of these methods (Andrews, 1984). Suppose a child is conceived from sperm and egg of anonymous donors, carried by a surrogate mother and raised by a family that is biologically not even related. Should the child be told about such things? What will the child's reaction be if he or she finds out?

Sex Therapy   Sex therapy is being used to help couples with nonphysical problems that affect their sex life and their ability to conceive. Obviously, intercourse
is necessary for conception to occur. But if a couple is having problems with
premature ejaculation, impotence, or lack of sexual enjoyment, they may avoid
having intercourse.

Sex therapists usually use techniques devised by Masters and Johnson and
others to guide the couple to a more satisfactory sexual relationship. (See Leiblum
and Pervin, 1980, for a fuller discussion of these techniques.) In general the
couple is seen together. To reduce their performance expectations and fear of
sexual failure, they are prohibited from having intercourse for a period of time.
The therapists give them a series of exercises, which they perform at home and
then discuss with the therapists. The discussions also deal with sexuality in general
and with the couple's specific problems. In the exercises they learn to explore
each other in sensual rather than specifically sexual ways. They learn not only to
give and receive pleasure but also what gives the partner pleasure. As they
become more knowledgeable and relaxed about sexuality, they are led, through
further structured exercises, to increased comfortableness with intercourse.

Sex therapy has suffered from a sudden popularity that is leading to ethical
problems. For example, some therapists have been known to have intercourse
with their clients in the name of therapy. Others are using sexual surrogates
(substitute partners) to help their clients overcome sexual problems (see Kaplan,
1979; Pope et al., 1986). Although such practices might be justified on theoretical
grounds, ethical and moral questions are involved. Masters and Johnson have
commented that they think only half a dozen of the many sex therapy clinics are
legitimate, using well-trained staff and proven procedures (Masters et al., 1980).
To help rectify abuses, they organized a series of multidisciplinary meetings to
identify and discuss the primary ethical issues pertinent to sex therapy and
research. From the proceedings, published in 1977 as *Ethical Issues in Sex
Therapy and Research*, came a set of ethical guidelines for sex therapists, counselors, and researchers (Masters et al., 1980). Recently several state legislatures
have considered licensure regulations for sex counselors. In California, for example, sex counselors are required to have master's degrees and supervised
training.

Despite ethical and moral problems, sex therapy is a breakthrough in the
treatment not only of infertility problems resulting from impotence and frigidity,
but also of other sexual problems. In the past, for example, an impotent male
had little chance to overcome his problem because he failed every time he
attempted intercourse. Getting and maintaining an erection is a complex interaction
between a man's chemistry and his psychological state of being. No matter how
physically healthy a man is, if he is psychologically "in the wrong place," he will
not become erect. Failure causes worry and fear that he will fail again. Such
worry and fear work against achieving an erection and thus complete a vicious
circle. As success declines, the man often loses his sexual desire. Sex therapy
can break this pattern of fear, failure, and more fear by setting up situations in
which the man can be successful, thus lessening his fears, increasing his future
chances of success, and rekindling his sexual desire.

Much the same is true for the nonorgasmic woman. In her case failure to
achieve orgasm does not hinder her ability to become pregnant, but it may lead
to lack of interest in and/or fear of sex and thus lower her frequency of intercourse,
which will reduce her chances of becoming pregnant.

Summary

Family planning is an important part of marriage. The decision to have children should be made rationally by the couple. Yet many pregnancies are unplanned, the resultant children unwanted, and the consequences to the marriage often devastating. The couple should ask themselves if they can help all their children grow into adulthood in the most healthful possible manner. They should not only want the children they have but also be healthy and economically equipped to feed, clothe, and educate their children.

Birth control has a long but until quite recently somewhat unsuccessful history. Technological advances have led to more reliable contraceptive methods, though the perfect contraceptive has yet to be invented. The pill, IUD, condom, and diaphragm are all popular and effective methods of birth control.

Sterilization as a form of birth control also became increasingly popular during the 1970s. Although usually irreversible, advances in technique are increasing the possibility of reversible sterilization procedures.

Abortion laws have been revised, making abortion on demand a reality. The revisions have generated a great amount of controversy, and it is quite possible that more restrictive laws may again be introduced. Be that as it may, abortion is a presently available method of birth control, though it requires much thought before using it.

Family planning also helps couples have children when fertility problems exist. Increased understanding of reproduction has helped solve some of the problems that cause infertility. Probably 15 to 20 percent of American couples have some infertility problem. Beginning with the 1970s, in addition to correction of physical problems such as low sperm count, failure to ovulate, blocked Fallopian tubes, and so on, efforts have been made to help couples who have sexual problems that stem from their upbringing or from some psychological problem. The couple who cannot successfully have sexual relations will not be able to have children, unless by artificial insemination. Sex therapy, although controversial, is proving helpful to such couples.

In general the couple who plan their family realistically and who control reproduction increase their chances of having a happy sex life and a fulfilling marriage. To leave reproduction to chance too often leads to problems and unhappiness.

Children Having Children

Before the baby came, her bedroom was a dimly lighted chapel dedicated to the idols of rock'n'roll. Now the posters of rock stars are gone and the walls painted white. Angela's room has become a nursery for six-week-old Corey. Angela, who just turned 15, finds it hard to think of herself as a mother. "I'm still just as young as I was. I haven't grown up any faster." Indeed sitting in her parents' living room, she is the prototypical adolescent, lobbying her mother for permission to attend a rock concert, asking if she can have a pet dog, and so forth. The weight of her new responsibilities is just beginning to sink in. "Last night I couldn't get my homework done," she laments with a toss of her blond curls. "I kept feeding him and feeding him. Whenever you lay him down, he wants to be picked up." "Babies are a big step, I should have thought more about it," she says.

Each year more than a million American teenagers will become pregnant, four out of five of them unmarried. Together they represent a distressing flaw in the social fabric of America. Many become pregnant in their early or mid-teens, some 30,000 under the age of fifteen. If present trends continue, researchers estimate, fully 40 percent of today's fourteen-year-old girls will be pregnant at least once before the age of twenty.

Teenage pregnancy has been around as long as there have been teenagers, but the dimensions and social costs of the problem are just beginning to be appreciated. In November of 1985 Wisconsin passed landmark legislation designed to combat unwanted teen pregnancies. The law provides funds for sex education in public schools, repeals restrictions on the sale of nonprescription contraceptives and provides funds for counseling pregnant adolescents. It

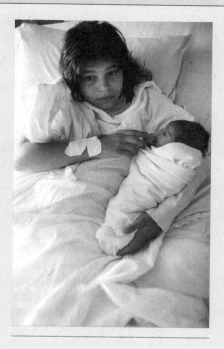

also takes the unusual step of making grandparents of babies born to teenagers legally responsible for the babies' financial support. Other states are trying to start birth control clinics in high schools. These are just some of the attempts to combat the growing problem of teenage pregnancy.

Such strong and controversial measures reflect the magnitude of the problem. Teen pregnancy imposes lasting hardships on two generations: parent and child. Teen mothers are, for instance, many times as likely as other mothers with young children to live below the poverty level. According to one study, only half of those who give birth before eighteen complete high school (as compared to 96 percent of those who postpone childbearing). On the average they earn half as much money and are far more likely to be on welfare: 71 percent of females under thirty who receive Aid

to Families with Dependent Children had their first child as a teenager.

As infants, the offspring of teen mothers have high rates of illness and mortality. Later in life they often experience educational and emotional problems. Many are the victims of child abuse at the hands of parents too immature to understand why their baby is crying or has developed a will of its own. Finally these children are prone to dropping out and becoming teenage mothers themselves. According to one study, 82 percent of girls who gave birth at age fifteen or younger were daughters of teenage mothers.

With disadvantage creating disadvantage, it is no wonder that teen pregnancy is widely viewed as the very hub of the U.S. poverty cycle. Much of the so-called feminization of poverty starts off with teenagers having babies.

Among the urban ghettos, the trends are especially disturbing. Nearly half the black females in the United States are pregnant by age twenty. The pregnancy rate among those aged fifteen to nineteen is almost twice what it is among whites. Worse still, nearly 90 percent of the babies born to blacks in this age group are born out of wedlock; most are raised in fatherless homes with little economic opportunity. Teenage pregnancy ranks near the very top of issues facing black people as far as many black leaders are concerned.

The shocking prevalence of teenage pregnancy among white as well as black Americans was brought to light when the Alan Guttmacher Institute released the results of a thirty-seven country study in 1985. Its findings: The United States leads nearly all other developed countries in its incidence of pregnancy among girls aged fifteen through nineteen. Looking in detail at Sweden, Holland, France, Canada, and Britain, the researchers found that American adolescents were no more active than adolescents in these countries but they were found to become pregnant in much greater numbers.

To understand the nature of the problem, one must look beyond the statistics and examine the dramatic changes in attitudes and social mores that have swept through American culture during the past thirty years. The teenage birth rate was actually higher in 1957 than it is today, but that was an era of early marriage when nearly a quarter of eighteen- and nineteen-year-old females were married. The overwhelming majority of teen births in the fifties thus occurred in a connubial context, and mainly to girls over seventeen. Twenty to thirty years ago, if an unwed teenager should, heaven forbid, become pregnant, chances are her parents would see that she was swiftly married off in a shotgun wedding. Or if marriage was impractical, the girl would discreetly disappear during her confinement, the child would be given up for adoption, and the matter would never again be discussed in polite society. Abortion, of course, was out of the question because it was illegal at the time.

All of this has changed. Today if a girl does not choose to abort her pregnancy (and some 45 percent of teenagers do not), chances are she will keep the baby and raise it without the traditional blessings of marriage. With teen marriages two or three times more likely to end in divorce, parents figure, "Why compound the problem?" In 1950 fewer than 15 percent of teen births were illegitimate. By 1983 more than

50 percent were, and in some regions the figure exceeds 75 percent.

Unfortunately unwed motherhood may even seem glamorous to impressionable teens. They see Jerry Hall on TV flinging back her hair, talking about having Mick Jagger's second (out-of-wedlock) child and saying what a wonderful life she has. But if unwed motherhood has lost much of its notoriety, premarital sex over the same period has become positively conventional. Like it or not, American adolescents are far more sexually active than they used to be. A 1982 survey conducted by Johns Hopkins Researchers found that nearly 20 percent of fifteen-year-old girls admitted that they had already had intercourse as did nearly 33 percent of sixteen-year-olds and 43 percent of seventeen-year-olds.

Social workers are almost unanimous in citing the influence of the popular media— television, rock music, videos, and movies—in propelling the trend toward precocious sexuality. It's obvious from Bruce Springsteen's lyrics in *She's the One*, that each girl must be a scheming seductress chasing innocent boys.

The girl in the song has "killer graces" and "secret places" that are too large for any boy to fill. Although the boy tries to resist her, he doesn't have a chance because of her lovely french cream complexion and her dreamlike qualities. Her French kisses and her long, falling hair and her eyes that shine like a midnight sun seduce the innocent boy into a sexual relationship. The fact that a sexual relationship may lead to pregnancy or sexually transmitted disease never seems to be mentioned in most popular lyrics pushing sex.

Instead, our young people are bar-

raged by the message that to be sophisticated and hip they must be sexually experienced.

And yet for all of their early experimentation with sex, their immersion in heavy-breathing rock and the erotic fantasies on MTV, one thing about American teenagers has not changed: They are in many ways just as ignorant about the scientific facts of reproduction as they were in the days when Doris Day, not Madonna, was their idol. For example, studies show that teenagers wait about 12 months after first becoming sexually active before they seek contraception. Unable to grasp the situation when they become pregnant, they often wait too long to consider an abortion. The gravity of the situation completely avoids them. "I was going to have an abortion, but I spent the money on clothes."

For many young girls there is another, less tangible factor in the sequence of events leading to parenthood: a sense of fatalism, passivity, and, in some cases, even a certain pleasure at the prospect of motherhood. "Part of me wanted to get pregnant. I liked the boy alot and he used to say he wanted a baby." For young girls trapped in poverty, life offers few opportunities apart from getting pregnant. Pregnancy brings recognition. In Bill Moyers's television special on the black family (CBS Reports: *Vanishing Family Crisis in Black America*, January 25, 1986) all the young women either pregnant or with a child out of wedlock reported that being a mother made them someone: It gave them an identity, if not prestige. "Before I was pregnant, I was nothing. Now I'm somebody, I'm a mother." No wonder teenage pregnancies have reached epidemic proportions in some ghetto areas. According to Gutt-macher statistics, black American teenagers have the highest fertility rate of any teenage population in the entire world. One in four black babies is born to a teen mother, most of them unwed. The National Urban League has declared teenage pregnancy its primary concern. Says league president John Jacob, "We cannot talk about strengthening the black community and family without facing up to the fact that teenage pregnancy is a major factor in high unemployment, the numbers of high school dropouts, and the numbers of blacks below the poverty line."

Needy girls, black or white, who imagine that having a baby will fill the void in their lives are usually in for a rude shock. Hopes of escaping a dreary existence, of finding direction and purpose, generally sink in a sea of responsibility. With no one to watch the child, school becomes impossible, if not irrelevant. And despite the harsh lessons of experience, many remain careless or indifferent about birth control. About 15 percent of pregnant teens become pregnant again within one year; 30 percent do so within two years.

The problem faced by children of such parents begin before they are even born. Only one in five girls under age fifteen receives prenatal care at all during the vital first three months of pregnancy. The combination of inadequate medical care and poor diet contributes to a number of problems. Teenagers are 92 percent more likely to have anemia and 23 percent more likely to have complications related to prematurity, than mothers aged twenty to twenty-four. All of this adds up to twice the normal risk of delivering a low-birth-weight baby (one that weighs under 5.5 pounds), a category that puts an infant in danger of serious mental, physical, and developmental problems that may require costly care.

Speaking of cost, it is estimated that overall the United States spends $8.6 billion on income support for teenagers who are pregnant or have given birth.

What Do You Think?

- If American society is now so hip about sex, why do these girls fail to use contraceptives?
- Do you think that the mass media has much influence over teenagers?
- What are the messages about sexuality given out in popular music and videos?
- How are women viewed by popular music and videos?
- If you are a woman and contemplating a date, do you go prepared (with contraceptive precautions) to have sex?
- If a situation in which you could engage in sexual intercourse arose unexpectedly, would you put the behavior on hold until prepared contraceptively?
- What do the answers to the above two questions tell you about your attitudes toward sexual activity?
- Why do research studies of college women (not young teenagers) indicate that most say they will use contraception if they have sexual intercourse, but most also report not using anything when indeed they did have intercourse?

Source: Adapted in part from Wallis, 1985, pp. 78–90.

Pregnancy and Birth

Contents

We have great strengths when we bear children—but we also have great needs.

- *Love;*
- *Enough money and/or community support to care for ourselves;*
- *Nourishing food in adequate amounts;*
- *Sufficient rest;*
- *A skilled, wise practitioner whom we trust and like, a place of birth that feels comfortable and safe, and continuity of care throughout the childbearing process;*
- *Confidence in our ability to give birth well;*
- *People around us who respect us, who have confidence in us and patience with the natural unfolding of our labor;*
- *After the baby is born, the opportunity to be with her or him whenever we want and a helping hand during the days and weeks that follow birth.* *

Despite all the talk about effective birth control methods, zero population growth, and low birthrates, most Americans do have children, and most of the children are desired, cared for, loved, and a source of happiness (along with some heartache) to their parents. Indeed the birthrate has risen from a low of 14.5 babies per thousand population in 1975 to approximately 15.8 per thousand in 1986 (National Center for Health Statistics, 1986). Examining the birthrate per thousand fertile women (women aged eighteen to forty-four years) rather than per thousand population (for the year 1985) finds sixty-five births for white women, seventy-two births for black women, and eighty-six births for Hispanic women (U.S. Bureau of the Census, 1985; National Center for Health Statistics, September 19, 1986). Relatively few American women remain childless throughout their lives. In this century the highest proportion of women having no children was 15 percent among women born between 1920 and 1924. These women reached the peak of their childbearing years during the Great Depression and World War II when many factors combined to increase the likelihood of childlessness (U.S. Bureau of the Census, December 1980).

For a mother listening to her six-foot son discuss the finer points of football, for a father escorting his lovely twenty-two-year-old daughter down the aisle, it may be difficult to remember the beginnings: the love-making; the missed menstrual period that led mother to think, "Maybe I'm pregnant"; the thrill of feeling a tiny, unseen foot kick; the scary feelings when labor started; the dramatic rush to the hospital; holding the red, wrinkled seven-pound newborn son or daughter and counting all of the fingers and toes to make sure they are all there; the long discussion over the name; the wet spot on dad's suit after hugging the baby goodbye before going to work; the first tooth, the first sickness, the first bicycle, the first day of school, the first date, high school graduation, and now marriage— and perhaps soon the new cycle when suddenly a little one hugs them and says "Hi grandad, hi grandma."

All of us, with our billions and billions of cells and complex organs, have grown from the union of two microscopic cells: the ovum, or egg cell (about 0.004 inch

*Adapted from *The New Our Bodies, Ourselves,* by The Boston Woman's Health Book Collective, 1984, p. 327.

Figure 12-1 Sperm wander aimlessly when no egg is present (a), but all move toward the egg when it is present (b).

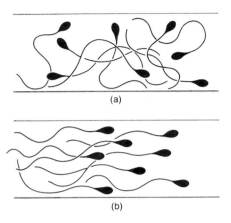

(a)

(b)

Conception
Fertilization of the egg by the sperm to start a new human life

in diameter), and the sperm (about 0.00125 inch in diameter). We weighed only 0.005 of a milligram or one 20-millionth of an ounce at conception!

The possibility of **conception** begins with ovulation, the release of one mature egg (containing twenty-three chromosomes, fat droplets, protein substances, and nutrient fluid, all surrounded by a tough gelatinous substance or membrane) that must find its way to the Fallopian tube and begin a three-day journey to the uterus. Fertilization must occur within twenty-four hours of ovulation, or the egg will die and be expelled.

A sperm cell, the other necessary ingredient for conception, like the egg contains twenty-three chromosomes within its nucleus (the head), but it also has a tail that gives it mobility. There are about 200 to 400 million sperm in an average ejaculation. They are so minute that enough of them to repopulate the earth could be stored in a space the size of an aspirin tablet.

When sperm are deposited in the vagina after an ejaculation, they are affected by the presence of an egg. If an egg isn't present, sperm will swim erratically in all directions. But if an egg is present, they will swim directly toward it (see Figure 12-1). By using their tails, they can swim at a rate of three to four centimeters an hour. Their great numbers are necessary because the job of reaching the egg is so arduous that only a few thousand will reach the Fallopian tube that contains the egg. Many will die in the acidic environment of the vagina. Many will also go up the wrong tube or get lost along the way. Those that do reach the egg will have to overcome another obstacle: the tough outer membrane of the egg. Each sperm that reaches the egg will release a bit of enzyme to help dissolve the egg's membrane. Finally, one sperm will manage to enter the egg and will fertilize it. Once this occurs, the egg will become impervious to all remaining sperm and they will die.

Sperm remain viable within the female reproductive tract for about forty-eight hours; the egg remains viable for about twenty-four hours. Their lives may be slightly shorter or longer depending in part on the chemistry of the reproductive system of the woman at a given time. Thus conception can only occur during approximately three days of each twenty-eight-day cycle. For example, if intercourse occurs more than forty-eight hours before ovulation, the sperm will die, and if it occurs more than twenty-four hours after ovulation, the egg will have died. The rhythm method of birth control is based on this fact (see Chapter 10).

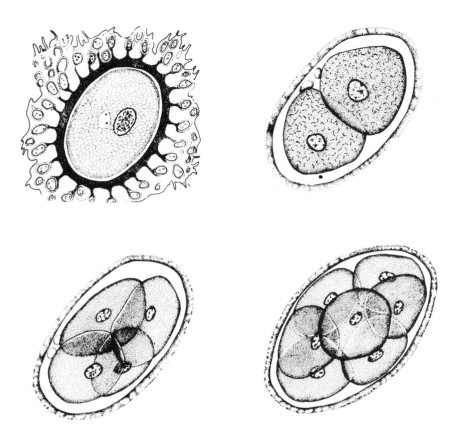

Figure 12-2 Cell division after conception.

Within thirty-six hours after fertilization, the egg divides in half, and then divides again. The dividing continues as the egg moves down the Fallopian tube, with the cells getting smaller with each division (see Figure 12-2). By the time the floating mass of cells reaches the **uterus** (in about three to four days), it will contain about thirty-six cells. This cluster, called a *blastocyst*, then becomes hollow at the center. The outermost shell of cells, called the *trophoblast*, multiplies faster, attaches the blastocyst to the uterine walls, and eventually becomes the placenta, umbilical cord, and amniotic sac. The inner cells separate into three layers. The innermost layer (the *endoderm*) will become the inner body parts; the middle layer (the *mesoderm*) will become muscle, bone, blood, kidneys, and sex glands; and the outer layer (the *ectoderm*) will eventually become skin, hair, and nervous tissue (see Table 12-1). On the sixth or seventh day after fertilization, the blastocyst will be implanted in the uterine wall and the cells will begin to draw nourishment from the uterine lining.

Uterus
The hollow, pear-shaped organ in females within which the fetus develops; the womb

Boy or Girl?

Sex determination takes place at conception. The female egg always carries an X chromosome. The sperm, however, may be either of two types, one carrying an X chromosome and the other a Y chromosome. If the egg has been fertilized by an X sperm, the child will be female (XX). If, on the other hand, the egg has been

_____ **Table 12-1** _____

Prenatal Development

Time Elapsed	Embryonic or Fetal Characteristics	Illustrations
28 days 4 weeks 1 month	¼–½ inch long. Head is one-third of embryo. Brain has lobes, and rudimentary nervous system appears as hollow tube. Heart begins to beat. Blood vessels form and blood flows through them. Simple kidneys, liver, and digestive tract appear. Rudiments of eyes, ears, and nose appear. Small tail.	
56 days 8 weeks 2 months	2 inches long. 1/30 of an ounce in weight. Human face with eyes, ears, nose, lips, tongue. Arms have pawlike hands. Almost all internal organs begin to develop. Brain coordinates functioning of other organs. Heart beats steadily and blood circulates. Complete cartilage skeleton, beginning to be replaced by bone. Tail beginning to be absorbed. Now called a fetus. Sex organs begin to differentiate.	
84 days 12 weeks 3 months	3 inches long. 1 ounce in weight. Begins to be active. Number of nerve-muscle connections almost triples. Sucking reflex begins to appear. Can swallow and may even breathe. Eyelids fused shut (will stay shut until the 6th month), but eyes are sensitive to light. Internal organs begin to function.	
112 days 16 weeks 4 months	6–7 inches long. 4 ounces in weight. Body now growing faster than head. Skin on hands and feet forms individual patterns. Eyebrows and head hair begin to show. Fine, downylike hair (lanugo) covers body. Movements can now be felt.	

Table 12-1
continued

Time Elapsed	Embryonic or Fetal Characteristics	Illustrations
140 days 20 weeks 5 months	10–12 inches long. 8–16 ounces in weight. Skeleton hardens. Nails form on fingers and toes. Skin covered with cheesy wax. Heartbeat now loud enough to be heard with stethoscope. Muscles are stronger. Definite strong kicking and turning. Can be startled by noises.	
168 days 24 weeks 6 months	12–14 inches long. 1½ pounds in weight. Can open and close eyelids. Grows eyelashes. Much more active, exercising muscles. May suck thumb. May be able to breathe if born prematurely.	
196 days 28 weeks 7 months	15 inches long. 2½ pounds in weight. Begins to develop fatty tissue. Internal organs (especially respiratory and digestive) still developing. Has fair chance of survival if born now.	
224 days 32 weeks 8 months	16½ inches long. 4 pounds in weight. Fatty layer complete.	
266 days 38 weeks 9 months	Birth. 19–20 inches long. 6–8 pounds in weight (average). 95 percent of full-term babies born alive in the United States will survive.	

Figure 12-3 Microscopic view showing the difference between X-bearing sperm (with larger, oval-shaped head) and Y-bearing sperm (with smaller, wedge-shaped head and longer tail).

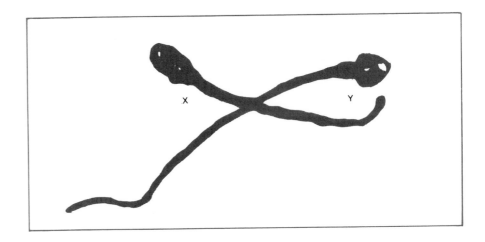

fertilized by a Y sperm, the child will be male (XY) (see Chapter 7 for a complete discussion). It is believed that Y sperm (androsperm) have a small wedge-shaped body with a long tail and that X sperm (gynosperm) have a larger oval-shaped head and a shorter tail (Figure 12-3). These differences have not yet been proved conclusively (McCary & McCary, 1982).

Many more males are conceived than females. In fact, approximately 140 males are conceived for every 100 females. However, only 106 males are born for every 100 females. We do not know why this is so. Some suggest that the Y sperm move more quickly than the X sperm and thus reach the egg earlier. Perhaps, it is because the male is the weaker sex as far as survival is concerned. In all age groups up to age eighty, males perish at a greater rate than females. For example, in the age bracket fifteen to twenty-four years, 277 males die for every 100 females who die; in the age bracket thirty-five to forty-four years, 161 males die for every 100 females who die.

Multiple Births

The human female normally conceives only one child at a time, so multiple births have always been unusual. Twins occur about once in every 90 births, triplets once in 9000 births, and quadruplets once in 500,000 births among American whites. Twins occur once in every 70 births among American blacks (Papalia & Olds, 1986, p. 44). Mortality rates are significantly higher for multiple births. Twins are often born somewhat prematurely and are usually smaller than normal in size.

Most twins are *fraternal*, which means they developed from two separate eggs that were fertilized simultaneously. Such twins are no more similar in physical characteristics than are any other siblings (brothers or sisters). Such twins could also each have a different father if the mother had sexual intercourse with two different men at about the same time, and each egg was fertilized by a sperm from a different partner. About a third of twins are *identical*, which means they developed from the subdivision of a single fertilized egg, and usually shared a common placenta. Unlike fraternal twins, their genetic makeup is identical, so they have very similar physical characteristics and are always the same sex.

Recently, the so-called fertility drugs have contributed to the multiple birth phenomenon (see p. 389). In such cases women who fail to ovulate properly have been given a gonadotropin to stimulate proper ovulation. In numerous instances the use of these hormones has caused multiple births. In one case an Australian woman gave birth to nine infants, none of whom survived. With increased understanding of the reproductive functions, the risk of multiple births may be reduced when fertility drugs are used.

Pregnancy

How does a woman know if she is pregnant? Because the union of the egg and the sperm does not produce any overt sensations, the question "Am I pregnant?" isn't easy to answer in the early stages of pregnancy. What are some common early symptoms of pregnancy?

- *A missed menstrual period.* Although pregnancy is the most common reason for menstruation to stop suddenly in a healthy female, it is certainly not the only reason. For example a woman may miss a period because of stress, illness, or emotional upset. In addition about 20 percent of pregnant women have a slight flow or spotting, usually during implantation of the fertilized egg into the uterine wall (Pincus & Wolhandler, 1984, p. 342; Schulz, 1979).
- *Nausea in the morning (morning sickness).* Early in the first trimester a pregnant woman often experiences nausea in the morning, although vomiting usually doesn't occur. The nausea usually disappears by the twelfth week of pregnancy.
- *Changes in shape and coloration of breasts.* The breasts usually become fuller, the areolae (the pigmented areas around the nipples) begin to darken, and veins become more prominent. Sometimes the breasts tingle, throb, or hurt because of the swelling.
- *Increased need to urinate.* The growing uterus pressing against the bladder and the hormonal changes that are taking place may cause an increase in the need to urinate. Somewhere around the twelfth week of pregnancy, the uterus will be higher in the abdomen and will no longer press against the bladder, so urination will return to normal.
- *Feelings of fatigue and sleepiness.* Because of the hormonal changes that are taking place some women find that they are always tired during the first few months of pregnancy and need to sleep more often and for longer periods.
- *Increased vaginal secretions.* These may be either clear and nonirritating or white, slightly yellow, foamy, or itchy. Such secretions are normal.
- *Increased retention of body fluids.* Increased body fluids are essential to pregnant women and growing babies, thus some swelling of the face, hands, and feet is normal during pregnancy. (Olds, London & Ladewig, 1984).

Some women do not experience any of these symptoms; some experience only a few; few experience them severely.

Pregnancy may also have some cosmetic effects. Skin blemishes often abate, leaving the complexion healthy and glowing. In the latter stages of pregnancy pink stretch marks may appear on the abdomen, although most of them will disappear after birth.

Figure 12-4 Negative and positive pregnancy test reactions. In a negative test agglutination (clumping) will be visible within two minutes. In a positive test no agglutination will occur at two minutes.

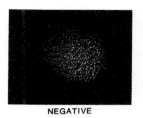

NEGATIVE   POSITIVE

Pregnancy Tests

Usually a physician can tell if a woman is pregnant by a simple pelvic examination. It is possible to feel the uterine enlargement and softening of the cervix by manual examination after six to eight weeks of pregnancy. However, because most women want to know if they are pregnant as soon as possible, chemical tests are used to discover pregnancy earlier.

Doctors usually perform a test of agglutination, the clumping together of human chorionic gonadotropin (HCG), to assess whether pregnancy has occurred. This process takes only a few minutes and can be used one to fourteen days after menstruation should have started. The test involves taking a morning urine specimen, placing a drop of it on a slide, and adding the proper chemicals. In a negative reaction agglutination will be visible in two minutes. If the woman is pregnant, no agglutination will occur at two minutes (see Figure 12-4).

Several tests examine the woman's blood serum, also seeking changed levels of HCG. One is called radioimmunoassay (RIA). This test takes about one hour to complete and becomes positive a few days after presumed implantation. A newer test, the Biocept-G technique, has reduced the necessary incubation period to thirty minutes and gives accurate results within a few days after a missed menstrual period. In this case a blood sample is mixed with radioactive iodine with which the HCG will react if present.

The tests are considered 95 to 98 percent accurate but can give inaccurate results if they are performed too early (before enough hormone shows up in the urine) or if there are errors in handling, storing, or labeling the urine (Boston Women's Health Book Collective, 1984; Nass, Libby & Fisher, 1981). Sometimes it may take several tests to determine if a woman is pregnant because she may produce very low levels of hormone and there may not be enough in her urine to give a positive result even though she is pregnant. It is rare for a pregnancy test to give a positive result when the woman is not pregnant.

False pregnancy (pseudocyesis) in which the early physical signs are present though the woman is not really pregnant, is also possible. Inexpensive pregnancy tests clarify the situation and usually end the symptoms (unless there is a physical problem causing them).

Because the menstrual cycle is easily affected by one's emotions, uneasiness about engaging in sexual activity may disrupt a woman's monthly cycle enough to delay her period or even cause her to skip a period altogether. Unfortunately, emotional reaction and physical reaction interact to increase her problems in this case. For example, if a woman has sex and worries that she might be pregnant, the worry may actually postpone her period, causing her further worry, which further upsets her menstrual timing, and so on. A pregnancy test is one way to resolve the worry over possible pregnancy.

Since 1976 a number of home pregnancy-test kits have come on the market, selling for around $10. They work on the same system as the HCG tests we have already discussed and may be used from seven to ten days after a menstrual period is missed. The accuracy of these tests is high if they are used correctly. The false positive rate is plus or minus 5 percent, while the false negative rate is plus or minus 20 percent (Pritchard & MacDonald, 1980). Of course misuse increases the error rate.

Doctors fear that diagnostic errors with home pregnancy tests may lead to serious health hazards. For example, the early stages of uterine cancer may produce a false positive reading and thereby delay treatment of the cancer. Assured by a false negative that she is not pregnant, a woman might continue to take drugs or smoke, thereby threatening the well-being of her unborn child. A doctor's visit costs money, but it is well worth the precaution if pregnancy is a possibility. There are also clinics, such as those run by Planned Parenthood, that give pregnancy tests for a minimal charge or free.

The following comments capture some of the feelings that a woman may have as the early signs of pregnancy begin to appear.

> Your period is late.
>
> Well, there's nothing unusual in that, you tell yourself. You just need a good night's sleep, or maybe you're catching a cold.
>
> After a few days, you say, "It's late because I'm anxious." You try to think about something else. You try so hard you can hardly bring yourself to wake up in the morning—as long as you stay asleep, you don't have to think about anything at all. "I'm exhausted," you say, "that's why it's late."
>
> After a week has gone by, it begins to look as if your period is not just late, it is altogether absent.
>
> Even that is not so unusual. You have heard of many women who have skipped periods completely during times of stress or illness. You begin to search your memory for other things you have heard—about hot baths that bring on delayed menstruation, about running up five flights of stairs, jumping off porches, taking laxatives. But mixed in with the hearsay and old wives' tales, you cannot force out of your mind one hard fact:
>
> You had intercourse last month, so the odds are more than even that you are pregnant.
>
> This is somehow unthinkable if you have not planned to be pregnant, and especially if you have never been pregnant before. It is *your* body, known, familiar; you realize in an abstract way that it is equipped for pregnancy, but the idea that it should suddenly begin to function in this strange and unfamiliar way without your willing or intending it seems utterly unreasonable. How can it happen to you? (Guttmacher, 1973, pp. 1–2)

The average duration of pregnancy is 266 days, or thirty-eight weeks, from the time of conception. For the first two months the developing baby is called an **embryo**; after that it is called a **fetus**. The change in name denotes that all of the parts are now present. The sequence of its development is shown in Table 12-1.

Environmental Causes of Congenital Problems

Although the developing fetus is in a well-protected environment, negative influences from outside may still affect it. Sometimes these outside elements cause

Embryo
The developing organism from the second to the eighth week of pregnancy, characterized by differentiation of organs and tissues into their human form

Fetus
The developing organism from the eighth week after conception until birth

---

Inset 12-1

Cocaine Babies

A pattern of abnormalities and suffering endured by cocaine babies is beginning to emerge. Many of these babies begin life in an agonizing state of withdrawal that may last up to three weeks. Such babies now make up more than one-half of the drug-associated births reported to the Los Angeles Department of Children's Services.

At eight months, Aaron is about the size of an infant half his age. Listless and uncoordinated, he has yet to sit up by himself. His eyes are red-rimmed and appear unable to focus on anything for any length of time. It may be that he is partially blind.

One study done at Northwestern Memorial Hospital in Chicago found that coke users had an extremely high incidence of miscarriage (38 percent). In some cases spontaneous abortion occurred immediately following use of cocaine (Chasnoff et al., 1985). In addition, since the drug causes dramatic fluctuations in blood pressure, it may deprive the fetal brain of oxygen or cause fragile vessels to burst, the prenatal equivalent of a stroke.

Cocaine babies seem to have higher than normal rates of respiratory and kidney troubles, and some suspect a link with sudden infant death syndrome.

It is clear that with an estimated 5 million Americans using cocaine on a regular basis, more and more cocaine-addicted and/or damaged infants will be born. As one researcher warns, "For pregnant women, there is no such thing as 'recreational' drug use" (Chasnoff et al., 1985).

Source: Adapted from *Time*, 1986.

Congenital defect
A condition existing at birth or before, as distinguished from a genetic defect

Genetic defect
An abnormality in the development of the fetus that is inherited through the genes, as distinguished from a congenital defect

Umbilical cord
A flexible cordlike structure connecting the fetus to the placenta and through which the fetus is fed and waste products are discharged

Placenta
The organ that connects the fetus to the uterus by means of the umbilical cord

birth defects, which are called **congenital defects**. (These should not be confused with **genetic defects**, which are inherited through the genes.)

The developing fetus gets its nourishment from the mother's blood through the **umbilical cord** and **placenta**. There is no direct intermingling of the blood, though some substances the mother takes in can be transmitted to the fetus. When you consider the extremely small size of the fetus during its early months, you can see how a small amount of a substance can do a lot of harm.

Drugs   If the mother uses narcotics, such as heroin (and also methadone) or cocaine (see Inset 12-1), the child will be born addicted and will suffer withdrawal symptoms if it is not given the drug and then gradually withdrawn from it.

Furthermore, most common prescription drugs affect the fetus. According to The Boston Women's Health Book Collective (1984, pp. 33–40), some antihistamines may produce malformations. General anesthetics at high concentrations may also produce malformations. Cortisone crosses the placenta and may cause alterations in the fetus. Antithyroid may cause goiter in infants, and tetracycline may deform babies' bones and stain teeth.

Among other drugs thought to damage the human fetus are the antibiotics streptomycin and sulfonamides taken near the end of pregnancy; excessive amounts of vitamins A, D, B_6, and K; certain barbiturates, opiates, and other central nervous system depressants when taken near the time of delivery; and the synthetic hormone progestin, which can masculinize the female fetus. The most commonly prescribed tranquilizers, chlordiazepoxide (Librium) and meprobamate (Equanil and Miltown), and diazepam (Valium) may cause defects when taken early in pregnancy (for a more complete discussion of the effects of drugs on the fetus, see Olds, London, & Ladewig, 1984, pp. 360–362). The most widely publicized

instance of drug-related birth defects came from the widespread use of thalidomide in Europe. Thalidomide was a very effective sleeping pill and tranquilizer,
believed to be safer than most other sedatives. It was widely used in Europe
during the 1960s and was sampled by many women in the United States before
cases of seriously deformed babies began to receive attention. Many of these
children had only small, flipperlike appendages attached to their shoulders rather
than arms and hands. Others had stunted arms and legs.

Infectious Diseases   Certain infectious diseases contracted by the mother, especially during the first three months of pregnancy, may harm the developing
fetus. The best known of these is German measles (rubella), which can cause
blindness, deafness, or heart defects in the child. Some women who contract
German measles elect to have an abortion rather than risk having a deformed
child.

Sexually transmitted diseases also affect the fetus. Herpes (see p. 348), for
example, can cause a spontaneous abortion, inflammation of the brain, or other
brain damage. Sexually transmitted diseases can be contracted by the newborn
baby. If the mother has syphilis, the baby will have the symptoms of the second
and last syphilitic stages (see p. 348). Gonorrhea can affect the newborn's eye-
sight; as a precaution, silver nitrate or another prophylactic agent is applied to the
eyes of all newborns. This safeguard has almost totally eradicated the problem.
AIDS can also be passed on to the unborn child by an infected mother (see pp.
351–355). There is some question that AIDS might be passed on to an infant
through the infected mother's milk as well although little research has yet been
done on this topic.

Smoking   Smoking adversely affects pregnancy. It increases the risk of spontaneous abortion, of premature birth, and of low birth weight in babies carried to
term. Premature birth and low birth weight increase the chances of infant sickness
and death. Babies of smoking mothers also remain smaller for some time than
babies of nonsmoking mothers. Pregnant women are advised to cut down on
their smoking or stop altogether (U.S. Surgeon General, 1985).

Cigarette smoking by the father may also have adverse effects on the fetus.
First, the mother may inhale smoke secondarily when the father smokes. Second,
there is some evidence that male cigarette smokers are more apt to produce
abnormal sperm, which in turn can produce an abnormal fetus (*Science News*,
1981).

Alcohol   Fetal alcohol syndrome (FAS), first identified in 1973, affects a large
proportion of babies born to chronically alcoholic mothers. In fact the U.S. Public
Health Service suggests that FAS is now the leading cause of birth defects in the
United States (U.S. Public Health Service, 1984). FAS includes retarded growth,
subnormal intelligence, and lagging motor development. Affected infants also
show alcohol withdrawal symptoms such as tremors, irritability, and spontaneous
seizures. Even when the children are of normal intelligence, they often have a
disproportionate amount of academic failure (Shaywitz, Cohen & Shaywitz, 1980).

What about moderate drinking during pregnancy? Even moderate occasional
social drinking has been shown to have possible harmful effects. In a study of
over 30,000 women, researchers found that those who drank as few as one to
three drinks per day had a higher risk of miscarriage during the second trimester

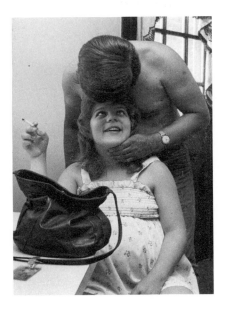

than women who did not drink (Harlap & Shiono, 1980). Another study found that only 8.1 percent of nondrinking mothers miscarried, whereas 17 percent of women who drank twice a week or more miscarried (Kline et al., 1980).

Radiation   Radiation, of course, penetrates the mother's body, so it will also reach and affect the fetus. The worst abnormalities occur if the mother is X-rayed during the first three months of pregnancy, when the embryo's major organs are developing. Even one pelvic X ray can cause gross fetal defects during this period. Thus, if pregnancy is suspected, a woman should avoid all X rays, even dental X rays, especially early in the pregnancy.

Rh factor

An element found in the blood of most people that can adversely affect fetal development if the parents differ on the element (Rh negative versus Rh positive)

Rh Blood Disease   The **Rh factor** (named for the rhesus monkey, in whose blood it was first isolated) is a chemical that lies on the surface of the red blood cells in most people. People with the chemical are considered Rh positive; those without are Rh negative. Only about 15 percent of white and 7 percent of black Americans are Rh negative. If a child inherits Rh positive blood from the father but the mother is Rh negative, the fetus's Rh positive factor is perceived as a foreign substance by the mother's body. Like a disease, it causes the mother's body to produce antibodies in her blood. If these enter the fetus through a capillary rupture in the placental membrane, they destroy red blood cells, which can lead to anemia, jaundice, and eventual death unless corrective steps are taken. Only small amounts, if any, of the child's antibody-stimulating Rh factor reach the mother through the placenta during pregnancy, so the first child is usually safe. However, during delivery the afterbirth (placenta and remaining umbilical cord) loosens and bleeds, releasing the Rh positive substance into the mother, which causes her system to produce antibodies. Once these are produced, she is much more easily stimulated to produce them during future pregnancies involving Rh positive children. Each succeeding child will be more affected than the previous one. With complete replacement of the child's blood at birth, many can be saved. An even better treatment is now available that essentially eradicates Rh problems. An Rh immunoglobulin that blocks the mother's immune system can be injected into the mother, thereby preventing production of the antibodies that attack the red blood cells of the fetus. (See Olds, London & Ladewig, 1984 for a more complete discussion.)

Controlling Birth Defects

Once a woman learns that she is pregnant, she should arrange for regular visits to a physician. Regular prenatal care will help avoid birth defects and dispel any fears she may have.

Diet   The expectant mother should eat a well-balanced diet with plenty of fluids. Inasmuch as the mother's diet has a direct effect on the fetus, she should consult her doctor if there is any doubt about the adequacy of the diet. Protein and vitamin deficiencies can cause physical weakness, stunted growth, rickets, scurvy, and even mental retardation in the fetus (Boston Women's Health Book Collective, 1984, pp. 329–332). Poor diet can also cause spontaneous abortions and stillbirths. The pregnant woman may find that she cannot eat large meals early in pregnancy if she feels nauseous. In late pregnancy the uterus takes up so much room that she may again be unable to eat large amounts. In both cases she should eat small amounts more often and avoid going for long periods without food.

An inadequate diet leaves the mother more prone to illness and complications during pregnancy, both of which may cause premature birth or low birth weight. As we have seen, premature and low-birth-weight babies are more prone to illness and possible death than normal-term babies. Women whose finances are inadequate for them to eat well during pregnancy and nursing can get help from the Women, Infants, and Children program (WIC), a supplemental food program sponsored by the government. This program provides milk, fruit, cereal, juice, cheese, and eggs. (Contact your local public health office for information about this program.)

In the past women have attempted to limit weight gain during pregnancy to some specified amount such as twenty pounds. Since each woman's metabolism is different, it is impossible to forecast just how much weight a given woman should gain to remain healthy. Certainly pregnancy is not the time to diet.

Amniocentesis   A test has been developed for detecting genetic defects, such as Down's syndrome (formerly called mongolism), amino acid disorders, hemophilia, and muscular dystrophy. The procedure, called **amniocentesis**, involves taking a sample of the amniotic fluid and studying sloughed-off fetal cells found in it. Amniocentesis should be done between the fourteenth and sixteenth weeks of pregnancy. The test can be performed in a doctor's office, though the laboratory work will take another fourteen to eighteen days to complete. The test also reveals the fetus's sex.

It is well to have the test if you have already had a child with a hereditary biochemical disease, if you are a carrier of hemophilia or muscular dystrophy, if you have already had a child with a genetic abnormality, and if you are over forty because the risk of having a child with a genetic abnormality increases with age. If the test indicates the presence of a birth defect, the woman, her husband, and the doctor can discuss their options, including possible abortion.

Amniocentesis is not risk-free. The technique can induce miscarriage, but this occurs in less than 1 percent of cases. Other problems such as infection and injury to the fetus also occur in about 1 percent of cases (Olds, London & Ladewig, 1984, p. 381).

Ultrasound in Obstetrics   **Ultrasonography,** generally considered safe and non-invasive, has become a major means of obtaining data about the placenta, fetus, and fetal organs during pregnancy. It can replace the X ray as a method of viewing the developing child in the uterus, thus avoiding radiation exposure for both mother and child (Hobbins, 1982; Olds, London, & Ladewig, 1984). It is also simpler than X rays because the picture is immediately available.

Ultrasound works on the principle that different tissues give off different-speed echoes of high-frequency sound waves directed at them. Moving a transducer (sound emitter) across the mother's abdomen creates an echogram outline of the fetus and its various organs (see Figure 12-5). Using a "real time" transducer that gives off several simultaneous signals from slightly differing sources, will produce a picture showing movement of the different organs, such as the heart. The echogram allows the physician to learn about the position, size, and state of development of the fetus at any time after about the first ten weeks of pregnancy. For example, the procedure can tell a physician if the fetus will be born in the normal headfirst position or in some problem position.

Amniocentesis
A prenatal diagnostic procedure in which a long hollow needle is inserted through the mother's abdomen into the amniotic sac to obtain a sample of amniotic fluid, which is analyzed for signs of defect or disease

Ultrasound
Sound waves directed at the fetus that yield a visual picture of the fetus; used to detect potential problems in fetal development

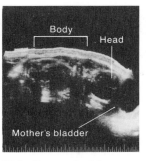

Figure 12-5   Sonograph of fetus.

Figure 12-6 The fetoscopy procedure.

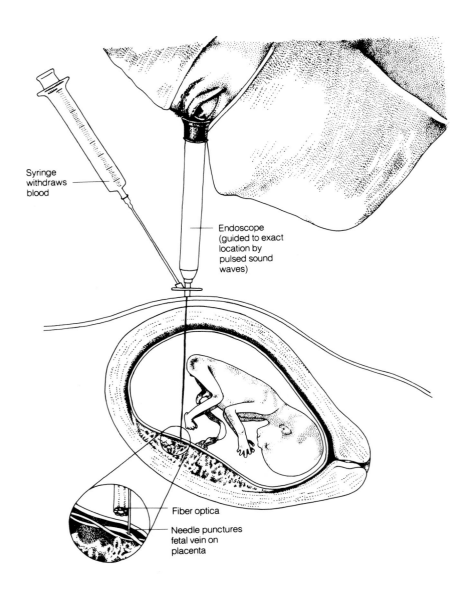

Syringe
withdraws
blood

Endoscope
(guided to exact
location by
pulsed sound
waves)

Fiber optica

Needle punctures
fetal vein on
placenta

Fetoscopy

Examining the fetus through a small viewing tube inserted into the mother's uterus

Fetoscopy Fetoscopy, a delicate procedure usually performed some fifteen to twenty weeks into pregnancy, allows direct examination of the fetus. First, an ultrasound scan locates the fetus, the umbilical cord, and the placenta. The physician then makes a small incision in the abdomen and inserts a pencil-lead-thin tube into the amniotic sac. The tube contains an endoscope with fiber-optic bundles that transmit light. This light-containing tube enables the physician to see tiny areas of the fetus. By inserting biopsy forceps into the tube, the physician can take a 1 mm skin sample from the fetus. A blood sample can also be drawn by inserting a needle through the tube and puncturing one of the fetal blood vessels lying on the surface of the placenta (see Figure 12-6). The technique induces miscarriage in about 5 percent of cases, while the rate for amniocentesis is less than 1 percent. Since ultrasound has come into use, the need for this procedure has lessened (Olds, London, & Ladewig, 1984, p. 388). It is still used to diagnose various skin malformations and some diseases such as sickle-cell anemia (Hobbins, 1982).

Intercourse during Pregnancy

Although some people regard intercourse during pregnancy with suspicion, research indicates that it is usually not harmful (Olds, London, & Ladewig, 1984, pp. 263–265; Boston Women's Health Book Collective, 1984, pp. 348–349). Indeed, couples should not lose the close contact as well as physical enjoyment afforded through intercourse. There is evidence that for some women erotic feelings increase during the second trimester of pregnancy. By the third trimester, however, most women lose sexual interest to a degree.

Couples should exercise some care to avoid excessive pressure on the woman's abdomen, deep penile penetration, and infection. Because the uterine contractions of orgasm are similar to labor contractions, intercourse should be avoided during the last three weeks of pregnancy. Spotting, bleeding, or pain also contraindicates intercourse. In the later stages of pregnancy, the rear entry position with the woman lying on her side is usually the most comfortable (McCary & McCary, 1982).

If a woman has miscarried or has been warned that she is apt to miscarry, she should avoid intercourse during the first three months of pregnancy, especially around the time her period would be due. In most normal pregnancies, however, intercourse poses no real threat. Indeed, some doctors suggest that the contractions of orgasm are helpful to pregnancy because they strengthen the uterine muscles. Intercourse also provides exercise for the muscles of the pelvic floor. And focusing on the feelings of complete relaxation after orgasm can help one learn to relax during labor contractions.

Many women report that sex is important to them during pregnancy. They believe that continued sexual contact maintains close emotional ties with their husbands. To them their husbands' interest shows acceptance of the pregnancy and of their changing body shape. In other words, sexual contact means tenderness, caring, sharing, and love. Many women also feel freer in their sexual behavior because they obviously no longer need fear pregnancy. To hold one another, to caress, to be intimate is important as birth draws near. It will help allay anxieties and let both partners know that they are not alone but have loving support.

Birth

By the time nine months have passed, the mother-to-be is usually anxious to have her child. She has probably gained twenty to twenty-five pounds. This extra weight is distributed approximately as follows:

Amniotic fluid: 2 pounds

Baby: 7 to 8 pounds

Breast enlargement: 2 pounds

Placenta: 1 pound

Retained fluids and fat: 6 + pounds

Uterine enlargement: 2 pounds

There are two objections to gaining too much weight during pregnancy: Excessive weight can strain the circulatory system and heart, and many women find it difficult to lose the extra weight after the baby is born. On the other hand, dieting during pregnancy to remain within an arbitrary weight-gain limit is also risky because, as we pointed out earlier, good nutrition is important during pregnancy.

Although 266 days is the average length of time a child is carried, the normal range varies from 240 days to 300 days. It is therefore difficult for the physician to be exact when estimating the time of delivery. In fact, there is only about a 50 percent chance that a child will be born within a week of the date the doctor determines. In general the expected birth date will probably come and go without any sign of imminent birth. This can be wearisome for the expectant mother, but it is perfectly normal.

Perinatal Mortality

Perinatal deaths refer to the sum of spontaneous fetal deaths occurring after twenty weeks gestation plus infant deaths occurring during the first twenty-seven days following birth. Between 1950 and 1981 the perinatal mortality rate in the United States declined 61 percent, from 32.5 to 12.6 per 1000 live births and fetal deaths. This decline was generally continuous throughout the period.

Perinatal mortality differentials between white and all other populations remained relatively constant over the 1950 to 1981 period, reflecting similar percentage decreases for other groups. In 1981 the ratio of rates was 1.55 or half again higher for other groups compared to whites. This is probably accounted for by the generally better prenatal care that whites enjoy compared to other groups.

The sex differential in perinatal mortality declined between 1950 and 1981. For all races combined, approximately 130 males died for every 100 females in 1950, compared to only 119 in 1982. (All statistics in this section are from National Center for Health Statistics, March 31, 1986.)

Labor

Three to four weeks before birth, the fetus "drops" slightly lower in the uterus (called lightening) and is normally in a headfirst position (see Figures 12-7 and 12-8). The cervix (the opening to the uterus) begins to soften and dilate (open). There may be occasional contractions of the uterus, which women pregnant for the first time may mistake for labor (false labor). These early contractions are irregular and are usually not painful.

Essentially, there are three stages of **labor**. The first two are illustrated in Figure 12-8. The *first stage* is the longest, lasting eight to twenty hours on the average for the first child and three to eight hours for subsequent children. During this time the cervix must dilate enough for the baby to pass through. (The contracted and closed cervix has held the baby in the uterus until now.) The sac of **amniotic fluid**, a salt solution that suspends, cushions, and maintains the embryo at an even temperature, will break some time during the labor process, except in about 10 percent of women who experience breaking shortly before labor begins. The uterine contractions become more frequent and longer lasting until the baby finally descends into the birth canal (vagina). During this first stage there is little the mother can do except rest, try to relax, and remain as comfortable as possible.

Labor
Changes in a woman's body as it prepares to deliver a child, consisting mainly of muscle contractions and dilation of the cervix

Amniotic fluid
The fluid that surrounds and insulates the fetus in the mother's womb

Figure 12-7 The position of the fetus before birth.

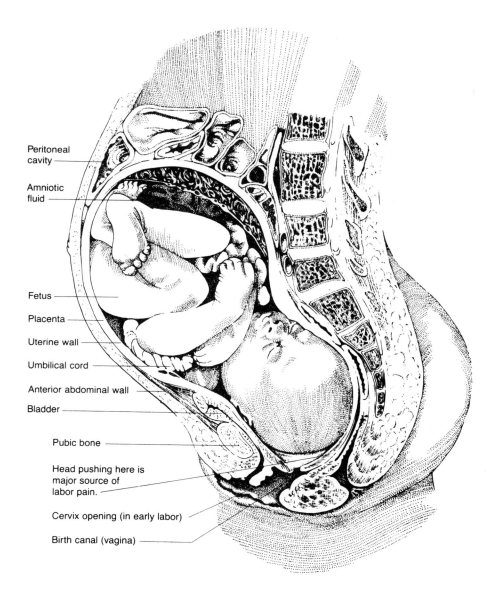

Peritoneal
cavity

Amniotic
fluid

Fetus

Placenta

Uterine wall

Umbilical cord

Anterior abdominal wall

Bladder

Pubic bone

Head pushing here is
major source of
labor pain.

Cervix opening (in early labor)

Birth canal (vagina)

At first the contractions may be thirty minutes apart, but gradually they will
come more often until they occur every few minutes. The expectant mother
should go to the hospital as soon as she ascertains that she is having regular
labor pains (see Inset 12-2).

Transition is the term used to describe the baby coming through the cervix
and the commencement of the *second stage* of labor. In the second stage the
uterine contractions push the child down through the vagina into the outside world
with about a hundred pounds of force. During this stage the mother can actively
help the process by pushing or bearing down, thereby adding another fifteen
pounds or so to the pressure created by the uterine contractions. This stage may
be as short as fifteen to twenty minutes or can last an hour or two.

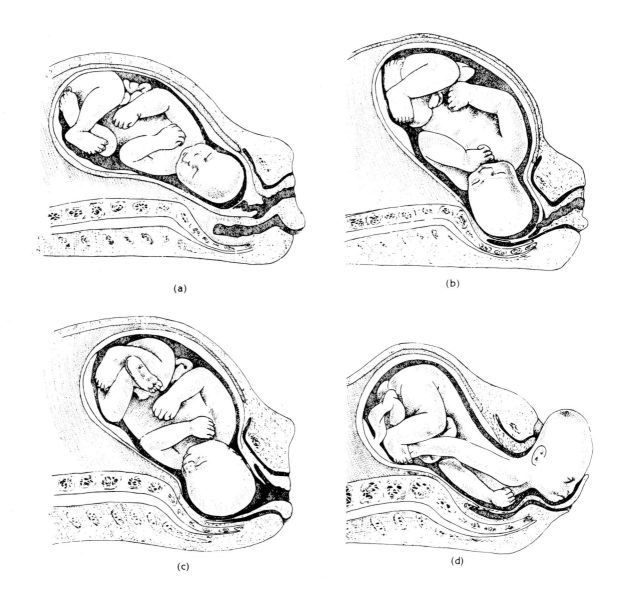

(a)

(b)

(c)

(d)

Figure 12-8 Events in the birth process:
(a) before labor begins; (b) early stages of
labor, dilation of cervix begins; (c) cervix
completely dilated; baby's head starts to
turn; (d) late stage of labor; baby's head begins to emerge.

The *third stage* is delivering the afterbirth or detached placenta, which occurs
five to twenty minutes after the birth of the child. During this time the uterus
contracts and begins to return to its normal size, and there is minor bleeding.
Normally this stage lasts for only a few minutes.

Although there is a certain amount of pain connected with a normal birth,
knowledge of the birth process and the source of labor pain and a relaxed and
confident mental attitude will reduce such pain to a minimum. It is wise for both
expectant parents to take childbirth preparation classes. Local Red Cross units,
county health facilities, and adult education programs usually offer such courses.
As mentioned earlier, prenatal care from a doctor should be sought as soon as
one becomes pregnant. Although most births are normal, a small number will

---

Inset 12-2

Guide to First-Stage Labor Progress

Signs of Labor

1. Bloody show/mucous plug
2. Gush of water
3. Contractions

Real labor will include item 3 and may or may not include items 1 and 2. You may have "false labor" for days or weeks before the onset of real labor. Your due date is not always the best guide to when labor will start.

Ways to Check for Real Labor

1. Change of activity does not change contractions.
2. Contractions increase in length.
3. Contractions become closer together.
4. Contractions increase in intensity.

Call the Doctor When

1. Contractions are ten minutes apart or less, lasting forty-five to sixty seconds or more for one hour.
2. Bag of water breaks.
3. Anything more than a bloody show appears from vagina.
4. Anything unusual happens.

Early Labor

1. The cervix is thinning and opening or dilating slightly.
2. Labor is generally easy at this point and spirits high.
3. Continue your activities and pay attention—it's fun.

It's the Real Thing

1. Contractions are regular now and the cervix is opening.
2. Spirits are high, but the realization that labor is work is starting to dawn.
3. Relax and use slow easy abdominal breathing. Going to bed is not necessary unless desired.

Late Labor

1. This is really hard work. Contractions are intense and close.
2. It takes real concentration on relaxation and abdominal breathing.
3. Birth is getting near.

Transition

1. Confusion is perhaps the best definition. Changing gears going from first-stage contractions to second-stage contractions.
2. Contractions may get closer together or farther apart.
3. Ride with each contraction; it may be your last in first stage.
4. The urge to push signals second stage.

---

be abnormal, such as when the child presents buttocks first (breech presentation) rather than head first (see Figure 12-9). In many cases the doctor can recognize the potential problem and be prepared ahead of time.

Fetal Monitoring

Within the past few years **fetal monitoring** during birth has become specialized. During labor electronic sensors are placed on the mother's abdomen, and in the second stage of birth an electrode is attached to the baby's scalp. These electrodes record the baby's heartbeat as well as the uterine contractions. Ultrasound techniques also display a picture of the baby and offer another measure of heartbeat.

Fetal monitoring
Using various instruments to measure the vital signs of the fetus during the birth process

Figure 12-9 Atypical fetal positions at birth: (a) breech presentation, with fetus in buttocks-first position; (b) transverse position, with fetus's head at one side of the uterus and its buttocks at the other.

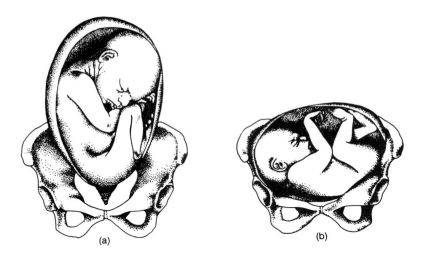

(a)   (b)

These monitoring techniques allow the physician to monitor the baby's condition closely. Fetal distress can be recognized more quickly than in the past when only external monitoring methods were used.

Considerable criticism has been aimed at this kind of technical monitoring, mainly because it is associated with increased cesarean births. However, many claim that such monitoring has reduced infant mortality rates. For example, in 1950 California had an infant death rate of 24.9 per thousand live births. By 1984 that rate had dropped to 9.7 infant deaths. It seems obvious that monitoring of both mother and baby during birth can be important to successful birth. Whether monitoring leads to unnecessary cesarean births, as some critics claim, is a separate question that should be investigated rather than put forward as an argument to cease monitoring.

Cesarean Section

Cesarean section
The delivery of a baby by means of a surgical incision through the mother's abdominal and uterine walls

From as early as 1882, under certain circumstances, such as when a baby is too large to pass through the mother's pelvis or when labor is very long and hard, the baby has been removed via a **cesarean section**. In this operation an incision is made through the abdominal and uterine walls and the baby is removed. The recovery period is longer than for a normal birth. Although many people believe to the contrary, it is possible for a woman to have several babies in this manner or to have one by cesarean section and the next normally.

The popular but erroneous legend that Julius Caesar was delivered surgically gives the operation its name. Probably the term *cesarean* originated from an ancient Roman law, which was later incorporated into a legal code called the Lex Caesarea. This statute, aimed at trying to save the child's life, made it mandatory that an operation be performed on a woman who might otherwise die in the advanced stages of pregnancy (McCary & McCary, 1982).

Recently the percentage of cesarean section births has increased, rising to around 20 percent of all births (Blakeslee, 1985) and even higher in specific hospitals. This represents a fourfold increase in the past decade. This has led to controversy because the cesarean section is more traumatic to the mother's body than natural birth. Of course it is far less traumatic to the child because there is no prolonged pressure on the child as there is in the normal birth process.

Hospitals contend that better monitoring of the child just before birth and throughout the procedure leads to early recognition of possible problems and that many of these can be headed off by a cesarean section. They admit that monitoring has led to a higher proportion of cesareans but point out that it has also reduced infant mortality. However, it appears that some of the increase in cesarean births stems from the desire of parents to have a "perfect" baby and the ensuing fear on the part of the delivering doctor that legal action will be taken against him if the baby is less than "perfect."

The incidence of infection associated with cesarean delivery is about five to ten times higher than with vaginal deliveries (Hawrylyshyn et al., 1981). Many women's groups criticize the increasing use of cesarean delivery, feeling that most are unnecessary and are not done in the best interests of the mother (Boston Women's Health Book Collective, 1984, pp. 384–386).

Birth Pain

The uterine contractions, which are simple muscle contractions, usually don't cause pain, though prolonged or overly strong contractions can cause cramping. The majority of pain arises from the pressure of the baby's head (the largest and hardest part of the baby at the time of birth) against the cervix, the opening into the birth canal. In the early stages of labor, the contractions of the uterus push the child's head against the still-contracted cervix and this point becomes the major source of pain. By trying to relax at the onset of a contraction, by breathing more shallowly to raise the diaphragm, and by lying on her side with knees somewhat drawn up, a woman can reduce labor pain to a minimum.

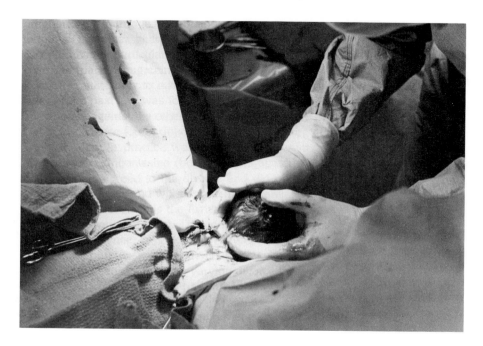

Once the child's head passes through the cervix, there is little or no pain as it passes on through the vagina. Hormonal action has softened the vagina to such an extent that it can stretch up to seven times its normal size. An additional difficulty may occur at birth as the child passes out of the mother into the outside world. There is often a slight tearing of the perineum, or skin between the vaginal and anal openings, because the skin may have to stretch beyond its limits to allow the infant to exit. In most cases the doctor will make a small incision called an *episiotomy* so that the skin does not tear. The incision is sewn after the delivery. Sometimes massage can be used to stretch the skin enough so tearing will not occur, especially if the infant is small.

Natural Childbirth

Natural childbirth
Birth wherein the parents have learned about the birthing process and partici-pate via exercises such as breathing techniques so as to minimize pain

In recent years many women have sought an alternative to the automatic use of anesthesia and the rather mechanical way many American hospitals have handled childbirth. Many years ago (1932) Grantly Dick-Read coined the phrase **natural childbirth** and suggested in his book *Childbirth without Fear* that understanding of birth procedures by the mother could break the pattern of fear, tension, and pain too often associated with childbirth (Dick-Read, 1972). Natural childbirth thus means knowledgeable childbirth, not simply childbirth without anesthesia or at home.

General anesthesia for childbirth has become much less popular, even in hospitals, because it slows labor and depresses the child's activity, making the birth more difficult even though less painful. All systemic drugs used for pain relief during labor cross the placental barrier by simple diffusion. Although such drugs affect the fetus, so do pain and stress experienced by the mother. With-holding medication from tense, anxious laboring women may not accomplish the intended goal of reducing fetal problems (Olds, London, & Ladewig, 1984, p. 511). Generally, however, using systemic drugs with women in labor should be mini-mized. The caudal or spinal block is another method used to ease maternal discomfort during childbirth. The spinal block produces a temporary loss of feeling below the waist. It is normally given in stage two of labor, when the baby has passed into the birth canal or vagina. Advocates of natural childbirth question the value of this procedure because most of the mother's pain is over once the child is in the birth canal.

More common today is paracervical anesthesia, which involves injection of novocaine or a similar pain-killing substance into the area around the cervix. This quickly deadens the area, blocking out the pain. It is similar to being injected in the gums around a tooth that is to be filled. The anesthetic action is localized and has little if any effect on the baby, and the mother is completely conscious and able to participate in the birth.

Hypnosis is also being used more frequently during labor and delivery to help relax the mother and reduce her sensations of pain. It is particularly useful for women who cannot tolerate the drugs used in anesthesia. It cannot be used with everyone and requires a knowledgeable doctor. Those who use it report relaxed and relatively uncomplicated deliveries.

Today, more and more physicians are letting the woman decide whether she wants an anesthetic and if so, what type. It is important that the expectant mother is informed of the benefits and disadvantages of the available forms of anesthesia so that she can make her choice intelligently.

A couple interested in natural childbirth will find that numerous sources of training and information are available. (There are a number of sources of free information on natural childbirth. You can write to the American Society for Psychoprophylaxis in Obstetrics, 36 West 96th Street, New York, NY 10025; the Association of Mothers for Educated Childbirth (concerned with home delivery), Box 9030, Far Rockaway, NY 11691; and the International Childbirth Education Association/Education Committee, Box 22, Hillside, NJ 07205.)

As mentioned earlier, Red Cross facilities, county medical units, and evening adult schools often provide childbirth preparation classes. The classes provide information on the birth process, what to expect, and how to facilitate the natural processes. The woman is also taught physical exercises that will help prepare her body for the coming birth. She learns techniques of breathing to help the natural processes along and to reduce the amount of pain she would otherwise experience.

We have already noted that one of the basic principles underlying natural childbirth is that knowledge reduces fear and reduced fear means less tension and pain. The other basic principle of natural childbirth is to make the mother and father active participants in the birth of their child rather than passive spectators. For instance, controlled breathing (with the father helping to pace the breathing) supplies the right amount of oxygen to the working muscles, giving them the energy they need to function efficiently. Voluntarily relaxing the other muscles helps to focus all energy on the laboring muscles. Another aspect of breathing exercises is to focus attention on responding to the contractions, which keeps attention from focusing on the pain. The Boston Women's Health Book Collective notes that selective attention doesn't

> give our minds time or room to register that we might be feeling pain. As a result, some women say they never really felt any pain during labor; others say that feelings of pain kept surfacing but that they were almost always able to control those feelings with increased concentration on the breathing techniques. One woman wrote that there was a kind of beauty in her acceptance of the pain she felt: "I don't think pain is necessarily bad. I had a short, hard labor, and it was clear to me that the incredible euphoria that I experienced afterward was in part a function of the fact that it was very painful. It really was almost positive pain, really worth it in retrospect." (1976, p. 275)

Inasmuch as the couple has decided to have the child together, it is also important that they learn together about the processes involved and that the father is not simply a spectator during labor and delivery. The couple will want to know if the hospital they plan to use will allow the father into the labor and delivery rooms so that he can be there to give psychological support and comfort to the mother. During the early stages of labor, he will be able to remind her of what to do as the contractions increase. He can keep track of the time intervals between contractions, monitor her breathing, remind her to relax, massage her (if she finds that a help), and keep her informed of her progress. In other words, he can help by *sharing* the experience. Several birthing methods (including Bradley and Lamaze) urge the father to learn about the birth process and actively participate. This also facilitates father-child bonding.

Once the baby has passed through the cervix into the birth canal (vagina) and

Inset 12-3

Birth without Violence: The Leboyer Method

What makes being born so frightful is the intensity, the boundless scope and variety of the experience, its suffocating richness.

People say—and believe—that a newborn baby feels nothing. He feels everything.

Everything—utterly, without choice or filter or discrimination.

Birth is a tidal wave of sensation, surpassing anything we can imagine. A sensory experience so vast we can barely conceive of it.

The baby's senses are at work. Totally.

They are sharp and open—new.

What are our senses compared to theirs?

And the sensations of birth are rendered still more intense by contrast with what life was before.

Admittedly, these sensations are not yet organized into integrated, coherent perceptions. Which makes them all the stronger, all the more violent, unbearable—literally maddening. (Leboyer, 1975, pp. 15–16)

Many theorists have hypothesized that the trauma of birth leaves an indelible mark on human personality. One of Freud's early followers, Otto Rank, suggested that the birth trauma is the major source of later problems that center around insecurity, because this trauma marks humans with a basic anxiety about life. . . .

The child emerges out of the quiet, warm, dark, secure environment of the womb into a bright, loud, cooler world, and its source of oxygen and nutrition, the umbilical cord, is immediately severed. The child is hung upside down, slapped, cleaned, and made to function immediately on its own. Little won-

der that the child screams, clenches its fist, and has an agonized look on its face. The sensation of the air rushing into its lungs for the first time must be a searing experience. Add to this all of the other new experiences, and life must seem a cacophony of terrifying intensity.

Frederick Leboyer simply tells us to listen to the child. Let the child guide us through the first few minutes after birth. Leboyer's four basic steps are simple. First, once delivery is imminent, reduce the light and be quiet. The infant's vision and hearing will then not be immediately assaulted. Second, as soon as the infant is out, place it comfortably on the mother's warm abdomen, which will serve as a nest for the child. Let the child retain the prebirth curved position of the spine until ready of its own accord to straighten and stretch. Third, do not cut the umbilical cord until the child's own systems are functioning smoothly, six to ten minutes after birth. This way the child is doubly supplied with oxygen and there will be no period of possible deficit and related alarm reaction and ensuing terror. During this time the mother and doctor gently massage the child, simulating the environmental contact the child has so long enjoyed within the mother. Fourth, once the cord stops pulsating, cut it and bathe the baby in water similar in temperature to the familiar environment from which it recently emerged. During this time also hold the baby and massage it gently. The hands make love to the child, not briskly rubbing nor timidly caressing, but deeply and slowly massaging just as the child felt

within the womb. The child makes contact with the world at a pace that is comfortable for it. And how long might this be? Perhaps ten to twenty minutes is all. Is this too much to ask for a child at this most eventful time in its life?

And what of the Leboyer-born children's later personalities? It might be too early to tell, but they seem noticeably different, especially in their unusually avid interest in the world around them. Does fear and terror at birth cause many of the problems felt by adult humans? Will reducing the impact of birth on the child help that child become an adult with fewer problems? Only time will tell. But shouldn't we try to reduce birth trauma and see what happens?

On the other hand, there are many doctors who feel that the Leboyer method does nothing. A study conducted at McMaster University Medical Centre in Hamilton, Ontario, compared twenty-eight infants delivered by the Leboyer method with twenty-six who had routine deliveries. The study reported no differences between the infants (Associated Press, 1980).

the doctor is present, things happen so fast and the woman is so involved with the imminent birth that the father's presence and help is less important.

Rooming-In

More and more hospitals are allowing **rooming-in**, which means that the mother is allowed to keep her baby with her, rather than having the child remain in a nursery. Rooming-in is especially helpful to the breastfeeding mother. Both mother and newborn benefit from the physical closeness, and the child will cry less because it will get attention and be fed when hungry. Many hospitals are planning for rooming-in by connecting the nursery to the mother's room, allowing her free access to her infant. In these hospitals the baby is placed in a drawerlike crib that the mother may pull into her room whenever she wants. If she is tired, she simply places the child in the drawer and pushes the infant back into the nursery where it is cared for.

Rooming-in
The practice of placing the newborn in the mother's room after delivery so that the mother (and father) can care for it

Alternative Birth Centers

Some hospitals have created **alternative birth centers**, homelike settings for child-birth. Relatives and friends are allowed to visit during much of the childbirth process. Barring complications, childbirth takes place in the same room that the mother is in during her entire stay at the center. Couples interested in such birth centers usually must apply in advance. The mother-to-be must be examined to be as certain as possible that she will have a normal delivery. In addition, the birth center usually requires that the couple attend childbirth classes. Birth centers are a compromise between normal hospital birth and home birth. It is part of the continuing trend by hospitals to make childbirth less mechanical and help couples participate as fully as possible. There are also numerous out-of-hospital birth centers now operating (Echegaray, 1982).

Alternative birth center
A special birth center that creates a homelike atmosphere for birth

Home Births

Some women prefer **home birth** to having their children in a hospital. At home the woman is in familiar surroundings, can choose her own attendants, and can follow whatever procedures soothe and encourage her (have music playing, for example). At home, birth is also a family affair.

The immediate question that comes to mind is, how safe is home birth? In Europe where home birth is common, statistics indicate that home birth is just as safe as hospital birth (Boston Women's Health Book Collective, 1984). American doctors do not agree and cite many instances of tragedy with home birth that could have been avoided in a hospital. The amount of risk can be reduced by careful prenatal screening of the mother and by providing backup emergency care. If the prenatal screening indicates conditions that might involve a complicated delivery, the woman should have her baby in a hospital that has the facilities to deal with possible problems.

The emergency backup for a home delivery should include a doctor, para-professional, nurse, or midwife to deal with any unforeseen problems. In the future it may be possible to set up some kind of mobile birth unit staffed by trained personnel. The unit, perhaps housed in a converted motor home, could either be parked outside the home or brought to the house by calling an emergency

Home birth
Giving birth at one's home rather than in a hospital

Midwife

A person, usually a woman, trained to assist in childbirth or, in some countries, to perform delivery

number. In case of emergency, the mother could be quickly shifted to the unit, which would contain any necessary equipment. Remember, though, that birth is a normal process; 85 to 95 percent of births do not involve any difficulties (Boston Women's Health Book Collective, 1984).

The **midwife** is an honored professional used by 80 percent of the world's population to attend childbirth (Olds, London, & Ladewig, 1984, p. 5). Midwives are used in home delivery in many modern countries such as Sweden and the Netherlands and were used in our country until the turn of the century, yet the organized medical profession and many others believe that delivery in the hospital by doctors is much safer. In addition, they believe that it would be difficult to enforce standards of competence if home delivery by midwives became widespread. England, on the other hand, has set high standards and has trained midwives since 1902. About 80,000 women are registered as midwives in England, of which about 21,000 are actively practicing. In 1970 about 75 percent of all births were midwife-assisted (*British Birth Survey 1970*, 1975). In England the obstetrician is the leader of the birth team and the midwife does the practical work. In Holland about 35 percent of Dutch women now choose to have their babies at home. Home birth is considered so safe that the national health insurance scheme, which pays for most births, will not pay for a hospital birth unless medically indicated (*Santa Barbara News Press*, August 1985).

In the United States certified nurse-midwives (CNM) are registered nurses who practice legally in the hospital setting. In 1982 there were 2598 CNMs in the United States (Olds, London, & Ladewig, 1984, p. 7). Some states do not allow them to perform home births. (For information on your state's midwife regulations and a list of CNMs in your area, contact The American College of Nurse-Midwives, 1522 K Street NW, Suite 1120, Washington, DC 20005.)

As interest in home births increases and as hospital costs soar (it now costs over $3000 to have a baby with standard hospitalization and delivery), the idea of midwifery is returning in the United States. Some states now have licensed training programs for midwives.

Breastfeeding

Attached to the natural childbirth philosophy is a strong emphasis on breastfeeding. There are many reasons for this emphasis, such as the fact that breastfeeding is more natural. The major reason that psychologists advocate breastfeeding, however, is that it brings the mother and child into close, warm physical contact. Inasmuch as feeding is the infant's first social contact, many experts, such as Erik Erikson (1963) and Ashley Montagu (1972), believe that this loving contact is necessary to the development of security and basic trust in the infant. Another advantage of breastfeeding derives from the secretion of colostrum. This substance is present in the breast immediately after birth and is secreted until the milk flows, usually three to four days after birth. It has a high protein content, but, most important, it is high in antibodies and helps make the child immune to many infectious diseases during infancy. Breastfeeding also causes hormones to be released that speed the uterus's return to normal. One should also count the warm, loving feelings that arise in the nursing mother as an advantage of breastfeeding.

The new mother needs to prepare for breastfeeding as well as understand the natural process if she is to be successful. Her breasts will be engorged, congested,

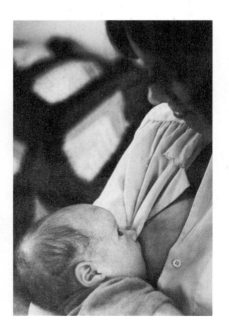

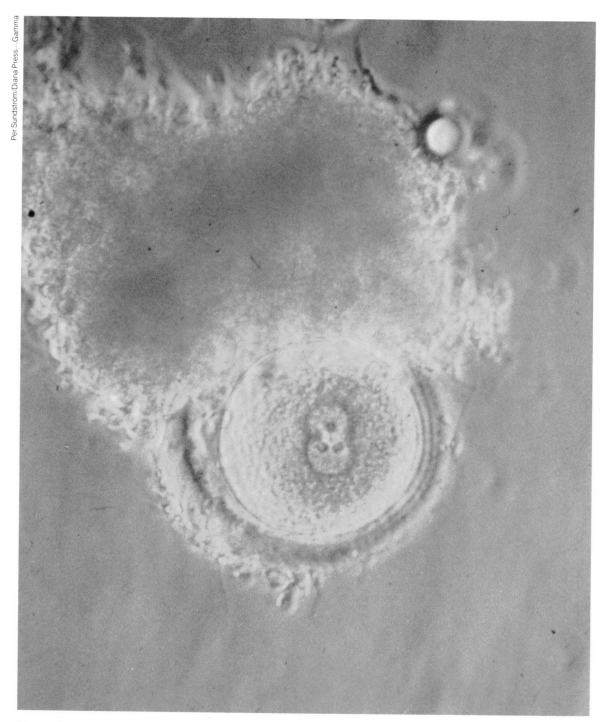

The round egg can be seen emerging from a group of cumulus-corona cells, which at ovulation completely surround the egg. On the egg's surface are thousands of spermatazoa, which look like small needles. The egg has been fertilized, and the two round structures in the center contain the chromosomes from the mother and father.

Spermatozoa in early stages of penetration on the moonlike landscape of the egg's shell.

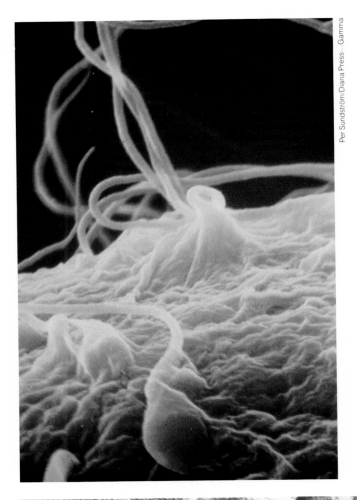

The womb (uterine wall) is prepared for implantation of the embryo. The surface is folded and consists of many kinds of blood-enriched cells.

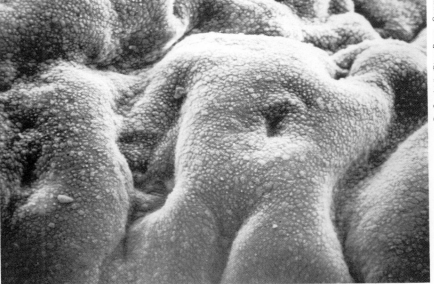

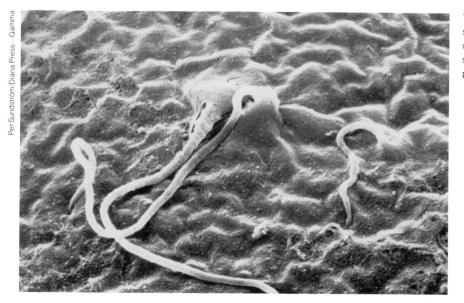

Three spermatozoa in different stages of penetration. Only part of the tail is seen of the leading spermatozoa (to the right of the photograph).

Human embryo in amniotic sac, approximately 8 weeks old.

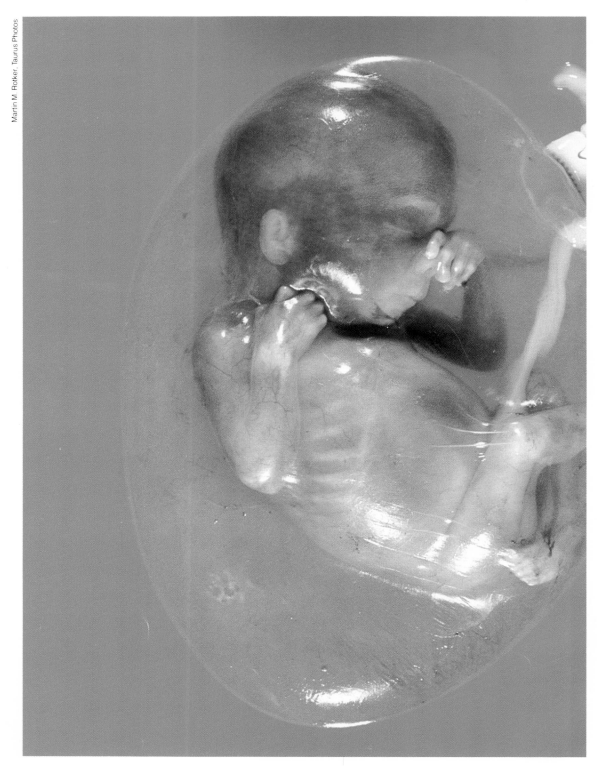

A 16-week-old fetus in amniotic sac.

Inset 12-4

Some Speculations about Breastfeeding and Sex

Only in the 1960s and 1970s did breastfeeding come back into vogue after forty years of unpopularity. One might ask why breastfeeding fell into disrepute. Although some new mothers claim that they can't breastfeed, investigation reveals few women who, for physiological reasons, cannot breastfeed. Rather it appears to be a problem of attitude or lack of knowledge.

One reason for a poor attitude may be the close association that has developed between a woman's breasts and her sexuality. Breast size and shape have, since World War II, be-come increasingly important to attractiveness and sexuality. But one need only remember the popularity of the flat-chested look of the 1920s flapper era to realize that large breasts have not always implied sexuality. In fact, in most primitive societies the breasts are left exposed because their primary function is for feeding rather than sexual arousal.

Because of the association between breasts and sexuality, some women may be afraid that breastfeeding will ruin their figure and decrease their sex appeal. In reality this need not happen. If the new mother exer-cises and watches her diet, she should be able to return her figure to normal within a reasonable time.

The woman who thinks of breasts only in sexual terms may also feel guilty about the pleasurable sensations she feels when her child nurses. She may confuse the maternal feelings elicited by the nursing with sexual feelings and feel guilt because of the deeply ingrained taboos surrounding incest.

Why do you think American women abandoned breastfeeding for so many years?

---

and painful for the first few days after birth. However, mothers who have rooming-in and who begin to breastfeed the baby from birth onward (the sucking reflex of a baby born to an unanesthetized mother is very strong), on the baby's demand, usually do not experience engorgement. The act of breastfeeding itself soon relieves the congestion. Before birth it is helpful if the mother massages her nipples to prepare them for the child's sucking. Otherwise, the nipples sometimes become chafed and sore. If this happens, exposing the nipples to the air will help.

Milk normally begins to flow between the third and fourth day. The baby is biologically prepared to maintain itself during these days, because it normally has a little surplus fat that sustains it until milk flow begins. Thus the mother does not need to worry that she will not be able to satisfy the infant's hunger during the first few days. (For more information on breastfeeding, contact La Leche League International, 9616 Minneapolis Avenue, Franklin Park, IL 60131).

In the words of Ashley Montagu, women should remember that "Over the five or more million years of human evolution, and as a consequence of seventy-five million years of mammalian evolution, breastfeeding has constituted the most successful means of administering to the needs of the dependent, precariously born human neonate" (1972, p. 80).

Although about 60 percent of American mothers breastfeed (up from 25 percent in 1970), many new parents decide to bottle feed (Parachine, 1985). With bottle feeding it is important to make sure the baby receives the holding and close bodily contact that breastfeeding supplies. The father can participate as well, in providing holding and physical contact for the baby.

At times the father is a forgotten person immediately after birth. Not only does

the mother occasionally suffer mild depression after birth, but the father may also suffer feelings of neglect, jealousy, and simply "being left out" after childbirth. The more of a partnership, the more sharing a couple can have in the whole process of conception, pregnancy, and childbirth, the more satisfaction both the father and mother will receive.

Postpartum Emotional Changes

The first few weeks and months of motherhood are known as the postpartum period. About 60 percent of all women who bear children report a mild degree of emotional depression ("baby blues") following the birth, and another 10 percent report severe depression (Clark, 1983; Boston Women's Health Book Collective, 1984, p. 397).

> Some of us are high, some are mellow, some of us are lethargic and depressed, or we are irritable and cry easily. Mood swings are common. We are confused and a little scared, because our moods do not resemble the way we are accustomed to feel, let alone the way we are expected to feel. If this is our first baby we may feel lonely and isolated from adult society. The special attention and consideration many of us receive as expectant mothers shift to the baby and we too are expected to put the baby's needs before our own. (Boston Women's Health Book Collective, 1973, p. 207)

Most women experience this mild postpartum depression between the second and fourth days after delivery. This may be due in part to the changing chemical balance within the woman's body as it readjusts to the nonpregnant state. This readjustment takes about six weeks. For most this depression passes quickly. The general emotional reactions to parenthood, especially with the first child, continue for a much longer period.

Summary

Pregnancy and childbirth are an integral part of most marriages. Despite the drop in the birthrate, and the increasing number of couples expressing the desire to remain childless, childbearing and rearing will be a part of the majority of people's lives. Knowledge of pregnancy and the birth process is important to the act of birth itself. Those who are knowledgeable stand a better chance of having a simple, uncomplicated childbirth.

Both the egg and sperm cells are among the smallest in the body, yet they contain all of the genetic material necessary to create the adult human being. Both contribute the same number of chromosomes, twenty-three, but the sperm is responsible for the sex of the child. There are two kinds of sperm, an X sperm, which creates a female, and a Y sperm, which creates a male. Many more males are conceived than females, but by the end of the first year of life, there are almost equal numbers of males and females. This is because the death rate for males at all stages of life after conception is higher than the rate for females.

Pregnancy takes several weeks before it becomes recognizable, though some pregnancy tests can determine pregnancy by the end of the third week. A missed menstrual period is usually the first sign. Other signs might be breast tenderness and coloration change, slight morning sickness, and the necessity for more frequent urination.

The average pregnancy is 266 days, or thirty-eight weeks. During this time the mother should eat a good diet and be under the care of a physician. She should avoid medicines and being X-rayed, as well as stressful life events, if possible. The developing fetus can be affected by the environment. If the mother is addicted to narcotics, has an infectious disease such as German measles or STD, or is a heavy smoker, for example, the child may be damaged. Any resulting defects in the child are called congenital defects. Genetic defects are caused by the chromosomes and genes. By removing a small amount of amniotic fluid—a process termed *amniocentesis*—doctors can analyze it to discover any genetic defects, such as Down's syndrome, before birth.

The birth process is generally divided into three stages. The first is the labor stage, during which the cervix relaxes and opens and the uterus contracts periodically in an effort to push the infant into the birth canal (vagina). In the second stage these contractions, with help from the mother, push the child through the birth canal into the outside world. The third stage comes shortly after the baby has been delivered when the placenta or afterbirth is expelled.

In recent years more and more emphasis has been placed on having the mother and father participate as much as they can in the birth of the child. Natural childbirth means knowledgeable childbirth, with the use of drugs reduced to a minimum. Breastfeeding is being encouraged, as is rooming-in, or keeping the baby with the mother immediately after birth rather than removing it to the hospital nursery.

Philosophically, those encouraging natural childbirth believe that for a couple to share the miracle of creating life can be an emotional high point. They suggest that care and planning be made a part of pregnancy so that the birth process will function smoothly and the parents will be able to derive the most pleasure and satisfaction from the entire process of bringing a child into the world.

The Secret Life of the Unborn Child

Several years ago I spent a weekend with some friends in the country. Helen, my hostess, was seven months pregnant, and in the evening I would find her sitting alone in front of the fireplace, softly singing a beautiful lullaby to her unborn child.

After the birth of her son, Helen told me that the same lullaby had a magical effect on him. No matter how hard he was crying, he would calm down when the song was sung. As a psychiatrist with a special interest in prenatal experience, I was intrigued. I wondered if a woman's actions, perhaps even her thoughts and feelings, might be able to influence her unborn child.

From my investigation and search of the scientific literature a new portrait of the unborn child emerged, one fundamentally different from the passive, mindless creature of the traditional pediatrics text:

■ The unborn child is an aware, reacting being who from the sixth month on—perhaps even earlier—leads an active emotional life.
■ The fetus can see, hear, experience, and, on a primitive level, even learn.
■ Whether a child becomes happy or sad, aggressive or meek, secure or anxiety-ridden may depend, in part, on what messages the fetus receives in the womb.
■ This new knowledge has enormous implications for parents. It suggests they have a greater influence over the unborn child than ever before imagined.

Many studies suggest that the unborn child is not just conscious and aware, but sensitive to remarkably subtle emotional nuances. Precisely at what moment the brain cells ac-

quire this ability is still unknown. However, most of what is known with some research support suggests that the child from the sixth month in utero onward has such skills.

To illustrate, consider the sensation of anxiety. What could produce a deep-seated anxiety in an unborn child, one that could have long-term effects? One possibility is his mother's alcohol consumption or smoking. Studies have shown the profound effects of maternal cigarette smoking on the fetus: a sharp increase in the rate of heartbeat, a decrease in the oxygen supply, and a reduced birth weight. It is possible that some of these effects are stress related.

Naturally the fetus has no way of knowing the mother is smoking or thinking about it, but the fetus is developed enough to react to the unpleasant sensation it produces, which is caused by a drop in the oxygen

supply. Possibly even more harmful are the psychological effects of maternal smoking. Periodic reduced oxygen might thrust the fetus into a chronic state of uncertainty and fear, never knowing when that unpleasant physical sensation will recur or how painful it will be when it does.

Another happier kind of learning goes on in utero through hearing. Our speech patterns are as distinct as our fingerprints. Apparently the learning of these speech patterns is influenced by our mothers even before birth. In addition, acute hearing allows the fetus to react to music. A six-month-old fetus definitely responds to the sound and melody. Put Vivaldi on the phonograph and even the most agitated baby relaxes. Put on hard rock and most fetuses start kicking violently.

Even something as mundane as the mother's heartbeat has an effect. It is an essential part of the unborn child's life-support system. The child does not know that, but it does seem to sense that the reassuring rhythms of its beat is one of the major constellations of its universe. This was demonstrated a few years ago when a hospital piped a tape of a maternal heartbeat into a nursery filled with newborn babies. The researchers assumed that if the sound had any emotional significance, the babies on the day the tape was played would behave differently than on days when it wasn't played.

And so they did, to a degree that stunned the investigators. In virtually every way the heartbeat babies did better, apparently reassured by the comforting rhythm. They ate more, weighed more, slept more, breathed better, and cried and got sick less.

Although much more difficult to assess, psychologist Monika Tomann-Specht concluded that the mother's attitude toward her child had the greatest single effect on how an infant turned out. In her study she followed 235 women through pregnancy and birth. The children of accepting mothers, who looked forward to having a family, were much healthier, emotionally and physically, at birth and afterward, than the offspring of rejecting mothers.

What about a father's influence? Few things affect the mother as deeply as worries about her partner, and his support is important to her and the child's well-being. Conversely, perhaps nothing is more dangerous to a child, emotionally and physically, than a father who abuses or neglects his pregnant wife. A study done in the early 70s indicates that a woman locked in a stormy marriage may run a 100 percent greater risk of bearing a psychologically damaged child than a woman in a secure, nurturing relationship.

This underscores the father's important part in the prenatal equation, but studies suggest another dimension to his supportive role. It appears that a child learns to identify the father's voice in utero. There are also indications that the newborn, hearing that voice, may respond to it, at least physically. If crying for instance, the child may stop at the familiar soothing sound of the father's voice.

Today men should be thoughtfully involved in their children's lives from the very beginning. The sooner this bonding based on love and care begins, the more each child is likely to benefit.

If, in fact, the child can respond in utero, then pregnancy becomes an important part of the environmental influence on that child in more ways than we had previously realized.

Source: Adapted from *The Secret Life of the Unborn Child* by Thomas Verny, M.D., and John Kelly (New York: Simon & Schuster, 1981).

What Do You Think?

- Do you think that a fetus can respond to its environment before birth?
- What might this mean in the case of an abortion?
- What effect might an unwanted pregnancy have on the unborn child?
- What effect might a parental fight or breakup have on the unborn child?
- Since an increasing number of pregnancies occur outside of marriage where fathers are apt to be less involved with the mother, might this have an effect on the unborn child?
- When a pregnancy occurs outside of marriage, what are the chances of the mother being happy and accepting of the baby compared to a pregnancy within marriage?

Chapter 13

The Challenge of Parenthood

Contents

And a woman who held a babe against her bosom said,
Speak to us of Children.
And he said:
Your children are not your children.
They are the sons and daughters of Life's longing for itself.
They come through you but not from you,
And though they are with you yet they belong not to you.
You may give them your love but not your thoughts,
For they have their own thoughts.
You may house their bodies but not their souls,
For their souls dwell in the house of tomorrow, which you cannot visit, not
even in your dreams.
You may strive to be like them, but seek not to make them like you.
For life goes not backward nor tarries with yesterday.
You are the bows from which your children as living arrows are sent forth.
The archer sees the mark upon the path of the infinite, and He bends you
with
His might that his arrows may go swift and far.
Let your bending in the archer's hand be for gladness;
For even as He loves the arrow that flies, so He loves also the bow that is
stable.

Kahlil Gibran, *The Prophet*

Marriage and parenthood have often seemed synonymous in the past. Having children was the major goal of marriage. Many popular assumptions supported this goal:

- Marriage means children.
- Having children is the essence of woman's self-realization.
- Reproduction is woman's biological destiny.
- It is the duty of all families to produce children to replenish the society.
- Children prove the manliness of the father.
- Children prove the competence and womanliness of the mother.
- Be fruitful and multiply.
- Having children is humanity's way to immortality; children extend one into the future.
- Children are an economic asset, needed hands for necessary labor.

The beliefs of the past often remain to encumber the present long after the original reasons for the belief have disappeared. So it is with reproduction and parenthood. For thousands of years humans had to reproduce—had to be parents—if the species was to survive. And they had little choice in the matter because the pleasure of sexual relations often meant pregnancy.

Historically marriage has implied having and rearing children. Indeed the primary function of the family was to provide a continuing replacement of individuals so that the human species and the particular society continued to exist.

Yet the dogma of the past has quietly become the liability of the present for uncontrolled reproduction today means the ultimate demise of the species, not its survival. In the past high infant mortality, uncontrolled disease, and war meant that society had to press all families to reproduce at a high level in order to maintain the population. Women were pregnant during most of their fertile years. Even today in many underdeveloped countries, infant mortality runs as high as

200 per 1000 live births, and because of malnutrition and disease many women see fewer than half of their children reach maturity.

In developed countries, however, the infant mortality rate has been cut to less than 15 per 1000 live births. The infant mortality rate in the United States has dropped from 14 per 1000 live births in 1977 to 10.5 per 1000 live births in 1986, the lowest ever recorded (U.S. Department of Health, 1986, p. 1).

Children by Choice

Reduced infant mortality through greater control of disease and pestilence has removed the necessity for most American families to have large numbers of children. Because a much larger percentage of children now reach adulthood, a family may safely limit the number of children they produce to the number they actually desire. Hence the historical pressure on the family to reproduce continuously is no longer necessary.

The problems of overpopulation pose a great threat to the survival of the human species, thus necessitating the limitation of reproduction. Let's take a look at how population has increased. The human population did not reach one billion until 1830. But by 1930—just 100 years later—another billion had been added. The fourth billion was reached in 1975, and by the end of the century it is predicted that we will be adding a billion persons to the world population every five years.

Knowledge of overpopulation dangers, improved and readily available birth control methods, and legal abortions have combined to give newly married American couples greater freedom from unwanted pregnancy. Although the social expectation to have children remains, couples are less likely to be thought of as selfish hedonists or as infertile if they remain childless. America's birthrate today is near its lowest point, approximately two children per marriage, or 15.7 births per 1000 population in 1986 (U.S. Department of Health, 1986, p. 1). Many underdeveloped countries, on the other hand, have birthrates of 40 to 50 per 1000 population. If America's birthrate continues at the zero population growth level, the population will reach a high in the year 2015 and start downward around 2020, depending on the amount of immigration.

The number of children overwhelmingly preferred by Americans today is two (Glick, 1979; David & Baldwin, 1979; U.S. Bureau of the Census, 1983). In 1945 only 23 percent of the public stated one or two as the ideal number of children. Larger numbers of young educated women are stating a "no children" preference today than at any time in the past. However, stating such a preference and living by it are two different things. According to Ira Reiss (1980), childlessness among married couples is actually not increasing much, although there is some increase among college-educated partners. In fact, many young women who stated a "no children" preference in the early 1970s are now reproducing. The only age group that experienced an increase in fertility between 1980 and 1984 was women 30 to 34 years of age. In 1984 the fertility rate for these women was 72.2 per 1000, up from 60 per 1000 in 1980 (U.S. Bureau of the Census, 1985) (these rates appear much higher because they measure only women in this age group and not the entire population). American families are still having children but fewer of them per family.

A couple's conscious or unconscious reasons for having children strongly affect the way the child is treated and reared. Because species survival, political reasons, and economic factors are no longer relevant to having children in modern society, people's personal reasons for wanting children have become much more important. Many of the personal reasons have a selfish element. It is this selfish element that, when frustrated by the child, so often leads to feelings of disappointment and failure on the part of parents. Bernard Berelson (1972) lists six basic personal reasons for having children; each has a large selfish component.

Why Are Children Wanted?

1. Children give parents *personal power*. First, there is the power over the children, which during the early years of childhood is absolute. Second, having children sometimes gives one parent power over the other. Either partner may use the children to hold the other. Children can also represent increased political and/or economic power as in societies where marriage alliances are arranged to control power. In America the Kennedy or Rockefeller families come to mind when we think of children as potential power.
2. Children offer proof of *personal competence* in an essential human role. "Look what I can do; see how virile I am; see how fertile I am."
3. Parenthood confers *personal status*. "I have contributed to the society; I can produce and achieve."
4. Children are a form of *personal extension*, immortality, life after death. "After all, my children are a part of me, both biologically and psychologically."
5. The *personal experience* of having children is rewarding. A parent can feel: "the deep curiosity as to how the child will turn out; the renewal of self in the

Inset 13-1

"Right" and "Wrong" Reasons to Have a Baby

"Wrong" Reasons

1. To save or strengthen the marital relationship.
2. To please your parents or friends.
3. Because everyone you know has children.
4. To escape from the outside working world.
5. To relieve the fear of being alone in old age, the fear of what you may be missing out on, the fear of what people may think of you, and so forth.
6. Because you've been mothering your mate and think a real baby would be more fun.
7. To prove to the world you are a real woman or man.
8. To become somebody important.
9. To do a better job than your parents did with you.

"Right" Reasons

1. Both you and your mate want and choose to have a child.
2. Your aim is to give, rather than to get.
3. Your relationship and lives are established so that you give from your excess and do not need to take from your lives.
4. You are going to be available to your child and not always busy and preoccupied with other things.
5. You want the challenge of rearing a child into a healthy productive adult.
6. You are looking forward with pleasure to rearing a child.

Source: Adapted from Brinley, 1984.

---

second chance; the reliving of one's own childhood; the redemptive opportunity; the challenge to shape another human being; the sheer creativity and self-realization involved."

6. The experience of having children can produce *personal pleasure*, the love involved in having wanted children, caring for them, and enjoying them.

Of course, there are many other personal reasons for having children. For example: "Children will make me an adult." "I'll have something of my own." (Note in the Chapter 11, Scenes from Marriage, most of the teenage mothers give this as their major reason for having a child.) "People will pay attention to me." "I'll have someone to help and to love." "A child will save my marriage," and so on. As we shall see in the next section, the idea that children will save a marriage is erroneous. The increased complications of parenthood usually hasten the end of a troubled marriage.

To know and understand our reasons for having children is a small step in the right direction. And to understand that the resultant child is an individual in his or her own right and that this new individual has no responsibility to fulfill our needs and reasons for producing him or her is a big step in the direction of enlightened childrearing.

What Effects Do Children Have on a Marriage?

The most often heard words from parents to couples thinking about becoming parents are, "Your life will never be the same again." "We know, we know," replies the couple contemplating parenthood. "Oh no you don't," reply the parents. And the parents are right. Parenthood is constant. It is demanding. You can divorce a problem spouse but you can't divorce a problem child. It lasts to the end of your life.

> *Russ received an urgent call from his thirty-five-year-old son living 1000 miles away asking him to come over as soon as possible as he and his wife were breaking up and he needed his dad's help and support. Fortunately Russ was retired so he left the next day. He arrived just in time to see the wife and her brothers driving off with all the furniture that Russ had given to his son and daughter-in-law for their wedding gift. He and his son ended up sleeping on the floor in the empty house for a week until the son got things sorted out.*

The point of this story is that parenting does not end when a child is twenty-one years of age, or when they are married, or when they live at some distance from their parents. Parenthood is a lifetime commitment and obligation.

The effects that children have on a marriage is a complicated question involving many factors. Certainly, the readiness of the couple for pregnancy and ensuing parenthood is crucial. We have already discussed the importance of planning parenthood so that the child is wanted. Yet even parents who want a child will experience ambivalence toward actually having one. Are we *really* ready? How much freedom will I lose? Can we afford a child? Will I be a successful parent? Such questions will arise continually for any expectant parent.

Unplanned pregnancies make such questions infinitely more difficult. Couples often feel trapped into parenthood by an unexpected pregnancy. They are not ready for, and have not consented to, parenthood. They are often angry and resentful, especially the prospective father because he has the least control over the pregnancy. An unwed father, for example, has virtually no legal rights in deciding what shall be done about an unwanted pregnancy. Yet he is legally responsible for the newborn child.

In studying readiness for fatherhood, researchers have identified four major factors that men think are most important in making the decision to become a parent (May, 1982). The most basic factor is whether a man has ever wanted to become a father. If he has always thought that he would one day have children,

the transition to actual fatherhood is easier. The second factor is whether he regards the overall stability of the couple's relationship as important. Researchers have found that the husband's positive perception of marital adjustment was strongly associated with high pregnancy acceptance on his part (Porter & Demeuth, 1979). The third major factor is whether he believes the couple is relatively secure financially. If a man perceived that, as a couple, they were doing about as well as could be expected and if their situation was similar to his expectation of acceptable financial position, then he felt much more ready for parenthood. The couple's objective financial picture proved less important than these more subjective evaluations. The last factor was whether a man felt he had completed the childless part of his life. If the man had set certain life goals for himself, ones that would best be met before starting a family, then completion of most of these enhanced a feeling of readiness for fatherhood.

Men may have more trouble working out parenthood readiness questions than women. This is because they rarely seek out support or help in dealing with such questions (Tognoli, 1980). They are more prone than women to keep their concerns to themselves. They are reluctant to discuss them with their pregnant spouses for fear of upsetting them and "making matters worse" (May, 1979; Roehner, 1976).

Although women seem better at handling readiness for parenthood, they too must confront meaningful life choices. In years past there was not much choice for women; the parenting/homemaking role was often the only role open to them. In those days, however, the homemaking role was a much larger and more varied role than it is today. Women were productive members of farm and craft teams along with their husbands. Children either shared in the work of the household or were left to amuse themselves. These mothers were usually not lonely or isolated because the world came into their homes in the form of farmhands, relatives, customers, and so on. Such women had no reason to complain of the boredom and solitude of spending ten-hour days alone with their children. In addition to being mothers, they contributed to their family and their society in other important and productive ways.

Today the homemaking role has been drastically reduced in scope. The general affluence—especially of the American middle-class family—the small nuclear family structure, the trend toward women's liberation, and the removal of eco-nomic production from the home into the factory all combine to decrease the satisfactions derived from a now narrow and exaggerated maternal/homemaking role. The modern woman has many other choices available to her, which make readiness for parenthood an increasingly difficult choice for her to make. (See Chapters 7 and 9.)

Today, the idea that a mother must remain continually at home with her children is losing credence as more and more mothers join the workforce. The supposedly negative effects that absent mothers, baby-sitters, and child-care centers have on children have not been found when good child care is available (Nye & Hoffman, 1974; Belsky, Lerner, & Spanier, 1984; Cochran & Gunnarsson, 1985; Smith, 1979). The key word here is *good*. Unfortunately good child-care for working mothers has not kept pace with the need. Neglected and uncared for children (latchkey children) are now more of a problem than ever before (*U.S. News and World Report*, 1982; Hechinger, 1986, A-11) (see Chapter 7).

Regardless of the state of parenthood preparation and readiness, the actual

transition to parenthood does involve a number of costs to the parents. First, the physical demands associated with caring for the child are usually far greater than the parents anticipated. Second, unforeseen strains are placed on the husband-wife relationship. Many recent studies suggest that the presence of children in the family on the average lowers the marital happiness or satisfaction of the parents (Glenn & McLanahan, 1981; Campbell, 1981; Miller & Sollie, 1980; Glenn & Weaver, 1977; Waldron & Routh, 1981; Belsky, Spanier, & Rovine, 1983; Belsky, Lang, & Rovine, 1985). Many couples report that their happiest time in marriage was before the arrival of the first child and after the departure of the last (Bell, 1975). The trends reported by these studies are not new. For example, study of the research done during the 1960s on family stability and happiness also indicates that children more often detract from than contribute to, marital happiness (Hicks & Platt, 1970). Of course, most of this research involves group data and averages. The effect that children will have on your own marital relationship will depend on your understanding and tolerance of the natural demands and strains that the presence of children creates. The effects that children have on a marriage also vary greatly with the ages of the children (see "The Growing Child in the Family," p. 454).

A third cost to parenthood appears to be that the personal elements of the marital relationship—friendship, romance, and sex—tend to become less satisfying as the marital relationship becomes focused more on the instrumental functions (day-to-day obligations, managing and running the family, integrating family routine and work schedules, and so on) and less on emotional expression. The time that has been used by the childless couple to nurture their personal emotional relationship is displaced by the time demands of the child.

A fourth set of negative feelings experienced by new parents involve opportunity, costs, and restrictions. New parents complain about the limits placed on their social lives, particularly their freedom to travel or decide to do something on the spur of the moment.

Despite the negativeness of some research findings, most parents express overall satisfaction with children and the parenting role (Chilman, 1980a). In one large national survey of parents with children under age thirteen, 73 percent of the fathers and mothers expressed satisfaction with the fun and enjoyment they derived from family life, and 90 percent of the parents said they would have children again (Yankelovich et al., 1977). These findings were replicated in 1982 by George Gallup when a remarkable 79 percent of those polled indicated that they were highly satisfied with their family life.

Miller and Sollie (1980) have identified several positive themes in new parent's lives. Parents derive emotional benefits from the joy, happiness, and fun that accompanies child care. New parents often report self-enrichment and feelings of personal development when undertaking the parental responsibilities. Parents also report an increased feeling of family cohesiveness and strengthened relationships between themselves and the extended family. Miller and Sollie suggest that the transition to parenthood is a good time for the couple to work to build the family strengths discussed in Chapter 1.

At first glance it may seem that parents' expression of satisfaction with their children and family life contradicts the general evidence of reduced marital satisfaction when children enter the family. The answer to this apparent contradiction is that both negative and positive expressions are genuine. Parenthood, in many ways, is a paradox (Hoffman & Manis, 1978). On the one hand are the problems of contending with a demanding child. On the other hand are the joys of having and caring for another person. The paradoxical character of parenthood is not simply a function of the fact that both of these experiences are part of parenthood, but that the "lows" and "highs" are so extreme and so intense that you want to cry at one moment and laugh at the next.

Colleen *(Monday afternoon):   I never realized that an infant could be so demanding. I never get a moment's peace when she's awake, not even to go to the bathroom. I can't even say "wait a minute" because she is too young to understand (10 months). I feel like my whole life has been taken over by a tyrant. All she does is demand—me! me! me! I've lost my identity, my individuality, to a word—"mother."*

Colleen *(Tuesday morning):   I'm glad I have her. It's neat to know she is a part of me and of Bob. She is a real little person who is perfect and loves me and needs me. She makes me feel successful at something, helping another. It makes me feel good to know that I was able to produce a child and be a parent. (LaRossa & LaRossa, 1981, p. 177)*

The fact is that children add enormously to the complexity of family relationships. For example, a couple must contend with communication in only two directions.

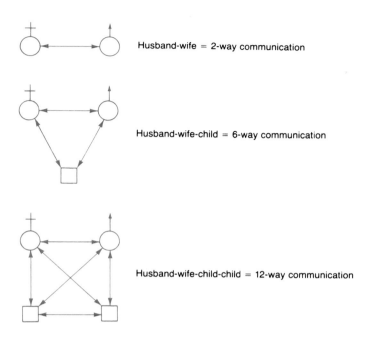

Husband-wife = 2-way communication

Husband-wife-child = 6-way communication

Husband-wife-child-child = 12-way communication

Figure 13-1 Adding children complicates communication.

Add one child and this becomes six-way communication; add two children, and there is now twelve-way communication (see Figure 13-1).

Prospective parents can become better-prepared parents by reading and taking classes about parenthood. Yet even with a thorough preparation, bringing the first new baby home is an exciting, happy, and frightening experience for new parents. No matter how much learning about children they have done, they can never be sure that what they are doing is correct. If the baby cries, they worry. If it doesn't cry, they still worry. They will have to adjust to the feeding routine. The mother cannot venture far from the baby, especially if she is breastfeeding. The father has to adjust to taking second place in the wife's time and attention. An infant is demanding of both of these if nothing else.

Prospective parents sometimes forget that children will be with them for perhaps twenty or more years, and that their effect on the marriage will be profound. A spouse who becomes unpleasant or a marital relationship that sours can be left behind via divorce. But you cannot divorce a child who is unpleasant and frustrating. Parents are morally and legally responsible to provide care and shelter until the children are of age.

Traditionalization of the Marital Relationship

Examining a couple's relationship after a child enters the family points clearly to the overriding change that occurs. In almost all cases—except for two-career families that can afford to place child care almost fully in the hands of others— the parents' relationship moves in the traditional direction. The mother assumes most of the parenting and household roles (even if she works), while the father turns toward the work world. This occurs even when the couple believe in and work for an egalitarian homemaking relationship (Entwisle & Doering, 1980; LaRossa & LaRossa, 1981). Both of the Belsky (1983, 1985) studies found that the changes in the marital relationship were more pronounced for wives.

Several theories try to account for this traditionalization phenomenon. Alice Rossi (1977, p. 17) argues for a physiological theory in which hormonal changes in women during pregnancy, birth, and nursing establish "a clear link between sexuality and maternalism." New mothers receive "erotogenic pleasure" from nursing their infants, which means, according to Rossi, that "there may be biologically based potential for heightened maternal investment in the child, at least through the first months of life, that exceeds the potential for investment by men in fatherhood" (p. 24). Implicitly answering the traditionalization question, Rossi goes on to say that "significant residues of greater maternal than paternal attachment may then persist into later stages of the parent-child relationship."

Personality theories of socialization can be used to account for traditionalization. Early sex role socialization can also be used as an explanation. Such socialization, usually modeled from one's parents, is deeply ingrained. Because our society gives little or no formal education for parenthood, we tend to act out these parenting models when we have our own children. As young people we may be egalitarian in philosophy, among our peers and early in marriage before parenting becomes part of our relationship. But when children arrive, we fall into behavior patterns to which we were early socialized and which, in most cases, tend to be traditional.

A sociological explanation of traditionalization can also explain much by examining the social constraints placed on parenting by the general society in relation to the nature of the human infant. As we discussed in Chapter 2 (p. 38), the human infant is born in the most dependent state of any animal. A human baby is so dependent that without continuous care from an adult, it will not survive. The infant's demands are also nonnegotiable: It cannot be told to "wait until tomorrow." Thus in the early life of the child there must be continual adult supervision. This demand clashes with the social realities. As we saw in Chapter 9 (p. 288), economic reality for most couples is that the man can earn more money. The coming of a child increases the economic burden on the family. If the husband can earn more than the wife, who will go out to work and who will stay home to care for the child? The answer is obvious.

If mother breastfeeds and the society frowns on breastfeeding in public, social pressure keeps her at home with her infant. If workplaces do not have infant-care facilities, as most do not, how can a mother go to work? If she does, much of what she earns is taken by the costs of outside child care (Chapter 9, p. 294).

Continuous adult care of the infant also means that one partner's "winning" (being free to pursue his or her own interests outside of parenting) means that the other must "lose" (forgo his or her interests for the sake of the baby). It is this constant time demand of the young child that causes much of the conflict between parents. As Ralph and Maureen LaRossa state: "It is this basic pattern—child dependency resulting in continuous need for care, which means scarcity of time, which leads to conflicts of interest and often conflict behavior—that cuts across the experiences of all couples in our sample" (1981, p. 47).

It is the loss of free time that bothers new parents the most.

What Do You Think?

1. In what ways have you caused trouble between your parents?
2. How could they have avoided any of these problems?
3. Overall, do you think that having children improved your parents' marriage? How?
4. Harmed your parents' marriage? How?
5. Assuming that you have children, what do you think are some of the ways that they might positively influence your relation with your spouse? Negatively influence your relationship?

> Colleen: *I do still have some time to myself, for example, when she is taking her nap. But it isn't really totally free time for me to use any way I wish. I'm still "on call." Bob tries to give me free time by staying home with her and letting me go out. But if he has been at work all day, he also needs some free time so it is hard for him too.*

The Father's Role in Parenting

Colleen touches on a basic conflict between most new fathers and mothers. How much do they share the parenting duties? The movement toward traditionalization in new parents' relations means that the ideal of sharing (if it was an ideal before birth) is slowly lost. If the new mother stops work and remains home to parent, the father assumes few of the childrearing duties once the "baby honeymoon" passes (Cordell et al., 1980). Mothers claim that the period of help given by the father when the new baby arrives home ends quickly (usually within a few months).

Even when the mother goes back to work after the birth, studies have found that the wife's employment has a negligible impact on the husband's housework and child-care responsibilities (Berk-Fenstermaker, 1985; Barnett & Baruch, 1983; Pleck & Rustad, 1980; Blumstein & Schwartz, 1983). Most fathers, even those who share childrearing obligations, fail to appreciate the everyday life of a mother with small children. They help, but as an appreciated helper who never really assumes full responsibility. In a sense mothers feel more trapped than fathers because they have no one to hand their job to, whereas fathers do—mother. Robinson (1977) found that housewives spend seven times as much time as employed men in child-care activities, and employed mothers twice as much. Even this is misleading because 50 percent of men's care activities involve play with the child.

Many fathers indicate that their work in supporting the family is the most important part of their parenting role and so feel that they need to do little else with the children, especially if their wives are not working.

> *Jean and Jim have two children, a boy age ten and a girl age eight. Jim believes that because he is at work all day, it is Jean's duty to keep the children "out of his hair" when he gets home so that he can relax and recuperate. Jean resents this, believing that she, too, has worked all day. She has also had full responsibility for the children since school was out. She has asked Jim to watch the children occasionally on Saturday or Sunday so that she may have a day off, but he thinks weekends should be a family time.*

Even if such attitudes represent the new father's viewpoint, he is still faced with a number of tasks (Barnhill, Rubenstein, & Rocklin, 1979).

1. *Decision-making*: The father must make the decision to accept the reality of having a child.
2. *Mourning*: While the new father gains the role of father, he also undergoes a substantial loss. He loses personal and economic freedom, some of his wife's attention, and much of their relationship's flexibility.
3. *Empathic responding*: The husband who participates in the pregnancy and birth will feel more closely involved with his wife and hence with the new child. This developmental task may be missed by the noninvolved father. Such fathers often feel unknowing about and later somewhat alienated from their children.
4. *Integrating*: The child must be integrated into the spatial, temporal, and social life of the family. The question of how much time the husband spends with his wife and how much with the mother of his child is answered by the way in which the father integrates these "fathering" and "husbanding" responsibilities.
5. *Establishing new family boundaries*: The new father must now also alter his role as an individual in his extended family. He has moved between generations, becoming primarily a parent rather than a son. In addition, he becomes connected in a whole new series of family relationships transforming his siblings into aunts and uncles, his parents into grandparents, etc.
6. *Synergizing*: The father's last task is developing a sense of trust in the adequacy of the child, the marriage, the family, and himself. This includes integration of the previous five tasks into a coherent lifestyle, along with the acceptance of his own imperfections and those of his family. Synergizing refers to a state of enhancement that occurs if the father is able to achieve this new husband-father level and function successfully in it.

Even though the American father has not shared equally in the parenting role, recent social changes indicate that he may be participating more in the future. The historical characterization of the harsh, austere, disciplinarian father is being replaced by a more humanistic, affectionate, caring kind of father. Liberation of the woman's role also works to liberate the father's traditional role, freeing him to be more loving than he has been in the past. Paternal participation in childbirth is now more and more encouraged (Chapter 12). Fathers that do participate in childbirth tend to hold and rock their infants more. The experience seems to lead to earlier bonding between a father and his newborn. As more women move into careers, more men will have to share a larger portion of the parenting role. A few men are experimenting with fulfilling the home and parent role that used to be limited to their wives while their wives move out into the work world. Although these examples are limited, they are indicative of a trend to bring more parenting into the father's role (Ricks, 1985). Most experts agree that this would be rewarding to all concerned.

Fathering is drastically reduced when families break up. In most cases children go with their mother, and their father's contact with them is greatly reduced. Many former husbands are just as happy to escape their parental duties. Many wish to maintain their father role, but the logistics of being with the children enough to remain effective defeat many absent fathers. Contact with the children usually means contact with the former wife, which may be painful. The father's living

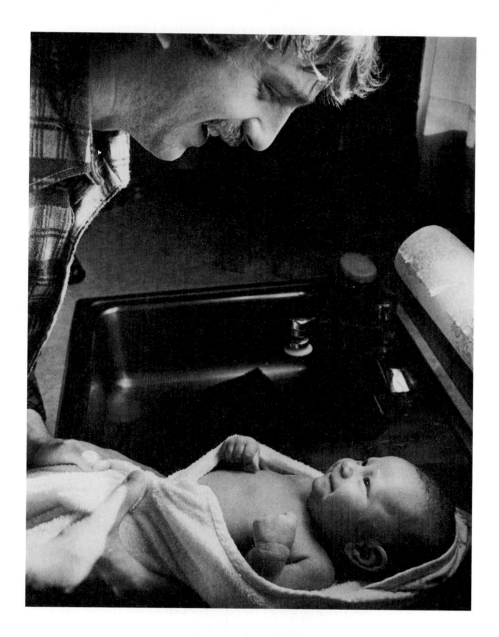

situation is often unconducive to having the children stay with him. New commitments limit his time. In most cases even when the father desires to retain his role with the children, studies indicate that his contact with the children declines rapidly.

For a few fathers the breakup of the marriage means coming to know their children better. (About 11 percent of families are single-family, man-headed.) When they have the children, they are prepared in advance and so devote time to them, whereas they might not have when the family was intact. More fathers (although very few percentagewise) are obtaining custody of their children, and

What Do You Think?

1. Do you want children at some time in the future? Why or why not?
2. If you want to have children, how many do you want? Why?
3. In what ways do you think your parents were successful in their parenting? In what ways were they unsuccessful?
4. How would you change the ways in which your parents raised you? Why?

for them parenting becomes a central responsibility. (For further reading on the father's role in child development, see Parke, 1981; LeMasters & DeFrain, 1983.)

Parental Effectiveness

Most people take on the job of parenthood assuming they will be successful: "Of course, we can be good parents." Yet raising children is an extremely demanding job. Certainly it is time-consuming, lasting for twenty years or more. What qualifications do expectant parents consider themselves to have? They all have parents, and all have been children. But, as we know from our own experience as children, all parents fail in their job to some degree. Some failure, especially in the eyes of one's children, seems to be an integral part of parenting.

> There is no question but that your parents failed you as parents. All parents fail their children, and yours are no exception. No parent is ever adequate for the job of being a parent, and there is no way not to fail at it. No parent ever has enough love, or wisdom, or maturity, or whatever. No parent ever totally succeeds. (Close, 1968)

Because of this phenomenon, great amounts of advice flow from grandparents, doctors, clergy, popular magazines, and child experts, all describing how best to rear children. Benjamin Spock, known to millions of parents for his advice about childrearing (*Baby and Child Care* has sold more volumes than any other book except the Bible), has observed:

> A great many of our efforts as professionals to help parents have instead complicated the life of parents—especially conscientious and highly sensitive parents. It has made them somewhat timid with their children—hesitant to be firm. They are a little scared of their children because they feel as parents they are being judged by their neighbors, relatives, and the world on how well they succeed. They are scared of doing the wrong thing. (Spock, 1980)

And of course a great deal of advice comes from the children themselves who are as yet unblessed with their own children. What fifteen-year-old doesn't know exactly how bad his or her parents are and how to be the perfect parent?

The problem with all this advice is that there is little agreement about the best method of rearing children. In a sense children come to live with their parents; their parents do not go to live with them. Parents need not think they must relinquish their lives completely in favor of the child's development. Parental growth and development go hand in hand with child growth and development.

Good parents love their children but are also honest enough to know that there will be days when they are angry with them, unfair with them, and in other ways terrible with them. Secure children will survive such episodes.

There is no single correct way to rear children. If children are wanted, respected, and appreciated, they will be secure. If they are secure, they usually will also be flexible and resilient. What is important is for the parents to be honest and true to themselves. Small children are very empathetic; that is, they have the ability to feel as another is feeling. They respond to their parents' feelings as well as to their actions. Parents who are naturally authoritarian will fail in coping with their children if they attempt to act permissively because they have read that permissiveness is a beneficial way of interacting with children. The children will feel the tension in their parents and will respond to that rather than to the parents' overt actions. Thus parents who attempt to be something other than what they are—no matter how theoretically beneficial the results are supposed to be —will generally fail. Parental sincerity is one of the necessary ingredients of successful childrearing. By and large, the pervasive emotional tone used by the parents in raising children affects subsequent development more than either the particular techniques of childrearing (e.g., permissiveness, restrictiveness, punishment, and reward) or the cohesiveness of the marital unit (whether it is stable or broken by divorce or death).

Overconcern and overprotection can also cause problems for children. Children need increasing degrees of freedom if they are to grow into independent adults. This means that they must have freedom to fail as well as to succeed. They need to experience the consequences of their actions, unless, of course, the consequences are dangerous to their well-being. Consequences teach children how to judge behavior. Parents who always shield children from failure are doing them a disservice. The children will not be able to modify their behavior to make it more successful because they will be ignorant of the results.

Overprotection can sometimes even be dangerous. For example, children taken to beach resorts need to know about and have water skills as soon as possible. Knowledge and skill are the best protection against accidents. Parents who take their children to the beach and then scream hysterically at them the moment they start toward the water are doing only one thing, teaching them to fear the water. Any lifeguard knows that fear of the water may lead to panic if there is trouble and that panic is the swimmer's worst enemy. It is true that parents need to be aware of small children's activities on the beach. But concern should be shown by helping them learn about the river, lake, or ocean and by showing them how to have fun in the water and gain confidence in their abilities rather than making them fearful. The best protection for children at a beach is early swimming lessons and then unobtrusive watchfulness to make sure they are not too far out.

It is also important to remember that the family and the child are not isolated from the broader society. Parents are the first to be blamed for their children's faults. Yet the influences on the child from sources outside the family become increasingly powerful as the child grows older. School, peers, friends, and the mass media all exert influence on both parents and children. For example, it is difficult for parents to enforce a rule against marijuana use when their teenager's friends are using it and the media present numerous experts giving opinions that it is not as detrimental to health as either alcohol or tobacco. But if their child is caught using it, most often the parents are blamed, not peers or media.

Parents have the most difficult task in the world—to rear happy, healthy children into competent and successful adults—and they must do this in an incredibly complex environment. The vast majority of parents love their children and do the best job they can. Our society puts the tremendous responsibility of childrearing almost totally on the parents, even though parents in reality are only one among many influences on the development of children. Our economic system, schools, religious organizations, mass media, and many other institutions and pressure groups impinge on the child's world. Often these influences are positive and help the parent in the task of rearing and socializing children. Unfortunately, these influences can sometimes be negative, countering the direction parents wish their children to take (LeMasters & DeFrain, 1983).

Parenting then is not something done only by parents. How parenting is accomplished and the results of the parenting are influenced both by the family

and the larger society. Parents must pay attention to the society as well as to their children. To expect children to become adults reflecting only the values and behaviors of their immediate family is unrealistic. The effective parent must also be a concerned citizen and work to better the society at large.

| **Stimulation and Development** | Belsky, Learner, and Spanier (1984, pp. 41–48) identify several key dimensions of mothering: physical contact, attentiveness, verbal stimulation, material stimulation, responsive care, and some restrictiveness. Note that all of these involve stimulation of the child. |

Stimulation is necessary for the development of basic behavioral capacities. Early deprivation of stimulation generally produces slower learning later in life. Early stimulation, on the other hand, enhances development and later learning. For example, various research evidence suggests that

> given the present state of our knowledge, the best physical environment in which to rear a child is one that gives him experience with a variety of physical objects which he can manipulate and control freely with minimal restriction. Experiences will give him an opportunity to develop basic motor skills which he can later apply to more specific learning situations. (Scott, 1968, p. 114)

However, overstimulation of the child such as is found in some accelerated learning programs may have negative effects (Berger, 1986, pp. 192–195).

The emphasis on early childhood education and intervention, beginning with the Head Start program in the early 1960s, reflects recognition of the importance of early environmental stimulation for children. Although there is controversy over the effects of Head Start experiences and the contribution to lasting change in the child made by such experiences, there is little doubt that the preschool years are important to the cognitive development of the child (Weinberg, 1979).

Some stress in childhood—which is a kind of stimulation—may also be related to achievement. In a study of over 400 famous twentieth-century men and women (Goertzel & Goertzel, 1962), two conclusions seemed to indicate that a child need not be protected from all stress and strain; that, indeed, some manageable stress stimulates achievement.

1. Three-fourths of the children were troubled by poverty; a broken home; rejecting, overpossessive, estranged, or dominating parents; financial ups and downs; physical handicaps; or parental dissatisfaction over the children's school failures or vocational choices.
2. Handicaps such as blindness; deafness; being crippled, sickly, homely, undersized, or overweight; or having a speech defect occurred in the childhoods of over one-fourth of the sample. In many of these individuals the need to compensate for such handicaps was seen by them as a determining factor in their drive for achievement.

This doesn't mean that parents should deliberately introduce stress into their children's lives. Rather, it means that parents may relax and be less concerned if their children are placed in a stressful situation. Children who are secure in the love and warmth of their parents will be able to survive and, in fact, grow in the face of stress. For example, moving away from a neighborhood, from places of familiarity and friends, can be upsetting. Yet studies of the effect of long-distance moves on children show little negative effect. The children seem to make friends easily, the school change is not difficult, and any disturbance in their behavior dissipates quickly (Barrett & Noble, 1973).

Belsky, Learner, and Spanier (1984) concluded from their review of infant stimulation research that parents who promote optimal cognitive development during the infancy years function effectively as *sources of stimulation*, by speaking to and by playing with the infant. Parents also function as *mediators or filters of stimulation*, by directing infant attention to objects and events in the child's world and by restricting the toddler from engaging in dangerous activities. In other words, successful parents moderate and control the amount of stimulation and stress experienced by their infants.

Childrearing, Discipline, and Control

For many parents control of their children is accomplished in a haphazard manner. If parents liked their own parents, they tend to copy their childrearing methods. If parents disliked their own parents' methods, they tend to do the opposite. In either case parents' own experiences as children influence how they themselves parent. The General Mills American Family Report indicates that most parents overwhelmingly use negative techniques to control their children. Table 13-1 shows the percentage of parents reporting use of various disciplinary methods.

Unfortunately, negative control methods tend to have negative side effects because they serve as model behaviors. A child who is screamed at tends to become a child who screams to get his or her way. A child who is treated negatively tends to become a negative child. A child who is punished violently tends to learn that violence is how to change another's behavior. Hostility, low self-esteem, feeling

Table 13-1

Percentage of Parents Using Various Disciplinary Methods

Method	Percentage
Yelling at or scolding children	52
Spanking children	50
Making children stay in their rooms	38
Not allowing children to play	32
Not letting children watch television	25
Making children go to bed	23
Threatening children	15
Giving children extra chores	12
Taking away an allowance	9

Source: Adapted from General Mills, 1977.

of inferiority and insecurity are frequent reactions of children who are reared by basically negative methods.

Rather than having only a few control techniques, automatically used, parents must work toward having a variety of well-understood childrearing methods. Each child and each situation will be somewhat unique. Therefore, parents should try to react in accordance with each situation. First one tries to understand the child and the problem, then one tries to identify what changes are necessary, and finally one attempts to accomplish the changes in the best possible manner. Thus childrearing becomes a rational, thoughtful, directive process, as opposed to an irrational, reactive process.

In general children can be controlled by using many different methods that vary in intensity from mild to strong. Many parents use a strong method such as punishment when, in fact, a mild method such as distraction might have worked equally well. By first trying milder methods, many of the negative side effects of punishment can be eliminated or at least reduced. Table 13-2 outlines a continuum of mild to strong methods. One must consider the age of the child when using this table. Two-year-olds will not understand item 3c, an appeal to their sense of fair play, because this ethical concept has not yet been grasped.

Directing a child's behavior ahead of time is preferable to and much easier than being unprepared and surprised by a child's behavior and then trying to react properly. For example, if you give a child a difficult task, stay close (1b, proximity control) so that you can offer help if it is needed (2a).

Firm routines (2c) reduce conflict and the number of overt decisions necessary. For example, an orderly routine at bedtime accomplishes tooth brushing, elimination, getting into pajamas, story reading, and lights off. In a sense the child is on automatic pilot, and little conflict arises once the routine is established. Such routines are only helpful in certain areas of life and probably work best with the preschool and early school child. Distraction (2b) is helpful with small children;

Inset 13-2

Using Discipline and Punishment Effectively

Whether one agrees with the use of punishment as a means of teaching children, studies of parental control indicate that it is still the major method used by most parents. Unfortunately, punishment does not always work, and it has negative side effects such as anger and hostility.

If punishment is used, the parent needs to understand a few simple principles that help maximize its usefulness and minimize the negative side effects. If mild punishment is to be effective, there needs to be alternative behavior open to the child. For example, if a child is punished for turning on the television rather than dressing for school, the punishment will work better if the child knows when he or she can watch TV. In this case the child knows that there is another way to do what he or she wants that will not result in punishment. In addition punishment works best if the child is not highly motivated. For example, a child eats just before dinner. If the child missed lunch, chances are she or he is very hungry (highly motivated), and punishment will probably not be very effective in keeping the child from eating. If there are alternatives and if the child is not highly motivated, then following the guidelines based on psychological learning theory set forth here will help achieve desired goals while keeping punishment to a minimum.

1. Consider the individual child and the potential negative side effects. *Example*: Randy reacts strongly to punishment, and the reaction lasts for a considerable length of time. He is bet-

ter controlled by reward or distraction. If punishment is used, it is mild. Michelle is not at all sensitive to punishment. She can be punished, her behavior will change, and there are no lasting side effects.

2. Punish as soon after the act as possible. *Example*: Children are bright, but it is hard for them to associate an act with punishment that comes many hours after the act. The mother who at 10 A.M. tells the child to "Just wait until your father comes home, you will get it," does little more than turn father into an ogre. By the time the father arrives home, little change of behavior will be derived from punishment.

3. If possible let the punishment flow from the act. *Example*: A child is constantly warned when he reaches toward a hot stove, but behavior change will take time. The child who touches the hot stove is immediately punished by his own action, understands what the word *hot* means, and has learned in one trial. Obviously, one cannot always set up a situation where punishment flows from the act, but when possible it is more efficient.

4. Make the punishment educational and be sure that children understand what their alternatives are. *Example*: Many young children really do not understand exactly what they have done and what new behavior is desired. Mary was punished when her mother found her at the cookie jar before dinner. Later Mary found some cookies on the counter and was again punished. Mary did not understand that she was being punished for eating cookies the first time. She thought her mother did not want her around the cookie jar for fear

she might break it. Also, she did not understand that she could have cookies after dinner.

5. Keep the punishment as mild as possible and keep it devoid of emotion. *Example*: Jimmy's mother became so exasperated that she lost her temper and spanked him. By losing her own temper, she increased the emotional atmosphere, causing Jimmy to become even more upset. She also modeled overt anger.

6. Try to punish the act, not the child. *Example*: "You are a bad boy. We don't love you when you are bad." This is a threatening and upsetting statement to a child and really is unnecessary. Generally, it is the particular act that is bad rather than the child. When the child changes the behavior, there is no longer a need for punishment, hence the child's relationships should immediately return to normal. By directing punishment at only the act, the child will not continue to be punished by thinking he or she as an individual is bad and unworthy of love ("I don't like your behavior so please change it. I like you, however.")

What Do You Think?

1. What were the major methods of control used by your parents when you were a child?
2. How did you react to these methods as a child?
3. What do you think of them as an adult? Did they work? Why or why not?
4. Which methods would you use with your children? Why?
5. What will you do if you and your spouse disagree on control methods?

Table 13-2

Mild-to-Strong Child Control Methods

---

1. Supporting the child's self-control
   a. Signal interference (catch the child's eye, frown, say something)
   b. Proximity control (get physically close to the child)
   c. Planful ignoring (children often do "bad" things to get attention, and if they don't get it, they will cease the behavior because they are not getting what they want)
   d. Painless removal (remove the child from the problem source)

2. Situational assistance
   a. Giving help
   b. Distraction or restructuring a situation
   c. Support of firm routines
   d. Restraint
   e. Getting set in advance

3. Reality and ethical appraisals
   a. Showing consequences to behaviors
   b. Marginal use of interpretation
   c. Appealing to sense of reason and fair play (not useful until child is intellectually able to understand such concepts)

4. Reward and contracting
   a. Rewards (payoffs) should be immediate
   b. Initial contracts should call for and reward small pieces of behavior (a reward for picking up toys, rather than a reward for keeping room clean for a week)
   c. Reward performance after it occurs
   d. Contract must be fair to all parties
   e. Terms of contract must be clear and understood
   f. Contract must be honest
   g. Contract should be positive
   h. Contract must be used consistently
   i. Contract must have a method of change to cope with failures

5. Punishment: See Inset 13-2

---

they usually have short attention spans, and they are easily shifted from one focus to another. Saying "no" to a child immediately creates a confrontation. ("Don't touch the expensive art book.") However, presenting an alternative and saying "do this" does not necessarily create such a confrontation. ("Why don't you look at this coloring book?"—while handing it to the child.)

The Growing Child in the Family

The essence of children is growing, changing, maturing, and becoming, rather than sameness. Parents must themselves constantly change in their relationship to the growing child. Just about the time they have adapted and learned to cope with a totally dependent child, they will need to change and learn to deal with a suddenly mobile, yet still irresponsible two-year-old. Then the school years follow, when the increasing influence of peers signals declining parental influence. Puberty and adolescence are the launching stage for once small, dependent children to go into the world on their own to establish new families and repeat the cycle. As the child grows and changes, the family also changes. For example, the mother usually remains close to the child during its infancy. During elementary school

Stages

1 Infancy Oral-sensory 1st year	Trust versus Mistrust (mothering, feeding)							
2 Toddler Muscular-anal 2 to 3 years		Autonomy versus Shame, Doubt (toilet training, self-control)						
3 Early Childhood Locomotor-genital 4 to 5 years			Initiative versus Guilt (increased freedom and sexual identity)					
4 School age Latency 6 to 11 years				Industry versus Inferiority (working together, school)				
5 Puberty and Adolescence 12 to 18 years					Identity versus Role-Diffusion (adult role)			
6 Young adulthood						Intimacy versus Isolation (love and marriage)		
7 Adulthood, middle age							Generativity versus Self-Absorption (broadening concerns beyond self)	
8 Maturity, old age								Integrity versus Despair

Figure 13-2 Erikson's eight developmental stages.

the parents often become chauffeurs, taking the child to a friend's home, music lessons, after-school sports, and so on. Change and growth in the child means parental and family change.

One way of viewing these changes is to see them as a series of social and developmental situations involving problematic encounters with the environment. These situations involve normal "problems" children must "solve" if they are to function fully. This section will focus on psychosocial stages rather than biological developmental stages, though the two are interrelated.

Erik Erikson (1963) identifies eight psychosocial developmental stages, each with important tasks, that describe the human life cycle from infancy through old age (Figure 13-2). Erikson's stages are theoretical, of course, and though there is controversy over the exact nature of developmental stages, the idea of stages is useful in helping parents understand the changing nature of the growing child and themselves. In each of these stages children must establish new orientations to themselves and their environment, especially their social environment. Each stage requires a new level of social interaction and can shape the personality in either negative or positive ways. For example, if children cope successfully with the problems and stress in a given stage, they gain additional strengths to become fully functioning. On the other hand, if children cannot cope with the problems of a particular stage, they will, in effect, invest continuing energy in this stage, becoming to some extent fixated, or arrested in development. For example, an adult who always handles frustration by throwing a temper tantrum has failed to move out of the early childhood stage when temper tantrums were the only manner of handling frustration. Such an individual is not coping successfully with the stress and problems of adult life.

Notice in Figure 13-2 that each stage can be carried down the chart into adulthood. For example, trust versus mistrust influences all succeeding stages. A person who successfully gains basic trust is better prepared to cope with the ensuing developmental stages. The reverse is also true. A mistrusting individual will have more trouble coping with ensuing stages than a trusting person. Let's now take a closer look at the first six stages.

Infancy: The Oral-Sensory Stage—Trust versus Mistrust (First Year)

Human beings undergo a longer period of dependence than any other species (see Chapter 2). In the first years children are completely dependent on parents or other adults for survival and are unable to contribute to the family because their responses to the environment are quite limited. Thus their development of trust depends on the quality of care they receive from their parents or the adults who care for them. The prolonged period of dependence makes the child more amenable to socialization (learning the ways of the society). Sometimes, however, a child will be too strongly or wrongly socialized in the early stages and thus will suffer from needless inhibitions as an adult. Such inhibitions are easily recognized by modern youth as "hang-ups."

The first year, when the infant must have total care to survive, is a difficult adjustment for many new parents because they have enjoyed relatively great personal freedom as well as time to devote to one another. Overnight a newcomer usurps that freedom and has first call on their time. Not only does the infant demand personal time and attention, but also many other considerations arise. To go to a movie now means the additional time and cost involved in finding and paying a baby-sitter. To take a Sunday drive means taking along special food, diapers, car seat, and so forth. But for the couple who really want children, the challenge and fun of watching a new human grow and learn can offset many of the problems entailed in the new parental roles.

During this first year the husband must make the adjustment to sharing the wife's love and attention. This can be difficult for a husband who is accustomed to being the center of "his" wife's life. Now suddenly the baby takes priority. As we mentioned earlier, it is not uncommon for a new father to feel some resentment and jealousy over this change in his position. Although most couples are financially strained at this time in their marriage, it is important that they arrange times to be by themselves and that they remember to pay attention to their own relationship. In the past this was easier to do because often relatives were close by who could watch the infant. Today getting time together usually means paying someone to take care of the child. Such money is well spent if it gives the couple an opportunity to improve their own relationship. Their relationship is the primary one, and if it is good the chances are greater that the parents-children relationship will be good also.

Children learn trust through living in a trusting environment. This means that their needs are satisfied on a regular basis and that interactions with the environment are positive, stable, and satisfying. Parents who have a good relationship are better able to supply this kind of environment.

The term *oral-sensory* derives from the fact that eating and the infant's mouth and senses are its major means of knowing the world at this stage.

Toddler: The Muscular-Anal Stage—Autonomy versus Shame and Doubt (Two to Three Years of Age)

As children develop motor and mental capacities, opportunities to explore and manipulate the environment increase. From successful exploration and manipulation emerges a sense of autonomy and self-control. If the child is unsuccessful or made to feel unsuccessful by too-high parental expectations, feelings of shame and doubt may arise. This is a time of great learning. Children learn to walk, to talk, to feed and dress themselves, to say "no," and so forth. If parents thought the infant demanding, they learn what "demanding" really can be with their two- and three-year-olds. It seems there is not a minute's peace. The relationship between the parents can suffer during this time because of the constant demands and ensuing fatigue and frustrations engendered by the child's insatiable demands. On the other hand, it is exciting to see the child's skills rapidly developing. First steps, first words, and curiosity all make this period one of quick change for child and parent alike.

During this stage parents should try to create a stimulating environment for the child. As we mentioned earlier, stimulation appears to enhance learning skills. Alphabet books, creative toys that are strong enough to withstand the rough treatment given by most two- and three-year-olds, picture books, and an endless answering of questions all help stimulate the child. Toilet training, which also occurs during this period, needs to be approached positively and with humor if it is to be easily accomplished. The achievement of toilet training is a great relief to parents since the messy job of diaper changing and cleaning is over.

The name of this stage denotes the increasing activity of the child and the toilet-training tasks.

Early Childhood: The Locomotor-Genital Stage—Initiative versus Guilt (Four to Five Years of Age)

Children become increasingly capable of self-initiated activities, which is a source of pride for parents. It is exciting to see children's capabilities increase. With each passing month they seem to be more mature, have more personality, and become more fun to interact with. As their capabilities and interests expand, so must the parents'. Where children's energy comes from is a constant source of amazement and bewilderment to often-tired parents. However, school is just around the corner and with it comes a little free time.

Children who do not increase their capabilities, perhaps because of accident or illness, may feel guilty and inadequate about their chances of success in school.

Locomotor indicates that the child is now very active in the environment; *genital* refers to sex-organ interest and exploration.

School Age: The Latency Stage—Industry versus Inferiority (Six to Eleven Years of Age)

At last the children are in school and for a few hours a day the house is peaceful. Now the children's peers begin to play a more active part in the family's life. Relationships broaden considerably as parents also become PTA members, den mothers,. or Little League coaches. This is often a period of relative family tranquility as far as the child is concerned.

The children's increasing independence also affects the parents. They find that what other parents allow their children to do becomes an important influence on their own children. "Mom, everyone else can do this, why can't I?" becomes a major protest of children trying to get their own way.

The children have new ideas, a new vocabulary, and broader desires, all of which can conflict with parental values. Reports about the children's behavior may also come from other parents, teachers, and authorities. How the children are doing at school becomes a source of concern.

Children become increasingly expensive as they grow. They eat more, their clothes cost more, and more money is needed for school and leisure activities. For many parents this becomes a time of juggling schedules to meet the demands of after-school sports, PTA meetings, Little League, and music lessons.

Yet for most families the elementary school years go smoothly. Children become more interesting, more individual, and increasingly independent. More important for the parents is their own increased freedom because the children are now away from home for part of the day.

During this time it is especially important for parents to work together in childrearing. By this time children are aware and insightful and can work their parents against one another to achieve their ends unless the parents coordinate. Children can cause conflict between their parents, particularly if the parents differ widely in their philosophy of childrearing. Often a well-functioning supportive husband-wife relationship can serve to buffer or inhibit the negative impact of a difficult child. Couples that do not enjoy a supportive relationship may find that fighting about the children is one of the major points of disruption in their relationship (Belsky, Learner, & Spanier, 1984, p. 129).

Latency refers to the general sexual quietness of this stage, although there is more sexual activity than Erikson thought.

Puberty
Biological changes a child goes through to become an adult capable of reproduction

Adolescence
The general social as well as biological changes a child experiences in becoming an adult

The Puberty-Adolescence Stage: Identity versus Role Diffusion (Twelve to Eighteen Years of Age)

The tranquility of the elementary school years is often shattered by the arrival of puberty. The internal physiological revolution causes children to requestion many earlier adjustments. **Puberty** signifies the biological changes every child, regardless of culture, must pass through to mature sexually. **Adolescence** encompasses puberty as well as the social and cultural conditions that must be met to become

TRY TO SEE IT MY WAY. I AM NEARLY TWENTY AND IF I WAS EVER GOING TO MAKE THE BREAK NOW WAS THE TIME TO DO IT IMAGINE HALF MY GIRL FRIENDS WERE ALREADY SEPARATED FROM THEIR HUSBANDS AND HERE I WAS STILL LIVING AT HOME!

SO I TOLD MY PARENTS I WAS MOVING OUT

YOU CAN'T IMAGINE THE YELLING AND SCREAMING MY FATHER SAID "YOU'RE BREAKING YOUR MOTHER'S HEART!" MY MOTHER SAID "WHAT WAS MY CRIME? WHAT WAS MY TERRIBLE CRIME?"

AND BEFORE I KNEW IT WE WERE IN THE MIDDLE OF A BIG ARGUMENT AND I TOLD THEM THEY BOTH NEEDED ANALYSIS AND THEY TOLD ME I HAD A FILTHY MOUTH AND SUDDENLY I WAS OUT ON THE STREET WITH MY RAINCOAT, MY SUITCASE AND MY TENNIS RACKET BUT I HAD NO PLACE TO MOVE!

SO I LOOKED AROUND DOWNTOWN AND EVERYTHING WAS TOO EXPENSIVE AND EVENING CAME AND ALL MY GIRL FRIENDS HAD RECONCILED WITH THEIR HUSBANDS SO THERE WAS ABSOLUTELY NO PLACE I COULD SPEND THE NIGHT

WELL, FRANKLY WHAT ON EARTH COULD I DO? I WAITED TILL IT WAS WAY PAST MY PARENTS BEDTIME. THEN I SNEAKED BACK INTO THE HOUSE AND SET THE ALARM IN MY BEDROOM FOR SIX THE NEXT MORNING.

THEN I SLEPT ON TOP OF THE BED SO I WOULDN'T WRINKLE ANY SHEETS, SNEAKED SOME BREAKFAST IN THE MORNING AND GOT OUT BEFORE ANYONE WAS UP.

I'VE BEEN LIVING THAT WAY FOR TWO MONTHS NOW.

EVERY NIGHT AFTER MIDNIGHT I SNEAK INTO MY BEDROOM, SLEEP ON TOP OF THE BED TILL SIX THE NEXT MORNING, HAVE BREAKFAST AND SNEAK OUT

AND EVERY DAY I CALL UP MY PARENTS FROM THE DOWNSTAIRS DRUGSTORE AND THEY YELL AND CRY AT ME TO COME BACK. BUT, OF COURSE, I ALWAYS TELL THEM NO.

I'LL NEVER GIVE UP MY INDEPENDENCE.

an adult. The adolescent period in Western societies tends to be exaggerated and prolonged, with a great deal of ambiguity and marked inconsistencies of role. Adolescents are often confused about proper behavior and what is expected of them. They are not yet adults, but at the same time they are not allowed to remain children. For example, an eighteen-year-old boy may enter the armed services and participate in battle, yet in many states he may not legally drink beer. The fact that prolonged adolescence is a cultural artifact does not lessen the problems of the period.

The problems of puberty and adolescence fall into four main categories:

1. Accepting a new body image and appropriate sexual expression
2. Establishing independence and a sense of personal identity
3. Forming good peer group relations
4. Developing goals and a philosophy of life

During this stage peer influence becomes stronger than parental influence. What friends say is more important than what parents say. The major problem facing parents now is how to give up their control, how to have enough faith in the child to "let go."

Parents, entering middle age, are also facing problems of requestioning and reordering their lives (see Chapter 14). They must begin to think about coping with the "empty-nest" period of their lives as their adolescent children grow into young aadulthood and leave home to establish their own families. Most research suggests that this is the stage of greatest family stress (Olson, 1986).

The Young Adulthood Stage: Intimacy versus Isolation

Although some children leave the family in their late teens, many remain longer, especially if they choose to go on to higher education. Seeking a vocation and a mate are the major goals of this period. In the past, success in these two tasks ended children's dependence on the family. Today, however, parents often continue to support their children for several more years of schooling and may sometimes support a beginning family if a child marries during school. This can be a financially strained period for the family. In addition, studies indicate that the presence in the home of unmarried sons and daughters over eighteen can be a strain on their parents' relationship. Both husbands and wives often report that this period when older children are living at home is a dissatisfying time in their marriage (Glick & Lin, 1986).

John is twenty, living at home with his parents, William and Jan. John works and contributes a little toward the food budget. However, his parents find that his living at home strains their relationship. John has a new car and insists that because it is new, it should have a place in the garage. His father often transports clients in his car, and though it is older he feels that it must be parked inside so it remains clean. Jan often intercedes in her son's behalf, "Oh, William, it's his first car, let him use the garage."

> *This angers William, and he sometimes feels as though it's two against one. He also has wanted a den for years and would like to convert John's bedroom into one. When he encourages John to look for his own place, Jan feels that he is "just throwing him out." "We should be happy that he wants to be with us." However, Jan does find it difficult when John has his friends over. They take over the living room and television, leaving her and William with little to do but retreat to their bedroom.*

Ideally, by the time their children are grown, parents like and love them and take pride in a job well done. Now, after twenty or more years the marital relationship again concerns just two people, husband and wife. Sometimes parents discover that their relationship has been forfeited because of the urgency of parenthood. In this case they face a period of discovery and rediscovery, of building a new relationship, or of emptiness. Parents must work to maintain their relationship all through the period of childrearing. If they fail to do this, their relationship may become simply "for the children." In this case when the children leave, there may be no relationship between the husband and wife (see Chapter 14).

Broader Parenting

Perhaps the dissatisfaction and decreased marital happiness felt by some parents result from the American nuclear family where one father and one mother are expected to give a child total parenting: all the care, love, and attention that is necessary for healthy growth. But most societies do not expect one father and one mother to supply 100 percent of a child's needs. Grandmothers and grandfathers, aunts and uncles (blood relatives or not), older siblings, and many others also supply parenting to children.

In many American suburban families, children and their parents (especially children and their mothers) are basically alone together. The parents cannot get away from the small child for a needed rest and participation in adult activities, and the child cannot get away from the parents. The nuclear family is often too isolated from friends and relatives who might occasionally serve as substitute parents.

> *Susan and her mother have always disagreed but recently, with puberty, the conflict has intensified to such a point that the entire family is in constant turmoil. Susan and her mother simply cannot communicate at this time. Susan feels that her mother doesn't understand her, and her mother feels that Susan is too defensive to talk to and won't listen. Susan says her mother is old-fashioned and behind the times. Her mother feels that Susan lacks respect for her elders and is insensitive to others in general.*
>
> *Susan relies on her girlfriends for advice. Yet she needs a female adult with whom she can communicate her fear and anxieties about becoming an adult and from whom she can learn. In the past Susan could have turned to a grandmother or an aunt who lived in the family or nearby.*

What if parents find they can't be good parents for a particular child? The child will be trapped in the setting for years. In the past this child could possibly have lived with relatives who might be better suited to act as his or her parents. Children were sometimes traded between families for short periods, spent summers on a farm, were helped to grow by numerous adults and older children. This extended family meant that no one person or couple was responsible for total parenting. Some critics of the nuclear family suggest that the nuclear family pattern of parents and children always alone together creates problems in children rather than preventing them. Inasmuch as the reality of the nuclear family is the only reality small children may know, they cannot correct misperceptions. Because they have no other basis by which to compare how adults act, it is difficult for them to recognize problems and reorient themselves.

Broader parenting might be supplied by trading care of children with other families, volunteer community nursery schools, business-supplied day-care centers for workers, and expanding the nuclear family to include relatives. Volunteering to work in a community nursery is also a way for prospective parents to gain experience with children.

Parents Without Pregnancy: Adoption

We usually think of adoption as the resort of a couple who cannot conceive children. However, there are many other reasons for adoption. A couple may not be able to care for their children, for example, so friends or relatives may adopt the children in order to give them a home. Or a couple may feel strongly about the problems of overpopulation and decide to adopt rather than add to the population. Or a husband or wife may wish to adopt their spouse's other children by a prior marriage in order to become their legal parent as well as their stepparent.

The choice to adopt a child is just that, a reasoned decision, a choice made by a couple after a great deal of deliberation and thought. As such the decision-making process leading to adoption makes an ideal model that all couples desiring children can follow. Adoption takes time, and certain requirements such as family stability, finances, and housing must be met by the prospective parents. Costs of adoption range from $500 to $3000.

Although there are many older children and children with special problems available for adoption, infants are in short supply. In the past, most infants available for adoption were supplied by mothers having children out of wedlock. However, as America's sexual mores relaxed, the stigma of out-of-wedlock birth also lessoned. Today approximately 75 percent of white children and 94 percent of black children born out of wedlock are kept by their mother (Belsky, Learner, & Spanier, 1984, p. 32). In California, for example, there are approximately twenty-five couples seeking each adoptable infant (Cohen, 1986).

Adoptive parents have some advantages as well as disadvantages compared with natural parents. For example, adoptive parents may choose their child. To some degree they can pick genetic, physical, and mental characteristics of the child. They can bypass some of the earlier years of childhood if they desire. On the other hand, they do not experience pregnancy and birth, which help focus a couple on impending parenthood. Of course, some may consider this another advantage of adoption.

A unique parenting problem faced by adoptive parents is that of deciding whether and when to share the knowledge of adoption with the child. Experts believe the best course is to inform the child from the beginning, but this is sometimes difficult for parents to do. They may fear that such information will affect the child's love for them. They may want to tell them but simply keep avoiding it until it seems too late. Most adoption agencies, such as The Children's Home Society, supply counseling to prospective adoptive parents on how to handle telling the child. The problems created for both parents and children if the children find out about their adoptive status from others are usually greater and often harm the parent-child relationship. The basic trust of the children in their parents may be weakened or perhaps even destroyed if the parents aren't the ones to tell them.

At some time in their lives many adoptive children feel the need to know something about their natural parents. In most legal adoptions, however, records identifying the true parents are unavailable. At this time only the state of Kansas has open adoption records, although adoptees are pressuring all states to make information about their real parents available. Because adoption records are often unavailable to the adoptee, there can be problems in getting passports and other situations where a valid birth certificate is necessary. Adoption records have been closed in the past to avoid the situation in which a biological parent regrets the decision to give up the child and seeks to get the child back at some later date. The heartache possible for both biological and adoptive parents in such a situation is well documented.

Although seldom mentioned, parents who give up their child for adoption also sometimes feel the need to know what has become of their child. Parents who give a child up to an adoption agency rather than using a direct adoption may never know if the child is actually adopted.

For many years legal adoption was a drawn-out process wherein prospective parents went through a strenuous screening process to establish their parental suitability. Recently such screening has been minimized. In a few cases, especially with older children, single persons are being allowed to adopt. Cooperative adoption, in which the biological parents and the adoptive parents mutually work out the adoption, is also being tried. The idea is that the child is gaining a family rather than losing a family when adoption occurs. Needless to say such cooperative adoptions must be entered carefully so that problems do not arise later between the two sets of parents.

Adoption gives parentless children a home and family as well as giving childless couples children. Unfortunately, not all parentless children are easily adoptable. Many minority children are never adopted. However, those adopted into white families seem to adjust well (*Los Angeles Times*, 1985, p. 11). Children with defects and health problems are seldom sought by prospective adoptive parents. For the most part such children are reared in various kinds of institutions or by a series of short-term foster home placements.

The Single-Parent Family

The single-parent family is the fastest growing family form in the United States. The fact that for many single parents the situation is only temporary does not minimize the dramatic change in American family life brought about by this phenomenon.

Single-Parent Family Statistics

- One in every five families with children under eighteen years old is a one-parent family, up from one in every ten in 1970.
- From 1970 to 1984, the number of one-parent families more than doubled (from 3.2 million to 6.7 million).
- From 1970 to 1980, all families with children under eighteen increased by only 8 percent while similar two-parent families actually declined by 5 percent.
- Mother-child families comprise 88 percent of one-parent families.
- Mother-child families are disproportionately concentrated among blacks. About one-third of all mother-child families with children under eighteen are maintained by black women. Of all black families with children under eighteen 50 percent are mother-child families. Of white families with children under eighteen 15 percent are mother-child families.
- The fewer years of schooling a parent has completed, the greater the likelihood that the parent will be maintaining a one-parent family. Of single parents under forty-five years of age with children under eighteen years of age 28 percent had not received a high school diploma and only 9 percent had a college degree. In two-parent families, only about 15 percent of husbands had no high school degree but 25 percent had college degrees.
- Mother-child families with children under eighteen are economically worse off than other family forms. In 1984 two-parent families had a median income of $28,165, father-child families $19,950, mother-child families $9,153.
- Only 24 percent of all children under eighteen but 60 percent of children in mother-child families lived in families below the poverty level in 1983.
- If the various trends in divorce, unwed pregnancies, etc. hold, 60 percent of all children born today may expect to spend one year or longer in a one-parent family before they reach eighteen years of age. (All of the above statistics are from Norton & Glick, 1986).

Single-parent families derive from a number of sources. The largest percentage of one-parent families result from divorce. In 1984 42 percent of all one-parent families were maintained by a divorced parent; 24 percent by never-married mothers (a 500 percent increase since 1970); 8 percent by widows; and 23 percent by a separated parent (U.S. Bureau of Census, 1985). See Figure 13-3 for a comparison of the sources of one-parent families between 1970 and 1984.

The increase in single-parent families is due mainly to the rapid increase in divorce rates over the past decade. The number of children with divorced mothers has doubled since 1970. Although the actual number of children is far smaller, the number with a never-married mother has tripled. This dramatic change is not really a great increase in illegitimacy but rather a dramatic increase in the number of unwed mothers who opt to keep their child (94 percent of adolescent unwed mothers). The so-called teenage pregnancy epidemic of the 1970s turns out to be more of a teenage baby-keeping epidemic (Scharf, 1979; see Scenes from Marriage, Chapter 11). And because these mothers had been a major source of babies for adoption agencies, such agencies are now having a difficult time finding enough children to keep up with the demand as we saw.

As we have noted, the rising divorce rate has been the major contributing factor to the increase in single-parent families. Beginning in 1980, however, the divorce rate began to level out (Chapter 15), so we can expect the rate of increase of

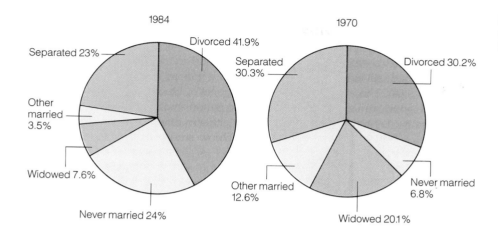

1984

1970

Separated 23%

Divorced 41.9%

Separated
30.3%

Divorced 30.2%

Other
married
3.5%

Never married
6.8%

Widowed 7.6%

Other married
12.6%

Never married 24%

Widowed 20.1%

Figure 13-3 Children living with one parent, by marital status of parent; 1984 and 1970.

single-parent families also to slow. Remember also that single-parent families tend to be transitional because marriage rates for single parents are high (Reiss, 1980; Norton & Glick, 1986).

Although family form (single-parent, nuclear, three-generation, foster, and so forth) affects children, the old idea that only the traditional two-parent, father-mother family does a good job in rearing children is passing (Marotz-Baden et al., 1979). However, there is little doubt that single parenting has more inherent problems than two-parent childrearing. In many ways the problems of the single-parent family are exaggerated duplicates of the working mother's problems.

The majority of single-parent families are women and their children. Thus for them all of the problems encountered by the working mother are present (see Chapter 9). Low pay, child-care problems, overburden caused by working and continuing to shoulder household and childrearing duties face the single mother. The single father may face these same problems, except that his pay is usually much better. A problem that most fathers face is that the home and child-care burdens are new and often frightening at first.

Single-parent families headed by women with small earning power suffer numerous logistic problems. Finding child care that is not exorbitant in cost is a major concern. Finding adequate housing in a satisfactory neighborhood is often impossible. Even in small cities female-headed families are concentrated in less desirable blocks of the city (Roncek, Bell & Chaldin, 1980; Norton & Glick, 1986). Larger amounts of welfare aid go to these families than to any others, which is indicative of the financial difficulties they face.

Social isolation is one of the problems faced by any single parent. Juggling work, home maintenance, and child-care duties usually leaves one little time for either social interaction or self-improvement activities. Emotional isolation is a second major problem. Having no other adult in the home with whom to interact often leads to feelings of loneliness and a sense of powerlessness. If one is a separated, divorced, or unmarried parent, emotional isolation may be increased by the social stigma sometimes attached to these statuses. The early widowed parent, on the other hand, will experience sympathy and support from society.

Many single parents attempt to alleviate isolation and reduce living expenses by making greater use of shared living arrangements. One study indicates that

---

The Single-Parent Family Can Do as Good a Job Rearing Children as the Two-Parent Family

The single-parent family is no less a family than the two-parent family. It is simply a different family structure for carrying out family functions. As Parents Without Partners (America's largest self-help group for single parents) points out, "It is the quality of parenting, not the quantity of parents, that counts most in rearing children."

Two-parent families in which both parents work, or in which there is a great deal of conflict, may offer little quality time to their children. Thirty minutes of quality time with a child is worth more than hours of nonattentive time such as when the parents are preoccupied with their work or with watching television. Quality time includes the element of mutual response, attending fully to the child, talking to, playing with, expressing affection for the child and these can all be offered to the child by a single parent.

Although quality time cannot be dictated, the parent needs to plan some time alone with children. Here single parents have a decided advantage in that they are 100 percent in charge of their free time and do not have to share it with a spouse. Total attention can be directed at the child rather than only partial attention as when some attention must be reserved for the spouse in the two-parent family.

Choose activities that both you and the child enjoy. If you also enjoy the activity, your enthusiasm will interact with that of your child to create quality time. Again it is easier for a single parent since the single parent does not have to find an activity that both the child and the spouse enjoy.

Don't try for quality time when you first arrive home from work. Allow yourself time to relax and be honest with your child if you are too tired for active play. You need energy to create quality time, so give yourself time to build up energy after a long day's work. Again the single parent has an advantage over the two-parent family spouse in that energy does not have to be shared with another adult. If one is tired, the little energy available can be used to create quality time with your child.

Since the single parent does not have to share emotional resources with a spouse, it is clear that with some planning and a strong commitment to making quality time available for parent-child interaction, the single parent can be an effective parent.

---

23 percent of the single-parent sample had a second adult (usually a relative) living in the household, whereas only 9 percent of the two-parent families shared their household with another adult (Smith, 1980).

It will be a long time before all of the evidence is in about the ability of the single-parent family to rear children successfully. There is no doubt that the job is much harder for the single parent, but whether this will result in increasing numbers of problem children and hence problem adults is still debatable. In 1965 Patrick Moynihan suggested that the American family, especially the black family was in serious trouble. He was roundly criticized for his viewpoint. In 1986, in

---

The Single-Parent Family Has Too Many Difficulties to Do a Good Job of Childrearing

It is clear from looking at the statistics on single-parent families that such a family has many more obstacles to overcome to find success in childrearing. It is also clear that most single parents must work, which necessitates leaving their children with caretakers for most of the day. Also for mother-child families (88 percent of all single-parent families) simply surviving financially is a difficult task. Survival difficulty makes it likely that single parents are worried, frustrated, monetarily unfree, and unable therefore to give their best to their children.

Also the single parent must bear all responsibilities without support from another adult. There is little chance of escape for the tired, depressed, financially strapped single parent since there is usually no other adult to assume responsibility for the children during the single parent's free time. Also for the working single parent to place the children with a caretaker during free time is difficult psychologically. After all, the child is with a caretaker all day long. The simple logistics of the single parent's situation makes quality time with children almost impossible to create.

Character formation is the essential family task, for the obvious reason that children are first formed by families. If the family does not lay the needed psychic foundation, it falls to the schools to try to do it. To date, however, the schools have not been an adequate substitute for the family in the forming of basic character in the young.

For the educational mission of the family, character formation, it is essential to have active and involved parenthood, accorded sufficient time and commitment, at least for the children's formative years, especially from birth until age six but preferably until the end of adolescence. What children require above all are parents who care, educate, have a commitment to parenting and the energy to back up their commitment, and have a relationship to emulate. Hence parents who are overworked, habitually tired, or consumed by their own personal problems are unable to provide effective basic parenting.

Because of the difficult logistical situation of the average single parent, basic parenting often is nearly impossible. It is estimated that there were more than 6.5 million "latchkey kids" in 1983. These are children who must fend for themselves because they have no parenting adults at home much of the time (Long, 1983). Some suggest that the full impact of the dramatic changes in childrearing (working mothers, single-parent families, etc.) will show up in increasing neglect of American children (*U.S. News and World Report*, 1982).

As part of the ideology that tries to legitimate absent parenting, it has been argued that "quality" counts; that if you cannot spend much time with your child, you can make up for this by making the minutes you do provide "count." Pop psychologists who promote this notion do not cite any data to show that one can make minutes into quality time on order. Indeed, it is more plausible that quality time occurs when one has longer stretches of "quantity" time. Most important, there is no evidence that quality time can make up for long stretches of no time (Etzioni, 1983).

In general the increasing numbers of single-parent families mean that the chances for successful parenting are reduced and that lack of character development in America's children may soon become the nation's number one problem if it isn't already.

---

his book *Family and Nation*, Moynihan again reviewed the American family and discovered that much of what he predicted about family problems had come true. In this case, his views found general acceptance among many family scholars. According to federal estimates 8 to 10 million American youngsters age six and under are in child-care situations. Latchkey children on the average spend two and one-half hours a day without adult supervision (Turkington, 1983, p. 19). A combination of divorce, unmarried births, dual-worker families, and a preoccupation with self may mean that more American children are indeed neglected children.

Summary

Parenthood remains one of the major functions of marriage. Despite decreasing emphasis on it and more tolerance of childlessness for married couples, the majority of married couples will become parents.

Planning for parenthood, improving parenting skills, working as a parent team, and understanding the course of development a child passes through in becoming an adult are all important to successful parenting. In addition, understanding how children will affect the parental relationship is crucial. No one method has yet been discovered whereby parents can assure the successful upbringing of their children. The fact is that parenthood is a difficult and ever-changing job that demands intelligence, flexibility, emotional warmth, and stability, as well as a good portion of courage.

Children will affect their parents in many ways. Bringing the first baby home immediately changes the lifestyle of the parents. Suddenly they have a dependent and demanding person to take care of who contributes little to the family. Not only is room taken up in the family's living place, but additional funds are needed to care for the new family member. Dad and Mom will both come second to the infant's demands. Although one can divorce a troublesome spouse, there is little that parents can do to escape a troublesome child. Legally and morally, children are the parents' responsibility until they reach legal adulthood. Even then parents in many cases will still shoulder responsibility for their children, for example when they go to graduate school.

Erik Erikson identifies eight psychosocial developmental stages that describe the human life cycle from infancy through old age. The first six are important to parents. They are the oral-sensory stage (first year), the muscular-anal stage (two to three years), the locomotor-genital stage (four to five years), the latency stage (six to eleven years), the puberty-adolescence stage (twelve to eighteen years), and the young adulthood stage (eighteen to thirty, approximately). Each stage has certain tasks that the child must accomplish to become a successful adult. By knowing what stage a child is passing through and the kinds of tasks that characterize the stage, parents can better understand the child and plan helpful activities.

Broader parenting would help parents do a better job. Having alternative sources of parenting available would serve a number of helpful purposes. Parents would have time-out periods from their children. This would allow them to concentrate for a short period on themselves and their relationship and would give them a respite from the burdens and responsibilities of the children. The children would have a broader set of influences and greater stimulation. They would also learn to cope with new and different kinds of people. In general their experience base would be broader.

Adoption is another avenue to parenthood. It has the advantages of contributing to population control as well as allowing parents greater choice in selection of the children they want. It does, however, involve the difficulty of having to tell the children that they are adopted.

The single-parent family, although usually transitory, is more common today than ever before. Such a family faces many problems, but with support is capable of doing a good childrearing job. Adolescent parents also face special problems, the main one being that the parents themselves are still in the process of becoming fully functioning adults and parenthood makes this job harder.

Parenthood is an important part of most marriages. Good planning will help make parenthood a positive factor in marriages.

Television as a Surrogate Parent

In most American homes three parents mind the children: the father, the mother, and television. Indeed with the increasing incidence of single-parent (especially mother only) families, television has perhaps replaced father for a good many children. Certainly it can be said of the generations born in the 1960s or later that they are the product of the television age.

By age sixteen most children have spent more time watching television than going to school (Singer, 1983). A Nielson survey in 1984 found that preschool children watched television on the average of twenty-seven hours and nine minutes each week or an average of three hours and forty minutes per day (re:act, 1984).

What effect does all of this TV viewing have on children? Most researchers feel that the effects are negative yet they have been hard-pressed to document their feelings. Essentially three major problems are cited: the effect of commercials, the content of programs, especially violence, and the time spent in passive observation.

Small children accept commercial messages uncritically because their thinking processes are not advanced enough to make judgments about truth and fantasy. Because young children believe everything they see in commercials, they are easily manipulated into wanting everything they see. The parents are therefore placed in the position of resisting the constant demands of their children or succumbing and buying everything from expensive toys that soon become boring or broken to sugared cereals and drinks that promote tooth decay (Berger, 1986, p. 334).

The content of television programs is even more controversial. As early as 1952, congressional hearings investi-

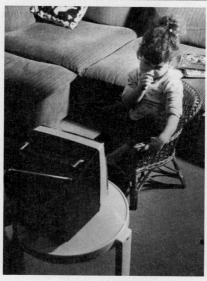

gated the amount of violence on TV. Over the years there has been a great deal of research on the violence question and yet the answers remain somewhat clouded. For instance, recent research (Singer & Sherrod, 1979; Singer & Singer, 1981) on three- and four-year-olds attending nursery school correlated their imaginativeness, emotionality, aggression, cooperation, interaction, and mood with their parents' reports of television watching by the child. A strong relationship was found between frequent physical aggression and frequent viewing of all

but educational children's programs. Viewing of the latter programs, on the other hand, was found to be related to prosocial behavior and to using mature language in school. This research example reflects the mixed findings about television viewing that often emerge from the research. However, as far as violence viewing on television is concerned, most researchers now conclude that there is at least a moderate causal relationship between television violence and later aggressive behavior (Pearle, 1984). Certainly all researchers agree that television is indeed an important influence on children and is *perhaps* as influential as parents themselves (Rubinstein, 1983).

It is also clear that television is affecting the whole American society, not just the children. For example, in a recent Florida murder case a young man was convicted of killing his elderly neighbor despite the plea of "involuntary subliminal television intoxication." On a worldwide level it is obvious too that many terrorist acts are perpetrated to bring media attention to the people or "cause" espoused by the terrorist group (Schorr, 1981).

Aside from violence, the content of television allows children access to all of the social and human problems from which they were shielded to some extent in the past. Postman (1982) suggests that television is doing away with childhood. What makes one group (adults) different from another group (children) is the knowledge they possess. When knowledge was gained through the written word, a child had to learn to read before newspaper stories of violence or corruption could be understood. Today, via picture and word, understanding for children can be immediate. The constant reporting of all of the negative happenings in the world leads to skepticism about the worth of the adult society. Children who view a great deal of television are more likely to view the world as a mean and scary place. To what extent does viewing so much that is negative about the world undermine a child's belief in adult rationality, in the possibility of an ordered world, in a hopeful future? Without such hopes and beliefs, there is little chance that a person will work to better the human condition.

Also the way in which television content is presented leads to difficulty for the child. Everything is handled quickly. For example, there may be ten books and hundreds of research papers on AIDS, but when television does an "in-depth" study of the AIDS epidemic, it lasts forty-five seconds for each of four different nights. Thus a major social problem is condensed into three minutes interspersed among commercials. How important can it be?? Some suggest that watching television is like attending a party populated by people you don't know. Every few seconds you are introduced to a new person as you move through the room. The general effect is one of excitement, but in the end it is hard to remember the names of the guests or what they said. It is of no importance that you do, in any case. Tomorrow there will be another party. Why bother to concentrate on one person or a topic when by tomorrow there will be all new people and topics? The classroom

teacher who must ask pupils to concentrate in order to learn is hard put to compete against the excitement and constant change of the television set. Many teachers report that holding students' attention has become their major classroom problem.

Hours of passive observation deprive the child of social interaction as well as of the physical activity necessary to grow in a healthful manner. Many children now enter school without any social skills because they have had so little social interaction. Many children also appear in poor physical condition, apparently because they have little active play time. Some families who voluntarily gave up television viewing reported that their children played and read more, that siblings fought less, that family activities became more common, and that mealtimes were longer (Chira, 1984).

Because television viewing has a strong impact on viewers, especially children, it is important for parents to consider its place in their home. How can it be used to promote prosocial rather than antisocial behavior? How can it improve children's cognitive development rather than retard it? A few concerned parents who object to the negative influence of television opt to have no television. Yet as children grow and begin to visit friends, this strategy can backfire because the children end up watching at friends' houses, thus limiting parental control over television input. Inasmuch as 95 percent of American homes contain television, the

best course of action for parents is to set up supervised viewing for their children. First, parents will need to consider the role of television in their own lives. For instance, if a mother has the TV turned on all day for company while she is alone at home, she will need to decide whether she wants to continue this.

Once parents determine their own preferences about television's role in their lives, they will need to set appropriate ground rules for their children. These rules should include:

1. How much time per day and per week the children may devote to television
2. The actual time of the day or evening that television may be watched
3. The kinds of programs that may be watched
4. The amount of adult attention and discussion to be given during and after TV viewing (such parental interaction with the child has been found to mitigate the negative effects we have been discussing)
5. How much to use television as a reward in order to influence other kinds of behavior besides television viewing

Parents who are unwilling or unable to control their children's use of television abrogate parental responsibility, thus leaving television as the main parent influencing their children's development.

Chapter 14

Family Life Stages: Midlife Crises to Surviving Spouses

Contents

Blush   *Donna and Bill spend a great deal of time romancing one another. Candlelight dinners, interesting evenings at musical and/or dramatic events, lots of hugging and loving. They have been married two years and are still in the honeymoon stage.*

Blur   *Donna and Bill spend a great deal of time talking about Little League baseball, driving children to music lessons, hearing about each other's work experiences and wondering if they will ever find time to hug and love again. They have been married fifteen years (childrearing stage).*

Backlash   *The travel folders and maps are out and Donna and Bill are planning their first vacation alone together in twenty years. Goodness, they even hugged and loved last Sunday morning without fear of interruption. You guessed it, they have been married twenty-five years and the last child has left home. They are reawakening to one another (middle-age stage).*

Balance   *Donna and Bill love and respect one another and are enjoying their lives, their children, their grandchildren, and Bill's retirement. They often look at one another and say, "What do you know, we really survived all of the ups and downs and made it." They have been married forty years and are 90 percent sure they will reach their "golden" wedding anniversary, health permitting (retirement stage).*

Donna and Bill may be the same people (at least in name) as when they first married, but it is clear that they have been through a number of different marriages, even if each marriage was to one another.

The flush of love and the excitement of exploring a new relationship effectively keep most newly married couples from thinking about later stages of their relationship. After all who can think about children leaving home when no children have yet arrived? What possible relevance can retirement have for a twenty-three-year-old man receiving his first job promotion? And what newly married woman can be thinking about the very real likelihood that she will spend the last ten to fifteen years of her life as a widow, alone and without this man she now loves so much?

Yet these are important questions with which almost all married couples must come to grips at some time in their lives. Perhaps one way that you can make such questions relevant is to consider them in the context of your parents' and grandparents' lives. We cannot expect to live our lives identically to our relatives' because we are different individuals and live in changing times. Yet their lives may serve as a preview for some of the changes that will come into our own lives.

If you have children, the day will come when your children leave home. This is a change that you will have to face as did your parents and their parents before them. The couple who thinks about and prepares for these inevitable family life changes before they occur stands a better chance of adapting to them in a creative and healthy manner.

Any family relationship can change, just as individuals within the relationship can and do change. Change does not mean the end of the relationship. Indeed, lack of change over time is usually unhealthy and may ultimately lead to the demise of the relationship.

Marriage changes, just as people change. In a sense Donna and Bill had many different marriages over the course of their lives together. Change can be for better or worse. If a marriage changes too much for the worse, it may end. On the other hand, individuals and families can grow in positive directions to become stronger, more intimate, more communicative, more need fulfilling, more supportive, and more loving. Because change cannot be avoided, the real question to answer becomes, "Will I cope with the changes in my life and family in a positive and healthy manner?" To answer this question, we must first consider the changes that can be expected.

An Overview of Family Life Stages

Dividing family life into stages will help us gain better understanding of the changes that people go through as they move from birth to death. A developmental stage approach has long been taken in studying children, as we saw in Chapter 13. The prenatal stage, infancy, preschool, school, prepuberty, puberty, adolescence, and young adulthood are all well-known developmental stages in the life of the maturing human.

What about stages in the life of a maturing marriage? If we examine the general kinds of problems faced at various marital stages, we find that for the average American couple there are six important periods in a long-term marriage: (1) newly married, (2) early parenthood, (3) later parenthood, (4) middle age (empty nest), (5) retirement, and (6) widowed singleness.

The problems of the *newly married* stage revolve around adjusting to each other, establishing a home, setting directions to the relationship, learning to confront the world as a pair rather than as individuals, and learning to work together to achieve mutually accepted goals. These problems have already been discussed in various parts of preceding chapters.

The arrival of children places a couple in the parental role. This change will compound the problems of a newly married couple, especially if children arrive shortly after marriage, before the couple has had much time to work out the problems of the first stage.

Early parenthood covers pregnancy, birth, infants, toddlers, preschoolers, and elementary school children. When puberty arrives and the children move into junior and senior high school, college, and the young adult world, the problems parents face change drastically. So drastic are the changes that it is worthwhile to examine this period in marriage separately—hence the third stage, *later parenthood*. As we saw in Chapter 13, adolescence is actually a combination of puberty—the biological maturing of the child—and the social expectations placed on the child to behave in an adult manner. America, like many western cultures, does not sharply define entrance into adulthood. In fact, the adolescent period in America is nebulous, conflicting, and confused because it extends well beyond the achievement of biological maturity. Because of this, many parents find later parenthood a trying time. Children become increasingly independent, yet parents are still legally and ethically responsible for their children's actions. Finances can be strained, especially if the children go on to higher education. Parents also have to begin adjusting to their children's adult sexuality and mate selection process, which culminates in the acceptance of a new family as the children marry and reproduce.

The remaining three stages, middle age, retirement, and widowed singleness have all been greatly affected by increased life expectancy. In 1900 life expectancy for white males was 48.2 years and for white females 51.1 years. By 1985 the figures were 72 years and 79 years respectively. Peter Uhlenberg (1980) suggests a number of family effects when increased life expectancy and declining mortality are combined:

- Decreased infant and childhood mortality encourages a stronger emotional bond between parents and children and reduces fertility since it is no longer necessary to have two babies to produce one adult.
- The number of living grandparents is greatly increased for children and thus three-, four-, and even five-generation families are more common.
- Marriages potentially can last much longer so that more couples experience middle age and prolonged retirement together or divorce.
- Greater survival advantages for women relative to men have increased the period of widowhood at the end of the life course.
- The number of elderly persons depending on middle-aged children is increasing.

Thus, the final three family life stages take on a new and important significance as life expectancy increases.

The *middle-aged (empty nest)* stage begins when the last child leaves home. However, for many couples the parental role continues in that they may still give monetary and psychological support to their newly independent or married children. Even in the grandparent role parents often continue many parental behaviors because children are still part of the couple's lives at times. For others, especially traditional child-centered mothers, the empty nest stage can be one of loneliness and loss if the children move far away or reject continued parenting. New interests and goals must be developed to replace the lost parenting functions. The husband may need to help his wife reorient her life away from the children and this in turn will usually influence his own life. Fathers or career-oriented mothers survive this stage more easily than traditional mothers, because many of their goals and fulfillments lie outside the family. Their feelings of loss when the children leave are usually less severe.

The husband and wife may draw closer during the middle-aged stage. In earlier marital years many wives devoted their energies to the children, and their husbands devoted themselves to their work. Husband and wife may well have grown emotionally apart. When the children are gone a couple may renew their life together, reinvest in one another, and lay the foundation to the next marital stage, *retirement.*

Increasing life expectancy, automation, and America's emphasis on youth have combined almost to double the length of retirement in the average worker's life during this century. Torry (1982) estimates that people now spend at least a quarter of their adult lives in retirement. The retiring worker faces the problem of adjusting to leisure after years of basing much of his or her self-worth on working and income production. In addition our work ethic says that stature is gained by a work orientation, not leisure. Retirement equals obsolescence in the view of American society. For the productive worker retirement presents a choice: adjust or be miserable.

In a sense retirement for a worker is similar to the empty nest stage for the traditional child-centered wife. The retiree must cope with lack of purpose and feelings of uselessness. Those who cannot find substitute goals find retirement an unhappy period. For some it is literally a short-lived period; death often arrives shortly after retirement for those who cannot adjust. On the other hand, especially for those that have been financially successful, retirement may mean rebirth rather than death. It may signal a new beginning, expanding interests, and rediscovery of the marital partner. Poor health and poverty are the two greatest enemies of the retired. Indeed economic necessity forces some 30 percent of men to continue working after age sixty-five.

Inevitably one of the marital partners dies, and so the final marital stage is usually a return to *widowed singleness.* In 1984 there were about 9.4 million widows in the United States, approximately six times the 1.7 million widowers (U.S. Bureau of the Census, April 1985, p. 200). These statistics point clearly to the fact that widowhood is a far greater possibility than becoming a widower. Although the percentage of widowed persons in the general population has dropped this century, the number of years that widowed singleness may be expected to last has risen dramatically. For example, half the women widowed at age sixty-five can expect fifteen more years of life. Thus this final marital stage can be especially lengthy for women.

Being widowed is predominantly an older person's problem. Younger widowed persons tend to remarry but remarriage becomes increasingly remote with advancing age. In 1981 only 1 percent of brides and 2 percent of grooms were sixty-five or older (U.S. National Center for Health Statistics, 1984, p. 8). For the widowed person who does remarry, being widowed may not be the last stage of marriage. Remarriage will reinstate an earlier marital stage.

Because we have discussed in earlier chapters the first three family life stages—newly married and early and later parenthood—we will devote the remainder of this chapter to the last three stages, middle age, retirement, and widow/widowerhood.

Middle Age (The Empty Nest)

For most couples middle age starts when the children become independent and ends when retirement draws near. Although these figures are arbitrary, most people are in this stage between the ages of forty and sixty-five.

The U.S. Census Bureau uses the age of forty-five to denote the onset of middle age. It is better, however, to delimit this stage by the kinds of changes and problems that occur. For example, a very young mother might face empty nest changes by the time she is thirty-five.

Historically, middle age is a relatively new stage in marriage. Due to the much shorter life spans before 1900 most wives buried their husbands before the last child left home. As Paul Glick points out, "In 1890 women bore their last child at thirty-two, buried their husband at age fifty-three and attended their last child's wedding at age fifty-five" (1955, p. 4). Thus for most marriages before 1900, there was no period of return to simply being a couple again. Yet today such a period is very likely, and the chances are great that it will last for fifteen to twenty-five years.

The changes faced during middle age can be somewhat different for men and women. If the woman has not had a career, her adjustment centers on no longer being needed by her children, whereas the man's problems usually revolve around his vocation and feelings of achievement and success.

For both partners, however, middle age reactivates many of the questions that

each thought had been answered much earlier in their lives. Indeed many of the questions that arise resemble those struggled with when the partners were adolescents: Who am I? Where am I going? How will I get there? What is life all about? How do I handle my changing sexuality? Hence the term **middlescence** has been coined to describe this stage.

Writers who compare middle age with adolescence and who discover an identity crisis in both periods disagree about what this crisis means (Kerckhoff, 1976). Some see middle age characterized by trying to avoid the recurring bizarre, irrational, sexually confused questions that first occurred at adolescence (Mc-Morrow, 1974). Others suggest that although middle age may be frustrating and upsetting, such problems can also produce growth. Still others deny that there is a real identity crisis during middle age (Skolnick, 1978, p. 265; 1983).

Those suggesting that the crisis of middle age does indeed exist and is useful say:

> Middlescence is the opportunity for going on with the identity crisis of the first adolescence. It is our second chance to find out what it really means to "do your own thing," to sing your own song, to be deeply true to yourself. It is a time for finding one's own truths at last, and thereby to become free to discover one's real identity. (LeShan, 1973)

In describing the pain and danger that middle-aged people will experience in reexamining their identities, Eda LeShan compares the process with a lobster's periodic shedding of its shell: It makes the lobster vulnerable, but allows it to grow.

Middlescence
The second adolescence, experienced in middle age, usually involving reevaluation of one's life

For some, then, it is no wonder that they choose to use their marriage as an escape from facing the existential challenges of middle age. They do not want to ask the important questions because it is safer to assume that marriage is answer enough.

Who am I?
I am Mr. or Mrs. Jones.

What is my life all about?
I am a wife or husband.
I do my duty to the family and help keep it running smoothly.

Where am I going?
We hope to take a trip to Cape Cod next summer.

What is life all about?
My marriage is the answer to all existential questions.
My marriage is my existence.

But to the couples who take the risk, the crisis of middle age can offer a chance to grow, and its problems can become a vehicle for growth. Marriage enrichment for the middle-aged couple is not to be focused on the improvement of marriage so much as on the improvement of the humans in it. It is not so much what actually happens to us in middle age as it is our attitude about it that really counts. We all experience some kind of crisis in this as in other stages, but how do we use the crisis? If we use it for further growth and expansion of our lives, our marriages, our relationships, and ourselves may all benefit and make the second half of our lives even more fulfilling than the first half.

The Authenticity Crisis of Midlife

Midlife crisis
The questioning of one's worth and values, usually beginning sometime in one's forties or early fifties

Speaking of the **midlife crisis** Gail Sheehy writes (1977, p. 350):

Deep down a change begins to register in those gut-level perceptions of safety and danger, time and no time, aliveness and stagnation. I start with a vague feeling. . . .

I have reached some sort of meridian in my life. I had better take a survey, reexamine where I have been, and reevaluate how I am going to spend my resources from here on. Why am I doing all this? What do I really believe in?

Underneath this vague feeling is the fact, as yet unacknowledged, that there is a down side to life, a back of the mountain, and that I have only so much time before the dark to find my own truth. As such thoughts grow, the continuity of the life cycle is disrupted. Somewhere between thirty-five and forty-five if we let ourselves, most of us will have a full-out authenticity crisis.

There is infinite variety in the way individuals face the questions that arise when they realize that life is finite. Some people simply look the other way and avoid the questions. Others try to change their external world by relocating, finding a new spouse or a new job. Others seek internal changes such as a new set of values or a new philosophy of life.

Obviously a person's life circumstances influence the questions and their answers. A child-centered mother out of the occupational world for twenty years may feel panic as she realizes that she will soon be unneeded by her children. Another mother who has always worked in addition to raising her children may be happy that her children will no longer need her, thus freeing some time to

---

Inset 14-1

Her New Life Begins on a Jarring Note

The morning after the wedding she found herself standing in her nightgown in the doorway of her daughter's room experiencing the void. "I almost feel as if she's died," the woman thought wryly. "Stop it. She's on her honeymoon, surely some of the happiest days of her life."

But later, as she packed away some childhood artifacts to be put in the attic for the grandchildren, the hollowness returned. Her daughter was not planning any babies right away. It would be a long time before she might need a grandmother's help.

The woman heard the question echoing in her head again: "Of what use am I, really? What's my function now?" She became angry at herself for permitting the question, in this form, and the anger diffused toward her husband.

Riding home in the car after the wedding, they'd had the worst fight of their marriage. "You're actually glad they're all gone," she had cried out.

"Of course. It's over—we've done our job," he had said.

"What's over?" she had flared. "You sound as if you're planning to cut our children right out of your life." She had known at the time that she was overstating; obviously he loved the kids.

But finally he had said those bitter words: "You became a different woman with the first baby. All those years you were a mother first and a wife second. Sometimes I felt I was at the bottom of your list, right after the dog."

Outrageous and cruel. Not true. Not true at all. He'd had too much champagne, and now suddenly he was like a wounded little boy: "You never had time for me. Your mind was always somewhere else. If a child sneezed you were out of my arms in a flash, like a mother bear defending her cubs in mortal danger."

Sex, that was it. "Yes, that is it," he had said. "But also when we were talking, or not talking. Or trying to do something together as adults, just the two of us. Evenings out, we'd talk about the kids. I couldn't get you off it. And we never took a vacation on our own."

"I thought you loved our family vacations," she had cried.

"I did. I do," he had groaned. "What's the use? A man can't ever fight Motherhood—all that virtue."

"What do you want from me?" she had finally asked in a small, tight voice.

"I want us to be lovers again, the way we were before the kids came. There's only the two of us now. We've got the rest of our lives to live together, alone. And it's got to get better than it has been—or else."

Suddenly now, just thinking about that brutal threat, she became weak and had to sit down. Yes, it happened all the time: Men and their midlife crises. Looking for young bodies, young women to flatter their egos.

And yes, in all those frenzied months of the wedding preparations, he had become distant. Maybe he already had a mistress. She tried to think when they had last made love. Was it possible that something terrible was about to happen to her?

No, surely not. Surely he knew how much she loved and respected him. He looked so sad that morning when he left for work, so tired. He wasn't a young man anymore. "But he's right," she thought, "I can be a better wife to him. If it isn't too late."

At the bottom of her despair that morning in the kitchen she unscrewed her jar of instant coffee, and found inside his scrawled note: "Dear Wife, grow old with me. The best is yet to be, the last of life, for which the first was made.—Robert Browning & Your Husband."

She read it again and again. Then, when she had exhausted her tears, she reached eagerly for the phone to begin her new life.

Source: Sanderson, 1982.

---

pursue long-neglected interests. Because of these individual differences, our discussion of the midlife changes must remain general. Some individuals will experience the things we discuss, others may not, and still others may experience things that are not discussed. Despite these limitations it is worthwhile to examine the middle years of life, because we will all pass through them.

For the traditional wife and mother, the midlife crisis will revolve around the growing independence of her children and finally their move from home. She has to face her partial failure as a parent. She faces feelings of loss and uselessness because she is no longer needed. She may have general feelings of marital and life dissatisfaction and periods of increased introspection as she seeks new life goals (Reinke et al., 1983). Her feelings are somewhat akin to a worker's feelings on retirement. She often faces reentry to the work world where she may not have used her skills for twenty years. She faces a renewal of her earlier "pair" relationship. She faces the biological boundary of the end of her childbearing years. "No more children even if I wanted them." This and the accent on youth in America will cause her to reevaluate her sexuality, asking: Am I still attractive to men? Is there more to sex than I have experienced? She, as well as her husband, will become aware of death in a personal way as one-by-one their parents die. This event causes many people to direct their thoughts for the first time to the inescapableness of death, to realize that their lives are finite. Today women must also face the questions of changing identity and roles aroused by the women's movement.

Thus we see that the midlife changes faced by women are broad and profound. And both the woman and her husband face the turmoil within each other created by this stage. If her husband is unhappy and dissatisfied with his work, this adds to a woman's crisis. If she decides to return to college, this may add to her husband's stress and strain.

The typical husband's midlife crisis revolves around his work rather than his family. This is particularly true for the highly successful man. In a competitive economic society such as ours, a person must devote a great deal of energy to his or her work to achieve success. The male is often forced to handle two marriages, the first to his work and the second (in importance also) to his family.

Thus a husband's midlife crisis centers around letting go of the impossible dream of youth. He begins to recognize that not all of his dreams will be achieved. For those few men who have fulfilled their dreams, the midlife question becomes, What do I do now? Most men, however, must cope with disillusionment: the feeling that the dream was counterfeit, the vague feeling of having been cheated—that the dream isn't really what they thought it would be—and the growing awareness that perhaps they won't ever achieve their dreams.

America's emphasis on youth will also cause the man problems. Younger competitive men become a threat to job security. Subtle comments about retirement may take on a personal significance.

Unfortunately, this dream disillusionment usually carries over into the man's family. He doubts himself, he doubts his family. He may even blame them for his failure to achieve the dreams of his youth.

Along with general self-doubts come doubts about sexuality. Unlike his wife's, though, these doubts usually revolve less around physical attractiveness than performance. His wife's sexuality is at its highest peak and women's liberation may have influenced her to be more aware and assertive of her own sexuality. This can make his self-doubts extremely strong. Self-doubt can be a man's greatest enemy to satisfactory sexual relations. The "other woman" often becomes a problem at this time as the man may use her to prove his sexuality (see Inset 14-3).

In some cases a rather interesting partial exchange of roles takes place at this time of life. The woman becomes more interested in the world outside her family and more responsive to her own aggressiveness and competitive feelings. She returns to the work world, to school, or to an interest in public affairs and causes.

Inset 14-2

Changing Careers at Midlife

Five years ago Jane and Bill Smith and their two older children left their home in Santa Barbara where they were a mathematician and a teacher, respectively. Now they're back as a physician and lawyer-to-be. Bill, an internist with a local medical group, used to be a systems analyst with a large research and development firm. Jane is scheduled to take her bar exam early this year after having taught elementary school for years.

"I read about a program at the University of Miami where they retrain people with Ph.D.s in the biological sciences to become M.D.s," said Bill. "There was at the time a plethora of Ph.D.s and a lack of M.D.s. Then they let a few people in with degrees in the physical sciences"—he has a doctorate in math—"and discovered that they did just as well."

He spent two years in the accelerated medical school program, which he calls the time of "learning the language," then three years in a Veteran's Administration hospital for his internship and residency, "where I really learned to be a doctor."

Bill said he'd never been exposed much to the hospital environment until he began singing in a barbershop quartet, which was often invited to en-

tertain in rest homes and hospitals. He said he'd had the field of medicine "in the back of my mind" for a long time before he applied. He thought that medicine would be a more self-sufficient career than computers.

"I enjoy the work itself. I never took math home. Nobody cares about the answers except people in the field. However, I never get tired of medicine. When I get home, I get out the medical journals and the texts."

"I knew there'd be 700 applicants and only 28 selected so I didn't get my hopes up. They called for an interview, and three weeks later called again to say that I was 29th, the 'first alternate.' I figured that they told this to many people, so we bought a ping-pong table and settled back into our old routine."

Classes began in Miami on July 1. On July 5, after an afternoon of tennis, the couple arrived home to a telephone call from Miami asking, "Can you come tomorrow?" A student had dropped out making room for the first alternate.

Making a quick decision, he packed up and left the next day, leaving Jane to sell the house and furniture plus complete a summer job that she had undertaken.

Bill said the only courses he had in undergraduate school that applied to medical school were a year in chemistry and a course in physiology. But based on his medical school test scores, the lack of preliminary courses wasn't too difficult a problem. "Math training involves more rational thought and medicine is simply more memorization at first."

During his residency his wife took the opportunity to go to law school. When they returned to Santa Barbara she did some volunteer work in the consumer fraud division of the district attorney's office. "Now I'm spending all my time studying for the bar," she said.

As a teacher Jane said she "was always interested in the political side of teaching. I'm interested in educational law—children's rights, parents' and teachers' rights. I don't think anyone is working in that area here." She said that she was considering this career change even before Bill made his change.

For both spouses to make such dramatic midlife changes is certainly unusual. Yet this true story points out that families can make major and dramatic changes and survive and be rejuvenated.

Her husband becomes more receptive to his long-repressed affiliative and loving urges. He renews his interest in the family and in social issues outside his work. He becomes more caring in the way that his wife has been caring within the family. Unfortunately, the children are not very receptive to his newfound parental caring since they are busy seeking their own independence (Zube, 1982), and a mother's new interests in the world outside her family may be impeded by the fact that the "empty nest" is increasingly refilled by returning adult children or the couple's elderly parents.

Young adults (eighteen to thirty-four years old as defined by the U.S. Census)

Inset 14-3

Midlife Crisis: The Other Woman

The wives of men in midlife crisis are usually enraged at the "other women" who may enter their husband's lives at a vulnerable point. For many of these wives the midlife crisis can have only one meaning: a married man having an affair, usually with a younger woman.

Although the midlife crisis is much broader than that, it is important that the voices of distressed wives and former wives be heard. One irate woman wrote following an article on the problems of single women dating married men, "I am greatly annoyed at your considerable sympathy for the single woman involved with the married man. What about the wife, after twenty or more years of marriage, having this turbulence thrust upon her? No matter how good the marriage, living with another person is never perfect. When he meets a new woman it builds his ego to know that she finds him interesting and attractive. The wife has probably already gone through her midlife crisis with little or no support from him, and now he is shattering their marriage and creating emotional havoc for her and the children. Invariably the man is looking for change and not open to counseling."

"Six months ago my husband left our twenty-year marriage to have space to work out his problems. Of course, there's more to it than that: including an eighteen-month extramarital relationship. It's a shame that he couldn't put more effort into his marriage."

Others wrote of their self-doubts: "Did I do something wrong? Did I care too much? Did I overprotect and let him get away with too much? Did I nag?" And many talked of their dismay at having to face a future so different from the one they envisioned: "Now at fifty-plus I must find a new way of life and a job to support myself in the manner I have been accustomed to. Great way to start my senior years!"

The letters from single women who are dealing with men in their midlife crisis proclaim that it's no picnic for them either.

One such woman wrote that the man she had a "flirtation" with suddenly ended his marriage. He told her he had been unhappily married for years. He then pursued her ardently, had her give up her apartment and move into a house for the two of them. After she moved in, he decided to reconcile with his wife and moved her out again.

But none of the single women addressed the questions frequently asked by angry wives: "Don't these women care that they are entering a man's life when he's extremely vulnerable, and that they are breaking up a longstanding marriage and family? Aren't they at all concerned about the wife?"

"Other women" seem to care a little and feel somewhat guilty, but not enough to end the relationship. There are several reasons:

■ The "other woman" often does not enter the relationship wanting the man to leave his wife and commit himself to her. This is particularly true now, when affairs with married men are much more common than they were in the past (Richardson, 1986).
■ The "other woman" usually knows the wife only through the husband's words, and she often hears how bad things are, that he hasn't loved his wife in years, and that his wife is terrible.

■ The man tells her how much he values her, that she makes him happy, etc. The "other woman" begins to think of his wife as the past and herself as his future.
■ She truly feels that she is good for the man and believes that it would be a tragedy for herself and for him if he goes back to his wife.

Because of these beliefs and feelings, her own powerful attachment to the man and the "all is fair" attitude that seems to exist because of the scarcity of single men, the "other woman" is not usually deterred by sympathetic feelings for the wife.

Source: Adapted from Halpern, 1986.

in 1984 were more likely than young adults in 1970 to be living in the homes of their parents. Indeed the proportion of eighteen- to twenty-four-year-old men in parental homes increased from 54 percent in 1970 to 62 percent in 1984. For young adult women the figures are 41 percent and 47 percent respectively. Young adults between twenty-five and thirty-four years of age showed the same pattern. In 1970 10 percent of young adult men and 7 percent of young adult women were living with their parents, while in 1984 13 percent of young men and 8 percent of young women were doing so (U.S. Bureau of the Census, July 1985, p. 6).

The higher percentage of men living at the parental home is probably accounted for by the later age of marriage for men than for women. The vast majority of young adults who lived with their parents were not living as a subfamily (that is, they had no spouse or children living with them).

A number of factors probably contribute to the higher proportion of young adults living with their parents. Marriage is being postponed, there is an increasing emphasis on advanced education, housing costs are high, and during 1981–1983 the economy was in a recession and unemployment was high. The high divorce rate also prompts increased numbers of adult children to return home, at least temporarily.

Research indicates that a young adult in the home contributes to a high level of parental dissatisfaction (Spanier et al., 1975; Rollins & Cannon, 1974). Figure 14-1 indicates that marital satisfaction increases sharply as children leave home. With more young adults remaining or returning home, their parents, instead of being alone and able to concentrate on themselves and their relationship, find themselves having to share their home and lives with other adults. The continuing lack of privacy and their children's failure to contribute monetarily or share in the day-to-day running of the home are parent's major complaints about having adult children living at home. In turn, the young adults complain about lack of freedom and parental interference.

Increased life expectancy has increasingly led to a middle-aged couple's "empty nest" being refilled by aging parents (Beck & Beck, 1984). Even if elderly parents do not actually live with the couple, the couple must concern themselves with caring for and helping their parents. The number of persons over sixty-five years of age doubled between 1950 and 1980 and is predicted to double again by 2020. In addition, modern medicine is keeping older people with chronic illnesses like Alzheimer's disease alive for years longer. Thus the chances of a couple needing to help care for aging parents will continue to increase.

Caring for the elderly has traditionally been women's work, a natural extension of their role as homemakers and nurturers. One study found that 33 percent of the elderly surveyed received help from a daughter, compared to 17 percent who received help from a son (Hull, 1985).

For the woman joining the workforce (Chapter 9) or renewing her interest in the world outside of the family once the children leave home, it can be particularly frustrating to shoulder the burden of caring for elderly parents. One study found that 28 percent of nonworking women had quit their jobs to care for their parents (Hull, 1985).

However, most children are loath to put their aging parents into institutional homes. Despite the public stereotype of the elderly all living in nursing homes, only .3 percent of men and .5 percent of women over 65 years of age live in institutions (U.S. Bureau of the Census, 1985a).

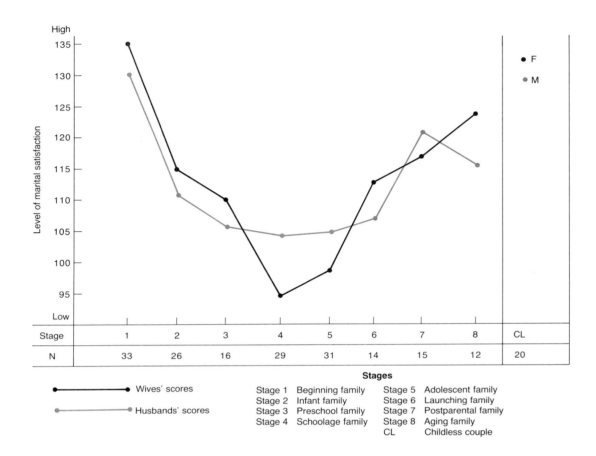

Stage	1	2	3	4	5	6	7	8	CL
N	33	26	16	29	31	14	15	12	20

Stages

Wives' scores

Husbands' scores

Stage 1	Beginning family	Stage 5 Adolescent family
Stage 2	Infant family	Stage 6 Launching family
Stage 3	Preschool family	Stage 7 Postparental family
Stage 4	Schoolage family	Stage 8 Aging family
		CL Childless couple

Figure 14-1 Spouses' mean scores on the Locke-Wallace Marital Adjustment Scale by stage in the family life cycle (Spanier et al., 1975).

Thus middle age may mean an "empty nest" and a renewed emphasis on the primary couple, or it may not. However, for both men and women, midlife usually means rethinking and reevaluating life. It is a time of restructuring. The resulting turmoil may threaten the marriage and family, or it may result in a revitalized marriage. By recognizing and squarely confronting the issues of midlife, the chances increase that the results will be positive and growth producing rather than negative and destructive.

Retirement

Retirement usually signals the beginning of disengagement. In many nonindustrialized societies this is a gradual process. The hardest physical labor is performed by young men and women at the peak of their physical condition. As they age and their own offspring grow to maturity, they assume more administrative and supervisory duties while their children take on the harder physical labor. This gradual tapering off of duties and the smooth transition of tasks from one generation to the next was done to some extent on the farm in rural America.

By contrast, in the American urban setting retirement is usually abrupt, based on reaching a certain arbitrary age or having worked for some specified number of years. In a sense age categories of employability are created. For example, child labor laws hold children out of the labor force, whereas mandatory retirement plans force older workers out of the labor market at an arbitrary age. In 1986 changes in retirement laws did away with mandatory retirement age.

The abruptness of retirement can cause severe adjustment problems for the newly unneeded worker. The woman in the traditional mothering role faces her retirement at the earlier "empty nest" stage. Her retirement comes gradually as her children gain independence one by one. Working spouses, on the other hand, are suddenly placed in a totally new role. After forty to fifty years of going to work, they receive a gold watch and pats on the back and are told to go fishing and enjoy their new leisure time. They are thrust into a new lifestyle that for most retirees is characterized by less income, declining health, and increasing loneliness. They miss their colleagues and the status that was derived from their job. The common question asked by a new acquaintance, "What do you do?" is now answered by, "Nothing, I'm retired." Because so much of the career person's self-image is defined by work identity, retirement often means some kind of identity crisis. Because retirement comes abruptly for many Americans, it is necessary to prepare ahead, both economically and psychologically.

A few retirees seem able to find happiness in the "doing nothing" role. "It's great not to have to get up every morning and go to work." Yet most cannot "do nothing" easily and happily after years of working. Many retirees continue to do odd jobs or continue as part-time employees if their occupation permits. For example, a retired school teacher may occasionally do substitute teaching. Some retirees change activities entirely and start a new vocation or avocation. They may decide to open their own business or actively pursue some long-suppressed interest such as writing or painting. Perhaps they busy themselves with volunteer work. There are numerous examples of people retiring and then returning to the work world. Konrad Adenauer assumed the leadership of postwar Germany at the age of seventy-three and actively guided Germany to a powerful world position for fourteen years until the age of eighty-seven.

Making specific plans for one's newly acquired leisure time is of great help psychologically to the new retiree. To wake up each morning having something to do rather than wondering what to do is an important goal for successful adjustment to retirement.

Those who had broad interests or are able to develop new interests generally make the quickest and best adjustment to retirement. People who age optimally are those who stay active and manage to resist shrinkage of their social world. They maintain the activities of middle age as long as possible and then find substitutes for the activities they are forced to relinquish: substitutes for work when forced to retire, substitutes for friends and loved ones lost to death.

Elizabeth Hill and Lorraine Dorfman (1982) investigated the reactions of housewives to the early years of their husbands' retirement. Table 14-1 lists some of the positive and negative aspects mentioned by these wives. In addition the researchers asked what suggestions these wives had for other women whose husbands were soon to retire. The most frequent suggestions were:

- Wives should try to keep their husbands busy in retirement.
- Wives should try to continue their own preretirement activities.
- Couples should do more together.
- Wives should plan to maintain some privacy.

Table 14-1

Reaction of Housewives to the Retirement of Their Husbands

Positive Aspects of Retirement	Percentage of Wives Mentioning	Negative Aspects of Retirement	Percentage of Wives Mentioning
Time available to do what you want	81	Financial problems	36
Increased companionship	67	Husbands not having enough to do	31
Time flexibility	33	Too much togetherness	22
Increased participation of husbands in household tasks	28		
Decrease in own household responsibilities	22		
Husbands happier	22		

Source: Hill and Dorfman, 1982.

Although most of the literature on retirement concerns men, questions of retirement are becoming more important for women as well. As we saw in Chapter 9, more and more women are entering the work force. Past research (Lowenthal, Thurnher & Chiriboga, 1975) has indicated that retirement does not hold the significance for women it does for men even when the woman has worked full-time for most of her life. One reason postulated for retirement's being less significant for working women is that many women experience several roles (wife, mother, homemaker) throughout their life cycle that they perceive to be as important as the role of worker. However, this aspect may well change as more and more women seek lifelong careers. Just as men must prepare for retirement, so must working women (Johnson & Price-Bonham, 1980).

Money and health seem to be the two most important factors influencing the success not only of retirement but also of general adjustment to old age. It takes a great deal of money to live free of economic worries. Generally the retiree's income is more than halved on retirement. The stereotype of the older retired person fighting off poverty has largely been replaced especially since Social Security and many pension plans have been indexed to the inflation rate. Moynihan (1986, p. 94) points out that in the past ten years poverty among America's elderly has been largely defeated. In 1959 35.2 percent of people aged 65 and over lived in poverty. By 1983 that figure was down to 14.1 percent (O'Hare, 1985, p. 5). However, for those who still suffer financially in retirement, it is ironic that when they finally retire and get enough free time to do the things they want they have little money available to pursue desires other than those of subsistence. Financial status directly creates the quality of life for the retired couple. Can they travel, indulge their hobbies, and eat as well as the television ads depict? They can, only if they are financially well off.

The retiree not only must have planned well economically for retirement but also must have planned for a potentially long period due to increased life expectancy. As we saw earlier, people may now live up to 25 percent of their lives in retirement. Inflation is the retired person's greatest enemy. Those retired on an essentially fixed income fall further and further behind with each passing day of inflation. A retiree may be financially well off at retirement but may have dropped into poverty ten years later because of continued inflation and the shrinking value of the dollar. Indexing of retirement income works to cancel this trend toward poverty caused by inflation.

Health is the other major influence on people's adjustment to retirement and old age. About 40 percent of those over sixty-five have long-term chronic conditions such as high blood pressure that interfere to some degree with their daily activities (U.S. Office of Human Development, 1976). Although government programs such as Medicare help the elderly cope financially with health problems, such benefits need to be supplemented monetarily. Thus lack of money may compound health problems and further reduce the quality of life for the retired. Given the high costs of medical care, there are few people who can be completely safe from financial disaster brought on by prolonged or severe health problems.

Assuming that monetary and health problems are not overwhelming, many couples report that the retired period of their lives is one of enjoyment and marital happiness. They are able, often for the first time, to be together without jobs and children placing demands on them. They can travel and pursue hobbies and long-neglected interests. They can attend to one another with a concentration not available since they first dated. In some ways a successful retirement is like courting. After years of facing the demands of work and family and growing apart in some ways, retirement provides the time needed to renew the relationship, make discoveries about each other, and revive the courtship that first brought the couple together (see Inset 14-3).

Loss of a Spouse: A Return to Singleness

One can be faced with the death of a spouse at any stage of marriage. A spouse can die of disease or accident at any time. But the problems of the young widower or widow are much different from the problems spouses face when they lose their partner at the end of their lives and find themselves alone after many years of marital partnership. The young person who loses a spouse generally remarries (see Inset 14-4), but among those over sixty-five only about 2 percent of men and 1 percent of women remarry.

Regardless of age, loss of a spouse involves all the processes that occur whenever one loses a loved one. Grief, feelings of guilt, despair, anger, remorse, depression, turning away and at the same time toward others are all normal reactions. Given time, most of us can overcome our emotional distress at losing a spouse and go on with our lives. For a few long-married couples death of one precipitates the death of the other. This often occurs when a woman has taken most of her self-identity from her husband (see Inset 14-5).

Widowedness as the Last Stage of Marriage

As we saw in the overview of family life stages, the last stage of marriage is overwhelmingly one of widowhood. Of women between sixty-five and seventy-four 62 percent are widowed, while only 2.1 percent of men in this age range are (U.S. Bureau of the Census, July, 1985, p. 49).

Widowers generally exhibit more severe problems of disorganization. They

---

Inset 14-4

Death of a Wife: A Young Father Alone

Jim was only twenty-eight when Jane was killed in an auto accident while returning from her job. He was left with his son, Mike, who was four years old.

"At first, everyone rushed over and wanted to keep Mike for me. Some of our friends almost couldn't accept 'no' for an answer. Yet I felt that Mike needed to be with me and certainly I needed him.

"It is also amazing to remember who came over the first few days. People that we had hardly known brought food. At first when they asked what they could do, I replied, 'Nothing.' Yet they were so obviously disappointed that I finally tried to think of something for them to do. This seemed to make them feel better, although I'm not sure it helped me. In a way I needed things to do, things to distract me from my grief at least for a short time.

"Although I certainly mourned at first, I found that I was often too angry to mourn. I wanted revenge on the other driver, and I was particularly mad at the city for allowing such a dangerous intersection to exist without stop signs. At times I was even angry at my wife for driving so poorly, but this always made me feel guilty. Actually I think I was angry at the whole world. Why did events conspire to take her away from me?

"I had a lot of remorse for things I had put off doing with and for Jane. We really should have spent the money and gone home to see her parents last Christmas. Why hadn't I told her I loved her more often? In many ways at first I felt I had failed her.

"However as time passed I realized that perhaps she had failed me just a little also. At first I could only think of the good things. To think of bad things between us when she wasn't there to defend herself just seemed terrible. Gradually though I have been able to see her, our relationship, as it really was, with both good and bad. I want

to preserve her memory for myself and our son, but I want it to be a realistic memory, not a case of heroine worship. I do fantasize about her, especially when I'm alone, and it really helps me to relive some of the memories, but I know that they can't substitute for the present. I must keep living and carrying forward for myself and our son.

"Although I'm not dating yet, I will in the future. She'd not want me to remain alone the rest of my life. Right now, though, I prefer to be alone with our son, with my thoughts and memories. I need time to understand what has happened, time to be sad. I need time for grief, time to adjust to my new single-parent role, time to ease the pain. I'll be ready for a new relationship only after I have laid the old one gently and lovingly to rest. When the time comes, I will look forward to marrying again."

---

have higher rates of suicide, physical illness, mental illness, alcoholism, and accidents (*U.S. News & World Report*, 1974). One study also shows that their overall mortality rate was 26 percent higher than that for matching (age, schooling, smokers, nonsmokers, and so forth) married men. For widows the mortality rate was only 3.8 percent higher than for matching married women. It is interesting to note that there was no evidence that either men or women were significantly more likely to die in the early months of bereavement. Rather, death resulted later and seemed related to the stressful life situation of the widowed person rather than to an immediate reaction to the death of the spouse. Another interesting discovery was that remarriage by widowers dramatically lowered their mortality rates. In men under fifty-five who remarried (about half of them did) the death rate was 70 percent lower than for those who did not remarry. In men aged fifty-five to sixty-four, the death rate was 50 percent lower. Such data tend to support our assumption that marriage can promote health (Chapter 2). One finding of this same study that applies to both widowers and widows was the dramatic rise (three to four times) in mortality rates if a widowed person moved into a retirement or nursing home because of illness or inability to live with other family members (*Time*, 1981). Despite these negative findings about the problems of widowers, the social problems caused by aging center on the far larger numbers of widows in the American society.

In 1984 there were about 9.4 million widows, and about 7.5 million of them were over sixty-five; only 1.7 million men were widowers, and about 1.3 million of them were over sixty-five (U.S. Bureau of the Census, April 1985). About 76 percent of men and 39 percent of women over age sixty-five still live with a spouse (U.S. Bureau of the Census, 1985a). The problems of widowhood are for the most part the same problems generally faced in old age but faced alone without a spouse.

In rural America many retired parents received monetary and housing support from their grown children. A century ago people tended to grow old on the farm within the family setting. Grandparents gradually turned the farm over to their children, remaining on the farm, giving advice, fulfilling the grandparent role, and being active family members until they died. As America urbanized, however, children tended to move away from their parents and establish independent households within the cities. Often both partners worked at jobs that took them out of the home. Living space diminished so that no room was available for other than the immediate nuclear family. As the children who had moved to the cities grew older, there was no farm to which they could return, and thus urbanization slowly moved the care of the elderly out of the children's reach.

Today many Americans own their homes, which often gives them refuge and a major asset in their later years. More than two-thirds of the elderly remain in their home until death (Streib, 1972). Another 25 percent over sixty-five live with a child. Despite the large amount of generally negative publicity about institutional care for the elderly, only about 1 percent of those in their late sixties and over live in institutions such as nursing homes (U.S. Bureau of the Census, 1985a). The remaining elderly live in a variety of circumstances: with relatives other than children, with roommates, and in rented quarters. Perhaps half a million are well enough off monetarily to buy or lease living quarters in exclusive retirement communities such as Arizona's Sun City or California's Leisure World.

Elderly parents who live with their children put their children in the position of "parenting their parents." This role reversal is difficult for both the elderly parents and their children. Also the frustration that often results when elderly parents live with their children brings about the possibility of elder abuse (Pedrick-Cornell & Gelles, 1982).

The increasing longevity of Americans has created the phenomenon of the four-generation family. It is estimated that half of all persons over sixty-five with living children are members of four-generation families. This does not mean that they live with their families, but they are great-grandparents. This role is relatively new in society. Great-grandchildren can be as great a source of joy and fulfillment as grandchildren. On the other hand, the generational gap is so large that great-grandchildren can also be a source of bewilderment as their lifestyles become increasingly different from those of the oldest generation (Shanas, 1980).

The fact that children no longer automatically care for their aging parents means that governmental agencies have had to be created to help the elderly. Government-regulated retirement programs and social security have been established to help economically. Medicare and nutrition programs such as Meals on Wheels

have been established to help in the area of health. The National Council on Aging publishes a directory of special housing for the elderly. Licensing and supervision of institutional facilities for the aged is being tightened. The elderly themselves are organizing as a power bloc (the Grey Panthers, for example) to work toward improvement of care and opportunities for people in their later years. Programs such as the Retired Senior Volunteer program, which pays out-of-pocket expenses to those involved in community activities and projects, and the Senior Corps of Retired Executives, which pays them to counsel small businesses, are springing up to keep the elderly active and useful. All of these things bode well for us as we move into the later years of our lives. The majority of the elderly report that they are satisfied with their family relations (Seelbach & Hansen, 1980). Yet the question remains: If possible isn't the bosom of the family—the center of intimate relationships—the place to age gracefully and die with dignity and care? Fortunately, current research supports earlier work that reported that older persons are not abandoned by their families. Rather, contact between older parents and their adult children is often frequent and supportive (Sanders et al., 1985, p. 93).

Inset 14-5
Doctor's Wife

My grandmother died only a few months after my grandfather did even though she was in good health and had seldom been sick in her life. My grandfather was a strong independent man who worshipped my grandmother and took especially good care of her. He never allowed her to work or to want for anything and remained much in love with her, often publicly displaying his affection, until he died.

He was an old-fashioned family doctor who made house calls and thought of his patients as his family. My grandmother's entire identity revolved around being "doctor's wife" (that is how she often referred to her-

self). Her life was his life, and in hindsight I realize she never developed any of her own interests. In fact, she seemed to have no interests outside of his interests. As "doctor's wife" she took care of him, the family, and the house. When the children became independent, she became even more attentive to him and didn't develop any other interests to replace the missing children.

With the arrival of grandchildren, she became the happy mother all over again, caring for the grandchildren as often as she could. When grandfather died, we all tried to visit her often and invited her to visit our families. She

told us to give her a little time to adjust and that for the present she preferred to stay home. About three months later I found her lying in grandfather's bed having passed away from an apparent heart attack. In retrospect I think that she had died in spirit when grandfather passed away. The death certificate indicates "heart attack" as the cause of death.

When I think about it, I had no grandmother. My grandmother was "doctor's wife." When he died, her identity died and soon thereafter her body. I prefer to substitute "broken heart" for "heart attack" on the death certificate.

We pointed out earlier that most people finally do make an adjustment to the death of a loved one. In her study of elderly Chicago widows, Helena Lopata (1979) reports the figures for adjustment periods shown in Table 14-2. A few widows reported that they would never be able to establish a new life, but only time will tell if their feeling is correct. Lopata makes several interesting points about her sample that probably hold true for many widows. Many of them had never been alone in a home, having gone from the home of their parents directly into one established with marriage. Many of them had no occupational skills, never having worked other than perhaps in a few odd jobs before marriage. Their traditional socialization was to be passive about the world outside of their home environment. They had always depended on a family support system. Thus their socialization and consequent life experiences did not adequately prepare them to start a new life alone.

These factors should diminish as more and more women enter the workforce and establish a more independent lifestyle. The women's movement's emphasis on individual identity for all women, even when married, should also help negate the factors Lopata found.

The upsurge of interest in death and bereavement has also helped widows and widowers cope with their new roles. More understanding and empathy has been extended to them. For example, programs using widows to counsel other widows have been helpful in reducing the adjustment period.

Remarriage is perhaps the best solution for the widow or widower. Yet few over

---

Table 14-2
Time Necessary for Elderly Widows to Adjust and Begin Developing a New Life after the Death of a Spouse

Time Needed	Percentage
2–11 months	25
One year	20
1–2 years	23
Over 2 years	16
Other	16

sixty-five actually remarry. For widows the lack of available older men is the major obstacle. Some researchers (Lasswell, 1973; Duberman, 1977) suggest that polygyny might be an appropriate solution. If the few available older men were allowed more than one wife, remarriage opportunities would be more abundant for older widows. Another way to alleviate the problem would be for women to marry men eight to ten years younger than themselves (Glick, 1979), but this would require a change in the long-standing American tradition of women marrying men one to two years older than themselves.

Some of the elderly do live with other people of both sexes out of necessity. About 7.6 percent of men and 19.9 percent of women over sixty-five years of age live with someone other than their spouse (U.S. Bureau of the Census, 1985a). Some 5 percent of people cohabitating are over the age of sixty-five, and about 6 percent of them are widowed (U.S. Bureau of the Census, July 1985, p. 7).

It is important to plan ahead against the loss of a spouse regardless of age. Yet few of us do it probably because it means contemplating the death of someone we love, and this is always unpleasant and usually avoided.

Married people need to be able to answer a number of practical questions if their spouse should pass away.

- Is there a will, where is it, and what are its contents?
- Is there life insurance, how much is it, and how does one get it to pay off?
- What are your financial liabilities and assets?
- Do you have access to safety deposit boxes and where are the keys?
- How much cash can you raise in the next sixty days to keep the family going?

If one can answer such questions as these, the practical transition to widowhood can be greatly eased. This, in turn, allows one more time to deal with the emotional and psychological transition.

The Grandparenting Role

Many people speak nostalgically of the extended family of rural nineteenth century America. Parents, grandparents, and grandchildren happily living and working together on the farm is a wonderful romantic ideal. Yet the short life expectancy of 100 years ago made this arrangement relatively rare. Today, although most Americans no longer live on the farm, the chances of children having living grandparents is far higher than it was 100 years ago. Between 1900 and 1980, the probability of three or four grandparents being alive when a child reaches age fifteen increased from .17 to .55 (Uhlenberg, 1980).

Greater life expectancy has also drastically changed the picture of grandparent. Grandparents are no longer the little white-haired lady or man sitting contentedly in his or her rocking chair. (The author's seventy-two-year-old mother, grandmother of two, recently eloped.) Grandparents are often still actively employed, living full and active lives of their own.

For many retired, widowed, and elderly persons, however, fulfilling the role of grandparent can bring back many of the joys and satisfactions of family life. Grandchildren can mean companionship, renewal of intimate contact, the joy of physical contact, and the fulfillment of being needed and useful. One source of family strength reported by older couples was the support offered to them by their children and grandchildren (Sanders et al., 1985, p. 89).

Like the retirement and widowed stages of marriage, grandparenting has been greatly extended by increased life expectancy. Most children have a relationship with one or more grandparents throughout their youth. It is quite possible today for a person's period of grandparenting to be longer than the period in which their own children were at home. Of course, younger grandparents, still married, employed, and living in their own homes do not have the same needs to grandparent as older, retired, and perhaps widowed grandparents.

For older grandparents the role might be described as "pleasure without responsibility." They can enjoy the grandchildren without the obligation and responsibilities they had to shoulder for their own children. The grandparent role gives some a chance to be an even better parent, especially for men. "I can be, and I can do for my grandchildren things I could never do for my own kids. I was too busy to enjoy my own, but my grandchildren are different." Association with grandchildren can yield a great deal of physical contact for the widow or widower. This is one of the things most often reported missed after one's spouse dies.

In the past the stereotype of the elderly person has excluded the close physical contact of sexual activity. We know today that this is erroneous. Physical contact is an important source of intimacy and emotional gratification, regardless of age. Much physical warmth can be had with grandchildren. Hugging, kissing, and affection gained from grandchildren can go a long way toward replacing the physical satisfaction earlier had in marriage.

Many grandparents also report feelings of biological and psychological renewal from interacting with their grandchildren: "I feel young again." "I see a future."

This picture of grandparenting is only one of many pictures. There is great variation in the kinds of relationships that grandparents have with their grandchildren. Much of the relationship depends on how close grandparents and grand-children live to one another. If a grandchild lives far away there may be no relationship. If one set of grandchildren live nearby and all the others live at some distance, there may only be a relationship with those close by. Some grandchildren may live with parents who don't get along with the grandparents or may no longer be living with the grandparent's son or daughter as a result of divorce so again there may be little or no relationship.

After interviewing 510 grandparents of a national sample of children, Cherlin and Furstenberg (1985, p. 102) divided grandparenting into three styles: *detached* (26 percent) where there was little or no contact, *passive* (29 percent) where grandchildren were seen once or twice a week but the relationship was shallow and ritualistic, and *active* (45 percent) where there was a deep meaningful ongoing relationship. It is obvious from the figures that only a portion of grandparents derive the pleasures and satisfactions from their grandchildren that we have described.

Cherlin and Furstenberg also point out that there is often *selective investment* in grandchildren (1985, p. 110). Even active grandparents may be only selectively relating to one or two of many grandchildren, being detached or passive from the others. Also there will be differences between the kinds of relationships established by grandmothers as compared to grandfathers.

We have discussed the kinds of satisfactions grandparents can derive from their grandchildren. However, grandparents can give a lot to their grandchildren and to the overall family as well. Bengtson (1985, p. 21) suggests that just "being there" is an important grandparenting function. Family members can draw support and feelings of well-being just by knowing that their grandparents are alive and available. They can provide a buffer against family mortality; act as a deterrent against family disruption; serve as arbitrators in family disputes; and provide a place to go to escape marital difficulties. Children whose parents divorce can seek support and permanence with their grandparents (Troll, 1983). Grandparents can become surrogate parents for grandchildren who don't get along with their parents or where a parent is missing because of death or divorce. Since grandparents are not normally responsible for grandchildren and therefore do not have to set all of the rules and administer punishment, they can become friends and sometimes allies of their grandchildren.

Increased life expectancy and the high divorce rate combine to add a number of new dimensions to the grandparenting role. Increasing life expectancy means that more and more grandparents have their own elderly parents still living and perhaps will have to shoulder some responsibility for them.

Divorce of grandparents or death of one and remarriage of the other may mean new stepgrandparents for grandchildren. Also, especially for a grandfather re-marrying, it could mean new children for the grandparents. Of course, remarriage of grandparent's own children may mean relating to a new set of stepgrandchildren.

Also divorce brings up visitation rights of grandparents as well as spouses. Since children go with the mother in 90 percent of divorces, it is the paternal grandparents who usually lose contact with grandchildren. For detached or passive grandparents this may be no problem. For active grandparents enforced separa-tion from grandchildren can be devastating. By 1986 fourteen states had enacted some type of grandparent visitation rights legislation (*Santa Barbara News Press*, 1986).

It is clear that with increased longevity the grandparenting role is increasingly important and complex. Fortunately more and more researchers are studying grandparenting (Bengtson & Robertson, 1985) as more and more people become grandparents for longer and longer portions of their lives.

Summary

Families, like the people within them, span a long period of time. As individuals change over time, so do families. In this chapter we have tried to trace what some of the common changes might be. Because most of the book is concerned with the early family stages, we have examined only the middle and later stages in this chapter.

When the last child leaves home, the middle-aged (empty nest) stage begins. This is usually a time of reassessment for both husband and wife of how their lives will change now that the children are gone. What will they do with the time that used to be devoted to mothering and fathering? How have they lived their lives to date; how do they want to live them in the future? What new directions should they undertake? What will be their relationship with their adult children? Between themselves? How will they fulfill the grandparent role? What role will sexuality play in their middle years?

Retirement enters one's thoughts during the middle years. When it finally comes, the family will have adjustments to make. Time demands will change abruptly; monetary circumstances may shift downward; and feelings of uselessness may have to be coped with by one or both of the spouses leaving the world of work that has for so long been part of their identity.

At the last, death must be faced as one spouse, usually the husband, dies. For many there is a return to singleness in the later years. In fact the period of widowhood may be increasingly longer as life expectancy continues to rise.

The grandparenting role is taking on more importance as life expectancy increases. The role is also becoming more complex as families divorce and remarry.

Despite the death of one spouse, the family often remains active. Grandparenting can bring small children back into one's life and yield new satisfactions to those aging within the family. For some, however, old age may mean being without family for the first time.

The Widow and How She Copes

Lois Chambliss-McClellan was nine months pregnant when her husband Robert, 31, died of a heart attack in their Morristown, N.J., home two years ago.

"It was a Sunday morning," she recalls. "He put his arms around me and said, 'Do you think we're going to have the baby today?' He was teasing." Minutes later, Robert went into the couple's bedroom, where he collapsed and died.

When Colleen McClellan, now 2, asks about her father, "I don't know how I'm going to answer her," the mother says.

McClellan, 32, is one of more than 11 million American women who have been forced to pick up the pieces—emotionally and financially—after the death of their spouses. The number of widows may grow beyond 15 million in the next decade because of greater longevity, particularly among women.

Each no doubt has a different story to tell, yet most share common problems that follow the loss of a spouse.

First Stages: Shock, Denial

For most widows, the first reaction to a husband's death is shock, then numbness. Comments such as "She is holding up well" are frequently heard from relatives, who don't realize her husband's death still has not sunk in.

Counselors say some women resent their husbands for dying. Others hold back their feelings, denying to themselves that their partners are gone. Some start feeling guilty, believing they could have gotten their husbands to the hospital earlier or forced them to take better care of themselves.

To help these women, the American Association of Retired Persons has a Widowed Persons Service in 170 lo-

cations nationwide. The AARP will send a volunteer who has gone through the same experience to talk to the new widow about problems she may face.

Learning to Live Alone

"You feel like a fool driving home in an evening gown by yourself," comments Margaret DeGrace, 55, a Detroit museum administrator whose husband William died of throat cancer three years ago.

As widowhood stretches into years, a problem for many is losing close friends as well as husbands. Long-time companions find it depressing to be around them. With a husband gone, some consider the widow a different person.

Six months to a year after a death, friends figure a widow doesn't need

help any more, and that's often when she needs help the most. New Beginnings in Detroit offers a six-week course for widows and other bereaved people; it tells them what to expect in the recovery period. The organizer, Robert Weikart, an Episcopal priest, says widows are not encouraged to join until several months after the funeral because at first "it doesn't really register that their spouse is gone."

The program, like others across the country, offers a twenty-four-hour hot line for widows. Some groups feature guest speakers such as policemen who explain how to secure doors or accountants who discuss Social Security.

Another Mate?

Many women feel undue pressure to begin dating again when they are still grieving. But once they are ready, they often have trouble meeting men. Younger women find they are too busy on their jobs to date extensively or are burdened with children.

Above age sixty-five, there are three women for every two men, and society expects men to take the initiative. Because the average widow is fifty-six years old, she faces an average of twenty-two years of being single unless she remarries.

Many older women are not interested in remarrying because they nursed incapacitated husbands before they died. Alice Quinlan of the Older Women's League says: "If I were a widow, I would think twice about going through that all over again."

Widow groups advise the bereaved to go to events they can attend without escorts at first. Many widows rush into a new marriage, then are disappointed when they compare the new husband with the deceased spouse.

The Financial Maze

Experts say that once a widow is ready to deal with finances, the first step is to find important papers and be sure savings are intact. Then she must contact insurers, Social Security and, in many cases, veterans' offices. Next, she should write her husband's employer about survivor benefits available and advise creditors that he died.

Legal and accounting advice is often essential. "The common problem is that well-meaning relatives and friends give all sorts of worthless advice," says Houston investment counselor Gordon Wise. He recommends professional management for estates of $500,000 and up. Below that, he recommends investing in a good mutual fund with enough flexibility to switch investments if a widow's objectives change.

Dealing with Children

"All through my life I hoped and prayed that this wouldn't happen to my kids," remarks Arlene Kuby, 42, of Chicago, a mother of four whose husband died two years ago.

Kuby, whose own father died when she was six, would rather stay home with her children but will have to increase her workweek from two to three days.

For many widowed parents who go back to work, the biggest problem is locating good child care. Some find day-care centers, others pay neighbors, and a few leave older children by themselves.

A widow also must deal with the grief of her children and grandchildren in addition to her own. "Give them an opportunity to talk, but do not insist that they share their grief," says Ruth Loewinsohn, author of the AARP's *Survival Handbook for Widows*.

A widow is sometimes pressured by her grown children to move out of her home and live with them. Most authorities counsel a widow to consider whether she can adapt to a living arrangement in which she is no longer the boss. It is not wise, they say, to move quickly to a new environment.

Future Plans

Many widows who have been homemakers all of their lives suddenly find themselves out looking for jobs. Some are able to parlay their experience in helping their husbands or working with volunteer groups into productive jobs, but for others it is an enormous struggle.

Those who don't work find getting credit and insurance particularly hard. A woman in her fifties or early sixties who looks for health insurance on her own often pays twice as much and gets half the benefits, widows' groups say.

Many who expect to receive pensions find that their husbands neglected to get survivor-benefit protection as part of their pension plans. Congress tried to remedy this situation in 1984 when it required both spouses to sign the document if one of them wants to waive this coverage.

For advice on jobs and careers, a major resource is the Displaced Homemakers Network, 1010 Vermont Avenue, N.W., Washington, D.C. 20005. Local chapters of the group conduct workshops designed to ease the problems of getting back into the workforce.

Whether dealing with a widow's finances or her emotional problems, the main advice is not to rush her. Some suggestions: Call a widow often, avoid pitying her, and don't treat her like a child. "The kindest thing you can do is call up and ask them out to dinner," says Illinois widow June Steele. "Friendship is so important at the time of rebuilding."

Source: Adapted from Doan, M., and Collins, D., "11 Million Widows—Here's How They Cope," *U.S. News and World Report*, 28 October 1985, 56–57.

The Dissolution of Marriage

Contents

"In sickness and in health, till death do us part." This traditional part of the marriage ceremony might well be changed to the following in modern America: "In happiness and in good health, till divorce do us part."

A hundred years ago in this country, 30 out of every 1000 marriages were ended each year by the death of one of the spouses. Only 3 marriages in 1000 were ended by divorce. Today divorce, separation, and desertion rather than death finish most marriages.

Let No Man Put Asunder

It seems obvious that the "love match" marriage based on romance, self-gratification, and happiness—in other words, on the fulfillment of all one's needs—must suffer from a high rate of failure. In the past, a good marriage was measured by how well each spouse fulfilled the socially prescribed roles of husband and wife. Today Americans ask a great deal more of marriage, and the higher the stakes the higher the chances of failure.

In addition, the greatly increased life span (since 1900, an additional twenty-four years for men and twenty-eight years for women, see p. 475) means that marriages are now expected to endure for much longer than ever before. How realistic is it to ask a marriage to last for fifty to sixty years?

The rate of divorce in this country has been rising throughout the century. In 1900 there was about one divorce for every twelve marriages. By 1922 there was one divorce for every eight marriages, and in the late 1940s there was approximately one divorce for every three and a half marriages. This peak was probably caused by the dislocations arising from World War II. From 1950 to 1964, the ratio of divorce to marriage leveled off at approximately one divorce for every four marriages. But the divorce rate started to rise again in 1967, and by 1984 there was approximately one divorce for every two marriages. The median duration of marriage is approximately seven years (U.S. National Center for Health Statistics, December 26, 1985).

However, divorce statistics do not yield a complete picture of the incidence of broken marriage. Legal separation claims another 3 percent of all marriages. Desertion, another manner of breaking a marriage, is especially prevalent among the poor, although obtaining statistics on desertion is difficult because such facts do not often appear in any records. Usually it is the husband who leaves, although more wives are now deserting than in the past.

In any case it appears that dissolution of American marriages is relatively commonplace and becoming more so in the 1980s. Some family experts have begun to call American marriages "throwaway marriages." A better name is **serial marriages**; that is, Americans tend to marry, divorce, and remarry. Of all American couples married during 1983 45 percent had divorce in the background of one or both partners (U.S. National Center for Health Statistics, May 2, 1986, p. 11). A high divorce rate apparently does not mean that Americans are disenchanted with marriage, because the divorced remarry in great numbers and relatively quickly (see Chapter 16).

It is important to remember that statistics on divorce and separation must be interpreted cautiously. For example, the crude divorce rate—the ratio of divorces to each 1000 persons within the population—is greatly influenced by birthrate (Table 15-1). A decrease in birthrate will produce a higher percentage of divorce, presuming the total number of divorces remains stable. Thus the fact that the birthrate is at an all-time low in America accounts for some of the increase in the

Serial marriage
Marrying, divorcing, and marrying again; a series of legal marriages

---

Table 15-1

Number of Divorces and Divorce Rates

Year	Number of Divorces	Percent Change from Previous Year	Rate per 1000 Total Population	Rate per 1000 Married Women 15 Years and Over
1986	1,192,000	+ .01	5.0	—
1985	1,172,000	+ .01	4.9	—
1984	1,156,000	− .005	4.9	21.3
1983	1,158,000	− .01	4.9	21.3
1982	1,170,000	− .03	5.0	21.7
1981	1,213,000	+ .03	5.3	22.6
1980	1,182,000	.00	5.2	22.6
1979	1,181,000	+ .04	5.3	22.8
1978	1,130,000	+ .03	5.1	21.9
1977	1,090,000	+ .006	5.0	21.3
1976	1,083,000	+ 4.5	5.0	27.7
1975	1,036,000	+ 6.0	4.9	20.3
1974	977,000	+ 6.8	4.6	19.3
1973	915,000	+ 8.3	4.4	13.2
1972	845,000	+ 9.3	4.1	17.0
1971	773,000	+ 9.2	3.7	15.8
1965	479,000	+ 6.4	2.5	10.6
1960	393,000	− .5	2.2	9.2
1955	377,000	− .5	2.3	9.3
1950	385,144	− 3.0	2.6	10.3
1946	610,000	+ 25.8	4.3	17.9
1941	293,000	+ 11.0	2.2	9.4

Sources: U.S. National Center for Health Statistics, December 26, 1985, p. 5; *Population Today.* December, 1986, p. 6.

crude divorce rate. To conclude that the institution of marriage and the family is in a state of decay and breakdown based on divorce statistics is not valid. "Divorce statistics tell us very little about the institution of marriage except that some people choose to dissolve their marriage and others have this choice made for them by their spouses" (Crosby, 1980, p. 57).

Reasons for America's High Divorce Rate

The reasons for America's high divorce rate are many and varied. There are the personal reasons that divorcing couples give, such as communication breakdown, sexual failure, or overuse of alcohol. More important, though, are the overriding influences that affect all marriages. The general social problems that have their roots deeply in American society and philosophy affect all relationships.

As we have mentioned, Americans ask a great deal of modern marriage, perhaps too much. High expectations often lead to disappointment and failure. Ask nothing, receive nothing, then "nothing" is not disappointing. Ask a great deal, receive a little, and unhappiness often follows. Divorce in this context may mean not the failure of the institution of marriage but an attempt to improve one's marriage, to improve the institution.

Tied closely to Americans' high expectations of marriage is the relative freedom of individuals to make marital choices. The first basic assumption of this book—that a free and creative society will offer many structural forms by which family functions can be fulfilled—is a second cause for America's high divorce rate.

Many choices breed a certain amount of dissatisfaction. Is the grass greener on the other side of the fence? Might some alternative be better than what I have? Being surrounded by married friends who see marriage as you do and who are committed to it adds strength and durability to one's own marriage. Being surrounded by those who don't support your concept of marriage, who suggest or live alternate life styles, and who deride and chide the kind of marriage you have is disruptive of your own marital patterns. Although such disruptions might lead to a better present marriage, they are just as apt to lead to marital complications.

Changing sex roles are part of the American interest in the general concept of change and its benefits. All those who question traditional sex roles place pressure on the institution of marriage. For example, a woman who decides that the role of mother is not for her, seeks a career, and leaves the care of their children to her husband is bound to face some disapproval from her family and friends. Certainly the same holds true for the husband who decides at forty to quit his job as an accountant, cease supporting his family, and begin writing adventure stories. Although the end result of sex role changes may be "people liberation," transitory results will continue to be marital disruption for some. Because the changing roles of women and men are listed as a major cause of divorce does not mean that such change will not in the long run be good for the family. Certainly many of those advocating change believe the family will benefit.

Another reason for the high divorce rate is America's heterogeneity. There are so many kinds of people, so many beliefs, attitudes, and value systems that family and marriage mean many and differing things to various Americans. Even though people tend to marry people with similar backgrounds, there will still be differences in belief and attitude. For example, consider the situation of a female college graduate interested in pursuing both a family life and a career; she marries an engineer from a traditional family background who believes the wife's place is in the home. Conflict seems inevitable.

Also stemming from America's heterogeneity is the higher incidence of mixed marriages. People of differing marital and family values and philosophies are more apt to marry in America simply because they are here and freedom of marital choice is encouraged. When such persons marry, building a successful and enduring marriage is more difficult because of their many differences.

The general mobility of Americans may also cause increased marital breakup. By moving often, a family may not create a network of support. Other married friends, relatives, and membership in institutions such as churches (Chapter 1) all tend to support a marital relationship. A high degree of mobility tends to weaken such supports.

A list of the general reasons for marital failure would be incomplete if it failed to include social upheaval, economic problems, and the general state of health of the society. Certainly the stresses and strains brought on by the Vietnam War took their toll of marriage. Spouses were separated, children disagreed with their parents about the war, and there were periods of riot and social disorganization, all of which strained the family institution.

Continuing economic worries have also brought failure to many American marriages. Marital failure is highest among the poor, becoming progressively lower as economic status rises. Also, as noted, desertion tends to be high among the poor since it does not entail the costs of a divorce.

Acceptance of divorce by Americans is another important factor in the rising

Table 15-2
Perceived Causes of Marriage Breakdown

Causes[a]	% of All Respondents (n = 335)	% Men (n = 102)	% Women (n = 233)
Sexual incompatibility	45	56	40
Lack of communication[b]	40	41	40
Husband's lack of time at home	40	28	46
Financial	32	24	36
Husband's association with another woman[c]	31	17	37
Husband's drinking[d]	30	17	36
Husband's cruelty[e]	26	37	4
Wife's lack of interest[f]	26	25	26
Friction with relatives	23	29	21
Disagreements over children	20	22	19
Wife's association with another man[c]	19	35	12
Husband's lack of interest[f]	13	15	12
Wife's ill health	13	13	13
Inadequate housing	9	4	13
Religious differences	5	5	5
Husband's gambling	5	3	7

Note: Percentages do not add up to 100. Multiple complaints are included.
[a]Causes mentioned by less than 5% are not included.
[b]Includes lack of common interests.
[c]No homosexual relationships were mentioned.
[d]Includes husband's alcoholism.
[e]Includes wife's perception of husband as having sadistic, cruel, or brutal personality.
[f]Includes statement of resentment about the lack of stimulation.

Source: Burns, 1984, p. 551.

divorce rates. The stigma of divorce has largely vanished over the past thirty years. In fact, a forty-year-old divorcée is probably less stigmatized than a forty-year-old man or woman who has never been married. General social acceptance is also noticeable in the trend toward more lenient divorce laws and increased provision of economic alternatives to marital dependency via various forms of government assistance (Furstenberg & Spanier, 1984, p. 48).

Last on our list of reasons for increasing marital failure are the personal inadequacies, failures, and problems that contribute to each individual divorce. Regardless of the magnitude of social problems and pressures that disrupt marriage, the ultimate decision to end a relationship is made by one or both spouses. The specific reasons given for divorce by individuals are listed in Table 15-2.

Emotional Divorce and the Emotions of Divorce

Paul Bohannan (1970) has described what he terms the "six stations" of divorce. First is the *emotional divorce*, which centers on the problem of the deteriorating marriage. It begins before the second station, the *legal divorce*, and may go on long after the legal divorce. It brings forth the kind of thinking and questioning described in Inset 15-1 and may go on for several years. It is only when one finally lets go of the former spouse emotionally that one really becomes free. Yet the third and fourth stations, the *economic* and *coparental divorce*, may mean restraints on freedom for years. The fifth station is the *community divorce*, the

---

Inset 15-1

Divorce: A Personal Tragedy

How can I be missing her after all of the fighting and yelling we've been doing the past year or two? It's so nice to be in my own place and have peace and quiet. Damn, it sure is lonely. It's great to be a bachelor again, but after fifteen years of married life, who wants to chase women and play all those games? Wonder why the kids don't call? Keeping house is sure a drag. I wonder what she's doing. Do you suppose she is nicer to her dates than she was to me?

What really went wrong? Two nice kids, a good job, nice home, and I certainly loved her when we married. But she has been so unaffectionate and cold over the years. She never seemed to have time for me. Or was it that I never had time for her? When we dated, she was so flexible. She'd do anything with me, but after our first child she seemed to become so conservative. She wouldn't do anything daring. I had so little leisure time what with working so hard to give the family a good life. Why couldn't she do what I wanted when I was free? It's really all her fault. Of course, I could have included her more in my work world. Maybe if I had shared more of my business problems with her, she'd have been more understanding. It's true I am awfully short-tempered when the pressure is on. Certainly I didn't listen to her much any more. It seemed as if she only bitched and complained. I get enough of that at the office. You don't suppose there was another person? Maybe it was all my fault. A failure at marriage, that's me. Never thought it could happen to me. When did it start? Who first thought of divorce? Maybe the idea came because all our friends seemed to be divorcing.

On and on the thoughts of this newly divorced man go. Anger, guilt, frustration, conflict, insecurity, and emotional upheaval are the bedmates of divorce. "Our culture says that marriage is forever and yet I failed to make a go of it. Why?" The whys keep churning up thoughts, and endless questioning follows marital breakdown. There are so many questions, doubts, and fears.

---

reactions of friends and the community to the divorce. The last station is the *psychic divorce*, where the major task is regaining individual autonomy.

Divorce is not a spontaneous, spur-of-the-moment act as marriage can be. In most cases dissolution occurs slowly, and divorce is the culmination of a prolonged period of gradual alienation (Spanier & Thompson, 1984, p. 46). In many cases several years elapse between a couple's first serious thought of divorce and the decree (Melichar & Chiriboga, 1985). Willard Waller (1967) delineates the following aspects in the alienation process:

1. Early in the process there is a disturbance in the sex life and affectional response. Rapport is lost, with an attempt to compensate for its lack in some cases. Emotional divorce begins here.
2. The possibility of divorce is first mentioned. This tends to clarify the relationship somewhat, with the initiator taking the lead and the partner remaining passive through the divorce cycle.
3. The appearance of solidarity is broken before the public. The fiction of solidarity is important as a face-saver. Once it is broken, the marriage cannot be the same again.
4. The decision to divorce is made, usually after long discussion, although at times it is made without forethought.
5. A severe crisis of separation follows. Severing a meaningful relationship is a traumatic experience at best, even if it is felt to be the only alternative.

6. Final severance comes with the actual divorce. This may come after a long period of delay and separation. While it is usually thought of as closing the case, the actual legal procedure is necessary before the next stage of the final adaptation can begin.

7. A period of mental conflict and reconstruction closes the case. The former partners enter new social worlds and full estrangement takes place.

Thus long before legal divorce a couple may find themselves beginning the process of emotional divorce. Often the beginnings of the process are not noticeable. What usually happens involves such things as a subtle withdrawal of one partner from the other, the erection of barriers that shield each from hurt by the other, a gradual shift of concern from "us" to "me," the tendency to meet more and more psychological needs outside of marriage, and finally the erosion of the couple's sex life. The actual facts or events that lead up to divorce are as varied as the individuals who marry, but one thing that always happens is that each begins to concentrate on the other's weaknesses, shortcomings, and failures rather than on their strengths. The "20 percent I hate you" becomes the point of attention, rather than the "80 percent I love you" (see Chapter 5, pages 151–153). The inability to accept the partner the way he or she is or to accept unwanted change in the partner is at the root of most emotional divorces.

Although many breakups occur during the first few years of marriage, with the peak occurring about three years after marriage, nearly 40 percent of all broken marriages have lasted ten or more years. The median duration of a marriage at the time of divorce in the United States is approximately seven years (p. 501). A couple usually decide on a legal divorce only after years of worsening relations.

Once legal divorce is initiated, many emotions will be experienced—essentially the emotions of loss, the grief felt at the death of a loved one, the loss of feelings of psychological well-being. For a lucky few—perhaps those divorcing quickly after marriage—grief and mourning will not occur. For a very few happiness and joy over regaining freedom may be the major emotions experienced (see Table 15-3). But for most there will be a period of denial—it really isn't happening—followed by grief, mourning, and a mixture of the following:

- *Self-pity*: Why did this happen to me?
- *Vengeance*: I'm going to get even!
- *Despair*: I feel like going to sleep and never waking up again.
- *Wounded pride*: I'm not as great as I thought I was.
- *Anguish*: I don't know how I can hurt so much.
- *Guilt*: I'm really to blame for everything.
- *Loneliness*: Why don't our friends ever call me?
- *Fear*: No one else will want to marry me.
- *Distrust*: He (or she) is probably conniving with attorneys to take all the property.
- *Withdrawal*: I don't feel like seeing anyone.
- *Relief*: Well, at least it's over, a decision has finally been made.
- *Loss of feelings of psychological well-being*: I feel awful, depressed, nervous, suicidal.

There is some evidence that the lowered feelings of psychological well-being on the part of at least one partner may actually exist early in the relationship of those who subsequently divorce. At least one study (Erbes & Hedderson, 1984)

Table 15-3

Characterization of the Divorce Experience and Perceptions of "Best" and "Worst" Periods

	Combined Sample	Female	Male
Characterization of Divorce Experience			
Traumatic, a nightmare	23%	27%	16%
Stressful, but bearable	40%	40%	40%
Unsettling, but easier than expected	20%	19%	24%
Relatively painless	17%	13%	20%
Most Difficult Period			
Before decision to divorce	55%	58%	50%
After decision, but before final decree	22%	20%	25%
Just after the divorce	21%	19%	23%
Now	3%	3%	3%

Source: Adapted from Albrecht, 1979.

found that even years before separation and divorce the divorced men scored significantly lower in measures of psychological well-being than stably married men. This brings up the question of whether such feelings contribute to marital failure or whether they are only the result of marital failure.

Unfortunately our society offers no ritual, no prescribed behaviors, for the survivor of divorce. The community does not feel it necessary to help as it does in bereavement. Indeed the fact that the spouse still lives often denies the divorced person the opportunity to come to a final acceptance of the breakup because there is always a chance, no matter how small, of recovering the spouse. For some rejected spouses this little chance is exaggerated and becomes the sustaining theme of their lives for a long time after the legal divorce. Children and monetary involvement are often reasons for continued association. Even in cases where marital breakup is hostile and bitter, the loneliness following the breakup may spur a mate to wish the spouse were home, even if only to fight with and ease the loneliness.

No matter how much one thinks about and prepares for a separation, there is still a shock when the actual physical separation occurs. A very common reaction for many persons to the initial separation, especially for the person left, is the sudden panic of abandonment.

> It's the same feeling you had as a child when you got separated from your mother in the supermarket. Although separation panic comes in many forms, most people experience it as apprehensiveness or anxiety. They feel physically and psychologically shaky, and have great difficulty concentrating on any complex task. As a thirty-five-year-old insurance agent described it, "I felt an alertness and constant vigilance. I had to be busy all the time but I couldn't concentrate on anything. I'd start to make a sandwich, only to forget it halfway as I began pacing through the house. I felt that something awful would happen, that I'd get sick or get too nervous to work. (Mckay et al., 1984, p. 11)

Such feelings will recede but a divorced spouse may later feel a resurgence of hurt, hostility, and rejection on learning of the former spouse's new relationships. To hear that one's former mate is remarrying is often upsetting and may arouse past hostilities and regrets even if considerable time has passed.

It is probably important that anger be a part of divorce, for it is anger that will finally break the emotional bonds that remain between the former spouses. Not until these bonds are finally broken will each be free. Fortunately for most divorcing couples a turning point comes when their energies can finally turn from destruction to construction once again.

Creative Divorce and Rebirth

Divorce is the death of a relationship, but it can also be the rebirth of an individual. Just as death is difficult, so is rebirth. Once the mourning and grief begin to subside, the newly divorced individual faces important choices about life directions. What does one do when newly alone? Seek the immediate security of a new marriage? Prepare to live alone the rest of one's life? Make all new friends or keep old friends? Maintain ties to the past relationship? Escape into the work world? Seek counseling? Experiment with sexual involvements? More and more professionals as well as divorced persons themselves are saying, "Use the pain and suffering of divorce to learn about yourself. Seek the rebirth of a new, more insightful, more capable person out of the wreckage of failure."

The phrase "creative divorce" was popularized by Mel Krantzler (1973) in his book of that name, and it has come to stand for a movement that declares:

> Divorce is not an end, it is a new beginning. Divorce does not mean the decay and destruction of marriage and the family in America, rather it means renewed effort to improve marriage and the family. Divorce is the beginning of a new enriching and enlivening voyage of self-discovery that makes me a happier and stronger person than I was before. Through divorce, a painful and emotional crisis, I learned that what I went through was what all divorced people go through—first a recognition that a relationship has died, then a period of mourning, and finally a slow, painful emotional readjustment to the facts of single life. I experienced the pitfalls along the way—the wallowing in self-pity, the refusal to let go of the old relationship, the repetition of old ways in relating to new people, the confusion of past emotions with present reality— and I emerged the better for it. (p. 30)

Such attitudes are a far cry from the feelings most persons initially experience at the breakup of their marriage. Yet it makes a great deal of sense to use divorce as a learning opportunity rather than seeing it only as a failure from which nothing good can be derived (see Inset 15-2). If a divorce is not used to gain insight into oneself and past relationships, one is doomed to make the same relational mistakes as before.

Many groups have sprung up to help the newly divorced move in a positive direction. We Care is an organization of volunteers who do just what their name implies: care and help those in mourning, whether it be over the death of a loved one or the death of a relationship. Parents Without Partners (PWP) is a nationwide organization whose goal is to help alleviate some of the isolation that makes it difficult for single parents to provide a reasonably normal family life for themselves and their children. Many adult education facilities, churches, and other service-oriented organizations offer workshops and group experiences for the newly divorced.

A word of warning is in order, however. Recently a myth of romantic divorce has appeared, perhaps a defense against guilt on the part of the growing numbers of divorced people in American society. In essence it stresses only those things

---

Inset 15-2

Getting On with Your Life

Just how long it takes to make the decision to get on with your life will vary, but inevitably this step must come. Each person must do it in his or her own way, at his or her own speed, and stumble over the obstacles as best he or she can. It's tough, but you must keep moving forward.

The following are tools that can be used effectively. Remember, determination is the key.

1. Be good to yourself; protect the inner child. Turn on your childlike personality; do things to make your inner self feel good.

2. Stay away from guilt trips—he said this, she said that, my fault, his fault, and so on—stay out of that deadly trap. The relationship is over, the marriage didn't jell. Remember the good times, and let go.

3. Avoid bitterness and hostility at all costs. They will only hurt you.

4. Take a realistic appraisal of yourself: Focus on your good points; stay out of self-recrimination; keep reminding yourself that you are lovable, worthwhile, unique, special—there has never been nor shall there ever be one exactly like you.

5. Stay in the now. Plan time and activities for your internal child. The childlike portion of you is dependent on approval from yourself and others, so give it permission to cry, to express the hurt, and then to laugh and be free.

6. Reach out to others, don't close yourself off—turn on, be excited, get into other people, and find something good about them.

7. Make a list of short-range and long-range goals, and do something to activate them.

8. Recognize fear as a useful tool. Fear gives you caution, with caution there is discrimination, and with discrimination there are useful decisions.

9. Trust your intuitional hunches, be spontaneous; have faith and trust in yourself. Try not to rule out the possibility that all that has happened has a purpose, that in every negative there is a positive to be learned.

---

perceived as positive about divorce. It tries to make divorce an exciting romantic adventure in the ongoing stream of life. However this myth, which stresses only the joys of greater freedom and the delights of self-discovery, hardly prepares the divorcing couple for the traumas and stresses they will find in reaching these goals. Nor does it prepare people to reevaluate both their broken marriages and themselves in order to make more successful future marriages.

> The hooker in divorce is that in order to get over a marriage, you have to go back to it. To go forward to a new life, you have to go backward to the past. That's the agony of breaking up a marriage. It's not over yet, even after divorce. . . .
>
> From what you see on television and in the movies, you'd think that getting a divorce was some yellow brick road to personal growth and happiness; all those stories of personal freedom, the joys of being single, the good sex out there; the jokes about falling off the marriage merry-go-round and having fun. The Great New Life.
>
> But ask someone who's been through it. There is nothing funny or easy about divorce. It is a savage emotional journey. Where it ends, you don't know for a long time (Trafford, 1984, pp. 1, 19).

What Do You Think?

1. What do you think is the single most important thing that a newly divorced person should avoid doing if he road to recovery? Why?

2. What are some things the newly divorced person should avoid doing it he or she wants to speed recovery?

3. If you were advising a newly divorced person, what would you tell him or her? Why?

The major dangers facing the newly divorced are prolonged retreat from social contact, jumping quickly into a new marriage, leading a life based on hope that the spouse will return, or leading a life based on hostility and getting back at the

Problems of the Newly Divorced

former mate. Certainly the first step after any loss may be one of momentary retreat, turning inward, contemplation, and avoidance of all situations reminding one of the hurt, disappointment, guilt, and shame of failure. Unfortunately though, some divorced people make such a reaction their lifestyle. In essence such people die psychologically and end their lives in every way but physically.

A larger group of divorced people seek a new relationship as quickly as possible. Discounting those who had a satisfying relationship with someone else before their divorce and are now fulfilling it as soon as possible, there are many who can't stand the thought of failure or being alone and thus rush into the first available relationship. These people usually have not had time to reassess themselves or their motives. The idea of facing themselves and the challenges of becoming an independent person are simply too frightening. These are often people who have never really been alone. They married early, and in a sense they may never have grown up psychologically. Even though their first marriage may have been unsatisfying, marriage is still preferable to assuming responsibility for oneself. Rushing into a new marriage they will likely make the same mistakes again.

We have already looked at some of the problems of attempting to hold onto a past relationship. Living by false hope only locks one into a kind of prolonged alternation of hope and disappointment. However, a life based on continuing anger and harassment of a former spouse may be the most destructive of all, because the former spouse is harmed as well as the mate seeking revenge. The horror stories connected with this reaction to divorce are enough to keep people from ever marrying. The stories usually involve one spouse taking the divorced spouse back to court time and again in an effort (conscious or unconscious) to punish him or her. Fortunately few divorced persons react in this fashion for long.

Community divorce, Bohannan's fifth station of divorce, describes problems and changes in one's lifestyle and in one's community of friends that occur on

divorce. When one marries, single friends are gradually replaced by married couple friends. When one divorces, there is usually another change of friends. Unfortunately changes of friendship after divorce tend to be more complicated both for the person newly divorced and for the couple's friends. Some friends may side with one or the other person when a couple divorces. Remaining friends with a newly divorced person is difficult for at least two reasons. The divorcing couple cause their married friends to reexamine their own marriages. Often a divorcing couple will inadvertently cause trouble in the marriages of their friends. There is conflict over with which partner to remain friends. The newly single person may also be viewed as a threat or at least as a "fifth wheel" by still-married friends. Generally the newly divorced person will find that old friendships tend to fade and be replaced by new friendships, often ones in which the new friends share some of the same kinds of problems as the newly divorced.

Most divorced people start to date within the first year after their separation. The new dating partners bring with them a new circle of friends. Thus most divorced people will experience a gradual change in their larger community of friends and contacts.

Economic Consequences

The bottom line is that divorce brings about severe financial changes for the divorcing couple. For many divorcing couples with children, the man becomes single, but the woman becomes a single parent, and poverty often begins with single parenthood. More than half the poor families in the United States are headed by single mothers (Ehrenreich & Piven, 1984, p. 162).

Lenore Weitzman (1985, p. 323) found that divorced men experience an average 42-percent rise in their standard of living in the first year after divorce, while divorced women (and their children) experience a 73-percent decline. Two factors tend to account for this disparity. First, men have always earned more than women (Chapter 9). This fact does not affect married women since they traditionally share in the man's resources. Once a woman is divorced, however, she no longer shares the man's higher earning power and must rely on court-ordered child or spousal support to make up the difference between her earning power and her former husband's.

The second factor that accounts for the divorced woman's relatively poorer economic condition is that courts don't always order child or spousal support payments, and even if they do former husbands often fail to pay. Interestingly enough, the women's movement has actually reduced the number of child or spousal support payments ordered by the courts. "No-fault" divorce means that a spouse cannot be awarded monetary help as punishment against the guilty spouse; monetary support must be tied to the ability of the divorced spouses to support themselves. If women have equal rights to men theoretically they should be able to support themselves, and this tends to be the rationale on which the courts now base spousal support after divorce. This would be fine if women were indeed able to earn as much as men, but that is not yet the case, particularly for women who must care for children (Chapter 9). Courts now award spousal or child support in about half of all divorce cases.

In the cases where support is awarded, more than half (53 percent) of the women do not receive it (U.S. Bureau of the Census, 1983). Thus, in actuality only about 25 percent of divorced women receive any additional support from their former husbands to make up for the disparity between men's and women's earning powers. Hence, as Weitzman pointed out, divorce usually means a drastically reduced standard of living for women, especially if they have custody of the children, which in 90 percent of the cases they do.

These facts have led to a large increase in child poverty in the United States paralleling the increased number of divorces. Weitzman (1985, p. 352) reports that the percentage of American children living in poverty increased from 14.9 percent in 1970 to 21.3 percent in 1983. At the current rate of divorce it appears that about 60 percent of children born today will spend some of their childhood in a single-parent family, which increases their chances of living in poverty for at least that period of their lives.

In light of the poor child and spousal support payment records of noncustodial spouses, both state and local governments as well as the federal government have tried to enforce such payments through legislation. In 1984 Congress unanimously approved legislation to strengthen child support collection through mandatory income withholding and the interception of federal and state income tax refund checks to cover past due support. Earlier (1982) law established a federal Parent Locator Service that allows custodial parents access to various federal records, such as IRS information, to find an errant spouse, which is, of course, the first step in enforcing support payments. In addition the 1984 legislation allowed states to provide information to consumer credit agencies on past due child support when the arrears are more than $1000. Late payment penalties of between 3 and 6 percent may also be applied. Payments may be made through a state agency if requested by either parent. All these enforcement tools have helped increase support payments. In those few jurisdictions that have jail sentences for errant noncustodial parents there seems to be quick compliance with the court-ordered payments.

The single-parent family created either by divorce or having a child out of wedlock has not only economic problems but also severe time problems (Sanick & Mauldin, 1986). To work and rear children successfully without an additional adult requires an almost superhuman effort. The complex logistics of working and providing childcare at the same time, especially when money is in short supply, make it difficult for the single-parent family to function. Fortunately the single-parent family tends to be temporary. As we shall see in Chapter 16, the majority of divorced people remarry. In fact approximately 50 percent of divorced people remarry within three years. Although it might seem that having children would make it harder to remarry, studies show that this is not true.

Children and Divorce

The first problem for parents contemplating divorce is telling the children. There is no easy way to do this. Wallerstein and Kelly (1980; 1984) reported that 80 percent of the children studied were completely unprepared for their parents' separations. In a disturbingly high number of cases, a parent would simply disappear while a child was sleeping or away from home. It is an unpleasant task to share an impending separation with one's children, but it is important to the child's well-being that it be done (see Inset 15-3).

It has generally been thought that divorce always has negative effects on the

---

Inset 15-3

Guidelines for Telling the Children

Matthew Mckay and his colleagues (1984, pp. 142–144) suggest the following guidelines for telling children about an impending separation:

1. Tell children as clearly as you can what divorce means and be prepared to repeat this information several times for younger children.
2. Describe some of your attempts to protect and improve your marriage.

3. Emphasize that both parents will continue to love and care for the children.
4. Do not assess blame. You can share your unhappiness and anger, but when you assess blame you are asking the children to take sides.
5. Try to describe any changes the children may expect in their day-to-day experiences.
6. It is important to emphasize that

the children in no way caused the divorce and are not responsible for problems between the parents. You are divorcing one another, not the children.
7. Assure the children that they will always be free to love both parents.
8. Encourage your children to ask questions throughout the process of divorce and adjustment.

---

children involved. Because of this belief many couples remained together "for the sake of the children" or postponed divorce until the children were grown. Yet the effects of divorce on children are not at all clear. There is no doubt that the immediate effects are unsettling. Long-term effects are probably mixed. Some children may suffer long-term damage. Others may be much better off after a divorce than they were when the conflicting parents were together. An unhappy marriage is an unhappy home for children; if divorce promotes parental happiness, the children should also benefit. Although this folk wisdom sounds reasonable, long-term study of divorced families only partially supports it.

Judith Wallerstein and Joan Kelley (1980; 1984) did a long-term study of sixty families that had gone through divorce. They interviewed them close to the time of divorce and at eighteen months, five years, and ten years after the divorce.

> Our overall conclusion is that divorce produces not a single pattern in people's lives, but at least three patterns, with many variations. Among both adults and children five years afterward, we found about a quarter to be resilient (those for whom the divorce was successful), half muddling through, coping when and as they could, and a final quarter to be bruised: failing to recover from the divorce or looking back to the predivorce family with intense longing. Some in each group had been that way before and continued unchanged; for the rest, we found roughly equal numbers for whom the divorce seemed connected to improvement and to decline. (1984, p. 67)

What factors appear associated with the 25 percent who adapted well to the divorce? Not surprisingly, children with strong, well-integrated personalities who were well adjusted before the divorce were making the best adjustments. Children also did significantly better when both parents continued to be a part of their lives on a regular basis. This was true only when the parents themselves were able to work out a satisfactory and nondestructive postdivorce relationship. Aside from these two factors, it was difficult to predict which children would do well and which would not.

One thing is clear: Divorced parents who fight via their children will probably cause their children harm. One parent may try to turn the children against the

Child snatching
The taking of children from the custodial spouse by the noncustodial spouse after a divorce

former spouse. Visitation rights may become attempts by the visiting parent to lure the child away from the custodial parent. The "Disneyland Dad" syndrome, in which the visiting parent indulges the child, may cause conflict with the custodial parent, who thinks that the "ex" is spoiling the children. Parents need to speak openly about the divorce but without speaking negatively about the former mate. Unless divorced parents can work out some mutually acceptable relationship that holds conflict to a minimum, adjustment will remain difficult for the children. In extreme cases recurring court battles may be fought over the children. Or **child snatching** may occur, which is frightening, confusing, and possibly dangerous to the child.

Although we have been discussing the general effects of divorce on children, it is important to realize that both the age and the sex of the child must be considered to understand divorce effects. Younger children seem to have more severe reactions to the divorce of their parents than adolescent children. Preschoolers (two to six years old) react to divorce with fright, confusion, and self-blame. Children seven to eight years old seem to blame themselves less but express feelings of sadness and insecurity. They have a problem expressing anger and a strong desire for parental reconciliation. Nine- to ten-year-old children can express their anger better, but they feel a conflict of loyalty, are lonely, and are ashamed of their parents' behavior. Adolescents express their anger, sadness, and shame most openly and seem better able to dissociate themselves from the parental difficulties (Lowery & Settle, 1985).

Boys typically show more maladjustment and more prolonged problems than girls. Increased aggression, dependency, disobedience, and regressive behaviors are observed among more boys than girls (Lowery & Settle, 1985).

Although not much studied, the role of former grandparents can also be important to children. Divorce removes the children not only from one parent but also from at least one set of grandparents. Moreover grandparents who have close and ongoing relationships with their grandchildren and then, because of divorce, are denied access to them are also victims of divorce (although generally unnoticed). Grandparents are one step removed from the conflicts of a divorce and therefore may be able to offer their grandchildren relative security and affection during the trying times. By 1983 recognition of the grandparent-grandchild relationship had led forty-three states to recognize grandparent visitation rights (Press, 1983).

Studies comparing adults from divorced (when the person was a child) and intact families find that the adults from divorced families more often characterized their childhoods as unhappy (Wallerstein & Kelley, 1980, 1984). They are more likely to suffer from feelings of worthlessness, guilt, and despair. Yet such feelings might be caused by their parents' bad relationship before the divorce rather than the divorce itself.

At this time we do not fully understand the effects of divorce on children. The immediate effects, usually negative, vary from child to child. Some children will be affected even as adults (Magrab, 1978). It is also clear that the divorced family is usually less adaptive economically, socially, and psychologically to the raising of children than the two-parent family. The one-parent family lacks the support and buffering effect of another adult (Wallerstein & Kelley, 1980, 1984).

Fortunately most divorced people remarry, thereby reconstituting the two-parent family. Of course in this case children must establish a new successful relationship with the stepparent, which is another problem (Chapter 16).

Despite the general acceptance of divorce in our society, it remains an unpleasant and traumatic experience for most parents and a trying and difficult time for most children.

Types of Child Custody   Courts have four choices when awarding custody of children in a divorce proceeding. The most common is *sole custody* (65 to 70 percent). In this case the children are assigned to one parent, generally the mother (90 percent), who has sole responsibility for physically raising the children.

Another choice is joint custody, in which the children divide their time between the parents, who share the various decisions about their children. At present there is an increasing trend for courts to award joint custody. In 1980 California became the first state to institute a statute favoring joint custody with its appealing promise that the children of divorce could "keep both parents" (Weitzman, 1985, p. 245). The perceived advantages are: Both parents continue parenting roles; the arrangement avoids sudden termination of a child's relationship with one parent; and it lessens the constant child-care burden experienced by most single parents. Joint custody, however, forces the parents to maintain a relationship; if they cannot do this successfully, there are negative effects on the children (Abarbanel, 1979; Benedek & Benedek, 1979).

A third choice is split custody, in which the children are divided between the parents. In most cases the father takes the boys and the mother the girls. This method has the major drawback of separating the children from one another. It does, however, reduce the burden on the parent who might otherwise have sole custody of all the children.

The fourth choice is to award custody to someone other than a parent or parents. This is seldom done unless both parents are highly incompetent or offer such a poor environment for the children that the court decides parental custody would be harmful. In most such cases grandparents or other near relatives gain custody of the children.

Custody and visitation plans often cause conflict between the divorcing couple. Yet in practice most children are still placed in the physical custody of their mother. Noncustodial fathers tend to drop gradually out of their children's lives. Frank Furstenberg and his colleagues (1983) found that only 16 percent of children from divorced families saw their father at least once a week. Another 16 percent saw their fathers at least once a month and 15 percent saw them at least once a year. The remaining 53 percent of the children had had no contact with their fathers in the past year.

For many years couples with children tended to avoid or at least postpone divorce until the children were grown. This is no longer true, and, with America's high divorce rate, increasing numbers of children will go through the divorce experience. Estimates based on the divorce rate suggest that from 59 to 66 percent of the children born in 1983 are likely to experience disruption of their parents' marriage by age seventeen (Weitzman, 1985, p. 215).

What Do You Think?

1. Of the various types of child custody, which do you think would have been best for you if your parents divorced when you were six years old?
2. Should parents stay together for the sake of the children?
3. If a noncustodial parent does not pay court-ordered child support, what do you think should be done?
4. If a parent denies visitation rights to his or her ex-spouse, what do you think should be done?
5. If the above occurs and the noncustodial parent snatches his or her child away without permission, what do you think should be done?

Historically, the American attitude toward divorce has been negative, stemming mainly from the majority Christian heritage. The stigma has a long history. Until the advent of Christianity there was no regulation (at least in Western countries) of marriage and divorce. As soon as the Church was established, however, divorce

Divorce: The Legalities

was formally forbidden and made legally impossible. (There was no civil marriage or civil divorce until recent centuries.) To this day civil divorces of Catholics, even in non-Catholic countries, are not recognized by the Catholic church, and those Catholics who obtain such a divorce and remarry are considered to be in a state of sin and therefore ineligible for communion, although they are no longer excommunicated.

Italy allowed divorce for the first time in December 1970. Italy's divorce law is hardly liberal, yet it took years of effort to gain any kind of divorce law. Couples seeking divorce must be legally separated for at least five years when separation is mutual and for six or more years when one partner is opposed. Other grounds cited in the new law are: foreign divorce or remarriage by one spouse, long prison sentences, incest, attempted murder of family members, criminal insanity, and nonconsummation of the marriage. Adultery is not included as a ground for divorce. Ireland remains one of the few countries without legal divorce, having voted down a divorce statute in 1986.

The attitudes of many Americans, however, have changed; divorce is now a legitimate option. It is even considered a right and proper way to end an unsuccessful marriage.

The Conservative versus Liberal Battle over Divorce

Divorce laws vary from extreme restriction, such as in Ireland where no divorce is allowed, to extreme permissiveness, such as in Japan where divorce is granted simply on mutual consent. Even within the United States there is great variety because divorce, like marriage, is regulated by individual states. For example, until 1949 divorce was not allowed in South Carolina. Until 1966 adultery was the only grounds for divorce in New York, a situation that led to the creation of businesses that planned and documented "adulterous" situations for couples seeking divorce but uninvolved in real adultery. Since 1969 California has allowed divorce essentially by mutual consent, having dropped the old idea of adversary proceedings in which one member of the marriage had to be proved guilty of behavior that would give the other partner some state-defined ground for divorce.

The reason for such variety in divorce laws is the old philosophic battle between those who believe that stringent divorce laws will curtail marriage failure and those who believe that marriages fail regardless of the strictness of divorce legislation. The latter also believe that unrealistic laws do more harm than good.

Until the advent of Christianity, governments in the Western world did not regulate marriage or divorce. In republican Rome, for example, it was customary to marry simply by living together with the stated intention of becoming husband and wife. No ceremony was required. The Roman state recognized a marriage as dissolved when the parties separated.

The Christians, partly in reaction to the hedonistic Roman society, advocated strict control of sexuality and hence strict regulation of marriage and divorce. In the Christian ethic marriage became indissoluble except by death. Sexual intercourse was permitted only within marriage and was therefore limited to one partner. Marriage was not only an assumption of responsibility for spouse and offspring but also a sacrament by which the marriage partners acknowledged their belief in and responsibilities to God and their faith in Christ. The Protestant Reformation reestablished the idea of divorce when Martin Luther claimed that marriage was not a sacrament but a "worldly thing." He considered it justifiable for a husband to leave his wife if she committed adultery. This viewpoint brought back the idea of permissible divorce, but along with it came the idea that one spouse had to be proved a transgressor, thus introducing the adversary approach to divorce that has remained in the Western world to this day. Because religion and government were closely related, laws concerning marriage and divorce were soon enacted.

Thus the state laid down certain grounds for divorce, rules that if broken by one spouse allowed the other to divorce. And because one spouse had to be proved a wrongdoer, punishments were often established. For example, in the American colonies it was common to deny the guilty spouse the right of remarriage if a divorce was granted. In the past, payment by one spouse to the other (alimony) was sometimes used to punish the guilty spouse rather than simply to help a spouse become reestablished.

The adversary/punishment approach to divorce remained the only approach in America until 1969 when California passed the first "no-fault" divorce law. Thus the idea that a marriage might be terminated simply because it had broken down, without placing blame on one party or the other found its way into both the law of the books (how the laws are written) and the law of action (how laws are actually applied). It is interesting that this first "no-fault" divorce law was passed under the conservative governor of California, Ronald Reagan, who subsequently became the first divorced person to be elected president of the United States.

The Legal Sham of Past Divorce Laws

All states set grounds on which a divorce can be granted. Some of these grounds have been adultery, mental or physical cruelty, desertion, alcoholism, impotence, nonsupport, insanity, felony conviction or imprisonment, drug addiction, and pregnancy at marriage. To obtain a divorce in the past, one of the partners had to prove the other guilty of having transgressed in at least one of the areas accepted by the particular state in which they lived. In addition, all states banned *collusion* (partners agreeing and working together to obtain a divorce) or moving to another state only to take advantage of more lenient divorce laws. Thus if the letter of the past law was followed, divorce would have to be an action taken by one spouse against the other, who would have to be proved guilty of conduct the state of residence found unacceptable and therefore grounds for divorce.

Yet the law in practice was often quite different. Some 85 to 90 percent of divorces were uncontested (both partners agreed to the divorce). And as long as both partners agreed to the divorce and did not fight it in court, divorces were granted fairly freely and without much substantiation of charges, regardless of the laws on the books. Thus the American divorce system was restrictive in writing and permissive in practice. The courts usually did not inquire into questions of collusion, residence, or grounds. They accepted the word of the party in court and did not pursue such questions unless asked to do so by the parties and their lawyers. In a sense America's varying divorce laws were a true democratic compromise. The conservatives had strict laws on the books, and the liberals had permissive courts.

All states attach residency requirements to divorce. Each state now recognizes

divorce in every other state if the other state's residency requirements have been met. And this "if" is not checked in the usual uncontested divorce. Theoretically states do not recognize foreign divorces unless one party actually lives or has lived in the foreign country. But the formal law again differs from the informal action, and the state will do nothing about a foreign divorce, even if neither party lives abroad, unless a complaint is received. However, if a complaint is received and the divorce is contested, states may invalidate a divorce where residency requirements have not been met. In cases of remarriage spouses have sometimes been prosecuted for bigamy when the divorce to the former spouse has been invalidated. (See Appendix B for state divorce requirements.)

The Move toward No-Fault Divorce

For many years the Interprofessional Commission on Marriage and Divorce Laws advocated elimination of the "proof of guilt" (adversary) procedure and substitution of "the best interests of the family."

California led the way in doing this when it passed a "dissolution of marriage" law (Senate Bill 252) in 1969 that became the model for other states to follow. The law removed fault: the question of who was to blame. Grounds were reduced to (1) irreconcilable differences that have caused irremedial breakdown of the marriage or (2) incurable insanity. Section 4507 of the bill defined irreconcilable differences as those grounds that are determined by the court to be substantial reasons for not continuing the marriage and that make it appear that the marriage should be dissolved.

The no-fault law also simplified property allocation by dividing property equally under most circumstances. Child support remained the responsibility of both husband and wife. By 1986 all states except South Dakota had enacted some type of **no-fault** or modified-fault divorce proceedings.

No-fault divorce
Divorce proceedings that do not place blame for the divorce on one spouse or the other

Although from a legal view the two grounds are quite vague and open to varied interpretation, in practice this has meant that the courts simply ask the petitioner if his or her marriage has broken down because of irreconcilable differences. The court does not inquire into the nature of the differences, though the court can order a delay or continuance of not more than thirty days if in its opinion there is a reasonable possibility of reconciliation. The no-fault law has a unique section that bars evidence of misconduct on the part of either spouse:

> In any pleadings or proceedings for legal separation or dissolution of marriage under this part, . . . evidence of specific acts of misconduct shall be improper and inadmissible, except where child custody is in issue and such evidence is relevant. (*West's Annotated California Codes*, Section 4509, 1983, p. 280)

To date the last point has been ignored by the courts.

Because misconduct of one partner or the other is no longer considered, property settlements, support, and alimony awards are no longer used as punishment. There are now seven states in which all property acquired during the marriage is considered community property belonging equally to each spouse. The states are Alaska, California, Idaho, Louisiana, Nevada, Texas, and Washington. As long as the parties to the divorce agree and have divided their community property approximately evenly, the courts do not involve themselves in property settlements. The courts do set up support requirements for minor children, deeming such minors the responsibility of both parents until they are of age. In practice this generally means that the children live with the mother and the father pays support.

Although fault is no longer determined, the judge still has the right to award alimony, though not as punishment for wrong-doing.

> In any judgment decreeing the dissolution of a marriage or a legal separation of the parties, the court may order a party to pay for the support of the other party any amount, and for such a period of time, as the court may deem just and reasonable having regard for the circumstances of the respective parties, including duration of marriage, and the ability of the supported spouse to engage in gainful employment without interfering with the interests of the children. (*West's Annotated California Codes*, section 4801, 1983, p. 629)

In most cases the wife will receive alimony until she is able to get on her feet financially. Often the wife who has devoted herself exclusively to the family for years has lost what marketable skills she may once have had, and if she is older finding a job is even more difficult. The judges are tending to award limited-term alimony on the basis of need. In one case the court awarded a wife funds for a college education on the grounds that she had provided such an education for her husband by working to put him through school when they first married, and now it would be fair for him to do the same for her. A number of courts are using the following rough guidelines in awarding alimony. If the marriage has lasted less than twelve years, the period of support will not exceed half the duration of the marriage. In marriages of twenty years or more, awards of support may be given until remarriage. Generally, under no-fault proceedings the amount and duration of alimony have been drastically reduced (Williams, 1977; Weitzman, 1985).

The simplified no-fault laws have encouraged a new "do-it-yourself" trend in divorce. Retaining an attorney in order to obtain a divorce was mandatory in the past, if for no other reason than to help interpret complicated divorce laws. Although many attorneys work hard as marriage counselors and do all they can to minimize the problems of divorce, others seem to intensify problems rather than minimize them:

> And because these divorce proceedings are handled by two lawyers, each of whom is being paid to demonstrate his/her own abilities, what is fair is often completely overlooked in favor of what can be gotten away with. Too many lawyers representing husbands feel they can justify their fees only by working out arrangements by which the husband pays too little. Too many wives' lawyers feel satisfied only when they can point out how little the husband has left. (Sheresky & Mannes, 1972, p. x)

The structure of the legal profession links attorneys to individual clients and rewards them for representing their client's interests. One example of this reality involved an attorney who was struggling with the question of a wealthy doctor's support for his college-age children. While the doctor could well afford to support his children through college and graduate school, and was ready to sign an agreement to do so, the attorney had the professional responsibility to tell the doctor that the law did not require him to support his children past eighteen (Weitzman, 1985, p. 400). In fact, his obligation to get the best possible deal for his client made it necessary for the attorney to try and talk the doctor out of signing such an agreement.

Recently divorced people often express negative sentiments about attorneys. It may be that the lawyer has simply become a scapegoat. On the other hand, the legal profession may need clearer guidelines for handling divorce as well as some training in counseling and interpersonal relations. Regardless of whether attorneys are involved or not, the couple that can work out differences before approaching a lawyer and the court is in a much better position to obtain a fair and equitable divorce. Without such agreement, a couple put themselves in the hands of a judge who knows little or nothing of their personal situation. Certainly a judge's decision will be more arbitrary than a mutual decision by the divorcing couple.

It is important that attorneys who handle divorce cases (1) realize that there are psychological as well as legal factors to the termination of marital contracts and (2) attend to these factors as they process their cases. Failure to recognize the psychological aspects in this area of law can lead to a multiplicity of problems and further complicate an already difficult situation. This is not to suggest that lawyers become marriage counselors but to point out the nonlegal issues that directly affect a divorce action.

Many people are going directly to the courts, following simplified procedures from guidebooks written by sympathetic lawyers or knowledgeable citizens, and obtaining their own divorces for the cost of filing ($100 to $300). However, a do-it-yourself approach to divorce is not recommended unless the partners are relatively friendly; agree on all matters, including child support; and do not have large assets.

Strict versus Liberal Divorce Laws

Those favoring strict divorce laws claim that such laws act to strengthen marriage by forcing couples to work out their problems and assume responsibility for making their marriage work. Such persons consider divorce a sign of individual

---

Inset 15-4

Humanizing Divorce Procedures

Because the courts have for so long considered divorce an adversary procedure, it has been difficult for those in the legal profession to think in no-fault terms. Most of the legal terminology of divorce is derived from criminal law, thus the language used by attorneys and the courts is derived from that same background (see Table 15-4).

A lawyer is also traditionally trained to take the side of his or her client and to do the best possible for them. Thus it is difficult for many lawyers to let go of that training (in fact, unethical to do so) and concern themselves with the entire family unit. Perhaps not every lawyer should handle divorces. Family law specialization is already a reality in many states. Such a specialization should lead the lawyer to think in terms of protecting all members of the family. The family law attorney must think beyond the divorce, especially if children are involved, inasmuch as "parents are forever." All divorce really does is rearrange family relationships, not end them.

The family law attorney should encourage self-determination on the part of the divorcing couple. They each have strengths and weaknesses and are often better judges of how to change

Table 15-4

Legal Terminology of Divorce Derived from Criminal Law

Term	Criminal Meaning	Divorce Meaning
Custody	Holding of a criminal in jail	Giving of a child to a parent by the courts
Custodian	Prison guard	Parent having legal custody of the child after a divorce
Visitation	Friends and relatives visiting the person jailed	The noncustody parent visiting his or her child
Defendant	Person against whom legal action is taken	Person being sued for divorce
Plaintiff	Person or state taking legal action against defendant	Person suing for divorce
Suit	Legal action to secure justice	Legal action to secure divorce

their relationship than attorneys and courts. The traditional attorney is trained to do everything for the client rather than encourage the client to take control of the process as much as possible. The family law attorney must learn to become a facilitator to the couple, complementing their strengths and weaknesses.

Emotions are not permissible facts in a court of law. Yet emotions are facts in most divorce proceedings. They must be considered because the close intimacy of marriage usually cannot be dissolved without them.

In recent years the law has recognized the need for family support dur-

ing the crises of divorce. No-fault divorce, conciliation courts, joint child custody, and family law specialization for attorneys are all steps in the direction of humanizing divorce. The changes in the law are not enough; we must also work to bring the ideas of no fault and family well-being into the consciousness of those working in the legal system.

Source: Adapted from "Drawing Individual and Family Strengths from the Divorce Process," a talk given by Meyer Elkin, California conciliation court pioneer, at the California Council on Family Relations Annual Conference held in Santa Barbara, California, September 26–28, 1980.

---

failure in marriage. However, in reality divorce per se is not the problem; the problem is marital breakdown. Laws may preclude divorce, but they cannot prevent marriage breakdown; they may deny the freedom to remarry, but they cannot prevent a man and a woman from living together. Those favoring more liberal divorce laws accuse strict laws of creating undue animosity and hardship, of leading to perjury and the falsification of evidence, and of simply being unenforceable (Rheinstein, 1972; Weitzman, 1981).

Rather than using strict divorce laws to maintain marriage, a better approach might be to make marriages harder to enter. The waiting period between the issuance of a marriage license and the actual marriage could be longer. Premarital counseling could be required. Trial marriages could be sanctioned. More couples seem to be forsaking formal marriage and simply living together, at least for a while, in what appears to be a trial union. This trend might lead to lower divorce rates, although research to date does not support this supposition (Chapter 4).

The real issue is whether the law can make marriage successful. It seems doubtful. This does not mean there should be no state involvement in marriage. Certainly assigning responsibility for children, assuring some order in property inheritance, and guarding against fraud and misrepresentation are legitimate state concerns. But beyond those concerns, states' efforts to legislate successful marriage have not worked. Laws that support good human relations might be more helpful. For example, if a couple finds insurmountable obstacles to success in their marriage, the laws should support their efforts to dissolve the marriage in the most amicable and beneficial manner to both partners.

Some Cautions about No-Fault Divorce

There is little question that the implementation of no-fault divorce procedures has eased the immediate trauma of divorce by focusing on the demise of the marriage rather than on the guilt of one of the spouses. The fear that easier divorce laws would lead to skyrocketing divorce rates has not proved to be absolutely true (Dixon & Weitzman, 1980). Divorce rates have increased since the first no-fault law in 1969, but many factors have contributed.

The enthusiasm for no-fault and do-it-yourself divorces, however, must be tempered. Divorce for most people is traumatic and involves many negative consequences, even under the best of circumstances.

Although on first appearance a divorce settlement that splits assets and responsibilities equally between the couple seems fair and equitable, it favors the man in the majority of cases. This is because the woman's earning power is usually less than the man's. Due mainly to the growing divorce rates, female-headed families with children have increased greatly, in 1985 representing about 23 percent of all families (Norton & Glick, 1986). As a group these families have the hardest time financially. Approximately 50 percent live below the official poverty line. About 40 percent spend some time on welfare. Perhaps economic settlements should not be evenly divided at the time of divorce but should take into consideration the lower earning power of the woman, especially if she assumes custody of the children, as occurs in most cases.

Lenore Weitzman (1985) makes a strong case that the no-fault divorce laws have in practice caused a large proportion of divorced women and their children severe economic hardship. For example, "equal" division of marital property stipulations have caused a dramatic increase in the sale of the family home. Since the home is the major asset of most couples it is impossible to divide property equally unless the home is turned into cash via sale. Court orders to sell the family home ran about one in ten in 1968 before no-fault divorce laws. By 1977 such orders were issued in one out of three divorce cases (Weitzman, 1985, p. 31). Sale of the family home adds additional stress and disorganization to the divorcing family as all parties must now find new housing. Because of inflation, new housing is usually more expensive than the home that must be sold. In

What Do You Think?

1. How hard do you think it is for a father to have a relationship with his children after divorce?

2. How do you think the father in the first story should handle the situation?

3. What should the former wife do to get Bill to visit more often and make payments on time?

4. In your experience which of the two cases seems to occur more often? Why?

Inset 15-5

Divorce and Dad

Pay but Don't Interfere

I left home because it seemed easier for Elaine and the kids. After all, I was but one person, they were three. The children could remain in their schools with their friends and have the security of living in the home they had grown up in. I figured I'd come to visit often. I hoped that our separation and divorce would have minimal impact on the children and felt that the family remaining in our home was the way to achieve this.

It certainly hasn't worked out as I first imagined. Visiting the children often is no simple matter. Elaine has a new husband, the children have their friends and activities. And I seem to be busier than ever.

At first I'd just drop by to see the children when time permitted, but this usually upset everyone concerned. Elaine felt I was hanging around too much and even accused me of spying on her. Actually there might have been a little truth in this accusation, especially when she started dating. The children usually didn't have time for me because they had plans of their own. I felt rejected by them.

Next, Elaine and I tried to work out a permanent visitation schedule. I was to take the children one evening a week and one weekend a month. Then she accused me of rejecting the children because I wouldn't commit more time to them. But my work schedule only had a few times when I was sure I would be free and thus able to take the children.

At first, the set visiting times worked out well. I'd have something great planned for the children. Soon, however, Elaine told me that I was spoiling them. She said that they were always upset and out of their routine when I brought them home. Would I mind not doing this and that with them. Gradually the list of prohibitions lengthened. She had the house, the children, and my money to support the kids, yet I seemed to have fewer and fewer rights and privileges with them.

Be sure child-support payments arrive promptly but please leave the children alone became more and more Elaine's message.

Since she remarried, my only parental role seems to be financial. I really have no say on what the children do. I feel like I'm being taken every time I write a child-support check.

The Missing Dad

When Bill and I divorced, I wanted him to see our two children as often as possible and told the judge that he could have unlimited visitation rights. Bill seemed happy and said he looked forward to seeing the children often, both at my place and in his new home. A year has now gone by and Bill almost never visits the children. Each time I ask him about it, he has another excuse. At first he told me that he was too busy getting moved into his place. Then he was working a lot of overtime and was just too pooped to visit. Later, he said his new girlfriend was not comfortable with his visiting here. When I suggested that he take the children to his place, he told me that they did not allow children, something he hadn't realized when he moved in, he said.

I think that the children really need their dad. It is important to them, and they miss him. They ask where he is and why he doesn't come more often. I'm embarrassed when they ask since I don't know what to tell them. I really think he just doesn't care.

Even though the court ordered him to pay $200 a month for child support, he is very irregular about the payment, and often I have to remind him that it is due. This makes it very uncomfortable, too. Between asking him to visit the children more often and reminding him to send the child-support payment, all I seem to do is nag him. In fact, he accuses me of being a worse nag than when we were married, but what can I do?

Divorced Dad Wins $25,000 from Ex-Wife

In a verdict described as precedent setting, a divorced father has been awarded $25,000 because of the serious emotional problems he claims were caused by his ex-wife's refusal to permit visits with their daughters.

A Fairfax County Circuit Court jury of three men and four women made the award to Harold H. Memmer, a civilian Army worker at Fort Belvoir in northern Virginia. Legal experts believe the verdict is the first of its kind.

Memmer claimed that his ex-wife, who has since remarried and lives in Evansville, Indiana, had encouraged the girls, aged thirteen and twenty, not to talk to him.

Source: Santa Barbara News Press, 8 August 1980.

addition if the family must move to a new neighborhood, children's schooling and friendships will be disrupted at the very point at which they most need continuity and stability. In many states the divorce judge can award temporary use of the home to the custodial party when children are involved, but judges have seldom taken this step.

Property settlements agreed to by the divorcing couple under no-fault rules have been found to be incomplete and at times grossly unfair to one of the pair (Weitzman, 1981). An amicable agreement reached by a divorcing couple based on present circumstances may be totally inappropriate at some time in the future (Leslie, 1979). Studies of property settlements in California have suggested that divorcing mothers are faring more poorly under the no-fault system than they did under the former system (Seal, 1979; Dixon & Weitzman, 1980, 1982). However, Welch and Price-Bonham (1983) found that there were few changes in how mothers fared in Georgia and Washington after no-fault systems were instituted, although this study was limited to one county in each state.

Another major factor working against custodial parents and their children is the reduction of the age of majority (legal adult status) from twenty-one to eighteen. As a consequence, college students who are over eighteen are no longer considered children in need of support. Thus when expenses are apt to be greatest for custodial parents, there is no legal necessity for the noncustodial parent (the father in most cases) to help financially.

It is interesting to note that in the past divorce proceedings have been instituted primarily by women. However, several studies indicate that after no-fault divorce legislation becomes law, more men than women file for divorce (Gunter, 1977; Gunter & Johnson, 1978). Although the studies do not suggest the reasons for this reversal, it may be that equal property division does in fact favor the male as we have suggested (Weitzman, 1981, 1985).

Many of the sex-based assumptions ridiculed by feminists a decade ago—assumptions about women's economic dependence, their greater investment in children, their need for financial support from their ex-husbands—were ironically not so ridiculous after all. Rather they reflected, even as they reinforced, the reality of married women's lives, and they softened the economic devastations of divorce for women and their children. In the early days of the women's movement there was a rush to embrace equality in all its forms. Some feminists thought alimony was a sexist concept that had no place in a society in which men and women were to be treated as equals. Alimony was an insult, a symbolic reflection of the law's assumption that all women were nonproductive dependents. But it soon became clear that alimony was a critical mechanism for realizing the goal of fairness in divorce. To a woman who had devoted twenty-five years of her life nurturing a family and at age fifty had no job, career, pension, or health insurance, alimony was not an insult but a lifeline (Weitzman, 1985, pp. 359–360).

Such cautions about no-fault divorce are not meant to negate the advantages and the basic civility that no-fault divorce laws have brought to the procedure. They are simply meant to warn the reader that divorce under any circumstances is difficult. If it is not a legal trial, it is certainly an emotional one.

Divorce but Not the End of the Relationship

Many people who contemplate divorce see it as ending their misery, ending forever a relationship that has become intolerable. Yet this is not always true; it is certainly almost never true if children are involved. Divorced people often remain bound to one another by children, love, hate, friendship, business matters, dependence, moral obligations, the need to dominate or rescue, or habit (Price-Bonham et al., 1983). It is increasingly recognized that divorce does not necessarily dissolve a family unit and, in the case of children, may result in a **binuclear family**.

Every state has provisions for modifying judgments made by the court at the time of divorce. Requests for change of custody, of support, or of alimony can be made by either spouse at any time. If you believe marital problems end with divorce, you should attend "father's day" in court. Many larger cities set aside specific days when motions are heard relative to an errant father's neglect in paying child support or to a mother's refusal to permit her former husband to visit their children. Sometimes these hearings are emotionally packed scenes, replete with name calling, charges, and countercharges.

On the positive side many former spouses become good friends after the pain of divorce fades. Some divorced couples remain business partners. Even after remarriage of one or both, there may be friendly interaction between the couples and the new spouse or spouses. Children usually tie a couple together long after divorce. Divorce thus may not be an end to a relationship at all but may only mean that the relationship has changed. Those who look to divorce as a final solution to their marital problems will probably be in for a surprise, especially if children are involved and the marriage is of relatively long duration.

Ann Goetting's (1979) study of 180 divorced and remarried men and women emphasized the lack of prescribed roles for former spouses. Respondents indicated a high degree of consensus about the following:

1. Former spouses should inform one another of emergency situations involving the children.
2. Former spouses should not discuss current marital problems.
3. It is appropriate for a spouse periodically to request and be given extra time with his or her children.

In contrast there was low consensus regarding: (1) extra financial support, (2) willingness to socialize, (3) perpetuation of rapport, (4) reciprocal influence in childrearing behavior, and (5) the former husband caring for the children (Price-Bonham et al., 1983).

Some professionals discourage relationships with former spouses. They contend that these continuing attachments drain energies that could be more productively spent in forming new relationships. They argue that the best policy for childless couples is to sever all ties.

In general it must be remembered that one's former spouse still has all the characteristics that attracted one to him or her in the first place. Therefore it seems unrealistic to expect that one will totally and forevermore dislike the spouse one is divorcing. Some suggest that the best divorce adjustment is probably gained through an "amicable divorce" (Blood & Blood, 1979). This offers a minimum of conflict and develops through a process of gradual deescalation from a marital to a friendship relationship.

Binuclear family
A family that includes children from two nuclear families; occurs when one or both of the divorced parents remarry

Numerous sociologists have proposed theories to explain why marriages are sometimes dissolved. Although we cannot cover the great volume of marriage

Toward a Model of Marital Dissolution

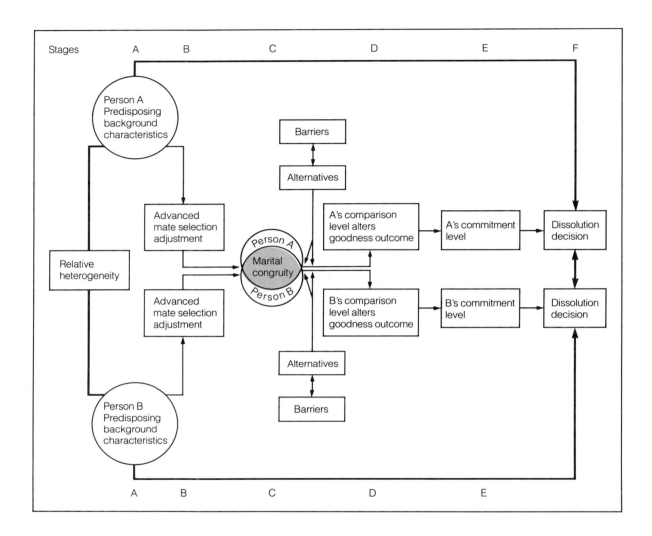

Figure 15-1 A social-psychological model of the dissolution decision (adapted from Edwards & Saunders, 1981)

stability and instability data from which the theorists draw, it is worthwhile to examine at least one theory of marital dissolution. Edwards and Saunders (1981) propose a model of the marital dissolution decision that incorporates much of the previous research on divorce.

First, they point out that each marriage exists within a social context that influences the decision to terminate a marriage. Such social factors become part of the predisposing background characteristics each person brings to marriage. In general the largest and most consistent body of research dealing with marital dissolution indicates that the greater the discrepancy between individual background characteristics of the partners, the greater the chance of divorce. It is interesting to note that our socialization as men or women greatly influences our expectations about marriage. The expectations are sometimes so different between the sexes that some researchers have suggested, "There are two marriages in every marital union, his and hers" (Bernard, 1972, p. 15).

These predisposing background characteristics of each marital partner represent stage A in the model diagram in Figure 15-1. Stage B is represented by the degree of adjustment achieved by the partners during their courtship. Essentially it means that the better the mate selection process, the greater the chances of a successful marriage. Stage C represents the state of the marital relationship. Marital congruity means that the couple is in agreement on most aspects of their relationship. To have high congruity in a marriage does not necessarily mean the relationship is conflict free. If both spouses agree that conflict is an acceptable part of their relationship, then conflict will not cause them great marital problems. Essentially the idea of congruence relates to our earlier discussion of a couple's expectations (Chapter 5). If expectations are realistic and similar between spouses, there is high congruence, and the likelihood of divorce diminishes.

Stage D represents the spouses' evaluation of their relationship, the perceived barriers to divorce, and the perceived goodness of their alternatives to the present relationship. If a relationship is judged highly satisfactory, if there are many barriers to divorce, and if there are few attractive alternatives, the chance of divorce is slight (Levinger, 1965; Levinger & Males, 1979; Udry, 1981).

On the other hand, when these factors are reversed, the chance of divorce increases. Richard Udry's (1981) research indicates that marital alternatives in today's society may be a better predictor of divorce than marital satisfaction. This conclusion seems to support the idea (Farber, 1964) that our marriage system is one in which we are all permanently available as a spouse. In other words, even if we are married, we remain partially open to a new relationship. Udry (1981) suggests that in arriving at an assessment of personal alternatives, individuals are in some way taking inventory of their resources and are considering what kind of life the alternatives would provide them if they were cut off from their present spouses. But they are also making an assessment of the value of their spouses—that is, those qualities, skills, or contributions the spouses bring to the marriage. Could they get someone better? It might be supposed that individuals consider among their own assets their education, income-producing capacity, sexual attractiveness, age, and number of children. But they must also consider their spouse's assets and wonder if they could command more or less than their present partner in today's marriage market. This line of reasoning leads to the hypothesis that the greater a person's resources, the greater his or her perception of marital alternatives, while the lower the person's resources, the greater the other's marital alternatives.

For divorce to occur, the advantages of the perceived alternatives would have to outweigh the strengths of the barriers to divorce. Barriers include such things as moral proscriptions, family pressure, feelings of obligation, concern for one's children, religious directives, divorce laws, and general level of community acceptance of divorce. During the past twenty years we have witnessed a lessening of the barriers to divorce and an increase in the demand for personal satisfaction and fulfillment. It is little wonder, if this divorce model be correct, that the perceived alternatives have become a strong influence toward divorce. "Maybe I can do better with a new spouse" becomes an increasingly attractive thought.

Stage E represents one's commitment to the marriage. It indicates the extent to which one's personal needs and self-interests are bound up in and met by a particular relationship and no other. Commitment is the determination to continue a relationship, an attitude that may or may not be shared equally by the pair (Reiss, 1980). In the face of America's high divorce rate, it is little wonder that more and more Americans are talking about lack of commitment as one of the great ills of our society (Etzioni, 1983).

Stage F represents one's decision whether to remain in a given marriage. A model of divorce such as this is useful in helping us realize that many factors influence marital stability. Looking for a single cause of marital disruption, as many of the state laws have done in the past, is too simplistic.

Divorce Counseling and Mediation

As we pointed out, to go to court means to give up control of your relationship to a third party, namely the court. Generally, a good court settlement is one in which both parties will feel shortchanged. In other words, each party will be accepting a settlement to which they probably don't fully agree. Divorce mediation on the other hand tries to provide a setting in which the divorcing couple can meet, communicate and negotiate with professional help, and thereby reach their own settlement, which can then be presented to the court. In most cases, the court will accept such settlements. There are several advantages. Financial costs are far less than in a contested divorce. Emotional costs are also reduced since mediated divorce focuses on compromise rather than confrontation and seeks the best for all members of the family. By laying the groundwork for mutual cooperation in working out the postdivorce relationship (custody, visitation, support, etc.), divorce mediation reduces the chances of postdivorce conflict (McKay et al., 1984). Perhaps most important, the decisions are made by family members rather than forced on them by the court.

Divorce mediation involves one or two professional mediators (a lawyer and/or a mental health worker) who meet with both husband and wife to help them resolve conflicts, reach decisions, and negotiate agreements about the dissolution of their marriage (Ruman & Lamm, 1983). Such counseling is gaining popularity, especially since no-fault divorce proceedings have replaced adversary methods. Usually the first phase is predivorce counseling, which centers on the decision to divorce. At this point there is still a possibility of saving the marriage. The counselor acts as an objective third party (mediator) to help the couple contemplating divorce come to a good decision. The mediator acts as a neutral advisor, an expert source of information who suggests options from which the couple is free to choose. The spouses do not abdicate the decision making but are helped to decide for themselves (Coogler, Weber & McKenry, 1979; Haynes, 1981; McKay et al., 1984). Divorce counseling per se begins when the decision is made and lawyers and/or legal proceedings enter the picture. Such counseling can help the individuals cope with their conflicting feelings and understand the legalities and alternatives available. It is important that both partners be willing to consent to full disclosure if mediation is to work.

The third phase of divorce counseling occurs after the divorce is final and is aimed at helping the person get life started again. In a few states some divorce counseling is available through the courts, and occasionally courts require such counseling. Conciliation courts usually attempt to ameliorate the negative effects of marital failure. Their first goal is to save the marriage, but failing that they try to ensure an equitable divorce, "to protect the rights of children and to promote the public welfare by preserving, promoting, and protecting family life and the institution of matrimony, and to provide means for the reconciliation of spouses and the amicable settlement of domestic and family controversies" (*West's Annotated California Codes*, 1983, p. 72).

Those seeking counseling should not expect to find support for their side or simple advice that will resolve their problems. They should also not expect to see and feel immediate improvement in themselves and their relationship with the former spouse. Rather they will find clarification and help in assessing strengths and weaknesses so they can move toward better understanding and clearer communication. The better the couple's communication and understanding, the less traumatic the divorce will be, for both themselves and their children if there are any.

After a thorough review of American marriage and divorce statistics, Paul Glick (1975) lists a number of steps that might reduce divorce. He suggests first that more effective marriage and family training be given at home and in the schools. Certainly such courses in the schools are increasingly popular, and it is hoped that such an interest by young persons will lead to sounder partner choices and improved marriages.

Glick also advocates more scientific methods of mate selection than the current haphazard system based largely on emotion. Periodic marital checkups through visits to trained marriage counselors should be encouraged. As pointed out earlier, by the time most couples in difficulty seek help, their marriage is beyond help. Facing problems before they are insoluble, building problem-solving techniques into marriage, heading off divorce with help, if necessary, are needed elements in American marriage. Changing marriage laws to encourage couples to take their entry into marriage more seriously would also help reduce the necessity of divorce.

California took a step in the direction of stricter marriage laws in Assembly Bill 402 (*West's Annotated California Codes*, 1983), which became effective in 1970. This law, the first of its kind, empowers the courts to require premarital counseling of any couple applying for a marriage license if either party is under eighteen years of age and the court deems such counseling necessary. In Los Angeles County the courts made such counseling mandatory (Elkin, 1977).

Child-care centers would help give working couples with young children more time for one another and more time to work positively on their marriage. Many couples simply do not have time for their marriage in the early childrearing, work-oriented years. When the children are finally capable of independence and economic stability has been achieved there is often not enough left of the marriage to be salvaged, much less improved.

Certainly we need to give at least as much time to the good aspects of marriage as we do to the negative aspects. Giving publicity to ways in which marriage can be improved and the strengths found in successfully married couples (see Chapter 1) and concentrating on relationship improvement will be of more value than exaggerating the problems inherent in marriage.

Reducing Divorce Rates

Summary

A means of dissolving marriage exists in almost every society. Divorce is America's mode of ending unsatisfactory marriages. The divorce rate has increased drastically during this century, probably reflecting Americans' changing expectations for marriage and increasing tolerance of change.

There are many reasons for the high divorce rate in the United States. Americans ask a great deal of marriage, and the more we ask of an institution, the more apt it is to fail. Changing sex roles, emphasis on the individual, heterogeneity of population, mobility, and poverty all affect marriage and increase the chances for divorce.

The decision to divorce is usually reached slowly and involves emotions much like the feelings that one goes through after the death of a loved one. Indeed long before legal divorce and perhaps long after it as well, a couple will go through the suffering of an emotional divorce. Divorce is complicated by the presence of children and/or considerable property.

Most divorced persons eventually remarry. In order for the remarriage to be successful, it is necessary for divorcing people to learn from their past mistakes. The divorce must act as a catalyst to further self-insight. Divorced people have numerous problems with which to cope. They must make changes in their economic situation, in their living situation and in their relations with family, friends, children, and coworkers.

In the past few years all states have instituted some form of no-fault divorce. In these proceedings neither party has to be proved guilty of breaking some rule leading to grounds (a legal reason) for divorce. The only thing that must be proved is that the marriage has suffered an irremediable breakdown. Doing away with fault finding has considerably simplified divorce procedures. Unfortunately "no-fault" divorce is not perfect; it has often caused the divorced mother severe economic hardship.

Divorce does not necessarily mean the end of a relationship, especially if children are involved. Visitation and financial obligations usually mean that the man and woman will have considerable interaction even after divorce. Such association may be difficult. Divorce counseling and mediation before as well as after divorce can help couples make satisfactory adjustments to the change in their lives.

Joint Custody: Does It Work?

Joint custody, or mutual sharing of parental rights and responsibilities after divorce, has always been possible for "consenting parents," but until lately has seldom been a reality.

In the past three years, however, since California—always in the vanguard of family law—enacted its joint-custody provision, followed a year later by mandatory mediation, the picture has changed dramatically. Today at least half the states have jumped on the joint-custody bandwagon. (Some specify a difference between joint *legal* custody where parents share all important decisions and joint *physical* custody where both share an equitable but not necessarily equal time with the child.) Coparenting or shared parenting (the broader terms many experts prefer) has achieved almost fad status. Although currently in 90 percent of divorced families the mother still has sole legal custody, joint custody has been declared "the wave of the future."

Parents all over the country are trying every form of physical joint custody possible: alternate days or alternate weeks (which one father calls his "Daddy Week" and his "Single Week") to alternate months or years. There's also weekday versus weekends, school year versus school vacations, and "the bird's nest"—where the family home is kept for the kids while the parents move in and out. In some cases there's even a "parents' apartment" with two separate bedrooms that the former husband and wife take turns using. But whether the kids are shared while parents live across the street or across the country, two main ingredients are crucial: close contact with both parents and keeping the kids out of the divorce conflict.

Even leading advocates of volun-

tary coparenting warn, however, that it's not a panacea, and not for everyone. More important, the ramifications of some of the new joint custody laws, which "presume" joint custody to be the "preferred" choice for all families, could be harmful to children and to mothers; in fact, they could be devastating.

When *Does* It Work?

"Where parents are able to do it, it's the best arrangement. . . . Women who have careers and trust the father like it very much, but I never said it should be imposed by the court if the parents disagree," vows Dr. Judith Wallerstein, whose five-year landmark study with former colleague Joanan Kelley is the

most quoted research in support of joint custody. "To say it's the preferred way to go for all children is really to experiment with the children of this country."

Wallerstein, a leading advocate for voluntary coparenting, says she is now "scared and worried" that important social policy is being formed before adequate research is done, making some children victims by asking them to travel "a no-child's land" between two hostile parents.

"I've been hoping women's groups would get into this with a voice that's loud," she adds, warning of the mixed hidden agendas of the father's rights groups. "Some of it may be backlash, economically based . . . men hoping to pay less child support when women still earn only fifty-nine cents on the dollar."

For many feminist leaders, Wallerstein's battle cry is most welcome. "Joint custody is being used to hold women hostage," says Joanne Schulman, staff attorney for the National Center on Women and Family Law, who compares joint custody to no-fault divorce, which sounds good, but is intended and used to harm women. "The practical effect is devastating. There's no way you can go to court and force a father to be responsible, to pick up his end of the visitation, much less to engage him in joint custody when two-thirds of the fathers fail to pay child support now, and the courts do very little about it.

"It's not a coincidence that joint custody legislation and the Moral Majority are the current vogue. Joint custody merely takes this patriarchal control one step further—to controlling ex-wives and children *post-divorce*," Schulman proclaims.

Nancy Polikoff, staff attorney for the

Women's Legal Defense Fund, worries about "the friendlier parent" interpretation—when the parent who asks for joint custody is considered to be more cooperative and, hence, awarded sole custody.

"This is an incredibly insidious provision because it means that by asking for joint custody, you sound like the good guy," says Polikoff. "I don't know how we got to the point where the parent who opposes joint custody looks like the bad guy. It's ludicrous in any case, and especially where there's spouse abuse."

She cites West Virginia's "primary caretaker" philosophy as a good example of responsible custody case law. The state allows joint custody when both parents agree voluntarily. When they don't, custody is awarded to the primary caretaker *before* the split, ensuring some continuity for the children and some protection for the nurturer. "Not only is that parent likely to be the financially disadvantaged parent and therefore have less funds to go through a contested divorce, but she or he would have the most invested in keeping the child and be more likely to trade away all sorts of benefits."

Although some parents find joint custody a helpful way to renegotiate old arrangements, Schulman reports that many women, after they traded everything and moved into a small apartment to keep the children, "find three years down the road that he's remarried, making more money, has a 'family home' and goes in for 'modification' [in the custody agreement]. He can give the child a better lifestyle financially and he wins physical custody."

"I'm scared to death that ten years from now, someone will do research and discover that joint custody is disastrous for the children because kids are going to get shifted back and forth and nobody's going to know who's in charge," sighs Judith Avner, staff attorney for the NOW Legal Defense and Education Fund. (Both California and New York NOW state chapters have opposed presumption of joint custody.)

Dr. Serena Stier, an attorney/clinical psychologist researching mediation, sees joint custody as a "legal handle" that could hinder a mother's ability to make decisions. "One thing mothers used to have even if the father wasn't seeing the children or paying child support was that they could say, 'At least, he's not interfering with the way I raise them.'"

Many critics worry that mothers are asked to give up their strongest and sometimes only bargaining chip, likely custody of the children. California psychologist and divorce mediator Marilyn Ruman sees how joint custody could take away a lot of leverage from women if there is not "a process of mediation to balance the terrible inequity and power distribution found in most relationships."

While joint custody is clearly not a panacea, research shows that children of divorce crave conflict-free contact with both parents. The trick remaining is how to create that "demilitarized zone" around the kids and yet let each parent get on with a new life.

Perhaps what parents, judges, lawyers, and now mediators are really grappling with is the basic reevaluation of, "What is a family?" Our children are trying to tell us: a family, a parent, is forever—whether we like it or not. And joint custody is the expression of that hope to keep the family going long after the marriage is over.

Source: Scott, Gail. *Ms.*, April 1983. © by Gail Scott. Reprinted by permission.

Remarriage: A Growing Way of American Life

Contents

"It seems to me that John and Helen were just divorced, and here's an invitation to Helen's wedding." "Not only that, but I met John and his new girlfriend at lunch yesterday and from the way they were acting, I'll bet we'll soon get an invitation to their wedding." "It's hard to understand. They were so eager to escape their marriage and now it seems they can hardly wait to get back into another marriage."

Divorced people as a group are not against marriage. For every age group remarriage rates are higher than first marriage rates, remarriage rates for men are higher than for women, and remarriage rates for the divorced are higher than for the widowed. Statistically there are few single divorced people in America's population. Four out of five divorced men remarry and three out of four divorced women remarry (Furstenberg & Spanier, 1984, p. 37). Not only do divorced persons remarry in large numbers but also they tend to remarry quickly. Approximately 50 percent of divorced people remarry within three years and about 66 percent are remarried within five years. Today, about 45 percent of America's marriages in a given year are a remarriage for at least one of the new mates. Overall about 25 percent of American families are **blended** or **reconstituted** families (National Center for Health Statistics, May 2, 1986, p. 11).

Age differences between remarried spouses tend to be greater than age differences between first-married couples. For first-married couples the age difference has consistently been two years. However, in marriages between never-married women and divorced men, the age difference averages seven years. For remarriages of both spouses the age difference is four years. The only category for which brides are generally older than their grooms (approximately one year) are marriages of previously married women to never-married men (National Center for Health Statistics, May 2, 1986, p. 3).

May–December marriages, marriages between an older man and much younger woman are more common among divorced men than among men entering their first marriage. Although we have little empirical data on the success of such marriages, many such couples express high levels of marital satisfaction. The women appreciate the security and stability that an older man can often offer. The men express pleasure with the generally high energy level and flexibility of their younger wives.

From remarriage statistics we can conclude that divorce serves not so much as an escape hatch from married life but as a recycling mechanism permitting individuals a chance to upgrade their marital situation (Furstenberg & Spanier, 1984, p. 53). Considering the rise in divorce rates, the lengthening life span, and the younger ages at which Americans divorce (about 33 percent of divorcing husbands and 44 percent of the wives are in their twenties at the time of divorce; National Center for Health Statistics, December 26, 1985, p. 11) it appears that the incidence of remarriage will remain high in the future. What Americans experience is not monogamy, but serial monogamy—that is, several spouses over a lifetime but only one at a time.

Historically, remarriage is not new or novel. But the early death of one spouse has been the reason for remarriage in the past. Today it is divorce. Although the widowed do continue to remarry, they stay single longer than the divorced and their remarriage rates are lower.

Blended or reconstituted family
Husband and wife, at least one of whom has been married before, and one or more children from previous marriage

Many people married for some time, burdened with the responsibilities of a growing family and missing the flush of romance that brought them together with

Returning to Single Life

their mate, feel pangs of envy when their friends divorce and reenter the singles world. Remembering their dating and courting days, they relive nostalgic memories of the excitement of the "new date" and the boundless energies that one expended as a young person pursuing and being pursued. Except for a few, such dreams on the part of married people are just that, dreams.

The return to the singles world can be frightening for both men and women and especially for those married for some years. "Can I be successful as a single person?" is a question that cannot be answered at first. Most people have experienced a severe blow to their self-esteem with the divorce (Chapter 15), and they are reluctant to face the potential rejections involved with meeting new people. For some the idea may be so threatening that they don't return to the single life but remain hidden in the safety of their own aloneness until remaining alone the rest of their life appears to be even more threatening, and they eventually venture out into the singles world.

Just when divorced persons are ready to return to the single social life varies greatly. For most it takes about one year after divorce to get themselves emotionally back together again. Those who had an ongoing extramarital relationship are in a different position and often remarry as soon as legally possible.

Learning to date and relate to the opposite sex as a single person is especially difficult for anyone who has been married for a long time because his or her self-image has for so long been that of one part of a couple. Once the divorced (or widowed) persons reenter the social world, though, they are often surprised at the number who share their newly single status. Except for the very young divorced, most reenter a world of single but formerly married people rather than one of never-married people. This eases the transition inasmuch as those they meet have also experienced marital collapse. There is a certain empathy, which helps them feel more acceptable. In fact, the discovery that they can meet and interact with people of the opposite sex in their new single role can be exciting and heartening. "Maybe I'm not such a failure after all," is a common response.

Initial sexual experimentation is often a reaction of the newly divorced person, especially a person who was rejected by the spouse and did not want a divorce. To be desired sexually is a boost to shattered self-esteem. To be close to another person physically, to be held, touched, and sexually pleasured makes the rejected person feel loved and cared for as well as verifying his or her sexual desirability. For these reasons newly divorced persons are sometimes easily available for sexual encounters. Therefore the newly divorced person must guard against sexual exploitation and not make the error of equating sex with love.

Although dating has already been discussed in Chapter 4, it is important to realize that the dating practices of the divorced or widowed person will tend to be different from the dating practices of the young unmarried individual. For example, the divorced have more problems meeting new people than the young never married. Sometimes friends, relatives, and business associates supply new acquaintances. Organizations such as Parents Without Partners and We Care become meeting places. Often the lofty educational and helping goals of these groups are secondary to their social functions. The lofty goals may make it easier for people to join activities without appearing to be "mate hunting."

Many singles clubs make introductions to others their major purpose. Such clubs sometimes frighten and intimidate those just recuperating from marital failure. Many are uncomfortable with attending singles parties that have a "meat market" atmosphere.

Although long used in Europe, the personal newspaper advertisement is relatively new in the United States. Discounting the ads for sexual partners in underground newspapers, there is a growing use of legitimate classified advertising to seek desirable companions and potential mates, especially by divorced persons.

ATTRACTIVE refined widow seeks real gentleman, 60s. Home loving, likes music, trips, books, gardening; financially secure; who wants to enjoy lasting companionship.

EXPERIENCED sailboat skipper, fifties, single, yacht club member, wants to meet compatible outdoor gal who would like to go sailing.

MAN seeking intelligent, independent, intuitive female companion (21–35) for social events. Send photo.

MALE 39, desires pleasant, attractive easy-going female. Enjoys good home life, occasional outdoor activities, flying, fishing, ghost towning. Photo & phone.

RETIRED lady loves nature, fine music. Sincere, kind, honest, sense of humor; wants same as bus travel companion or share your trans. No smoking.

Those using such ads should take precautions to make sure that the person one decides to meet is sincere. Using a post office box or telephone number rather than one's home address and arranging for the first meeting to be in a public place are sensible safeguards.

Technology has found a place in the formerly marrieds' new single life in the form of computer dating. For a fee information is fed into a large bank of personal information on many single clients and a match is made from stated interests, hobbies, habits, education, age, and so on. The pair then meet. Some agencies

What Do You Think?

1. What do you think the major dating problems would be for the newly divorced man?
2. For the newly divorced woman?
3. If you were newly divorced, how would you go about meeting potential dates?
4. Would you use a dating service? Why or why not?
5. Would you place a newspaper personal ad seeking friends? Why or why not?

estimate that about 25 percent of their clients eventually marry someone they met through the computer's selection. Other agencies make a videotape interview with each client. Questions are asked about background, interests, feelings about sexual relations, and the qualities sought in prospective dates. The client then has the opportunity to look at videotapes of people who share interests and/or meet their qualifications. Videotapes have the advantage in giving an overall impression of the person before any meeting.

There are many other ways to meet new people. The major factor in meeting new people is the active participation of the newly divorced in the singles' world. Unless one is out in society, meeting new people is difficult. Probably the newly divorced person in a small town setting stands the poorest chance of meeting someone new.

Dating among divorced and widowed persons often involves children as part of the dating equation. Approximately 54 percent of divorcing couples have children under eighteen years of age. Of divorcing couples with children, 26 percent have one child, 20 percent have two children and 9 percent have three or more children (National Center for Health Statistics, December 26, 1985, p. 1).

The romantic rendezvous for two more and more often includes three or four. With the high divorce rate and increased numbers of single-parent families, many singles now find that dating someone new means getting acquainted with the date's children. "I recently started dating Jean. When I went to pick her up for our first date, I rang the bell and put on my best smile. But it wasn't Jean who opened the door, it was a ten-year-old kid. He seemed to be checking me out the way date's fathers used to when I was a teenager."

Regardless of how meeting people is done, the high remarriage rates indicate that meeting new prospective mates is accomplished by most people who divorce. And the new mate tends to be in the same situation; that is, divorced people marry divorced people. Dates often come from the person's present group of acquaintances.

Remarriage: Will I Make the Same Mistakes Again?

As noted earlier high remarriage rates among divorced people indicate that the divorced are still interested in marriage and the role of "being married." The fact is that most activities in the American culture, for better or worse, revolve around the married pair, the couple. High remarriage rates seem to suggest that it is important to have someone with whom to share, to be intimate, to feel closeness, and to experience a part of something larger than oneself.

To love and be loved are important to most Americans. As unhappy as a marriage may have been, for most there was a time when love and closeness were experienced. Indeed, loss of this intimacy may have been a major part of the decision to leave the marriage. Certainly, finding intimacy is a factor in most remarriages just as it was in the first marriage.

The route to marriage for young unmarried Americans is fairly clear (see Chapters 3 and 4). You date, you fall in love, you become engaged, you marry. In second marriages, though, the simplicity of ignorance has been replaced by the knowledge and, for some, the anxiety of past experience.

Those divorcing react to the idea of remarriage in many different ways. There are those who remarry quickly because they already have another relationship in place at the time of divorce. There are also those who remarry quickly on the rebound, out of loneliness, out of insecurity, or simply because they know no other way of life but married life. Such persons often married young, going straight from their parents' homes into marriage and thus have had no practice in being a single adult.

A minority of divorced persons (approximately 20 percent of divorced men and 25 percent of divorced women) do not remarry. Their reasons are many. Perhaps some simply enjoy the autonomy and independence of single life. Others may want to remarry but fail to find an acceptable mate. Still others may have been so hurt in their first marriage that they avoid relationships that might lead to remarriage. A few who choose not to remarry may be unable psychologically to give up their lost spouse. This is especially true of the widowed, who sometimes feel disloyal to the deceased spouse if they form a new relationship. Sometimes the children of a widowed spouse discourage remarriage of their remaining parent for fear that the stepparent may take what they feel is rightfully theirs.

However, the most common reaction tends to be a careful, cautious relationship-testing period leading to remarriage. For persons approaching remarriage slowly, the risk of a second mistake is their focal concern. Most divorced persons believe that they were deluded in their first marriage and therefore approach a second marriage with extra care, no longer naive about the difficulty of achieving a successful marriage. They realize that they must work out the problems of their first marriage and establish a new independent and strong self-image. In this way they hope that their new relationship will be more mature and one of equality in contrast to their first immature relationship. They realize that without such care and work remarriage will be a triumph of hope over experience and very apt to fail.

The partners in a remarriage must deal with all the problems any newly married pair faces. In addition they must deal with attitudes and sensitivities within themselves that were fostered by their first marriage. They may enter remarriage with many prejudices for and against the marital relationship. They need to divest themselves of these if they are to face the new partner freely and build a new relationship that is appropriate to both. In a remarriage the mate is new and must be responded to as the individual she or he is, not in light of what the past spouse was. An additional task in every remarriage, then, is the effort partners must make to free themselves from inappropriate attitudes and behaviors stemming from the first marriage. In essence second marriages are built on top of first marriages (Furstenberg, 1979, p. 16).

> *Bob had been married for twelve years to Alice, had two children by the marriage, and was established economically when his marriage ended in divorce. Two years later he married Carol, eight years his junior, who had one child by her previous husband, Ted.*
>
> *Bob and Carol both approached their marriage carefully, giving much thought to their relationship. Both agree that their new marriage is a big improvement over their past marriages. They find that their biggest problem is making sure they react to one another as individuals rather than on the basis of their past relationships. This is not always easy.*
>
> *Bob's past wife, Alice, is emotionally volatile, which both attracted and repulsed him. He liked Alice's displays of happiness and enthusiasm but hated her temper fits and general unhappiness.*
>
> *Carol is placid and even-tempered. In fact these personality characteristics were in part what drew him to her. However, when they do things together, he keeps asking her if she is having fun, is she enjoying herself? He asks her so often that Carol is bugged by what she considers to be his harassment of her. One day she blew up at him over this. He reacted strongly to her negative emotional display. Once everything was calm again, they both discovered that the problem grew out of his past marriage. Bob simply expected Carol to show her enjoyment in the same way Alice had. He was not relating to Carol as an individual but was reacting in light of his past experiences with Alice. When Carol blew up at him, his reaction was much larger than necessary. Her emotional blast activated all of his past dislike of Alice's temper fits.*

Inasmuch as most divorced persons marry other divorced persons, the story about Bob and Carol clearly shows that another couple is involved in such remarriages, namely the former spouses. This phantom couple often dictates to the newly remarried pair, if not directly through the courts and divorce settlements, then indirectly via years of previous interaction.

A remarriage between divorced persons is more difficult than a first marriage for a number of reasons besides the influence, often negative, of past spouses:

1. Each mate may have problems of low self-esteem stemming from the divorce.
2. The divorced are less apt to tolerate a poor second marriage. They have been

through divorce and know that they have survived. Life after divorce is not an unknown any longer and is therefore less threatening than before. Divorced persons tend to end an unhappy remarriage more quickly than they ended their first marriage (Furstenberg & Spanier, 1984, p. 183).

3. The past relationship is never really over. Even if the Bob, Carol, Ted, and Alice kind of dynamics are successfully overcome, the past marriage can still directly affect the new marriage. For example, payments to a former spouse may be resented by the new spouse, especially if the current marriage seems short-changed monetarily. First marriages also indirectly affect remarriage. Although remarried couples go to considerable lengths to differentiate marital styles between their first and second relationships, this very effort to change relationship styles suggests that the second relationship is influenced by reactions to their first marriage.

4. If children are involved in the remarriage, there will be a great many more complications, as we shall see in the next section. Family law is also inadequate in dealing with the blended family. For example, there are no provisions for balancing husbands' financial obligations to spouses and children from current and previous marriages. What are the support rights of stepchildren in stepfamilies or in stepfamilies that end in divorce (Kargman, 1983)?

5. The society around the remarrying person tends to expect another failure. "He (she) couldn't make it the first time, so he'll (she'll) probably fail this time, too." "After all, most divorced people don't learn, they usually remarry the same kind of person as their earlier spouse." "Once a failure always a failure." This lack of support can create a climate of distrust in the minds of the remarried couple themselves.

Despite such problems many remarriages do last. Only a small percentage of Americans divorce more than once. What are the statistics on success and failure of second marriages? Unfortunately, the statistics do not present a clear picture. Some studies comparing the divorce rates of first marriages with those of second marriages do report that a remarriage is more likely to break up than a first marriage (McCarthy, 1978; Becker, Landes & Michael, 1976; Cherlin, 1977, 1978; Bumpass & Sweet, 1977). The differences are small. Paul Glick (1984) estimates that 49 percent of men and women will divorce but 54 percent of women and 61 percent of men who remarry will divorce a second time. But these studies do not take into account the small group of divorce-prone people who marry and divorce often and who in the course of these repeated divorces tend to overinfluence the remarriage-divorce figures. Other studies find that remarriages are no more likely to end in divorce or separation than first marriages (Riley & Spreitzer, 1974; Weed, 1980).

Perhaps more important than divorce-rate comparisons are the subjective evaluations made by those remarrying. A comparison of the reported marital happiness of divorced and never-divorced white respondents to three national surveys revealed little difference between the two groups. The comparison concluded that remarriages of divorced persons that do not end quickly in divorce are probably, as a whole, almost as successful as intact first marriages (Glenn & Weaver, 1977). Stan Albrecht (1979) also found that remarriages were happy marriages. However, none of the variables that had often been noted in the past as good predictors of marital satisfaction among first married couples (presence of children, age at marriage, social class, and similarity of religion) seemed to be strongly related to remarriage satisfaction. Remarriages seem to be judged by different criteria than first marriages, perhaps because they are based on different factors. (Perhaps the romantic illusion is gone for those remarrying.) Glenn and Weaver (1977) conclude that divorce and remarriage seem to have been effective mechanisms for replacing poor marriages with good ones and for keeping the level of marital happiness fairly high.

Furstenberg and Spanier (1984) find that those in successful remarriages repeatedly state that their marriage is different from their first marriage. Most important is that they feel they have married the *right* person, that is, "someone who allows you to be yourself" (p. 83). In other words, they have chosen a better mate for themselves. Because of this better choice, they feel that their remarriage is better than their first marriage. They feel this is true because they have learned to communicate differently and now handle conflicts more maturely. Better communication also leads to better decision making. Because both partners feel they are more equal in their remarriage (p. 71) the division of labor in remarriage tends to be more equitable.

Furstenberg and Spanier (1984) also point out that hostility toward the remarried couple's former spouses tends to be a part of the successful remarriage.

> Most interviews yielded liberal expressions of hostility displayed toward former partners. . . . Repudiating the former spouse heightens solidarity in the new relationship. Expressions of hostility serve to demonstrate loyalty to the new spouse, thus reducing the potential for jealousy. The couple could unite in outrage over past injustices inflicted by a former spouse. In the in-depth interviews, a partner would sometimes tell stories that had become a part of the lore of their marriage. In recounting such incidents, the current spouse can provide reassurance that things really are different now. The husband or wife hearing his or her biography replayed can affirm just how much change has occurred and usually responds by declaring that he or she is married to the right person this time. Through this dramatic interplay, assurance is provided that the second marriage is essentialy different from the first. (p. 65)

Although such hostility may be helpful in cementing the remarried couple's relationship, it can make coparenting of a divorced couple's children much more difficult.

Even though the statistics are mixed on the success of remarriages, it is clear that a great many are successful despite the extra problems involved. As divorce becomes more prevalent and acceptable, the problems facing those wishing to remarry may diminish. Perhaps social support for remarriage will be greater in the future as more and more people marry more than once during their lifetimes.

His, Hers, and Ours: The Stepfamily

For many years children in the home precluded the parents' divorcing. Everyone "knew" the dire consequences to children if divorce occurred. Many couples stayed together for years after their marriage had failed in order to spare the children the trauma of divorce.

But staying together for the children's sake is no longer as prevalent as it once was. Some people are reasoning that strain and conflict are as harmful to children as divorce. Those persons in discordant marriages who divorce and remarry are often taking positive steps to improve their home situation and provide a healthier environment for children than was possible within the original family.

Many people believe that the divorced person who has custody of the children stands much less chance of remarriage. In actuality, if age is held constant, having children does not seem significantly to influence one's chances of remarriage (Spanier & Glick, 1980; Koo & Suchindran, 1980). In fact, remarriages may well involve at least three different sets of children. Both spouses may bring their own children into the new marriage, and in addition they may decide to have children together. Hence his, hers, and ours is often a correct description of the children in a reconstituted family.

Literature is replete with many examples of the poor treatment accorded stepchildren. The ogre **stepparent** is a popular stereotype in fairy tales and other children's stories. Yet there is little evidence to support this stereotype in reality. Certainly the transition to a new parent is not always easy. Generally children remain with their biological mother and the stepparent is a new father. Because ties are usually closest to the mother, this is probably an advantage for most children. A frequent impression drawn from mass media stories is that more children are now being placed in the custody of the father. In absolute numbers this is true (1,378,000 children living with the father only in 1984 compared with 748,000 in 1970). But the same rate of increase has occurred for children living with a divorced mother. Consequently, over the years a fairly constant 10 percent of all children living with a divorced parent live with the father (U.S. Bureau of the Census, July 1985).

Stepparent
The husband or wife of one's parent by a later marriage

The research on the effects of remarriage on children is mixed. For example, though there is some conflicting evidence, children in stepfamilies don't appear to differ significantly in self-image or personality characteristics from children in their original families (Ganong & Coleman, 1984 [a review of approximately forty studies]; Robinson, 1984; Pink & Wampler, 1985).

However, counselors and therapists report that stepchildren and stepparents do have a great deal of trouble in their relationships. Stepparents often feel confusion over the roles they must fulfill, children feel loyalty conflicts, and co-parenting of children with former spouses may split parental authority (Ganong & Coleman, 1986, p. 313). Perhaps the reason the data on stepchildren are mixed is that each situation is unique and one cannot generalize about the effects of divorce or a stepparent on children. It may well be that a child who is well adjusted and has a healthy personality will cope successfully with the family breakup and become a more mature, independent child. If the child is unstable, divorce may cause even greater maladjustment.

To learn what effect divorce and remarriage have on a child, we need to know the answers to the following questions: What were the preconditions to the divorce (much fighting; calm, quick decision; long, slow decision; emotional; rational, and so on)? How well adjusted was the child? What age was the child? With which parent did the child go? Did the child want to go with that parent? What kind of person is the stepparent? How long was the child given to adjust to the stepparent? How many siblings went with the child into the remarriage? Were other children present from the stepparent? What sort of family atmosphere was created? Did the natural parent support or disrupt the child's adjustment? With so many questions to answer, it is not so surprising that the research findings are mixed. The only valid conclusion is that some children suffer more than others from divorce and remarriage.

For divorcing parents who want and need to know how to reduce the negative

---

Inset 16-1

The Ten Commandments of Stepparenting

The natural family presents hazards enough to peaceful coexistence. Add one or two stepparents, and perhaps a set of ready-made brothers and sisters, and a return to the law of the jungle is virtually ensured. Some guidelines for survival include the following advice for stepparents:

1. *Provide neutral territory.* Just as the Romans had gods that lived in the house and protected it, stepchildren have a strong sense of ownership. The questions: "Whose house is it? Whose spirit presides here?" are central issues. Even the very young child recognizes that the prior occupation of a territory confers a certain power. When two sets of children are brought together one regards itself as the "main family" and the other as a subfamily, . . . and the determining factor is whose house gets to be the family home. One school of thought suggests that when a couple remarries they should move to a new house, even if it means selling the family heirlooms. If it is impossible to finance a move to neutral territory, it is important to provide a special, inviolate place which belongs to each child individually.

2. *Don't try to fit a preconceived role.* When dealing with children the best course is to be straight right from the start. Each parent is an individual with all his or her faults, peculiarities and emotions, and the children are just going to have to get used to this parent. Certainly a stepparent should make every effort to be kind, intelligent, and a good sport, but that does not mean being saccharine sweet. Children have excellent radar for detecting phoniness, and are quick to lose respect for any adult who will let them walk all over him or her.

3. *Set limits and enforce them.* One of the most difficult areas for a natural parent and stepparent living together is to decide on disciplinary measures. The natural parent has a tendency to feel that the stepparent is being unreasonable in demands that the children behave in a certain way. If the parents fight between themselves about discipline, the children will quickly force a wedge between them. It is important that the parents themselves work out the rules in advance and support one another when the rules need to be enforced. . . .

4. *Allow an outlet for feelings by the children for natural parents.* It is often difficult for the stepparent to accept that his or her stepchildren will maintain a natural affection for their natural parent who is no longer living in the household. The stepparent may take this as a personal rejection. Children need to be allowed to express feelings about the natural parent who is absent. This needs to be supported in a neutral way so that the children do not feel disloyal.

5. *Expect ambivalence.* Stepparents are often alarmed when children appear to show both emotions of strong love and strong hate toward them. Ambivalence is normal in all human relationships, but nowhere is it more accentuated than in the feelings of the stepchild toward the stepparent.

6. *Avoid mealtime misery.* For many stepfamilies meals are an excruciating experience. This, after all, is the time when the dreams of blissful family life confront reality. Most individuals cling to a belief in the power of food to make people happy. . . . Since it is the stepmother who is most often charged with serving the emotionally laden daily bread, she often leaves the table feeling thoroughly rejected.

---

consequences of divorce and remarriage on their children, probably the single best thing they can do is maintain a reasonable relationship with the divorced mate. Fighting over children or using them against a former spouse will lead to negative consequences for the child.

Stepparents face additional problems beyond those of natural parents. To begin with they must follow a preceding parent. If the child and the natural parent had a positive relationship, the child is apt to feel resentful and hostile to the stepparent. The child may also feel disloyal to the departed parent if a good relationship is established with the stepparent. Often a child feels rejected and unloved by the parent who leaves the household. In this case the child may cling more tightly to the remaining parent as a source of security and continuity. The remaining parent's

If the status quo becomes totally unbearable, it is forgivable to decide that peace is more important and turn a blind eye, at least temporarily, to nutrition. Some suggested strategies include: daily vitamins, rid the house of all "junk" foods, let the children fix their own meals, eat out a lot, and/or let father do some of the cooking so he can share in the rejection. Stepfathers tend to be less concerned about food refusal but more concerned about table manners.

7. *Don't expect instant love.* One of the problems facing a new stepparent is the expectation of feeling love for the child and for that love to be returned. It takes time for emotional bonds to be forged, and sometimes this never occurs. All stepparents must acknowledge that eventuality.

Alternately, nonacceptance by the children is often a major problem. Some children make it very clear that "You are not my mother or father!" This can be very painful or anger provoking, especially if it is the stepparent who is doing the cooking and laundry, and giving allowances. Most children under three have little problem adapting with relative ease. Children over five have more difficulty. . . .

8. *Don't take all the responsibility. The child has some too.* Ultimately, how well the stepparent gets along with the stepchild depends in part upon the kind of child he or she is. Children, like adults, come in all types and sizes. Some are simply more lovable than others. If the new stepmother has envisioned herself as the mother of a cuddly little tot and finds herself with a sullen, vindictive twelve-year-old who regards her with considerable suspicion, she is likely to experience considerable disappointment. Like it or not, the stepparent has to take what he or she gets. But that doesn't mean taking all the guilt for a less than perfect relationship.

9. *Be patient.* The words to remember here are "things take time." The first few months and often years have many difficult periods. The support and encouragement of other parents who have had other similar experiences can be an invaluable aid.

10. *Maintain the primacy of the marital relationship.* It has been our experience that most stepparenting relationships have resulted from divorce by one or both members of the couple. There is a certain amount of guilt left over about the breakup of the previous relationship which may spill over into the present relationship and create difficulties when there are arguments. The couple needs to remember that their relationship is primary in the family. The children need to be shown that the parents get along together, can settle disputes, and most of all will not be divided by the children. While parenting may be a central element in the couple's relationship, both partners need to commit time and energy to the development of a strong couple relationship; this bond includes, but is greater than, their parental responsibilities.

Source: Turnbull & Turnbull, 1983.

subsequent remarriage can be threatening to such a child. "This stepparent is going to take my last parent away from me." The stepparent may be met with anger and hostility. When the child's relationship with the departed parent was not good, hostility remaining from this prior relationship can be displaced onto the stepparent.

Because of the constant comparison made by children between biological parents and stepparents, many stepparents make the mistake of trying too hard, especially at first. Usually it is better for the stepparent to move slowly, because it takes time for the child to adjust to the new situation and to reevaluate the past parental relationship (see Inset 16-1). It is also important to the child to figure out just what the remaining parent's feelings are toward the new mate. Making this adjustment is even more difficult when the stepparent tries to replace the natural parent, especially if the child is still seeing his or her real parent. Probably the best course for the stepparent is to take on a supplemental role, meeting the needs of the child not met by the noncustodial parent. In this way the stepparent avoids direct competition with the natural parent.

When a remarried family has children of its own, additional problems may arise with stepchildren. The stepchild may feel even more displaced and alienated. The remaining parent may seem to have been taken away first by the new stepparent and now by their new child. At least some evidence refutes this idea. Of remarried families who had children together, 78 percent rated their relationships with stepchildren as excellent, whereas only 53 percent of those who did not have children together rated their stepchildren relationships as excellent (Duberman, 1973). Perhaps having brothers or sisters takes the focus off the stepchild, allowing a more natural adjustment for both parent and child. A new child can be a source of integration in a stepfamily, as everyone finally has someone to whom all are related (Papernow, 1984).

The role of parent is often difficult. The role of stepparent can even be more difficult, yet an empathic, caring stepparent can give a great deal to a child. The stepparent can be an additional source of love and support. The stepparent can supply friendship and, by making the family a two-parent family again, solve some of the childrearing problems of the single parent. When a stepparent enters a child's life when the child is young, it is possible and often happens that the child comes to look on the stepparent as his or her real parent, which alleviates the child's feelings of loss.

One of the most difficult issues for stepfamily members to deal with is sexuality. It has been suggested that there is a loosening of sexual boundaries (Perlmutter et al., 1982). This is related to the nonbiological and nonlegal structure of the stepfamily, which has not had the advantage of a long developmental period to form intimate parent-child ties. Emotional attachments can grow over time yet incest taboos are not necessarily strong in the stepfamily. The increase in the affectionate and sexual atmosphere in the home during the time that new couples are more romantically involved may also contribute to the loosening of sexual boundaries. It is not unusual for stepfamily members to experience sexual fantasies, increased anxiety, distancing behavior, or even anger in response to and in trying to cope with these sexual issues. In more extreme circumstances, a sexual relationship can develop between a stepparent and stepchild or between stepsiblings (Covi & Robinson, 1985, p. 123). Although all states have laws governing sexual relations between blood relatives, most states do not cover sexual relations between members of reconstituted families.

The New Extended Family

Although we have spoken only of stepparents, it is important to realize that the blended family will bring another set of kin into the relationships. By and large, new kin do not replace old kin but add to those from the first marriage. For example, there will now be stepgrandparents. There will probably be the new spouse of the noncustodial parent. A blended family's immediate family tree can be unimaginably complex. As an extreme imagine the many relationships of the following blended family:

> *Former husband (with two children in custody of their natural mother)*
> *marries new wife with two children in her custody. They have two chil-*
> *dren. Former wife also remarries man with two children, one in his cus-*
> *tody and one in the custody of his former wife, who has also remarried*
> *and had a child with her second husband who also has custody of one*
> *child from his previous marriage. The former husband's parents are also*
> *divorced and both have remarried. Thus when he remarries, his children*
> *have two complete sets of grandparents on his side, plus one set on the*
> *mother's side, plus perhaps two sets on the stepfather's side.*

The example could go to any level of complexity; indeed trying to sort out all of the relationships in some blended families is an impossible task. When one considers the complexities of the blended family, it is surprising that as many remarriages are as successful as they seem to be.

The immediate effect of divorce on relative interaction is that it intensifies contacts between blood relatives while relations with former in-laws are curtailed. Unless the relatives (mainly grandparents) of the noncustodial parent make real efforts to maintain contact with their grandchildren, contact is slowly lost just as it is with the noncustodial parent (Furstenberg & Spanier, 1984, pp. 92–100). However, with remarriage the children's circle of relatives suddenly expands greatly, especially if they have been able to maintain contact with relatives of the noncustodial parent. Whether or not such expansion occurs depends in part on the proximity of relatives. If a remarried family lives at great distance from one set of relatives, that set tends to have less contact with the family than those relatives who live close by.

Furstenberg and Spanier (1984) found that:

> What remarriage does is not to subtract but to add relatives. Contrary to our expectation, contact with biological and with stepgrandparents were not inversely related. Contact with stepgrandparents did not diminish the child's interaction with the family of his or her noncustodial biological parent. . . . Individuals have the option but never the obligation to define people as relatives when they are not closely related by blood. Kinship is often achieved rather than ascribed. Remarriage illustrates this principle by creating an enlarged pool of potential kin. To a large extent, it is up to the various parties involved to determine the extent to which potential kin will be treated as actual relatives. (pp. 160–161)

In the past remarriage was brought about far more often by death than by divorce. Remarriage after death, of course, meant the replacement of a parent, rather than the addition of a parent as remarriage after divorce means. Today remarriage most often means the addition of a parent plus all of the stepparent's relatives. In a way remarriage has brought the idea of extended family (granted not blood relatives) back into American society. It becomes quite possible for a child in a remarried family to have many, many sets of grandparents as we saw in the example. They may have two sets of biological grandparents and four sets of stepgrandparents if both their biological parents remarry. If all these grandparents live close by and maintain relationships with the blended family, holidays such as Christmas can become logistical feats. On the other hand, maintaining a wide circle of relatives can also offer much support and love to children in the blended family.

Building Stepfamily Strengths

A review of popular literature about stepfamilies (Coleman et al., 1985, 1986) found the following potential strengths discussed:

- Stepchildren learn problem solving, negotiation, and coping skills as well as becoming more flexible and adaptable.
- The presence of more adults adds support and exposure to a wider variety of people and experiences.
- Stepfamilies are better for children than single-parent families.
- More parental models are available.
- Stepparents try harder to be good parents.

Although there is little empirical evidence to support the extent of such supposed advantages for stepchildren and their families, it is worthwhile to examine potential strengths that can be built up in blended families. Naturally all of the family strengths enumerated in Chapter 1 will be equally or even more important to the blended family since the blended family tends to be more complicated organizationally than a first marriage family. It also lacks the societal support usually afforded intact nuclear families.

One positive step toward building blended family strength is for society to recognize the blended family as a legitimate alternative to the nuclear family (Wagner, 1984). This will help to do away with the "wicked stepparent" myth that can cause harm to the stepfamily. This will also facilitate the creation of model roles and rules for the functioning of the stepfamily. Inset 16-1 makes a number of other suggestions for the building of strong stepfamilies.

Summary

High remarriage rates indicate that the high divorce rates do not necessarily mean that Americans are disenchanted with marriage as an institution. They may simply indicate that Americans have high expectations for marriage as well as the freedom to end marriage when their expectations are not fulfilled.

The majority of divorced persons remarry, most of them within a few years of divorce. A few remarry as soon as possible, but the rest usually remain single for at least a short period of time. The adjustment to single life is often difficult, especially for those who have been married a long time. Learning to date and interrelate with the opposite sex as a single person after many years of marriage is especially difficult because the newly single person's self-image has for so long been that of a married person, part of a couple. The newly single person may also be insecure and may suffer from feelings of failure and guilt. These feelings make it hard to relate to new people.

Remarriage is sought by most divorced people. Yet this is often a difficult choice because the idea of marriage evokes negative attitudes based on a negative experience with marriage. People marrying for a second time carry with them attitudes and expectations from their first marital experience. In many cases they also continue to have to cope with their first family. Visiting children, child support, and alimony payments may add to the adjustment problems in the second marriage.

Children from prior marriages often add to the responsibilities of second marriage. Becoming a stepparent to the new spouse's children is not easy. A second family may have children from several sources. Each spouse may have children from his or her previous marriage and in time they may have children together. Children from previous marriages often mean continued interaction between the formerly married couple when the former mate visits with or takes the children periodically. Many remarriages, especially when children from the previous marriage are present, actually involve relationships among four adults. The remarried pair naturally have their own relationship, but in addition each will have some level of relationship with the divorced spouse.

About 20 to 25 percent of those divorcing never remarry. For these single life becomes permanent. However, as divorce rates rise, the likelihood of remarriage rises because there are more potential partners. At present about one in four American marriages involves at least one person who was formerly married. Remarriage, then, has definitely become a way of life for a significant number of Americans.

Remarriage Myths

The Role of Myths in Marriage and Family Life

A *myth* has been defined as "an ill-founded belief held uncritically, especially by an interested group" (*Webster's New Collegiate Dictionary*, 1979), and as "a recurring theme . . . that appeals to the consciousness of a people by embodying its cultural ideals or by giving expression to deep, commonly felt emotions" (*American Heritage Dictionary*, 1973). Myths are oversimplified, but firmly held, beliefs that guide perceptions and expectations. Bernard (1981) pointed out that myths usually incorporate an element of truth, noting that, "If there were not some truth in a cultural myth, it would quickly lose its power" (p. 67). That myths are generally unfounded does not reduce their power to influence both attitudes and behavior. Problems develop when myths serve as blinders to actual experience and lead people into painful situations that could have been prevented. . . .

Remarriage Myths

1. *Things must work out.* For some couples the goal of remarriage is to "get it right" this time. Everything will work out because this time it is *really* love. Those who had a simple first wedding ceremony may opt this time for multiple bridesmaids, a long, white gown, and other trappings of a traditional wedding. Those who had a traditional first wedding ceremony may choose something simpler or just different in an attempt to change their luck and get it "right." This approach merely incorporates the original marriage myth, with a note of added intensity or desperation.

2. *Always consider everybody first.* The remarriage version of the second myth may take several forms. Variations may include "always consider yourself first," "always consider the other person first," "always consider your marriage first," "always consider yourself and *your* children first" (as compared to your spouse and his or her children), and finally, "always consider everybody first." These mutually exclusive myths may all be operating at one time. . . .

People who had few financial resources as single parents may have felt deprived. If they developed an assertive style of obtaining resources for themselves and their children during this period, then they may continue to use that style on behalf of their children after remarriage; however, they may feel guilty for not trusting their spouses and putting them first. Those

in the legal professions contribute to this problem by encouraging people to consider themselves and their children first legally and financially and by advising them to arrange antenuptial agreements, marriage contracts, and trusts.

Stepfamilies often consist of a man living with a woman and her children. The stepfather is faced with the task of joining a single-parent family system that may have been functioning for some time. The woman, who is trying to put her children first, may feel protective and interfere when the stepfather disciplines them (Mowatt, 1972). She may then feel guilty because she has failed to consider her husband first (the original marriage myth). The children may resent having to share their mother's attention with the stepfather, and she may feel guilty about giving them less attention. Thus, trying to juggle everyone's needs is not only stressful, it is impossible. . . .

An alternative myth often fostered by counselors—"always consider the marital relationship first" (Visher & Visher, 1979)—is related to the first remarriage myth: If the relationship does not come first, then the marriage may fail, and it *must* succeed. There is empirical evidence, however, supporting the idea that satisfaction with stepparent-stepchildren relationships is more important to family happiness than is satisfaction with the marital relationship (Crosbie-Burnett, 1984).

3. *Keep criticism to oneself and focus on the positive.* Some remarried partners believe that if they had adhered to this myth in their first marriage they might still be married. Consequently, they return to this myth with a vengeance in remarriage. It may be even more difficult to adhere to in remarriage, however, because there often are more people and things to criticize (i.e., stepchildren, former spouses, former in-laws, new in-laws). This myth also incorporates the pseudomutuality that arises because of the intense fear of failure. The marriage remains frozen and static because poking and prodding might uncover a fatal flaw. Children also may support this myth by becoming overtly upset if their parents and stepparents argue or by being unnaturally "good" around stepparents.

Few would fault a couple who show strong determination to make their remarriage work. The problems occur when an intense fear of failure interferes with direct, open communication between the partners (Jacobson, 1979). Intimate relationships normally involve disagreements and conflict. It would be impossible to totally avoid conflict, yet to the person overly concerned with becoming a two-time loser, conflict may create extreme anxiety. The result is often a style of adaptation called *pseudomutuality*. Pseudomutuality among remarried people and stepfamilies is defined as the tendency to deny history, ambivalence, and conflict (Sager et al., 1983). . . .

4. *If things are not going well, focus on what went wrong in the past and make sure it does not happen again.* This myth again pushes for pseudomutuality and denial rather than honest communication. It is a reworking of the old relationship to "get it right" instead of an attempt to build a new and unique relationship. A corollary myth is to "criticize the past and focus on the future." Couples who convince themselves that everything was negative in their previous marriages (proof of which is that the marriage failed) and that everything is going to be per-

fect in their new marriage are building a relationship based on denial. The first sign of any pattern resembling that of the previous marriage may cause panic. . . .

5. *See oneself as part of the couple first, as an individual second; see oneself as an individual first, as part of a couple second.* This myth is actually a combination of two myths. The first version is identical to the marriage myth and is held by remarried persons who are attracted to the sense of security they perceive as a benefit of being married. These individuals may have rushed quickly into remarriage following divorce (or even following death of a spouse).

The second version is identical to the divorce myth and is held by remarried persons who consider themselves sadder but wiser after their first marriages—the major lesson they learned is that one must look out for oneself. . . .

6. *What is mine is mine, what is yours is yours.* This myth tends to move developmentally through family stages from marriage ("what is mine is yours"), to divorce ("what is yours is mine"), to single parenthood ("what is mine is mine"), to remarriage ("what is mine is mine, what is yours is yours"). A problem with this myth is the lack of an "ours" orientation. There may be good reason to maintain some individual control of financial assets, but establishing intimacy in an atmosphere of a business corporation may be difficult, if not impossible.

Stepfamilies tend to organize their finances in one of two ways: *common pot* or *two pot*. In the common pot, family resources are pooled and distributed based on perceived or expressed needs. There is no distinction

between yours and mine. The two-pot stepfamily continues the single-parent family theme "what is mine is mine," and the remarriage is often preceded by the involvement of lawyers, antenuptial agreements, and contracts.

Fishman and Hamel (1983) found the two-pot agreement to be satisfactory when both partners were contributing approximately equal resources to the household. They found it to be much less satisfactory when contributions were blatantly unequal and one set of children was obviously "richer" or "poorer" than the other. They also found that a couple's economic stability was a matter of perspective; sometimes one spouse perceives the family's economic stability as solid and the other views it as shaky. They believed that a shared perspective of the family financial situation was an important factor in stepfamily unity and that neither the common pot nor the two-pot approach would guarantee a remarriage free of conflict over financial resources. . . .

7. *Marriage makes people significantly happier.* This myth is dramatically reinstated at the time of remarriage. It is not only imperative that people be happy in their remarriages, but even happier than they were in their first marriages. A related remarriage myth is that if two people are happy and love each other enough, then everyone will be happy, including children, grandparents, and former spouses.

The myth of "instant love," or "if you love me you will love my children," often operates at the time of remarriage and can cause a great deal of grief and misunderstanding. The couple, caught up in the bliss of a new romantic love relationship, may at first be oblivious to the fact that other family members (e.g., children) are less enthralled. It takes extraordinary effort to love a stepchild who blatantly ignores your existence or who is cleverly rude. . . .

The wise couple may decide they cannot ensure the happiness of their children in the stepfamily. Rather than concentrating on making the children "happy," they should concentrate on providing structure and reasonable rules and limits so that the children are at least aware that they will not be allowed to dominate the family with their unhappiness.

There is evidence from clinical literature that the remarriage of one spouse rekindles the animosity of the former spouse created by the breakup of the previous marriage (Visher & Visher, 1979). Instead of being happy about the remarriage, the former spouse becomes more intrusive, jealous, and difficult (although some former spouses may be happier). Previous agreements may have to be renegotiated, including legal arrangements such as visitation and child support.

Remarriage may make the remarried couple significantly happier, but they may find their circle of marital bliss surrounded by unexpected ripples of discontent and unhappiness on the part of others. If the remarriage does not result in happiness quickly enough or great enough, believers in this myth may seek someone to blame (stepchildren are good candidates for scapegoats) or may begin to plan or anticipate the dissolution of the marriage.

8. *What is best for us must be harmful for the children.* The final remarriage myth is a watered-down version of the divorce myth. Although the effects of parental remarriage on children are typically not perceived as negative as are the effects of parental divorce on children, there is clearly a widespread belief in our society that all stepchildren have a difficult time. . . . The empirical research on stepchildren, however, does not support the view that parental remarriage has harmful effects on children (Ganong & Coleman, 1984).

Paradoxically, many remarrying parents entertain both this myth and myths that seem to be diametric opposites. "Having a 'real' family again is best for everyone" and "what is best for us is best for the children" are remarriage myths that essentially are denials of the notion that children will have to make adjustments and experience stress when parents remarry. Adherents to these myths may really believe that their children have been harmed by their changing family structure but react by convincing themselves that a two-parent family is a panacea.

Finally, it should be noted that the list of remarriage myths discussed here is not exhaustive. There are probably hundreds of fallacies related to remarriage and hundreds more related to broader stepfamily issues. Counselors must keep their eyes and ears open for other potential myths that disrupt the lives of their clients.

Source: Adapted from Coleman & Ganong, 1985.

Actively Seeking Marital Growth and Fulfillment

Contents

We began our journey of marriage and family study by examining the characteristics of strong, successful families. Although recognizing that these six characteristics were described ideally, they give us a goal, a direction to take as we seek successful intimate relationships for ourselves.

Can we commit ourselves to relationships in which we appreciate our mates and they us, in which we develop good communication patterns so that the time we spend together is fulfilling and growth producing? Can we develop a value system and problem-solving skills that will allow us to deal positively with crises and stress? If we can do these things we stand a good chance of creating a strong family for ourselves and loved ones.

One of the basic assumptions on which this book is based is that the fully functioning family can act as a buffer against mental and physical illness (Chapter 2). What can we do to make our intimate relationships more fully functioning? Although everything we have discussed thus far bears on this question, this concluding chapter will specifically attend to the goal of seeking marital growth and fulfillment.

The American scenario of marriage has always included "and they lived happily ever after." This meant that once you found the right person, fell in love, and married all your problems would be over. Of course this is a fairy tale. We know that all married couples will face problems.

Yet the persistence of this fairy tale, even if only at the unconscious level, hampers many Americans' efforts to realize the fullest possible potential in their marriages. To find out if this fairy tale influences you, examine your reaction to the following statement: "All married couples should periodically seek to improve their marriage through direct participation in therapy, counseling, or marriage enrichment programs."

What do you think? Following are some typical reactions:

- It might be a good idea if the couple is unhappy or having problems.
- I know couples who need some help, but Jane and I are already getting along pretty well. It wouldn't help us.
- We already know what our problems are. All we need to do is. . . .
- I'd be embarrassed to seek outside help for my marriage. It would mean I was a personal failure.
- We're so busy now, what with work, the children, and social engagements, we wouldn't have time for any of those things.
- John is a good husband [Mary is a good wife]. I really couldn't ask him [her] to participate in anything like that. He [she] would feel I wasn't happy with him [her] or our marriage.
- I could be happier, but overall our marriage is fine.

It is true that not all married couples need to seek counseling. But it is also true that marriage needs to be more than just maintained to be successful.

Although an analogy between marriage and the automobile is superficial and a gross oversimplification, it may clarify this point. An unmaintained car quickly malfunctions and wears out; a well-maintained car gives less trouble and lasts longer. However, over and beyond maintenance a car can be improved (by buying better tires, or changing the carburetion, exhaust, compression, gearing, and so on) and thereby modified to run better (faster, smoother, and more economically). Most Americans spend most of their adult lives married. Yet they spend little time

and energy improving their marriage. At best they often just maintain it. If the marriage becomes too bad, they leave it to seek a new marriage that will be better. The new marriage (car) may be better for a while, but without maintenance and improvement, it too will soon malfunction.

Some Americans expend a fair amount of energy seeking a new mode of marriage. Perhaps communes are the answer. Maybe just living together and avoiding legal marriage is the answer. Yet disenchantment quickly grows with the "improved" alternatives to marriage. The new commune member who had communication problems with his or her spouse finds that communicating intimately with seven other people is even more difficult. The cohabiting couple who thought that limited commitment was the way to avoid the humdrum in their life together soon find that a prolonged lack of commitment leads to increasing insecurity and discomfort. *Perhaps the energies spent seeking some ideal alternative to marriage might be better spent working on marriage itself.*

After all most of us marry the people we do because we love them, want to be with them, and want to do things for them. We marry by our own decision in most cases. We start out supposedly with the best of all things going for us, "love." Where does it go? Why isn't it able to conquer all of our problems? Might it be that the fairy tale, "and they lived happily ever after" keeps us from deliberately building a better marriage? Do we think that love will automatically take care of everything?

In reality a number of factors combine to keep most Americans from taking a more active part in improving their marriages. The fairy tale we have been discussing has been called the "myth of naturalism" (Vincent, 1973). This is the feeling that marriage is "natural" and will take care of itself if we select the right partner. That is, many people believe that outside forces may support or hinder their marriage but that married couples need do little for marriages to function well, especially when the outside forces are good (full employment, little societal stress, and so on).

Another factor is the general "privatism" that pervades American culture. "It's nobody else's business" is a common attitude about problems in general and marriages in particular. It's bad taste to reveal our intimate and personal lives publicly. Seeking outside activities to improve marriage means sharing personal information, which is an invasion of privacy.

A third factor is the cynicism that treats marriage as a joke and thus heads off attempts to improve it (Mace & Mace, 1974). "You should have known better than to get married. Don't complain to me about your problems." This attitude contradicts the romantic concept of marriage but acts just as strongly to keep people from deliberately seeking to improve their marriages. "Why would anyone want to improve this dumb institution?" Even though American society is marriage oriented, there is still a great deal of ridicule of "the ball and chain." Facing up to and countering the antifamily themes found in American society is an important step toward revitalizing marriage and the family (Etzioni, 1983).

Despite these factors there is a growing trend toward actively seeking marriage improvement. For example, more than 1.5 million couples have participated in the Roman Catholic Marriage Encounter program since it started in 1967 (Garland, 1983). Although created for Catholics, it is open to all couples who wish to participate. Such programs indicate that the idea of marriage improvement is finding a place in society.

In order to improve a marriage, it is necessary to believe that relationships can be improved. In other words, the myth of naturalism must be overcome. A marriage will not just naturally take care of itself. In addition, the privatism and cynicism that surround marriage must be reduced if effective steps are to be taken to enrich a marriage.

To improve their marriage, a couple must work on three things: (1) themselves as individuals, (2) their relationship, and (3) the economic environment within which the marriage exists. We have already looked at these elements. For example, in Chapter 5 we discussed the self-actualized person in the fully functioning family; in Chapter 8 we examined marriage as an economic institution and found that the economics of one's marriage will drastically affect the marital relationship; in Chapter 6 we looked at ways to improve communication within a relationship.

This final chapter stresses the idea that every person has the ability to improve his or her marriage. Marriages tend to get into trouble because many people believe that they can't do much about their marriages and because many of us simply don't take the time to nourish our marriage and make it healthier. We also tend to get into trouble because security and comfort may lull us into avoiding risks, and we must remain willing to risk if we expect to grow and maintain positive movement in our lives and relationships.

Although this chapter deals specifically with activities designed to improve marital relationships, it is important that a couple work to improve the other two influences on marriage: themselves as individuals and their economic situation. Neglect of any of these influences or emphasis on only one can lead to marital failure. In fact, a couple can be extremely successful in one of the three areas and still fail miserably at marriage, as the two following cases demonstrate.

> *Bill and Susan both worked to buy the many things they wanted: a house, fine furnishings, nice clothing, a fancy car, and so on. Bill even held two jobs for a while. Certainly no one could fault their industriousness and hard work. In time their marital affluence became the envy of all who knew them. After seven years of marriage they divorced. Their friends were surprised. "They had everything, why should they divorce?" Unfortunately they didn't have much of a relationship other than to say hello and goodby as each went off to work. In addition each worked so hard that neither had time for self-improvement. No self-improvement means no growth or change; this eventually leads to boredom with the relationship, and boredom often portends failure.*

Bill and Susan were successful with their marital economic environment but did not pay enough attention to improving themselves as individuals or to improving their relationship.

> *Jack and Mary believed that the key to successful marriage was self-improvement. Both took extension classes in areas of their own interest. They attended sensitivity training groups and personal expansion workshops. Unfortunately they could seldom attend these functions together because of conflicting work schedules. Soon they were so busy improving themselves that they had little time for one another. The house was a shambles, the yard was weeds, and their relationship disappeared under a maze of "do-your-own-thing" self-improvement.*
>
> *After seven years they divorced. Their friends were surprised. "After all, they're so dynamic and interesting, why should they divorce?" They had become so self-oriented that their relationship had disappeared and their living environment had become unimportant.*

Jack and Mary worked so hard to improve themselves individually that they had no time for each other or for their home.

Both of these scenarios happen every day. The second is becoming more prevalent with the growing interest in the human potential movement. The very concepts used in this book—self-actualization, self-fulfillment, and human growth orientation—can all be taken to such an individual extreme that marriage is disrupted.

> A possible fallacy of the human potential movement is making self-fulfillment the central goal, while seemingly ignoring the fact that the human being is essentially a relationship-oriented and interactional creature. If an educational or therapeutic goal is to unlock human potential, there must be a corresponding focus on marriage and family relationships. (Cromwell & Thomas, 1976, p. 15)

More and more family researchers as well as general observers of American society see excessive hedonism as America's greatest enemy. Stressing individuality at the expense of mutuality overlooks the importance of successful human relationships, which many see as a basic human need, even for successful individual functioning. Amitai Etzioni (1983) suggests that mutuality, the basic need for interpersonal bonds, is not something each person creates on his or her own and then brings to the relationship. Rather it is constructed by individuals working with one another. It is this working together that is the essence of the healthy family.

To make marriage as rewarding and fulfilling as possible, a couple must be committed first to the idea that "effective family relationships do not just happen, they are the result of deliberate efforts by members of the family unit" (Cromwell & Thomas, 1976). Then they must be prepared to work on all three facets of marriage: to improve themselves as individuals, to improve their interactional relationship, and to improve their economic environment. These three areas encompass developing oneself in the physical, social, emotional, intellectual, and spiritual realms.

Such a commitment helps a couple anticipate problems before they arise rather than simply reacting to them. When there is commitment to active management and creative guidance of a marriage, the marriage can become richly fulfilling and growth enhancing, both for the family as a social unit and for the individuals within the family.

Marriage Improvement Programs

Many helping techniques are now available to families. Some aim at solving existing problems, others aim at general family improvement. We will briefly examine some of these techniques, in the hope of accomplishing two goals:

1. To help families seek experiences that benefit them.
2. To alert families to some of the possible dangers involved in unselective, nondiscriminative participation in some of the popular techniques.

Help for family problems in the past has usually come from relatives, friends, ministers, and family doctors. The idea of enriching family life and of improving already adequate marriages simply did not occur to most married people. Marriage traditionally was an institution for childrearing, economic support, and proper fulfillment of marital duties defined in terms of masculine and feminine roles. If there were problems in these areas, help might be sought. If not the marriage was fine.

Marriage in modern America, however, has been given more and more responsibility for individual happiness and emotional fulfillment. The criteria used to judge a marriage have gradually shifted from how well each member fulfills roles and performs proper marital functions to the personal contentment, fulfillment, and happiness of each individual in the marriage.

Marital complaints now concern sex role dissatisfaction, unequal growth and personal fulfillment opportunities, feelings of personal unhappiness, and feelings that the marriage is shortchanging the individual partners. That is, more and more marriage problems revolve around personal dissatisfactions than around traditional marital functioning. The "me" in today's marriages often seems more important than the "us."

A successful family is able to find a balance between personal freedom and happiness and family support and togetherness. The "me" and the "us" come into an acceptable balance. Such a balance will vary with each family. One end of the continuum will find *joint conjugal relationships* where the balance favors the "us." These are couples that are close emotionally and share most areas of their lives. Their leisure activities almost always involve one another and their outside friendships are almost always couple friendships. At the other end of the continuum are *separated conjugal relationships* where the balance favors the individual. Such couples usually have separate leisure activities and friends.

It is interesting to note that the two ends of this "togetherness" continuum have related loosely to economic levels in the past. Those at higher economic levels tended to emphasize togetherness while those on the lower economic levels tended to emphasize individuality. Today with so many wives in the workforce, the women's liberation movement, and the general social support for individual growth and fulfillment the differentiation between economic classes has lessened. The lifestyles of most American families have moved slowly toward separated conjugal relationships.

Emphasis on emotional fulfillment as the most important aspect of marriage makes an enduring marital union much more difficult to attain. According to one authority, "Emotional fulfillment has always occurred in the family; probably more so in the past than is usual today. But it was never before seen as the primary function of the family. It was a lucky 'by-product' " (Putney, 1972). For example, when Australia was first colonized by male convicts, there was a brisk trade in mail-order wives because there were no available women in the country. Most of these marriages seem to have been successful for the simple reason

> that the prospective husband and wife expected things of each other that the other could provide. The man needed assistance and companionship of a woman in the arduous task of making a farm, and he wanted sons to help him. He expected certain skills in his wife, but all girls raised in rural England were likely to have them. Her expectations were similarly pragmatic. She expected him to know farming, to work hard, and to protect her. Neither thought of the other as a happiness machine. If they found happiness together more often than American couples do, it may have been they were not looking so hard for it. They fulfilled each other because they shared a life; they did not share a life in the hope of being fulfilled. (Putney, 1972)

The search for emotional fulfillment has led to many new methods to gain this end. Sensitivity training, encounter groups, family enrichment weekends, sex therapy, sexuality workshops, communication improvement groups, massage and bodily awareness training, psychodrama, women's and men's liberation groups, and many other experiential activities have sprung up in recent years to help Americans enrich their lives.

Although this chapter's overview cannot hope to do justice to the many marriage improvement techniques that are emerging, let's take a brief look at some typical ones before we examine marriage enrichment in more detail.

1. *Courses on marriage and the family:* These are offered by most colleges. They aim to help people better understand the institution of marriage. Many

schools offer even more specialized courses, often in the evening, on marital communication, economics of marriage, childrearing, and so on.

2. *Encounter groups*: These consist of group interactions, usually with strangers, where the masks and games used by marital partners to manipulate one another and conceal real feelings are stripped away. The group actively confronts the person, forcing him or her to examine some problems and the faulty methods that might have been used to solve or deny problems. A great deal of emotion is released by such groups. Couples contemplating attending an encounter group should carefully consider the guidelines on page 563.

3. *Family enrichment weekends*: These involve the entire family in a retreat setting where they work together to improve their family life. The family may concentrate on learning new activities to share. They may listen to lectures, see films, and share other learning experiences. They may interact with other families and learn through the experiences of others. They may participate in exercises designed to improve family communication or general family functioning (see Inset 17-1).

4. *Women's and men's consciousness raising groups*: These groups center their discussions and exercises on helping people escape from stereotypical sex roles and liberate the parts of their personalities that have been submerged in the sex role. For example, women who believe that the typical feminine role has been too passive may work to become more assertive. On the other hand, men who feel the typical masculine role has repressed their ability to communicate feelings may work to become more expressive.

5. *Married couples' communication workshops*: These workshops may be ongoing groups or weekend workshops in which communication is the center

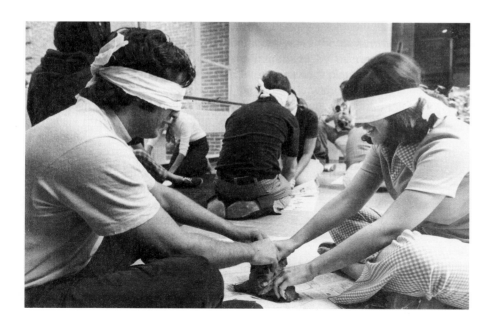

Inset 17-1

A Family Life Enrichment Weekend

Mr. and Mrs. Smith have been married for fifteen years. They have two children, Colin, thirteen, and Beth, ten. Their church recently started a series of family retreat weekends at a nearby mountain camp. After some discussion, the family agreed that it would be fun and rewarding to go on one of the weekends.

Early Saturday morning they arrive at the camp and move into one of the cabins. Inasmuch as nothing is scheduled until lunch, the family explores the camp and surroundings. There is a small lake with boating and fishing, a tennis court, volleyball court, and plenty of hiking trails.

At noon the twenty families gather in the cafeteria/meeting hall for lunch. Everyone is given a name tag and the leaders are introduced. After lunch each family introduces themselves. Much to the children's delight, there are many other children present. The leaders assign each family to one of five family subgroups. After lunch the family groups meet and the four families become better acquainted. The group leader then introduces the first work session, entitled "Becoming More Aware." There are exercises in identification of feelings, and attention is given to feelings the participants would like to have more of and those they would like to experience less.

After a break the group leader discusses methods the families might use to reduce unwanted feelings and increase desired feelings. Each family then practices some of these methods while the others observe. After a family finishes, there is a general critique of their experience.

The families are free after the work session until dinner. After dinner short movies on various developmental problems are shown to the children. At the same time the parents attend a sexuality workshop. The parents are shown massage techniques designed to relax and give physical pleasure. They are asked to practice the techniques in their individual cabins. They are assured of privacy because the children will be occupied for at least another hour. The children meanwhile are asked to form small groups and discuss how the children shown in the films can be helped to meet the developmental problems portrayed.

Next morning, the first work session is devoted to the theme "Being Free." This involves learning openness to experiencing each other. The children of the four families talk to one another about things they like and don't like while the parents sit and listen. Then the roles are reversed. Afterward, each family exchanges children. They are then given a hypothetical problem to solve. Each newly constituted family has a half hour to work on the problem while the other families observe.

At noon each family group eats together and then uses the hour recreational period to do something together, such as hiking, boating, or fishing.

The afternoon work session again separates the parents and children. In each case the assignment is the same. The children are asked to form family groups where some children play the parents' roles. They are given problems to work out as a family unit. The parents also form family groups with some parents taking children's roles.

In the final dinner meeting all of the families come together. Both the families and the leaders try to summarize the experiences of the weekend and their significance. Then the leaders outline several homework assignments, one of which each family has to choose and promise to work on at home.

What Do You Think?

1. What do you see as the major benefits such an experience could provide a family?

2. Would you be willing to participate with your family in such an experience? Why or why not?

3. Do you have any friends who have participated in any kind of marriage enrichment experience? How did they respond to it?

of attention. Role playing, learning how to fight fairly, understanding communication processes, and actively practicing in front of the group all help the couple toward better communication. An important aspect of this is the critique made by the group after a couple communicates about something that causes a problem for them.

6. *Massage and bodily awareness training*: This training is often a part of sexuality workshops. It is aimed at developing the couple's awareness of their own bodies and teaching them the techniques involved in physically pleasuring each other through massage. The art of physical relaxation is part of bodily awareness training.

7. *Psychodrama*: This is a form of psychotherapy developed by J. L. Moreno. It is used to dramatize problems by acting them out with other group members as the players. In the case of marriage enrichment, it is used to help individuals in the family better understand the roles of other family members. This understanding is accomplished mainly through timely changes of role by the individuals participating in the drama under the direction of the group leader. Shifting roles also helps each player understand how the other person in the drama feels and sees the situation.

8. *Sensitivity training*: This training consists of exercises in touching, concentrating, heightening awareness, and empathizing with one's mate. The exercises increase each mate's self-awareness and sensitivity to the other.

9. *Sex therapy and sexuality workshops*: These focus on a couple's sexual relationship. Sex therapy is used to overcome sexual problems. Sexuality workshops are designed more to help couples improve this aspect of their relationship than to cure severe problems. Such a workshop assumes that there are no major sexual problems. The goal is to heighten sexual awareness so that the couple's sexual relations may be enriched. Films, discussion, mutual exploration, sensitivity, and massage and bodily awareness techniques are all used to reduce inhibitions and expand the couple's sexual awareness.

10. *Marriage counseling and family service organizations*: Both of these services are aimed more at the couple with real marital and family difficulties. For example, Parents Without Partners (PWP) is an active volunteer organization to help and support single parents. Planned Parenthood helps families with reproductive problems such as finding the best contraceptive. The American Association of Marriage and Family Counselors will help a couple find a reputable marriage counselor.

Guidelines for Choosing Marriage Improvement Programs

Unfortunately the large demand for marriage improvement programs has brought some untrained and unscrupulous people into the fields of marriage counseling and marriage enrichment. For example, it is relatively simple as well as monetarily rewarding to run a weekend encounter group of some kind. All you need is a place where the people can meet. Some participants have found that not all such experiences are beneficial or even accomplish what is claimed. In a minority of cases, unexpected repercussions, such as divorce, job change, and even hospitalization for mental disturbance, have occurred after some supposedly beneficial group experience. Consider what happened to the following couple because one partner could not tolerate the intensity of the group experience.

John and Mary have been married for eleven years and have two children. He has always been shy and uncomfortable among people, but despite this he has worked out a stable, satisfying relationship with Mary. She is more socially oriented than John. She began to attend a series of group encounter sessions out of curiosity. As her interest increased, she decided that John would benefit from a group experience. She asked him to attend a weekend marathon. Unfortunately the group turned its attention too strongly toward John's shyness, causing him acute discomfort that finally resulted in his fleeing from the group. He remained away from his home and work for ten days. On returning he demanded a divorce because he felt that he was an inadequate husband. Fortunately psychotherapeutic help was available and John was able to work out the problems raised by the group encounter.

Evaluation studies of the Marriage Encounter program (a popular church-sponsored enrichment program) indicate that only about 10 percent of the participants experience potentially harmful effects (Dohery & Lester, 1982, p. 9). But since there are possible negative effects, it is worthwhile to list what they might be:

1. The perceived benefits might be illusory or at best temporary.
2. The stress on the relationship might tend to deny individual differences.
3. There might be divisive influences on the couple's relationship with other family members.
4. The communicative techniques taught might rigidify the couple's communication patterns, and failure to practice the techniques might lead to guilt or resentment. (Dohery, McCabe, & Ryder, 1978, pp. 104–105)

Because marriage enrichment experiences can be so beneficial to couples, it is important to reduce the potential negative aspects to a minimum. Couples seeking marital enrichment or help for marital problems are advised to check out the people offering such services. They should also discuss the kind of experiences they want and make sure that they are the experiences offered. For example, if a couple decides that they would like to improve their sexual relations and can do so by seeking some general sensitivity training (learning to feel more comfortable with their bodies, be more aware, and give and accept bodily pleasure), they might be rudely shocked if the group leader has a nude encounter group with the goal of examining each person's emotional hang-ups about sex.

Couples who have a reasonably satisfactory marriage can use the following guidelines in choosing a marriage enrichment activity:

1. Choose the activity together and participate together if possible.
2. If only one mate can participate, do so with the consent of the other and bring the other into the activity as much as possible by sharing your experiences.
3. In general avoid the one-shot weekend group; it is often too intense and no follow-up is available if needed.
4. Never jump into a group experience on impulse. Give it a lot of thought, understanding that experiences leading to growth may be painful.

5. Do not participate in groups where the people are friends and associates if the group's goal is total openness and emotional expression. What occurs in a group session should be privileged information.
6. Don't remain with a group that seems to have an ax to grind, that insists that everybody be a certain type of person or that all must participate in every activity.
7. Participate in groups that have a formal connection with a local professional on whom you can check. The local professional is also a source of follow-up if necessary.
8. A group of six to sixteen members is optimum size. Too small a group may result in scapegoating; too large a group cannot operate effectively.

Such cautions are not meant to dissuade couples from trying to improve their marriages. They are simply meant to help couples select experiences that are beneficial and supportive rather than threatening and disruptive. Legitimate marriage counselors throughout the United States are working to upgrade their profession and tighten the rules guiding counseling practices. Many states now have licensing provisions for marriage and family counseling.

Whenever seeking help, regardless of recommendations, always check credentials. The foremost organization in the nation for accrediting and certifying marriage counselors is The American Association of Marriage and Family Therapists, 225 Yale Avenue, Claremont, California 91711. At no charge it will supply a list of three or more accredited marriage counselors in your area. Psychologists are also active in marital counseling and enrichment training. Membership in the American Psychological Association (APA) indicates that the member has met minimum training requirements and has agreed to abide by a strict set of ethics in client relationships. The American Association of Sex Educators and Counselors has established certification standards for sex therapists. You can receive a copy of these standards and a list of certified sex therapists by writing to Sex Therapy Certification Committee, American Association of Sex Educators and Counselors, Suite 304, 5010 Wisconsin Avenue N.W., Washington, D.C. 20016. In addition more than 350 marriage-and-family-oriented nonprofit social service organizations throughout the nation are affiliated with the Family Service Association of America, 44 East 23d Street, New York, N.Y. 10010, and the National Association of Social Workers, Suite 600, 1425 H Street N.W., Washington, D.C. 20005. Many churches also offer family counseling and enrichment programs. In fact, some churches have been pioneers in the marriage enrichment movement.

An Ounce of Prevention Is Worth a Pound of Cure: Marriage Enrichment

Only recently have those working in the field of marriage and family counseling turned their attention away from marital problems and focused on marriage enrichment. "What we are now seeking to do, late in the day when the scene is already strewn with marital wrecks, is to equip married couples with the insight and training that will keep their marriages in such good order that the danger of going on the rocks will be as far as possible avoided" (Mace & Mace, 1974, p. 133).

Past marital services have been remedial in nature. When a couple had a marital problem, they could seek help from numerous sources. Marriage enrichment places the emphasis on the preventive concept of facilitating positive growth. In other words, the goal is to help couples with "good" marriages further improve their relationship.

Marriage enrichment programs are for couples who perceive their marriage as functioning fairly well and wish to make it even more mutually satisfying. Because the emphasis is on education and prevention rather than on therapy these programs are not for couples with serious problems in their marriage. Enrichment programs are generally concerned with enhancing the couple's communication, emotional life, or sexual relationship; fostering marriage strengths; and developing marriage potential while maintaining a consistent and primary focus on the relationship of the couple (Otto, 1975, p. 137).

> The purpose of marriage enrichment is to teach couples attitudes, communication behaviors, and knowledge about family and marital relationships. This education is designed to help them develop relationships that meet personal needs and enhance individual development. This is education in the best sense of the term—experiencing new ideas and new approaches to relating, not just learning about them. It is education that enables spouses to change the way they think, what they feel, and how they care for each other. (Garland, 1983, p. 217)

Some people in the field make a distinction between marriage enrichment and family life enrichment programs. The latter involve not only the primary couple but the entire family in the program. They are designed for families without severe problems.

If couples are to direct and improve their marriage, they must increase their awareness. You can't improve anything unless you recognize what is taking place. It is helpful to organize awareness into four subcategories (Hill, 1961): topical, self, partner, and relationship. Marriage enrichment programs usually spend a great deal of time helping couples or families to become more aware in each of these categories.

For example, sensitivity training exercises help you focus on your internal sensory, thinking, and emotional processes. A realistic picture of yourself, openness to your feelings, minimal defensiveness, and eliminating some emotional hang-ups are goals sought by enrichment programs in the category of self-awareness.

Partner awareness involves knowing accurately what your partner is experiencing in terms of his or her own self-awareness (Miller et al., 1975). How does this behavior affect my partner? Is my partner happy, sad, or indifferent? How can I best communicate with my partner? What does my partner think or feel about this? Answering such questions accurately is the goal of partner awareness training.

Relationship awareness shifts the focus from the behavior of one individual to the interactional patterns of the couple or the entire family. For example, who starts an argument, who continues it, and who ends the interaction? Does each individual contribute self-disclosures, feeling inputs, negative and positive communications? Does the couple play unproductive games? If so, who initiates the game? What are the rules by which the family interacts?

Every interrelationship has boundaries, constraints that either encourage or discourage certain types of awareness and various types of behavior. These rules are usually outside our direct awareness but they create and maintain meaning and order. We like to conceptualize rules in terms of who can do what, where, when, how, and for what length of time. This can be applied to any issue in a relationship (Miller et al., 1975, p. 147). For example, is personal criticism allowed in a family? Who is allowed to criticize, when, and to what degree? What is a family's mode of handling conflicts? Some talk directly about issues and try actively to solve them. Other families pretend that conflicts don't exist and ignore them, hoping they will go away. Others deal with the issue in some stereotypical manner that usually fails to solve the conflict but allows the ventilation of hostility.

Topical awareness is less important than the three we have just discussed. Topical awareness encompasses references to events, objects, ideas, places, and people, topics that constitute most of everyday conversation. By increasing topical awareness, the couple can focus on their interests, where they differ and where they coincide. They can find areas in which they can work and play together. They can recognize and tolerate areas of their spouse's interests that they don't share.

Another purpose of marriage enrichment programs is to help couples and families develop a game plan for handling disputes and conflicts. What are the rules, how are they clarified, and what procedure can change them? "If you haven't a set of rules before the game starts, the game is likely to degenerate into a series of arguments and squabbles, and so it is with relationships" (Miller et al., 1975, p. 147). Thus most marriage enrichment programs spend a great deal of time on the development of communication skills. For example, identifying problem ownership, self-assertion, empathic listening, negotiation, and problem solving are all emphasized. The kinds of skills discussed in Chapter 6 are generally taught and practiced in enrichment programs.

Esteem building is another area of concern in enrichment programs. Better communication can equip a person to be more destructive as well as constructive. We sometimes forget this when lauding the improvement of communication skills. Emphasizing esteem building, making the intent or spirit with which something is said positive, and valuing both the self and the partner make communication constructive and growth enhancing. Esteem building is particularly difficult for a partner who feels devalued and inferior, thus enrichment programs stress the importance of building a relationship that negates such feelings and supports valued, positive, high-esteem feelings in family members.

The fact that a family is interested in and open to the idea of marriage enrichment is an extremely important strength. Certainly the kinds of goals sought in the marriage enrichment movement are worthwhile. These goals, however, are not as important as the family's general attitude toward marriage. The family that takes an active role in guiding, improving, and working to better family relations is the family that stands the greatest chance of leading a long, happy, and meaningful life.

Marriage with Purpose: Effective Management

Popular lore has it that the love marriage simply happens (the myth of naturalism that we discussed earlier). If we are in love, then the other factors necessary to a successful relationship and marriage will fall into place automatically, magically. There is no reason to worry about problems ahead of time. Of course there will be differences, but they can be worked out successfully by any couple truly in love.

It is almost a sacrilege to suggest that people entering love relationships should make a conscious effort to guide and build their relationship. In fact, many argue that attempted guidance and control of a relationship will ruin it. Their advice is to "relax and let it happen." This attitude implies a great tolerance on the part of each individual, because what happens may not be something the other wants. How tolerant are we? Does love mean that we must never judge our mate? Are we to accept any behavior from our mate in an effort to "let it happen"?

Most people are tolerant only up to a given point, after which certain behavior becomes unacceptable. Most of us are tolerant in some areas of our life and intolerant in other areas. Of course everyone can learn to be more tolerant, but total tolerance of all things is probably impossible. People have many and varying standards. The point is that when we let a relationship "just happen," it usually isn't long before we discover some of our intolerances. Then we try to make changes in our relationship or mate. Conflict usually follows because our mate may not want to change or have the relationship change in the direction we desire. Without mutually acceptable ways of handling conflict, unconscious games and strategies may take over, and soon communication will be lost.

Marriage and family require management skills. Work, leisure, economics, emotions, interests, sex, children, eating, and maintaining the household all require effective management in the fully functioning family. We have discussed most of these matters elsewhere in the book, but it seems a proper ending to tie them all together under the concept of effective management.

"Surely you can't be serious? Effective management belongs in business, not in my marriage." Yet every married couple, especially if they have children, is running a business. For example, just planning what the family will eat for the next week, buying it, preparing it, and cleaning up afterward requires management and organizational skills, especially if money is in short supply. There are also recurrent personal and family crises that throw off schedules and plans.

In addition to day-to-day management is the planning necessary to achieve long-range goals. Some families seem to move from catastrophe to calamity and back again. Other families seem to move smoothly through life despite the crises that arise periodically. What is the difference? Often it is one of efficient planning and management versus lack of planning and management. Look at the different attitudes toward money of the following two couples:

Jim and Marge went to college with Bill and Sally. They remained close friends after college, as both Jim and Bill got jobs with the same company. Each couple has two children. Marge works periodically and the money she earns is always saved or used to achieve some specific goal such as a trip to Europe or an addition to the house. Sally works most of the time also, but she and Bill don't care much about things such as budgeting. As long as there is enough money to pay the bills, nothing else matters.

"You and Jim are always so lucky. Bill and I have wanted to add an extra master bedroom for ourselves so we could have a retreat away from the children, but we'll never be able to afford it," complains Sally.

> *"Luck has nothing to do with it. Jim and I have planned to add the bedroom for a number of years. We always budget carefully so our monthly expenses are covered by Jim's salary. That way all of the money I earn less child-care costs goes into savings. The new bedroom represents my last three years of work. I'd hardly call it luck."*

Naturally Sally isn't interested in hearing Marge's response. "Luck" is an easier way to explain her friend's new bedroom. Besides, what Marge is telling her is, "Be a better money manager, and you, too, can add a new bedroom." This advice will only make her feel guilty and inadequate. "It isn't worth all the trouble to budget money and be tightwads to get a new bedroom," Sally will probably think to herself.

Creative family management in all areas helps the family run smoothly and achieve its desired goals. This reduces frustrations and conflicts because it gives family members a feeling of success. Careful planning also helps a family maintain the flexibility necessary to cope with unforeseen emergencies. Such flexibility gives family members a feeling of freedom, of being able to make choices rather than having choices forced on them by events beyond their control.

The entrapment that many married persons feel occurs in some cases because they do not take the initiative to plan and guide their lives but simply react to circumstances. Of course there are times and situations when one can do nothing but react. The poor in particular often have so little control over their lives that they give up planning altogether and live by luck and fate.

Family control and rational planning become more difficult as social institutions multiply and infringe on family responsibilities. Some of these external stresses on the family have emerged out of necessity. When society begins to develop beyond a primitive level, its members soon find that many tasks are better performed by agencies other than the family. Priests take over the job of interceding with the supernatural; police forces, armies, and fire brigades take over the job of protecting the family from physical harm; and schools undertake to educate children. In the complex modern world the family often has little voice in what kind of work its members will perform, or where, or for how long; all these matters are decided by impersonal forces of the marketplace or by distant corporations, unions, or government bureaus (Wernick, 1974, p. 112).

It becomes even more important that planning, foresight, and management be an integral part of family life to cope successfully with such outside pressures. The family that actively takes control of its destiny is most often the family that grows and prospers, thereby helping every member toward self-fulfillment.

The Family Will Remain and Diversify

Many try to predict the future of the American family. Their predictions vary from an early death to visualizing new and improved families that will be havens of fulfillment for their members. It is unlikely that families will disappear or that there is any ideal single family structure. All families face both external environmental pressures and internal stresses and strains. Older generations will probably always see what seems to them to be family deterioration because their children

choose different lifestyles from their own. Yet difference in lifestyle and in family structure does not necessarily mean deterioration. Perhaps with increased affluence and education each individual will be able to choose from a wider acceptable variety of lifestyles, thereby increasing the chances that the family will be satisfying and fulfilling to its members.

The family has always been with us and always will be. And it will also always change. Family flexibility allows it to survive. The family is flexible because humans are flexible and build institutions that meet their purposes at a given time. When we forget the basic flexibility of humans, we see changes in institutions as threatening, even when they may in fact be changes that help people meet their needs.

The concept of family has always been controversial, but it is always one of the central concepts whenever people congregate into a society. Change is an integral part of the concept of family. As Elise Boulding has suggested: "The family has met fire, flood, famine, earthquake, war, economic and political collapse over the centuries by changing its form, its size, its behavior, its location, its environment, its reality. It is the most resilient social form available to humans" (1983, p. 259).

Summary

The American dream "and they lived happily ever after" remains only an unfulfilled dream unless the newly married couple commit themselves to the idea of working not only to maintain but also to improve their relationship. Unfortunately a number of factors work against such commitment. First there is the myth of naturalism that claims love will take care of any problems that arise if you marry the "right" mate. Second is the general "privatism" that pervades American culture and precludes sharing of the very intimate problems that arise in marriage. The third factor is the cynicism that often surrounds the idea of marriage.

In order to improve an intimate relationship, a couple must work on three things: (1) themselves as individuals, (2) their relationship, and (3) the economic environment within which their relationship exists. If any of these is ignored, the chances that the relationship will experience problems increase.

There are now many marriage improvement programs from which couples may choose. However, couples need to use caution in choosing such programs. As beneficial as most programs are, there is always the potential for damage to the relationship if the couple is unprepared for the experience or if the particular program is poorly presented.

Marriage and/or family enrichment programs are planned for the family that does not have serious problems. Enrichment programs are for families that are getting along pretty well but want to improve their relationships and the quality of their lives.

As unromantic as it may sound a fulfilling marriage and family life is largely based on good management. The family that remains in control of its day-to-day life as well as its future is most apt to be successful. Good planning and follow-through are essential to maintaining such control.

Although the family faces many problems just as it has in the past, the flexible nature of the family allows it to survive as the major institution for intimate interaction. Just what form it will take in the future remains to be seen, but it will survive as it always has.

Appendix A

Marriage Requirements By State*

Marriageable age, by states, for both males and females with and without consent of parents or guardians. But in most states, the court has authority to marry young couples below the ordinary age of consent, where due regard for their morals and welfare so requires. In many states, under special circumstances, blood test and waiting period may be waived.

State	With Consent		Without Consent		Blood Test		Wait for License	Wait after License
	Men	Women	Men	Women	Required	Other State Accepted		
Alabama(b)	14	14	18	18	Yes	Yes	none	none
Alaska	16(m)	16(m)	18	18	No	No	3 days	none
Arizona	16(g)	16	18	18	Yes	Yes	none	none
Arkansas	17	16(h)	18	18	Yes	No	3 days	none
California	18(g)	18	18	18	Yes	Yes	none	none
Colorado	16	16	18	18	Yes	. . .	none	none
Connecticut	16	16(j)	18	18	Yes	Yes	4 days	none
Delaware	18	16(k)	18	18	No	No	none	24 hrs.(c)
District of Columbia	16	16	18	18	Yes	Yes	3 days	none
Florida	17	17	18	18	Yes	No	none	none
Georgia	16(g)	16(g)	18	18	Yes	Yes	none(k)	none
Hawaii	16	16	18	18	Yes	Yes	none	none
Idaho	16	16	18	18	No	Yes	none	none
Illinois(a)	16	16	18	18	Yes	Yes	none	1 day
Indiana	17(k)	17(k)	18	18	Yes	No	72 hours	none
Iowa	(k)	(k)	18	18	No	Yes	3 days	none
Kansas	(k)	(k)	18	18	No	No	3 days	none
Kentucky	(k)	(k)	18	18	Yes	No	3 days	none
Louisiana(a)	18(k)	16(h)	18	16	Yes	No	none	72 hours
Maine	16(h)	16(h)	18	18	No	No	5 days	none
Maryland	16	16	18	18	none	none	48 hours	none
Massachusetts	(k)	(k)	18	18	Yes	Yes	3 days	none
Michigan(a)	16	16	18	18	Yes	No	3 days	none
Minnesota	16(e)	16(e)	18	18	none	. . .	5 days	none
Mississippi(b)	17(l)	15(l)	21	21	Yes	. . .	3 days	none
Missouri(b)	15	15	18	18	none	Yes	3 days	none

Many states have additional requirements; contact your individual state. (a) Special laws applicable to nonresidents.
(b) Special laws applicable to those under 21 years: Ala., bond required if male is under 18, female under 18.
(c) 24 hours if one or both parties are resident of state; 96 hours if both parties are non-residents.
(d) None, but both must file affadavit.
(e) Parental consent plus court's consent required.
(f) As of 8/85, there is a bill on the governor of New York's desk that would eliminate the premarital exam and reduce the 3-day waiting period to 24 hours.
(g) Statute provides for obtaining license with parental or court consent with no state minimum age.
(h) Under 16, with parental and court consent.
(i) If either under 18, wait full three days.
(j) If under stated age, court consent required.
(k) If under 18, parental and/or court consent required.
(l) Both parents' consent required for men age 17, women age 15; one parent's consent required for men 18–20 years, women ages 16–20 years.
(m) Parental and court consent required if 14 or over, but under 16.

*As of 1985

State	With Consent		Without Consent		Blood Test		Wait for License	Wait after License
	Men	Women	Men	Women	Required	Other State Accepted		
Montana	15	15	18	18	Yes	Yes	none	3 days
Nebraska	17(h)	17	18	18	Yes	Yes	2 days	none
Nevada	16(h)	16(h)	18	18	none	none	none	none
New Hampshire(a)	14(e)	13(e)	18	18	No	No	3 days	none
New Jersey(a)	16(g)	16(g)	18	18	Yes	Yes	72 hours	none
New Mexico	16	16	18	18	Yes	Yes	none	none
New York	16	14(e)	18	18	Yes	No	none	24 hrs.(f)
North Carolina(a)	16	16	18	18	Yes	No	none	none
North Dakota(a)	16	16	18	18	Yes	. . .	none	none
Ohio(a)	18	16	18	18	Yes	Yes	5 days	none
Oklahoma	16	16	18	18	Yes	No	none	none
Oregon	17	17	18	18	Yes	No	3 days	none
Pennsylvania	16	16	18	18	Yes	Yes	3 days	none
Rhode Island(a)(b)	14	12	18	18	Yes	No	none	none
South Carolina	16	14	18	18	none	none	24 hrs.	none
South Dakota	16	16	18	18	Yes	Yes	none	none
Tennessee(b)	16	16	18	18	Yes	Yes	3 days	none
Texas	14(k)	14(k)	18	18	Yes	Yes	none	none
Utah	14	14	18	18	Yes	Yes	none	none
Vermont(a)	18	16	18	18	Yes	. . .	none	5 days
Virginia(a)	16	16	18	18	No	No	none	none
Washington	17	17	18	18	(d)	. . .	3 days	none
West Virginia	18	16	18	18	Yes	No	3 days	none
Wisconsin	16	16	18	18	Yes	Yes	5 days	none
Wyoming	16	16	19	19	Yes	Yes	none	none
Puerto Rico	18	16	21	21	Yes	none	8 days	none
Virgin Islands	16	14	18	18	none	none	8 days	none

Divorce Requirements By State*

State	Breakdown of Marriage, Incompatibility	Cruelty	Desertion	Nonsupport	Alcohol &/or Drug Addiction	Felony	Impotency	Insanity	Living Separate and Apart	Other Grounds	Residence Time	Time Between Interlocut'y and Final Decrees
Alabama	X	X	X	X	X	X	X	X	2 yrs.	A-B-E	6 mos.	none-M
Alaska	X	X	X	...	X	X	X	X		B-C-F	none	none
Arizona	X	...	...	...	...	...	...	...			90 days	none
Arkansas	...	X	X	X	X	X	X	X	3 yrs.	C-I	3 mos.	none
California[2]	X	...	...	...	...	...	...	X			6 mos.	6 mos.
Colorado[2]	X	...	...	...	...	...	...	...			90 days	none
Connecticut	X	X	X	X	X	X	...	X	18 mos.	B	1 yr.	none
Delaware	X[4]	...	...	...	...	...	...	...	6 mos.		6 mos.	none
District of Columbia	...	...	...	...	...	...	...	...	6 mos.-1 yr.		6 mos.	none
Florida	X	...	...	...	...	...	...	X			6 mos.	none
Georgia	X	X	X	...	X	X	X	X		A-B-F	6 mos.	L
Hawaii	X	...	...	...	...	...	...	...	2 yrs.	K	3 mos.	none
Idaho	X	X	X	X	X	X	...	X	5 yrs.	H	6 wks.	none
Illinois	...	X	X	...	X	X	X	...		I-J	90 days	none

Adultery is either grounds for divorce or evidence of irreconcilable differences and a breakdown of the marriage in all states. The plaintiff can invariably remarry in the same state where he or she procured a decree of divorce or annulment. Not so the defendant, who is barred in certain states for some offenses. After a period of time has elapsed even the offender can apply for permission.

(1) Generally 5 yrs. insanity but: permanent insanity in Ut.; incurable insanity in Col.; 1 yr. Wis.; 18 mos. Alas.; 2 yrs. Ga., Ha., Ind., Nev., N.J., Ore., Wash., Wy.; 3 yrs. Ark., Cal., Fla., Md., Minn., Miss., N.C., Tex., W. Va.; 6 yrs. Ida.; Kan.: Incompatibility by reason of mental illness or incapacity.

(2) Cal., Colo., and Ore., have procedures whereby a couple can obtain a divorce without an attorney and without appearing in court provided certain requirements are met.

(3) Other grounds existing only in N.H. are: Joining a religious order disbelieving in marriage, treatment which injures health or endangers reason, wife without the state for 10 years, and wife in state 2 yrs. husband never in state and intends to become a citizen of a foreign country.

(4) Provable only by fault grounds, separation for some period, generally a year, proof of marital discord or commitment for mental illness.

(A) Pregnancy at marriage.

(B) Fraudulent contract.

(C) Indignities.

(D) Consanguinity.

(E) Crime against nature.

(F) Mental incapacity at time of marriage.

(G) Procurement of out-of-state divorce.

(H) Gross neglect of duty.

(I) Bigamy.

(J) Attempted homicide.

(K) Separation by decree in Conn.; after decree: one yr. in La., N.Y., Wis.; 18 mos. in N.H.; 2 yrs. in Ala., Ha., Minn., N.C., Tenn.; 3 yrs. in Ut.; 4 yrs. in N.J., N.D.; 5 yrs. in Md.

(L) Determined by court order.

(M) 60 days to remarry.

(N) One yr. to remarry except Ha. one yr. with minor child; La. 90 days.

(O) 6 mos. to remarry.

(P) Adultery cases, remarriage in court's discretion.

(Q) Plaintiff, 6 mos.; defendant 2 yrs. to remarry.

(R) No remarriage if an appeal is pending.

(S) Actual domicile in adultery cases.

(U) Abuse and neglect of child; physical or mental injury to child. **Enoch Arden Laws.** disappearance and unknown to be alive—Conn., S.C., Va., Vt., 7 yrs. absence; Ala., Ark., N.Y. 5 yrs. (called dissolution); N.H. 2 yrs.

N.B. Grounds not recognized for divorce may be recognized for separation or annulment. Local laws should be consulted.

*As of 1985

State	Breakdown of Marriage, Incompatibility	Cruelty	Desertion	Nonsupport	Alcohol &/or Drug Addiction	Felony	Impotency	Insanity	Living Separate and Apart	Other Grounds	Residence Time	Time Between Interlocut'y and Final Decrees
Indiana	X	...	...	...	...	X	X	X			6 mos.	none
Iowa	X	...	...	...	...	...	...	...			1 yr.	none-N
Kansas	X	...	...	...	...	...	...	...		H	60 days	none-M
Kentucky	X	...	...	...	...	...	...	...	1 yr.		180 days	none
Louisiana	...	X	X	X	X	X	...	...	1 yr.	C-J-K	12 mos.	none-N
Maine	X	X	X	X	X	...	X	X		H	6 mos.	none
Maryland	...	X	X	...	...	X	X	X	1-3 yrs.	D-I	1 yr.	none
Massachusetts	X[4]	X	X	X	X	X	X	...	6 mos.-1 yr.		1 yr.	6 mos.
Michigan	X	...	...	...	...	...	...	...			180 days	none
Minnesota	X	...	...	...	...	...	...	...		K	180 days	none-O
Mississippi	X	X	X	...	X	X	X	X		A	6 mos.	none-P
Missouri	X[4]	...	...	...	...	...	...	...			90 days	none
Montana	X	...	...	...	...	...	...	...			90 days	none
Nebraska	X	...	...	...	...	...	...	...			1 yr.	6 mos.
Nevada	X	...	...	...	...	...	...	X	1 yr.		6 wks.	none
New Hampshire[3]	X	X	X	X	X	X	X	...	2 yrs.	K	1 yr.	none
New Jersey	...	X	X	...	X	...	...	X	18 mos.	E-K	1 yr.	none
New Mexico	X	X	X	...	...	...	...	...			6 mos.	none
New York	...	X	X	...	...	X	...	...	1 yr.	K	1 yr.	none
North Carolina	...	...	...	...	...	...	X	X	1 yr.	A-E	6 mos.	none
North Dakota	X	X	X	X	X	X	X	X		H-K	12 mos.	none
Ohio	X	X	X	...	X	X	X	X	2 yrs.	B-G-H-I	6 mos.	none
Oklahoma	X	X	X	X	X	X	X	X		A-B-G-H	6 mos.	none
Oregon[2]	X	...	...	...	...	...	...	...		B	6 mos.	30 days
Pennsylvania	X	X	X	...	...	X	X	X	3 yrs.	C-D-I	6 mos.	none
Rhode Island	X	X	X	X	X	X	X	...	3 yrs.		1 yr.	3 mos.
South Carolina	...	X	X	...	X	...	...	...	1 yr.		3 mos.	none
South Dakota	X	X	X	X	X	X	...	...			none	none
Tennessee	X	X	X	X	X	X	X	...		A-H-I-J-K	6 mos.	none
Texas	X	X	X	...	...	X	...	X	3 yrs.		6 mos.	none-O
Utah	...	X	X	X	X	X	X	X		K	3 mos.	3 mos.
Vermont	...	X	X	X	...	X	...	X	6 mos.		6 mos.	3 mos.
Virginia	...	X	X	...	...	X	...	...	6 mos-1 yr.	E	6 mos.	3 mos.
Washington	X	...	...	...	...	...	...	...			none	none-R
West Virginia	X	X	X	...	X	X	...	X	1 yr.	U	1 yr.	none
Wisconsin	X	...	...	...	...	...	...	...	1 yr.	K	6 mos.	none-O
Wyoming	X	...	...	...	...	...	...	X	2 yrs.		60 days	none

Glossary

A

Abortion Induced or spontaneous termination of a pregnancy before the fetus is capable of surviving on its own.

Abstinence One of several premarital sexual values, based on the belief that sexual intercourse between unmarried men and women is wrong.

Adolescence The general social as well as biological changes a child experiences in becoming an adult.

Agapé Greek term for spiritual love.

Alienation A feeling of not being a part of a society.

Alternative birth center A special birth center that creates a homelike atmosphere for birth.

Ambivalence Simultaneous liking and disliking of an object or person.

Amniocentesis An important prenatal diagnostic tool. A long hollow needle is inserted through the mother's abdomen and into the amniotic sac, where a sample of the amniotic fluid is drawn off. This fluid contains sloughed-off cells from the fetus that may be examined microscopically for signs of disease or birth defects, enabling early treatment to be instituted. This technique may also determine the baby's gender.

Amniotic fluid The fluid that surrounds and insulates the fetus in the mother's womb.

Anaphrodisiac A drug or medicine that reduces sexual desire.

Androgen The dominant male hormone, which is thought to have an effect on aggression.

Androgynous The quality of having both masculine and feminine personality characteristics.

Aphrodisiac A chemical or other substance used to induce erotic arousal or to relieve impotence or infertility.

Areola The pigmented area surrounding the nipples of the breasts, a significant erogenous zone for about half of the male and female population.

Artificial insemination Induction of semen into the vagina or uterus by artificial means.

B

Bankruptcy Being financially insolvent, unable to pay one's bills.

Bigamy Being married to two people at the same time.

Binuclear family A family that includes children from two nuclear families; occurs when one or both of the divorced parents remarry.

Birth control Deliberate limitation of the number of children born.

Bisexuality Having sexual relationships with partners of the same and opposite sex.

Budget A plan for balancing expenses with estimated income.

C

Cesarean section The delivery of a baby by means of a surgical incision through the mother's abdominal and uterine walls. Cesareans are generally performed when the physical condition of the mother or the fetus is such that one or both might not survive the stress of vaginal delivery.

Child snatching The taking of children from the custodial spouse by the noncustodial spouse after a divorce.

Clitoris The small organ situated just under the upper portion of the labia minora of the female genitalia. It is the homologue of the male penis, consists of a shaft and a glans, and becomes erect with sexual arousal. It is also the chief organ for erotic arousal in most women.

Cluster family An artificially contrived family group that meets for companionship, recreation, and other meaningful experiences without the members actually living together.

Cohabitation A man and woman living together in an intimate relationship without being legally married.

Common-law marriage A marriage that becomes legally recognized after the woman and man have lived together for some time as though they were wife and husband.

Commune A group of people who live together by choice rather than because of blood or legal ties. Also referred to as an intentional community.

Conception Fertilization of the egg by the sperm to start a new human life.

Condom Also known as a "rubber" or "prophylactic," the condom is a thin sheath, usually made of rubber, which is rolled over and down the shaft of the erect penis prior to intercourse. While used primarily as a method of contraception, it also protects against venereal disease.

Congenital defect A condition existing at birth or before, caused by the intrauterine environment; as distinguished from a genetic defect.

Consumer Price Index (CPI) A sample of costs of goods and services collected by the Bureau of Labor Statistics, which are then compared with some arbitrarily set base period (now set at 1967).

Contraception A deliberate action to prevent fertilization of the ovum as a result of copulation.

Contraceptive Any agent used to prevent conception.

Credit buying Purchasing goods by making payments for them over a period of time.

Cunnilingus Oral contact with female genitalia.

D

D&C (dilatation and curettage) A procedure usually used to induce an abortion during the first twelve weeks of pregnancy. It involves dilating (stretching) the cervix and scraping away the contents of the uterus with a sharp instrument (curette). The operation requires no incision, recovery is usually rapid, and most patients are in the hospital only overnight. (Used as a diagnostic procedure, a D&C is performed to determine the cause of abnormal menstrual bleeding or to determine the cause of bleeding after the menopause.)

Dating Social interaction and activity with a person of the opposite sex.

DES Abbreviation for diethylstilbestrol, known as the morning-after pill. It contains high doses of estrogen and terminates a pregnancy if taken within twenty-four hours of intercourse.

Diaphragm A contraceptive device consisting of a circular piece of thin rubber that is fitted by a physician so that it spans the back of the vagina and covers the cervix. Spermicidal jelly often is used in conjunction with the diaphragm.

Discount interest Interest paid on the full amount initially borrowed even though some of the loan is repaid each month.

Double standard Different standards of appropriate sexual behavior for men than for women; the acceptability for men but not for women of all types of sexual behavior.

Douche   Flushing the vagina with water or with a spermicidal agent after intercourse. A relatively unreliable method of contraception.

Dual-career family   A marriage in which both spouses pursue their own careers.

E

Ejaculation   The expulsion of semen by the male during orgasm.

Embryo   The developing organism from the second to the eighth week of pregnancy, characterized by differentiation of organs and tissues into their human form.

Empty-nest stage   Period in a marriage that begins when the last child leaves home and continues until either spouse retires or dies.

Enculturation   The process of learning the mores, rules, ways, and manners of a given culture.

Endogamy   The inclination or the necessity to marry within a particular group.

Engagement   The final courtship stage before marriage; characterized by public knowledge of the coming marriage.

Episiotomy   A surgical incision made in the mother's perineum during childbirth in order to prevent tearing of the vaginal tissues.

Eros   The physical, sexual side of love; termed "Cupid" by the Romans.

Estrogen   Often called the "female hormone," it is active in many important ways, such as directing the differentiation of embryonic tissue into female genitalia, directing the differentiation of prenatal brain tissue that governs various female physiological functions, and directing the development of female secondary sexual characteristics at puberty. It is produced chiefly in the ovaries and adrenal cortex of the female and, to a lesser extent, in the testicles and adrenal cortex of the male.

Exogamy   The inclination or the necessity to marry outside a particular group.

Extended family   A nuclear or polygamous family and the parental generation. The typical extended family includes the husband, wife, their children, and the parents (or aunts/uncles) of the spouses.

F

Fallopian tubes   The two tubes in the female reproductive system which link the ovaries to the uterus. Eggs released from the ovaries move down these tubes to the uterus.

Family   A group of two or more persons who are related by blood, marriage, or adoption (U.S. Census definition). The term usually implies the presence of children, a common residence, and economic cooperation.

Family enrichment programs   Groups of three to five families who meet together for mutual care and support and for the development of family potential.

Family life cycle   A model designed to explain the behavior patterns of married couples. It divides marriage into various stages according to the number, age, and health of a married couple's children.

Family of orientation   The family into which an individual is born or adopted.

Family of procreation   The family which one begins by marrying andd having one's own children.

Family planning   Controlling the number and spacing of children through systematic use of contraceptive methods.

Fellatio   Oral contact with male genitalia.

Fetal monitoring   Using various instruments to measure the vital signs of the fetus during the birth process.

Fetoscopy   Examining the fetus through a small viewing tube inserted into the mother's uterus.

Fetus   The name given to the developing human organism from eight weeks after conception until birth.

G

Gender   Attitudes and behavior associated with each of the two sexes.

Genes   The subcellular structures within the chromosomes in the cell nucleus that contain the DNA molecules and determine the traits of the differentiating cells of the organism.

Genetic defect   An abnormality in the development of the fetus that is inherited through the genes, as distinguished from a congenital defect.

Genitalia   The external reproductive organs.

Genotype   The underlying genetic trait that, in contrast to the *phenotype*, is not readily observable.

Gonorrhea   A venereal disease caused by gonococci. Unlike syphilis, which typically involves the entire body, gonorrhea usually remains localized in the genitalia and is self-limiting, although it may persist and cause serious and permanent damage, including sterility. Symptoms are common in men, but the disease is often asymptomatic in women and difficult to detect.

Gross National Product (G.N.P.)   Total value of a nation's annual output of goods and services.

H

Halo effect   The tendency for a first impression to influence subsequent judgments about something.

Hermaphrodite   A person who has both male and female organs, or organs that are indeterminant (such as a clitoris that resembles a penis).

Heterogamy   The mutual attraction and compatibility of persons with opposite and complementary personality traits—for example, dominance-submission, nurturance-dependence, achievement-vicarious.

Home birth   Giving birth at one's home rather than in a hospital.

Homogamy   The strongly practical attraction of persons who share similar objective characteristics, such as race, religion, ethnic group, intelligence, education, social class, age, and interests and skills.

Hysterectomy   A surgical procedure which removes a woman's uterus. While hysterectomies result in sterility for the woman, they are usually conducted because of a malignancy.

I

Impotence   The inability of a man to experience erection. It may be caused by either physical or psychological factors and is usually temporary.

Incest   Copulation between closely blood-tied relatives. The degree of closeness that is considered incestuous depends on social attitudes, but all societies proscribe sexual relations between parents and children and between siblings.

Infanticide   The deliberate killing of infants as a measure to control population or for some other socially accepted purpose.

Infertility   Inability to produce children.

Inflation   A sustained rise in the average of all prices.

Inflationary recession A falling off of business activity at the same time that prices are rising.

Intimacy Experiencing the essence of oneself in intense intellectual, physical, and/or emotional relationships with others.

Intrauterine device Known as the IUD, it is a small object that a physician inserts into a woman's uterus to prevent conception from occurring.

Investment Use of money to earn more money, such as putting it in a business or in stocks.

J

Jealousy The state of being resentfully suspicious of a loved one's behavior toward a suspected rival.

L

Labor Changes in a woman's body as it prepares to deliver a child, consisting mainly of muscle contractions and dilation of the cervix.

Laparoscopy A sterilization procedure for females involving the use of a telescope instrument (laparoscope) to locate the Fallopian tubes, which are then cauterized.

Legal separation A legal decree that forbids cohabitation by husband and wife and provides for separate maintenance and support of the wife and children by the husband. A legally separated couple is still bound by the marital contract and may not remarry.

M

Marriage contract A written agreement between married partners outlining the responsibilities and obligations of each partner.

Masturbation Any voluntary erotic activity that involves self-stimulation.

Menopause The cessation of ovulation, menstruation, and fertility in the woman. It usually occurs between ages forty-five and fifty.

Menstruation The discharge of blood and the unfertilized ovum from the uterus through the vagina; normally occurs every twenty-eight days in women from puberty to menopause.

Mental health A mode of being in which a person is free of mental problems and/or disease.

Middlescence The second adolescence experienced in middle age, usually involving reevaluation of one's life.

Midlife crisis The questioning of one's worth and values, usually beginning sometime in one's forties or early fifties.

Midwife A person, usually a woman, trained to assist in childbirth or, in some countries, to perform delivery.

Miscarriage A spontaneous abortion.

Miscegenation Marriage or interbreeding between members of different races.

Modeling Learning vicariously by observing others' behavior.

Monogamy The state of being married to one person at a time.

N

Natural childbirth Birth wherein the parents have learned about the birthing process and participate via exercises such as breathing techniques so as to minimize pain.

Naturalism, myth of The belief that two people will naturally get along in marriage if they love each other.

No-fault divorce Divorce proceedings that do not place blame for the divorce on one spouse or the other.

Norm Accepted social rules for behavior.

Nuclear family A group of persons, consisting of a married couple and their children, who live by themselves. The children may be natural or adopted by the couple.

O

Open marriage A relationship that emphasizes role equality and the freedom for each partner to maximize his or her own potential; may or may not involve extramarital sex.

Oral contraceptive Hormonal materials (in pill form) that suspend ovulation and therefore prevent conception.

Orgasm The climax of excitement in sexual activity.

Ovaries The female sex glands in which the ova (eggs) are formed.

Ovulation The regular monthly process in the fertile woman whereby an ovarian follicle ruptures and releases a mature ovum (egg).

Ovum The female reproductive cell (egg) that when fertilized develops into a new member of the same species.

P

Paracervical anesthesia Injection of a pain killer, such as Novocain, into the cervix to reduce pain during childbirth.

Phenomenology The study of how people subjectively experience their environment.

Philos Greek term for the love found in deep, enduring friendships; a general love of mankind.

Placenta The organ that connects the fetus to the uterus by means of the umbilical cord.

Polyandry A form of marriage in which one woman has more than one husband.

Polygamy Marriage with multiple spouses (as opposed to *monogamy*, with one spouse).

Polygyny A form of marriage in which one man has more than one wife.

Postpartum depression Also known as the blues, it is a feeling of depression, after giving birth, characterized by irritability, crying, loss of appetite, and difficulty in sleeping. Such feelings are thought to be a result of numerous physiological and psychological changes that occur as a result of pregnancy, labor, and delivery.

Premature ejaculation The inability to delay ejaculation as long as the male or his partner wishes.

Prenatal Existing or occurring before birth.

Propinquity Nearness in time or place.

Puberty Biological changes a child goes through to become an adult capable of reproduction.

R

Recession A temporary falling off of business activity.

Reconstituted family A husband and wife, at least one of whom has been married before, and one or more children from previous marriage(s).

Rh factor An element found in the blood of most people that can adversely affect fetal development if the parents differ on the element (Rh negative versus Rh positive).

Rhythm method   A birth-control method involving avoidance of sexual intercourse when the egg is in the Fallopian tubes. The "calendar method" and the "temperature method" are used to predict this time. The rhythm method is a relatively unreliable contraceptive technique.

Role   Particular type of behavior one is expected to exhibit when occupying a certain place in a group.

Romantic love   Love at first sight, based on the ideas that there is only one true love and that love is the most important criterion for marriage.

Rooming-in   The practice of placing the newborn in the mother's room after delivery so that the mother (and father) can care for it.

S

Saline abortion   An abortion-inducing procedure in which a salt solution is injected into the amniotic sac to kill the fetus, which is then expelled via uterine contractions.

Self-actualization   The process of developing one's cognitive, emotional, social, and physical potential.

Semen   The secretion of the male reproductive organs that is ejaculated from the penis during orgasm and contains the sperm cells.

Sensitivity training   Training in learning to understand and be more aware of one's body, its feelings and functioning.

Serial marriage   The process of having a series of marriages, one after the other.

Sex therapy   Therapy of any kind designed to help persons overcome sexual problems.

Sexually transmitted disease (STD)   Any contagious disease communicated mainly by sexual interaction.

Simple interest   Interest paid only on the unpaid balance of a loan.

Socialization   The process of a person's learning—from parents, peers, social institutions, and other sources—the skills, knowledge, and roles necessary for competent and socially acceptable behavior in the society.

Spermaticides   The chemical substances that destroy or immobilize sperm and are used as contraceptives.

Stepparent   The husband or wife of one's parent by a later marriage.

Sterility   The permanent inability to reproduce.

Sterilization   Any procedure (usually surgical) by which an individual is made incapable of reproduction.

Surrogate mother   A woman who becomes pregnant and gives birth to a child for another woman who is incapable of giving birth.

Swinging   Agreement by married couples to swap mates sexually.

Syphilis   A venereal disease caused by a microorganism called a *spiro-*

chete. Syphilis goes through four stages, each with separate and distinct characteristics, and can involve every part of the body. It is transmitted by contact of mucous membrane or broken skin with an infectious syphilitic lesion.

T

Testosterone   An important component of the male sex hormone androgen. It is responsible for inducing and maintaining the male secondary sexual characteristics.

Transsexualism   A compulsion or obsession to become a member of the opposite sex through surgical changes.

Transvestism   A sexual deviation characterized by a compulsive desire to wear garments of the opposite sex.

Trial marriage   Cohabitation between two people who intend to marry.

Tubal ligation   A sterilization procedure for females in which the Fallopian tubes are cut or tied.

U

Ultrasound   Sound waves directed at the fetus that yield a visual picture of the fetus; used to detect potential problems in fetal development.

Umbilical cord   A flexible cordlike structure connecting the fetus to the placenta and through which the fetus is fed and waste products are discharged.

Uterus   The hollow, pear-shaped organ in females within which the fetus develops; the womb.

V

Vacuum aspiration   An abortion-inducing procedure in which the contents of the uterus are removed by suction.

Vasectomy   A sterilization procedure for males involving the surgical cutting of the vas deferens.

Virginity   Not having experienced sexual intercourse.

W

Withdrawal   Removing the penis from the vagina before ejaculation. A relatively unreliable method of contraception.

Bibliography

Abarbanel, A. "Shared Parenting After Separation and Divorce: A Study of Joint Custody." *American Journal of Orthopsychiatry*, April 1979, 320–329.

Adams, B. *The Family: A Sociological Interpretation*. New York: Harcourt Brace Jovanovich, 1986.

Adams, D., Gold, A., and Burt, A. "Rise in Female-Initiated Sexual Activity at Ovulation and Its Suppression by Oral Contraceptives." *New England Journal of Medicine* (November 23, 1978): 1145–1150.

Adams, V. "Getting at the Heart of Jealous Love." *Psychology Today*, May 1980.

Addiego, F., et al. "Female Ejaculation?" *Medical Aspects of Human Sexuality*, August 1980, 99–103.

Advertising Age, September 4, 1986.

Albrecht, S. "Correlates of Marital Happiness Among the Remarried." *Journal of Marriage and the Family*, November 1979, 857–867.

American Friends Service Committee. *Who Shall Live?* New York: Hill and Wang, 1970.

Andrews, L. B. "Yours, Mine and Theirs." *Psychology Today* (December 1984): 20–29.

Archer, J. "Gender Roles as Developmental Pathways." *British Journal of Social Psychology* 23 (1984): 245–256.

Archer, J., and Lloyd, B. *Sex and Gender.* Cambridge, England: Cambridge University Press, 1985.

Associated Press. "No Differences Seen in Childbirth Methods." *Santa Barbara News Press*, April 15, 1980, A-5.

Avioli, P. S. "The Labor Force Participation of Married Mothers of Infants." *Journal of Marriage and the Family* 47 (August 1985): 739–745.

Baca Zinn, M. "Political Familism: Toward Sex Role Equality in Chicano Families." *Journal of Social Sciences and Arts*, Winter 1975, 13–26.

———. "Chicanas: Power and Control in the Domestic Sphere." *DeColores*, Fall 1976, 19–31.

———. "Employment and Education of Mexican-American Women: The Interplay of Modernity and Ethnicity in Eight Families." *Harvard Educational Review*, February 1980, 47–62.

Bach, G., and Deutsch, R. *Pairing*. New York: David McKay, 1974.

Bach, G., and Wyden, P. *The Intimate Enemy.* New York: Avon, 1968.

Bachrach, C. A., and Mosher, W. D. "Voluntary Childlessness in the United States: Estimates from the National Survey of Family Growth." *Journal of Family Issues* (December 1982).

Bader, E., et al. "Do Marriage Preparation Programs Really Help?" Paper presented at the National Council on Family Relations Annual Conference. Milwaukee, Wis., October 1981.

Baker, L. "In My Opinion: The Sexual Revolution in Perspective." *Family Relations*, April 1983.

Baker, R. *Growing Up*. New York: New American Library, 1982.

Ball, R. E., and Robbins, L. "Marital Status and Family Life Satisfaction Among Black Americans." *Journal of Marriage and the Family*, May 1986, 389–394.

Bandura, A. *Principles of Behavior Modification*. New York: Holt, Rinehart and Winston, 1969.

Bane, M. *Here to Stay: American Families in the Twentieth Century.* New York: Basic Books, 1976.

Barclay, A. M. "Biopsychological Perspectives on Sexual Behavior." In *Sexuality: A Search for Perspective*, edited by D. Grummon and A. Barclay. New York: Van Nostrand Reinhold, 1971, 52–54.

Barnett, R., and Baruch, G. "Women Still Do the Majority of Childcare and Housework." Report on their study by Susan Cunningham (staff writer) found in *Monitor*. Washington, D.C.: American Psychological Association, November 1983, 16.

Barnhill, L. "Healthy Family Systems." *Family Coordinator*, January 1979, 94–100.

Barnhill, L., Rubenstein, G., and Rocklin, N. "From Generation to Generation: Fathers to Be in Transition." *Family Coordinator*, April 1979, 229–235.

Barocas, R., and Karoly, P. "Effects of Physical Appearance on Social Responsiveness." *Psychology Report* 31 (1972): 495–500.

Barrett, C., and Noble, H. "Mother's Anxieties versus the Effects of Long-distance Move on Children." *Journal of Marriage and the Family*, May 1973, 181–188.

Barrett, K. "Date Rape: A Campus Epidemic." *Ms*, September 1982.

Barrett, N. "Women in the Job Market: Unemployment and Work Schedules." In *The Subtle Revolution: Women at Work*, edited by R. Smith. Washington, D.C.: The Urban Institute, 1979.

Beck, S. H., and Beck, R. W. "The Formation of Extended Households During Middle Age." *Journal of Marriage and the Family*, May 1984, 277–287.

Becker, G. E., Landes, E., and Michael, R. "Economics of Marital Instability." Working paper no. 153. Stanford, California: Bureau of Economic Research, 1976.

Beeson, B., and Williams, A. Research reported in the *Santa Barbara News Press*, 10 October 1983, C-10.

Bell, C. "Comparable Worth: How Do We Know It Will Work?" *Monthly Labor Review.* Washington, D.C.: Bureau of Labor Statistics, December 1985, 5–12.

Bell, R. *Marriage and Family Interaction*. Homewood, Ill.: Dorsey, 1975.

Bell, R., and Coughey, K. "Premarital Sexual Experience among College Females, 1958, 1968, and 1978." *Family Relations*, July 1980, 353–357.

Bell, S. "Birth Control." In *The New Our Body, Ourselves*. Boston: Women's Health Book Collective, 1984.

Belsky, J., Lang, M. E., and Rovine, M. "Stability and Change in Marriage Across the Transition to Parenthood: A Second Study." *Journal of Marriage and the Family*, November 1985, 855–865.

Belsky, J., Learner, J., and Spanier, G. B. *The Children in the Family.* Reading, Mass.: Addison-Wesley, 1984.

Belsky, J., Spanier, G. B., and Rovine, M. "Stability and Change in Marriage Across the Transition to Parenthood." *Journal of Marriage and the Family*, August 1983, 567–577.

Benedek, E., and Benedek, R. "Joint Custody: Solution or Illusion." *American Journal of Psychiatry*, December 1979, 1540–1544.

Bengtson, V. "Diversity and Symbolism in Grandparental Roles." In *Grandparenting*, edited by Y. L. Bengtson and J. F. Robertson. Beverly Hills, Calif.: Sage, 1985, 11–25.

Bentler, P., and Newcomb, M. "Longitudinal Study of Marital Success and Failure." *Journal of Consulting and Clinical Psychology* 46 (1978): 1053–1070.

Berelson, B. *The Population Council Annual Report*. New York: Population Council, 1972.

Berger, D., and Wenger, L. "How Close Is the Pill for Men?" *Parade*, 8 September 1985, 18, 20. (For more information, write to Dr. C. Alvin Paulsen, University of Washington, % Pacific Medical Center, Dept. P, 1200 12th Ave. South, Seattle, Washington 98144.)

Berger, K. *The Developing Person Through Childhood and Adolescence.* New York: Worth, 1986.

Berk, R., and Berk, S. *Labor and Leisure at Home.* Beverly Hills, Calif.: Sage, 1979.

Berk-Fenstermaker, S. *The Gender Factory: The Apportionment of Work in American Households.* New York: Plenum Press, 1985.

Bernard, J. *The Future of Marriage.* New York: World, 1972.

Bernard, J., et al. "Courtship Violence and Sex Typing." *Family Relations* 34 (1985): 573–576.

Bernard, M., and Bernard, J. "Violent Intimacy: The Family as a Model for Love Relationships." *Family Relations* 32 (1983): 283–286.

Bernard, S., et al. "Courtship Violence and Sex-Typing." *Family Relations*, October 1985, 573–576.

Bianchi, S., and Farley, R. "Racial Differences in Family Living Arrangements and Economic Well Being: An Analysis of Recent Trends." *Journal of Marriage and the Family* (August 1979): 537–551.

Biddle, B. *Role Theory: Expectations, Identities, and Behaviors.* Chicago: Dryden, 1976.

Bienvenu, M. "Measurement of Marital Communication." *The Family Coordinator*, January 1970, 26–31.

Blake, J. "Is Zero Preferred? American Attitudes toward Childlessness in the 1970s." *Journal of Marriage and the Family* 41, no. 2 (1979): 245–257.

Blakeslee, S. "Caesarean Section Choice for 1 out of 5 Births." *Santa Barbara News Press*, March 24, 1985, A-14.

Blau, F. D., and Ferber, M. A. "Women in the Labor Market: The Last Twenty Years." In *Women and Work: An Annual Review*, edited by L. Larwood, et al. Beverly Hills, Calif.: Sage, 1985, 19–49.

Blizard, D. A. "Sex Differences in Running-wheel Behavior in the Rat: The Inductive and Activational Effects of Gonadal Hormones." *Animal Behavior* 31 (1983):378–384.

Blood, R. O., and Blood, M. C. "Amicable Divorce." *Alternative Lifestyles* 2, no. 4 (1979): 483–498.

Blumstein, P., and Schwartz, P. *American Couples.* New York: Pocket Books, 1983.

Bohannan, P. *All the Happy Families.* New York: McGraw-Hill, 1984.

———. *Divorce and After.* Garden City, N.Y.: Doubleday, 1970.

Borland, D. "An Alternative Model of the Wheel Theory." *Family Coordinator* 24 (1975): 289–292.

Boston Women's Health Book Collective. *The New Our Bodies, Ourselves.* New York: Simon & Schuster, 1973, 1976, 1984.

Boulding, E. "Familia Faber: The Family as Maker of the Future." *Journal of Marriage and the Family*, May 1983, 257–266.

Brinley, M. "Should You Have a Baby?" *McCall's*, January 1984, 28.

British Birth Survey 1970. London: William Heinemann Medical Books, 1975.

Brody, J. "Vasectomy Procedure Gains Favor among American Men." *Santa Barbara News Press*, 19 November 1979, F-20.

Bruck, C. "Menopause." *Human Behavior*, April 1979, 195–201.

Budd, L. "Problems Disclosure and Commitment of Cohabiting and Married Couples." Ph.D. diss., University of Minnesota, 1976.

Bumpass, L., and Sweet, A. "Differentials in Marital Instability, 1970." *American Society Review*, December 1977, 754–766.

Burk, R., and Weir, T. "Relationship of Wife's Employment Status to Husband, Wife and Pair Satisfaction and Performance." *Journal of Marriage and the Family* 38 (May 1976): 279–287.

Burns, A. "Perceived Causes of Marital Breakdown and Conditions of Life." *Journal of Marriage and the Family*, August 1984, 551–562.

Business Week. "Women at Work." 28 January 1985, 80–85.

Calderone, M. "Love, Sex, Intimacy, and Aging as a Life Style." In *Sex, Love, and Intimacy—Whose Life Styles?*, edited by M. Calderone. New York: SIECUS, 1972.

California Commission on the Status of Women. *Status of Women.* Sacramento, Calif.: 1986.

Campbell, A. *The Sense of Well-Being in America.* New York: McGraw-Hill, 1981.

Canfield, E. "On the Sex Education Frontiers." Talk given at the California Council on Family Relations Annual Conference, Anaheim, Calif., 18–20 October 1979.

Carlson v. Olson, 256 N.W.2d 249 (1977).

Cash, T., and Janda, L. "The Eye of the Beholder." *Psychology Today*, December 1984, 46–52.

Cash, T., Winstead, B., and Janda, L. "The Great American Shape-up." *Psychology Today*, April 1986, 30–37.

Casler, L. "This Thing Called Love." *Psychology Today*, December 1969.

Cavanagh, J. "Rhythm of Sexual Desire in Women." *Medical Aspects of Human Sexuality*, February 1969, 29–39.

Chafetz, J. *Masculine/Feminine or Human?* Itasca, Ill.: Peacock, 1974.

Chasnoff, I. J., et al. "Cocaine Use in Pregnancy." *New England Journal of Medicine*, September 12, 1985, 666–669.

Chassler, S. "Men Listening." *Ms*, August 1984.

Cherlin, A. *Marriage, Divorce, Remarriage.* Cambridge, Mass.: Harvard University Press, 1981.

———. "Remarriage as an Incomplete Institution." *American Journal of Sociology* 84, no. 3 (1978): 634–650.

———. "The Effects of Children on Marital Dissolution." *Demography*, August 1977, 265–272.

Cherlin, A., and Furstenberg, F. "Styles and Strategies of Grandparenting." In *Grandparenting*, edited by V. L. Bengtson and J. F. Robertson. Beverly Hills, Calif.: Sage, 1985, 97–116.

Chillman, C. "Parent Satisfactions, Concerns, and Goals for Their Children." *Family Relations*, July 1980a, 339–346.

Chira, S. "Town Experiment Cuts TV." *New York Times*, 11 February 1984.

Clark, C., et al. "Path-analytic Model of Postpartum Depression and Somatic Complaints." Paper presented at the American Psychological Association annual convention, Anaheim, Calif., August 26–30, 1983.

Clark, H. *Cases and Problems on Domestic Relations.* 3d ed. St. Paul, Minn.: West, 1980.

Clark, J. *The Importance of Being Imperfect.* New York: McKay, 1961.

Clatworthy, N., and Scheid, L. "A Comparison of Married Couples: Premarital Cohabitants and Non-premarital Cohabitants." Ohio State University, 1977. Manuscript.

Clayton, R., and Bakemeier, J. "Premarital Sex in the Seventies." *Journal of Marriage and the Family* (1980): 759–775.

Close, H. "To the Child: On Parenting." *Voices*, Spring 1968.

Cochran, M. M., and Gunnarsson, L. "A Follow-up Study of Group Day Care and Family-based Childrearing Patterns." *Journal of Marriage and the Family*, May 1985, 297–309.

Cohen, A. "Building New Families: Current Issues in Adoption." Talk given at the International Conference of Family Strengths at Los Angeles, 20–22 April 1986.

Coleman, M., and Ganong, L. H. "Remarriage Myths: Implications for the Helping Professions." *Journal of Counseling and Development*, October 1985, 116–120.

Coleman, M., et al. "Stepfamily Strengths: A Review of Popular Literature." *Family Relations*, October 1985, 583–588.

———. "Strengths of Stepfamilies Identified in Professional Literature." In *Family Strengths 5: Vital Connections*, edited by S. Van Zandt, et al. Lincoln, Neb.: University of Nebraska Press, 1986.

Coogler, O. S., Weber, R., and McKenry, P. "Divorce Mediation: A Means of Facilitating Divorce and Adjustment." *Family Coordinator*, April 1979, 255–259.

Cordell, A. S., et al. "Fathers' Views on Fatherhood with Special Reference to Infancy." *Family Relations*, July 1980, 331–338.

Corder, J., and Stephan, C. "Females' Combination of Work and Family Roles: Adolescent's Aspirations." *Journal of Marriage and the Family*, May 1984, 391–402.

Council of Economic Advisors. *Annual Economic Report to the President: 1984.* Washington, D.C.: U.S. Government Printing Office, 1985.

Coveney, L., et al. *The Sexuality Papers.* London: Hutchinson, 1984.

Coverman, S., and Sheley, S. F. "Change in Men's Housework and Child-care Time, 1965–1975." *Journal of Marriage and the Family*, May 1986, 413–422.

Covi, R. B., and Robinson, B. E. "Stepfamilies: A Review of the Literature with Suggestions for Practitioners." *Journal of Counseling and Development*, October 1985, 121–125.

Cox, F. "Premarital Sex and Religion." Unpublished study, Santa Barbara City College, 1978.

Cozby, P. W. "Self-Disclosure: A Literature Review." *Psychological Bulletin*, July 1973, 73–91.

Cramer, D. W., et al. "Tubal Infertility and the Intrauterine Device." *New England Journal of Medicine* 312, no. 15 (1985): 941–947.

Cromwell, R., and Thomas, V. "Developing Resources for Family Potential: A Family Action Model." *The Family Coordinator* 25 (January 1976): 13–22.

Cromwell, V., and Cromwell, R. "Perceived Dominance in Decision Making and Conflict Resolution Among Black and Chicano Couples." *Journal of Marriage and the Family*, November 1978, 749–759.

Crosbie-Burnett, M. "The Centrality of the Step Relationship: A Challenge to Family Theory and Practice." *Family Relations* 33 (1984): 459–464.

Crosby, J. "A Critique of Divorce Statistics and Their Interpretation." *Family Relations*, January 1980, 51–58.

———. *Reply to Myth: Perspectives on Intimacy.* New York: John Wiley & Sons, 1985.

Crowe, M. "Toxic Shock Syndrome (TSS): A Newly Recognized Disease." In *The New Our Body, Ourselves*, by The Boston Women's Health Book Collective. Boston: Simon & Schuster, 1984.

Curran, D. *Traits of a Healthy Family.* New York: Ballantine, 1983.

Cutler, B. R., and Dyer, W. G. "Initial Adjustment Process in Young Married Couples." *Social Forces,* December 1966, 195–201.

Daling, J. R., et al. "Primary Tubal Infertility in Relation to the Use of the Intrauterine Device." *New England Journal of Medicine* 312, no. 15 (1985): 938–940.

Dalton, K. *Once a Month.* Pomona, Calif.: Hunter House, 1979.

Darnley, F. "Adjustment to Retirement: Integrity or Despair." *The Family Coordinator*, April 1975.

David, H., and Baldwin, W. "Childbearing and Child Development: De-mographic and Psychosocial Trends." *American Psychologist*, October 1979, 866–871.

Davis, K. E. "Near and Dear: Friendship and Love Compared." *Psychology Today*, February 1985, 22–28, 30.

Dean, P. "Women in the Air Force." *Los Angeles Times*, 2 February 1986, VI-1, 12, 13.

DeBoer, L., and Seeborg, M. "The Female-Male Unemployment Differential: Effects of Changes in Industry Employment." *Monthly Labor Review.* Washington, D.C.: Bureau of Labor Statistics, November 1984, 8–15.

DeLamater, J., and MacCorquodale, P. *Premarital Sexuality: Attitudes, Relationships, Behavior.* Madison, Wis.: University of Wisconsin Press, 1979.

DeMaris, A. "A Comparison of Remarriages with First Marriages on Satisfaction in Marriage and Its Relationship to Prior Cohabitation." *Family Relations* 33 (1984): 443–449.

DeMaris, A., and Leslie, G. "Cohabitation with the Future Spouse: Its Influence Upon Marital Satisfaction and Communication." *Journal of Marriage and the Family* 46 (1984): 77–84.

Diamond, S. S. "Women on the Job: Surge Widely Felt." *Los Angeles Times*, 9 September 1984.

Dick-Read, G. *Childbirth without Fear.* 4th ed. New York: Harper & Row, 1972.

Dion, K., Berscheid, K., and Walster, E. "What Is Beautiful Is Good." *Journal of Personality and Social Psychology* 24 (1972): 285–290.

Dixon, R., and Weitzman, L. "Evaluating the Impact of No-Fault Divorce in California." *Family Relations*, July 1980, 297–307.

———. "When Husbands File for Divorce." *Journal of Marriage and the Family*, February 1982, 103–115.

Doherty, W. J., and Lester, M. E. "Casualties of Marriage Encounter Weekends." *Family Therapy News* 13 (1982): 4, 9.

Doherty, W. J., McCabe, P., and Ryder, R. G. "Marriage Encounter: A Critical Appraisal." *Journal of Marriage and Family Counseling* 4 (1978): 99–106.

Doress, P. B. "Women Growing Older." In *The New Our Body, Ourselves*, by the Boston Women's Health Book Collective. Boston: Simon & Schuster, 1984.

Dreskin, W., and Dreskin, W. *The Day Care Decision: What's Best for You and Your Child.* New York: M. Evans, 1983.

Duberman, L. *Marriage and Its Alternatives.* New York: Praeger, 1974, 1977.

———. "Step-Kin Relationships." *Journal of Marriage and the Family*, May 1973, 283–292.

Easley, E. B. "Sexual Effect of Female Sterilization." *Medical Aspects of Human Sexuality* 6 (February 1972).

Echegaray, M. "Having a Baby without a Doctor: The Rebirth of Midwives." *McCalls*, April 1982, 37–38.

Edwards, J. N., and Saunders, J. M. "Coming Apart: A Model of the Marital Dissolution Decision." *Journal of Marriage and the Family*, May 1981, 379–389.

Ehrenreich, B. *The Hearts of Men.* New York: Doubleday, 1983.

Ehrenreich, B., and Piven, F. "The Feminization of Poverty: When the Family Wage System Breaks Down." *Dissent*, Spring 1984.

Ekman, P. *Telling Lies: Clues to Deceit in the Marketplace, Politics and Marriage.* New York: W. W. Norton, 1985.

Elkin, M. "Premarital Counseling for Minors: The Los Angeles Experience." *The Family Coordinator*, October 1977, 429–443.

———. "Drawing Individual and Family Strengths from the Divorce Process." Talk given at the California Council on Family Relations Annual Conference. Santa Barbara, Calif., 26 September 1980.

Engebretson, J. "Stepmothers as First-time Parents: Their Needs and Problems." *Pediatric Nursing* 8 (1982): 387–390.

English, V. "The War Against Choice: Inside the Abortion Movement." *Mother Jones*, February/March 1981.

Entwisle, D. R., and Doering, S. G. *The First Birth*. Baltimore, Md.: Johns Hopkins University Press, 1980.

Erbes, J. T., and Hedderson, S. C. "A Longitudinal Examination of the Separation/Divorce Process." *Journal of Marriage and the Family*, November 1984, 937–941.

Erikson, E. H. *Childhood and Society*. 2d ed. New York: Norton, 1963.

Etzioni, A. *An Immodest Agenda: Rebuilding America Before the 21st Century*. New York: McGraw-Hill, 1983.

Family Planning Perspectives. "No Atherosclerosis Risk in Vasectomized Men, Preliminary Studies Find." 13, no. 6 (1981): 276.

Farber, B. *Family Organization and Interaction*. San Francisco: Chandler, 1964.

Ferber, M. A. "Labor Market Participation of Young Married Women: Causes and Effects." *Journal of Marriage and the Family* 44, no. 2 (1982): 457–475.

Field, M. "California Poll on Women." *San Francisco Chronicle*, 13 February 1986, 1.

Finkelhor, D. "The Prevention of Child Sexual Abuse: An Overview of Needs and Problems." In *Siecus Report*. New York: Sex Education and Education Council of the U.S., September 1984, 1–5.

Fisher, K. "Parents at Work: Please Yield." *Monitor*, October 1985, 8.

Fishman, B., and Hamel, B. "The Economic Behavior of Stepfamilies." *Family Relations* 32 (1983): 359–366.

Ford, D. A. "Wife Battery and Criminal Justice: A Study of Victim Decision-making." *Family Relations*, October 1983, 463–475.

Freidan, B. *The Second Stage*. New York: Summit Books, 1981.

———. *The Feminine Mystique*. New York: Dell, 1963.

Friedrich, O. "A Legal Moral Social Nightmare." *Time*, 10 September 1984, 54–56.

Friday, N. *My Secret Garden: Women's Sexual Fantasies*. New York: Simon & Schuster, 1974.

Fromm, E. *The Art of Loving*. New York: Harper & Row, 1956.

Fullerton, H. N. "The 1995 Labor Force: BLS's Latest Projections." *Monthly Labor Review*. Washington, D.C.: Bureau of Labor Statistics, November 1985, 117–125.

Furstenberg, F. F., and Spanier, G. *Recycling the Family: Remarriage After Divorce*. Beverly Hills, Calif.: Sage, 1984.

———. "Recycling the Family." *Marriage and Family Review*. 2, no. 3 (1979).

Furstenberg, F. F., et al. "The Life Course of Children of Divorce: Marital Disruption and Parental Contact." *American Sociological Review*, October 1983, 656–668.

Galbraith, J. K. *The Affluent Society*. Boston: Houghton Mifflin, 1958.

Gallup, G. "What Americans Think About Their Lives and Families." *Families*, June 1982.

Gallup Poll. "Public Remains Closely Divided Over High Court's Abortion Ruling." *Santa Barbara News Press*, 31 July 1983, A-9.

Galvin, K. M., and Brommel, B. J. *Family Communication: Cohesion and Change*. Glenview, Ill.: Scott, Foresman, 1982.

Ganong, L. H., and Coleman, M. A. "A Comparison of Clinical and Empirical Literature on Children in Stepfamilies." *Journal of Marriage and the Family*, May 1986, 309–318.

———. "The Effects of Remarriage on Children: A Review of the Empirical Research." *Family Relations*, July 1984, 389–406.

Gardner, J. W. *Self-Renewal: The Individual and the Innovative Society*. Rev. ed. New York: W. W. Norton, 1981.

Garland, D. "Training Married Couples in Listening Skills: Effects on Behavior, Perceptual Accuracy and Marital Adjustment." *Family Relations*, April 1981, 297–306.

———. *Working with Couples for Marriage Enrichment*. San Francisco: Jossy-Bass, 1983.

Gary, L. et al., "Strong Black Families: Models of Program Development for Black Families." In *Family Strengths 7: Vital Connections*, edited by S. Van Zandt, et al. Lincoln, Neb.: Center for Family Strengths, 1986, 453–468.

General Mills. "American Families at Work." *The General Mills American Family Report 1980–81*. Minneapolis, Minn.: General Mills, 1981.

———. "Raising Children in a Changing Society." *The General Mills American Family Report, 1976–1977*. Minneapolis, Minn.: General Mills, 1977.

Gibran, K. *The Prophet*. New York: Knopf, 1923.

Gilbert, S. J. "Self-Disclosure, Intimacy and Communication in Families." *The Family Coordinator*, July 1976, 221–231.

Giles-Sims, J. "A Longitudinal Study of Battered Children of Battered Wives." *Family Relations*, April 1985, 205–210.

Glenn, N., and McLanahan, S. "The Effects of Offspring on the Psychological Well-being of Older Adults." *Journal of Marriage and the Family*, May 1981, 409–421.

Glenn, N., and Supancic, M. "The Social and Demographic Correlates of Divorce and Separation in the United States: An Update and Reconsideration." *Journal of Marriage and the Family*, August 1984, 563–575.

Glenn, N., and Weaver, C. "The Marital Happiness of Remarried Divorced Persons." *Journal of Marriage and the Family*, May 1977, 331–337.

Glick, P. "A Demographer Looks at American Families." *Journal of Marriage and the Family* 37 (February 1975): 15–27.

———. "American Household Structure in Transition." *Family Planning Perspectives* 16 (1984): 205–211.

———. "Black Families." In *Families*, edited by H. McAdoo. Beverly Hills, Calif.: Sage, 1981.

———. "Marriage, Divorce and Living Arrangements: Prospective Changes." *Journal of Family Issues* 5 (1984): 7–26.

———. "Prospective Changes in Marriage, Divorce, and Living Arrangements." *Journal of Family Issues* 1 (1984).

———. "The Future Marital Status and Living Arrangements of the Elderly." *The Gerontologist* 19 (1979): 3.

———. "The Life Cycle of the Family." *Marriage and Family Living* 17 (1955): 3–9.

Glick, P., and Lin, S. "More Young Adults Are Living with Their Parents: Who Are They?" *Journal of Marriage and the Family*, February 1986, 107–112.

Glick, P., and Norton, A. "Marrying, Divorcing, and Living Together in the United States Today." *Population Bulletin* 32, no. 5 (1979).

Glick, P., and Spanier, G. "Married and Unmarried Cohabitation in the United States." *Journal of Marriage and the Family* 42 (1980): 19–30.

Glick, P., and Sung-Ling, N. "Recent Changes in Divorce and Remarriage." *Journal of Marriage and the Family*, November 1986, 737–748.

Goetting, A. "The Normative Integration of the Former Spouse Relationship." *Journal of Divorce* 2 (Summer 1979): 395–414.

Goertzel, V., and Goertzel, M. *Cradles of Imminence*. Boston: Little, Brown, 1962.

Gold, D., and Andres, D. "Developmental Comparisons Between 10-year-old Children with Employed and Nonemployed Mothers." *Child Development* 49 (1978): 75–84.

Goldstine, D., et al. *The Dance-away Lover and Other Roles We Play in Love, Sex and Marriage.* New York: Morrow, 1977.

Goleman, D. "Special Abilities of the Sexes: Do They Begin in the Brain?" *Psychology Today*, November 1978.

Goodman, E. "Maternity Leave Is Never Enough." *Santa Barbara News Press*, 4 February 1986, A-17.

Gordon, T. *Parental Effectiveness Training.* New York: Peter Wyden, 1970.

Gotwald, W. H., and Golden, G. *Sexuality: The Human Experience.* New York: Macmillan, 1981.

Goy, R., and McEwan, B. *Sexual Differentiation in the Brain.* Cambridge, Mass.: MIT Press, 1980.

Greenblat, C. "The Salience of Sexuality in the Early Years of Marriage." *Journal of Marriage and the Family* 45 (1983): 289–299.

Greenhaus, J., and Beutell, N. "Sources of Conflict Between Work and Family Roles." *Academy of Management Review* 10 (January 1985).

Greer, G. *Sex and Destiny.* New York: Harper & Row, 1984.

Griffitt, W., and Hatfield, E. *Human Sexual Behavior.* Glenview, Ill.: Scott, Foresman, 1985.

Gross, H. "Dual-Career Couples Who Live Apart: Two Types." *Journal of Marriage and the Family* 42 (August 1980): 565–576.

Gunter, B. "Notes on Divorce Filing as Role Behavior." *Journal of Marriage and the Family*, February 1977, 95–98.

Gunter, B., and Johnson, D. "Divorce Filing as Role Behavior: Effect of No-Fault Law on Divorce Filing Patterns." *Journal of Marriage and the Family*, August 1978, 571–574.

Guttentag, M., and Secord, P. *Too Many Women.* Beverly Hills, Calif.: Sage, 1983.

Guttmacher, A. *Abortion: A Woman's Guide.* New York: Abelard-Schuman, 1973.

————. *Birth Control and Love.* New York: Macmillan, 1969.

————. *Pregnancy, Birth and Family Planning.* New York: New American Library, 1984.

Hager, P. "Medical Gains Stir Debate on Abortion Ruling." *Los Angeles Times*, 9 September 1985.

Hales, D., and Hales, R. "Testosterone: The Bonding Hormone." *American Health*, November/December 1982.

Halpern, H. "Midlife Crises: Frontline Dispatches." *Los Angeles Times*, 12 May 1986, V-2.

Hanna, S., and Knaub, P. "Cohabitation Before Marriage: Its Relationship to Family Strengths." *Alternative Lifestyles* 4 (1981): 507–522.

Hannan, M., and Tuma, N. "Income and Marital Events: Evidence from an Income-Maintenance Experiment." *American Journal of Sociology*, May 1977, 1186–1211.

Haney, D. "Study Suggests IUD Causes Infertility in 80,000." *Santa Barbara News Press*, 11 April 1985, D-5.

Hansen, G. "Reactions to Hypothetical Jealousy Producing Events." *Family Relations*, October 1982.

Harlap, S., et al. "A Prospective Study of Spontaneous Fetal Losses After Induced Abortions." *New England Journal of Medicine* 301 (1979): 677–681.

Harlap, S., and Shiono, P. "Alcohol, Smoking, and Incidence of Spontaneous Abortions in First and Second Trimester." *The Lancet*, 26 July, 1980, 173–176.

Harper, P. "Baby Born to Infertile Couple." *Santa Barbara News Press*, 25 February 1986, A-1, 16.

Hartman, W., and Fithian, M. *Treatment of Sexual Dysfunction.* Long Beach, Calif.: Center for Marital and Sexual Studies, 1972.

Hatcher, R., et al. *Contraceptive Technology 1984–1985.* 12th ed. New York: Irvington Publishers, 1984.

Hatfield, E., and Walster, G. *A New Look at Love.* Reading, Mass.: Addison-Wesley, 1978.

Hawkes, G., and Taylor, M. "Power Structure in Mexican American Farm Labor Families." *Journal of Marriage and the Family*, November 1975, 807–811.

Hawrylyshyn, P., et al. "Risk Factors Associated with Infection Following Cesarean." *American Journal of Obstetrics and Gynecology*, February 1981, 294.

Haynes, J. *Divorce Mediation.* New York: Springer, 1981.

Hechinger, F. "Children in U.S.: Victims of Self-serving Population." *Santa Barbara News Press*, 9 May 1986, A-11.

Hefferan, C. "Financial Stresses and Opportunities for Families in the 1980's." In *Family Strengths 5*, edited by G. Rowe, et al. Newton, Mass.: Education Development Center, 1984.

Heiman, J. "Women's Sexual Arousal—The Physiology of Erotica." *Psychology Today*, April 1975, 91–94.

Helfer, R., and Kempe, C. *The Battered Child.* Chicago: University of Chicago Press, 1974.

Henshaw, S. "Legal Abortions—Estimated Number, Rate, and Ratio, By Race: 1972 to 1982." In *Statistical Abstracts of the United States.* 105th ed. Washington, D.C.: U.S. Government Printing Office, 1985.

Hicks, M., and Platt, M. "Marital Happiness and Stability: A Review of the Research in the Sixties." *Journal of Marriage and the Family*, November 1970, 553–574.

Hill, E. A., and Dorfman, L. T. "Reaction of Housewives to the Retirement of Their Husbands." *Family Relations*, April 1982, 195–200.

Hill, W. *Hill Interaction Matrix Scoring Manual.* Los Angeles: University of Southern California, Youth Studies Center, 1961.

Hite, Shere. *The Hite Report: A Nationwide Study of Female Sexuality.* New York: Macmillan, 1976.

————. *The Hite Report on Male Sexuality.* New York: Knopf, 1981.

————. Basic Lecture Series, Institute for Advanced Study in Human Sexuality. San Francisco, Calif., October 1979.

Hobbins, J. "Fetoscopy." In *Protocols for High Risk Pregnancies*, edited by J. T. Queenan and S. E. Hobbins. Oradell, N.J.: Medical Economics Co., 1982.

Hoffman, L. "Effects of Maternal Employment on the Child—A Review of the Research." *Developmental Psychology* 10 (1974): 204–228.

Hoffman, W., and Holmes, J. "Husbands, Wives, and Divorce." In *Five Thousand Families*, edited by G. Duncan and J. Morgan. Ann Arbor: Institute for Social Research, University of Michigan, 1976.

Hoffman, W., and Manis, J. "Influences of Children on Marital Interaction and Parental Satisfactions and Dissatisfactions." In *Child Influences and Family Interaction: A Life-Span Perspective*, edited by R. M. Lerner and G. B. Spanier. New York: Academic Press, 1978.

Hogue, C. "An Evaluation of Studies Concerning Reproduction after First Trimester Induced Abortion." *International Journal of Gynecology and Obstetrics* 15 (1977): 167–171.

Hogue, C., et al. "Impact of Vacuum Aspiration on Future Childbearing. A Review." *Family Planning Perspectives* 15 (1983): 119–126.

Honeycutt, J., Wilson, C., and Parker, C. "Effects of Sex and Degrees of Happiness on Perceived Styles of Communicating in and out of the

Marital Relationship." *Journal of Marriage and the Family* (May 1982): 395–406.

Hopson, J., and Rosenfeld, A. "PMS: Puzzling Monthly Symptoms." *Psychology Today*, August 1984, 30–35.

Hornung, A., and McCullough, B. "Status Relationships in Dual-Employment Marriages: Consequences for Psychological Well-Being." *Journal of Marriage and the Family*, February 1981, 125–141.

House Hearings on Child Support Enforcement Legislation Before the Subcommittee on Public Assistance and Unemployment Compensation of the Committee of Ways and Means of the U.S. House of Representatives on July 14, 1983. Washington, D.C.: U.S. Government Printing Office, 1984, 13.

Houseknecht, S. "Childlessness and Marital Adjustment." *Journal of Marriage and the Family*, May 1979, 259–265.

Houseknecht, S., and Macke, A. "Combining Marriage and Career: The Marital Adjustment of Professional Women." *Journal of Marriage and the Family*, August 1981, 651–661.

Hull, J. "Women Find Parents Need Them Just When Careers Are Resuming." *Wall Street Journal*, 9 September 1985.

Hunt, M. *Sexual Behavior in the 1970s.* Chicago: Playboy Press, 1974.

———. *The Natural History of Love.* New York: Knopf, 1959.

Hupka, R. "Societal and Individual Roles in the Expression of Jealousy." In *Sexual Jealousy*, chaired by H. Sigall. Symposium presented at the meeting of the American Psychological Association, San Francisco, August 1977.

Huston, T., and Levinger, G. "Interpersonal Attraction and Relationships." *Annual Review of Psychology, 1978.* Palo Alto, Calif.: Annual Reviews, 1978.

Insel, P. M., and Roth, W. T. *Health in a Changing Society.* Palo Alto, Calif.: Mayfield, 1976.

Jacobs, P. "First Successful Transfers of Human Embryos Revealed." *Los Angeles Times*, 22 July 1983, Part 1–1, 21.

Jacobson, D. "Stepfamilies: Myths and Realities." *Social Work* 24 (1979): 202–207.

Jacques, J., and Chason, K. "Cohabitation: Its Impact on Marital Success." *The Family Coordinator*, January (1979): 35–39.

Johnson, C. K., and Price-Bonham, S. "Women and Retirement: A Study and Implications." *Family Relations*, July 1980, 381–385.

Johnson, M. "Commitment: A Conceptual Structure and Empirical Application." *Sociological Quarterly* 14 (1973): 395–406.

Johnson, R. "A Study of Extramarital Sex." In *Beyond Monogamy*, edited by L. Smith and J. Smith. Baltimore, Md.: Johns Hopkins University Press, 1974.

Johnson, S. "Many Child Abuse Reports Unfounded, Expert Claims." *Santa Barbara News Press*, 18 December 1985, B-11.

Jones, E., and Jones, H. *Sensual Drugs.* New York: Cambridge University Press, 1977.

Jones, E., and Wortman, C. *Ingratiation: An Attributional Approach.* Morristown, N.J.: General Learning, 1973.

Jorgenson, S., and Gaudy, J. "Self-disclosure and Satisfaction in Marriage: The Relationship Examined." *Family Relations*, July 1980, 281–287.

Jourard, S. *Personal Adjustment.* New York: Macmillan, 1963.

Kahn, H., and Weiner, A. "The Future Meanings of Work: Some 'Surprise-free' Observations." In *The Future of Work*, edited by F. Best. Englewood Cliffs, N.J.: Prentice-Hall, 1973.

Kaplan, H. *Disorders of Sexual Desire.* New York: Brunner-Mazel, 1979.

Kargman, M. "Stepchild Support and Obligations of Stepparents." *Family Relations*, April 1983, 231–238.

Keller, D. "Women's Attitudes Regarding Penis Size." *Medical Aspects of Human Sexuality* (1976): 178–179.

Kerckhoff, A., and Davis, K. "Value Consensus and Need Complementarity in Mate Selection." *American Social Review* 27 (1962): 295–303.

Kerckhoff, R. "Marriage and Middle Age." *The Family Coordinator*, January 1976, 5–11.

Kerr, C. *Sex for Women That Want to Have Fun and Loving Relationships with Equals.* New York: Grove Press, 1977.

Kieffer, C. "Consensual Cohabitation: A Descriptive Study of the Relationships and the Sociocultural Characteristics of Eighty Couples in Settings in Two Florida Universities." Master's thesis, Florida State University, 1972.

———. "New Depths in Intimacy." In *Marriage and Alternatives: Exploring Intimate Relationships*, edited by R. Libby and R. Whitehurst. Glenview, Ill.: Scott, Foresman, 1977.

Kimura, D. "Male Brain, Female Brain: The Hidden Difference." *Psychology Today*, November 1985, 50–58.

Kinsey, A., et al. *Sexual Behavior in the Human Female.* Philadelphia: Saunders, 1953.

———. *Sexual Behavior in the Human Male.* Philadelphia: Saunders, 1948.

Kirschner, B., and Wallum, L. In *Contemporary Families and Alternate Life Styles*, edited by E. Macklin and R. Rubin. Beverly Hills, Calif.: Sage Publishing, 1983.

Kitano, H. H., et al. "Asian-American Interracial Marriage." *Journal of Marriage and the Family*, February 1984, 179–190.

Kline, J., et al. "Drinking During Pregnancy and Spontaneous Abortion." *The Lancet*, July 26, 1980, 176–180.

Knox, D. *Human Sexuality.* St. Paul, Minn.: West, 1984.

———. *Choices in Relationships.* St. Paul, Minn.: West, 1985.

Knox, D., and Wilson, K. "Dating Behavior of University Students." *Family Relations* (1981): 255–258.

———. "Dating Problems of University Students." *College Student Journal* 17 (1983): 225–228.

Kogan, B. A. *Human Sexual Expression.* New York: Harcourt Brace Jovanovich, 1973.

Kolodny, R., et al. "Depression of Plasma Testosterone Levels after Chronic Intensive Marijuana Use." *New England Journal of Medicine* 290 (April 18, 1974): 872–874.

———. Masters and Johnson Institute Seminar on Human Sexuality, Los Angeles, 6–7 December 1982.

Koo, H., and Suchindran, C. "Effects of Children on Women's Remarriage Prospects." *Journal of Family Issues* 1 (1980): 497–515.

Kosteic, J., and Preti, G. "Birth Control Through Saliva Changes." *Science Digest*, December 1982, 91.

Krantzler, M. *Creative Divorce.* New York: Evans, 1973.

LaRossa, R., and LaRossa, M. *Transition to Parenthood.* Beverly Hills, Calif.: Sage, 1981.

Lasswell, M. "Looking Ahead in Aging: Love after Fifty." In *Love, Marriage, Family*, edited by M. Lasswell and T. Lasswell, Glenview, Ill.: Scott, Foresman, 1973.

Lasswell, M., and Lobsenz, N. *Styles of Loving.* Garden City, N.Y.: Doubleday, 1980.

Latham v. Latham, 274 Ore. 421, 541 P.2d 144 (1976).

Lauer, J., and Lauer, R. "Marriages Made to Last." *Psychology Today*, June 1985, 22–26.

Lear, H. "Vasectomy—A Note of Concern." In *Vasectomy: Follow-up of 1000 Cases, Simon Population Trust–Sterilization Project*. Cambridge, England: Simon Population Trust, 1969.

Leboyer, F. *Birth Without Violence*. New York: Knopf, 1975.

Lederer, W., and Jackson, D. *The Mirage of Marriage*. New York: W. W. Norton, 1968.

Lee, G., and Stone, L. "Mate-selection Systems and Criteria: Variation According to Family Structure." *Journal of Marriage and the Family* 42 (1980): 319–326.

Leiblum, S., and Pervin, L., eds. *Principles and Practice of Sex Therapy.* New York: Guilford Press, 1980.

LeMasters, E. E., and DeFrain, J. *Parents in Contemporary America*. Homewood, Ill.: Dorsey Press, 1983.

Leo, J. "On the Trail of the Big O." *Time*, March, 3, 1986, 12.

———. "The Revolution Is Over." *Time*, 9 April 1984, 74–84.

Leonard, G. "Rediscovering True Love." *Cosmopolitan*, January 1984.

LeShan, E. J. *The Wonderful Crisis of Middle Age*. New York: David McKay, 1973.

Leslie, G. "Personal Values, Professional Idealogies and Family Specialists: A New Look." *The Family Coordinator*, April 1979, 157–162.

Leslie, L., et al. "Parental Reactions to Dating Relationships: Do They Make a Difference?" *Journal of Marriage and the Family* 48 (1986): 57–66.

Lessard, S. "Aborting a Fetus: The Legal Right, the Personal Choice." *The Washington Monthly* 4 (August 1972): 29–37.

Levin, A., et al. "Induced Abortion: The Risk of Spontaneous Abortions." *Family Planning Perspective* 11 (1978): 39–40.

Levinger, G. "Marital Cohesiveness and Dissolution: An Integrative Review." *Journal of Marriage and the Family*, January 1965, 19–28.

Levinger, G., and Moles, O. C., eds. *Divorce and Separation: Context, Causes and Consequences*. New York: Basic Books, 1979.

Lewis, J. *How's Your Family: A Guide to Identifying Your Family's Strengths and Weaknesses*. New York: Brunner-Mazel, 1979.

Lewis, R., and Spanier, G. "Theorizing about the Quality and Stability of Marriage." In *Contemporary Theories about the Family*, edited by W. Burr et al. Vol. 1. New York: Free Press, 1979.

Lewis, R., et al. "Commitment in Married and Unmarried Cohabitation." Paper presented at the annual meeting of the American Sociological Association, San Francisco, 1975.

Libby, R. "Creative Singlehood as a Sexual Lifestyle: Beyond Marriage as a Rite of Passage." In *Marriage and Alternatives: Exploring Intimate Relationships*, edited by R. Libby and R. Whitehurst. Glenview, Ill.: Scott, Foresman, 1977.

Life. "Having Babies." March 1986, 33.

Lindemann, B. "The Sex Role Revolution." In *American Marriage: A Changing Scene?* by F. Cox. Dubuque, Iowa: Wm. C. Brown, 1976.

Linton, R. *The Study of Man*. New York: Appleton, 1936.

Long, T. "Interviews with 300 Latchkey Children: Results and Implications for Service." Paper presented at the American Psychological Association Annual Convention, Anaheim, Calif., 26 August 1983.

Lopata, H. Z. *Women as Widows*. New York: Elsevier, 1979.

Los Angeles Times. "Birth Control by Computer Works." 13 October 1982.

———. "Nonwhite Children Adjust Well when Adopted by White Families, Study Reports." 26 December 1985, Part 1, 11.

Lothstein, L. "Sex Reassignment Surgery: Historical, Bioethical and Theoretical Issues." *American Journal of Psychiatry* 139 (1982): 417–426.

Lowenthal, M. F., Thurnher, M., and Chiriboga, D. *Four Stages of Life: A Comparative Study of Women and Men Facing Transitions*. San Francisco: Jossey-Bass, 1975.

Lowery, C. R., and Settle, S. A. "Effects of Divorce on Children: Differential Impact of Custody and Visitation Patterns." *Family Relations*, October 1985, 455–463.

Lyness, J., Lepetz, M., and Davis, K. "Living Together: An Alternative to Marriage." *Journal of Marriage and the Family* 34 (1972): 305–311.

MaCadam, M., and Meadows, F. "Company-supported Child Care." *Business to Business*, April 1985, 69–73.

MacDonald, P. C. "Estrogen Plus Progestin in Post-menopausal Women." *New England Journal of Medicine*, 31 December 1981.

Mace, D. "Strictly Personal." *Marriage and Family Living*, September 1980.

Mace, D. (ed.). *Prevention in Family Services: Approaches to Family Wellness*. Beverly Hills, Calif.: Sage, 1983.

Mace, D., and Mace, V. *We Can Have Better Marriages*. Nashville: Abington, 1974.

———. "Counter-Epilogue." In *Marriage and Alternatives: Exploring Intimate Relationships*, edited by R. Libby and R. Whitehurst. Glenview, Ill.: Scott, Foresman, 1977.

———. "Family Wellness: Wave of the Future." In *Family Strengths 6*, edited by R. Williams et al. Lincoln, Neb.: University of Nebraska, 1985.

Macklin, E. "Nonmarital Cohabitation." *Marriage and Family Review* (1978a): 1–12.

———. "Nonmarital Heterosexual Cohabitation: An Overview." In *Contemporary Families and Alternative Lifestyles*, edited by E. Macklin and R. Rubin. Beverly Hills, Calif.: Sage, 1983.

MacLeod, J. S. "How to Hold a Wife: A Bridegroom's Guide." *The Village Voice*, February 11, 1971.

Madden, J. "The Persistence of Pay Differentials: The Economics of Sex Discrimination." In *Women and Work: An Annual Review*, edited by L. Larwood et al. Beverly Hills, Calif.: Sage Publications, 1985.

Magrab, P. "For the Sake of the Children: A Review of the Psychological Effects of Divorce." *Journal of Divorce* 1 (1978): 1424–1432.

Makepeace, J. "Courtship Violence Among College Students." *Family Relations* 30 (1981): 97–102.

Malatesta, V., et al. "Alcoholic Effects on the Orgasmic-Ejaculatory Response in Human Males." *Journal of Sex Research* 15 (1979): 101, 107.

———. "Acute Alcohol Ingestion and Female Orgasm." *Journal of Sex Research*; research referred to by R. C. Kolodny at Masters and Johnson Institute Seminar on Human Sexuality, Los Angeles, December 6–7, 1982.

Mall, J. "Report on Child-rearing: Job Aims to Aid Families." *Los Angeles Times*, 2 February 1986, VI-9.

Maloney, E. *Human Sexuality*. New York: McGraw-Hill, 1982.

Maret, E., and Finlay, B. "The Distribution of Household Labor Among Women in Dual-Earner Families." *Journal of Marriage and the Family*, May 1984, 357–364.

Markowski, E., and Johnson, M. "Behavior, Temperament, Perceived Temperament and Idealization of Cohabiting Couples Who Married." *International Journal of Sociology* 10 (1980): 115–125.

Marotz-Baden, R., et al. "Family Form or Family Process? Reconsidering the Deficit Family Model Approach." *The Family Coordinator*, January 1979, 5–14.

Marvin v. Marvin, 18 Cal.3d 660, 134 Cal. Rep. 815, 557 P.2d 106 (1976).

———. *Family Law Reporter* 5 (1979): 3109.

———. *Family Law Reporter* 7 (1981): 2661.

Maslow, A. *Toward a Psychology of Being*. 2d ed. Princeton, N.J.: Van Nostrand, 1968.

———. *The Farther Reaches of Human Nature*. New York: Viking, 1971.

Masnick, G., and Bane, M. *The Nation's Families: 1960–1980*. Boston: Auburn House, 1980.

Masters, W., and Johnson, V. Masters and Johnson Institute Seminar on Human Sexuality, Los Angeles, Calif., 6–7 December 1982.

————. *Human Sexual Response*. Boston: Little, Brown, 1966.

————. "Sex and the Aging Process." *Journal of American Geriatrics Society*, September 1981, 385–390.

Masters, W., et al., eds. *Ethical Issues in Sex Therapy and Research*. Vol. 11. Boston: Little, Brown, 1980.

Maugh, T. "Marijuana: New Support for Immune and Preproductive Hazards." *Science* 190 (1975): 865–867.

May, K. "Factors Contributing to First-time Fathers' Readiness for Fatherhood: An Exploratory Study." *Family Relations*, July 1982, 353–362.

————. "Management of Detachment and Involvement in Pregnancy by First-time Expectant Fathers." Doctoral dissertation, University of California, San Francisco, 1979.

May, R. *Love and Will*. New York: W. W. Norton, 1970.

McCarthy, J. "A Comparison of the Probability of the Dissolution of First and Second Marriages." *Demography* 15, no. 3 (1978): 345–359.

McCary, J., and McCary, S. *Human Sexuality*. Belmont, Calif.: Wadsworth, 1982.

McGinnis, A. *The Friendship Factor*. Minneapolis, Minn.: Augsberg, 1979.

McKay, M., et al. *The Divorce Book*. Oakland, Calif.: New Harbinger Publications, 1984.

McKean, K. "Closing in on the Herpes Virus." *Discover*, October 1981, 75–78.

McMorrow, F. *Middlescence: The Dangerous Years*. New York: Strawberry Hill, 1974.

Mead, Margaret. "Jealousy: Primitive and Civilized." In *Woman's Coming of Age*, edited by S. Schmalhausen and V. Calverton. New York: Morrow, 1948, 1968.

Mehren, E. "Employers and Their Pregnant Employees." *Los Angeles Times*, 6 May 1986, V-1.

————. "Working Wives: Negative Effect on Husbands." *Los Angeles Times*, 31 March 1986, Part V, 1, 4.

Melichar, J., and Chiriboga, D. "Timetables in the Divorce Process." *Journal of Marriage and the Family*, August 1985, 701–708.

Mellon, S. "Legal Issues as They Relate to All Members of the Families." Paper presented at the Iowa Conference on Blended Families, Iowa City, Iowa, February 1984.

Mendelson, J. H. "Marijuana and Sex." *Medical Aspects of Human Sexuality*, November 1976, 23–24.

Miller, B., and Sollie, D. "Normal Stresses during the Transition to Parenthood." *Family Relations*, October 1980, 459–465.

Miller, H., and Siegel, P. *Loving: A Psychological Approach*. New York: Wiley, 1972.

Miller, M., and Revinbark, W. "Sexual Differences in Physical Attractiveness as a Determinant of Heterosexual Liking." *Psychology Report* 27 (1970): 701–702.

Miller, R. *Economic Issues for Consumers*. St. Paul, Minn.: West Publishing, 1984.

————. *Personal Finance Today*. St. Paul, Minn.: West Publishing, 1983.

Miller, S., et al. "Recent Progress in Understanding and Facilitating Marital Communication." *The Family Coordinator* 24 (April 1975): 143–152.

Mirande, A. "The Chicano Family: A Reanalysis of Conflicting Views." *Journal of Marriage and the Family*, November 1977, 747–756.

Mishell, D. "Current Status of Intrauterine Devices." *New England Journal of Medicine* 312, no. 15 (1985): 984–985.

Money, J., and Ehrhardt, A. *Man and Woman, Boy and Girl: The Differentiation and Dimorphism of Gender Identity from Conception to Maturity*. Baltimore, Md.: Johns Hopkins University Press, 1972.

Montagu, A. *Touching: The Human Significance of Skin*. New York: Harper & Row, 1972.

Montague, M. *Prenatal Influences*. Springfield, Ill.: Charles C Thomas, 1962.

Montgomery, B. "The Form and Function of Quality Communication in Marriage." *Family Relations*, January 1981, 21–30.

Monthly Labor Review. Bureau of Labor Statistics. Washington, D.C.: U.S. Government Printing Office, August 1966.

Mooney, D. *Blush, Blur, Backlash, and Balance* were terms for family life stages described in an article by N. Hellmich, "Marriage: Don't Call it Unpredictable." *USA Today*, 9 May 1986, 7D.

Moore, C. "Bye-bye, Ms American Pie." *Washington Post Magazine*, 27 November 1983, 10, 11, 16–19.

Moore, K., and Hofferth, S. "Effects of Women's Employment on Marriage: Formation, Stability and Roles." In *Marriage and Family Review* 2, no. 2 (1979).

Morris, D. *Intimate Behavior*. New York: Random House, 1971.

Morris, J. *Conundrum*. New York: Harcourt Brace Jovanovich, 1974.

Mosher, W., and Hendershot, G. "Religion and Fertility: A Replication." *Demography* 21, no. 2 (1984): 185–191.

————. "Reproductive Impairments Among Currently Married Couples: United States, 1976." *Advance Data*. U.S. National Center for Health Statistics, H.E.W., no. 55, 24 January 1980.

Mowatt, M. "Group Psychotherapy for Stepfathers and Their Wives." *Psychotherapy: Theory, Research and Practice* 9 (1972): 328–331.

Moynihan, P. *Family and Nation*. New York: Harcourt Brace Jovanovich, 1986.

Ms. "Pay Equity: The Battle Heats Up." November 1985, 19.

Murdock, G. "Sexual Behavior: What Is Acceptable?" *Journal of Social Hygiene* 36 (1950): 1–31.

————. *Social Structure*. New York: Macmillan, 1949.

Murguia, E., and Frisbie, W. P. "Trends in Mexican-American Intermarriage: Recent Finding in Perspective." *Social Science Quarterly*, December 1977, 374–389.

Murstein, B. *Love, Sex, and Marriage through the Ages*. New York: Springer, 1974.

————. "Mate Selection in the 1970s." *Journal of Marriage and the Family* (1980): 777–792.

Myricks, N. "The Law and Alternative Lifestyles." In *Contemporary Families and Alternative Lifestyles*, edited by E. Macklin and R. Rubin, Beverly Hills, Calif.: Sage, 1983.

————. "'Palimony': The Impact of Marvin v. Marvin." *The Family Coordinator*, April 1980, 210–215.

Nass, G. D., Libby, R., and Fisher, M. *Sexual Choices*. Monterey, Calif.: Wadsworth, 1981.

National Center for Health Statistics. "Births, Marriages, Divorces & Deaths for Nov. 1985." *Monthly Vital Statistics Report*. Washington, D.C.: U.S. Government Printing Office, February 20, 1986.

————. "Perinatal Mortality in the United States: 1950–1981." *Monthly Vital Statistics Report*. Washington, D.C.: U.S. Government Printing Office, March 31, 1986.

————. "Advance Report of Final Marriage Statistics: 1983." *Monthly Vital Statistics Report*, Vol. 35, no. 1, supp. Hyattsville, Md.: 2 May 1986.

————. "Advance Report of Final Divorce Statistics: 1983." *Monthly Vital Statistics Report*, Vol. 34, no. 9, supp. DHHS Pub. No. (PHS) 86-1120. Hyattsville, Md.: December 26, 1985.

————. "Advance Report of Final Marriage Statistics: 1981." *Monthly Vital*

Statistics Report, Vol. 32, no. 11, supp. DHHS Pub. No. (PHS) 84-1120. Hyattsville, Md.: 1984.

———. "Advance Report of Final Marriage Statistics: 1983." *Monthly Vital Statistics Report*, Vol. 35, no. 1, supp. DHHS Pub. No. (PHS) 86-1120. Hyattesville, Md.: May 2, 1986.

———. "Annual Summary of Births, Marriages, Divorces, and Deaths: United States, 1985." *Monthly Vital Statistics Report*. Washington, D.C.: U.S. Department of Health and Human Services, September 19, 1986.

National Institute of Mental Health. "Admission Rates of Outpatient Psychiatric Services per 100,000 Population Eighteen Years and Over by Marital Status." Washington, D.C.: U.S. Government Printing Office, 1973. *NCFR Report* 30, no. 4 (December 1985): 14.

Nelson, P., and Banonis, B. "Family Concerns and Strengths Identified in Delaware's White House Conference on Families." In *Family Strengths 3: Roots of Well-Being*. Lincoln, Neb.: University of Nebraska Press, 1981.

Newsweek. "Home Tests for Pregnancy." September 3, 1979, 69.

Nieva, V. F. "Work and Family Linkages." In *Women and Work: An Annual Review*, edited by L. Larwood et al. Beverly Hills, Calif.: Sage, 1985.

Nock, S., & Kingston, P. "The Family Work Day." *Journal of Marriage and the Family*, May 1984, 333–343.

Norton, A., and Glick, P. "One-parent Families: A Social and Economic Profile." *Family Rrelations* (January 1986): 9–17.

Nye, F. "Emerging and Declining Family Roles." *Journal of Marriage and the Family* 36 (1974): 238–244.

Nye, F., and Hoffman, L., eds. *The Employed Mother in America*. Chicago: Rand McNally, 1974.

O'Hara, K. "IUDs: Problem-Free Users Are New Kind of Victims." *Santa Barbara News Press*, 18 May 1986, E1 and 6.

O'Hare, W. "Poverty in America: Trends and New Patterns." *Population Bulletin*, Vol. 40, no. 3. Washington, D.C.: Population Reference Bureau, 1985.

Olds, S., London, M., and Ladewig, P. *Maternal Newborn Nursing*. 2d ed. Reading, Mass.: Addison-Wesley, 1984.

Olson, D. "What Makes Families Work?" In *Family Strengths 7: Vital Connections*, edited by S. Van Zandt et al. Lincoln, Neb.: University of Nebraska Press, 1986, 1–12.

Olson, D., and Markoff, R. *Inventory of Marriage and Family Literature*. Vol. XI (1984). Beverly Hills, Calif.: Sage, 1985.

Olson, D., et al. *Families: What Makes Them Work?* Beverly Hills, Calif.: Sage, 1983.

O'Neill, N., and O'Neill, G. *Open Marriage*. New York: Avon, 1972.

Oppenheimer, V. "Divorce, Remarriage and Wives' Labor Force Participation." Paper presented at the annual meeting of the American Sociological Society, Chicago, 1977.

Orlinsky, D. "Love Relationships in the Life Cycle: A Developmental Interpersonal Perspective." In *Love Today: A New Exploration*, edited by H. Otto. New York: Dell, 1972.

Otto, H. "Marriage and Family Enrichment Programs: Report and Analysis." *The Family Coordinator* 24 (April 1975): 137–142.

Packard, V. *The Hidden Persuaders*. New York: Pocket Books, 1958.

Papalia, D., and Olds, S. *Human Development*. New York: McGraw-Hill, 1986.

Papernow, P. "A Baby in the House." *Stepfamily Bulletin*, Winter 1984.

Parachine, A. "Breastfeeding, Once on the Rise, Is Slowing." *Los Angeles Times*, 20 December 1985, A-14.

Parke, R. D. *Fathers*. Cambridge, Mass.: Harvard University Press, 1981.

Pearle, D. "Violence and Aggression." *Society*, September 1984, 17–22.

Pedrick-Cornell, C., and Gelles, R. J. "Elder Abuse: The Status of Current Knowledge." *Family Relations*, July 1982.

Perlmutter, L. H., et al. "The Incest Taboo: Loosened Sexual Boundaries in Remarried Families." *Journal of Sex and Marital Therapy* 8 (1982): 83–96.

Pennar, K., and Merrosh, E. "Women at Work." *Business Week*, 28 January 1985, 80–85.

Peplau, L., Rubin, Z., and Hill, C. "Sexual Intimacy in Dating Relationships." *Journal of Social Issues* 33 (1977): 86–109.

Perry, J. D., and Whipple, B. "Pelvic Muscle Strength of Female Ejaculation: Evidence in Support of a New Theory of Orgasm." *Journal of Sex Research* 17 (1981): 22–39.

Peterman, D., et al. "A Comparison of Cohabiting and Noncohabiting Students." *Journal of Marriage and the Family* 36 (1974): 344–355.

Peters, M. F. "Black Families: Notes from the Guest Editor." *Journal of Marriage and the Family*, November 1978, 655–658.

Piatrow, P., Rhinehart, W., and Schmidt, J. "IUDs—Update of Safety, Effectiveness, and Research." *Population Reports*, ser. B, no. 3 (May 1979).

Pierce, C., and Sanfaco, J. "Man/Woman Dynamics: Some Typical Communication Problems." In *Beyond Sex Roles*, edited by A. Sargent. St. Paul, Minn.: West, 1977.

Pincus, J., and Wolhandler, J. "If You Think You are Pregnant: Finding out and Deciding What to Do." In *The New Our Bodies, Ourselves*. New York: Simon & Schuster, 1984.

Pines, A. As reported in Turkington, C. "Finding What's Good in Marriage." *APA Monitor*, November 1985.

Pink, J. E., and Wampler, K. S. "Problem Areas in Stepfamilies: Cohesion, Adaptability and the Stepfather-Adolescent Relationship." *Family Relations*, July 1985, 327–335.

Pleck, J. H., and Rustad, M. "Husbands' and Wives' Time in Family Work and Paid Work in the 1975–1976 Study of Time Use." Working paper. Wellesley, Mass.: Wellesley College Center for Research on Women, 1980.

Pope, K. S., et al. "Sexual Attraction to Clients: The Human Therapist and the (Sometimes) Inhuman Training System." *American Psychologist* 41, no. 2 (1986): 147–157.

Popenoe, P. *Family Life*. Washington, D.C.: George Washington University Medical Center, 1974.

Porter, K. L., and Demeuth, B. "The Impact of Marital Adjustment on Pregnancy Acceptance." *Maternal-Child Nursing* 8, no. 2 (1979): 103–113.

Postman, N. *The Disappearance of Childhood*. New York: Delacorte, 1982.

Pratt, W., et al. *Understanding U.S. Fertility: Findings from the National Survey of Family Growth, Cycle III*. *Population Bulletin*, Vol. 39, no. 5. Washington, D.C.: Population Reference Bureau, 1984.

Prescott, J. "Early Somatosensory Deprivation as an Ontogenetic Process in Abnormal Development of the Brain and Behavior." *Medical Primatology* 21 (1970): 102–106.

———. "Developmental Neuropsychophysics." In *Brain Function and Malnutrition: Neuropsychological Methods of Assessment*, edited by J. W. Prescott et al. New York: Wiley, 1975.

———. "Phylogenetic and Ontogenetic Aspects of Human Affectional Development." In *Selected Proceedings of the 1976 International Congress of Sexology*, edited by R. Gemme and C. C. Wheeler. New York: Plenum, 1976.

Press, A. "Divorce American Style." *Newsweek*, 10 January 1983, 42–43.

Press, A., and Camper, D. "The Court Stands By Abortion." *Newsweek*, 27 June 1983, 62–63.

Price-Bonham, S., et al. "Divorce: A Frequent Alternative in the 1970s." In *Contemporary Families and Alternative Lifestyles*, edited by E. D. Macklin and R. H. Rubin. Beverly Hills, Calif.: Sage, 1983, 125–146.

Prince and The Revolution. "Darling Nikki." *Purple Rain.* Warner Bros. Records, 1984.

Pritchard, J., and MacDonald, P. *Obstetrics.* 16th ed. New York: Appleton-Century-Crofts, 1980.

Putney, S. *The Conquest of Society.* Belmont, Calif.: Wadsworth, 1972.

Queen, S., and Habenstein, R. *The Family in Various Cultures.* Philadelphia: Lippincott, 1974.

Radetsky, P. "The Rise and (Maybe Not the) Fall of Toxic Shock Syndrome." *Science,* 1985, 73–78.

Rallings, E. M., and Nye, F. I. "Wife-Mother Employment, Family and Society." In *Contemporary Theories About the Family.* Vol. 1, edited by W. R. Bevor et al. New York: Free Press, 1979: 203–206.

Ramey, J. Presentation to Groves Conference on Marriage and the Family, Mount Pocono, Penn., 1981.

Rank, M. "Determinants of Conjugal Influence in Wives' Employment Decision Making." *Journal of Marriage and the Family,* August 1982, 591–604.

Rapaport, R., and Rapaport, R. "Men, Women and Equity." *The Family Coordinator* 24 (1975): 421–432.

re:act. "Viewing Goes Up." *Action for Children's Television Magazine* 13 (1984): 4.

Reasoner, H. "Boys and Girls Together." *CBS Reports,* 8 February 1980.

Reinke, B., et al. A study of women at various ages reported by K. Fisher and S. Cunningham, "Birth, Departure of Children Mark Transitions for Women." *Monitor,* November 1983, 18.

Reiss, I. "Essay." In *Marriage: For and Against,* edited by H. Hart et al. New York: Hart, 1972.

———. "The Family in the 80's." Talk given at the National Council on Family Relations Winter Board Meeting, San Diego, 29 February 1980.

———. "Toward a Sociology of the Heterosexual Love Relationship." *Marriage and Family Living,* May 1960.

Rheinstein, M. *Marriage Stability, Divorce and the Law.* Chicago: University of Chicago Press, 1972.

Richardson, L. "Another World." *Psychology Today,* February 1986, 22–27.

Ricks, S. "Father-infant Interactions: A Review of Empirical Research." *Family Relations,* October 1985, 505–511.

Ridley, C., Peterman, D., and Avery, A. "Cohabitation: Does It Make for a Better Marriage?" *Family Coordinator* (1978): 135–136.

Riley, L., and Spreitzer, E. "A Model for the Analysis of Lifetime Marriage Patterns." *Journal of Marriage and the Family,* February 1974, 64–71.

Risman, B., et al. "Living Together in College: Implications for Courtship." *Journal of Marriage and the Family* 43 (1981): 77–83.

Robinson, B. "The Contemporary American Stepfather." *Family Relations* July 1984, 381–388.

Robinson, I., and Jedlicka, D. "Change in Sexual Attitudes and Behavior of College Students from 1965 to 1980: A Research Note." *Journal of Marriage and the Family* 44 (1982): 237–240.

Robinson, J. *How Americans Use Time: A Social Psychological Analysis of Everyday Behavior.* New York: Praeger, 1977.

Roehner, J. "Fatherhood in Pregnancy and Birth." *Journal of Nurse-Midwifery* 21 (1976): 13–18.

Rogers, C. "Communication: Its Blocking and Facilitation." Paper read at Centennial Conference on Communications, Northwestern University, 11 October 1951.

Rollins, B., and Cannon, K. "Marital Satisfaction over the Family Life Cycle." *Journal of Marriage and the Family* 36 (1974): 271–283.

Roncek, D., Bell, R., and Chaldin, H. "Female-headed Families: An Ecological Model of Residential Concentration in a Small City." *Journal of Marriage and the Family,* February 1980, 157–169.

Rosenthal, R., and Jacobson, L. *Pygmalion in the Classroom.* New York: Holt, 1968.

Rossi, A. "A Biosocial Perspective on Parenting." *Daedalus,* Spring 1977, 1–31.

———. "The Biosocial Side of Parenthood." *Human Nature,* June 1978, 72–79.

Rubin, E., et al. "Prolonged Ethanol Consumption Increases Testosterone Metabolism." *Science* 191 (1976): 563–564.

Rubin, Z. "Are Working Wives Hazardous to Their Husband's Health?" *Psychology Today,* May 1983.

———. *Liking and Loving.* New York: Holt, 1973.

———. "Seeking a Cure for Loneliness." *Psychology Today,* October 1979, 82–90.

Rubin, Z., and Levinger, G. "Disclosing Oneself to a Stranger: Reciprocity and Its Limits." *Journal of Experimental Psychology* 11 (1975): 233–260.

Rubinstein, C. "The Modern Art of Courtly Love." *Psychology Today,* July 1983, 40–49.

———. "Wellness Is All." *Psychology Today,* October 1982, 27–37.

Rubinstein, E. "Research Conclusions of the 1982 NIMH Report and Their Policy Implications." *American Psychologist,* July 1983, 820–825.

Rudolph, B. "Mounting Doubts About Debts." *Time,* 31 March 1986, 50–51.

Ruman, M., and Lamm, M. "Divorce Mediation: A Team Approach to Marital Dissolution." *Trial,* March 1983, 80–86.

Russell, B. "Our Sexual Ethics." In *Why I Am Not a Christian.* New York: Simon & Schuster, 1957.

Safran, C. "Why More People Are Making Better Marriages." *Parade Magazine,* 28 April 1985, 14.

Sager, C., et al. *Treating the Married Family.* New York: Brunner-Mazel, 1983.

Sanders. A. J. "Differentials in Marital Status between Black and White Males." *Population Today,* November 1986, 6–7.

Sanders, G. F., et al. "Family Strengths of Older Couples and Their Adult Children." In *Family Strengths 6: Enhancement of Interaction,* edited by R. Williams et al. Lincoln, Neb.: University of Nebraska Press, 1985, 85–98.

Sanderson, J. "Her New Life Begins on a Jarring Note." *Santa Barbara News Press,* 19 December 1982, D-13.

San Francisco Chronicle. "Device May Pinpoint Fertile Days." 24 December 1976.

Sanick, M., and Mauldin, T. "Single Versus Two Parent Families: A Comparison of Mother's Time." *Family Relations,* January 1986, 53–56.

Santa Barbara News Press. "Birth Contract Trial Hears of Joy, Grief." 7 January 1987. F-8.

Santa Barbara News Press. "Grandparents Rights Model Law Changes." 17 February 1986, A-6.

Santa Barbara News Press. "Spending Increase Outpaces Rise in Income." 23 January 1986, A-9.

Santa Barbara News Press. "Dutch Mothers Opt for Home Delivery." 22 August 1985, D-7.

Santa Barbara News Press. "Public Remains Closely Divided over High Court's Abortion Ruling." Gallup Poll. July 31, 1983, A-9.

Santa Barbara News Press. "Eighteen-Year-Old Sperm Used in Artificial Insemination." 12 August 1982, E-8.

Santa Barbara News Press. "Surrogate Mother Fighting to Keep Unborn Child." 22 March 1981, A-3.

Santa Barbara News Press. "Divorced Dad Wins $25,000 from Ex-wife." 8 August 1980, A-5.

Santa Barbara News Press. "No Differences Seen in Childbirth Methods." 15 April 1980, A-5.

Sattin, R. W., et al. "Oral Contraceptive Use and the Risk of Breast Cancer." *New England Journal of Medicine,* August 14, 1986, 405–411.

Saxton, L. *The Individual, Marriage, and the Family.* Belmont, Calif.: Wadsworth, 1986.

Scharf, K. F. "Teenage Pregnancy. Why the Epidemic?" *Working Papers for a New Society.* Center for the Study of Public Policy Inc., March/April 1979.

Schlesinger, B. "Lasting Marriages in the 1980s." In *Family Strengths 5: Continuity and Diversity,* edited by G. Rowe et al. Newton, Mass.: Education Development Center, 1984, 49–63.

Schorr, D. "Go Get Some Milk and Cookies and Watch the Murders on Television." *The Washingtonian,* October 1981.

Schultz, D. *Human Sexuality.* Englewood Cliffs, N.J.: Prentice-Hall, 1979.

Schultz, D., and Rodgers, S. *Marriage, the Family and Personal Fulfillment.* Englewood Cliffs, N.J.: Prentice-Hall, 1975.

Schuman, W., et al. "Self-disclosure and Marital Satisfaction Revisited." *Family Relations,* April 1986, 241–247.

Schwartz, M. F., Money, J., and Robinson, K. "Biosocial Perspectives on the Development of the Proceptive, Acceptive and Conceptive Phases of Eroticism." *Journal of Sex and Marital Therapy,* Winter 1981, 243–255.

Science News. "Smoking and Sperm," April 18, 1981, 247.

Scoresby, A. *The Marriage Dialogue.* Reading, Mass.: Addison-Wesley, 1977.

Scott, J. *Early Experience and the Organization of Behavior.* Belmont, Calif.: Brooks/Cole, 1968.

Seal, K. "A Decade of No-Fault Divorce: What It Has Meant Financially for Women in California." *Family Advocate* 1 (Spring 1979): 10–15.

Seelbach, W. C., and Hansen, C. J. "Satisfaction with Family Relations among the Elderly." *Family Relations,* January 1980, 91.

Seligman, C., Paschall, N., and Takata, G. "Effects of Physical Attractiveness on Attribution of Responsibility." *Canadian Journal of Behavioral Science* 6 (1974): 290–296.

Shanas, E. "Older People and Their Families: The New Pioneers." *Journal of Marriage and the Family,* February 1980, 9–15.

Shaywitz, M., Cohen, D., and Shaywitz, B. "Behavior and Learning Difficulties in Children of Normal Intelligence Born to Alcoholic Mothers." *Journal of Pediatrics* 96, no. 6 (1980): 978–982.

Sheehy, G. *Passages: Predictable Crises of Adult Life.* New York: Bantam Books, 1977.

Sheresky, N., and Mannes, M. *Uncoupling: The Art of Coming Apart.* New York: Viking, 1972.

Sherfy, M. *The Nature and Evaluation of Female Sexuality.* New York: Random House, 1972.

Sidel, R. *Families of Fengsheng.* Baltimore, Md.: Penguin, 1974.

Siegel, L. "Vasectomy, Later Disease Not Linked, Study Shows." *Santa Barbara News Press,* 24 August 1984, A-8.

Sigall, H., and Aronson, E. "Liking for an Evaluator as a Function of Her Physical Attractiveness and the Nature of the Evaluations." *Journal of Experimental Social Psychology* 5 (1969): 93–100.

Sing, B. "Baby Boomers, Few Cash in on Image of Affluence." *Los Angeles Times.* 14 February 1986, 1-1.

Singer, D. "A Time to Reexamine the Role of Television in Our Lives." *American Psychologist,* July 1983, 815–816.

Singer, J., and Singer, D. *Television, Imagination and Aggression: A Study of Preschoolers.* Hillsdale, N.J.: Erlbaum, 1981.

Singer, J., and Singer, I. "Types of Female Orgasm." *Journal of Sex Research* 8, no. 4 (1972): 255–267.

Singer, J., and Sherrod, L. "Prosocial Programs in the Context of Children's Total Pattern of TV Viewing." Paper presented at the biennial meeting of the Society for Research in Child Development, San Francisco, March 1979.

Skolnick, A. *The Intimate Environment: Exploring Marriage and The Family.* 2d & 3d eds. Boston: Little, Brown, 1978, 1983.

Skolnick, A., and Skolnick, J. *Family in Transition.* Boston: Little, Brown, 1986.

Smith, D. "Wife Employment and Marital Adjustment: A Cumulation of Results." *Family Relations* 34 (October 1985): 483–490.

Smith, D., et al. "Association of Erogenous Estrogen and Endometrial Carcinoma." *New England Journal of Medicine* 293, no. 23 (1975): 1164–1167.

Smith, M. "The Social Consequences of Single Parenthood: A Longitudinal Perspective." *The Family Coordinator,* January 1980, 75–81.

Smith, R., ed. *The Subtle Revolution: Women at Work.* Washington, D.C.: Urban Institute, 1979.

Sollie, D., and Miller, R. "The Transition to Parenthood as a Critical Time for Building Family Strengths." In *Family Strengths: Positive Models of Family Life,* edited by N. Stinnett et al. Lincoln, Neb.: University of Nebraska Press, 1980.

Spanier, G., and Glick, P. "Mate Selection Differentials Between Blacks and Whites in the United States." *Social Forces* 58 (1980): 707–725.

———. "The Life Cycle of American Families: An Expanded Analysis." *Journal of Family History* 5 (1980): 97–111.

Spanier, G., and Thompson, L. *Parting: The Aftermath of Separation and Divorce.* Beverly Hills, Calif.: Sage, 1984.

Spanier, G., et al. "Marital Adjustment over the Family Life Cycle: The Issue of Curvilinearity." *Journal of Marriage and the Family,* May 1975, 263–275.

Spock, B. "What about Our Children?" In *Family Strengths: Positive Models for Family Life,* edited by N. Stinnett et al. Lincoln, Neb.: University of Nebraska Press, 1980.

Springsteen, B. "Thunder Road." *Born to Run.* CBS Inc., 1975.

Stambul, H., and Kelly, H. "Conflict in the Development of Close Relationships." In *Social Exchange in Developing Relationships,* edited by R. Burgess and T. Huston. New York: Academic Press, 1978.

Starr, R. "Child Abuse." *American Psychology* (1979): 872–878.

Stein, H. "The Case for Staying Home." *Esquire,* June 1984, 142–149.

Stein, P. *Single Life.* New York: St. Martin's Press, 1981.

Steinem, G. "Steinem: Reproductive Freedom Basic Right." *Planned Parenthood Review* 2, no. 4 (1982): 5–6.

Steiner, G. "Family Stability and Income Guarantees." In *The Washington COFO Memo,* Vol. 2, no. 4. Washington, D.C.: Coalition of Family Organizations, 1979.

Steinmetz, S. *The Cycle of Violence: Assertive, Aggressive, and Abusive Family Interaction.* New York: Praeger, 1977a.

———. "The Use of Force for Resolving Family Conflict: The Training Ground for Abuse." *Family Coordinator,* January 1977b.

Steinmetz, S., and Straus, M. *Violence in the Family.* New York: Harper & Row, 1974.

Stephan, C., and Corder, J. "The Effects of Dual-Career Families on Adolescents' Sex-Role Attitudes, Work and Family Plans, and Choices of Important Others." *Journal of Marriage and the Family* 47 (November 1985): 921–930.

Sternlieb, G., and Hughes, J. "Demographics and Housing in America." *Population Bulletin*. Washington, D.C.: Population Reference Bureau, January 1986.

Stinnett, N. "In Search of Strong Families." In *Building Family Strengths*, edited by N. Stinnett, B. Chesser, and J. DeFrain. Lincoln, Nev.: University of Nebraska Press, 1979.

————. "Strengthening Families: An International Priority." Talk given at the International Conference on Family Strengths sponsored by Pepperdine College, Los Angeles, 20–22 April 1986.

Stinnett, N., and DeFrain, J. *Secrets of Strong Families*. Boston: Little, Brown, 1985.

Straus, M., and Gelles, R. "Societal Change and Change in Family Violence from 1975 to 1985 as Revealed by Two National Surveys." *Journal of Marriage and the Family*, August 1986, 465–479.

Straus, M., Gelles, R., and Steinmetz, S. *Behind Closed Doors: Violence in the American Family*. New York: Doubleday, 1980.

————. "Husbands and Wives as Victims and Aggressors in Marital Violence." Paper presented at the annual meeting of the American Association for the Advancement of Science. San Francisco, January 1980.

————. "Leveling, Civility, and Violence in the Family." *Journal of Marriage and the Family* 36 (1974): 13–29.

————. "Measuring Intrafamily Conflict and Violence: The Conflict Tactics (CT) Scales." *Journal of Marriage and the Family* 41, no. 1 (1979): 75–88.

Streib, G. "Older Families and Their Troubles: Familial and Social Responses." *The Family Coordinator* 21 (January 1972).

Strong, J. *Creating Closeness*. Ames, Iowa: Human Communication Institute, 1983.

Strube, M., and Barbour, L. S. "The Decision to Leave an Abusive Relationship: Economic Dependence and Psychological Commitment." *Journal of Marriage and the Family* (1983): 785–793.

————. "Factors Related to the Decision to Leave an Abusive Relationship." *Journal of Marriage and the Family* (November 1984): 837–844.

Sugimoto, E. *A Daughter of the Samurai*. Garden City, N.Y.: Doubleday, 1935.

Tavris, C. *The Longest War: Understanding Sex Differences*. 2d ed. New York: Harcourt Brace Jovanovich, 1984.

Tavris, C., and Sadd, S. *The Redbook Report on Female Sexuality*. New York: Redbook, 1977.

Tillich, P. *Dynamics of Faith*. New York: Harper & Row, 1957.

Time. "Cocaine Babies." 20 January 1986, 50.

————. "More and More, She's the Boss." 2 December 1985, 64–65.

————. "In Search of Sexual Desire." 4 April 1983, 80.

————. "Man Wins Office Sex Suit." 2 August 1982.

————. "The New Scarlet Letter." 2 August 1982, 62–66.

————. "How Long Till Equality." 12 July 1982, 20.

————. "Not So Merry Widowers." 10 August 1981, 45.

————. "IUD Debate." 26 May 1980, 60.

————. "Testing Fetuses." 24 March 1980, 48.

————. "The Battle Over Abortion." 6 April 1981, 20.

————. "The New Morality." 21 November 1977, 111.

————. "Doubts About IUDs." 15 July 1974, 81.

Tognoli, J. "Male Friendship and Intimacy across the Life Span." *Family Relations* 29 (1980): 273–279.

Torry, B. "The Lengthening of Retirement." In *Aging From Birth to Death: Vol. 11: Sociotemporal Perspectives*, edited by M. W. Riley et al. Boulder, Colo.: Westview, 1982.

Trafford, A. *Crazy Time: Surviving Divorce*. New York: Bantam Books, 1984.

Trafford, A., et al. "She's Come a Long Way: Or Has She?" *U.S. News and World Report* 97 (1984): 44–51.

Troll, L. "Grandparents: The Family Watchdogs." In *Family Relationships in Later Life*, edited by T. Brubaker. Beverly Hills, Calif.: Sage, 1983, 63–74.

Turkington, C. "Lifetime of Fear May Be the Legacy of Latchkey Children." *Monitor*. Washington, D.C.: American Psychological Association, November 1983.

Turnbull, S., and Turnbull, J. "To Dream the Impossible Dream: An Agenda for Discussion with Stepparents." *Family Relations*, April 1983, 227–230.

Udry, J. "Marital Alternatives and Marital Disruption." *Journal of Marriage and the Family*, November 1981, 889–997.

————. *The Social Context of Marriage*. 3d ed. Philadelphia: Lippincott, 1974.

Uhlenberg, P. "Death and the Family." *Journal of Marriage and Family History* 5, no. 3 (1980): 313–320.

Ullian, D. "The Development of Conceptions of Masculinity and Femininity." In *Exploring Sex Differences*, edited by B. Lloyd and J. Archer. London: Academic Press, 1976.

U.S. Bureau of the Census. "Fertility of American Women: June 1984." *Current Population Reports*, ser. P-20, no. 401. Washington, D.C.: U.S. Government Printing Office, November 1985.

————. "Persons 65 Years Old and Older—Characteristics by Sex: 1960–1983." *Current Population Reports*, ser. P-20, no. 389; ser. P-23, nos. 57, 59, 917, 949; ser. P-60, nos. 142 and 144. Washington, D.C.: U.S. Government Printing Office, 1985a.

————. "Marital Status and Living Arrangements: March 1985." *Current Population Reports*, ser. P-20, no. 410. Washington, D.C.: U.S. Government Printing Office, November 1985.

————. "Household and Family Characteristics: March 1984." *Current Population Reports*, ser. P-20, no. 398. Washington, D.C.: U.S. Government Printing Office, April 1985.

————. "Child Support and Alimony: 1981." *Current Population Reports*, ser. P-23, no. 124. Washington, D.C.: U.S. Government Printing Office, 1983.

————. "Fertility of American Women: June 1981." *Current Population Reports*, ser. P-20, no. 378. Washington, D.C.: U.S. Government Printing Office, 1983.

————. "Fertility of American Women." *Current Population Reports*, ser. P-20, no. 358. Washington, D.C.: U.S. Government Printing Office, 1980.

————. "Households, Families, Marital Status and Living Arrangements: March 1985." *Population Characteristics*, ser. P-20, no. 402. Washington, D.C.: U.S. Government Printing Office, October 1985.

————. "Marital Status and Living Arrangements: March 1984." *Population Characteristics*, ser. P-20, no. 399. Washington, D.C.: U.S. Government Printing Office, July 1985.

————. *Statistical Abstracts of the U.S. 1984*. 104th ed. Washington, D.C.: U.S. Government Printing Office, 1983.

————. "Households and Family Characteristics: March 1985." *Current Population Reports*, ser. P-20, no. 411. Washington, D.C.: U.S. Government Printing Office, September 1986.

U.S. Congress. House. Committee of Ways and Means. Subcommittee on Public Assistance and Unemployment Compensation. Hearings on Child Support Enforcement Legislation. 1983.

U.S. Department of Health and Human Services. *Monthly Vital Statistics Report* 35, no. 1 (April 21, 1986): 1.

———. "Trends in Contraceptive Practice: United States, 1965–1976." DHHS pub. no. (PHS) 82-1986. Hyattsville, Md.: U.S. National Center for Health Statistics, 1982.

U.S. Department of Labor. *Monthly Labor Review.* Washington, D.C.: Bureau of Labor Statistics, December 1985.

———. *Monthly Labor Review.* Washington, D.C.: Bureau of Labor Statistics, January 1985, 55–59.

———. *Monthly Labor Review.* Washington, D.C.: Bureau of Labor Statistics, March 1984.

———. *Monthly Labor Review.* Washington, D.C.: Bureau of Labor Statistics, November 1982.

U.S. National Center for Health Statistics. "Advance Report of Final Natality Statistics, 1980." *Monthly Vital Statistics Report,* Vol. 31, no. 8, supp. DHHS pub. no. (PHS) 83-1120. Hyattsville, Md.: U.S. Public Health Service, November 1982.

U.S. News and World Report. "Our Neglected Kids." 9 August 1982, 54–58.

———. "The Plight of America's Two Million Widowers." April 1974, 59–60.

U.S. Office of Human Development. Administration on Aging. Publication no. (OHD) 77-2006, Washington, D.C.: U.S. Government Printing Office, 1976.

U.S. Public Health Service. *Morbidity and Mortality Weekly Report.* Centers for Disease Control, Atlanta: U.S. Government Printing Office, 1984.

———. "Fetal Alcohol Syndrome." *Morbidity and Mortality Weekly Report* 33, no. 11. Atlanta, Ga.: Centers for Disease Control, January 13, 1984.

U.S. Surgeon General's Report on Health Risks of Smoking. Washington, D.C.: U.S. Government Printing Office, January 1985.

Verbrugge, L. "Marital Status and Health." *Journal of Marriage and the Family,* May 1979, 267–285.

Verbrugge, L., and Madans, J. "National Health Interview." *American Demographics,* March 1986.

Vickery, C. "Women's Economic Contribution to the Family." In *The Subtle Revolution: Women at Work,* edited by R. E. Smith. Washington, D.C.: Urban Institute, 1979.

Vincent, C. *Sexual and Mental Health.* New York: McGraw-Hill, 1973.

Vines, N. "Adult Unfolding and Marital Conflict." *Journal of Marital and Family Therapy* 5, no. 1 (1979): 5–14.

Viorst, J. "Happy Couples—What's Their Secret?" *Redbook,* December 1984, 100.

Visher, E. G., and Visher, J. S. *Stepfamilies: A Guide to Working with Stepparent and Stepchildren.* New York: Brunner-Mazel, 1979.

Wagner, F. "What We Know About Stepfamilies." In *Family Strengths 5: Continuity and Diversity,* edited by G. Rowe et al. Newton, Mass.: Education Development Center and the University of Nebraska, 1984.

Waldron, H., and Routh, D. "The Effect of the First Child on the Marital Relationship." *Journal of Marriage and the Family,* November 1981, 785–788.

Wall Street Journal, 10 May 1985, 22.

Wallenberg, B. "The Good News Is the Bad News Is Wrong." *Esquire,* November 1984.

Waller, W. *The Old Love and the New: Divorce and Readjustment.* Carbondale, Ill.: Southern Illinois University Press, 1967.

Wallerstein, J. "Children of Divorce—Preliminary Report of a Ten Year Follow-up of Young Children." *American Journal of Orthopsychiatry* 54, no. 3 (1984): 444.

Wallerstein, J., and Kelly, J. "California's Children of Divorce." *Psychology Today,* January 1980, 67–76.

Wallis, C. "The New Origins of Life." *Time,* 10 September 1984, 46–53.

———. "Children Having Children." *Time,* 9 December 1985, 76–90.

Wallis, L. "Can Hormone Therapy of the Menopausal Syndrome Be Made Safe?" Proceedings of the Women in Medicine Conference, Cornell Medical School, 1981, 89–92.

Watson, R. "Premarital Cohabitation vs. Traditional Courtship: Their Effects on Subsequent Marital Adjustment." *Family Relations* (1983): 139–147.

Weed, J. "National Estimates of Marriage Dissolution and Survivorship: United States." *Vital and Health Statistics,* ser. 3, no. 19. DHHS Publication No. (PHS) 81-1403. Hyattsville, Md.: National Center for Health Statistics, 1986.

Weinberg, R. "Early Childhood Education and Intervention." *American Psychologist,* October 1979, 912–916.

Weitzman, L. "Sex-role Socialization." In *Women: A Feminist Perspective,* edited by J. Freeman. Palo Alto, Calif.: Mayfield, 1975.

———. *The Divorce Revolution: The Unexpected Social and Economic Consequences for Women and Children in America.* New York: Free Press, 1985.

———. *The Marriage Contract.* New York: Free Press, 1981.

Welch, C., and Price-Bonham, S. "A Decade of No-fault Revisited: California, Georgia and Washington." *Journal of Marriage and the Family,* May 1983, 411–418.

Welles, G. "New Devices for Birth Control." *USA Weekend,* 20–22 September 1985.

Wernick, R., and Editors of Time-Life Books. *The Family.* New York: Little, Brown, 1974.

Westheimer, R. *Dr. Ruth's Guide to Good Sex.* New York: Warner Books, 1983.

West's Annotated California Codes: Civil Code, sections 4000–5099. St. Paul, Minn.: West, 1986.

White, B. *The First Three Years of Life: A Guide to Physical, Emotional and Intellectual Growth of Your Baby.* 2d ed. New York: Avon, 1984.

White House Conference on Families: Final Report. Washington, D.C.: U.S. Government Printing Office, 1981.

Whitehurst, R. "Sex Role Equality and Changing Meanings of Cohabitation." Paper presented at the annual meeting of the North Central Sociological Association, Windsor, Canada, May 1974.

Wilcox, D., and Hager, R. "Toward Realistic Expectations for Orgasmic Response in Women." *Journal of Sex Research* 16 (1980): 162–179.

Williams, R. "Alimony: The Short Goodbye." *Psychology Today,* July 1977, 71.

Willscher, M. K. "Reversing Vasectomy." *Medical Aspects of Human Sexuality,* 8 August 1980, 6.

Wilson, B. "Marriages Melting Pot." *American Demographics* (July 1984): 34–37, 45.

Wilson, E. *On Human Nature.* Cambridge, Mass.: Harvard University Press, 1978.

Wilson, G., and Abrams, D. "Effects of Alcohol on Sexual Arousal in Male Alcoholics." *Journal of Abnormal Psychology* 87, no. 6 (1978): 609–616.

Wilson, G., and Lang, R. "Sex Differences in Fantasy Patterns." *Personality and Individual Differences* 2 (1981): 243–246.

Wilson, G., and Lawson, D. "Expectancies, Alcohol and Sexual Arousal in Women." *Journal of Abnormal Psychology* 87, no. 3 (1978): 358–367.

Winch, R. *The Modern Family.* New York: Holt, 1971.

Wolfe, L. "The Sexual Profile of That Cosmopolitan Girl." *Cosmopolitan,* September 1980.

Wolfers, J. "Psychological Aspects of Vasectomy." *British Medical Journal* 4 (1970): 297, 300.

World Almanac. New York: Newspaper Enterprise Association, 1986, 787.

Yankelovich, D., et al. *Raising Children in a Changing American Society.* Minneapolis: General Mills, 1977.

Ybarra, L. "Conjugal Role Relationships in the Chicano Family." Ph.D. diss., University of California, 1977.

Yogev, S. "Dual-Career Couples: Conflict and Treatment." *The American Journal of Family Therapy* 11, no. 2 (1983): 38–44.

Yogev, S., and Brett, J. "Perceptions of the Division of Housework and Child Care and Marital Satisfaction." *Journal of Marriage and the Family*, August 1985, 609–618.

Zaidi, A., et al. "Gonorrhea in the United States: 1967–1979." *Sexually Transmitted Diseases* 10, no. 2 (1983): 72–76.

Ziel, H., and Finkle, W. "Increased Risk of Endometrial Carcinoma among Users of Conjugated Estrogens." *New England Journal of Medicine* 293, no. 93 (1975): 1167–1170.

Zilbergeld, B., and Evans, M. "The Inadequacy of Masters and Johnson." *Psychology Today*, August 1980, 29–43.

Zube, M. "Changing Behavior and Outlook of Aging Men and Women: Implications for Marriage in the Middle and Later Years." *Family Relations*, January 1982, 147–156.

Author Index

F

Farber, B., 527
Farley, R., 51
Ferber, M. A., 283, 284
Finkle, W., 326
Finkelhor, D., 197
Finlay, B., 297
Fisher, K., 222
Fisher, M., 408
Friedrich, O., 388
Friedan, B., 217, 230
Frieze, I., 213
Fromm, E., 41, 65, 71, 81, 85
Fullerton, N. H., 285
Furstenberg, F., 494, 504, 515, 535, 542, 547

G

Galbraith, J. K., 252
Gallup, G., 492
Galvin, K. M., 171, 176, 192, 194
Ganong, L., 543, 550–552
Gardner, J., 4
Garland, D., 186, 566
Gary, L., 57
Gaudy, J., 176
Geller, R., 197, 199, 489
Gibran, K., 435
Gilbert, S. J., 176
Glenn, N., 16, 441, 541, 542
Glick, P., 29, 57, 105, 234, 436, 460, 464, 476, 492, 522, 529, 541, 543
Goertzel, M., 451
Goertzel, V., 451
Goetting, A., 525
Gold, A., 335, 336
Gold, D., 302
Goldstine, D., 68
Goleman, D., 212, 213
Golden, G., 346
Goodman, E., 309
Gordon, T., 176
Gotwald, W. H., 346
Goy, R., 207
Greenblat, C., 342
Greenhaus, J., 305
Greer, G., 233
Gross, H., 307
Gunnarsson, L., 440
Gunter, B., 524
Guttentag, M., 57, 236
Guttmacher, A., 366, 409

H

Habenstein, R., 39
Hager, P., 382

Hager, R., 335
Halpern, H., 482
Hanna, S., 110
Hannan, N., 294
Hansen, C., 491
Hansen, G., 89
Harlap, S., 381, 412
Harper, P., 390
Hatcher, R., 370
Hatfield, E., 70, 72, 87, 126
Hawkes, G., 58
Hawrylyshyn, P., 421
Haynes, J., 528
Hechinger, F., 440
Hefferan, C., 242
Heiman, J., 334
Helfer, R., 198
Hendershat, G., 364
Hicks, M., 441
Hill, C., 124
Hill, E., 485
Hobbins, J., 413, 415
Hofferth, S., 293, 294, 301
Hoffman, L., 302, 440, 442
Hoffman, W., 294
Hogue, C., 380
Holmes, J., 294
Honeycutt, J., 171
Houseknecht, S., 302, 307, 363
Hornung, A., 293
Hughes, J., 269
Hull, J., 483
Hunt, M., 61, 157, 335
Hunt, R., 174
Huston, T., 127, 128

I

Insel, P. M., 373, 374, 376

J

Jacklin, C., 213
Jacobs, P., 390
Jacques, J., 108
Janda, L., 126
Jedlicka, D., 116, 524
Johnson, C., 486
Johnson, D., 524
Johnson, M., 107, 108
Johnson, R., 157
Johnson, S., 197
Johnson, V., 121, 317, 326, 327, 329, 330, 335, 345, 346, 347, 393
Jones, E., 127, 345
Jones, H., 345
Jorgensen, S., 176

K

Karoly, P., 126
Keller, D., 329
Kelly, H., 127
Kelly, J., 431, 512, 513
Kempe, C., 198
Kerckhoff, A., 124
Kerckhoff, R., 477
Kieffer, C., 42, 107
Kinsey, A., 49
Kimura, D., 207, 212, 213
Kirschner, B., 307
Kitano, H. H., 54
Kogan, B. A., 345, 373
Kolodny, R., 344, 345
Kosteic, J., 371, 377
Krantz, J., 133–135
Krantzler, M., 508
Knaub, P., 110
Knox, D., 98, 99, 332, 346, 349
Koo, H., 543

L

Ladewig, P., 407, 410, 413, 415, 422, 426
Lamm, M., 528
Landes, E., 541
Landers, A., 71, 340
Lang, M. E., 441
Lang, R., 335
LaRossa, M., 442, 444
LaRossa, R., 442, 444
Lasswell, M., 75, 492
Lauer, J., 149, 157, 166
Lauer, R., 149, 157, 166
Lawson, D., 344
Lear, H., 373
Leboyer, F., 424
Lee, G., 97
Leiblum, S., 393
LeMasters, E. E., 449
Leo, J., 330–331, 338, 339, 340, 341, 344
Leonard, G., 340
Lerner, J., 440, 441, 450, 451, 458, 462
LeShan, E., 477
Leslie, G., 97, 110, 524
Lessard, S., 381
Levin, A., 381
Levinger, G., 127, 128, 527
Lewis, R., 18, 107, 149, 302
Libby, R., 333, 334, 409
Lin, S., 460
Lindemann, B., 212, 229
Linton, R., 61
Lloyd, B., 205, 207, 210, 213
Lobsenz, N., 75

Subject Index

(*Acknowledgments continued*)

p. 435 Reprinted from *The Prophet* by Kahlil Gibran, by permission of Alfred A. Knopf, Inc. Copyright 1923 by Kahlil Gibran and renewed in 1951 by administrators C.T.A. of Kahlil Gibran estate and Mary G. Gibran.

p. 479 Reprinted by permission of Jim Sanderson and Sun Features, copyright 1982.

p. 526 Copyright May, 1981 by the National Council on Family Relations. Reprinted by permission.

pp. 531–532 Gail Scott © 1983, *Ms Magazine.* Reprinted by permission.

pp. 544–545 Copyright, April, 1983 by the National Council on Family Relations. Reprinted by permission.

pp. 550–552 Copyright AACD © 1985. Reprinted by permission.

Photo Credits

Chapter 1 **2** © Hella Hammid, Photo Researchers. **5** © David S. Strickler, The Picture Cube. **10** © Sally Weigland, The Picture Cube. **14** © David M. Grossman, Photo Researchers. **15** © Suzanne Szasz, Photo Researchers. **21** (top) © David Powers, Stock, Boston; (bottom) © Ellis Herwig, Stock, Boston.

Chapter 2 **26** © Nancy Durrell McKenna, Photo Researchers. **33** © Carol Palmer, The Picture Cube. **35** Andre Kilian. **41** © Jeffry W. Myers, Stock, Boston. **54** © Stock, Boston.

Chapter 3 **60** © Frank Siteman, The Picture Cube. **69** © Renee Lynn, Photo Researchers. **78** © Ulrike Welsch, Stock, Boston. **85** © Bill Bachman, Photo Researchers. **88** © Charles Harbutt, Archive Pictures. **91** © Renee Lynn, Photo Researchers.

Chapter 4 **94** © Jeffry W. Myers, Stock, Boston. **99** Kathryn O'Connor. **101** © Frank Siteman, The Picture Cube. **102** Frank Cox. **106** © Peter Simon, Stock, Boston. **115** © Martha Stewart, The Picture Cube. **121** © Jerry Howard, Stock, Boston. **129** © Leslie Starobin, The Picture Cube. **133** (top) © Frederick D. Bodin, Stock, Boston; (bottom) © Phyllis Graber Jensen, Stock, Boston.

Chapter 5 **138** © Chester Higgins, Jr., Photo Researchers. **142** © Katrina Thomas, Photo Researchers. **148** © Christopher S. Johnson, Stock, Boston. **155** © Susan Rosenberg, Photo Researchers. **159** © Takatsuno, The Picture Cube. **165** (top) © Frank Siteman, The Picture Cube; (bottom) © Nancy Durrell McKenna, Photo Researchers.

Chapter 6 **168** © Michael Hayman, Stock, Boston. **172** © Teri Leigh Stratford, Photo Researchers. **186** © Frank Siteman, The Picture Cube. **192** © Peter Vandermark, Stock, Boston. **196** (top) © Jeff Albertson, Stock, Boston; (bottom) © James R. Holland, Stock, Boston.

Chapter 7 **202** © George W. Gardner, Stock, Boston. **205** Michael Weisbrot, Stock, Boston. **218** Kathryn O'Connor. **225** © Robert Eckert, The Picture Cube. **236** Frank Cox.

Chapter 8 **240** © Bill Owens, Jeroboam. **245** © Jean-Claude Lejeune, Stock, Boston. **249** © Janice Fullman, The Picture Cube. **270** © Frederick D. Bodin, Stock, Boston. **276** © Peter Menzel, Stock, Boston.

Chapter 9 **282** © Teri Leigh Stratford, Photo Researchers. **286** © Donald Dietz, Stock, Boston. **299** © Richard Hutchings, Photo Researchers.

Chapter 10 **312** © Paul Fusco, Magnum. **339** © Teri Leigh Stratford, Photo Researchers. **347** © Frank Siteman, Stock, Boston.

Chapter 11 **358** © Peter Menzel, Stock, Boston. **361** © Betsy Cole, The Picture Cube. **378** © Eric A. Roth, The Picture Cube. **379** © Barbara Adler, Stock, Boston. **395** © Mary Ellen Mark, Archive Pictures.

Chapter 12 **400** Kathryn O'Connor. **101** Kathryn O'Connor. **411** © Polly Brown, Archive Pictures. **421** © Phaneuf/Gurdziel, The Picture Cube. **426** © J. Berndt, The Picture Cube. **428** © Nancy Durrell McKenna, Photo Researchers. **430** © Barbara Alper, Stock, Boston.